The Handbook of Measurement Issues in Criminology and Criminal Justice

Wiley Handbooks in Criminology and Criminal Justice

Series Editor: Charles F. Wellford, University of Maryland College Park

The handbooks in this series will be comprehensive, academic reference works on leading topics in criminology and criminal justice.

The Handbook of Law and Society
Edited by Austin Sarat and Patricia Ewick

The Handbook of Juvenile Delinquency and Juvenile Justice
Edited by Marvin D. Krohn and Jodi Lane

The Handbook of Deviance
Edited by Erich Goode

The Handbook of Gangs
Edited by Scott H. Decker and David C. Pyrooz

The Handbook of Criminological Theory
Edited by Alex R. Piquero

The Handbook of Drugs and Society
Edited by Henry H. Brownstein

The Handbook of Measurement Issues in Criminology and Criminal Justice
Edited by Beth M. Huebner and Timothy S. Bynum

The Handbook of Measurement Issues in Criminology and Criminal Justice

Edited by

Beth M. Huebner and Timothy S. Bynum

WILEY Blackwell

This edition first published 2016

Registered Office
John Wiley & Sons, Ltd, The Atrium, Southern Gate, Chichester, West Sussex, PO19 8SQ, UK

Editorial Offices
350 Main Street, Malden, MA 02148-5020, USA
9600 Garsington Road, Oxford, OX4 2DQ, UK
The Atrium, Southern Gate, Chichester, West Sussex, PO19 8SQ, UK

For details of our global editorial offices, for customer services, and for information about how to apply for permission to reuse the copyright material in this book please see our website at www.wiley.com/wiley-blackwell.

Library of Congress Cataloging-in-Publication data applied for

Hardback ISBN: 9781118868782

A catalogue record for this book is available from the British Library.

Cover image: Getty/Alvina_Denisenko

Set in 10.5/13pt Minion by SPi Global, Pondicherry, India
Printed and bound in Malaysia by Vivar Printing Sdn Bhd

1 2016

Contents

Notes on Contributors vii

Introduction 1
Beth M. Huebner and Timothy S. Bynum

Part I Measurement of Criminal Typologies 7

1 Violent Crime 9
Nicholas Corsaro

2 Cybercrime 29
Thomas J. Holt

3 Juvenile Crime and Bullying 49
Sean P. Varano and Joseph M. McKenna

4 Rape and Other Sexual Offending Behaviors 69
Wesley G. Jennings and Bryanna Hahn Fox

5 White-Collar and Corporate Crime 92
Michael L. Benson, Jay Kennedy, and Matthew Logan

6 Human Trafficking 111
Amy Farrell and Katherine Bright

7 Challenges in Measuring and Understanding Hate Crime 131
Jack McDevitt and Janice A. Iwama

Part II Offenders, Offending, and Victimization 157

8 Gangs and Gang Crime 159
Chris Melde

9 Gendered Pathways to Crime 181
Julie Yingling

10 Mental Health and Physical Studies 202
Daryl G. Kroner and Maranda Quillen

11 Rehabilitation and Treatment Programming 223
Faye S. Taxman and Brandy L. Blasko

12 Measuring Victimization: Issues and New Directions 249
Leah E. Daigle, Jamie A. Snyder, and Bonnie S. Fisher

Part III Criminal Justice Organizations and Outcomes 277

13 Community Policing and Police Interventions 279
Michael J. Kyle and Joseph A. Schafer

14 Measurement Issues in Criminal Case-Processing and Court Decision-Making Research 303
Brian D. Johnson and Christina D. Stewart

15 Sentencing Outcomes and Disparity 328
Jared M. Ellison and Pauline K. Brennan

16 Correctional Interventions and Outcomes 351
Eric Grommon and Jason Rydberg

17 How Theory Guides Measurement: Public Attitudes toward Crime and Policing 377
Jonathan Jackson and Jouni Kuha

18 Measuring the Cost of Crime 416
Matt DeLisi

19 School Crime and Safety 434
Thomas Mowen, John Brent, and Aaron Kupchik

20 Traffic Stops, Race, and Measurement 452
Kyle McLean and Jeff Rojek

Part IV Specialized Measurement Techniques 473

21 Self-Reported Crime and Delinquency 475
Scott Menard, Lisa C. Bowman-Bowen, and Yi-Fen Lu

22 Crime and the Life Course 496
Lee Ann Slocum

23 Conducting Qualitative Interviews in Prison: Challenges and Lessons Learned 517
Kristin Carbone-Lopez

24 Spatial Analysis of Crime 535
Steven M. Radil

25 Network Analysis 555
Owen Gallupe

Index 576

Notes on Contributors

Michael L. Benson is professor of criminal justice at the University of Cincinnati. He is a past president of the White-Collar Crime Research Consortium. He has published extensively in the areas of white-collar crime, intimate partner violence, and life-course criminology. With Francis T. Cullen, he authored *Combating Corporate Crime: Local Prosecutors at Work,* which received the Outstanding Scholarship Award in 2000 from the Crime and Delinquency Division of the Society for the Study of Social Problems. The second edition of his book *Understanding White-Collar Crime: An Opportunity Perspective* will be published in 2015. He is currently working on a book on emotions in crime and criminal justice.

Brandy L. Blasko is currently a postdoctoral research fellow at George Mason University. She received her PhD from the Department of Criminal Justice at Temple University. Her research focuses on how criminal justice workers and criminal justice-involved individuals perceive, understand, and negotiate formal and informal aspects of the corrections environment.

Lisa C. Bowman-Bowen received her PhD in criminal justice from Sam Houston State University in 2014; she has an MS in criminology from Indiana State University (2004) and BS degrees in criminal justice and behavioral science from Grace College (2000). Her research projects focus on survey methodology and self-report measures, specifically for adolescent and young adult problem behaviors. Her dissertation and publications focus on self-reported substance use and illegal behavior.

Pauline K. Brennan received her PhD in criminal justice from the University at Albany, SUNY, and is an associate professor and the Doctoral Program Chair for the School of Criminology and Criminal Justice at the University of Nebraska Omaha (UNO). She also serves as the director of the London Program for UNO and is the president of the Association of Doctoral Programs in Criminology and Criminal Justice. Her areas of research include inequity in court processing, correctional policy, and issues related to female offenders and victims.

John Brent is assistant professor at Georgia Southern University. His recent work focuses on the cultural and structural dynamics underpinning transgressive and criminal behavior, building a theoretical foundation for criminal justice theory, critically examining school discipline and security, and methodological approaches in criminology. He is the coauthor, with Peter B. Kraska, of *Theorizing Criminal Justice: Eight Essential Orientations* (2010), and his work can be found in a number of leading peer-reviewed journals, including the *British Journal of Criminology, Justice Quarterly,* the *Journal of Criminal Justice,* and the *Journal of Criminal Justice Education.*

Katherine Bright is research associate at the Institute on Race and Justice at Northeastern University. Her primary research interests include human trafficking, particularly the commercial sexual exploitation of domestic minors, expectant and parenting youth, and youth partnership models as successful intervention tools. Her recent research has focused on labor trafficking within the US, as well as on the intersection of teen pregnancy, homelessness, and commercial sexual exploitation in Massachusetts.

Timothy S. Bynum, PhD, is professor in the School of Criminal Justice at Michigan State University. He is the former director of the National Archive of Criminal Justice Data (NACJD) at the Inter-University Consortium on Political and Social Research at the University of Michigan. Professor Bynum's current research includes the study of community-based interventions to reduce gang and gun violence, the implementation and assessment of an innovative neighborhood approach to violence in nine communities, and an assessment of the impact of residency restrictions for sex offenders. He previously conducted research on reentry programs for offenders released from prison, programs to reduce school violence, community-based correctional alternatives for both adult and juvenile offenders, and gang intervention programs.

Kristin Carbone-Lopez is associate professor in the Department of Criminology and Criminal Justice at the University of Missouri, St. Louis. Her research focuses on gender and the connections between crime and victimization across the life course. Her recent publications appear in *Criminology*, the *Journal of Research in Crime and Delinquency*, the *Journal of Interpersonal Violence*, the *Journal of Quantitative Criminology*, and *Signs: Journal of Women in Culture and Society.*

Nicholas Corsaro, PhD, is assistant professor of criminal justice at the University of Cincinnati and research director at the Police Foundation in Washington, DC. Corsaro received his PhD from the School of Criminal Justice at Michigan State University. He has served as an external evaluation researcher on a number of local and national strategic policing initiatives; this includes his work on the Indianapolis Violence Reduction Partnership (IVRP), the national Project Safe Neighborhoods (PSN), gun violence reduction (and evaluation) strategy, and the Cincinnati Initiative to Reduce Violence (CIRV) focused deterrence strategy. His research interests focus on strategic partnerships with police agencies in order to identify and target crime problems, research methods, analyses, and evaluation designs intended to examine potential changes in gun, gang, and drug market violence.

Leah E. Daigle, PhD, is associate professor in the Department of Criminal Justice in the Andrew Young School of Policy Studies at Georgia State University. She received her PhD in criminal justice from the University of Cincinnati. Her most recent research has centered on repeat sexual victimization of college women and the development and continuation of victimization across the life course. She is coauthor of *Criminals in the Making: Criminality Across the Life Course* (2nd edn., 2014) and *Unsafe in the Ivory Tower: The Sexual Victimization of College Women* (2010), which was awarded the 2011 Outstanding Book Award by the Academy of Criminal Justice Sciences, and author of *Victimology: A Text/Reader and Victimology: The Essentials* (2013).

Matt DeLisi is professor and coordinator of criminal justice studies and affiliate with the Center for the Study of Violence at Iowa State University. Professor DeLisi is the editor-in-chief of the *Journal of Criminal Justice* and a fellow of the Academy of Criminal Justice Sciences. The author of more than 250 scholarly publications, Professor DeLisi is one of the most prolific and cited criminologists in the world.

Jared M. Ellison received his MS in criminal justice administration from Niagara University and is a third-year doctoral student in the School of Criminology and Criminal Justice at the University of Nebraska, Omaha (UNO). His research interests include court processing, the correctional system, inmate behavior, and community reentry.

Amy Farrell is associate professor of criminology and criminal justice at Northeastern University. Her scholarship seeks to understand arrest, adjudication, and criminal case disposition practices. Her recent research focuses on criminal justice system responses to new crimes such as human trafficking. She has led studies of police responses to human trafficking and state and local prosecution of human trafficking for the National Institute of Justice (NIJ). She has testified about police identification of human trafficking before the US House of Representatives Judiciary Committee. Farrell was a co-recipient of NIJ's W. E. B. DuBois Fellowship on crime, justice, and culture in 2006.

Bonnie S. Fisher, PhD, is professor in the School of Criminal Justice at the University of Cincinnati. She received her PhD in Political Science from Northwestern University in 1988. She served on the National Academy of Sciences Panel on Measuring Rape and Sexual Assault in Bureau of Justice Statistics Household Surveys during 2011–2013. In 2015 she was the Co-PI (with David Cantor at Westat) working with the American Association of University Campus Climate Survey on the Sexual Assault and Sexual Misconduct Design Team. Her published articles and chapters span the field of victimology, and her primary research area has been on violence against women, from domestic violence to stalking to sexual assault, with an emphasis on college women. She has coedited and coauthored a number of books, including the *Encyclopedia of Victimology and Crime Prevention* (2010); *The Dark Side of the Ivory Tower: Campus Crime as a Social Problem* (2013); *Unsafe in the Ivory Tower: The Sexual Victimization of College Women* (2010, with Leah Daigle; this book won the 2011 Outstanding Book Award by the ACJS); and *Campus Crime: Legal, Social and*

Policy Perspectives (3rd edn., 2007). In 2015 she coedited a volume entitled *Critical Issues on Violence against Women: International Perspectives and Promising Strategies* and coauthored a textbook entitled *Introduction to Victimology: Contemporary Theory, Research, and Practice*.

Bryanna Hahn Fox, PhD, is assistant professor in the Department of Criminology in the College of Behavioral and Community Sciences and holds a courtesy appointment in the Department of Mental Health Law and Policy at the University of South Florida. She received her doctorate in psychological criminology from the University of Cambridge, England. Her major research interests include violence, crime analysis, criminal careers, and experimental criminology, and her recent research has been published in some of top criminology and criminal justice journals such as *Social Forces* and *Criminal Justice & Behavior*.

Owen Gallupe, PhD, is assistant professor in the Department of Sociology and Legal Studies at the University of Waterloo. His recent work appears in venues such as *Journal of Criminal Justice*, *Crime and Delinquency*, *Journal of Youth Studies*, and *Rationality & Society*.

Eric Grommon is assistant professor in the School of Public and Environmental Affairs at Indiana University–Purdue University, Indianapolis. His research interests include research methods, the evaluation of correctional programs, policies, and operations, and prisoner reentry. His research can be found in such outlets as *Criminology and Public Policy*, *Journal of Experimental Criminology*, *Journal of Offender Rehabilitation*, and *Justice Quarterly*.

Thomas J. Holt, PhD, is associate professor in the School of Criminal Justice at Michigan State University and specializes in cybercrime, policing, and policy. He received his PhD in criminology and criminal justice from the University of Missouri-Saint Louis in 2005. He has published extensively on cybercrime and cyberterror; he has over 35 peer-reviewed articles in outlets such as *Crime & Delinquency*, *Sexual Abuse*, *Journal of Criminal Justice*, *Terrorism and Political Violence*, and *Deviant Behavior*.

Beth M. Huebner, PhD, is professor and director of graduate programs in the Department of Criminology and Criminal Justice at the University of Missouri, St. Louis. Her research interests include prisoner reentry, criminal justice decision-making, gendered perspectives on crime and justice, and public policy. She is the author or coauthor of several scholarly articles and book chapters, and her work on incarceration and marriage was honored with the Academy of Criminal Justice Sciences Donal MacNamara Award. She was also given the Michigan State University School of Criminal Justice Wall of Fame: Young Alumni Award.

Janice A. Iwama, MS, is a doctoral candidate at the School of Criminology and Criminal Justice at Northeastern University. Her dissertation research focuses on examining the community conditions and social processes that impact hate crimes, particularly against immigrants and Hispanics. Her work applies a theoretical framework to improving our understanding on hate crimes within a community context, given the increasingly diverse population of the United States. Her research interests involve the impact of communities on crime, disproportionate minority contact, prevalence of hate crimes, racial and ethnic issues, and the victimization of immigrants. She recently worked on a National Institute of Justice-funded study examining national trends in hate crimes against immigrants and Hispanic Americans and is currently working on a study that examines racial profiling at traffic stops in Rhode Island for the Rhode Island Department of Transportation, with the Institute on Race and Justice at Northeastern University.

Jonathan Jackson is professor of research methodology in the Department of Methodology at the London School of Economics (LSE) and a member of the LSE's Mannheim Centre for Criminology. His research interests include procedural justice, legitimacy, trust, fear of crime, and measurement. He would like to thank Yale School Law and Harvard Kennedy School for hosting him during research leave while he coauthored this chapter; he is also grateful to the UK's Economic and Social Research Council for funding that research leave (grant number ES/L011611/1).

Wesley G. Jennings, PhD, is associate professor, associate chair, and undergraduate director in the Department of Criminology, has a courtesy appointment in the Department of Mental Health Law and Policy, and is a Faculty Affiliate of the Florida Mental Health Institute in the College of Behavioral and Community Sciences at the University of South Florida. In addition, he also has a courtesy appointment in the Department of Health Outcomes & Policy and is a faculty affiliate of the Institute for Child Health Policy in the College of Medicine at the University of Florida. He received his doctorate degree in criminology from the University of Florida.

Brian D. Johnson is associate professor of criminology and criminal justice at the University of Maryland. His areas of expertise involve social inequality in the justice system, with a particular focus on racial disparities in criminal case-processing and sentencing. Much of his research examines contextual influences in punishment as well as the use of advanced statistical modeling techniques to study the criminal process. Dr. Johnson is the recipient of the 2008 ASC Ruth Shonle Cavan Young Scholar Award and the 2011 American Society of Criminology, DCS Distinguished New Scholar Award. He has delivered invited workshops to the American Society of Criminology (ASC) and the National Institute of Justice (NIJ) and has served as a research consultant for organizations like Weststat, the National Center for State Courts (NCSC), and the Vera Institute of Justice. He is currently a co-PI on the National Science Foundation, Research Coordination Network grant for Understanding Guilty Pleas, and his published work has appeared in peer-reviewed journals such as *Criminology*, *Journal of Quantitative Criminology*, and *Justice Quarterly*.

Jay Kennedy is assistant professor in the Center for Anti-Counterfeiting and Product Protection and the School of Criminal Justice, Michigan State University. His research addresses the multilevel antecedents of corporate crime, business ethics, and crimes committed against corporations, including employee theft and intellectual property theft. Dr. Kennedy received his PhD in criminal justice, as well as an MBA, from the University of Cincinnati.

Daryl G. Kroner, PhD, is associate professor in the Department of Criminology and Criminal Justice at Southern Illinois University. Prior to this position, he was employed as a correctional psychologist from 1986 to 2008. During this time he worked at maximum, medium, and minimum facilities delivering intervention services to offenders. His current research interests include risk assessment, measurement of intervention outcomes, interventions among offenders with mentally illness, and criminal desistance.

Jouni Kuha is associate professor of statistics and research methodology in the Departments of Statistics and Methodology at the London School of Economics. His research interests include model selection, measurement error, misclassification and missing data, latent variable modelling, and analysis of cross-national survey data.

Aaron Kupchik is professor of sociology and criminal justice at the University of Delaware. His work focuses on the policing and punishment of children in schools, courts, and correctional facilities. He is the author of *Homeroom Security: School Discipline in an Age of Fear* (2010) and *Judging Juvenile: Prosecuting Adolescents in Adult and Juvenile Courts* (2006).

Michael J. Kyle is a doctoral student in the Department of Criminology & Criminal Justice at Southern Illinois University, Carbondale. Prior to beginning his doctoral studies Michael served as a law enforcement officer in both Missouri and Kansas. His research interests include policing, police leadership and ethics, and police legitimacy.

Matthew Logan is a PhD candidate in the School of Criminal Justice at the University of Cincinnati. Prior to beginning the doctoral program, he completed his Master's in sociology and Bachelor's in criminology at the University of Western Ontario in Canada. His research interests include criminological theory, institutional corrections, white-collar crime, and violence and victimization. He is currently using nationally representative data on state and federal correctional facilities to study the prison experience of white-collar inmates on a host of negative and positive prison outcomes. In the past he has also examined the prison experience of other inmate groups, including those with military backgrounds and mental illnesses.

Jack McDevitt, PhD, is associate dean for research for the College of Social Sciences and Humanities at Northeastern University. Jack also directs the Institute on Race and Justice and the Center for Criminal Justice Policy Research. Jack is the coauthor of three books: *Hate Crimes: The Rising Tide of Bigotry and Bloodshed* (1998) *Hate Crime Revisited: American War on Those Who Are Different* (2002; both with Jack Levin) and *Victimology* (2002, with Judith M. Sgarzi). He has also coauthored a numerous articles and reports on hate crime, racial profiling, and human trafficking and a monograph for the US Department of Justice on local law enforcement experiences with cases of human trafficking. He was recently appointed by the Speaker of the Massachusetts House of Representatives to chair a gun violence commission to make recommendations on ways to reduce gun violence in the commonwealth. He has spoken on hate crime, racial profiling, human trafficking, and security, both nationally and internationally, and has testified as an expert witness before the Judiciary Committees of The US House of Representatives and as invited expert at the White House.

Kyle McLean is a doctoral student at the University of South Carolina. He received his Master's degree in criminology and criminal justice from the University of South Carolina. His research interests are in criminological theory, policing, and perceptions of crime and justice.

Joseph M. McKenna is associate director of research and evaluation for the Texas School Safety Center at Texas State University. He has an MS in criminal justice and is pursuing a PhD at Texas State University. His research interests include violence, school crime/disorder, policing, and public policy. His recent publications focus on the role of the conflict faced by police officers who work in school environments.

Chris Melde, PhD, is associate professor and coordinator of undergraduate studies in the School of Criminal Justice at Michigan State University. He received his PhD in criminology and criminal justice from the University of Missouri, St. Louis in 2007. His primary research interests include street gangs, the ecology of violence, program evaluation, the impact of violent offending and victimization on adolescent development, and individual and community reactions to victimization risk.

Scott Menard is professor in the Department of Criminal Justice and Criminology at Sam Houston State University. He received his AB from Cornell University and his PhD from the University of Colorado, both in sociology. His teaching and research interests and his publications are primarily in the areas of statistics and quantitative methods, criminological theory testing, and longitudinal research on delinquent and criminal behavior and victimization.

Thomas J. Mowen is assistant professor of Criminal Justice at the University of Wyoming. His recent work has explored the impact of school discipline and policy on families and youth, inequalities in school punishment, and the role of family in the process of reentry. His recent work has been published in a number of peer-reviewed outlets including *Justice Quarterly, Criminology & Public Policy, British Journal of Criminology, and Youth & Society.*

Maranda Quillen is currently a graduate student in the Department of Criminology and Criminal Justice at Southern Illinois University in Carbondale. She will graduate with her Master's degree in May 2016. Her research interests include criminogenic thinking; factors lead offenders to engage in crime as well as factors that influence successful desistance from criminal activity.

Steven M. Radil is assistant professor of geography at the University of Idaho. His work, situated within political and urban geography, focuses on power, territoriality, and violence and bridges the often separate domains of spatial analysis, geographic information science, and social theory. He has published widely on these and related themes in a range of journals, including the *Journal of Quantitative Criminology* and the *Annals of the Association of American Geographers*.

Jeff Rojek is associate professor in the Department of Criminal Justice at the University of Texas at El Paso. His primary research interests are in the area of police officer and organizational behavior. He has conducted the annual analysis for the Missouri Attorney General's Vehicle Stop Report since 2002, and has published multiple articles on racial bias in traffic stops.

Jason Rydberg is assistant professor in the School of Criminology and Justice Studies at the University of Massachusetts, Lowell. His research interests include prisoner reentry, community supervision, sex offenders and offenses, and the evaluation of criminal justice programs, particularly as it concerns community corrections and crime prevention. His research has appeared in a variety of outlets, including *Criminology and Public Policy*, *Homicide Studies*, *Police Quarterly*, and *Justice Quarterly*.

Joseph A. Schafer is professor and chair in the Department of Criminology and Criminal Justice at Southern Illinois University, Carbondale. His research focuses on policing, organizational change, leadership, citizen perceptions of police, the diffusion of innovation, critical incident response, and futures research in policing.

Lee Ann Slocum is associate professor in the Department of Criminology and Criminal Justice at the University of Missouri, St. Louis. She is interested in within-individual stability and change in offending and substance use and has published several manuscripts that examine this issue.

Jamie A. Snyder, PhD, is assistant professor in the Department of Criminal Justice at the University of West Florida. She received her PhD in criminal Justice from the University of Cincinnati. Her current research interests include the victimization of college students, victimization in the military, criminological theory, and problem-oriented policing. Her research has been published in peer-reviewed journals such as *The Journal of Interpersonal Violence*, *Violence against Women*, and *Women & Criminal Justice*.

Christina D. Stewart is a doctoral student in the Department of Criminology and Criminal Justice at the University of Maryland. Her research interests involve various aspects of courts and sentencing, including court actor decision-making under sentencing guidelines, extralegal disparity in court outcomes, and the role of case-processing attributes in punishment. She is the recipient of the 2014 American Society of Criminology (ASC) Division on Corrections and Sentencing (DCS) student paper award

Faye S. Taxman, PhD, is university professor in the Criminology, Law and Society department and director of the Center for Advancing Correctional Excellence at George Mason University. She is recognized for her work in probation and community corrections, including the RNR Simulation Tool and the development of seamless systems of care models that link the criminal justice system with other service delivery systems.

Sean P. Varano, PhD, is associate professor in the School of Justice Studies at Roger Williams University (Bristol, Rhode Island). Dr. Varano earned his doctorate from the School of Criminal Justice at Michigan State University. His areas of research include youth violence and gangs, policing, and community-based responses to youth violence. His recent publications include the role of collective efficacy in promoting healthy places in Miami neighborhoods.

Yi-Fen Lu, PhD, received her PhD from the Department of Criminal Justice and Criminology at Sam Houston State University in 2015. Her areas of interest are varied, but include testing criminological theories, biosocial criminology, gene–environment interactions, and quantitative methodology. Her research emphasizes the interplay of biology and environment in the explanation of criminal behavior. Her recent work has examined genetic variation in relation to variation in criminal behavior, as well as the interrelationship between heritability, intelligence, self-regulation, and antisocial behavior.

Julie Yingling received her PhD from Michigan State University's School of Criminal Justice. She is currently assistant professor in the Department of Sociology and Rural Studies at South Dakota State University. Her research interests are drug and methamphetamine markets, gender, domestic violence, and qualitative methods.

Introduction

Beth M. Huebner and Timothy S. Bynum

The concept of measurement is ubiquitous in criminology and criminal justice. In every aspect of our field there are challenges in finding the appropriate measurement of even the most basic concepts. *The Handbook of Measurement in Criminal Justice and Criminology* provides a comprehensive primer on existing best practice and emerging developments in the study of, and in design research on, crime and criminology. The work as a whole contains chapters on the measurement of criminal typologies, the offenders, offending and victimization, criminal justice organizations, and specialized measurement techniques. Each chapter is written by experts in the field, who provide excellent surveys of the literature in the relevant area. Importantly, each chapter offers a description of the various methodological and substantive challenges that present themselves to those who conduct research on these issues and suggests possible solutions to these problems. An emphasis has been placed on research carried out outside of the United States. This was designed to give the reader a broader, more global understanding of the social context of research in criminology.

The goal of this volume in the Handbooks in Criminology and Criminal Justice series is to be a definitive reference book for professionals in the field, researchers, and students. It aims to identify the principal topics and areas of research in this field. As stated in the previous paragraph, the authors provide in each chapter a summary of the prominent data collection efforts in their area, offer an overview of the current methodological work, discuss challenges in the measurement of central concepts in their subject area, and identify new or emergent horizons in data collection and measurement. We encouraged authors not only to review work conducted in an international context (as already mentioned), but also to incorporate

The Handbook of Measurement Issues in Criminology and Criminal Justice, First Edition.
Edited by Beth M. Huebner and Timothy S. Bynum.

discussion of qualitative methodologies whenever appropriate. In this way the book will be grounded in current knowledge of specific topics, yet will also have new, synthetic material that reflects knowledge related to the leading minds in the field. The book is organized into four parts:

- Part I: Measurement of Criminal Typologies (Chapters 1–7);
- Part II: Offenders, Offending, and Victimization (Chapters 8–12);
- Part III: Criminal Justice Organizations and Outcomes (Chapters 13–20);
- Part IV: Specialized Measurement Techniques (Chapters 21–25).

The measurement of crime has been an integral part of criminology and criminal justice since the inception of the field; however, the data and the techniques available for studying individual involvement and patterns of crime have grown exponentially in the past decade, largely spurred on by enhanced data collection efforts initiated by federal, state, and local governments. In Chapter 1 Nicholas Corsaro provides a thorough discussion of historical and recent federal efforts to document crime in the United States. Corsaro's contribution is unique in that it explicitly acknowledges the role of criminal justice interventions in understanding crime trends and indicates methods for modeling change.

Crime is often described as a monolithic concept, but there is substantial variation across types of crime. Sean Varano and Joseph McKenna (Chapter 3), Wesley Jennings and Bryanna Hahn Fox (Chapter 4), and Jack McDevitt and Janice Iwama (Chapter 7) provide cogent discussions of a sample of unique offender typologies. For example, Varano and McKenna unfold the challenges of collecting data on juvenile offenders and victims and describe in detail the work that has been done to measure trends in, and the incidence of, juvenile crime. As importantly, they use bullying behaviors as an illustration of the ways in which behavior and law interact to influence the types of crime that are measured by criminal justice agencies. In their chapter on sex crimes, Jennings and Hahn Fox summarize recent legislation directed at sex offender populations and their chapter provides a sophisticated and theoretically informed discussion of heterogeneity across these populations. McDevitt and Iwama discuss the role that the Hate Crime Statistics Act (HCSA) of 1990 had on the measurement and documentation of hate crime. They use various pictorial descriptors to illustrate the types of crime that fit under this umbrella, and they follow changes in hate crime trends over time. They also make a call for more training, for the purpose of achieving greater consistency in data collection—a policy call that can be heard across most chapters in this volume. Together, the chapters in this group illustrate the heterogeneity of offender subpopulations and show the centrality of legal mandates for better understanding the substantial variation that exists in the overall measurement of crime.

In addition to a discussion of more traditional typologies of crime, we commissioned articles that consider emerging trends in criminology. In Chapter 2 Thomas Holt, a leading expert in the field of cybercrime, provides a nuanced discussion of the literature on cybercrime and begins a conversation on how this type of crime could be best defined and measured. Importantly, he points out the challenges of collecting data on this phenomenon and concludes with recommendations on how to improve both data collection and data analysis. Although white-collar crime has been studied for decades, Michael Benson, Jay Kennedy, and Matthew Logan describe in Chapter 5 the conceptual and practical challenges of measuring criminal acts that are not officially recognized legal categories. The difficulties continue, given that few data have been collected on this kind of criminal behaviors. Both chapters 2 and 5 constitute a roadmap for scholars interested in working in these areas; at the same time they offer a sophisticated discussion of the greatest methodological difficulties to be encountered there.

Scholars have also expressed considerable interest in studying individual patterns of crime and victimization. Most work on offenders has been captured by using self-report surveys. Scott Menard, Lisa Bowman-Bowen, and Yi-Fen Lu (Chapter 21) provide a superb primer on self-report data collection. There has been considerable argument in criminology on the best manner in which to measure individual offending: some scholars have advocated for cross-sectional measurement or "snapshots" of crime, while others have defended the need to model change over time. Menard, Bowman-Bowen, and Lu provide a cogent methodological discussion of this debate and offer important suggestions for innovations in self-report in criminology. The material presented by Lee Ann Slocum in Chapter 22 enlarges the context of this discussion, as she explores the nuances of longitudinal data research and presents an important argument about how technology may be used in the future. This highly theoretical chapter is a superb primer for students of criminology and includes a sophisticated discussion of quantitative methods used to study crime over the life course. Chapter 23 on qualitative research, by Kristin Carbone-Lopez, provides a complement to Slocum's chapter. Carbone Lopez gives us a firsthand account of the lived experiences of individual offenders. Apart from insight into the use of qualitative methods, this account offers a discussion of the way in which she has overcome methodological challenges. The paired effect of these chapters broadens our understanding of individual-level crime; moreover, the two chapters together give us detailed information on the myriad ways in which data can be collected and analyzed.

Moving beyond the broader documentation of individual crime patterns, scholars also explore the specific risks and needs among offender populations. In Chapter 10 Daryl Kroner and Maranda Quillen provide a cogent discussion of the importance of mental and physical health among criminal justice populations and of methodological challenges associated with it. They do a particularly strong job of documenting the work that has been done outside of the United States. In Chapter 9 Julie Yingling discusses specific patterns of criminality among women and pays attention to the role of drug use and victimization as a pathway to criminality. She focuses on qualitative work in this area but balances this presentation with an excellent discussion of new quantitative methodologies such as life-event calendars, which can be used to study gender and crime.

This handbook pays great attention to crime victimization. Although most research on crime has centered on official crime trends and offender typologies, a substantial body of work on victimization has emerged. In Chapter 12 Leah Daigle, Jamie Snyder, and Bonnie Fisher document the existing empirical work on measurement in victimization. For scholars new to this area of research, the tabulation of common survey measures used to study the phenomenon is particularly helpful. The authors review the work that has been done in experimental and quasi-experimental research, but they make a call for future studies that should incorporate both quantitative and qualitative designs in order to better understand the extent and nature of victimization. As a subset of the broader work on victimization, Amy Farrell and Katherine Bright identify in Chapter 6 the challenges of examining human trafficking as an emerging area of study. This chapter is essential reading for new scholars to the field, as it provides a nuanced discussion of the challenges of estimating human trafficking, where victims are often hidden from traditional law enforcement surveillance.

Crime does not exist in isolation and does not always occur at the individual level; hence we commissioned several works that consider crime within the context of groups and communities. In Chapter 8 Chris Melde provides a theoretically nuanced and detailed discussion of gangs and of how their operationalization by researcher and by official criminal justice decision makers can have substantial implications for understanding the prevalence and composition of gangs. Melde also describes recent work that has begun to link youthful gang behaviors to the individual outcomes former gang members and their families. One avenue of research identified by Melde is the use of social network analysis. This topic is addressed by Owen Gallupe in Chapter 25, which describes new and emerging methods for linking groups together, theoretically and empirically, through social network strategies. Readers should pay careful attention to the detailed graphical depictions of group phenomena. Crime and criminality among individuals and groups are embedded in place. Stephen Radil's Chapter 24, devoted to the spatial analysis of crime, is a guidebook on the main analytic decisions to be made when studying the conjunction of crime and place.

Although most traditional volumes on methodology have focused centrally on victims and offenders, there is much to be learned about criminal justice organizations. Michael Kyle and Joseph Schafer describe methodological work in policing in Chapter 13, Brian Johnson and Christina Stewart on courts processes in Chapter 14, and Thomas Mowen, John Brent, and Aaron Kupchick on school crime in Chapter 19. Each chapter illustrates the role of historical and legislative changes in influencing how organizations function and collect data. Particularly timely is the material presented by by Mowen, Brent, and Kupchick, who describe several pivotal political and social events that have shaped the manner in which school data are collected. Kyle and Schafer provide a primer on measurement in policing studies, and their discussion of methodological approaches to, and limitations of, studying police–crime relationships is particularly insightful. Johnson and Stewart outline research and data collection on courts, but their work has broader implications for our understanding of criminal justice decision-making. After reading their chapter, the reader has a clearer understanding of the problems posed by measuring criminal cases that traverse multiple agencies and involve decisions made by multiple court actors.

The nexus between criminal justice agencies and citizens is important, and vital research has highlighted a disproportionate contact between the criminal justice system and select groups. In Chapter 17 Jonathan Jackson and Jouni Kuha provide a theoretically and empirically sophisticated discussion of the measurement challenges involved in understanding fear of crime and public attitudes toward the police. The authors' use of graphical displays and a broad discussion of international work in the area make this chapter unique in the volume. Jared Ellison and Pauline Brennan's Chapter 15 builds on this work through its discussion of the role of a defendant's race or ethnicity and gender in sentencing outcomes. The authors place particular emphasis on the role of official sentencing guidelines on disparate outcomes. Similarly, in Chapter 20 Kyle McLean and Jeff Rojek describe the interaction of policing and race. Although these topics are often controversial, the authors of these three chapters show us both the multitude of ways in which disparity can be described and measured and the importance of documenting the larger relationship between the criminal justice system and minority communities.

Lastly, it is equally important to study and measure the effectiveness of criminal justice interventions. Although focused primarily on correctional interventions, Faye Taxman and Brandy Blasko's Chapter 11 offers a primer on evaluation design. The authors discuss the challenges and multifaceted nature of necessary elements like treatment and rehabilitative programming; but, even more importantly, they consider the proximal indicators of success at the client and the organizational level. It is the global perspective on the design and measurement of programming that makes this a unique and timely addition to the literature. Eric Grommon and Jason Rydberg's Chapter 16 is a perfect complement to Taxman and Blasko's chapter. Within the framework of studying recidivism, they advocate for a detailed understanding of the underlying mechanisms of intervention and provide a graphical description of this process. The chapter also includes a broad discussion of the challenges of measuring recidivism; and its theoretical and empirical work is augmented with examples from the authors' own research. Scholars and practitioners alike have begun to estimate the costs of criminal justice interventions. In Chapter 18 Matt DeLisi does an excellent job of presenting to us the available literature and the prevailing formula for calculating costs. Equally importantly, he describes recent work that considers the costs of programming used to influence crime and criminality; and he tells us about future work of this type. Together, these chapters provide important insight into what works in criminal justice interventions. Given the recent focus on evidence-based interventions, this work is timely and useful for scholars, students, and practitioners alike.

We hope that you enjoy this book. Our summary of the chapters gives you only a taste of the detailed information you will find in the volume. Each chapter was written by one or more experts in the field – people with a rich experience of what works and (perhaps even more importantly) what does not work in the field of criminology and criminal justice. We hope that new students will use these chapters as primers for their own research, and that established scholars will use the new and emerging methodologies discussed here to improve their own work.

Part I

Measurement of Criminal Typologies

1

Violent Crime

Nicholas Corsaro

The empirical examination of criminal violence typically centers on four interrelated units of analysis: (1) individuals, (2) groups such as gangs and gang networks, (3) events, and (4) places. While there is certainly a high degree of overlap across each of these different units (e.g., gang members are more likely to target suitable victims in high-risk community contexts), the present chapter attempts to disentangle each of these various dimensions of violent crime. Its overall purpose is to help inform theory and practice and highlight the most promising violent crime prevention approaches that attempt to understand and address each of these various dimensions of violent crime.

The chapter is outlined as follows. First, a review of violent crime across individuals, groups, events, and places is provided. Second, for each of the various units of analysis, in-depth methodological and analytical discussions are presented regarding consistent findings in the literature as well as the latest developments in data analysis and research. Third, the chapter concludes with a discussion of promising police-led strategies designed to reduce violent crime that focus on places, incidents, individuals, and groups. Evaluation approaches used by researchers to test the utility of these police-led approaches are also highlighted.

Individual-Level Violence

A large body of research attempts to distinguish violent criminal behavior from more general forms of crime and deviance, while yet other research suggests that patterns in violence are simply a product of versatile criminal behavior (Osgood et al., 1988).

The Handbook of Measurement Issues in Criminology and Criminal Justice, First Edition.
Edited by Beth M. Huebner and Timothy S. Bynum.

These varying perspectives stem from a broader set of theoretical and analytical approaches, which attempt to explain antisocial behavior at the individual level. Gottfredson and Hirschi (1990) proposed that criminality is best explained by a general theory of crime, on the grounds that stable individual differences in criminal behavior are general rather than specific and are linked to low self-control and high impulsivity. From this perspective, those individuals who are more likely to seize the opportunity and commit criminal (and occasionally violent) acts are also more likely than most others to begin offending early on in their life, to offend more persistently, to engage in a variety of crimes, and to desist in later life (Dean, Brame, and Piquero, 1996; Hirschi and Gottfredson, 1995). In contrast to this perspective, some researchers have illustrated that offending patterns are dynamic rather than static.

For instance, Loeber (1990) argued that higher rates of overall offending predict an increased likelihood of violence. Farrington (1986) showed that the adolescent peak of offending within the age-crime curve reflects a temporary increase in the number of people involved in antisocial and delinquent behavior. Likewise, Moffitt (1993) proposed that there are two qualitatively distinct categories of individuals who engage in antisocial, delinquent, and criminal behaviors: adolescent-limited offenders and life-course-persistent offenders. Adolescent-limited offenders are offenders who tend to be temporarily involved in antisocial behavior during specific periods, calibrated with their own physical and social development. This larger group of individuals eventually age out. Comparatively, life-course-persistent offenders form a smaller group of individuals who engage in crime continuously. Figure 1.1 displays the average age–crime curve for all general arrests and violent arrests for 2000–2011 reported to the Federal Bureau of Investigations (FBI) (Bureau of Justice Statistics, 2014a).

Methodologically speaking, when researchers examine the intersection of age, race, gender, and offense-specific patterns of violence, it is important to understand that officially reported data such as arrests and crime incidents can be inherently biased (Cernkovich, Giordano, and Pugh, 1985). Arrests that serve as the starting point of official records of crime are funneled through police decision-making (Smith and Visher, 1981). Research indicates that police officers can observe similar patterns of behavior in different groups (e.g., males vs. females; blacks vs. whites) and then give different responses to similar incidents. For example, in a study that examined police officers' decisions to arrest in cases that involved physical violence between citizens, Smith (1987) specifically found that a number of contextual factors influenced police decisions to arrest, which included victim attributes (e.g., police were less likely to arrest in violent encounters involving black or female victims) and neighborhood context (e.g., police were more likely to arrest and less likely to use mediation in lower-status neighborhoods). Labeling theory helps explain social responses to crime and deviance. Sociologist Howard Becker (1963) argued that the application of a label to a person influences the way institutions of social control respond to that individual's behavior. In short, official arrest and incident data have the potential to be filtered through a lens of interpretation and decision-making processes that take place among police officers. Thus, while official data provide a

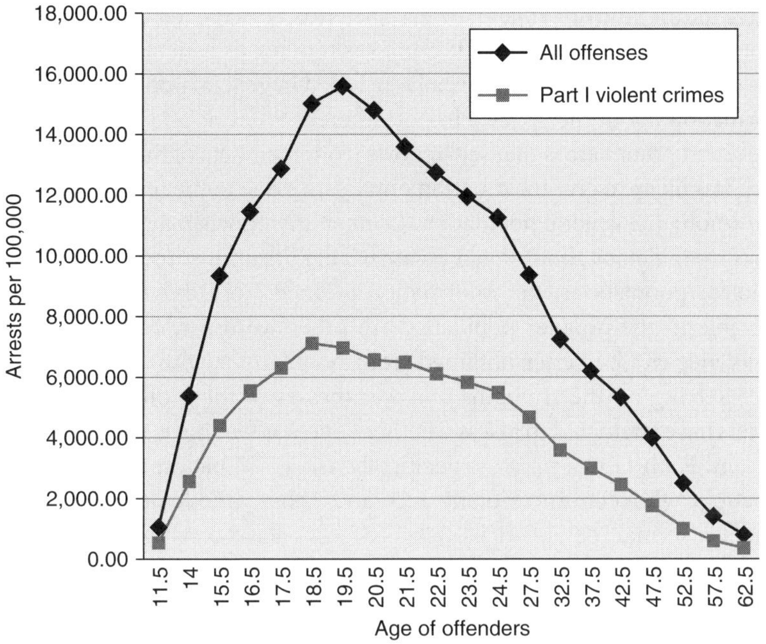

Figure 1.1 Age–crime curve for US arrests, 2000–2011.

relatively strong foundation for the measurement of criminal violence, such sources also have a number of serious limitations (e.g., unreported crimes; police officer decision-making; selection bias among citizens who report incidents) for those who attempt to more fully understand the nature and magnitude of violent crime. Indeed, data triangulation is a critical dimension for understanding individual patterns of offending over the life course.

Self-reported data provide more detailed information on behavioral patterns and are not influenced by the same potential biases as officially reported data. However, data from self-reports have an altogether different set of strengths and limitations. There are seemingly two important factors that researchers need to consider when examining self report data related to violence. First, does the analysis focus on gen eral crime and deviance or on specific crimes, such as violence and serious offenses? Analyses derived from data that focus only on more serious types of violence have the potential to ignore less serious and more typical types of crime (e.g., minor property offenses). Any theoretical test of violent offending should specifically model the causal processes that lead to violence; and those causal processes should be somewhat distinct from more general (and minor) offending patterns, if indeed offense specialization exists. Otherwise the sequencing of events may be quite similar, and violent crime is simply reflective of more general and more common types of crime.

Second, researchers must assess whether self-reports are drawn from institutionalized or noninstitutionalized populations. In the early 1990s, the National Research Council (NRC) argued that self-report studies from the general population are unsuitable for the study of violent crime. The NRC (1993) cited three reasons for this position: (1) the base rate of violent crimes is too low to generate reliable estimates; (2) truly violent persons are not typically included in general population samples; and (3) information about the sequencing of different types of offenses is not collected. The important point here is that self-reports from members of the general population are much less likely to give information on violence due to the relative infrequency of violence among the general population. Comparatively, when a richer context of violence and more details about it can be ascertained from institutionalized and previously violent populations, the information gleaned from these respondents is not generalizable to the broader population; in other words, more detailed narratives about violence can be better obtained from populations with a propensity toward violence. Relying on the strengths and weaknesses of these different data sources, researchers have attempted to assess whether violent offending is specialized in nature.

Reiss and Roth (1993, p. 381) specifically asked: "What are the differences between people who commit violent acts and those who commit more general, delinquent criminal, or antisocial acts?" Studies have consistently indicated that violent offenders tend to commit *more crimes* than nonviolent offenders. Thus, at the individual level, violent crimes seem to be a byproduct of overall offending patterns (simply put, they would be crimes at a higher overall rate). Additionally, there is no evidence that individual pathways to violence are empirically distinguishable from pathways that lead to general juvenile (and later adult) offending. Specifically, the family background and the childhood antisocial behavior of juveniles are quite similar for both high-frequency nonviolent and violent youths (Capaldi and Patterson, 1996; Piquero, 2000). Thus offense frequency accounts for most of the variation in violent offending for high-risk youths.

When examining individual-level correlates of violence, it is also necessary to analyze the role that victimization plays in the cycle of violence. Cohen, Kluegel, and Land (1981) argued that the probability of individual-level victimization is influenced by the following four factors: proximity to potential offenders; exposure to potential offenders; guardianship against victimization; and target attractiveness. From a violence-specific framework, guardianship and attractiveness usually refer to specific actions taken by victims that increase (or limit) their likelihood of victimization; such actions include deviant behaviors (Sampson and Lauritsen, 1990). The relationship between age and violent victimization risk is best described as a curve that peaks in the early to late teenage years, then drops precipitously through the remainder of the life course (Hirschi and Gottfredson, 1983). To illustrate this relationship, Figure 1.2 shows the average age and violent crime victimization risk for the period between 2000 and 2011 (Bureau of Justice Statistics, 2014b). Thus the violent crime age (Figure 1.1) and the violent victimization age (Figure 1.2) curves have considerable empirical overlap.

Individuals who are victimized during these critical developmental stages of adolescence are much more likely to suffer from a range of problems including depression, alcohol or drug dependence, phobic disorders, and more general forms of psychological distress (Robins and Rutter, 1990). Violent victimization during this

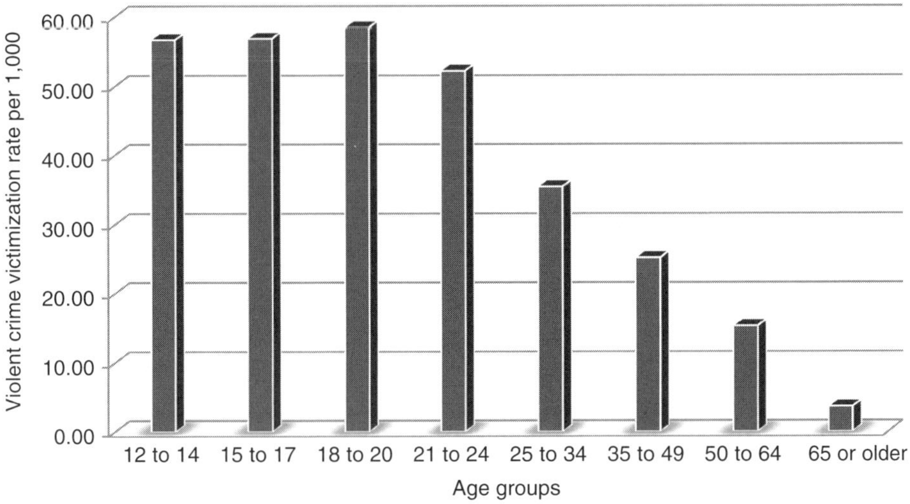

Figure 1.2 Violent crime victimization by age group, 2000–2011.

important time has long-term consequences such as disruption of social networks. In short, exposure to, and the consequences of, being a victim of physical, social, and psychological trauma as a teenager appear to potentially shape individuals' life-course trajectory, putting them at greater risk for both future victimization and future offending by disrupting stable transitions into adulthood. This also indirectly impacts opportunities for employment, normative beliefs, relationship stability, and support (Macmillan, 2001). Thus violent crime victimization and offending become cyclical in nature. Cycles of violence are perhaps best illustrated in group violence, particularly in the case of gangs.

Groups of Violent Offenders: The Case of Gangs

When high-risk individuals operate within, and are potentially influenced by, a network of offenders, the unit of analysis typically shifts to focus on group behavior – the most common of which is the focus on gangs. Certainly, it is possible to analyze gangs both at the individual level and at the macrolevel – in other words, it is possible to analyze individuals who are affiliated with gangs and broader social structures that facilitate gang membership. For the purpose of this discussion, the focus on gangs will be restricted to group-level processes (for a comprehensive review of prior gang research across multiple levels of analysis, see Decker, Melde, and Pyrooz, 2013). Gangs, and individuals within them, are at a substantially higher risk for violent offending and victimization (Short, 1997). However, the processes by which gang involvement influences violence are not always clear.

While gang membership is associated with an increased risk of violent offending and violent victimization, the extent to which gang membership plays a causal role in such changes in behavior is less clear (Thornberry et al., 1993). There are three theoretical frameworks that might explain how gang membership impacts delinquency and criminality: selection, facilitation, and enhancement. The selection model suggests that selection into a gang is the causal force behind the increased level of risk to gang members. Facilitation is a process whereby social learning, opportunity, and adaptation become primary reasons for increased risk to gang members. Enhancement is an intersection between selection and facilitation: the nature of the individual intersects with the nurture provided by the gang, which increases the predisposition (or penchant) toward violence in individuals who already have it. Melde and Esbensen (2013) found that gang membership has an independent effect on delinquency (even after controlling for selection effects), and that joining a gang is often associated with a reduction in informal social controls. Thus the group component of gang membership seemingly has an independent impact on individuals' levels of delinquency and violence.

There are also three potential mechanisms that likely lead to increased violence among gang members. First, the impact of group identity and collective orientation toward criminal involvement often facilitates group processes (Maxson and Esbensen, 2012). Specifically, individuals who adopt this orientation are more likely to obtain status within gangs. This is because gangs value a normative belief system that encourages and rewards toughness, power, and troublemaking (Miller, 1958). In short, advancing in a gang's hierarchy requires the willingness and capacity to resort to violence when this is deemed appropriate by the group.

Second, a gang's organizational structure also plays a role in violence, in that tightly woven organizations often help set and accomplish criminally oriented goals and can secure gang stability (Decker, Bynum, and Weisel, 1998). Gangs that are more loosely structured and less clearly defined have difficulty in obtaining status and accomplishing goals. Groups that are oriented toward violent crime from their organizational hierarchy will more likely resort to violence as a means of dispute resolution toward those goals.

Third, the intersection between self-identification and normative group orientation is perhaps the primary mechanism that explains gang violence at a group level. Decker et al. (2013) contend that the bonds between gang members are built on a normative orientation toward shared goals and interests, and those same bonds can serve as a catalyst for violence, for example in the form of response to a perceived insult or affront to face (Anderson, 1999). Likewise, Felson (2006) argues that gang members often engage in violence in order to protect themselves and because there are minimal sanctions that can be imposed upon them by agents of informal social control. Indeed, many gang members believe that they must utilize violence in response to symbolic threats to their status and that failure to do so would weaken individuals' normative orientations toward the gang – and the gang itself (Papachristos, 2009). From this perspective, direct victimization of an individual within the gang is shared indirectly among other members. This can have lasting consequences, due to the increased likelihood of a violent response.

A key methodological issue about gangs is that membership is often transient for many gang members (Thornberry et al., 1993). In order to capture the sequencing of life events that corresponds to behavior during membership phases, waves of surveys (self-report or victimization) are often utilized. However, repeated waves of cross-sectional surveys pose problems when one tries to disentangle the sequencing of life events from the actual change in behaviors. Stated simply, there is a gap between reported changes in behavior (as part of self-reported gang membership) and the reporting of those behaviors in surveys. Equal intervals of measurement are assumed for self-report analyses that use traditional regression-based methods. Additionally, more serious offenses are less frequent than minor offenses, which are difficult to parse out when attempting to examine offense frequency, severity, and specialization.

Understanding gang violence also requires an analysis of the microsocial contexts of group members. One common form of violence that occurs within gangs is retaliation (Decker, 1996). A review of the scholarly literature on homicides indicates that the majority of gang-related homicides are retaliatory, expressive, or spontaneous in nature (Klein and Maxson, 1989; Pizarro and McGloin, 2006). When one examines gang violence, incidents are often viewed through a lens that focuses on a contagion effect, where an initial incident can lead to a subsequent chain of violent incidents. This chain often sweeps up other high-risk individuals, as well as uninvolved bystanders caught up in the crossfire.

At a lower level, Hughes and Short (2005) illustrated that gang violence is often contextual and that pretexts for capturing gang incidents were critical to a more complete understanding of behavior. Specifically, the authors found that status concerns among gang members were the primary reason for violent responses to potential conflicts. These findings also highlight the need for violence research to analyze incidents (or events) as specific focal points.

Violent Crime Incidents

When critically examining violent crime incidents, it is imperative to understand the situational and contextual circumstances of the interaction between offender and victim, as well as its evolution. Cornish and Clarke (1986) proposed a rational choice perspective on criminality, according to which offenders weigh decision-making options differently across situationally and contextually different offense types. Thus, through this theoretical lens, violence looks different in nature from other, more general types of offending, because the motivations and circumstances for violent crime are different from the motivations and circumstances for other types of crime.

Incident-level analyses typically focus on exchanges between actors (i.e., victims, offenders, and third parties). An aggregate analysis conducted by Rand (1994) illustrates that, of the 1.4 million hospital emergency department patients treated for nonfatal injuries, 47 percent were most likely to be injured by someone known: a spouse, an intimate partner, a family member, a friend, or an acquaintance. Table 1.1 provides a breakdown of reported relationships between offenders and victims who

Table 1.1 Violent crime victim–offender relationships.

Relationship	*Offenses*	*Percent*
Unrecorded relationship	389,151	29%
Friend or acquaintance	308,644	23%
Stranger	308,630	23%
Parent, child, or relative	107,352	8%
Current boyfriend/girlfriend	134,190	10%
Spouse or former spouse	93,933	7%
Total	**1,341,900**	**100%**

sought hospital attention after violent victimization in 1994. Roughly half of all victims knew their assailants prior to their victimization. Indeed only 23 percent of all violent victimizations were reported as stranger-related.

In many cases violent events unfold as a result of "character contests" where there is a confrontation between actors to establish or save face in social occasions (Goffman, 1967). One of the most widely studied violent criminal events, homicide, has the lowest dark (or unknown) figure of crime. Thus, official records of homicide incidents tend to represent the actually known distribution of these events as they occur within a population. The analysis of situational transactions typically relies on a diverse range of methodological approaches such as ethnographies, in-depth respondent interviews, and various classifications of characteristics that occur in violent crime events. A number of different data collection approaches are used to obtain this type of detailed information, for instance participant observation, field notes, interviews, surveys, and coding of official records (e.g., police reports). The goal of these various methodological approaches is to collect data in such ways that the researcher imposes very little personal bias onto them and social meanings are perceived from the points of view of the research participants (Orbuch, 1997). In terms of criminal violence, situational analyses have been adapted to examine homicide incidents; and here two general findings have emerged (Luckenbill, 1977).

First, the majority of homicides occur during leisurely hours (between 6 p.m. and 2 a.m.), and particularly at the weekend (Messner and Tardiff, 1985). Homicide risk is also highest where informal affairs permit a wide range of acceptable (though illegal) activities among the various actors involved. Leisurely activities often include drinking, taking drugs, selling and purchasing sex, and gambling, to name a few. Of course, other homicides involve intimates such as spouses, family members, friends, or coworkers; and still a small proportion of homicides involve actors with little to no familiarity to one another.

Second, Luckenbill (1977) found that the majority of homicide incidents progressed through a series of stages or steps through which the victim – the person who gets killed – and the offender – the person who commits the killing – negotiate the event. These stages typically unfold as follows: (1) an initial (perceived) offense to face committed by one actor (typically, the homicide victim); (2) an interpretation by the other actor (typically, the eventual offender) that the transgression was personally offensive and requires a response; (3) a decision by the eventual offender to stand his or her ground, in an effort to reaffirm face; (4) a decision by the eventual victim whether to stand his or her ground or to apologize (and possibly lose face to the audience); (5) a battle where the lethal act takes place; and (6) the final stage, where the offender has to decide what to do and where to go after the victim was fatally injured. In short, most homicides examined by Luckenbill (1977) were not one-sided events with unwitting victims who assumed a passive role, but rather were likely to include dynamic interchanges between offenders, victims, and third parties.

Felson and Steadman (1983) extended situational event analyses to encompass both assaults and homicides. In their review of incidents, these authors found that casting a person into a negative situational role often resulted in retaliatory actions designed to demonstrate a more favorable identity (e.g., by counterthreating or counterattacking). Violent assaults and homicides often occur as a function of a perceived violation of conduct during a serious altercation or event. Felson and Steadman also found that, in the vast majority of homicides with witnesses, these third parties often served as antagonists rather than mediators. Thus the situational aspects of violence are complex in that witnesses often play some role in violent events.

Research also suggests that nonlethal violent events involving intimates (e.g., domestic violence assaults) are similar to fatal incidents. Dobash and Dobash (1984) illustrated that violent domestic events across various individuals seemingly display similarities in terms of sequencing. Often males with a propensity toward violence attempt to control their intimate partners and display behaviors associated with jealousy and possessiveness. Concerns about money and relationship stability are also typical triggers among high-risk actors. Female victims reported that offenders typically became physically violent when their authority was challenged or in situations of perceived loss of authority. Importantly, narrative interviews indicated that the violence rarely consisted of a single physical attack but rather involved a series of attacks (e.g., multiple slaps or blows). A common response by victims was to stop the argument, in an effort to deescalate the violence; likewise, a typical response by offenders was to act as though nothing happened, so that interactions typically returned to pre-violence level – until the next event.

From a methodological standpoint, early versions of situational crime research utilized official police records from assaults and homicides, though this data source had limited information in terms of unraveling the dynamic development of events. Interview and community participation methods are better suited to disentangle interactional and situational aspects of violence. For example, Straus (1979) relied on the conflict tactic scale (CTS) in order to empirically understand the dynamics of conflicts and subsequent violence. The CTS (and its later versions) typically involves a researcher's conducting an assessment with a victim or a perpetrator of prior violent activity (or with both) by asking and measuring how often in the past period of investigation (e.g., in the past year) that person discussed difficult issues with his/her spouse, insulted or swore at the spouse, smashed, hit, or kicked something (including his/her spouse), and feels in control of things happening to him/her

(Straus, 1979). Scoring takes place on three distinct parameters: prevalence (which establishes whether an assault, injury, or sexual coercion ever occurred); frequency (which establishes the number of times an event has occurred over a period of time, such as the past year), and severity (which can be nonexistent, minor, or severe). Detailed measurement tools like the CTS provide researchers with more explicit facts about how often violent events unfold and how serious they are. Likewise, there is a need to focus on the context in which violence occurs.

The Geography of Violent Crime

One of the most consistent findings in criminology is that crime and violence are not randomly distributed across geographic space. There are consistent structural correlates that correspond with violent crime at varying geographic levels: neighborhoods, cities, counties, standard metropolitan statistical areas, hot spots, and street segments. However, this seemingly commonsensical finding has actually resulted from a long and arduous research process, and the nuances of analysis are more complex than might otherwise appear. A place-based orientation to explaining violence has its roots in Shaw and McKay's (1942) modeling of juvenile delinquency, which contains their analysis of serious and violent juvenile offenses by place. The Chicago-based researchers argued that, at a geographical level, ethnic heterogeneity, residential instability, and poor economic status disrupted the social organization of communities, which led to high rates of crime and delinquency by juveniles across neighborhoods. In short, their analysis focused on the places that presented high rates of delinquency over time.

Likewise, Bullock (1955) examined homicide distributions across census tracts in Houston, Texas in the 1940s. As in earlier community level research, Bullock found that homicides were disproportionally more likely to occur in economically disadvantaged communities, which had high rates of unemployment combined with limited opportunities for social advancement. Similarly, Curry and Spergel (1988) found that a multidimensional measure of poverty – unemployment, people below the poverty level, and mortgage investment – simultaneously incorporated into a single item, had large and significant positive effects on gang-related homicide rates in Chicago in the late 1970s through the mid-1980s. Indeed, economic status (and strain) is almost always a significant associate of violence across the vast majority of studies.

Taylor and Covington (1988) found that changes in community structure, especially in neighborhoods that experienced declines in economic status and stability, were linked to increases in aggregate-level violence. In particular, they found that neighborhoods that experienced sharp increases in housing populations also experienced increases in violent crime. The authors argued that in underclass neighborhoods increases in violence were correlated with increases in deprivation, while in redeveloping neighborhoods violence was associated with broader community disorganization.

Researchers have worked to examine the specific influence of urban social structure on violence, and this has not been easy to disentangle. Multiple investigations often use different measures to capture similar social structural components (e.g., poverty, unemployment, and disadvantage), and these different variables are usually highly correlated. In the 1980s, when each measure was introduced separately and independently, inconsistent findings and biased results began to emerge in the literature.

In order to address this major methodological limitation, Land, McCall, and Cohen (1990) examined city- and state-level measures that correspond to violence from 1960 to 1980. While their study included data collected over a 20-year span, the analyses were conducted through a series of piecewise (or independent) cross-sectional statistical models (the 1960s' model; the 1970s' model; the 1980s' model). Land and colleagues specifically found that most of the following measures within cities and states were consistently represented across a host of different studies: population size and density; percentage of population living in poverty; unemployed people; black people; children living with a single parent; and median home income. Up to that point, scholars interested in a macrosocial explanation of violence most often attempted to assess the independent and unique influences on violence for these highly interrelated measures. Land and colleagues proposed the use of principal components analysis, which for their investigation collapsed this highly interrelated set of variables into two factors: population structure (population size and population density) and resource deprivation (measures of income inequality, percentage of poverty, and children living with single parents). By using this type of strategy, Land and colleagues were able to conduct an analysis that was more accurate and reduced the threat of model misspecification. They concluded that population structure, resource deprivation, and the proportion of divorced males in the population consistently correspond to homicide rates at a macrosocial level. Thus their study demonstrated the need for an analytic modeling of violence, designed to control for the high degree of interrelatedness between measures that basically capture similar social process. Land and colleagues' findings demonstrated that, taken together, the multiple dimensions of disadvantage (e.g., poverty, unemployment) illustrate how poor economic conditions, sources of strain, and blocked opportunities correlate to citywide levels of lethal violence over time. The use of principal components analysis to capture the combined variation of multiple indicators of a single concept has since become commonplace across scholarly research.

While research shows a relationship between social structure and violent crime in city neighborhoods, understanding why changes in poverty as well as population demography are related to violence at a structural level has been a key problem in criminological research. In agreement with a social disorganization framework and a cross-sectional research design, Krivo and Peterson (1996) found that higher rates of ethnic minorities often correlate to higher rates of violent crime. This more general finding has been established since the 1960s, and a number of sociological perspectives have attempted to explain it through a variety of theoretical perspectives, such as the theory of a subculture of violence (Wolfgang and Ferracuti, 1967) and the theory of neighborhood strain (Agnew 1992).

Liska and Bellair (1995) were among the first to challenge a key assumption that the relationship between ethnic minority levels and crime rates (including violent crime rates) occurred in a unilateral direction (i.e., that higher levels of minorities led to higher violent crime levels). In fact the authors concluded that a reverse relationship between ethnic minority levels and crime seems to exist. More specifically, in their city-level analysis Liska and Bellair found evidence that higher violent crime rates preceded changes in the racial and ethnic composition of cities (e.g., an exodus of white residents, combined with a growth of ethnic minorities, often occurred after crime had already began to increase). Moreover, Hipp (2011) relied on a longitudinal panel research design and extended this inquiry to the neighborhood level, where he found that white residents are seemingly more likely than minority residents to escape neighborhoods with increasing violent crime, and thus are more likely than ethnic minorities to avoid moving into neighborhoods with higher levels of violent crime. In short, white residents, according to Hipp (2011: 428) "avoid violent crime neighborhoods as much as possible," particularly by comparison with nonwhite residents.

The importance of this research from a measurement and analytic standpoint is that it demonstrates how sequential theories and explanations of violent crime that rely on the use of cross-sectional data (i.e., data taken at one point in time) have the serious potential to lead to inconclusive, ambiguous, and altogether biased conclusions. Thus the use of longitudinal data collection strategies, research methodologies, and analytic techniques has become quite commonplace in contemporary crime and place research. Perhaps nowhere is this better illustrated than in crime in microgeographic contexts such as hot spots and street segments.

The examination of microcrime contexts centers on the concentration of specific locations such as addresses, street segments, or crime clusters (i.e., hot spots) within larger social environments such as communities and neighborhoods. These places have been shown to make up a disproportionate level of criminal offending. Earlier cross-sectional research shows that a very significant clustering of overall crime occurs in a small number of areas. In Minneapolis for example, over half of all calls to police services were found to be concentrated in less than 5 percent of locations within the city (Sherman, Gartin, and Buerger, 1989). Extending the intersection between crimes and geographic context further, Sherman and Weisburd (1995) were also among the first to demonstrate the heterogeneous nature of crime at different places – namely that most locations have none to very few crimes, while certain locations consistently experience serious crime-clustering – including clusters of violent crime.

The practical and theoretical implications for focusing resources on hot spots was called into question by Spelman (1995), who argued that, if hot spots of crime simply shift rapidly from place to place over time, it is far too difficult to understand the process and focus crime control resources on such locations. From a methodological standpoint, the reliance on cross-sectional data would never allow for a more thorough understanding of the elements of stability and change in these social processes. Longitudinal research designs therefore became necessary in order for these empirical limitations to be addressed. Thus studies that focused on the intersection of crime and place began to utilize the same longitudinal and developmental-trajectory analytical methods that had been employed to assess individuals' risk of offending.

By drawing upon longitudinal data from over 14 years of crime incidents recorded in street segments in Seattle, Washington, Weisburd et al. (2004) found that roughly 84 percent of street segments had extremely stable trajectories of crime. Thus crime is not only concentrated at a small number of places, but also stable in most places as well. Additionally, Braga, Papachristos, and Hureau (2010) demonstrated the concentration of gun violence in microplaces by showing that, in over 30 years, less than 3 percent of street segments and intersections in the city accounted for over 50 percent of all gun violence incidents in Boston, Massachusetts. In essence, violent crime at microplaces does not appear to fluctuate in either a random or a systematic way; rather its underlying causes seem to facilitate similar levels of violence over time.

Many of the longitudinal studies of place relied on the use of growth curve estimation and group-based trajectory analysis (GBTA) as the analytic techniques that accounts for both change and continuity in behavior over time. The use of GBTA was first introduced by Nagin and Land (1993) in order to model developmental patterns of individual criminality. The primary assumption of GBTA is that patterns of observations of interest over time can be approximated with a discrete number of groups characterized by polynomial growth curves (Nagin, 2005). Specifically, GBTA is designed to identify latent groups of individuals (or places) with similar developmental pathways. When modeling the developmental pathways, GBTA allows individuals to follow different trajectories on the basis of observed values. This approach allows the researcher to approximate developmental processes in a dynamic way rather than in the traditional, static way, which makes GBTA quite attractive for researchers interested in understanding long-term trends. As an analytical approach, it allows researchers to compare differences in the stability and continuity of offending patterns over time, across individuals or across different geographic contexts. GBTA has been adapted to model in a similar way the distribution of crime at specific microplaces (Weisburd et al., 2004), as well as at large-scale macroplaces such as neighborhoods (Griffiths and Chavez, 2004) and cities (McCall, Land, and Parker, 2011).

We see both that violent crime is nonrandomly distributed over space and that the factors leading to violence appear to be quite stable across geographic contexts. Additionally, from a public policy standpoint, if violence is heavily concentrated and stable in specific places, implementing the most promising violence reduction strategies will often entail the use of a geographic component. Indeed, the most effective violent crime strategies attempt to disrupt the intersection of high-risk offenders and high-risk contexts.

Criminal Justice Strategies Designed to Reduce Violent Crime

While the evidence for crime prevention benefits across specific components of the criminal justice system has historically been mixed (Durlaf and Nagin, 2011), an emerging body of evidence has amassed that highlights the utility of strategic and focused policing interventions. In 2004 the National Academy of Sciences (NAS) reported that the strongest evidence for the impact of policing on crime relates to law enforcement strategies that are highly focused on specific crime problems (see Weisburd and Eck, 2004). A series of meta-analyses indicates that other types of highly diverse, concentrated, and comprehensive police-led strategies has the potential to significantly reduce the risk of violence in places that are high on crime and among groups of offenders with a propensity toward violence (Braga, Papachristos, and Hureau forthcoming; Braga and Weisburd, 2012; Weisburd et al., 2010).

A comprehensive violence reduction strategy requires the use of detailed data collection, analysis, and interpretation in order to guide the necessary planning phases that precede a specific focus on underlying violent crime problems. The present section highlights how police take into account information gleaned from the various overlapping units of analysis discussed earlier (incidents, places, individuals, and groups) in order to appropriately guide police strategies. Certainly, it is not feasible to review all known police-led initiatives that focus on these dimensions and aim to reduce violence. In order to illustrate how law enforcement has relied on data collection strategies for the reduction of violent crime risk, only a few prominent targeted strategies are highlighted here.

In New York City (NYC), CompStat was implemented in 1994 by then Chief William Bratton, in part as a possible approach to addressing the record number of homicides that the city experienced in the early 1990s. The NYC police department used crime mapping to identify locations within the city that were experiencing both serious (i.e., violent) and minor nuisance offenses. The organizational strategy held commanders in the various precincts accountable for developing solutions to serious crimes (Kelling and Sousa, 2001). The mapped data were intended to help officials develop coordinated plans for addressing those problems. Weekly CompStat meetings were attended by commanders of all precincts, police service areas, and operational unit divisions. During the presentation at the CompStat meetings, executive staff members probed commanders about crime and arrest activity as well as about specific cases (i.e., incident-based analyses), in order to assess whether there were underlying themes that linked different incidents to a deeper crime problem. The CompStat framework has since become widely adopted among urban US police agencies across the country (Kelling and Coles, 1996).

Kelling and Sousa (2001) found a relationship between misdemeanor arrests (a key component in the broader NYC police strategy of addressing minor offenses in order to reduce more serious types of crime) and decreases in violent crime. The authors also included measures of drug involvements, unemployment, and age composition changes in their analyses in order to assess whether any changes in violent crime in New York occurred above and beyond these other confounding factors and might have led to changes in crime. However, their evaluation design only looked at changes in crime observed in NYC.

Comparatively, Harcourt (2001) found that the change in NYC's violent crime rate was very consistent with similar reductions in violence encountered in San Diego, San Antonio, Houston, San Francisco, Los Angeles, and other large urban cities that had not implemented similar police reforms. A comparative analytical approach that relied on a quasi-experimental design – namely a comparison of crime trends in NYC with crime trends in other cities, which did not experience the same type of stop-and-frisk policing – was a strong methodological evaluation improvement. Ultimately the results obtained through this method called into question just how much of an effect CompStat policing had, when other cities registered declines in violence in the absence of the same police-led strategy. A host of additional studies have relied upon the counterfactual design when assessing the strategy and almost all agree that CompStat likely had some impact on overall NYC violence, although it remains unclear just how much (Harcourt, 2001; Rosenfeld, Fornango, and Baumer 2005; for a critical assessment of this evaluation approach, see Berk, 2005). Thus, when examining the impact of a police-led intervention within a targeted geographic context, it is important to assess whether comparable contexts minus some type of intervention also experienced similar changes in violence. Such a design provides more confidence that a given police-led approach was at least partially responsible for changes in violence.

Another police-led strategic approach to violence reduction that channels resources to underlying problems is the development of multiagency violent crime incident reviews. The NAS Panel on the Understanding and Control of Violent Behavior found through research on problem-oriented policing initiatives that modified places and changes in routine activities could contribute much to the understanding and control of violence (Reiss and Roth, 1993). Problem-oriented interventions arise from diagnoses of problems and from responses that are developed accordingly. Strategic problem analysis is a tool of problem-oriented policing and involves collecting and analyzing data on the nature of homicide and other types of interrelated violence in order to identify and understand event characteristics.

For example, in Boston, Massachusetts a working group of researchers, law enforcement officials, state and federal prosecutors, correctional officials, social service providers, and religious and community leaders worked in tandem to address youth gang homicide. More specifically, the Boston strategy was also designed to reduce gang and gun violence by using two deterrence-based strategies (Braga et al., 2001). First, target enforcement efforts were utilized against gun traffickers who were supplying illegal firearms in locations with a history of gun incidents. Second, highly active and violent youth gangs were summoned by the police to "call-in" sessions designed to make them aware of the specific penalties that would be leveraged against them individually (maximum prosecution, the use of federal prosecution where applicable, and no chance of community corrections) if any member of the group were to continue to engage in serious violence after the notification session.

As a way to convey the deterrent-laden message, law enforcement and prosecutors explained to groups of notified gang members that any further engagement in serious violence would force officials to "pull every lever" legally available in order to punish gang members (Kennedy, 1997, p. 463). These notification sessions were often held publicly in crime-stricken communities (e.g., neighborhood churches) in order to illustrate a collective public response to the violence (see Kennedy, 2009). The overall goal of Operation Ceasefire was to deter from violent crime by increasing the certainty and severity of punishment – but only in highly focused contexts, namely with chronic and violent groups of offenders.

The Boston Ceasefire strategy correlated with declines in citywide levels of youth homicide by roughly 63 percent after implementation (Braga et al., 2001). While some studies have questioned the specific magnitude of the Ceasefire effect on levels of youth homicide and gun violence within the city (Rosenfeld et al., 2005), a number of additional sites have since replicated the approach, and a series of evaluations have provided further evidence of a significant impact on violent crime (Braga et al., 2008; Engel, Tillyer, and Corsaro, 2013; McGarrell et al., 2006; Papachristos, Meares, and Fagan, 2007). Thus there is evidence that a comprehensive analysis of individuals, groups (gangs), places, and incidents can lead to promising results in terms of an impact on violent crime. In short, the various units of analysis presented here have the ability to inform theory as well as practice and policy.

Conclusion

Violent crime is a multidimensional concept. Violent crime incidents involve an intersection of people, groups, and places. Among individuals at risk for violence, there appear to be developmental pathways that lead to an increased likelihood of violent crime offending, as well as to other, more general types of crime. There is also a group dynamic to violence. High-risk individuals can be influenced by groups such as gangs, which cause the likelihood of both violent offending and victimization to increase exponentially while they are in a gang. At a geographic level, there are specific structural conditions such as resource constraints that correlate to violent crime incidents over time. Thus a contextual understanding of violence is critical. Theoretical explanations and practical policy approaches that aim to address violence must rely on a comprehensive analysis of incidents in order to assess the overlap among these various concepts. When this happens, we see strong evidence that analyzing detailed narratives about individuals, groups, places, and events can help law enforcement craft specific responses, which reduce the risk of violent crime. It is also highly likely that data collection strategies, measurement and analytical issues, and policy approaches that focus specifically on violent crime will continue to be at the forefront of future criminological research.

References

Agnew, R. 1992. Foundation for a general strain theory of crime and delinquency. *Criminology*, 30: 47–87.

Anderson, E. 1999. *Code of the street: Decency, violence, and the moral life of the inner city.* New York: Norton.

Becker, H. S. 1963. *Studies in the sociology of deviance.* New York: Free Press.

Berk, R. A. 2005. Knowing when to fold 'em: An essay on evaluating the impact of ceasefire, compstat, and exile. *Criminology and Public Policy*, 4: 451–466.

Braga, A. A., Kennedy, D. M., Waring, E. J., and Piehl, A. M. 2001. Problem-oriented policing, deterrence, and youth violence: An evaluation of Boston's Operation Ceasefire. *Journal of Research in Crime and Delinquency*, 38: 195–226.

Braga, A. A., Papachristos, A. V., and Hureau, D. M. 2010. The concentration and stability of gun violence at micro-places in Boston, 1980–2008. *Journal of Quantitative Criminology*, 26: 33–53.

Braga, A. A., Papachristos, A. V., and Hureau, D. M. Forthcoming. The effects of hot spots policing on crime: An updated systematic review and meta-analysis. *Justice Quarterly*.

Braga, A. A., Pierce, G. L., McDevitt, J., Bond, B. J., and Cronin, S. 2008. The strategic prevention of gun violence among gang-involved offenders. *Justice Quarterly*, 25: 132–162.

Braga, A. A., and Weisburd, D. 2012. The effects of focused deterrence strategies on crime: A systematic review and meta-analysis of the empirical evidence. *Journal of Research in Crime and Delinquency*, 49: 323–358.

Bullock, H. A. 1955. Urban homicide in theory and fact. *Journal of Criminal Law, Criminology and Police Science*, 45: 565–575.

Bureau of Justice Statistics, 2014a. Arrest data analysis tool. Accessed January 15, 2014. http://www.bjs.gov/index.cfm?ty=datool&surl=/arrests/index.cfm#.

Bureau of Justice Statistics, 2014b. National victimization analysis tool. Accessed January 23, 2014. http://www.bjs.gov/index.cfm?ty=nvat.

Capaldi, D. M., and G. R. Patterson. 1996. Can violent offenders be distinguished from frequent offenders? Prediction from childhood to adolescence. *Journal of Research in Crime and Delinquency*, 33: 206–231.

Cernkovich, S. A., Giordano, P. C., and Pugh, M. D. 1985. Chronic offenders: The missing cases in self-report delinquency research. *The Journal of Criminal Law and Criminology*, 76: 705–732.

Cohen, L. E., Kluegel, J. R., and Land, K. C. 1981. Social inequality and predatory victimization: An exposition and test of a formal theory. *American Sociological Review*, 46: 505–524.

Cornish, D., and Clarke, R. V. 1986. Introduction. In *The reasoning criminal*, edited by D. Cornish and R. V. Clarke, 1–16. New York: Springer.

Curry, G. D., and Spergel, I. A. 1988. Gang homicide, delinquency, and community. *Criminology*, 26: 381–406.

Dean, C. W., Brame, R., and Piquero, A. 1996. Criminal propensities, discrete groups of offenders, and persistence in crime. *Criminology*, 34: 547–575.

Decker, S. H. 1996. Collective and normative features of gang violence. *Justice Quarterly*, 13: 243–264.

Decker, S. H., Bynum, T. S., and Weisel, D. 1998. A tale of two cities: Gangs as organized crime groups. *Justice Quarterly*, 15: 395–425.

Decker, S. H., Melde, C., and Pyrooz, D. 2013. What do we know about gangs and gang members and where do we go from here? *Justice Quarterly*, 30: 369–402.

Dobash, R. E., and Dobash, R. P. 1984. The nature and antecedents of violent events. *British Journal of Criminology*, 24: 269–288.

Durlaf, S. N., and Nagin, D. S. 2011. Imprisonment and crime: Can both be reduced? *Criminology and Public Policy*, 10: 13–54.

Engel, R. S., Tillyer, M. S., and Corsaro, N. 2013. Reducing gang violence using focused deterrence: Evaluating the Cincinnati Initiative to Reduce Violence (CIRV). *Justice Quarterly*, 30: 403–439.

Farrington, D. P. 1986. Age and crime. *Crime and Justice: A Review of Research*, 7: 189–250.

Felson, M. 2006. *Crime and nature*. Thousand Oaks, CA: Sage.

Felson, R. B., and Steadman, H. J. 1983. Situational factors in disputes leading to criminal violence. *Criminology*, 21: 59–74.

Goffman, E. R. 1967. *Interaction ritual: Essays on face-to-face behavior*. New York: Anchor Books.

Gottfredson, M. R., and Hirschi, T. 1990. *A general theory of crime*. Stanford, CA: Stanford University Press.

Griffiths, E., and Chavez, J. M. 2004. Communities, street guns, and homicide trajectories in Chicago, 1980–1995: Merging methods for examining homicide trends across space and time. *Criminology*, 42: 941–978.

Harcourt, B. 2001. *Illusion of order: The false promise of broken windows policing*. Cambridge, MA: Harvard University Press.

Hipp, J. R. 2011. Violent crime, mobility decisions, and neighborhood racial/ethnic transition. *Social Problems*, 58: 410–432.

Hirschi, T., and Gottfredson, M. R. 1983. Age and the explanation of crime. *The American Journal of Sociology*, 89: 552–584.

Hirschi, T., and Gottfredson, M. R. 1995. Control theory and the life-course perspective. *Studies on Crime and Crime Prevention*, 4: 131–142.

Hughes, L. A., and Short, J. F. 2005. Disputes involving gang members: Micro-social contexts. *Criminology*, 43: 43–76.

Kelling, G., and Coles, C. M. 1996. *Fixing broken windows: Restoring order and reducing crime in our communities*. New York: Free Press.

Kelling G., and Sousa, W. H., Jr. 2001. *Do police matter? An analysis of the impact of New York City's police reforms*. Manhattan Institute Civic Report. Manhattan, NY: Manhattan Institute Center for Civic Innovation.

Kennedy, D. 1997. Pulling levers: Chronic offenders, high-crime settings, and a theory of prevention. *Valparaiso University Law Review*, 31: 449–484.

Kennedy, D. 2009. *Deterrence and crime prevention: Reconsidering the prospect of sanction*. New York: Routledge.

Klein, M. W., and Maxson, C. L. 1989. Street gang violence. In *Violent crime, violent criminals*, edited by M. Wolfgang and N. A. Weiner, 198–234. Beverly Hills, CA: Sage.

Krivo, L. J., and Peterson, R. 1996. Extremely disadvantaged neighborhoods and urban crime. *Social Forces*, 75: 619–650.

Land, K. C., McCall, P. L., and Cohen, L. E. 1990. Structural covariates of homicide rates: Are there any invariances across time and social space? *The American Journal of Sociology*, 95: 922–963.

Liska, A. E., and Bellair, P. E. 1995. Violent crime rates and racial composition: Convergence over time. *American Journal of Sociology*, 101: 578–610.

Loeber, R. 1990. Development and risk factors of juvenile antisocial behavior and delinquency. *Clinical Psychology Review*, 10: 1–41.

Luckenbill, D. F. 1977. Criminal homicide as a situated transaction. *Social Problems*, 25: 176–186.

Macmillan, R. 2001. Violence and the life course: Assessing the consequences of violent victimization for personal and social development. *Annual Review of Sociology*, 27: 1–22.

Maxson, C. L., and Esbensen, F.-A. 2012. The intersection of gang definition and group process: Concluding observations. In *Youth gangs in international perspective: Tales from the Eurogang program of research*, edited by C. L. Maxson and F.-A. Esbensen, 303–315. New York: Springer.

McCall, P. L., Land, K. C., and Parker, K. F. 2011. Heterogeneity in the rise and decline of city-level homicide rates, 1976–2005: A Latent Trajectory Analysis. *Social Science Research*, 40: 363–378.

McGarrell, E. F., Chermak, S., Wilson, J. M., and Corsaro, N. 2006. Reducing homicide through a "lever-pulling" strategy. *Justice Quarterly*, 23: 214–231.

Melde, C., and Esbensen, F.-E. 2013. Gangs and violence: Disentangling the impact of gang membership on the level and nature of offending. *Journal of Quantitative Criminology*, 29: 143–166.

Messner, S. F., and Tardiff, K. 1985. The social ecology of urban homicide: An application of the routine activities approach. *Criminology*, 23: 241–267.

Miller, W. B. 1958. Lower class culture as a generating milieu of gang delinquency. *Journal of Social Issues*, 14: 5–19.

Moffitt, T. E. 1993. Adolescence-limited and life-course persistent antisocial behavior: A developmental taxonomy. *Psychological Review*, 100: 674–701.

Nagin, D. S. 2005. *Group-based modeling of development*. Cambridge, MA: Harvard University Press.

Nagin, D. S. and Land, K. C. 1993. Age, criminal careers, and population heterogeneity: Specification and estimation of a nonparametric, mixed poisson model. *Criminology*, 31: 327–362.

National Research Council (NRC). 1993. *Losing generations: Adolescents in high-risk settings*. Washington, DC: National Academy Press.

Orbuch, T. L. 1997. People's accounts count: The sociology of accounts. *Annual Review of Sociology*, 23: 455–478.

Osgood, D. W., Johnston, L. D., O'Malley, P. M., and Bachman, J. G. 1988. The generality of deviance in late adolescence and early adulthood. *American Sociological Review*, 53: 81–93.

Papachristos, A. V. 2009. Murder by structure: Dominance relations and the social structure of gang homicide. *American Journal of Sociology*, 115: 74–128.

Papachristos, A. V., Meares, T. L., and Fagan, J. 2007. Attention felons: Evaluating project safe neighborhoods in Chicago. *Journal of Empirical Legal Studies*, 4: 223–272.

Piquero, A. 2000. Frequency, specialization, and violence in offending careers. *Journal of Research in Crime and Delinquency*, 37: 392–418.

Pizarro, J. M., and McGloin, J. M. 2006. Explaining gang homicides in Newark, New Jersey: Collective Behavior or Social Disorganization? *Journal of Criminal Justice*, 34: 195–207.

Rand, M. R. 1994. *Violence-related injuries treated in hospital emergency departments*. Washington, DC: Bureau of Justice Statistics.

Reiss, A. J., and Roth, J. A. 1993. *Understanding and preventing violence*. Washington, DC: National Academy Press.

Robins, L., and Rutter, M. 1990. *Straight and devious pathways from childhood to adulthood*. Cambridge: Cambridge University Press.

Rosenfeld, R., Fornango, R., and Baumer, E. 2005. Did ceasefire, compstat, and exile reduce homicide? *Criminology and Public Policy*, 4: 419–450.

Sampson, R. J., and Lauritsen, J. L. 1990. Deviant lifestyles, proximity to crime, and the offender–victim link in personal violence. *Journal of Research in Crime and Delinquency*, 27: 110–139.

Shaw, C. R., and McKay, H. D. 1942. *Juvenile delinquency in urban areas*. Chicago, IL: University of Chicago Press.

Sherman, L., and Weisburd, D. L. 1995. General deterrent effects of police patrol in crime hot spots: A randomized controlled trial. *Justice Quarterly*, 12: 625–48.

Sherman, L., Gartin, P., and Buerger, M. 1989. Hot spots of predatory crime: Routine activities and the criminology of place. *Criminology*, 27: 27–56.

Short, J. F. 1997. *Poverty, ethnicity, and violent crime*. Boulder, CO: Westview Press.

Smith, D. A. 1987. Police response to interpersonal violence: Defining the parameters of legal control. *Social Forces*, 65: 767–782.

Smith, D. A., and Visher, C. A. 1981. Street-level justice: Situational determinants of police arrest decisions. *Social Problems*, 29: 167–177.

Spelman, W. 1995. Criminal careers of public places. In *Crime and place: Crime prevention studies*, vol. 4, edited by J. E. Eck and D. Weisburd, 115–144. Monsey, NY: Willow Tree Press.

Straus, M. A. 1979. Measuring intra-family conflict and violence: The conflict tactics scale. *Journal of Marriage and the Family*, 41: 75–88.

Taylor, R. B., and Covington, J. 1988. Neighborhood changes in ecology and violence. *Criminology*, 26: 553–590.

Thornberry, T. P., Krohn, M. D., Lizotte, A. J., and Chard-Wierschem, D. 1993. The role of juvenile gangs in facilitating delinquent behavior. *Journal of Research in Crime and Delinquency*, 30: 75–85.

Weisburd, D., Bushway, S., Lum, C., and Yang, S.-M. 2004. Trajectories of crime at places: A longitudinal study of street segments in the city of Seattle. *Criminology*, 42: 283–321.

Weisburd, D., and Eck, J. E. 2004. What Can the Police Do to Reduce Crime, Disorder and Fear? *Annals of the American Academy of Social and Political Sciences,* 593: 42–65.

Weisburd, D., Telep, C. W., Hinkle, J. C., and Eck, J. E. 2010. Is problem-oriented policing effective in reducing crime and disorder? Findings from a Campbell systematic review. *Criminology and Public Policy*, 9: 139–172.

Wolfgang, M. E., and Ferracuti, F. 1967. *The subculture of violence: Towards an integrated theory in criminology*. London: Tavistock Publications.

Furter Reading

Bureau of Justice Statistics, 2014c. Gangs. Accessed February 14, 2014. http://www.bjs.gov/index.cfm?ty=tp&tid=36.

Cohen, J. 1986. Research on criminal careers. In *Criminal careers and career criminals*, vol. 1, edited by A. Blumstein, J. Cohen, and C. A. Visher, 292–418. Washington, DC: National Academy Press.

Miller, J. 2001. *One of the guys: Girls, gangs, and gender*. New York: Oxford University Press.

National Research Council (NRC). 2004. Effectiveness of police activity in reducing crime, disorder and fear. In *Fairness and effectiveness in policing: The evidence*, edited by W. Skogan and K. Frydl, 217–251. Washington, DC: The National Academies Press.

2

Cybercrime

Thomas J. Holt

Society has changed dramatically since the introduction of the home personal computer (PC) and telephone modem in the late 1970s. The rapid adoption of computers and of the Internet, particularly of computer-mediated communications (CMCs) methods like email and instant messaging, during the mid- to late 1990s has revolutionized the way in which individuals connect for social and financial transactions. Virtually all industrialized nations depend on computers, the Internet, and cellular technology in order to communicate, conduct business, and even support vital services like sewer, water, and power grids (Andress and Winterfeld, 2011; Wall, 2007). In fact there are now 2.8 billion Internet users worldwide, and 276.6 million of them reside within the United States (Central Intelligence Agency, 2015).

Barriers to technology are also dropping, a phenomenon that enables all members of society to gain access to the Internet and to CMCs. For instance, 71 percent of Americans use now video-sharing sites, particularly African American and Hispanic users, who increasingly have access to broadband Internet, smartphones, and mobile devices (Moore, 2011). A substantial proportion of Americans are also using the free Internet available in schools and libraries as a means to go online, increasing the general access to technology regardless of income (Zickuhr et al., 2013). In the United Kingdom, 42 percent of households have fiber optic or cable broadband Internet connections, which means that high-speed connectivity is somewhat common (Office for National Statistics, 2013). Over 80 percent of adults in the United States own a cell phone, and approximately one third of them own a smart phone that can be used to check their email or connect to the Internet (Smith, 2011).

The substantial benefits afforded by computer technology and by the Internet have also created unheralded opportunities for crime and deviance online and

The Handbook of Measurement Issues in Criminology and Criminal Justice, First Edition.
Edited by Beth M. Huebner and Timothy S. Bynum.

offline. For instance, sex workers and their clients now use cell phones, email, and website advertisements and reviews in order to identify, solicit, and arrange paid sexual encounters (Holt and Blevins, 2007; Milrod and Weitzer, 2012; Sharp and Earle, 2003). Similarly, pedophiles utilize the Internet to exchange images and videos of child pornography, much of which is produced by harming children and by documenting their abuse in the real world (Jenkins, 2001; Quayle and Taylor, 2002). Computers and the Internet have also facilitated new offenses that were not conceivable without them, such as the use of computer hacking techniques in order to illegally access computer systems and acquire sensitive information (see Holt, 2007; Taylor, 1999).

Criminologists have begun to examine the range of offenses facilitated by technology, as well as the utility of traditional theories of crime and deviance in virtual environments (see Higgins and Marcum, 2011; Holt and Bossler, 2014; Wall, 2007). There are, however, substantial limitations to our knowledge of the prevalence and incidence of these offenses. Many of these crimes are not captured in traditional crime metrics, whether through official sources or self-report surveys. As a result, researchers must consider how to improve our understanding of the dark figure of crime in the sphere of crimes enabled by technology.

This chapter will provide an overview of the various ways in which individuals utilize technology to engage in crime and deviance. Then the paucity of official statistics on the prevalence and incidence of cybercrime will be considered, along with alternative data collection methods currently employed to understand offender behavior. The chapter will conclude with recommendations for strategies designed to improve both the quality and quantity of statistical data on cybercrimes and our general ability to assess risks of offending and criminological theories of victimization.

Defining Cybercrime

The emergence of technology and its use in the facilitation of crime have led to a new lexicon for defining these activities. In the 1980s and through the mid-1990s, the term "computer crime" was used by both researchers and the popular media as a means to describe activities in which an individual used special knowledge of computers in order to offend (Furnell, 2002). During this period, to be used effectively, computers required specialized knowledge; and they were not commonly connected to other systems. As a result, most computer crimes were instances of computer-based fraud and theft committed by guessing individual passwords or by illegally accessing sensitive information, which the perpetrator did not have permission to use (Furnell, 2002; Wall, 2001).

The advent of the World Wide Web, easy to use computer operating systems, and large-scale Internet service providers (ISPs) like America Online (AOL) fundamentally changed the landscape for criminality (Brenner, 2008; Wall, 2001). As more individuals began to use the Internet, various CMCs became popular. In turn, people could use these technologies to communicate with others around the world. Specialized chat rooms and communities began to develop around various interests – particularly in sexual discussions that involved the exchange of pornographic content scanned from paper to digital formats (Quinn and Forsyth, 2005). Fraudsters also began to use email and other forms of CMC as a means to contact a global population of prospective victims with ease (James, 2005; King and Thomas, 2009; Wall, 2004).

The growth of the Internet and of cyberspace during the mid-1990s led to the development of the term "cybercrime," which designates acts "in which the perpetrator uses special knowledge of cyberspace" (Furnell, 2002, p. 21; Wall, 2001). For instance, sending threatening or harassing instant messages to an individual constitutes a form of cybercrime, since the sender is utilizing the Internet as a venue for hurtful activity. At the same time, computer hacks that may otherwise be considered computer crimes began to be referred to as cybercrimes, because the attackers utilized both computer technology and the Internet in order to remotely connect with computers around the world.

The phrase "computer crime" and the term "cybercrime" were used synonymously throughout the late 1990s and the first decade of the twenty-first century, although "cybercrime" became prevalent due to the fact that almost every computer and mobile device could go online through the use of wireless Internet connections (Brenner, 2008). As a result, there are likely few "pure" computer crimes – that is, crimes that exist simply as a result of the use of the Internet as a means to transmit, access, or share data (Wall, 2007). The term "cybercrime" will be used throughout this chapter to refer to the various offenses that stem either from the ability to access the Internet or from the use of technology to facilitate the offending act.

A Typology of Cybercrime

To refine our understanding of cybercrime, it is necessary to elaborate upon the various forms that a cybercrime may take in the real world. There are a number of cybercrime typologies that have been published (e.g., Pittaro, 2007; Rogers, 2000), though these are largely focused on single forms of cybercrime – a feature that limits their capacity to encapsulate all offenses that technology may enable. One of the best referenced and constructed cybercrime frameworks created to date is Wall's (2001) four-category typology, which identifies a wide range of technology-based crimes. Each category will be elaborated upon below, with the help of examples designed to clarify each form of cybercrime.

Cybertrespass

The first category of Wall's (2001) cybercrime typology is cybertrespass, which recognizes the crossing of invisible, though established boundaries of ownership online. Acts of cybertrespass are commonly attributed to computer hackers, as they utilize sophisticated knowledge of computer technology to gain access to systems they may or may not own (Furnell, 2002; Jordan and Taylor, 1998). Hacking is not, however, used solely for malicious activities. Individuals can utilize hacking techniques for the ethical protection of computer networks and systems (see Holt, 2007; Schell and Dodge, 2002). In fact the term "hacker" was originally used in the 1950s and 1960s to denote respect for skilled programmers who could make computers operate more efficiently (Holt, 2007; Jordan and Taylor, 1998).

The general public, and even local law enforcement authorities, tend to associate hacking with criminal activities such as large-scale data breaches and attacks against government and industry networks (Furnell, 2002; Schell and Dodge, 2002). Criminal hackers are also involved in the creation of malicious software programs – "malware" – that can be used to simplify and automate computer compromises and attacks (Furnell, 2002; Symantec Corporation, 2013). Malware takes a range of forms – for example of computer viruses, worms, and Trojan horse programs – that can be used to alter critical system functions and to add or delete files, and can be spread to other systems. An infection can cause substantial harm to email and network operations, computer software and hardware, and can facilitate identity theft and fraud through the loss of data or manipulation of information (Bossler and Holt, 2009; Ngo and Patternoster, 2011). There are millions of variants of malicious software circulating online, with new codes that are being identified on a daily basis (Symantec Corporation, 2013). Thus malware infections are a serious threat to Internet users around the globe that cannot be easily mitigated.

Cyberdeception/theft

Given the ways in which cybertrespass can be applied by malicious actors, the second category, cyberdeception/theft, contains the range of criminal acquisitions of data or materials online (Wall, 2001). Individuals around the world increasingly depend on the Internet and on CMCs both for engaging in financial transactions and for exchanging sensitive information, for example about sending state and federal tax returns (James, 2005). Hackers can acquire this information in a variety of ways, and this enables many forms of fraud and identity theft. For instance, customer payment information is transferred between companies at various points during financial transactions, in order to enable immediate payments for goods and services provided by retailers like Amazon, iTunes, and Target (Peretti, 2009). Attackers who can gain access to these data can quickly steal millions of customer records and credit or debit card details. This was evident when the US company Heartland Payment Systems announced that their system security had been compromised in 2008 by a small group of hackers. The company processes over 11 million credit and debit card transactions for over 250,000 businesses across the US on a daily basis (Verini, 2010). A group of hackers targeted its systems and were able to infiltrate and install malware that captured sensitive data in transit without triggering system security (Krebs, 2011). The hackers were able to acquire information from 130 million credit and debit cards processed by 100,000 businesses (Verini, 2010).

The quantity of information acquired by hackers through breaches has increased over the last decade (Symantec Corporation, 2013). In instances where millions of records are stolen, there is more information than any one person can use in a reasonable period of time. As a result, a black market for stolen data has emerged that enables cybercriminals to sell and buy information (Franklin et al., 2007; Holt and Lampke, 2010; Motoyama et al., 2011). Operating through forums and through the Internet Relay Chat (IRC), actors sell credit card and debit card account details, eBay and PayPal accounts, and supporting customer information obtained from victims around the world (Franklin et al., 2007; Holt and Lampke, 2010; Holt and Smirnova, 2014). In addition, individuals offer their services to obtain funds from stolen accounts through various money-laundering techniques involving online purchases or real-world money transfers (Franklin et al., 2007; Holt and Lampke, 2010; Holt and Smirnova, 2014). All of these services enable individuals to engage in high-tech credit card fraud and identity theft, whether or not the actor originally engaged in an act of trespass to acquire the data (Franklin et al., 2007; Holt and Lampke, 2010; Motoyama et al., 2011).

The capacity of the Internet and of CMCs to connect individuals also permits various forms of fraud that are otherwise common in the real world, such as stock scams, auction fraud, and work-at-home schemes (Grabosky and Smith, 2001; Newman and Clarke, 2003). One of the oldest and most prevalent forms of Internet fraud involves advance-fee email schemes (Internet Crime Complaint Center, 2013; Holt and Graves, 2007; Wall, 2004). The senders of these messages claim to reside in a foreign nation and may pose as deposed royalty, government employees, or attorneys (Holt and Graves, 2007; King and Thomas, 2009). They seek assistance in transfering a large amount of money out of some secret account and into a safe bank in the United States; and to that end they ask to use the recipient's account as a transition point. By way of recompense, the sender will share a portion of the total sum with the person who helps him or her (Holt and Graves, 2007). It is not known how many individuals receive these messages or respond to the sender, though there is limited evidence that victims lose thousands of dollars on average every year (Holt and Graves, 2007; Internet Crime Complaint Center, 2013).

Perhaps the most common form of cybertheft occurring around the world involves digital piracy, or the illegal copying of digital media – including computer software, sound recordings, and video recordings – without the explicit permission of the copyright holder (Gopal et al., 2004). Pirated materials are shared and distributed through various file-sharing services and Web sites, and virtually any form of digital content has been pirated. In fact, IDATE (2003) suggested that illegal file sharing accounts for over four times the amount of official sales of sound recordings worldwide. In addition, software piracy appears to be commonplace in all nations around the world, the greatest proportion being reported in Asia and Africa (Business Software Alliance, 2012). As a result, corporations and intellectual property holders lose billions of dollars every year in direct sales and taxes to governments

(Motion Picture Association of America, 2007; Siwek, 2007). Therefore piracy poses a serious threat to business and industry around the world.

Cyberporn and obscenity

The third category in Wall's (2001) typology comprises cyberporn and obscenity, which includes the various forms of sexual expression and materials available online. The legal criteria for porn and obscene content vary from nation to nation, which makes this category contentious in an international context (DiMarco, 2003; Wall, 2001). For instance, it is legal in the United States to consume pornographic images and video featuring consenting performers over the age of 18, though the same content is illegal when it features humans and animals. The latter is, however, legal in a number of nations such as Brazil, Cambodia, and Mexico (Brenner, 2011). The Internet makes it possible for individuals to distribute these images to international audiences regardless of the legal definitions of a given nation. In other words, technology has made it difficult to regulate and restrict access to pornographic content generally (Brenner, 2011).

The development of affordable high-definition digital cameras and video recording equipment, along with high-speed Internet connectivity, has also made it possible for amateurs to become lucrative pornographers (Edelman, 2009; Lane, 2000). In fact the pornography industry is intimately tied to the adoption and popularity of various forms of media, particularly video home system (VHS) and digital versatile disc (DVD) media, webcams, digital photography, and streaming Web content (Lane, 2000). For instance, estimates suggest that pornographic websites and services earn over $3,000 per second every day (Gobry and Saint, 2011).

The global communications potential of the Internet and World Wide Web has also led to the formation of communities that support various deviant sexual activities (Quinn and Forsyth, 2005). Forums, social networking sites, news groups, and blog spaces now exist for individuals interested in anything, from necrophilia to bondage, to connect and exchange information (Quinn and Forsyth, 2005). Virtual spaces allow individuals to share information anonymously, with minimal risk of embarrassment or shaming, which further allows them to feel validated and part of a community that is not otherwise possible in the real world (Quinn and Forsyth, 2005). As a result, there are now robust sexual subcultures operating for everything from sexual encounters with HIV-positive partners (Tewksbury, 2006) to sex with animals (Maratea, 2011) and sex tourism (Holt, Zeoli, and Bohrer, 2013; Hughes, 2003).

The ability to communicate anonymously with individuals around the world has also enabled the illicit sex trade to move online, with unique dynamics that affect both the clients and the sex workers (see Holt and Blevins, 2007; Hughes, 2003; Sharp and Earle, 2003; Soothill and Sanders, 2005). There are now websites, forums, and newsgroups designed to review the services of sex workers, including their motivations for soliciting and their experiences with streetwalking prostitutes, escorts, and massage-parlor workers (Holt and Blevins, 2007; Holt et al., 2008; Hughes, 2003; Sharp and Earle, 2003). For instance, there are Web forums operated by clients of sex workers that provide discussions on sexual services in every state in the United States and abroad and give these clients the ability to share information on their direct experiences with prostitutes, escorts, and strippers (e.g., Holt and Blevins, 2007). These sites enable clients to more easily avoid law enforcement detection and to solicit in areas they have minimal familiarity with in the real world (Holt et al., 2008). At the same time, some sex workers now utilize online vetting services and email in order to screen clients in advance of physical meetings and reduce their risk of harm (Cunningham and Kendall, 2010). A small proportion of sex workers have also used technology to transition from street prostitution to escort work, which increases their profit margins (Cunningham and Kendall, 2010).

One of the most heavily legislated against and reviled forms of online sexual expression involves sexual content featuring children (Jenkins, 2001; McKenna and Bargh, 2000). Almost all nations have criminalized the possession or creation of images, video, and in some cases drawings and literature that feature children engaged in sexual activities (Berson, 2003; McKenna and Bargh, 2000). As a result, the Internet has become a primary vehicle for the identification and anonymous distribution of pornographic and sexual materials featuring children – for example comic books, stories, pictures, and films (Durkin, 1997; Jenkins, 2001; Quayle and Taylor, 2002). The ability to conceal one's location and identity while online has also made it possible for individuals with an attraction to youth to contact and groom minors for sexual contact offline (see Wolak, Finkelhor, and Mitchell, 2004; Wolak, Mitchell, and Finkelhor, 2003).

Cyberviolence

The fourth and final category in Wall's (2001) typology of cybercrime consists of acts of cyberviolence. The Internet and computer technology provide a range of opportunities for individuals to spread emotionally damaging or injurious messages, or even to incite people to violence in the real world (Wall, 2001). In the last decade there has been substantial media and academic attention on the use of CMCs and mobile phones in harassing or bullying others through email and instant messaging (Marcum, 2013; Tokunaga, 2010). The popularity of social networking websites like Facebook and Twitter allows individuals to post, via text and video, embarrassing or hurtful messages that can be viewed by anyone (see Hinduja and Patchin, 2009). Estimates suggest that over the last decade there has been an increase in the proportion of youth populations experiencing some form of cyberbullying and harassment – an increase due in part to their substantial use of CMC (Jones, Mitchell, and Finkelhor, 2012). As a result of these experiences, victims also appear to report physical or emotional stress, sometimes in the form of school truancy, depression, and suicidal ideation (see Hinduja and Patchin, 2009; Tokunaga, 2010).

The global connectivity afforded by social media and the Internet has created opportunities for political and social expression that may lead to violence and harm. Political and social movements use social media platforms to spread their message directly to the target audience, in a way that may be more palatable, such as through music or video game content (Forest, 2009). As a result, extremist and terror groups frequently use the Internet as a means to attract individuals to their cause and to radicalize members toward violence. For instance, the terrorist group Al Qaeda in the Arabian Peninsula (AQAP) operates an English-language magazine called *Inspire*, which provides information on the perspectives of the group and the jihadist movement generally. An issue from March 2013 featured an article on the 11 public figures from the West who, according to its author, should be "wanted" (dead or alive) for crimes against Islam (Watson, 2013).

In addition, extremist groups and nation-states alike have begun to use hacking techniques to engage in attacks against governments and private industry targets around the world (Andress and Winterfeld, 2011). For instance, the activist group Anonymous has engaged in coordinated cyberattacks against various governments and corporations around the world to express its anger about corruption and unjust laws that restrict freedom of speech (Correll, 2010). In 2012 members of the group Izz ad-Din al-Qassam Cyber Fighters engaged in a series of denial-of-service attacks against major banks in the United States (Gonsalves, 2013). The attacks affected the Web sites of US Bankcorp, J. P. Morgan Chase and Co., Bank of America, PNC Financial Services Group, and SunTrust, keeping customers from accessing their account details for minutes to hours at a time (Gonsalves, 2013). These examples demonstrate the substantial risks that acts of cyberviolence pose to individuals, industry, and governments around the world.

Methodological Limitations of Cybercrime Research

Though research on cybercrime has improved over the past 10 years, there are still several major limitations that affect our knowledge of these offenses. Perhaps the greatest limitation is the lack of official data sources that can be used to estimate the prevalence or incidence of these offenses in the general population. In the United States, United Kingdom, and Canada, there are few if any reporting categories for cybercrime in the existing national-level data sources for crimes made known to the police. This information is notably absent from the FBI's Uniform Crime Reporting (UCR), which cover both serious and minor forms of crime to person and property. This may be due in part to the lack of both resources against and awareness of cybercrime among local law enforcement units, which may arbitrarily diminish civilians' willingness to report these offenses (Stambaugh et al., 2001).

In response to the limitations evident in the UCR's estimates of crime, the FBI developed the National Incident-Based Reporting System (NIBRS). The system was designed to help law enforcement agencies and academics understand the nature of criminal events through the collection of more detailed information regarding both completed and attempted crimes. Unlike the UCR, the NIBRS collects as much information about a criminal event as possible and covers over forty offense types. These include a category that specifies whether the offender was suspected of using a computer in the offense, and whether a computer was the object of the crime (Federal Bureau of Investigation, 2000). This is extremely valuable information, as it provides an initial estimation for the scope of cybercrimes reported to law enforcement.

The potential value of NIBRS data to assessing the state of cybercrime has not, however, translated into actual estimates of cybercrime. To date, there have been minimal studies examining cybercrimes with the help of NIBRS data (Finkelhor and Ornrod, 2004). This is due in part to the fact that law enforcement agencies must decide how they will classify cybercrime incidents. There is no category for cybercrime; hence responding agencies must list the offense either under an existing crime type or in the catchall category "all other offenses."

At present, the only forms of cybercrime that can be readily derived from NIBRS data are (1) sexual offenses against children and (2) various forms of fraud. For those instances where a computer was involved, there is the potential to capture the prevalence of these crimes (Finkelhor and Ornrod 2004). The errors otherwise present make it difficult to disaggregate these crime types from traditional offenses. Furthermore, the current reporting rate for NIBRS is approximately 25 percent of the total United States (Federal Bureau of Investigation, 2013). Thus these data are extremely unreliable as an estimate for the total incidence of any form of cybercrime in general. In fact recent research has surveyed law enforcement agencies regarding their arrests for child sexual exploitation crimes in order to create estimates rather than depending on official statistics (Mitchell and Jones, 2013).

Similar issues are evident in the other primary data sources on victimization collected in the United States and abroad. For instance, the National Crime Victimization Survey (NCVS) collects data from nationally representative samples of the US population in order to assess victimization and reporting; but it has not added cybercrime victimization to its main survey instrument. The NCVS has developed small supplemental studies to capture data on cyberstalking (Catalano, 2012) and identity theft (Baum, 2006; Harrell and Langton, 2013; Langton, 2011), but there is no consistency in these measures over time. The British Crime Survey, however, has begun to include measures for identity fraud (Reyns, 2012), and will add additional cybercrime measures over the next few years (Home Office, 2013).

Despite these advances, there are inherent errors in the measurement of cybercrime that make it difficult to discern the prevalence of certain forms of victimization. For instance, the National Crime Victimization Survey, Supplemental Survey (NCVS-SS) (Catalano, 2012) used a sample of 65,270 people collected in 2008 to assess the rate of cyberstalking. The survey found that 26.1 percent of those who reported being stalked were sent emails that made them feel fear (Catalano, 2012). These measures are, however, prone to error and must be carefully considered. Analyses of the NCVS-SS were revised in 2012 to exclude incidents of repetitive and unsolicited communication, which were actually spam messages incorrectly classified as either harassment or stalking. This correction did not dramatically decrease the rate of cyberstalking, though it demonstrates the challenges evident in measuring cybercrimes generally (Catalano, 2012).

In view of the lack of official statistics, a number of self-report measures have become key resources for estimating the scope of cybercrime. One of the most prominent self-report measures is produced by the Internet Crime Complaint Center (IC3). This agency is a joint effort by the FBI, the National White Collar Crime Center (NWC3), and the Bureau of Justice Assistance and was established in 2000. The IC3 is staffed with FBI agents, analysts, and technical support staff as well as supervisors from the NWC3. Victims of cybercrime can contact the IC3 and report their experiences by completing an online complaint form. The document asks a range of questions and collects information about the victim, the offender, and the offense. The IC3 staff then analyzes this information and forwards the relevant cases on to the appropriate local, state, or federal agency.

Variables such as the victim's and the offender's age and sex and the location of the offense are reported by the IC3 in its annual reports. Trends in Internet crime for specific jurisdictions can also be estimated from the IC3 database. For instance, over 262,813 complaints were received from victims in 2013, and they were associated with losses of over $781 million. By comparison with 2012, this represents a decrease in the number of complaints received, though a substantial increase in dollar losses. The majority of these complaints are about cases that involved some form of fraud, including auction-related counterfeit products and various email-based scams. Though these data are useful for understanding the scope of cybercrime, they only represent victims who are aware of the existence of the IC3. It is unclear how well known this resource is among consumers, the general population, or the law enforcement community. Given the circumstances, data from the IC3 should be viewed with a degree of skepticism.

In addition to the IC3, there are a number of self-report data sets that measure cybercrimes though they have substantial limitations. As a result, researchers have developed their own self-report survey data sets from college samples and juvenile populations (see Holt and Bossler, 2014 for a review). Many of these are specialized around a given topic, such as stalking (Finn, 2004), or are general cybercrime surveys with single-university samples (e.g. Higgins, 2005; Holt and Bossler, 2009). College samples in general are generated through either email-based solicitations to proportional samples of enrolled students or paper-based surveys distributed in large general-enrolment courses in order to capture as large a population as is possible. The questions typically address both offending and victimization, as well as general technology use. A small proportion of this research has also begun to include measures related to traditional offending and real-world environments, in order to provide a comparison between virtual and real behavior (see Holt, Turner, and Exum, 2014). As a result, these studies often lack statistical power or generalizability to larger populations (see Holt and Bossler, 2014, for review). In addition, the quantitative nature of these data sets do not allow for a robust understanding of the tactics or perceptions of offenders over time.

Though a number of cross-sectional data sets are available on cybercrime, few longitudinal samples exist. Despite the development of numerous longitudinal data sets in the United States – sets such as the National Longitudinal Survey of Youth (NLSY) and the National Youth Survey (NYS) – none includes measures for cybercrime. A nationally representative multiwave sample of US youth has been collected by researchers at the University of New Hampshire (see Jones et al., 2012). These data are not a true panel design, however, as the sample population changes with each successive wave. As a result, the data can only be used to assess trends and do not provide much by way of attitudinal or behavioral measures that could identify correlates in victimization or offending. Longitudinal data sources on cybercrime are emerging internationally; for example, the data from the Longitudinal Internet Studies for the Social Sciences (LISS) in the Netherlands capture identity theft, hacking, stalking, harassment, and malicious software infection victimization (see Van Wilsem, 2013). There have been few analyses of these data, which makes it difficult to assess their general value for our understanding of the risk factors associated with victimization.

There are industry sources that may also be used to assess the scope of cybercrime, though these tend to have substantial limitations. For instance, antivirus vendors collect data on malicious software infections that are provided on a quarterly and yearly basis (e.g., PandaLabs, 2007; Symantec Corporation, 2013). These estimates are particularly useful for documenting the presence of malware in the wild at any point in time and for identifying trends in common methods of attack. At the same time, the corporations that provide these statistics do not give much information on how the data are collected or on how representative the results may be. Typically, the data are generated from machines that use their software to provide an estimate of attacks (Symantec Corporation, 2013). This makes it difficult to extrapolate the findings to larger populations, as the latter may use different products – or no security tools whatsoever. In addition, the figures are only reflective of malware trends and give no information on identity theft or sex crime victimization.

Computer-Mediated Communications as a Data Source

In response to the lack of self-report data sets and generally low prevalence rates for serious cybercrime offending in college and youth samples (Holt and Bossler, 2014), in order to understand cybercrime some researchers have begun to use data developed from online environments such as Web forums, bulletin board systems (BBS), and archival Web sites (Hine, 2005; Holt, 2010). These sites allow individuals to communicate in near real time around the world through instant messaging systems or through asynchronous chat like blogs and email. Thus qualitative and quantitative researchers have begun to mine these communications for information on the social and behavioral practices of cybercriminals in a fashion similar to that of traditional ethnographies of real-world offenders.

Some of the most common resources for Internet-based research are forums (see Blevins and Holt, 2009; Holt, 2007, 2009; Holt and Blevins, 2007; Mann and Sutton, 1998; Malesky and Ennis, 2004; Taylor, 1999; Yip, Webber, and Shadbolt, 2013), BBSs (Jenkins, 2001; Landreth, 1985; Meyer, 1989), and newsgroups (Durkin and Bryant, 1999; Loper, 2000; Quayle and Taylor, 2002). These forms of CMC operate in asynchronous time, which means that individuals can post and respond to others at any time of day. They can post a comment, a question, or a point of interest, and others make their own posts in response to that originating post. The posts are all connected or threaded together, creating a single venue for multiple exchanges between participants.

The structure of threads in forums and BBSs makes them act as a sort of virtual discussion group where individuals engage in a naturally occurring conversation over an extended period of time (Holt, 2007; Mann and Sutton, 1998). Threads and posts are also typically archived, allowing researchers access to weeks, months, or even years of data at a time. This form of CMC is accessed in one of two ways online: open and closed-registration formats. Open forums allow anyone to view posts without being required to create a user account within the site (Cooper and Harrison, 2001; Mann and Sutton, 1998; Rutter and Smith, 2005). As a result, the contents of a forum may be captured by search engines like Google; therefore the participants' perceived degree of anonymity may be lower. A number of studies have utilized data derived from open forums to examine deviant communities such as digital pirates (see Cooper and Harrison, 2001; Holt and Copes, 2010), hacker communities (Holt, 2007; Mann and Sutton, 1998; Taylor, 1999), identity thieves (Franklin et al., 2007; Holt and Lampke, 2010; Motoyama et al., 2011; Yip et al., 2013), malicious software creators (Chu, Holt, and Ahn, 2010; Holt, 2013), pedophiles (Durkin and Bryant, 1999; Holt et al., 2010), self-injurers (Adler and Adler, 2007), and customers of sex workers (Blevins and Holt, 2009; Holt and Blevins, 2007; Holt et al., 2008; Milrod and Monto, 2012; Milrod and Weitzer, 2012).

Closed or registration-only forums do not allow people to view the content of posts until they have created a registered user account that has a username and password (Holt, Smirnova, and Chua, 2013; Jenkins, 2001; Landreth, 1985). Some of these forums require users to post at certain intervals in order to maintain an active account, which can limit the ability of researchers to collect data over time (Holt and Smirnova, 2014). Registration-only forums may also permit more illegal activity than open forums, which has led to the development of additional barriers to entry (see Holt and Smirnova, 2014). For instance, forums involved in the sale and distribution of stolen data implemented paid access and social vetting in order to regulate access strictly or give it only to known members of the community (see Holt and Smirnova, 2014). These practices raise ethical problems for researchers that may be absent from open forums – for example determining how the researcher will engage with forum users and how s/he will structure his or her online identity (see Hine, 2005; Rutter and Smith, 2005).

Considering the Future of Cybercrime Data Collection and Research

At this time there are no immediate solutions to the obvious challenges posed by measuring cybercrime. Although researchers have begun to shed light on the scope of these offenses and the complexity of empirical and law enforcement investigation, policymakers and the general public have not grasped this problem. This is evident in the lack of official statistics generated at the local level and in the absence of support for cybercrime investigation among local and state police agencies (Holt and Bossler, 2012; Stambaugh et al., 2001). Ever since the late 1990s researchers have called for a change in this respect, but there is minimal evidence that line officers or management place the investigation of cybercrime in the same context as that of street crime (Holt and Bossler, 2012; Senjo, 2004; Stambaugh et al., 2001). Therefore there is a great need for local police agencies to change their position by becoming more willing to respond to cybercrimes and to take reports of these offenses. Without such a change, there may never be sufficient support for the local reporting and investigation of cybercrimes (Stambaugh et al., 2001).

In much the same way, the general public must become more cognizant of the threat and severity of cybercrimes. There is some evidence that citizens either do not know whom to contact in the event that they experience cybercrimes or think that this experience may not be treated in the same fashion as being the victim of street crime (e.g. Stambaugh et al., 2001). Furthermore, many people may not even realize that they have been victimized until their personal information has been lost or their computer has been compromised (Holt and Lampke, 2010; James, 2005; Newman and Clarke, 2003; Wall, 2007). Public awareness campaigns targeting the general public are essential for ensuring that, in the event of becoming victims of cybercrime, citizens know what law enforcement agencies to contact and when (Stambaugh et al., 2001). Any campaign designed to ensure that individuals understand that they can contact law enforcement, and thereby to increase the likelihood of official statistics being generated around cybercrimes, would be inherently valuable.

There is also a need for resources capable of ensuring that cybercrimes can be properly investigated at all levels of law enforcement and of maintaining proper statistics for aggregation and empirical inquiry by researchers (Stambaugh et al., 2001). A paradigm shift of such magnitude as to change all of the above conditions is unlikely to occur within the next decade, due to the perception that drug crimes and terrorism are more serious offenses. There are, however, alternative strategies that could be employed in order to improve our knowledge of cybercrime offending and victimization. The development, through the National Institute of Justice (NIJ) and National Science Foundation (NSF), of grant-funding lines specifically dedicated to assessing cybercrime could provide a cost-effective means to acquire information (Stambaugh et al., 2001). For instance, a number of existing longitudinal large-scale population surveys that assess crime and delinquency could be easily adapted to include questions pertaining to cybercrime offending and victimization. Such a tactic would easily engender robust investigations of the correlates and predictors of the risk factors. Funding lines of research on alternative ways to measure cybercrimes, by using open-source data and automated mechanisms, may prove invaluable for expanding our knowledge of these offenses.

Finally, there is a need for the development and assessment of nontraditional data sources from online resources, including forums and other forms of CMC, in order to understand cybercrime at the micro- and macrolevel (see Holt and Bossler, 2014). At present, most of the research on cybercrime focuses on the level of the individual by using self-report data. This is helpful for understanding some prospective differences in risk factors for both victimization and offending (e.g. Bossler and Holt, 2009; Higgins and Marcum, 2011; Holt and Bossler, 2014; Ngo and Patternoster, 2011). The research that considers how macrolevel social and economic forces may – differentially – increase the risk of victimization at a country or regional level is, however, minimal (e.g., Kigerl, 2012). Such information could be tremendously valuable, given that cybercriminals are able to immediately affect victim populations outside of their country of origin.

Data from these sources can help fill a void left by the lack of reliable and accessible data from governmental and private sector sources. In addition, online data sources rely neither on governments to report their data nor on a country's residents to report offending or victimization that has occurred in that country. Such data are not yet commonly accepted among criminological researchers and are rarely published in key outlets in the field (see Holt and Bossler, 2014 for a review). Improved data collection and analysis techniques are thus required in order for the perceived value of online data to expand in the larger discipline. In turn, the field may be better able to document and triangulate the scope of cybercrimes occurring around the world.

References

Adler, P. A., and Adler, P. 2007. The demedicalization of self-injury: From psychopathology to sociological deviance. *Journal of Contemporary Ethnography*, 36: 537–570.

Andress, J., and Winterfeld, S. 2011. *Cyber warfare: Techniques, tactics, and tools for security practitioners*. Waltham, MA: Syngress.

Baum, K. 2006. *First estimates from the National Crime Victimization Survey: Identity theft, 2004*. Washington, DC: US Department of Justice, Office of Justice Statistics. Accessed April 15, 2007. http://www.ojp.usdoj.gov/bjs/pub/pdf/it04.pdf.

Berson, I. R. 2003. Grooming cybervictims: The psychosocial effects of online exploitation of youth. *Journal of School Violence*, 2: 5–18.

Blevins, K., and Holt, T. J. 2009. Examining the virtual subculture of johns. *Journal of Contemporary Ethnography*, 38: 619–648.

Bossler, A. M., and Holt, T. J. 2009. On-line activities, guardianship, and malware infection: An examination of routine activities theory. *The International Journal of Cyber Criminology*, 3: 400–420.

Brenner, S. W. 2008. *Cyberthreats: The emerging fault lines of the nation state.* New York: Oxford University Press.

Brenner, S. W. 2011. Defining cybercrime: A review of federal and state law. In *Cybercrime: The investigation, prosecution, and defense of a computer-related crime*, edited by R. D. Clifford, 3rd edn., 15–104. Raleigh, NC: Carolina Academic Press.

Business Software Alliance. 2012. *Shadow market: 2011 BSA Global Software Piracy study*. Accessed April 10, 2013. http://globalstudy.bsa.org/2011/downloads/study_pdf/2011_BSA_Piracy_Study-Standard.pdf.

Catalano, S. 2012. *Stalking victims in the United States, revised.* Washington, DC: US Department of Justice. Accessed January 14, 2013. http://www.bjs.gov/content/pub/pdf/svus_rev.pdf.

Central Intelligence Agency. 2015. *The world factbook, 2015.* Washington, DC: Central Intelligence Agency. Accessed December 20, 2015. https://www.cia.gov/library/publications/the-world-factbook/index.html.

Chu, B., Holt, T. J., and Ahn, G. J. 2010. *Examining the creation, distribution, and function of malware on-line.* Washington DC: National Institute of Justice. (NIJ Grant No. 2007-IJ-CX-0018.)

Cooper, J., and Harrison, D. M. 2001. The social organization of audio piracy on the Internet. *Media, Culture & Society*, 23: 71–89.

Correll, S. P. 2010. An interview with Anonymous. PandaLabs Blog. Accessed April 14, 2011. http://pandalabs.pandasecurity.com/an-interview-with-anonymous.

Cunningham, S., and Kendall, T. 2010. Sex for sale: Online commerce in the world's oldest profession. In *Crime online: Correlates, causes, and context*, edited by T. J. Holt, 2nd edn., 114–140. Raleigh, NC: Carolina Academic Press.

DiMarco, H. 2003. The electronic cloak: Secret sexual deviance in cybersociety. In *Dot.cons: Crime, deviance, and identity on the Internet*, edited by Y. Jewkes, 53–67. Portland, OR: Willan.

Durkin, K. F. 1997. Misuse of the Internet by pedophiles: Implications for law enforcement and probation practice. *Federal Probation*, 61: 14–18.

Durkin, K. F., and Bryant, C. D. 1999. Propagandizing pederasty: A thematic analysis of the on-line exculpatory accounts of unrepentant pedophiles. *Deviant Behavior*, 20: 103–127.

Edelman, B. 2009. Red light states: Who buys online adult entertainment? *Journal of Economic Perspectives*, 23: 209–220.

Federal Bureau of Investigation. 2000. *National Incident-Based Reporting System*, vol. 1: *Data collection guidelines.* Accessed June 15, 2014. http://www2.fbi.gov/ucr/nibrs/manuals/v1all.pdf.

Federal Bureau of Investigation. 2013. *Criminal Justice Information Services (CJIS) Division Uniform Crime Reporting (UCR) Program: National Incident-Based Reporting System (NIBRS) user manual.* Accessed December 28, 2015. https://www.fbi.gov/about-us/cjis/ucr/nibrs/nibrs-user-manual.

Finkelhor, D., and Ornrod, R. 2004. Child pornography: Patterns from NIBRS. *Office of Juvenile Justice and Delinquency Prevention Bulletin.* Accessed June 20, 2014. https://www.ncjrs.gov/pdffiles1/ojjdp/204911.pdf?q=pornography.

Finn, J. 2004. A survey of online harassment at a university campus. *Journal of Interpersonal Violence*, 19: 468–483.

Forest, J. J. 2009. Influence warfare: How terrorists and governments struggle to shape perceptions in a war of ideas. Westport, CT: Praeger.

Franklin, J., Paxson, V., Perrig, A., and Savage, S. 2007. An inquiry into the nature and cause of the wealth of Internet miscreants. Paper presented at the Conference on Computer and Communications Security 2007, October 29–November 2, Alexandria, Virginia.

Furnell, S. 2002. *Cybercrime: Vandalizing the information society*. Boston, MA: Addison Wesley.

Gobry, P. E., and Saint, N. 2011. *15 things you need to know about Internet porn*. Accessed June 1, 2013. http://www.sfgate.com/news/article/15-Things-You-Need-To-Know-About-Internet-Porn-2332518.php.

Gonsalves, A. 2013. Islamic group promises to resume US bank cyberattacks. *CSO Online*, February 28: 2013. Accessed March 5, 2013. http://www.csoonline.com/article/729598/islamic-group-promises-to-resume-u.s.-bank-cyberattacks?source=ctwartcso.

Gopal, R., Sanders, G. L., Bhattacharjee, S., Agrawal, M. K., and Wagner, S. C. 2004. A behavioral model of digital music piracy. *Journal of Organizational Computing & Electronic Commerce*, 14: 89–105.

Grabosky P. N., and Smith, R. 2001. Telecommunication fraud in the digital age: The convergence of technologies. In *Crime and the Internet*, edited by D. Wall, 29–43. New York: Routledge.

Harrell, E., and Langton, L. 2013. *Victims of identity theft, 2012*. US Department of Justice Bulletin (NCJ 243779). Accessed January 21, 2014. http://www.bjs.gov/content/pub/pdf/vit12.pdf.

Higgins, G. E. 2005. Can low self-control help with the understanding of the software piracy problem? *Deviant Behavior*, 26: 1–24.

Higgins, G. E., and Marcum, C. D. 2011. *Digital piracy: An integrated theoretical approach*. Raleigh, NC: Carolina Academic Press.

Hinduja, S., and Patchin, J. W. 2009. *Bullying beyond the schoolyard: Preventing and responding to cyberbullying*. New York: Corwin Press.

Hine, C., ed. 2005. *Virtual methods: Issues in social research on the Internet*. Oxford: Berg.

Holt, T. J. 2007. Subcultural evolution? Examining the influence of on- and off-line experiences on deviant subcultures. *Deviant Behavior*, 28: 171–198.

Holt, T. J. 2009. Lone hacks or group cracks: Examining the social organization of computer hackers. In *Crimes of the Internet*, edited by F. Smalleger and M. Pittaro, 336–335. Upper Saddle River, NJ: Pearson/Prentice Hall.

Holt, T. J. 2010. Exploring strategies for qualitative criminological and criminal justice inquiry using on-line data. *Journal of Criminal Justice Education*, 21: 300–321.

Holt, T. J. 2013. Examining the forces shaping cybercrime markets online. *Social Science Computer Review*, 31: 165–177.

Holt, T. J., and Blevins, K. R. 2007. Examining sex work from the client's perspective: Assessing johns using online data. *Deviant Behavior*, 28: 333–354.

Holt, T. J., Blevins, K. R., and Burkert, N. 2010. Considering the pedophile subculture online. *Sexual Abuse: Journal of Research and Treatment*, 22: 3–24.

Holt, T. J., Blevins, K. R., and Kuhns, J. B. 2008. Examining the displacement practices of johns with on-line data. *Journal of Criminal Justice*, 36: 522–528.

Holt, T. J., and Bossler, A. M. 2009. Examining the applicability of lifestyle-routine activities theory for cybercrime victimization. *Deviant Behavior*, 30: 1–25.

Holt, T. J., and Bossler, A. M. 2012. Police perceptions of computer crimes in two southeastern cities: An examination from the viewpoint of patrol officers. *American Journal of Criminal Justice*, 37: 396–412.

Holt, T. J., and Bossler, A. M. 2014. An assessment of the current state of cybercrime scholarship. *Deviant Behavior*, 35: 20–40.

Holt, T. J., and Copes, H. 2010. Transferring subcultural knowledge online: Practices and beliefs of persistent digital pirates. *Deviant Behavior*, 31: 625–654.

Holt, T. J., and Graves, D. C. 2007. A qualitative analysis of advanced fee fraud schemes. *The International Journal of Cyber-Criminology*, 1: 137–154.

Holt, T. J., and Lampke, E. 2010. Exploring stolen data markets on-line: Products and market forces. *Criminal Justice Studies*, 23: 33–50.

Holt, T. J., and Smirnova, O. 2014. *Examining the structure organization and process of the international market for stolen data*. National Institute of Justice: US Department of Justice. Accessed, July 1, 2014. https://www.ncjrs.gov/pdffiles1/nij/grants/245375.pdf.

Holt, T. J., Smirnova, O., and Chua, Y. T. 2013. An exploration of the factors affecting the advertised price for stolen data. In *Proceedings of the eCrime Research Summit (eCRS), 17–18 September*, 1–10. San Francisco, CA: IEEE Standards Association. doi: 10.1109/eCRS.2013.6805781

Holt, T. J., Turner, M. G., and Exum, M. L. 2014. The impact of self-control and neighborhood disorder on bullying victimization. *Journal of Criminal Justice*, 42: 347–355.

Holt, T. J., Zeoli, A. M., and Bohrer, K. 2013. Examining the decision-making processes of sex tourists using on-line data. *Journal of Qualitative Criminal Justice and Criminology*, 1: 122–151.

Home Office. 2013. *Cyber crime: A review of the evidence*. Accessed January 1, 2015. https://www.gov.uk/government/publications/cyber-crime-a-review-of-the-evidence.

Hughes, D. M. 2003. Prostitution online. *Journal of Trauma Practice*, 2: 115–131.

IDATE. 2003. Taking advantage of peer-to-peer: What is at stake for the content industry? Accessed January 7, 2009. http://www.idate.fr/an/_qdn/an-03/ IF282/index_a.htm.

Internet Crime Complaint Center. 2009. IC3 2008 Internet Crime Report. Accessed June 1, 2015. http://www.ic3.gov/media/annualreport/2008_IC3Report.pdf.

Internet Crime Complaint Center. 2013. IC3 2012 Internet Crime Report. Accessed June 1, 2015. http://www.ic3.gov/media/annualreport/2012_IC3Report.pdf.

James, L. 2005. *Phishing exposed*. Rockland, ME: Syngress.

Jenkins, P. 2001. *Beyond tolerance: Child pornography on the Internet*. New York: NYU Press.

Jones, L. M., Mitchell, K. J., and Finkelhor, D. 2012. Trends in youth Internet victimization: Findings from three youth Internet safety surveys, 2000–2010. *Journal of Adolescent Health*, 50: 179–186.

Jordan, T., and Taylor, P. 1998. A sociology of hackers. *The Sociological Review*, 46: 757–780.

Kigerl, A. 2012. Routine activity theory and the determinants of high cybercrime countries. *Social Science Computer Review*, 30 (4): 470–486.

King, A., and Thomas, J. 2009. You can't cheat an honest man: Making ($$$s and) sense of the Nigerian e-mail scams. In *Crimes of the Internet*, edited by F. Schmalleger and M. Pittaro, 206–224. Saddle River, NJ: Prentice Hall.

Krebs, B. 2011. Are megabreaches out? E-thefts downsized in 2010. *Krebs on security*. Accessed June 2, 2012. http://krebsonsecurity.com/tag/heartland-payment-systems.

Landreth, B. 1985. *Out of the inner circle*. Washington, DC: Microsoft Press.

Lane, F. S. 2000. *Obscene profits: The entrepreneurs of pornography in the cyber age*. New York: Routledge.

Langton, L. 2011. *Identity theft reported by households 2005–2010*. Washington, DC: US Department of Justice, Bureau of Justice Statistics.

Loper, D. K. 2000. The criminology of computer hackers: A qualitative and quantitative analysis. Unpublished doctoral dissertation, Michigan State University.

Malesky, L. A., Jr., and Ennis, L. 2004. Supportive distortions: An analysis of posts on a pedophile Internet message board. *Journal of Addictions and Offender Counseling*, 24: 92–100.

Mann, D., and Sutton, M. 1998. Netcrime: More change in the organization of thieving. *British Journal of Criminology*, 38: 201–229.

Maratea, R. J. 2011. Screwing the pooch: Legitimizing accounts in a zoophilia on-line community. *Deviant Behavior*, 32: 918–843.

Marcum, C. D. 2013. Examining cyberstalking and bullying: Causes, context, and control. In *Crime on-line: Correlates, causes, and context*, edited by T. J. Holt, 175–192. Raleigh, NC: Carolina Academic Press.

McKenna, K. Y. A., and Bargh, J. A. 2000. Plan 9 from cyberspace: The implications of the Internet for personality and social psychology. *Personality and Social Psychology Review*, 4: 57–75.

Meyer, G. R. 1989. The social organization of the computer underground. Master's thesis, Northern Illinois University.

Milrod, C., and Monto, M. A. 2012. The hobbyist and the girlfriend experience: Behaviors and preferences of male customers of Internet sexual service providers. *Deviant Behaviors*, 33: 792–810.

Milrod, C., and Weitzer, R. 2012. The intimacy prism: Emotion management among the clients of escorts. *Men and Masculinities*, 15: 447–467.

Motoyama, M., McCoy, D., Levchenko, K., Savage, S., and Voelker, G. M. 2011. An analysis of underground forums. *Proceedings of the 2011 Conference on Internet Measurement, November 2–4*, 71–79. Berlin: ACM.

Mitchell, K. J., and Jones, L. M. 2013. *Internet-facilitated commercial sexual exploitation of children*. Durham, NH: Crimes against Children Research Center.

Moore, K. 2011. *71% of online adults now use video-sharing sites*. Pew Internet and American Life Project. Accessed October 10, 2012. http://pewinternet.org/Reports/2011/Video-sharing-sites.aspx.

Motion Picture Association of America. 2007. 2005 Piracy fact sheet. Accessed December 12, 2007. http://www.mpaa.org/researchStatistics.asp.

Newman, G., and Clarke, R. 2003. *Superhighway robbery: Preventing e-commerce crime*. Cullompton, UK: Willan.

Ngo, F. T., and Paternoster, R. 2011. Cybercrime victimization: An examination of individual- and situational-level factors. *International Journal of Cyber Criminology*, 5: 773–793.

Office for National Statistics. 2013. *Internet access: Households and individuals, 2013*. Accessed January 20, 2014. http://www.ons.gov.uk/ons/dcp171778_322713.pdf.

PandaLabs. 2007. Malware infections in protected systems. Accessed November 1, 2007. http://research.pandasecurity.com/blogs/images/wp_pb_malware_infections _in_ protected_systems.pdf.

Peretti, K. K. 2009. Data breaches: What the underground world of "carding" reveals. *Santa Clara Computer and High Technology Law Journal*, 25: 375–413.

Pittaro, M. L. 2007. Cyberstalking: An analysis of online harassment and intimidation. *International Journal of Cyber Criminology*, 1: 180–197.

Quayle, E., and Taylor, M. 2002. Child pornography and the Internet: Perpetuating a cycle of abuse. *Deviant Behavior*, 23: 331–361.

Quinn, J. F., and Forsyth, C. J. 2005. Describing sexual behavior in the era of the Internet: A typology for empirical research. *Deviant Behavior*, 26: 191–207.

Reyns, B. W. 2013. Online routines and identity theft victimization: Further expanding routine activity theory beyond direct-contact offenses. *Journal of Research in Crime and Delinquency*, 50: 216–238.

Rogers, M. 2000. *A new hacker taxonomy.* Accessed June 20, 2014. https://www.cerias.purdue.edu/assets/pdf/bibtex_archive/2005-43.pdf.

Rutter, J., and Smith, G. W. H. 2005. Ethnographic presence in a nebulous setting. In *Virtual methods: Issues in social research on the Internet*, edited by C. Hine, 81–92. Oxford: Berg.

Schell, B. H., and Dodge, J. L. 2002. *The hacking of America: Who's doing it, why, and how.* Westport, CT: Quorum Books.

Senjo, S. R. 2004. An analysis of computer-related crime: Comparing police officer perceptions with empirical data. *Security Journal*, 17: 55–71.

Sharp, K., and Earle, S. 2003. Cyberpunters and cyberwhores: Prostitution on the Internet. In *Dot cons.: Crime, deviance and identity on the Internet*, edited by Y. Jewkes, 36–52. Portland, OR: Willan.

Siwek, S. E. 2007. *The true cost of sound recording piracy to the US economy.* Accessed January 9, 2009. http://www.ipi.org/ipi%5CIPIPublications.nsf. (PublicationLookupFullText/5C2EE3D2107A4C228625733E0053A1F4.)

Smith, A. 2011. *Smartphone adoption and usage.* Pew Internet and American Life Project. Accessed April 14, 2014. http://pewinternet.org/Reports/2011/Smartphones.aspx.

Soothill, K., and Sanders, T. 2005. The geographical mobility, preferences and pleasures of prolific punters: A demonstration study of the activities of prostitutes' clients. *Sociological Research Online* 10 (1). Accessed October 10, 2005. http://www.socresonline.org.uk/10/1/soothill.html.

Stambaugh, H., Beuapre, D. S., Icove, D. J., Baker, R., Cassady, W., and William, W. P. 2001. *Electronic crime needs assessment for state and local law enforcement.* Washington, DC: National Institute of Justice. (NCJ 186276.)

Symantec Corporation. 2013. *Symantec Internet security threat report*, vol. 18. Accessed June 23, 2013. http://www.symantec.com/threatreport.

Taylor, P. 1999. *Hackers: Crime in the digital sublime.* London: Routledge.

Tewksbury, R. 2006. Click here for HIV: An analysis of Internet-based bug chasers and bug givers. *Deviant Behavior*, 27: 379–395.

Tokunaga, R. S. 2010. Following you home from school: A critical review and synthesis of research on cyberbullying victimization. *Computers in Human Behavior*, 26: 277–287.

Van Wilsem, J. 2013. Bought it, but never got it: Assessing risk factors for online consumer fraud victimization. *European Sociology Review*, 29: 168–178.

Verini, J. 2010. The great cyberheist. *The New York Times.* Accessed November 14, 2010. http://www.nytimes.com/2010/11/14/magazine/14Hacker-t.html?_r = 1.

Wall, D. S. 2001. Cybercrimes and the Internet. In *Crime and the Internet*, edited by D. S. Wall, 1–17. New York: Routledge.

Wall, D. S. 2004. Digital realism and the governance of spam as cybercrime. *European Journal on Criminal Policy and Research*, 10: 309–335.

Wall, D. S. 2007. *Cybercrime: The transformation of crime in the information age.* Cambridge: Polity.

Watson, L. 2013. Al Qaeda releases guide on how to torch cars and make bombs as it names 11 public figures it wants "dead or alive" in latest edition of its glossy magazine. *Daily Mail*,

March 4. Accessed July 1, 2014. http://www.dailymail.co.uk/news/article-2287003/Al-Qaeda-releases-guide-torch-cars- make-bombs-naming-11-public-figures-wants-dead-alive-latest-edition-glossy-magazine.html.

Wolak, J., Finkelhor, D., and Mitchell, K. 2004. Internet-initiated sex crimes against minors: Implications for prevention based on findings from a national study. *Journal of Adolescent Health*, 35: 424e.11–20.

Wolak, J., Mitchell, K., and Finkelhor, D. 2003. *Internet sex crimes against minors: The response of law enforcement.* Washington, DC: Office of Juvenile Justice and Delinquency Prevention.

Yip, M., Webber, C., and Shadbolt, N. 2013. Trust among cybercriminals? Carding forums, uncertainty, and implications for policing. *Policing and Society*, 23: 516–539.

Zickuhr, K., Rainie, L., Purcell, K., and Duggan, M. 2013. *How Americans value public libraries in their communities.* Pew Internet and American Life Project. Accessed June 1, 2014. http://libraries.pewinternet.org.

Further Reading

Rosenmann, A., and Safir, M. P. 2006. Forced online: Pushed factors of Internet sexuality: A preliminary study of paraphilic empowerment. *Journal of Homosexuality*, 51: 71–92.

3

Juvenile Crime and Bullying

Sean P. Varano and Joseph M. McKenna

Introduction

Juvenile crime and delinquency have long captured the attention of the public, policymakers and scholars. The "scourge" of juvenile violence seems to be "rediscovered" every decade, as the public's attention waxes and wanes between hosts of headline-grabbing new stories. There is little doubt that, over much of the last fifty years, juvenile delinquency has made among the most salient news stories in the United States. During much of the 1990s, for example, youth violence regularly topped networks with the most important stories (Coalition for Juvenile Justice, 1997). This attention is indicative not only of an overall interest in violence on the part of the public, but of something peculiar about the interest in violent juveniles.

The attention given to juvenile violence and delinquency has been consequential. In fact, the perception that juvenile crime is on the rise and at unacceptably high levels has been one of the key drivers of criminal justice policy over much of the past century. Bernard and Kurlychek (2010) recognized that, throughout that period, there were predictable patterns to juvenile justice policy that were framed, at least in part, by vacillating perceptions about the extent and seriousness of juvenile delinquency. During such moments, when juvenile crime is culturally and politically deemed to be at unacceptably high levels, public bureaucracies and the public are often galvanized in ways that produce both the *resources* and the *will* to "do something" about the problem. From a long-term perspective, "doing something" generally amounts to the creation of additional laws and schemes that are punitive in nature.

While history is replete with examples of increases in youth violence and delinquency that drive public concern, there are eras when these concerns have

The Handbook of Measurement Issues in Criminology and Criminal Justice, First Edition.
Edited by Beth M. Huebner and Timothy S. Bynum.

been particularly powerful and effective in mobilizing collective action. The 1980s and 1990s can be described as a period when street crime, particularly youth-oriented street crime, emerged as a defining national problem across most communities in the United States, particularly larger urban jurisdictions. Violence was perceived to have reached epidemic levels, and much of the increase was, accurately or not, attributed to juveniles. Juveniles, for example, accounted for a substantial part of the growth in homicides between 1986 and 1993 (Snyder and Sickmund, 1999). There was a growing perception that youth culture had fundamentally changed in ways that created an institutionalized culture of violence (DiIulio, 1995). The apparent sharp increase in juvenile crime, coupled with the perception of a cultural shift that made violence more tolerated among young people, resulted in an unprecedented war on crime that reverberates even today.

Methodological issues about how juvenile crime is defined and measured are critical; both processes are impacted by *definitions* of crime, but also by how law is *enforced*. Like other complex social phenomena, delinquency and juvenile crime are exceedingly difficult to measure and fraught with methodological challenges. The intent of this chapter is to provide a detailed overview of the methodological problems that are pervasive in the area of juvenile delinquency. The chapter will first provide a more generalized discussion of the characteristics of juvenile delinquency that create measurement difficulties. While measurement is a challenge in all complex social phenomena, the argument will be made that features of juvenile delinquency and of the criminal justice system's response to it confound measurement in important ways. Focus will be given to the two primary types of data sources used to measure delinquency: official crime data and self-reported measures. The chapter will then give special notice to one type of juvenile delinquency that has garnered significant public attention in recent years, bullying, in an effort to show how public outrage about crime can change both definitions of crime and enforcement practices in ways that confound measurement.

Measurement Issues in Juvenile Delinquency

Like all areas of science, measurement in the social sciences identifies empirical indicators of abstract phenomena. Identifying empirical indicators subsequently permits measurement of the prevalence, causes, and consequences of the acts captured by the relevant concepts. Measurement is expected to provide an objective representation of complex phenomena, and although the limitations of particular measurement strategies are often discussed, social scientists treat concepts as if they have objective reality. Identifying data sources that provide reliable measures of juvenile delinquency can prove to be difficult, as many of the most commonly referenced data are beset by methodological problems that confound their interpretation. The section below provides detailed descriptions of the two mostly common types of delinquency measures: official crime and self-reported data.

Official data/Uniform Crime Report data

The Uniform Crime Report (UCR) is the most common data source used to compile national, state, and local crime statistics in the United States today. UCR data represent the universe of crimes that are *known* to the police and that they have *legally classified* as crimes (Black, 1980). They are typically comprised of two distinct, but related sets of elements: criminal *incident* and *arrest* data.[1] Crime incident data contain basic information about the criminal event itself, most notably its legal classification. Like offense data, arrest data include the legal classification of events, but also basic demographic components, most notably the age of the offender. Taken together, these two data sources yield the most comprehensive picture of criminal victimization (incident data) and offending (arrest data) in the United States.

It is the arrest segment of police data that provides measures of juvenile delinquency, since this is the only police data source that universally collects suspect demographic information. Arrests for *aggravated assault* in particular have traditionally been used to justify the conclusion of a spike in juvenile violence, and for two primary reasons (Howell, 2003). First, aggravated assault is generally considered a serious felony crime, indicative of violent offending. Thus it would be more appropriate to use measures of *aggravated* as opposed to *simple* assault on which to base conclusions about the prevalence of serious crime. Second, aggravated assaults occur with sufficient frequency to permit tracking and drawing conclusions. For example, the sheer volume of aggravated assaults helps to avoid the "tyranny of the small number" problem, whereby increases in the percentage of something that occurs with relative infrequency artificially create the image of an overwhelming problem.

UCR data have been used by some to the conclusion that there was a substantial juvenile crime wave during the 1980s and the early 1990s. Between 1989 and 1994, for example, the arrest rate for serious violent crime (murder, rape, robbery, and aggravated assault) increased by a whopping 46 percent among teenagers, by comparison to only about 12 percent for adults (Fox, 1996, p. 2). The number of juveniles identified as homicide offenders increased from just under 1,000 in 1984 to more than 2,500 ten years later, in 1994 (Fox, 1996, Figure 13). UCR data indicate that juveniles account for a disproportionate amount of all arrests. Although juveniles between the ages of 13 and 18, for example, made up approximately 8 percent of the US population, they accounted for nearly 20 percent of all individuals arrested (Bernard, 1999, p. 339). The proportion of homicides involving juvenile offenders increased from approximately 10 percent in 1965 to more than 15 percent in 1994, and the arrest rates for index crimes committed by juveniles aged 13–17 increased from 25 per 1,000 in 1965 to approximately 46 per 1,000 in 1995. Arrest rates of juveniles between the ages of 13 and 17 for violence also increased from approximately 2 per 1,000 in 1965 to nearly 8 per 1,000 in 1994 (Cook and Laub, 1998, pp. 36–40). Reputable scholars such as Cook and Laub (1998) noted that, after a period of relative stability in juvenile crime rates between the 1970s and 1980s, the potential for "trouble" was mounting; the authors referred to an "explosion in the rates in which adolescents commit and are victimized by serious crimes of violence" (p. 28).

While UCR data are regularly used as measures of crime and arrest data in social research, there may be important limitations that make comparisons among these data, both within and between communities, challenging at best (Eck and Maguire, 2000). When we interpret the meaning of crime data, it is important that we understand several caveats:

(a) Not all crimes are reported to the police. It is estimated that approximately 50 percent of serious crimes are never reported to the police (Skogan, 1977).
(b) Not all crimes reported to the police will appear in official crime databases (e.g., in the UCR). Police have the legal responsibility and authority to determine which crimes meet the basic requirements of a crime. It is estimated that between 6 percent and 65 percent of "reported" crimes (other than homicide) eventually make their way into official crime databases (Black, 1980; Klinger, 1997; Varano et al., 2009).
(c) Official UCR measures depicting "offenders" represent only those criminal events that have resulted in *arrests*. National data indicate that arrests are made in approximately 47 percent of violent crimes; and approximately 18 percent of property crimes (Federal Bureau of Investigations, 2014) are actually reported to the police.
(d) Criminal incidents might get more than one individual arrested for the event. When multiple offenders are involved in one crime, one single event may result in *multiple* arrests. Thus there is not necessarily a one-to-one relationship between incidents and arrest data.
(e) UCR arrest data do *not* represent the number of individuals arrested in a given year, but are best understood as the *total number of arrests* – adult, juvenile, or both – in a given year. This distinction recognizes that the same individuals can be arrested several times during one calendar year.
(f) Finally, when official UCR data are used to measure the prevalence of juvenile delinquency, it is the *arrest* segment of the data that is referenced. The arrest data include, for example, the age status (juvenile or adult) of the person(s) arrested, in addition to the crime classification.

The inherent challenges associated with using UCR data may be particularly relevant to measuring juvenile delinquency. Some have argued, for example, that UCR data present a misleading picture of juvenile involvement in crime (see Howell, 2003), because juveniles are more likely to commit crimes in groups (Warr, 2002). To the extent that group behavior is a common feature of juvenile delinquency, arrest data – the only kind of UCR data used to assess the extent of juvenile involvement in delinquency – might present a misleading picture of juvenile crime.

Juvenile delinquency is argued to be a *social* phenomenon by many criminologists. Since the earliest days of criminological research into the urban core, the group or gang was seen as a central component of delinquency (Thrasher, 1927). Elliot and Menard (1996) observed that peer networks are central to the onset and trajectory of criminal careers. Peers play a uniquely important role in the lives of young people and exert substantial influence over their behavior, presumably even over delinquent behavior (Brown, 1990). Summarizing this thesis, Stolzenberg and D'Alessio (2008) argue: "The basic premise is that individuals undergo a dramatic change in their exposure to delinquent peers during adolescence … that amplif[ies] group participation in illegal behavior" (p. 67). This evidence could lead one to reasonably conclude that, when arrests happen, those involving juvenile offenders are likely to be of more than one suspect. Analysis of crime data might suggest for example that, while the number, or even the proportion, of criminal *incidents* involving juveniles may remain static, the number of *arrests* of juveniles may actually rise. For these and other reasons, Howell (2003) cautioned against the exclusive use of UCR data for measuring trends in juvenile delinquency.

Recent research indicates that the influence of peers at individual and aggregate levels of delinquency is, however, far less clear than originally thought. Using data from the National Longitudinal Study of Adolescent Health, Haynie and Osgood (2005) found the impact of peers on patterns of delinquency to play a secondary role to other factors. When the relationship between peers and delinquency is considered in a representative sample of young people (as opposed to high-risk subpopulations), the influence of peer network takes a backseat (although it still remains a significant predictor), and *opportunity* emerges as one of the most salient predictors of delinquency. Also casting doubt on the role of peers in driving delinquency, Stolzenberg and D'Alessio's (2008, p. 79) analysis of National Incident-Based Reporting (NIBRS) data indicates that criminal offending is almost exclusively a solo enterprise until late adolescence, when *co-offending* finally kicks in. Interestingly, co-offending emerges, and ultimately becomes the dominant type of criminal offending, by and during the early twenties. In contrast to conventional wisdom, emerging research downplays the importance of co-offending on misrepresenting the picture of juvenile delinquency. So, while the utility of UCR data in providing an accurate measure of levels of juvenile delinquency is not necessarily clarified by this research, the research does nevertheless suggest that UCR data are likely not as confounded by the social nature of juvenile behavior as was previously thought.

Official data such as those supplied by the UCR might be problematic also because they are heavily influenced by discretionary decision-making among actors who work in the criminal justice system. Discretion, the heart of decision-making in the criminal justice system, has the potential to influence the picture of crime in ways that misrepresent the actual prevalence of crime. While all actors in the criminal justice system have discretion over how to leverage their legal authority, it is particularly important to pay attention to police discretion, because it occurs beyond the watchful eye of the public. As Goldstein (1960) observed: "These … decisions … are generally of extremely low visibility and consequently are seldom subject of review" (p. 543). Since police are generally more punitive or formal in their responses to criminal events involving juvenile suspects (Brown, Novak, and Frank, 2009; Smith, 1987), it is important to understand the impacts of changes in discretion on delinquency indicators.

Crime measures such as UCR data are *social products* influenced by a variety of factors, including the kinds of behavior that are defined as illegal and the ways in which actors in the criminal justice system such as police decide to *implement* the law. As Bernard (1999) noted, "changes in UCR data … may be a result of changes in [the application of law] rather than in offending" (p. 347). Even when legal definitions are consistent, *discretion* as to how law should be implemented can have a variable quality, which may vacillate between the formal (e.g., arrest) and the informal (reprimand and release). Although somewhat constrained by law, police use a variety of factors – such as seriousness of the offense, victim desires, offender cooperativeness, and organizational priorities – that help guide their decision-making (Black, 1980; Black and Reiss, 1970; McCluskey et al., 2004; Varano et al., 2009).

As the front line of the criminal justice system, the police retains an extraordinary amount of discretion in determining how the law gets applied via the arrest decision. Extralegal factors such as suspect age can function as conceptual "shortcuts" for dangerousness and thus explain how law is applied in practice. If there is in fact a perennial fear of youth, as suggested by Bernard and Kurlychek (2010), then differential enforcement practices may be a manifestation of that concern. Recent research supports the supposition that law is differentially enforced when it comes into contact with young people. Using systematic social observation data of police encounters with citizens in Cincinnati, Brown and colleagues (2009) reported that, other legal and extralegal factors aside, juveniles were significantly more likely to be arrested than adults (p. 206). The impact of age on police behavior appears to extend beyond the decision to arrest. Sobol, Wu, and Sun (2013), for example, measured "police vigor" in a broad context of police encounters by using data from the Project on Policing Neighborhoods (POPN) and reported that police generally used more formal levels of authority with juveniles than with adults – other situational and neighborhood-level factors being discounted (or controlled for). Police, it seems, treated juveniles in more punitive ways than their adult counterparts, even when controlling for legal factors such as crime seriousness.

If police are inclined to be more punitive toward juveniles than toward adults, then it is unclear to what extent local or national juvenile arrest data measure changes in *actual crime*, and not in *actual discretion*. This conclusion is based on the understanding that there is a certain amount of "actual" (or really existing) crime, and that actors in the criminal justice system can distort that picture depending on how they utilize discretion. If police have a greater tendency to handle crime informally (i.e., with no arrest), then traditional crime indicators such as arrest data would reveal lower levels of juvenile delinquency than expected. Discretion has a variable quality to it, and as such can be ratcheted up or down over time or across space, in order to achieve larger goals. Zero-tolerance policies, which are disproportionately applied to low-level crimes and to crimes involving juveniles (see Giroux, 2003), are a clear example of how shifts in policy may influence the picture of juvenile crime as measured with official crime data.

Using official data derived from the UCR to substantiate claims for a juvenile crime epidemic is, then, problematic. While the significance of group offending in misrepresenting the picture of juvenile delinquency is likely not as large as previously believed, there is evidence that shifts in discretion have impacted delinquency measures in recent decades. Aggravated assault, one category of crime often used to justify the conclusion that a juvenile crime wave exists (Fox, 1996), is particularly susceptible to shifts in discretion. Aggravated assault is considered among the most serious crimes (e.g., in the FBI Index or Part 1 crime) – those that warrant considerable public concern. Yet the actual level of physical injury encompassed in the category "aggravated assault" can range wildly between very serious (e.g., just short of murder) and relatively minor. One UCR data source that provides justification for the conclusion that there is an increase in juvenile crime is the category of juvenile arrests for murder. Due to the obvious seriousness of murders, there is no reason to believe that shifting levels of discretion would impact these data in any meaningful way. After hovering at approximately 6 per 100,000 between 1981 and 1987, rates of arrest for murder among young people aged between 10 and 17 began to increase dramatically around 1987, ultimately doubling to more than 12 per 100,000 in 1994 (Puzzanchera, 2013, p. 8). As rapidly as the arrest rate increased, this rate began a dramatic and steady decline in 1995, and eventually plateaued at about 4 per 100,000 – a rate also observed between the years 2000 and 2011.

Self-report data

In addition to UCR data and other "official" measures, self-reported data collected from both offenders and victims are often readily used to assess juvenile crime and delinquency. The attraction of such data sources lies in the ability of self-report measures to address some of the inherent limitations discussed earlier with regard to official measures (Krohn et al., 2010). For instance, self-report data allow for at least some of the crimes unreported to the police to be captured, as this information is collected directly from offenders and victims, regardless of whether any police report was filed or not. Similarly, self-report allows for crimes that do not result in an arrest to be included, especially relatively minor crimes or status offenses for juveniles. Ultimately, self-report measures of crime and delinquency are not impacted by the discretion of the criminal justice system, but rather rely on offenders' and victims' willingness to share accurate accounts of their experiences with crime. Therefore self-report data are often considered to give the most valid measures of delinquency (Dunford and Elliott, 1984). There are a number of self-report measures of juvenile crime and delinquency, some of which are discussed below.

Monitoring the Future The Monitoring the Future (MTF) project, which was first known as the National High School Senior Survey, began in 1975 and its aim is to understand the changes in beliefs, attitudes, and behaviors of young people in the United States over time (University of Michigan, 2014). Specifically, the project aspires to understand change on a number of diverse issues, such as government and politics, alcohol and drug use, gender roles, and protection of the environment.

This project is comprised of a series of surveys in which 8th, 10th, and 12th graders, college students, and young adults answer the same set of questions over a period of time, as part of an effort to assess change. Each spring, researchers use a multistage random sampling strategy to identify the national sample of students who will participate from each grade level. Each student who participates is then mailed a follow-up survey each year, until s/he becomes a young adult. Approximately fifty thousand students from over four hundred schools, both public and private, are surveyed each year (University of Michigan, 2014).

In terms of juvenile crime and delinquency, the MTF focuses on the beliefs, attitudes, and behaviors of students vis-à-vis alcohol, tobacco, and drug use. Considering the project's findings with regard to alcohol, there has been a steady decline since 1974 in the percentage of students in 8th, 10th, and 12th grade who reported using it in the 30 days prior to completing the survey (Johnston et al., 2014, Figure 1). For instance, the percentage of 12th graders who reported using alcohol in the 30 days prior to completing the survey was approximately 65 percent in 1974, while in 2014 this percentage fell to just under 40 percent (Johnston et al., 2014, Figure 1). Similar trends can be seen in both 8th and 10th graders, yet the percentages for these populations have been considerably lower than the percentages for 12th graders across time. This decrease in actual use has been accompanied by corresponding attitudes and beliefs. Since the early 1990s, there has been an increase in the percentage of students in 8th, 10th, and 12th grade who perceive *great risk* in having five or more drinks in a row (e.g., binge drinking) once or twice in a weekend (Johnston et al., 2014, Figure 1).

Despite an increase in the use of cigarettes by 8th, 10th, and 12th grade students in the mid- to early 1990s, which reached approximately 40 percent for 12th graders, the percentage of students who smoked cigarettes in the 30 days prior to taking the survey has decreased drastically since that year: the figure was lower than 20 percent for 12th graders in 2014 (Johnston et al., 2014, Figure 3). This decrease has been accompanied by an increase in the percentage of students in 8th, 10th, and 12th grade who see *great risk* in smoking a pack or more a day, as well as in the percentage of students who disapprove of smoking a pack or more a day (Johnston et al., 2014, Figure 3). Regarding the use of marijuana annually by students, trends have fluctuated to a certain degree over the past four decades. After a decrease in annual use of marijuana by 8th, 10th, and 12th grade students from the late 1970s up until the early 1990s, the annual use of marijuana increased until about 1997 (Johnston et al., 2014, Figure 6). Since that year, the use of marijuana by students in the same grades has remained relatively stable. But, despite this stability, the past several years have registered, among students of this group, a decrease in the perceived risks associated with marijuana use. In particular, the percentage of those who perceive *great risk* in using marijuana has decreased considerably since the mid-1990s (Johnston et al., 2014, Figure 6). Additionally, trends show that the availability of marijuana increases greatly with age. For instance, over 80 percent of 12th grade respondents in 2014 reported that it was *fairly easy* or *very easy* to get marijuana, while approximately 70 percent and 40 percent of 10th and 8th graders, respectively, reported such ease (Johnston et al., 2014, Figure 6).

The Youth Risk Behavior Surveillance System The Youth Risk Behavior Surveillance System (YRBSS) is similar to the MTF project in that it monitors changes in young people's behaviors over time. The YRBSS focuses on six types of health-risk behaviors that have been identified as the leading contributors to death and disability among youth. The Center for Disease Control conducts the survey every two years and uses a multistage cluster design to select a representative sample of students in 9–12 grade from public and private schools in the United States.

Many of the violence-related behaviors included in the YRBSS (i.e., carrying a weapon, carrying a gun, carrying a weapon on school property, being threatened or injured with a weapon on school property, being in a physical fight, being injured in a physical fight, and being in a physical fight on school property), have demonstrated steady decreases over time (Frieden et al., 2014). For instance, in 1991, 26.1 percent of students reported carrying a weapon at least once during the 30 days prior to the survey, whereas in 2013 this figured had dropped to 17.9 percent. Similarly, in 1991, 42.5 percent of students reported being in one or more physical fights during the 12 months before the survey; however, after a steady decrease through much of the 1990s and the first decade of the twenty-first century, this percentage has dropped to 24.7 percent. Nevertheless, not going to school because of safety concerns has increased slightly over time: in 1993, 4.4 percent of students reported having missed school for such reasons at least once during the 30 days before the survey, and in 2013 that figure increased to 7.1 percent.

Trends depicting decreases in many of the tobacco, alcohol, and drug-related variables included in the YRBSS are also apparent. Specifically, over time – namely over the period 1991–2013 – the number of youth reporting ever smoking cigarettes, smoking a whole cigarette before the age of 13, current cigarette use, current frequent cigarette use, smoking more than 10 cigarettes per day, smoking cigarettes on school property, buying cigarettes in a store or gas station, ever smoking cigarettes daily, currently smoking cigarettes daily, current cigar use, and current tobacco use has decreased (Frieden et al., 2014). For instance, in 1991, 70.1 percent of students reported ever trying cigarette smoking, while by 2013 this percentage had dropped to 41.1 percent. There has also been a decrease over time in youth who, at the time of the survey, had ever drank alcohol, drank alcohol before age 13 years, and reported either current alcohol use or having five or more drinks of alcohol in a row (Frieden et al., 2014). Similar trends are also seen in relation to drug use. Over time, marijuana use as well as the use of other illicit drugs has decreased (Frieden et al., 2014).

Other self-report measures Other self-report measures of juvenile crime and delinquency include the National Crime Victimization Survey (NCVS), specifically the School Crime Supplement (SCS), and the School Survey on Crime and Safety (SSOCS). The SCS to the NCVS is a national survey of approximately 6,500 students aged 12 through 18 in US public and private schools (National Center for Educational Statistics, 2014). The project aims to collect information regarding victimization, crime, and safety in schools. The survey is conducted every two years by the National Center for Education Statistics (NCES) and by the Bureau of Justice Statistics (BJS).

Similarly, the SSOCS is a nationally representative survey of approximately 3,500 public elementary and secondary schools (National Center for Education Statistics, 2014). This survey serves as the primary source of school-level data on crime and safety in the United States. The SSOCS is administered by the US Department of Education, National Center for Education Statistics (NCES) to public elementary, middle, and high school principals (as opposed to students) in the spring of even-numbered school years.

NCVS-SCS data indicate that overall rates of victimization for school-age children have steadily decreased since 1992. For instance, overall victimization rates for young people aged 12–18 were greater than 150 per 1,000 in 1992, yet in 2012 they were less than 50 per 1,000. The data do, however, suggest that victimization among young people aged 12–18 is more prevalent at school compared to other locations. The most recent *Indicators of School Crime and Safety* report, for example, indicates that approximately 1.36 million victimizations occurred in schools, by comparison to an estimated 991,200 that occurred outside school premises in 2012 (Robers et al., 2014). This translates into a victimization rate of 52 per 100,000 students in school, by comparison to 38 per 100,000 students outside of school. Increased victimization levels on school grounds was consistent across crime types. For instance, theft victimizations were higher at school (24 per 100,000) than away from school (18 per 100,000). Similarly, victimization levels for personal assaultive crime in 2012 were higher in school (24 per 100,000) than away from school (17 per 100,000) (Robers et al., 2014). These figures illustrate that, despite an overall decrease in victimization for school-aged children, victimization is now more likely to happen at school than away from school. However, much of this increased victimization is at least partially explained by the fact that young people spend a great deal of their time in the school environment.

In addition to victimization rates, school safety is also gauged in terms of the type and frequency of criminal and violent incidents that occur there. For instance, during the 2011–2012 school year, 88 percent of public schools reported at least one criminal incident each (Robers et al., 2014). The most prevalent criminal incidents were gang violence, drug crime, and simple assault. Approximately 20 percent of high school students indicated gang activity within their school, while 23 percent of high school students reported that drugs had been offered, sold, or given to them during the 2009–2010 school year. Additionally, 31 percent of high school students reported that they had been in a fight within the past 12 months.

Limitations to self-report measures of crime and delinquency Despite addressing some of the limitations associated with UCR data and other official measures of juvenile crime and delinquency, self-report measures have shortcomings of their own. Several of these shortcomings are associated with all self-report measures of crime, while others are unique to juvenile crime and delinquency.

First, self-report measures depend on offenders' and victims' willingness to report their experiences with crime; therefore, the possibility of respondents' not sharing these experiences is problematic. Thornberry and Krohn (2000), for example, argue that while the self-report method is an effective strategy for measuring delinquency over time, it does have its limitations particularly for longitudinal studies. Delinquency studies using self-report methods tend to be hampered by problems of instrumentation (instruments that change over time) and respondent fatigue. Lauritsen (1998) similarly warns that self-reported delinquency studies can be hampered by maturation effects that confound the accuracy of data over time.

Another limitation of self-reported delinquency research relates to the *location* of many of these studies. Major delinquency data collection efforts such as the MTF and the YRBSS are conducted in school settings. However, there are certain subpopulations of juveniles that are not included in self-report measures due to the fact that collection often occurs at school (Howell, 2003). These subpopulations include (1) students who are absent on the date of data collection, (2) students who have dropped out of school, and (3) students who are homeless and do not attend school regularly (McCord, Widom, and Crowell, 2001). It is possible that offenders or victims or both will not participate in data collection efforts for a number of reasons, and therefore their experiences of crime will not be captured. Just as official data are dependent upon police discretion, self-report data are largely dependent on potential respondents' willingness and availability to share their offenses or victimizations. Further, those who are available and agree to participate by sharing their experiences of crime may or may not do so accurately, which is a second potential limitation of self-report measures (Huizinga and Elliott, 1986; Thornberry and Krohn, 2000). Respondents to self-report surveys may over- or underreport their involvement in crime for a number of reasons. Thornberry and Krohn (2000) stated that although self-report measures appear to be reliable, there is evidence of a validity issue related to the underreporting of criminal involvement. This underreporting may be the result of deliberate falsification by, or on behalf of, the respondent or to recall problems associated with his or her criminal involvement. In addition to underreporting, Huizinga and Elliot (1986) discussed the potential for overreporting. However, given these biases and errors in official measures, the degree of over- and underreporting are difficult to determine.

A final limitation is that self-report measures and official measures tend to measure different types of crimes, and this makes comparison between them difficult (Hindelang, Hirschi, and Weis, 1979). Many of the self-report measures mentioned above focus on status offenses (e.g., tobacco and alcohol use) and relatively minor crimes, such as drug use, whereas the UCR and other official data collections tend to capture more serious crimes (Thornberry and Krohn, 2000). Research suggests that both measures provide an accurate depiction of their respective domains; however, these measures may not be evaluating the same domains (Hindelang et al., 1979).

Special issue in delinquency: Bullying

Juvenile delinquency, like many social problems, can be difficult to define and measure. As described above, juvenile delinquency measures are complicated by actual variation in behavior, changes in laws, and changes in how law is enforced via discretion. The interpretation of local, state, or even national juvenile delinquency is hampered by this reality. The issue of *bullying*, a contemporary problem that has received considerable attention from the public in recent years, is an important example of how behavior, law, and social control strategies intermix and make the measurement of social problems difficult. Although the public attention to bullying is relatively new, it is hardly a new problem.

Research indicates that prevalence rates of bullying victimization can vary quite wildly, from under 10 percent to over 50 percent (Atria, Strohmeier, and Spiel, 2007). In one 1995 study, young people aged 12–18 indicated that approximately 5 percent reported having been bullied in the previous six months while at school (Addington et al., 2002). Solberg and Olweus (2003) reported that approximately 10 percent of students across 37 schools in Norway were involved in bullying, either as victims or as offenders. Estimating bullying levels to be much higher, Nansel and colleagues (2001) reported that approximately 30 percent of youth experience moderate or frequent involvement in bullying. With such variation, making sense of the meaning of state- or federal-level statistics can be difficult. The difference in prevalence rates could be attributed to a multitude of factors, for example differences in sample demographics, the time reference point used to assess victimization or offending, the location reference point (e.g., whether the bullying episode occurred at school or elsewhere), and similar factors.

Although increased attention was given to bullying in the 1990s, the topic failed to draw sustained interest, particularly from policymakers. Something began to change in the period 2005–2010, when adolescent bullying, a problem acknowledged for generations, was not only (re)discovered, but argued to have reached epidemic levels and to indicate a public health crisis (Masiello and Schroeder, 2013). By the year 2007, for example, the Centers for Disease Control (CDC) identified bullying among young people as an emerging public health problem that required serious public attention. In 2010, the ABC News show *20/20* produced a detailed documentary on the problem of both traditional and online bullying and characterized it as an "epidemic that causes 160,000 children a day to stay home from school" (Dubreuil and McNiff, 2010). Fueled in part by an explosion in electronic communication and social media that has facilitated constant communication and by the attention given by the media to numerous teen suicides, bullying became one of the most highly debated areas of youth violence in more than a decade. But it was the tragic suicide of Phoebe Prince, a 15-year-old high school student from Hadley, Massachusetts, that captivated the public's attention and started a national discourse about bullying (Kennedy, 2010).

Phoebe Prince's death – and that of others, such as Carl Walker, a middle school student from Springfield, Massachusetts in 2009 (James, 2009), or Tyler Clementi, a student at Rutgers University (Foderaro, 2010) – propelled bullying into the national spotlight and compelled many states to take action and do something about bullying. Certainly this was not a new class of "delinquent" behavior; what changed was how the educational and legal systems chose to *respond* to the problem. In answer to growing levels of public outcry about bullying, legislators in some states introduced new legislation: they created laws that not only defined bullying as criminal behavior, but also compelled schools in particular to take action and implement more aggressive, zero-tolerance approaches to bullying. This relatively sudden and dramatic shift in attitude toward a behavior that has been well documented among young people and adults alike is important to consider.

New laws Like on the broader issue of juvenile delinquency discussed earlier in the chapter, it is the perception that dangerous and violent youth are involved that has the ability to drive quick and severe reactions from policymakers (see Bernard and Kurlychek, 2010). Never wanting to get caught flat-footed when a moral crisis puts questions of legality and governmental power into the national spotlight, many state legislatures responded to the perceived bullying crisis by implementing new laws. Much of the action to create or enhance laws was based on the perception that bullying, like other forms juvenile delinquency in the past, was at epidemic levels. Fears of bullying were exacerbated by arguments that social media had fundamentally altered the dynamics of bullying by extending the reach of bullies, who could harass now at all times and in all places (see Hinduja and Patchin, 2012). The growth in new state laws targeting bullying increased dramatically in the aftermath of the Columbine and Phoebe Prince tragedies. According to the US Department of Education, only one state, Georgia, had implemented bullying laws in 1999, but there was a steady increase in the number of states that created new bullying legislation; such legislation both refined legal definitions of bullying and implemented mandatory reporting requirements. Most states had implemented some sort of antibully laws between the years 2008 and 2010 alone. In a few short years, 46 states adopted bullying laws and 36 states adopted provisions pertaining to cyberbullying (Stuart-Cassel, Bell, and Springer, 2011). Of the 46 states that have adopted bullying laws, 29 have given a definition of bullying. For instance, Florida law defines bullying as:

> "Bullying" means systematically and chronically inflicting physical hurt or psychological distress on one or more students and may involve: (1) Teasing; (2) Social exclusion; (3) Threat; (4) Intimidation; (5) Stalking; (6) Physical violence; (7) Theft; (8) Sexual, religious, or racial harassment; (9) Public humiliation; or (10) Destruction of property. ("Bullying and harassment prohibited," 2005)

Texas law similarly defines bullying as:

> "Bullying" means ... engaging in written or verbal expression, expression through electronic means, or physical conduct that occurs on school property, at a school-sponsored or school-related activity, or in a vehicle operated by the district and that: (1) has the effect or will have the effect of physically harming a student, damaging a student's property, or placing a student in reasonable fear of harm to the student's person or of damage to the student's property; or (2) is sufficiently severe, persistent, and pervasive enough that the action or threat creates an intimidating, threatening, or abusive educational environment for a student. (b) Conduct

> described is considered bullying if that conduct: (1) exploits an imbalance of power between the student perpetrator and the student victim through written or verbal expression or physical conduct; and (2) interferes with a student's education or substantially disrupts the operation of a school. ("Bullying prevention policies and procedures," 2015)

It is important to note that not merely the *implementation* of new law is worthy of consideration, but the *substance* of the law as well. Bullying legislation and the attendant legal consequences can be differentiated from the more traditional legal code by how concepts of harm and prohibited behaviors are defined. Criminal law traditionally defines harm in explicit terms, which focus on *physical* aspects of harm – such as physical harm to the person (e.g., injury requiring medical attention), loss of property, or some sort of financial harm. Harm is traditionally defined in objective ways, which can be objectively identified and measured for the most part. In the case of bullying, harm goes beyond mere physical harm; and extends to emotional and social harm (National Bullying Prevention Center, 2014). The legal expansion of harm so as to include *emotional* harm creates a subjective framework for judging liabilities. That is, the same behavior might be legal or illegal depending on the victim's perceptions. Bullying legislation is also vague in terms of how it defines prohibited behavior. Instead of taking the more traditional legal route of creating specific categories of prohibited behavior, the new laws leave these categories vague and typically include behaviors that would be otherwise considered *legal*, were it not for the apparent harm. Massachusetts General Law (MGL) 71, Section 370, for example, prohibits *any* "verbal or electronic expression or a physical act or gesture or any combination thereof" that causes "physical or emotional harm" (Commonwealth of Massachusetts, 2011). These vague descriptions give broad discretion to alleged victims, school officials, and police or prosecutors to interpret the impact of specific behaviors on specific individuals when making judgments about legal culpability. In a practical sense, these new laws have the potential to *define in* or count among delinquency measures a broad grouping of behaviors that have traditionally been excluded.

A refined application of existing law In addition to the development of new law, the growing pressure to do something about the bullying problem resulted in the application of current laws in ways not traditionally done. Legal advocates, for example, have pushed for the application of federal civil rights charges under both Title VI and Title IX of the Civil Rights code (US Department of Education, 2010). The idea that accusations of federal civil rights violation could be applied to behavior traditionally viewed as otherwise "normal" among young people is notable. The push to enhance the application of existing laws has been a political priority also at the state and local levels (Toppo, 2012). The state of Georgia, for example, modified existing laws that prohibited disruption of or interference with the operation of a public school in order to address bullying. Still other states, such as Kentucky, Massachusetts, Missouri, and Nevada, have used existing laws prohibiting harassment as a way of tackling bullying. In addition to existing harassment laws, Massachusetts and Missouri have used existing stalking and witness intimidation legislation to go after alleged bullies (Sacco et al., 2012).

Legal restrictions on discretion The fight to combat perceived increases in bullying was also carried out by attempting to restrict the right to exercise discretion in schools and even in police departments that arguably did not respond to allegations with appropriate vigor. As part of the national dialogue on bullying, numerous accounts emerged of victims and parents who engaged school or police officials about the problem only to have their concerns rebuffed. A substantive part of the reform efforts in many states were directed at reducing the amount of discretion that both school administrators and the police could exercise (Sacco et al., 2012). By 2012, nine states passed legislation that *required* the reporting of alleged bullying incidents to police. The state of Kentucky law, for example, requires that "the principal shall file with the local school board and the local law enforcement agency or the Department of Kentucky State Police or the county attorney within forty-eight (48) hours of the original report a written report" (Sacco et al., 2012, p. A-34). The pressure to "crack down" on bullying and send a tough message to youth across the country is real and has serious consequences. State law not only directed schools to be more proactive in their reporting of behaviors to the police, but also extended the authority of the police over such matters. Missouri state law, for example, authorized police to make warrantless arrests of individuals suspected of violating aspects of the state's antibullying law (Sacco et al., 2012, p. A-48). Of particular concern is the finding that, when zero tolerance is implemented, particularly as it relates to less serious "crime" such as bullying, it is more likely to have a differential impact on young girls, by bringing a disproportionate number of them into contact with the juvenile court system (Chesney-Lind, Morash, and Irwin, 2010).

Bullying, a form of aggressive behavior mostly developed among young people, is an interesting comparison point, as it relates to juvenile delinquency. It represents a broad cross-section of behavior that falls on a continuum from the less to the more serious. Toward the more serious end of the scale are behaviors that stay within the framework of our existing legal codes such as criminal harassment, theft of property, and assault. There remains, however, toward the lower end of the spectrum, an entire class of behaviors that fall somewhere between behavioral infractions (when they happen in the context of schools) and lower level crimes. It is clear that, as the public's attention on the problem of bullying has increased, the arguments for schools and police to "do something" about the problem have intensified. The "do something," as is often the case, generally amounts to the passage of new laws and a restriction on discretion that creates an image of increasing crime levels. The impact of these changes on juvenile delinquency measures is unclear at this point, but there is little doubt that, as the focus on bullying becomes increasingly institutionalized, we would expect to see it manifest itself in aggregate juvenile delinquency measures.

Conclusion

As Kuhn (1970, p. 5) noted, "Normal science … is predicated on the assumption that the scientific community knows what the world is like." Measurement is an important component to this assumption and plays a central role in defining this shared understanding of the world in which we live. Measurement *is* the foundation of science; it presupposes patterns to the world that can be categorized, measured, and predicted. Creating shared agreement about how complex phenomena are conceptualized, operationalized, and measured is central to the scientific process. While those engaged in the scientific enterprise understand that conceptualization and measurement are not always as exact and specific as desired, *consumers* of science are often less critical and reflective of how measurement decisions impact science. Nowhere are measurement issues more challenging than in the social sciences, where the core concepts of interest are often less tangible and more subject to the *creation* of shared agreement than they are in the natural sciences.

The reliability and validity of measures in criminal justice and criminology are subject to these same concerns, which become particularly manifest in the area of juvenile delinquency. Like all questions of crime and justice, measurement concerns related to delinquency are confounded by shifts in evolution in law, policy shifts at varying levels of government, cultural shifts at the institutional level, among the various agencies responsible for implementing criminal justice, and individual decision-making among those responsible for enforcing the law. At their core, crime data must be understood as a social product created in a dynamic, political context. If crime data are the subject of measurement concerns, nowhere is this felt more than in the area of juvenile delinquency. To the extent that the public discourse about crime is shaped by apparent trends in juvenile offending (see Bernard and Kurlychek, 2010), data about juvenile crime can be considered the "canary in the cave," which experiences most directly and immediately shifts in culture and policy related to crime.

Consumers of official statistics such as the UCR data are encouraged to view the limitations of these sources with a degree of seriousness. Although countless articles have been written on the subject, consumers of official crime data, academics and policymakers alike, often do not give a proper voice to these concerns. It is critical to recognize that juvenile delinquency, along with related problems such as gangs or bullying, have a tendency to represent the worst fears of a society. The best way to avoid careless interpretation is vigilance in the use of mixed methods when measuring a problem. As juvenile delinquency is an abstract social concept prone to being unduly influenced by external factors, a mixed methods approach to measuring it offers the researcher an opportunity to provide the most reliable and valid measures. Use of "methodological pluralism" has important "pragmatic and epistemological implications" for measurement (Moran-Ellis et al., 2006). Bullying, a form of juvenile delinquency that has received substantial attention in recent years, provides an excellent example of why precise and accurate delinquency measures are desperately needed. In the absence of quality data that define a problem clearly, the public is likely to respond to the perception that problems have reached "epidemic levels" in ways not wholly consistent with the actual threat.

Note

1 Uniform Crime Report (UCR) data, which are maintained by the Federal Bureau of Investigations, are a complex compilation of the UCR and the National Incident-Based Reporting System (NIBRS). Both systems provide technical capacities for local jurisdictions to report their crime data to states' crime data repository – state police agencies in the cases discussed here. Once compiled at the state level, crime data are ultimately submitted to the FBI via electronic procedures. The NIBRS was developed in the early 1990s in an effort to *replace* the UCR system by collecting more detailed crime data pertaining to individual crimes. The rollout of the NIBRS system has gone much more slowly than expected, and hence the FBI maintains both crime-reporting processes. For purposes of providing national crime data, the FBI transforms NIBRS data into a format that allows for their integration with UCR data, in a more comprehensive picture of crime and crime trends (see Federal Bureau of Investigations, 2012).

References

Addington, L. A., Ruddy, S. A., Miller, A. K., and DeVoe, J. F. 2002. Are America's schools safe? Students speak out: 1999 School Crime Supplement. Statistical Analysis Report. Washington, DC: National Center for Educational Statistics.

Atria, M., Strohmeier, D., and Spiel, C. 2007. The relevance of the school class as social unit for the prevalence of bullying and victimization. *European Journal of Developmental Psychology*, 4 (4): 372–387.

Bernard, T. J. 1999. Juvenile crime and the transformation of juvenile justice: Is there a juvenile crime wave? *Justice Quarterly*, 16 (2): 337–356.

Bernard, T. J., and Kurlychek, M. C. 2010. *The cycle of juvenile justice*. New York: Oxford University Press.

Black, D. J. 1980. *Production of crime rates*. New York: Academic Press.

Black, D. J., and Reiss, A. J. 1970. Police control of juveniles. *American Sociological Review*, 35 (1): 63–77.

Brown, B. B. 1990. Peer groups and peer cultures. In *At the threshold: The developing adolescent*, edited by S. S. Feldman and G. R. Elliott, 171–196. Cambridge, MA: Harvard University Press.

Brown, R. A., Novak, K. J., and Frank, J. 2009. Identifying variation in police officer behavior between juveniles and adults. *Journal of Criminal Justice*, 37 (2): 200–208. doi: http://dx.doi.org/10.1016/j.jcrimjus.2009.02.004.

Bullying and harassment prohibited. 2005. Section 147 of Chapter 1006 (Support for learning) of Title 48 (Education code) in the 2015 Florida statutes. Accessed December 9, 2015. http://www.leg.state.fl.us/statutes/index.cfm?App_mode = Display_Statute&URL=1000-1099/1006/Sections/1006.147.html.

Bullying prevention policies and procedures. 2015. Section 0832 of Chapter 37 (Discipline, law and order) in Texas's Education code, 2G. Accessed December 9, 2015. http://www.statutes.legis.state.tx.us/Docs/ED/htm/ED.37.htm#37.0832.

Chesney-Lind, M., Morash, M., and Irwin, K. 2010. Policing girlhood. In *Fighting for girls: New perspectives on gender and violence*, edited by M. Chesney-Lind and N. Jones, 107–128. Albany, NY: SUNY Press.

Coalition for Juvenile Justice. 1997. *Annual report: False images? The news media and juvenile crime*. Washington, DC: US Government Printing Office.

Commonwealth of Massachusetts. 2011. Massachusetts General Law. Accessed December 3, 2015. https://malegislature.gov/Laws/GeneralLaws/PartI/TitleXII/Chapter71/Section37O.

Cook, P. J., and Laub, J. H. 1998. The unprecedented epidemic in youth violence. In *Youth violence*, vol. 24: *Crime and justice*, edited by M. Tonry and M. H. Moore, 27–64. Chicago, IL: University of Chicago Press.

DiIulio, J. 1995. The coming of the super-predators. *Weekly Standard*, 1 (11): 23–29.

Dubreuil, J., and McNiff, E. 2010. Bullied to death in America's schools. Accessed January 15, 2015. http://abcnews.go.com/2020/TheLaw/school-bullying-epidemic-turning-deadly/story?id = 11880841.

Dunford, F. W., and Elliott, D. S. 1984. Identifying career offenders using self-reported data. *Journal of Research in Crime and Delinquency*, 21 (1): 57–86.

Eck, J. E., and Maguire, E. 2000. Have changes in policing reduced violent crime? An assessment of the evidence. In *The crime drop in America*, edited by A. Blumstein and J. Wallman, 207–228. New York: Cambridge University Press.

Elliot, D. S., and Menard, S. 1996. Delinquent friends and delinquent behavior: temporal and developmental patterns. In *Delinquency and Crime*, edited by J. D. Hawkins, 28–67. New York: Cambridge University Press.

Federal Bureau of Investigations. 2012. National incident-based reporting system (NIBRS). Washington, DC: Federal Bureau of Investigations.

Federal Bureau of Investigations. 2014. Crime in the United States. Accessed December 18, 2014. http://www.fbi.gov/about-us/cjis/ucr/crime-in-the-u.s/2010/crime-in-the-u.s.-2010/tables/10tbl25.xls.

Foderaro, L. W. 2010. Private moment made public, then a fatal jump. *The New York Times*, September 29. Accessed December 7, 2015. http://www.nytimes.com/2010/09/30/nyregion/30suicide.html?pagewanted=all&_r=0.

Fox, J. A. 1996. Trends in juvenile violence: A report to the United States Attorney General on current and future rates of juvenile offending. Washington, DC: Bureau of Justice Statistics.

Frieden, T. R., Jaffe, H. W., Cono, J., Richards, C. L., and Iademarco, M. F. 2014. Youth risk behavior surveillance: United States, 2013. Atlanta, GA: Centers for Disease Control.

Giroux, H. 2003. Racial injustice and disposable youth in the age of zero tolerance. *International Journal of Qualitative Studies in Education*, 16 (4): 553–565. doi: 10.1080/0951839032000099543.

Goldstein, J. 1960. Police discretion not to invoke the criminal process: Low-visibility decisions in the administration of justice. *Yale Law Journal*, 69 (4): 543–594.

Haynie, D. L., and Osgood, D. W. 2005. Reconsidering peers and delinquency: How do peers matter? *Social Forces*, 84 (2): 1109–1130. doi: 10.1353/sof.2006.0018.

Hindelang, M. J., Hirschi, T., and Weis, J. G. 1979. Correlates of delinquency: The illusion of discrepancy between self-reported and official measures. *American Sociological Review*, 44: 995–1014.

Hinduja, S., and Patchin, J. W. 2012. *School climate 2.0: Preventing cyberbullying and sexting one classroom at a time*. Thousand Oaks, CA: Sage.

Howell, J. C. 2003. *Preventing and reducing juvenile delinquency: A comprehensive framework*. Thousand Oaks, CA: Sage.

Huizinga, D., and Elliott, D. S. 1986. Reassessing the reliability and validity of self-report delinquency measures. *Journal of Quantitative Criminology*, 2 (4): 293–327.

James, S. D. 2009. When words can kill: "That's so gay." ABC News. Accessed January 15, 2015. http://abucnews.go.com/Health/MindMoodNews/story?id = 7328091&page = 1.

Johnston, L. D., O'Malley, P. M., Bachman, J. G., Schulenberg, J. E., Miech, R. A., University of Michigan, ... United States of America. 2014. *Monitoring the Future national survey results on drug use, 1975–2013*, vol. 2: *College students and adults, ages* 19–55. Ann Arbor: Institute for Social Research, University of Michigan.

Kennedy, H. 2010. Phoebe Prince, South Hadley High School's' "new girl," driven to suicide by teenage cyber bullies. *New York Daily News*, March 29. Accessed December 9, 2015. http://www.nydailynews.com/news/national/phoebe-prince-south-hadley-high-school-new-girl-driven-suicide-teenage-cyber-bullies-article-1.165911.

Klinger, D. A. 1997. Negotiating order in patrol work: An ecological theory of police response to deviance. *Criminology*, 35 (2): 277–306.

Krohn, M. D., Thornberry, T. P., Gibson, C. L., and Baldwin, J. M. 2010. The development and impact of self-report measures of crime and delinquency. *Journal of Quantitative Criminology*, 26 (4): 509–525.

Kuhn, T. S. 1970. *The structure of scientific revolutions*, vol. 2. Chicago, IL: University of Chicago Press.

Lauritsen, J. L. 1998. The age crime debate: Assessing the limits of longitudinal self-report data. *Social Forces*, 77 (1): 127–154.

Masiello, M. G., and Schroeder, D. 2013. *A public health approach to bullying prevention*. Washington, DC: American Public Health Association.

McCluskey, J. D., Varano, S. P., Huebner, B. M., and Bynum, T. S. 2004. Who do you refer? The effects of a policy change on juvenile referrals. *Criminal Justice Policy Review*, 15 (4): 437–461.

McCord, J., Widom, C. S., and Crowell, N. A., eds. 2001. *Juvenile Crime, Juvenile Justice: Panel on Juvenile Crime: Prevention, Treatment, and Control*. Washington, DC: National Academy Press.

Moran-Ellis, J., Alexander, V. D., Cronin, A., Dickinson, M., Fielding, J., Sleney, J., and Thomas, H. 2006. Triangulation and integration: Processes, claims and implications. *Qualitative Research*, 6 (1): 45–59.

Nansel, T. R., Overpeck, M., Pilla, R. S., Ruan, W. J., Simons-Morton, B., and Scheidt, P. 2001. Bullying behaviors among US youth: Prevalence and association with psychosocial adjustment. *Jama*, 285 (16): 2094–2100.

National Bullying Prevention Center. 2014. Bullying info and facts: Defining bullying behavior. Accessed July 7, 2014. http://www.pacer.org/bullying/resources/info-facts.asp.

National Center for Educational Statistics. 2014. School crime supplement on the national crime victimization survey (SCS/NCVS). Accessed December 15, 2014. http://nces.ed.gov/programs/crime/surveys.asp.

Puzzanchera, C. 2013. *Juvenile arrests, 2011*. Washington, DC: Office of Juvenile Justice and Delinquency Prevention (OJJDP).

Robers, S., Kemp, J., Rathbun, A., and Morgan, R. E. 2014. *Indicators of school crime and safety, 2013*. NCES 2014-042/NCJ 243299. Washington, DC: National Center for

Education Statistics. Accessed December 14, 2015. http://www.bjs.gov/content/pub/pdf/iscs13.pdf.

Sacco, D. T., Silbaugh, K., Corredor, F., Casey, J., and Doherty, D. 2012. *An overview of state anti-bullying legislation and other related laws*. Cambridge, MA: Harvard University Press.

Skogan, W. G. 1977. Dimensions of the dark figure of unreported crime. *Crime and Delinquency*, 23 (1): 41–50. doi: 10.1177/001112877702300104.

Smith, D. A. 1987. Police response to interpersonal violence: Defining the parameters of legal control. *Social Forces*, 65 (3): 767–782.

Snyder, H., and Sickmund, M. 1999. *Juvenile offenders and victims: 1999 national report*. Washington, DC: Office of Juvenile Justice and Delinquency Prevention.

Sobol, J. J., Wu, Y., and Sun, I. Y. 2013. Neighborhood context and police vigor: A multilevel analysis. *Crime and Delinquency*, 59 (3): 344–368. doi: 10.1177/0011128712470348.

Solberg, M. E., and Olweus, D. 2003. Prevalence estimation of school bullying with the Olweus Bully/Victim Questionnaire. *Aggressive Behavior*, 29 (3): 239–268. doi: 10.1002/ab.10047.

Stolzenberg, L., and D'Alessio, S. J. 2008. Co-offending and the age–crime curve. *Journal of Research in Crime and Delinquency*, 45 (1): 65–86.

Stuart-Cassel, V., Bell, A., and Springer, J. F. 2011. *Analysis of State Bullying Laws and Policies*. Washington, DC. Accessed December 4, 2015. http://www2.ed.gov/rschstat/eval/bullying/state-bullying-laws/state-bullying-laws.pdf.

Thornberry, T. P., and Krohn, M. D. 2000. The self-report method for measuring delinquency and crime. *Criminal justice*, 4 (1): 33–83.

Thrasher, F. M. 1927. *The gang*. Chicago, IL: University of Chicago Press.

Toppo, G. 2012. Should bullies be treated as criminals? *USA Today*. Accessed December 4, 2015. http://usatoday30.usatoday.com/news/nation/story/2012-06-12/bullying-crime-schools-suicide/55554112/1.

US Department of Education. 2010. *Office of civil rights*. Washington, DC. Accessed December 10, 2015. http://www2.ed.gov/about/offices/list/ocr/letters/colleague-201010.pdf.

University of Michigan. 2014. Monitoring the future: A continuing study of American youth. Accessed December 15, 2014. http://www.monitoringthefuture.org.

Varano, S. P., Schafer, J. A., Cancino, J. M., and Swatt, M. L. 2009. Constructing crime: Neighborhood characteristics and police recording behavior. *Journal of Criminal Justice*, 37 (6): 553–563.

Warr, M. 2002. *Companions in crime: The social aspects of criminal conduct*. Chicago, IL: Cambridge University Press.

4

Rape and Other Sexual Offending Behaviors

Wesley G. Jennings and Bryanna Hahn Fox

Introduction

It is a well-known fact that in the United States sex offenders are considered some of the "worst of the worst" criminals, and a significant societal stigma is attached to anyone suspected of committing any of the crimes that fall under the broad "sex crimes" umbrella (Mancini, 2014). The basic definition of a sex crime, according to the US government, is any criminal offense that "has an element involving a sexual act or sexual contact with another" (Office of Justice Programs, 2014). Clearly, a wide range of offenses falls within this broad definition, for example rape and sexual battery, sexual assault, incest, child sexual abuse, indecent exposure, statutory rape, manufacturing, distributing, and accessing child pornography, and (most recently) "sexting" – that is, sending sexually explicit photos in text messages (Mancini, 2014).

Lawmakers, the media, and popular TV shows such as *To Catch a Predator* and *Law and Order: Special Victims Unit* have paid most attention to the "especially heinous … and vicious felonies" of sexual assault, rape, child molestation, sex trafficking, and sadistic sexual homicide. Not surprisingly, this intense focus on the most harmful and serious types of offenses has prompted the public and policymakers to lump together all forms of sex offending into one single unsavory cluster, and consequently to develop a one-size-fits-all "get tough" policy for all types of sex offending (Mancini, 2014).

As a result of the escalating attention and punishment doled out to sex offenders over the past two decades, an equal amount of research on the nature

The Handbook of Measurement Issues in Criminology and Criminal Justice, First Edition.
Edited by Beth M. Huebner and Timothy S. Bynum.

of and response to sex offending has been conducted by academics. The goal of the present chapter is to provide an overview of the extant literature on the causes, risk factors, recidivism, and typologies of sex offenders, as well as to review the studies conducted on the effectiveness and impact of recent sex offender policies.

Types of Sex Offenders

In general, any offense that "has an element involving a sexual act or sexual contact with another" constitutes a sex crime in the United States (Office of Justice Programs, 2014). For instance, inflicting serious bodily harm on another individual would be considered an assault in most states, unless unwanted touching or sexually threatening behavior against a nonconsenting person was involved in the act. In the latter case, the offense would be considered a sexual assault, which is classified as a sex crime instead of a violent offense. In some cases, the specific laws that define what counts as a sex offense may vary across states. For example, in states such as Virginia, it is illegal to have sexual contact with minors under the age of 15, while in other states the age limit is higher: in Tennessee it is illegal to have sexual contact with anyone under the age of 18 (Cocca, 2004).

Sexual assault

As stated, any act that involves the unwanted touching of another or sexually threatening behavior – including the threat to commit a sex act against a nonconsenting person – qualifies as sexual assault. While statutes differ on the exact criminal elements that define sexual assault across states, all deal with acts that fall just short of actual penetration, which constitutes a progressively more severe sexual offense.

Rape and sexual battery

In general, rape or sexual battery (or both) is defined as the vaginal, anal, or oral penetration of a nonconsenting individual, male or female. This final clause of the definition is important because, prior to the 1970s, most legal definitions for rape across the United States were gender-specific (Belknap, 2007) and often excluded offenses committed by husbands against their spouse (Finkelhor and Yllo, 1985). This means that an action fitting the legal definition of rape was not considered illegal if it was committed against a man, or if it involved a husband and wife. While the specific name of the offense – "rape" or "sexual battery" – still varies across states, the statute has now been changed to include all crimes committed against men, transgender persons, and women; and the marital exception has also been abolished. Nevertheless, there are states that have yet to completely adopt this gender-neutral language and that still maintain gendered legislation when it comes to rape.

Statutory rape

Unlike the definitions and laws pertaining to rape and sexual battery, which involve the sexual penetration of a nonconsenting individual, statutory rape laws prohibit any sexual activity between adults and juveniles who have not yet reached the legal age of consent, otherwise known as the "age of majority." While the age of majority varies from state to state, generally between the ages of 15 and 18, these offenses are distinct in that the act would not be criminalized if both parties were above the age of consent. There are exceptions to the statutory rape statute, as it does not apply to couples married legally and with parental permission, when one spouse is an adult and the other is under the age of majority (Cocca, 2004). It should also be noted that this is a gender-neutral offense, where both females and males can be the offender if they participate in a sexual act with someone under the legal age of consent.

Child sexual abuse

While all of the definitions reviewed thus far can apply to children if the person involved in the nonconsenting act is a minor, as children are considered a protected population, many states have created additional provisions to protect them specifically from sex crime (Mancini, 2014). For instance, an individual who commits sexual assault against a minor would not only be held responsible for the crime of sexual assault, but would also have committed child sexual abuse, as the initial sex crime involved a child. In some states, like Florida, additional child-specific offense categories have been created in order to further protect children from any type of sex act or sexual influence – for instance, "lewd and lascivious acts against minors." This kind of provision makes it illegal to commit a sexual act in front of a child, encourage or coerce a child to commit a sex act, and show a child any form of pornography (Florida Department of Children and Families, 2011).

Incest

Incest-related offenses have roots that go back as far as colonial times, when lawmakers made it illegal for an individual to have sexual relations with family members and people directly related to him or her (Groth, 1982). What is considered "directly related" has infamously varied from state to state. Nevertheless, when the sexual relationship takes place between a parent and a child, brother and sister, or first cousins, it is still considered incest. If the incest takes place between an adult and a child under the age of consent, the offense is also legally considered to be child sexual abuse.

Indecent exposure and public indecency

Unlike the other crimes outlined, indecent exposure and public indecency are non-contact crimes, as there is no physical contact between the offender and the victim of the offense. Common examples of indecent exposure and public indecency include frotteurism (or frottage), where an individual "flashes" his or her genitals or body parts to a nonconsenting party, and the more common act of "streaking," where a person appears in public in the nude.

Child pornography and technology-related offenses

The crimes of child pornography and other technology-related offenses are more recent developments, as the technology needed to commit these offenses has only developed and proliferated in the past few decades. For example, it is now illegal in most states to manufacture, distribute, access, and download images and videos of children in sexual situations, which are otherwise known as "child pornography" (Mears et al., 2008). As both the Internet and the number of individuals using it continue to grow, the number of states outlawing the creation, distribution, and use of child pornography will certainly increase as well. Finally, a relatively new development in sex offense definitions is the crime of sending of sexually explicit text messages or images via emails or cell phone text messages – a crime known now as "sexting." Adults who send or receive sexually explicit images of minors via cell phones can be prosecuted under existent state child pornography laws (Zhang, 2010), and the producers of such images, even if they are minors, may also be charged with violating child pornography laws, regardless of who the recipient may be (Humbach, 2010).

Typologies of Sex Offenders

Understanding the variation, or heterogeneity, of sex offending patterns has been the goal of a significant portion of recent sex offender research. Such understanding is extremely helpful for identifying the unique causes, interventions, and recidivism risk level for specific types of sex offenders. Although a variety of typologies have been created, either clinically or empirically, for an assortment of sex offenses, due to space limitations this chapter will review only the most prominent of sex offender typologies.

Groth and Birnbaum's child molester typology

One of the earliest sex offender typologies was Groth and Birnbaum's (1978) clinical classification of child molesters. According to this typology, offenders who commit crimes against children may be categorized as either fixated or regressed child molesters. The fixated offenders are socially and sexually preoccupied with children, gradually enticing them to engage in sexual activity through a long-term "grooming" process, by gaining the trust of their young victims and families (Edwards and Hensley, 2001). The regressed offenders prefer to have "normal" relationships with adults but become sexually interested in children after experiencing a negative life event, such as a breakup or loss of employment. Consequently the regressed offender's interest in children has been considered to be a coping mechanism or a crime of opportunity.

The Groth and Birnbaum typology is important because it laid the initial foundation for identifying, understanding, and evaluating the element of heterogeneity in a specific type of sex offender, namely child molesters. For instance, recent research has used the Groth and Birnbaum typology to examine variation in recidivism among child molesters, and this research has demonstrated that the fixated offenders are more likely to recidivate than regressed offenders (Terry and Tallon, 2004). Nevertheless, some academics have stated that the dichotomous typology oversimplifies the complex nature of child molesting (Simon et al., 1992).

Federal Bureau of Investigation (FBI) child molester continuum

The FBI aimed to develop its own classification of child molesters, on the basis of both the experiences of FBI agents and a review of relevant sex offender research (Lanning, 2001). The resultant typology categorized child molesters on a continuum between "situational" and "preferential" offenders, according to their motivation. This classification system is different from other typologies in that offenders do not need to fit squarely into one specific type or another. Instead, an offender may have some traits of a preferential offender but align substantially with situational-style offenses. In such cases the offender would not need to be placed exclusively into one category but would fall somewhere along the continuum: "it is a matter of degree" (Lanning, 2001, p. 25). The FBI's child molester continuum is also unique in that it describes the personality and demographic features of the offenders.

At the situational end of the continuum, offenders target child victims when opportunity and availability are present. Situational offenders are said to be of lower intelligence, lower socioeconomic status, and higher impulsivity and to present a high proclivity for violent pornography, a versatile criminal history, and a high likelihood of personality disorder diagnoses (e.g., antisocial personality disorder). At the opposite end of the spectrum, the preferential child molesters prefer to victimize children and are drawn to specific types of victims. Preferential child sex offenders are of higher intelligence and higher socioeconomic status, have specific offending histories (e.g., a history of crimes against children), are compulsive in their behavior, and may be diagnosed with forms of paraphilia or abnormal sexual disorders (e.g., pedophilia).

Research has generally been supportive of the FBI child molester continuum, as studies indicate that there is a broad range of motivations for child molestation and for fixation with children (Simon et al., 1992). In other words, the child molester's motivations and fixations are continuous, not dichotomous, and a continuum is therefore the ideal method of presenting, classifying, and understanding these types of offenders. Specifically, Simon and colleagues (1992) reviewed 136 consecutive cases of convicted sex offenders over a two-year period; these reviews included details of the offenders' pre-sentence data, Minnesota Multiphasic Personality Inventory (MMPI) results, case histories, and police reports. Applying the criteria, the team indicated that fixated versus regressed status yielded a unimodal and continuous distribution rather than the hypothesized bimodal distribution.

Knight and Prentky's Massachusetts Treatment Center Rapist Typology, Version 3 (MTC: R3)

Building upon Groth's (1979) original rapist typology – "anger rapists," "power rapists," and "sadistic rapists" – Knight and Prentky (1990) developed a multidimensional typology of rapists, which is known as MTC: R3. They used scientific empirical methods that resulted in nine subtypes of rapists, which in turn fall into four broad categories of themes: "opportunistic," "pervasively angry," "sexual gratification," and "vindictive" rapists. Within each of these four types there are multiple subcategories for those who wish to more effectively delineate and classify various offenders.

Opportunistic rapists are motivated by contextual or situational factors (e.g., encountering a victim during another offense, such as a burglary), which provide an offender with the opportunity to commit an impulsive sex offense. The MTC: R3 further delineates opportunistic rapists on the basis of their social competence (their interpersonal and communication skills, their assertiveness, etc.). Opportunistic and high social competence rapists are classified as type 1, while opportunistic and low social competence rapists are considered to be type 2.

Undifferentiated universal anger that pervades virtually all aspects of the offender's life is the primary feature of the "pervasively angry" rapist (Knight, 1999). Much like Groth's (1979) anger rapist, MTC: R3's pervasively angry rapists tend to be aggressive and physically violent when committing their offenses. No subcategories exist for this group, which leaves all pervasively angry rapists in one class. They are all classified as type 3 offenders.

The sexually motivated rapists are primarily motivated by the desire to fulfill personal sexual needs (Knight and Prentky, 1990). Unlike rapists in the prior categories, the sexually motivated rapists tend to be extremely preoccupied with their sexual fantasies and desires (e.g., by frequently fantasizing or by watching pornography). Sexually motivated rapists are further classified into four subtypes, depending on the sadistic or nonsadistic nature of their sexual fantasies. The sadistic rapists are then classified according to the explicitness of their sadistic behavior and dominance (overt vs. muted), and nonsadistic rapists are classified according to their level of social competence (low vs. high). Consequently, type 4 rapists are sexually motivated, sadistic, and overt offenders, type 5 rapists are sexually motivated, sadistic, and muted offenders, type 6 rapists are sexually motivated, nonsadistic, and high social competence offenders, and type 7 rapists are sexually motivated, nonsadistic, and low social competence offenders.

The last classification in the MTC: R3 concerns the vindictive rapists. While also angry, the vindictive rapists differ from pervasively angry offenders in that they are typically motivated by anger directed primarily at women – that is, misogynistic ("woman-hating") anger – and not by universal anger, directed at society in general. Once again, this category of offenders is sub-divided on the basis of social competence (low vs. moderate), so that type 8 rapists are vindictive and of low social competence and type 9 rapists are vindictive and of moderate social competence. According to Knight and Prentky (1990), vindictive rapists do not have a high level of social competence.

Attempts to validate the MTC: R3 typology by using a variety of samples have generally found that the classification system is a reliable method of identifying rapists by motivation (Knight, 1999; McCabe and Wauchope, 2005; Reid, Wilson, and Boer, 2010). For example, Reid and colleagues (2010) examined whether the MTC: R3 typology applied to a sample of 10 high-risk rapists from New Zealand. The results suggested that mean difference scores across the risk assessment items were able to differentiate rapists who evinced different patterns of risk and to yield distinct classifications.

Hazelwood and Warren's rapist typology

The final rapist typology was generated on the basis of Hazelwood and Warren's experiences as law enforcement officers and of their reviews of past research on sex offenders. As a special agent and profiler in the FBI's Behavioral Science Unit, Hazelwood was regularly consulted by state and local law enforcement agencies for investigative advice on serious sex-offending cases. On the basis of a body of scientific research and past experiences, Hazelwood and Warren suggested that male rapists fall into two categories: impulsive rapists and ritualistic rapists.

Impulsive rapists, much like Knight and Prentky's opportunistic rapists, are highly spontaneous and nonsophisticated offenders (Hazelwood and Warren, 2000). But Hazelwood and Warren further elaborate that impulsive rapists are generally unsuccessful at avoiding detection and apprehension by police, are antisocial, motivated by a sense of entitlement, anger, and control, but "lack criminal skills to control a person without resorting to violence" (Hazelwood and Warren, 2000, p. 271). The high level of underlying anger and potential hostility toward women closely aligns them with Knight and Prenty's pervasively angry and vindictive rapists, as well as with the anger rapists and power rapists in Groth's typology.

The ritualistic rapists, who are less common than the impulsive rapists, are more successful at avoiding detection but are also said to be motivated by power and anger toward the victim or toward society. However, in stark contrast to the impulsive rapist, ritualistic offenders will almost always demonstrate paraphiliac behavior in the offense. Ritualistic rapists are so motivated by their paraphilia that they will go to extreme ends to recreate a situation from their fantasies; this will often include offending against nonconsenting victims following very specific "scripts" in order to achieve idiosyncratic sexual fantasies and desires.

While Hazelwood and Warren's typology was not created through empirical methods, subsequent research that examined the validity of the typology – or "profile" – has found support for the dichotomy of a ritualistic and an impulsive rapist. Specifically, Goodwill and Allison (2007) studied 85 British rapists and concluded that these offenders fell into two groups: spontaneous–impulsive and ritualistic–methodical offenders. However, as Goodwill and Allison's study involved a relatively small sample size, future research with larger samples should be conducted to further investigate the validity of Hazelwood and Warren rapist typology.

Quadripartite model of sexual aggression

Hall and Hirschman produced a quadripartite model of sexual aggression against women (1991) and against children (1992) by using a psychological and intrapersonal approach, or an approach that accounts for the critical motivational factors behind sexual aggression without relying solely on statistically derived taxonomies, which may or may not be clinically meaningful. In this quadripartite model, four motivational precursors to sexually deviant behavior are outlined: physiological sexual arousal, cognitions justifying sexual aggression, negative affective state, and personality problems. Using these four motivational components, Hall and Hirschman developed a typology of sex offenders in which four key motivations served as the main or dominant theme and explained different types of sexual aggressors.

A high level of physiological sexual arousal, characterized by a deviant attraction to nonconsenting victims or children, is the main motivation underlying the "preferential" type of sex offender. Due to the physiological nature of their deviant sexual arousal, preferential-type sex offenders are known to have a large number of victims and constitute the most common subtype of sex offenders in this theoretical model.

The second subtype, the "incest" offender, possesses sufficient planning and self-regulatory skills, but is driven by strong cognitive motivations that justify sexual aggression and are coupled with incorrect interpretations of children's behaviors as sexual invitations. The third group in the model, the situational offenders, are driven by a negative affective state and are typically impulsive, opportunistic, and violent.

The final subtype identified in the quadripartite model consists of offenders who have difficulties establishing intimate adult relationships as a result of developmentally-based personality problems. Chronic offenders are typically found within this subtype, as these offenders are unable to effectively function in society. The quadripartite model is significant due to the breadth of its typology, which describes sex offenses against both children and women, and due to its ability to highlight the heterogeneity of the motivations and characteristics of many types of sex offenders.

Theoretical Explanations of Sex Offending

Although the Hall and Hirschman model has been said to have immense empirical scope and clinical value (Ward, Polaschek, and Beech, 2006), the model has also been criticized. Some of the criticisms revolve around its lack of adequate test validity in subsequent research and its insufficient explanatory value, as it is not clear whether the four factors outlined in the model are the underlying motivations of the sex offenders or just clusters of symptoms that result from other, more significant underlying causes. Consequently, other theoretically driven models of sexual offending and of the mechanisms underlying the motivations for sexual offending are relied upon as having greater explanatory power – models such as the ones reviewed below.

The four-factor model of child sexual abuse

Finkelhor's (1984) four-factor model of child sexual abuse is both the first multifactorial model of sex offending and one of the most widely accepted theories of sexually deviant behavior and offending against children (Elliott and Beech, 2009). In this integrated theory, four mechanisms are believed to be at the origin of child sexual abuse: emotional congruence, sexual arousal to children, blockage, and disinhibition. Emotional congruence refers to the relationship between the adult abuser's emotional needs and the child's personality traits: an abuser is drawn to children due to a perceived overlap between his/her own emotional needs and what a (sexual) relationship with a specific child could provide. In this vein, Finkelhor drew upon aspects of Bandura's (1968) psychological social learning theory to explain the development of sexual arousal in adults, stating that a child sexual abuser was likely molested as a child and that conditioning and reinforcement led him/her to find children arousing in adulthood. Blockage is the abuser's inability to have his or her needs met through appropriate relationships with adults. The blockage may arise as a result of poor social skills and lack of the self-confidence necessary to form effective intimate relations with other adults. Blockage could be chronic and constant or it could be situational – for example if a circumstance such as the loss of a relationship or some transitory crisis would lead to the temporary loss of the ability to form appropriate adult relationships. The final factor, disinhibition, draws upon cognitive behavioral theories to identify the factors that help a child molester overcome his/her inhibitions to the point where s/he allows him-/herself to molest a child. The factors that lower inhibitions and facilitate acting on the impulse to have inappropriate and illegal relations with a child include an abuser's personality traits, substance abuse, stress, cognitive distortion, and more. The first three factors of Finkelhor's integrated model (emotional congruence, sexual arousal to children, and blockage) explain why certain individuals become sexually interested in children, while the final factor (disinhibition) explains why this interest takes the form of sexually abusive behavior.

Finkelhor's four-factor model is unique in that it was the first to introduce multiple factors that lead to sexual offending, while also accounting for individual differences and circumstances that underline various sexual offenses and deviant behaviors. However, despite these strengths, a rigorous systematic evaluation has not been conducted on this model to date.

Integrated theory of sexual offending

Marshall and Barbaree (1990) developed an integrated and general theory of sexual offending. This theory suggests that the interaction of specific developmental and situational factors increases an individual's vulnerability to engaging in deviant and illegal sexual behaviors, which may then be reinforced by specific cognitive and psychological processes. According to these researchers, the negative developmental factors that predispose a person to commit a sexual offense include biological influences, traumatic and negative childhood experiences (such as child sexual abuse), poor socialization, inadequate parenting, ineffective self-regulation, low self-confidence, and low social competence. Individuals exposed to these negative developmental vulnerability factors may be less likely to solve problems adequately, feel included in the world, or regulate inappropriate feelings or sexual fantasies, and they may even feel that illegal and inappropriate sexual behaviors are rewarding. As such individuals transition from childhood to puberty, their distorted social expectations, in combination with a rise in sex hormones, increase the chances that these youngsters (and especially the young males among them) would satisfy their sexual needs through antisocial means. For many, engaging in a sexually deviant act not only provides sexual satisfaction and reduces sexual tension, but may help them meet a multitude of other needs as well.

Individuals exposed to many negative developmental vulnerability factors for sex offending may be able to monitor and restrain their behavior, unless specific situational factors – such as opportunity, sociocultural context, stress, or intoxication – disinhibit them and allow the illegal sexual behavior to occur. For people in this general theory, everyone has his/her own level of developmental vulnerability for sex offending, which is based upon the number and severity of developmental factors in the background. However, individuals with less developmental vulnerability may not easily be persuaded to offend in any given situation, while individuals with a high level of vulnerability may be less capable of dealing adequately with stress, sexual stimuli, disinhibition through intoxication, and so on and are more likely to commit a sexual offense. Then, after an individual engages in an illegal sexual act, the behavior may be reinforced through the development of cognitive distortions and through fixation on the rewarding effects of the sexually offensive activity (Marshall and Barbaree, 1990).

This theory is significant because it offers both a generalized model for the commission of all illegal sexual behaviors, across all types of individuals, and an integrated model that accounts for developmental, psychological, and situational influences. The idea of vulnerability factors was introduced by Marshall and Barbaree (1990) in this theoretical perspective, which has been particularly influential in the realm of treatment innovations, as it provides explanations for the development, onset, and maintenance of sexual offending (Parton and Day, 2002; Ward and Hudson, 1998; Ward and Siegert, 2002).

While the theories reviewed here aim to explain the general underlying causes of sex offending, they do not identify specific factors that increase the risk of offending or explain why certain individuals with certain risk factors present a higher risk of sex offending, recidivating, or committing specific types of sex offenses. Research on these risk factors is reviewed in the next section.

Risk Factors for Sex Offending

As delineated by the integrated theoretical models of sexual offending, risk factors for this behavior tend to deal with developmental and situational influences. The risk factors and the research examining these items span a variety of fields, which include criminology, psychology, sociology, and even medicine.

Developmental risk factors

In developmental and life-course criminology, one of the major risk factors for criminal behavior is an individual's age of criminal onset, chronic offenders being reported to begin their criminal career at an earlier age (often in childhood), whereas the more situational or temporary offenders begin offending during adolescence. Among sexual offenders, childhood and even adolescent onset is not a common occurrence, as the typical onset age for sex offending is in adulthood (Marshall et al., 1991; Smallbone and Wortley, 2004; Zimring, Piquero, and Jennings, 2007; Zimring et al., 2009; Lussier et al., 2010; see however, Prentky and Knight, 1993). The age of criminal onset has not been shown to significantly predict onset of sex offending in adulthood (Lussier et al., 2014).

Still, there may be a significant disagreement between the actual and the official age of onset for sex offending, and this could influence the findings of research that relies greatly upon official records (Prentky and Knight, 1993; Smallbone and

Wortley, 2004; Lussier, LeBlanc, and Proulx, 2005; Lussier and Mathesius, 2012). Limited research on the validity of official records in determining sex offending onset has shown that both official and self-report data suggest that adult-targeting sex offenders begin offending in their thirties but, while the first offense may occur in their early thirties, their first conviction occurs in the late thirties. This research indicates that there may be a gap of about seven years between actual and official onset of sex offending.

It should also be noted that this gap between actual and official onset may be even larger in the case of sex offenders targeting children, as the likelihood of an illegal act being identified and reported to the police, and consequently of the offender being apprehended, is significantly lower when victims are younger. In fact, by comparison to other types of sex offenders, those who abuse children typically avoid detection, on average, for more than a decade. The reason for this gap is twofold. First, child victims typically wait for several years, until they reach late adolescence or young adulthood, before they report their victimization to the police – if they ever do it (Lussier and Mathesius, 2012). Second, child victims may be even more vulnerable to victimization by offenders who are well known to them and have a position of trust and authority, which diminishes the chances of reporting and detection (Leclerc, Proulx, and McKibben, 2005). Still, research suggests that the most "successful" sex offenders in terms of time until detection were the least exclusive in terms of victim selection, as they often demonstrated no clear pattern in victim type (age, gender, relationship) and sexual preferences (Lussier et al., 2008; Lussier, Bouchard, and Beauregard, 2011).

Apart from age of onset, other developmental risk factors for sexual offending are hormone imbalances, traumatic and negative childhood experiences (such as child sexual abuse), poor socialization and parental attachment, ineffective self-regulation, low self-confidence, and deficits in emotional and social competence (Widom, 1989; Hanson and Harris, 2000, 2001; Beech and Ward, 2004).

Situational risk factors

The risk of sexual offending may also be increased by certain situational factors, which are often coupled with underlying developmental risk factors for illegal sexual behavior, as previously described. Specifically, opportunities may arise where a young person or an incapacitated or intoxicated adult would appear as an available sexual target. However, most individuals presented with such a situation would refrain from engaging in illegal sexual behavior. The exception is individuals with a vulnerability to commit such acts due to the developmental risk factors stated.

In addition to the opportunity to be exposed to sexual stimuli, drugs and alcohol may increase the likelihood of sexual aggression by increasing overall arousability (Seto and Barbaree, 1997). With sexual assault and rape, up to 50 percent of offenders have reported being intoxicated at the moment of the crime (Koss, Gidycz, and Wisniewski, 1987; Barbaree and Marshall, 1991). However, experiments examining the influence of drugs and alcohol have also reported conflicting results. For instance, Briddell and Wilson (1976) found that the expectation of alcohol consumption increased sexual arousal to rape in men, while an experiment conducted by Barbaree, Hudson, and Seto (1993) showed no effect for the expectation of alcohol consumption on arousal to rape. A more recent study using a randomized factorial design with male college students exposed to an audiotape of a date rape found that participants who consumed, or expected to consume, alcohol took significantly longer to determine that the man should refrain from attempting further sexual contact with the partner (Marx, Gross, and Adams, 1999).

High levels of anger, stress, and violent stimulation in a given situation could also impact the risk of an individual's committing a sexual offense. In 1984 Yates and colleagues examined the impact of anger on sexual arousal using an experimental design. In this study participants were divided into two groups. Those in the control group pedaled on a bike for one minute before submitting to a phallometric assessment designed to determine sexual arousal at that time. In contrast, the treatment condition, called the "anger" group, also pedaled on a bike for one minute before a female researcher made a disparaging remark about the subjects' biking performance; then they were immediately tested for phallomentic response. Results of the study showed that the participants in the anger condition had an equal sexual response for rape cues and for consenting cues, which indicated a complete lack of inhibition to violent, nonconsenting sexual arousal triggers.

Finally, watching pornography has been linked to an increased risk of sexual aggression (Malamuth, Addison, and Koss, 2000). The reason for this situational risk factor is theorized under the assumption that pornography fuels sexually aggressive attitudes, and may even represent a mental "training manual" for sexual aggression (see Hald, Malmuth, and Yuen, 2010). There is also a potential "imitation effect" when offenders mimic and try to re-create scenes witnessed in pornography (Kingston et al., 2008). However, some researchers note that pornography may be a cathartic factor, even protective against sexual offending, as exposure to it may release sexual aggression and reduce the risk of offending (Mancini, Reckdenwald, and Mears, 2012). More research is needed on the situational risk factors for sex offending, particularly pornography.

Specialization and Versatility in Sex Offending

Offense specialization is described as the tendency to repeat the same offense type in future arrests (Blumstein et al., 1986). With respect to sex offender specialization and versatility, Meithe and colleagues (2006) found that, among offenders released from prisons in a number of US states, only 5 percent could be characterized solely as sex offenders. Similarly, Sample and Bray (2003, 2006) analyzed the criminal careers of a large sample of sex offenders and reported that less than 7 percent committed the same type of sex offense in the five years following their initial sex offense. Therefore, contrary to popular belief (which is reflected in current laws and policies), research on offense specialization among sex offenders strongly suggests versatility rather than specialization in sex offenders' criminal behavior (see e.g., Hanson and Bussiere, 1998; Caldwell, 2002; Nisbet, Wilson, and Smallbone, 2004; Waite et al., 2005; Vandiver, 2006; Zimring et al., 2007; Zimring et al., 2009; Piquero et al., 2012).

It should be noted that, although specialization is not typical among the entire sex offender population, higher levels of specialization have been linked to particular types of illegal sexual acts, which once again suggests that sex offenders are not a very homogeneous group. For instance, Prentky and colleagues (1997) demonstrated that sexual recidivism rates were higher among child molesters than among rapists (52 percent vs. 39 percent) in their Massachusetts sample. Higher levels of specialization among child molesters were also reported in Harris, Mazerolle, and Knight (2009), in Miethe, Olson, and Mitchell (2006), and in Hanson, Scott, and Steffy (1995). Adding to these findings, Parton and Day (2002) found that child molesters tend to be more persistent offenders than rapists and other types of sex offenders, and Zimring and colleagues (2007) found that sex offenders tend to commit a high volume of general offenses, which minimize the specialized activity of sex offending. Together, this body of research suggests that sex offenders are in general versatile and frequent offenders, who "roll the dice more often, thereby increasing their chances of accumulating both sex and nonsex offenses in their career" (Zimring et al., 2007, p. 527; Zimring et al., 2009; Jennings et al., 2014; Smallbone, Wheaton, and Hourigan, 2003; Lussier et al., 2005; Magers et al., 2009; Piquero et al., 2012).

More recently, Piquero and colleagues (2012) used data from the Cambridge Study in Delinquent Development to examine the prevalence, specialization, frequency, recidivism, and continuity of sexual offending through age 50 in a sample of working-class males in London. Results of the study showed that, of the 405 men in the sample, only 10 (2.5 percent) had been convicted of a sex offense by the age of 50, and of those only 3 fitted the criteria for sex offending recidivism by having convictions for two or more sex offenses in their criminal career (Piquero et al., 2012). More research on risk factors for the related concept of sex offender recidivism is reviewed in the following section.

Sex-Offending Recidivism

Estimates of the rates of sex offender recidivism do vary by crime type, sample composition, and length of follow-up. For these reasons, Hanson and Bussiere (1998) conducted a meta-analysis of 61 studies that assessed the general rates of recidivism among adult sex offenders. A 36.3 percent overall recidivism rate was reported among the offenders in the meta-analysis (n = 19,374), when recidivism was defined as any reoffense. Similar results were obtained in a follow-up meta-analysis of adolescent and adult sex offender recidivism rates by Hanson and Morton-Bourgon (2005). Among the 29,540 offenders included in the 82 recidivism studies, researchers found an overall recidivism rate of 36.2 percent and a violent nonsexual recidivism rate of 14.3 percent (Hanson and Morton-Bourgon, 2005).

As stated, specialization in sex offenses is relatively rare among sex offenders; correspondingly, sex offenders' recidivism rate in sex offenses is also very low. For instance, in a recent study examining recidivism trajectories of sex and nonsex offenders, Jennings, Zgoba, and Tewksbury (2012) compared the 8-year recidivism trajectories of sex and nonsex offenders released from prison in the state of New Jersey. Results of this study showed that two types of recidivism trajectories exist: high risk and low risk. Among sex offenders, the vast majority (94.7 percent) fell under the low-risk trajectory, while a lower amount (72.8 percent) of nonsex offenders fell into the low recidivism risk trajectory after 8 years. Furthermore, approximately 5 percent of sex offenders were in the high-risk recidivism trajectory, as compared to 27 percent of nonsex offenders who were classified in that trajectory. The offenders in high-risk recidivism trajectories in both samples noticeably reoffend at high rates, particularly soon after their release from prison, and they maintain a non-zero recidivism rate throughout the 8-year observation period. Comparatively, the low-risk recidivism trajectory contain offenders who do not reoffend and some of the one-time recidivists.

Acknowledging that specific rates of sex-offending recidivism vary depending upon the type of study, sample, reporting mechanism, and analytical technique used in a given study, the prevalence of sex-offending recidivism among sex offenders is generally below 10 percent, as illustrated by the following findings: 4 percent (Vandiver, 2006), 4.7 percent (Waite et al., 2005), 6.5 percent (Sample and Bray, 2003), 9 percent (Nisbet et al., 2004), 9.7 percent (Sipe, Jensen, and Everett, 1998), 13 percent (Tewksbury, Jennings, and Zgoba, 2012), 13.4 percent (Hanson and Bussiere, 1998), and 13.7 percent (Hanson and Morton-Bourgon, 2005). Still, it is important to recognize the difficulty of measuring recidivism in general and sex recidivism specifically, since a considerable amount of sex crime goes unreported to law enforcement.

While a relatively small fraction of sex offenders appear to commit sexual offenses after conviction, variations in rates have been noted with regard to the type of sexual offense. Specifically, rates of reoffending among child molesters have been shown to be significantly higher than among nonsex offenders and rapists. For example, in their analysis of the crimes that 136 rapists and 115 child molesters committed after their sex offenses, Prentky and colleagues (1997) found recidivism rates near 50 percent for rapists and child molesters; but the child molesters' rates were higher than the rapists'. However, the higher recidivism rate among child molesters may be due in part to the high rate of sexual offenses committed by this group by comparison to the less frequently offending rapists (Parton and Day, 2002; Lussier et al., 2005). More research on these topics is needed.

With respect to specific risk factors for recidivism among sex offenders, Hanson and Bussiere (1998) stated that offenders with a history of prior offenses (of any kind), who victimized strangers and nonrelated victims, who showed an early onset of sexual offending, who were never married, who felt pervasively angry, and who had a personality disorder diagnosis were more likely to recidivate than other sex offenders. Additional research suggests that employment problems (McGrath, 1991; Maletzky, 1993), a sex-offending criminal history (Quinsey et al., 1993; Prentky et al., 1997), selecting nonfamilial victims (Hanson, Steffy, and Gauthier, 1993), and offending against older victims and male victims (Hanson and Bussiere, 1998) are all risk factors for sex offending recidivism. These findings have been corroborated by recent research (see e.g., Tewksbury et al., 2012).

Sex Offender Registry and Notification Laws and Consequences

The overwhelming public and political support for legislation aimed at protecting the public from sexual predators resulted in policies such as Megan's Law, Jessica's Law, and a variety of sex offender registry and notification (SORN) laws designed to confine, monitor, and deter sex offenders from future offending after a custodial sentence has been completed and the offender is released back into the public. These laws generally specify that convicted and registered sex offenders are prohibited from living within a 1,000 to 2,500 foot buffer zone from parks, schools, playgrounds, day-care centers, bus stops, or other places where children may congregate (Zgoba et al., 2008). Furthermore, the community notification aspect of the policy may require convicted and registered sex offenders to have their photos and crimes posted on a public website and to notify neighbors, via doorstep flyers, of their past crimes and current location in the neighborhood, or the police may notify neighbors, spreading this information through door-to-door visits in the community.

Despite these policies being seemingly noble in intention, recent research has shown little or no observable deterrent effects of SORN on sex offending (Schram and Milloy, 1995; Sample and Kadleck, 2008; Sandler, Freeman, and Socia, 2008; Vasquez, Maddan, and Walker, 2008; Zgoba et al., 2008; Letourneau et al., 2010; Tewksbury and Jennings, 2010; Tewksbury et al., 2012). In fact SORN does not appear to noticeably reduce either sex recidivism (Zgoba et al., 2008; Tewksbury and Jennings, 2010; Ragusa-Salerno and Zgoba, 2012) or general recidivism (Zgoba, Veysey, and Dalessandro, 2010; Jennings et al., 2012; Tewksbury et al., 2012) among convicted sex offenders. For example, in an analysis of recidivism rates of sex offenders both before (n = 247) and after (n = 248) SORN laws were implemented, Tewksbury and colleagues (2012) found a general recidivism prevalence of 51.4 percent among pre-SORN offenders and 48 percent among those released after SORN laws were implemented. In other words, no significant differences were observed.

However, recent research has noted that SORN may actually have some consequences, although these do not appear to be the effects that were intended by the policy. For instance, registered sex offenders abiding by SORN policies have been shown to have high rates of problems such as depression, difficulty maintaining employment and relationships, public recognition and harassment, and attacks (Simon, 1997; Zevitz and Farkas, 2000; Tewksbury, 2005; Levenson and Cotter, 2005; Burchfield and Mingus, 2008; Tewksbury and Lees, 2006; Tewksbury and

Mustaine, 2006; Mercado, Alvarez, and Levensen, 2008; Tewksbury and Zgoba, 2010) as well as difficulty finding and maintaining suitable housing (Grubesic, Murray, and Mack, 2007), limited access to social services and social support (Levenson and Hern, 2007), transiency (Levenson and Cotter, 2005; Mustaine, Tewksbury, and Stengel, 2006), and disproportionate residing in socially disorganized areas (Mustaine et al., 2006).

Given these collateral consequences, the significant costs of the policy, and the lack of evidence that SORN reduces the recidivism rates of sex offenders, it may be advisable for policymakers and practitioners to reconsider and revise the current policies. Future legislation may be more efficient by focusing on those types of sex offenders who are at higher risk of reoffending, rather than on all types. As demonstrated throughout this chapter and stated by Sample and Bray (2006), sex offenders are not a homogeneous group in terms of risk factors, specialization, or recidivism rates and therefore should not be treated homogeneously under the law.

Conclusion

In the end, this chapter offered an overview of the literature on the causes, risk factors, recidivism, and typologies of sex offenders, in addition to reviewing prior research that evaluates the effectiveness of recent sex offender legislation. What is clear is that there is wide variability in the estimates of the prevalence and frequency of sex offending and in the rates of recidivism. Recognizing this variability, it is important for future research to continue to examine these results from a wide variety of sources (official data, victimization reports, self-reports, polygraphs), in an effort at triangulation and at generating the most valid and reliable estimates. Additional work is also needed to further assess the validity and reliability of the various risk assessment instruments and proposed typologies in order to refine measurement and inform theory. Finally, future research needs to focus more directly on evaluating the effect of sex offender policies and legislation; it must rely on rigorous, quasi-experimental designs, which should enable more definitive statements to be made about the utility of these policies and laws.

References

Bandura, A. 1968. A social learning interpretation of psychological dysfunctions. In *Foundations of abnormal psychology*, edited by P. London and D. L. Rosenhan, 293–334. New York: Holt, Rinehart and Winston.

Barbarcc, H. E., Hudson, S. M., and Seto, M. C. 1993. Sexual assault in society: The role of the juvenile offender. In *The Juvenile Sex Offender*, edited by H. E. Barbaree, W. L. Marshall, and S. W. Hudson, 1–18. New York: Guilford Press.

Barbaree, H. E., and Marshall, W. L. 1991. The role of male sexual arousal in rape: Six models. *Journal of Consulting and Clinical Psychology*, 59: 621–630.

Beech, A. R., and Ward, T. 2004. The integration of etiology and risk in sex offenders: Atheoretical model. *Aggression and Violent Behavior*, 10: 31–63.

Belknap, J. 2007. *The invisible woman: Gender, crime, and justice*, 3rd ed. Belmont, CA: Wadsworth/Cengage.

Blumstein, A., Cohen, J., Roth, J. A., and Visher, C. A., eds. 1986. *Criminal careers and "career criminals,"* vol. 1. Washington, DC: National Academy Press.

Briddell, D. W., and Wilson, G. T. 1976. Effects of alcohol and expectancy set on male sexual arousal. *Journal of Abhorrent Psychololology*, 85: 225–234.

Burchfield, K. B., and Mingus, W. 2008. Not in my neighborhood: Assessing registered sex offenders' perceptions of local social capital and its limitations. *Criminal Justice and Behavior*, 35: 356–374.

Caldwell, M. F. 2002. What we do not know about juvenile sexual reoffense risk. *Child Maltreatment*, 7: 291–302.

Cocca, C. E. 2004. *Jailbait: The politics of statutory rape laws in the United States*. Albany, NY: SUNY Press.

Edwards, W., and Hensley, C. 2001. Contextualizing sex offender management legislation and policy: Evaluating the problem of latent consequences in community notification laws. *International Journal of Offender Therapy and Comparative Criminology*, 45 (1): 83–101.

Elliott, I. A., and Beech, A. R. 2009. Understanding online child pornography use: Applying sexual offense theory to Internet offenders. *Aggression and Violent Behavior*, 14: 180–193.

Finkelhor, D. 1984. *Child sexual abuse: New theory and research*. New York: Free Press.

Finkelhor, D., and Yllo, K. 1985. *License to rape: Sexual abuse of wives*. New York: Holy, Rinehart, and Winston.

Florida Department of Children and Families. 2011. *Florida sexual violence benchbook*. Tallahassee, FL: Florida Council against Sexual Violence.

Goodwill, A., and Allison, L. J. 2007. When is profiling possible? Offense planning and aggression as moderators in predicting offender age from victim age in stranger rape. *Behavioral Sciences and the Law*, 25: 823–840.

Groth, A. N. 1979. *Men who rape: The psychology of the offender*. New York: Plenum Press.

Groth, A. N. 1982. The incest offender. In *Handbook of clinical intervention in child sexual abuse*, edited by S. M. Sgroi, 215–239. Lexington, MA: Heath.

Groth, A. N., and Birnbaum, H. 1978. Adult sexual orientation and attraction to underage persons. *Archives of Sexual Behavior*, 36: 14–20.

Grubesic, T. H., Murray, A. T., and Mack, E. A. 2007. Sex offenders, residence restrictions, housing, and urban morphology: A review and synthesis. *Cityscape: A Journal of Policy Development and Research*, 13: 7–31.

Hald, G. M., Malmuth, N., and Yuen, C. 2010. Pornography and attitudes supporting violence against women: Revisiting the relationship in nonexperimental studies. *Aggressive Behavior*, 36: 14–20.

Hall, G. C. N., and Hirschman, R. 1991. Toward a theory of sexual aggression: A quadripartite model. *Journal of Consulting and Clinical Psychology*, 59: 662–669.

Hall, G. C. N., and Hirschman, R. 1992. Sexual aggression against children: A conceptual perspective of etiology. *Criminal Justice and Behavior*, 19: 8–23.

Hanson, R. K., and Bussiere, M. T. 1998. Predicting relapse: A meta-analysis of sexual offender recidivism studies. *Journal of Consulting and Clinical Psychology*, 66: 348–362.

Hanson, R. K., and Harris, A. J. R. 2000. Where should we intervene? Dynamic predictors of sexual offense recidivism. *Criminal Justice and Behavior*, 27: 6–35.

Hanson, R. K., and Harris, A. J. R. 2001. A structured approach to evaluating change among sexual offenders. *Sexual Abuse: A Journal of Research and Treatment*, 13: 105–122.

Hanson, R. K., and Morton-Bourgon, K. E. 2005. The characteristics of persistent sexual offenders: A meta-analysis of recidivism studies. *Journal of Consulting and Clinical Psychology*, 73: 1154.

Hanson, R. K., Scott, H., and Steffy, R. A. 1995. A comparison of child molesters and non-sexual criminals: Risk predictors and long-term recidivism. *Journal of Research in Crime and Delinquency*, 32 (3): 325–337.

Hanson, R. K., Steffy, R. A., and Gauthier, R. 1993. Long-term recidivism of child molesters. *Journal of Clinical and Consulting Psychology*, 61: 646–652.

Harris, D. A., Mazerolle, P., and Knight, R. A. 2009. Understanding male sexual offending: A comparison of general and specialist theories. *Criminal Justice and Behavior*, 36: 1051–1069.

Hazelwood, R. R., and Warren, J. I. 2000. The sexually violent offender: Impulsive or ritualistic? *Aggression and Violent Behavior*, 5: 267–279.

Humbach, J. A. 2010. "Sexting" and the First Amendment. *Hastings Constitutional Law Quarterly*, 37: 433–485.

Jennings, W. G., Piquero, A. R., Zimring, F. E., and Reingle, J. 2014. Assessing the (dis)continuity of sex offending from adolescence through early adulthood: Evidence from two large birth cohort studies. In *Sex offenders: A criminal career approach*, edited by A. Blokland and P. Lussier, 129–142. Oxford: Wiley Blackwell.

Jennings, W. G., Zgoba, K. M., and Tewksbury, R. 2012. A comparative longitudinal analysis of recidivism trajectories and collateral consequences for sex and non-sex offenders released since the implementation of sex offender registration and community notification. *Journal of Crime and Justice*, 35: 356–364.

Kingston, D. A., Fedoroff, P., Firestone, P., Curry, S., and Bradford, J. M. 2008. Pornography use and sexual aggression: The impact of frequency and type of pornography use on recidivism among sexual offenders. *Aggressive Behavior*, 34: 341–351.

Knight, R. A. 1999. Validation of a typology for rapists. *Journal of Interpersonal Violence*, 14: 303–330.

Knight, R. A., and Prentky, R. A. 1990. Classifying sexual offenders: The development and corroboration of taxonomic models. In *Handbook of sexual assault: Issues, theories, and treatment of the offender*, edited by W. L. Marshall, D. R. Laws, and H. E. Barbaree, 23–53. New York: Plenum.

Koss, M. P., Gidycz, C. A., and Wisniewski, N. 1987. The scope of rape: Incidence and prevalence of sexual aggression and victimization in a national sample of higher education students. *Journal of Consulting and Clinical Psychology*, 55: 162 – 170.

Lanning, K. V. 2001. *Child molesters: A behavioral analysis*, 4th ed. Alexandria, VA: National Center for Missing and Exploited Children.

Leclerc, B., Proulx, J., and McKibben, A. 2005. Modus operandi of sexual offenders working or doing voluntary work with children and adolescents. *Journal of Sexual Aggression*, 2: 187 – 195.

Letourneau, E. J., Levenson, J. S., Bandyopadhyay, D., Armstrong, K. S., and Sinha, D. 2010. Effects of South Carolina's sex offender registration and notification policy on deterrence of adult sex crimes. *Criminal Justice and Behavior*, 37: 537–552.

Levenson, J. S., and Cotter, L. P. 2005. The impact of sex offender residence restrictions: 1,000 fee from danger or one step from absurd? *International Journal of Offender Therapy and Comparative Criminology*, 49: 168–178.

Levenson, J. S., and Hern, A. 2007. Sex offender residence restrictions: Unintended consequences and community re-entry. *Justice Research and Policy*, 9: 59–73.

Lussier, P., Bouchard, M., and Beauregard, E. 2011. Patterns of criminal achievement insexual offending: Unravelling the "successful" sex offender. *Journal of Criminal Justice*, 39: 333–344.

Lussier, P., LeBlanc, M., and Proulx, J. 2005. The generality of criminal behavior: A confirmatory factor analysis of the criminal activity of sex offenders in adulthood. *Journal of Criminal Justice*, 33: 177–189.

Lussier, P., LeClerc, B, Healy, J., and Proulx, J. 2008. Generality of deviance and predation: Crime-switching and specialization patterns in persistent sexual offenders. In *Violent offenders: Theory, public policy and practice*, edited by M. DeLisi and P. Conis, 97–140. Boston: Jones and Bartlett.

Lussier, P., and Mathesius, J. 2012. Criminal achievement, criminal career initiation, and detection avoidance: The onset of successful sex offending. *Journal of Crime and Justice*, 35: 376–394.

Lussier, P., Tzoumakis, S., Cale, J., and Amirault, J. 2010. Criminal trajectories of adult sexual aggressors and the age effect: Examining the dynamic aspect of offending in adulthood. *International Criminal Justice Review*, 20: 147–168.

Magers, M., Jennings, W. G., Tewksbury, R., and Miller, J. M. 2009. An exploration of the sex offender specialization and violence nexus. *The Southwest Journal of Criminal Justice*, 6 (2): 133–144.

Malamuth, N. M., Addison, T., and Koss, M. 2000. Pornography and sexual aggression: Are there reliable effects and can we understand them? *Annual Review of Sex Research*, 11: 26–91.

Maletzky, B. M. 1993. Factors associated with success and failure in the behavioral and cognitive treatment of sexual offenders. *Annals of Sex Research*, 6: 241–258.

Mancini, C. 2014. *Sex crime offenders and society*. Durham, NC: Carolina Academic Press.

Mancini, C., Reckdenwald, A., and Mears, D. P. 2012. Pornographic exposure over the life course and severity of sexual offenses: Imitation and cathartic effects. *Journal of Criminal Justice*, 40: 21–30.

Marshall, W. L., and Barbaree, H. E. 1990. An integrated theory of the etiology of sexual offending. In *Handbook of sexual assaults: Issues, theories, and treatment of the offender*, edited by W. L. Marshall, 257–275. New York: Plenum Press.

Marshall, W. L., Jones, R., Ward, T., Johnston, P. and Barbaree, H. E. 1991. Treatment outcome with sex offenders. *Clinical Psychology Review*, 11: 465–485.

Marx, B. P., Gross, A. M., and Adams, H. E. 1999. The effect of alcohol on the responses of sexually coercive and noncoercive men to an experimental rape analogue. *Sexual Abuse: Journal of Research and Treatment*, 11: 131–145.

McCabe, M. P., and Wauchope, M. 2005. Behavioral characteristics of men accused of rape: Evidence for different types of rapists. *Archives of Sexual Behavior*, 34: 241–253.

McGrath, R. J. 1991. Sex-offender risk assessment and disposition planning: A review of empirical and clinical findings. *International Journal of Offender Therapy and Comparative Criminology*, 35 (4): 329–351.

Mears, D. P., Mancini, C., Gertz, M., and Bratton, J. 2008. Sex crimes, children, and pornography: Public views and public policy. *Crime and Delinquency*, 54: 532–559.

Mercado, C. C., Alvarez, S., and Levensen, K. 2008. The impact of specialized sex offender legislation on community reentry. *Sexual Abuse: A Journal of Research and Treatment*, 20: 188–205.

Miethe, T. D., Olson, J., and Mitchell, O. 2006. Specialization and persistence in the arrest histories of sex offenders: A comparative analysis of alternative measures and offense types. *Journal of Research in Crime and Delinquency*, 43: 204–229.

Mustaine, E. E., Tewksbury, R., and Stengel, K. M. 2006. Social disorganization and residential locations of registered sex offenders: Is this a collateral consequence? *Deviant Behavior*, 27: 329–350.

Nisbet, I. A., Wilson, P. H., and Smallbone, S. W. 2004. A prospective longitudinal study of sexual recidivism among adolescent sex offenders. *Sexual Abuse: A Journal of Research and Treatment*, 16: 223–234.

Office of Justice Programs. 2014. SMART: SORNA. Accessed June 14, 2014. http://ojp.gov/smart/sorna.htm.

Parton, F., and Day, A. 2002. Empathy, intimacy, loneliness and locus of control in child sex offenders: A comparison between familial and non-familial child sexual offenders. *Journal of Child Sexual Abuse*, 11: 41–57.

Piquero, A. R., Farrington, D. P., Jennings, W. G., Diamond, B., and Craig, J. 2012. Sex offenders and sex offending in the Cambridge Study in Delinquent Development: Prevalence, frequency, specialization, recidivism, and (dis)continuity over the life-course. *Journal of Crime and Justice*, 35: 412–426.

Prentky, R. A., and R. A. Knight. 1993. Age of onset of sexual assault: Criminal and life history correlates. In, *Sexual aggression: Issues in etiology, assessment, and treatment*, edited by G. C. Hall, R. Hirshchman, J. R. Fraham, and M. S. Zaragoza, 43–62. Washington, DC: Taylor and Francis.

Prentky, R. A., Lee, A. F., Knight, R. A., and Cerce, D. 1997. Recidivism rates among child molesters and rapists: A methodological analysis. *Law and Human Behavior*, 21: 635–659.

Quinsey, V. L., Harris, G. T., Rice, M. E. and Lalumière, M. L. 1993. Assessing treatment efficacy in outcome studies of sex offenders. *Journal of Interpersonal Violence*, 8: 512–523.

Ragusa-Salerno, L. M., and Zgoba, K. M. 2012. Taking stock of 20 years of sex offender laws and research: An examination of whether sex offender legislation has helped or hindered our efforts. *Journal of Crime and Justice*, 35: 335–355.

Reid, S. L., Wilson, N. J., and Boer, D. P. 2010. Application of the Massachusetts Treatment Center Revised Rapist Typology to New Zealand high-risk rapists: A pilot study. *Sexual Abuse in Australia and New Zealand*, 2: 77–84.

Sample, L. L., and Bray, T. M. 2003. Are sex offenders dangerous? *Criminology and Public Policy*, 3: 59–82.

Sample, L. L., and Bray, T. M. 2006. Are sex offenders different? An examination of rearrest patterns. *Criminal Justice Policy Review*, 17: 83–102.

Sample, L. L., and Kadleck, C. 2008. Sex offender laws: Legislator's accounts of the need for policy. *Criminal Justice Policy Review*, 19: 40–62.

Sandler, J. C., Freeman, N. J., and Socia, K. M. 2008. Does a watched pot boil? A time-series analysis of New York State's sex offender registration and notification law. *Psychology, Public Policy, and Law*, 14: 284–302.

Schram, D., and Milloy, C. D. 1995. *Community notification: A study of offender characteristics and recidivism*. Olympia: Washington Institute for Public Policy.

Seto, M. C., and Barbaree, H. E. 1997. Sexual aggression as antisocial behavior: A developmental model. In *Handbook of antisocial behavior*, edited by D. Stoff, J. Breiling, and J. D. Maser, 524–533. New York: Wiley.

Simon, L. 1997. The myth of sex offender specialization: An empirical analysis. *New England Journal on Criminal and Civil Confinement*, 23: 387–403.

Simon, L., Sales, B., Kazniac, A., and Kahn, A. 1992. Characteristics of child molesters: Implications for the fixated–regressed dichotomy. *Journal of Interpersonal Violence*, 7: 211–225.

Sipe, R., Jensen, E. L., and Everett, R. S. 1998. Adolescent sexual offenders grown up: Recidivism in young adulthood. *Criminal Justice and Behavior*, 25: 109–124.

Smallbone, S. W., Wheaton, J., and Hourigan, D. 2003. Trait empathy and criminal versatility in sexual offenders. *Sexual Abuse: A Journal of Research and Treatment*, 15: 49 – 60.

Smallbone, S. W., and Wortley, R. K. 2004. Criminal diversity and paraphilic interests among adult males convicted of sexual offenses against children. *International Journal of Offender Therapy and Comparative Criminology*, 48: 175–188.

Terry, K. J., and Tallon, J. 2004. *Child sexual abuse—A review of the literature: The nature and scope of the problem of sexual abuse of minors by priests and deacons, 1950–2002*. Washington, DC: United States Conference of Catholic Bishops.

Tewksbury, R. 2005. Collateral consequences of sex offender registration. *Journal of Contemporary Criminal Justice*, 21: 67–81.

Tewksbury, R., and Jennings, W. G. 2010. Assessing the impact of sex offender registration and community notification on sex-offending trajectories. *Criminal Justice and Behavior*, 37: 570–582.

Tewksbury, R., Jennings, W. G., and Zgoba, K. M. 2012. A longitudinal examination of sex offender recidivism prior to and following the implementation of SORN. *Behavioral Sciences and the Law*, 30: 308–328.

Tewksbury, R., and Lees, M. 2006. Perceptions of sex offender registration: Collateral consequences and community experiences. *Sociological Spectrum*, 26: 309–334.

Tewksbury, R., and Mustaine, E. E. 2006. Where to find sex offenders: An examination of residential locations and neighborhood conditions. *Criminal Justice Studies*, 19: 61–75.

Tewksbury, R., and Zgoba, K. M. 2010. Perceptions and coping with punishment how registered sex offenders respond to stress, Internet restrictions, and the collateral consequences of registration. *International Journal of Offender Therapy and Comparative Criminology*, 54: 537–551.

Vandiver, D. M. 2006. A prospective analysis of juvenile male sex offenders: Characteristics and recidivism rates as adults. *Journal of Interpersonal Violence*, 21: 673–688.

Vasquez, B. E., Maddan, S., and Walker, J. T. 2008. The influence of sex offender registration and notification laws in the United States: A time-series analysis. *Crime and Delinquency*, 54: 175–192.

Waite, D., Keller, A., McGarvey, E. L., Wieckowski, E., Pinkerton, R., and Brown, G. L. 2005. Juvenile sex offender re-arrest rates for sexual, violent nonsexual and property crimes: A 10-year follow-up. *Sexual Abuse: A Journal of Research and Treatment*, 17: 313–331.

Ward, T., and Hudson, S. M. 1998. The construction and development of theory in the sexual offending area: A meta-theoretical framework. *Sexual Abuse: A Journal of Research and Treatment*, 10: 47–63.

Ward, T., Polaschek, D. L., and Beech, A. R. 2006. *Theories of sexual offending*. Hoboken, NJ: John Wiley & Sons, Inc.

Ward, T., and Siegert, R. J. 2002. Toward a comprehensive theory of child sexual abuse: A theory knitting perspective. *Psychology, Crime and Law*, 8: 319–351.

Widom, C. S. 1989. Child abuse, neglect, and violent criminal behavior. *Criminology*, 27: 251–272.

Zevitz, R. G., and Farkas, M. A. 2000. Sex offender community notification: Managing high-risk criminals or exacting further vengeance? *Behavioral Sciences and the Law*, 18: 375–391.

Zgoba, K., Veysey, B. M., and Dalessandro, M. 2010. An analysis of the effectiveness of community notification and registration: Do the best intentions predict the best practices? *Justice Quarterly*, 27: 667–691.

Zgoba, K., Witt, P., Dalessandro, M., and Veysey, B. 2008. *Megan's Law: Assessing the practical and monetary efficacy*. Washington, DC: US Department of Justice.

Zhang, X. 2010. Charging children with child pornography: Using the legal system to handle the problem of "sexting." *Computer Law and Security Review*, 26: 251–259.

Zimring, F. E., Jennings, W. G., Piquero, A. R., and Hays, S. 2009. Investigating the continuity of sex offending: Evidence from the second Philadelphia birth cohort. *Justice Quarterly*, 26: 58–76.

Zimring, F. E., Piquero, A. R., and Jennings, W. G. 2007. Sexual delinquency in Racine: Does early sex offending predict later sex offending in youth and young adulthood? *Criminology and Public Policy*, 6: 507–534.

Further Reading

Jennings, W. G., Zgoba, K., Donner, C., Henderson, B., and Tewksbury, R. 2014. Considering specialization/versatility as an unintended collateral consequence of SORN. *Journal of Criminal Justice*, 42: 184–192.

Piquero, A. R., Jennings, W. G., and Barnes, J. C. 2012. Violence in criminal careers: A review of the literature from a developmental life-course perspective. *Aggression and Violent Behavior*, 17: 171–179.

5

White-Collar and Corporate Crime

Michael L. Benson, Jay Kennedy, and Matthew Logan

Introduction

Criminal behavior does not lend itself easily to quantification, and the difficulties involved in assigning numbers to behavior are especially pronounced in the case of white-collar crime and its theoretical sibling – corporate crime. These forms of crime pose conceptual and practical challenges with regard to measurement. Conceptually, one problem is that both white-collar crime and corporate crime are sociological constructs, not officially recognized legal categories. Thus, unlike in the case of many other forms of crime, such as robbery or burglary, which are well-defined legal categories with straightforward behavioral referents, it is often not clear what actions or activities should be included as part of the constructs of either white-collar or corporate crime. Indeed, debate over what should count as white-collar crime has continued to plague criminology since Sutherland (1940) first introduced the term (Geis, 1996; Shapiro, 1990; Braithwaite, 1985; Edelhertz, 1970; Tappan, 1947; Sutherland, 1945). This conceptual ambiguity has profound implications for measurement. Because researchers use varied definitions, they end up counting or measuring different things and sometimes drawing contradictory conclusions from their analyses.

Practical problems also complicate the quantification of white-collar and corporate crime. Although official data sources on street crime, such as the Uniform Crime Report (UCR) or the National Crime Victimization Survey (NCVS), never perfectly mirror the reality of what actually happens on the street, they do nevertheless constitute a nationally representative and centralized source of data concerning the extent, patterning, and trends of street crime and victimization. No such centralized

The Handbook of Measurement Issues in Criminology and Criminal Justice, First Edition.
Edited by Beth M. Huebner and Timothy S. Bynum.

data source exists for white-collar crime. Rather, official data on white-collar crime are scattered across a bewilderingly large number of law enforcement and regulatory agencies.

Even if a coherent official data infrastructure for white-collar crime were to magically appear, it almost certainly would vastly undercount the extent of white-collar crime, because white-collar crimes are meant to be hidden and to fail to come to light. Most street crimes, on the other hand, leave objectively verifiable evidence of their occurrence – a broken window, a bloodied body, or a loudly complaining victim – even if the perpetrator is never identified. However, because white-collar crimes are based on conspiracy, fraud, and deceit, they may go undetected, even by their victims, for long periods of time (Benson and Simpson, 2009). They are non-self-revealing (Sparrow, 1996). Thus the "dark figure" of white-collar crime is undoubtedly much larger than it is for other forms of crime.

This chapter summarizes information on the issues, challenges, and opportunities involved in measuring white-collar and corporate crime. It discusses the major conceptual and practical problems, identifies the data sources that are available on these types of crimes, and addresses the strengths and weaknesses of these sources. Although white-collar crime and corporate crime are related terms, they are not identical, and they pose different problems for measurement. Therefore we treat them separately, and we begin with white-collar crime.

Measuring White-Collar Crime

Definitions

There are two broad approaches to defining white-collar crime, and they are called "offender-based" and "offense-based." An offender-based approach (and definition) was originally proposed by Sutherland, who used the term white-collar crime to designate "a crime committed by a person of respectability and high social status in the course of his occupation" (Sutherland, 1949, p. 9). Others have proposed modifications to this definition; for example, Reiss and Biderman recommended the following:

> white-collar violations are those violations of law to which penalties are attached that involve the use of a violator's position of significant power, influence, or trust in the legitimate economic or political order for the purpose of illegal gain, or to commit an illegal act for personal or organizational gain. (Reiss and Biderman, 1981, p. 4)

The distinguishing characteristics of offender-based definitions are that they explicitly include selected social characteristics of the actor in the definition and they typically specify the occupational or institutional location of the act.

In contrast, offense-based definitions ignore the characteristics of the actor and focus on the nature of the illegal act in question (Edelhertz, 1970; Shapiro, 1990).

The most influential offense-based definition was developed by Edelhertz (1970, p. 3), who defined white-collar crime as "an illegal act or series of illegal acts committed by nonphysical means and by concealment or guile to obtain money or property, to avoid payment or loss of money or property, or to obtain business or personal advantage." Offense-based definitions are relatively easy to operationalize. To do so, researchers need only identify offenses that meet the criteria of being nonphysical property offenses committed by means of deceit or guile, then gather information on offenses of this kind that have come to the attention of the authorities. This approach has been used in a number of studies that investigate the sentencing of white-collar offenders in federal courts (Benson and Walker, 1988; Hagan, Nagel (Bernstein), and Albonetti, 1980; Wheeler, Weisburd, and Bode, 1982), as well as their experiences at other stages of the justice process (Benson, 1990; Cullen and Benson, 1993; Weisburd et al., 1991; Stadler, Benson, and Cullen, 2013) and in their criminal careers (Weisburd and Waring, 2001; Benson and Moore, 1992).

For measurement, the major implication of a distinction between offense-based and offender-based definitions is that the former include a much broader range of offenses and offenders than the latter. Thus the volume of white-collar crime expands considerably if researchers use an offense-based definition. For example, under an offense-based definition all offenses that are based on fraud are considered white-collar crimes, no matter how trivial or mundane they are or how lacking in respectability and high social status the perpetrators are. Crimes such as welfare fraud, personal income tax fraud, check fraud, and credit card fraud can be considered white-collar crimes according to Edelhertz's definition. However, because the people who commit these offenses rarely have high social status or significant power and because the offenses themselves are usually not occupationally based, these fraud-based crimes typically would not qualify as white-collar crimes according to Sutherland. Not only does the volume of white-collar crime expand if an offense-based definition is used; the seriousness of the offenses and the typical characteristics of the offenders also change. As Braithwaite (1985) has noted with regard to the use of offense-based definitions, the "practical consequences for empirical research have been that most white-collar criminals end up having blue collars," and the offenses become mundane and banal. In short, questions that are often asked about white-collar crime, such as "Who is the white-collar offender?" and "How much white-collar crime is there?" receive considerably different answers depending on which type of definition is used.

In the remainder of this section we identify and discuss data sources on white-collar offenders and offenses and on the victims of white-collar crime, keeping in mind that the usefulness of these sources for research purposes depends heavily on the definitional parameters discussed above. In addition, data on white-collar crime are often collected by official government agencies as part of routine record-keeping, which can limit its usefulness for research purposes. The following sections detail the strengths and weaknesses of using such data to assess and measure white-collar crime. This discussion will review official and unofficial sources for offenders, offenses, and victims.

Official sources

Official sources for data on white-collar crime include reports or surveys from various agencies – such as the Department of Justice (DOJ), the Federal Bureau of Investigation (FBI), the US Sentencing Commission (USSC), and the Government Accountability Office (GAO) – as well as from regulatory agencies such as the Environmental Protection Agency (EPA) and the Securities and Exchange Commission (SEC). In addition to detailing particular offenses, some of the reports and statistical series produced by these agencies allow researchers to glean information on the offenders that may contain relevant demographic characteristics. Below we examine official sources by using three examples: FBI data, sentencing data, and prison data.

FBI data One well-known but controversial source of information on white-collar crime is the FBI's Uniform Crime Report (UCR), which is based on the traditional Summary Reporting System (SRS) and uses an offense-based definition. Most white-collar crime researchers regard the traditional system as limited because it contains no information on the occupational status or socioeconomic position of the offender; it only includes data on age, race, and gender. Nor does the UCR include data on the types of white-collar crime that are of most interest to researchers; instead it covers only fraud, forgery and counterfeiting, embezzlement, and "all other offenses." Obviously, the category of "all other offenses" is problematic because it lumps together white-collar crimes with other crimes. In recent years, however, the FBI has made strides to improve its ability to measure white-collar crime – an effort largely credited to the implementation of the National Incident-Based Reporting System (NIBRS).

The utility of NIBRS data in measuring white-collar crime was evaluated by Barnett (2003) in a report to the DOJ. Barnett noted that NIBRS data provide a more comprehensive list of white-collar offenses than the traditional SRS. For example, under the SRS no distinction is made between the different types of fraud, whereas the NIBRS data present various subcategories of fraud, including false pretenses/swindle/confidence games, credit card and automatic teller machine (ATM) fraud, impersonation, welfare fraud, and wire fraud. In addition, the NIBRS data detail various offense characteristics that are not represented in the traditional system, such as: (1) whether the offender was suspected of using a computer during the commission of the offense; (2) where the offense took place (e.g., in commercial establishments vs. noncommercial public buildings); (3) the estimated cost of the offense to the victim and to the wider society; (4) the type of victim (e.g., financial institutions vs. individuals); (5) the age, sex, race, ethnicity, and residential status of the offender; and (6) the response of law enforcement to white-collar crime (e.g., clearance rates for specific white-collar offenses).

Despite these improvements over the SRS, there are also limitations to using NIBRS data in order to measure white-collar crime (Barnett, 2003). Among them is the fact that NIBRS data were originally designed according to the preferences and needs of the law enforcement community, whose primary emphasis is on gathering information on street crime at the local and state level. However, white-collar crime falls mainly under federal jurisdiction. Thus the NIBRS excludes specialized offenses that do not fit within the specific categories of fraud, embezzlement, counterfeiting, and bribery; these are at present the only white-collar crimes included in the NIBRS system. But, of course, the exclusion of other types of offenses leads to an overall underrepresentation of the crimes considered to be white-collar. In the same vein, a significant number of white-collar crimes are investigated by regulatory agencies or professional associations but are only reported to the UCR program if criminal charges are filed – which is extremely rare in the case of corporate malfeasance. The fact that the NIBRS is a voluntary program is also problematic, because agencies are neither obligated to submit statistics to the program nor financially compensated for doing so. A final limitation is that, with the exception of basic demographic characteristics, the data still omit important background characteristics, such as the offenders' level of education and income.

While the UCR and the NIBRS are the FBI's primary source of data on white-collar crime, information about white-collar offenses and offenders can also be gleaned from the agency's official Web site, which catalogues a number of reports – available as PDF documents – that are readily available to the general public. Among those listed are the Financial Crimes Report to the Public (2005–2011), the Financial Institution Fraud and Failure Report (2000–2007), and the Mortgage Fraud Report (2006–2010) – all of which detail and summarize significant cases for a given year that have been successfully prosecuted. While brief in nature and limited in scope, these reviews contain information regarding the nature of the offense, as well as the defendant's sex, age, and – sometimes – position within the company. The names of offenders are also released and – to the extent that they are discernibly foreign or domestic – may provide readers with information about their race or nationality. A similar protocol is followed by other agencies, such as the US Sentencing Commission's Annual Statistical Report, which publishes information on primary offense and offender characteristics for each offense category. While these Web sites constitute "official sources," they are also anecdotal and must be interpreted with caution when deciding whether the information they contain is relevant or reliable.

Data from research on sentencing As previously mentioned, the data from which inferences on white-collar offending are drawn are oftentimes created for other purposes. Despite this obvious limitation, many data sets are still useful for studying white-collar crime, as many of them contain relevant sociodemographic and offense-based variables. One of the best known data sets for studying white-collar offending was a large-scale study on the *Nature and Sanctioning of White Collar Crime* (Wheeler, Weisburd, and Bode, 2000 [1978]), from which the now famous Yale Studies on white-collar offending were derived (see Wheeler et al., 1982). These data, which are based on sentencing reports, are useful for two reasons: (1) they include offenses that most scholars would identify as white-collar-type crimes; (2) they include information on white-collar criminals that is based on reviews of conviction records and presentencing investigation reports across seven federal judicial districts.

The eight criterion offenses – as listed in the criminal code – are securities violations, antitrust violations, bribery, bank embezzlement, mail and wire fraud, tax fraud, false claims and statements, and credit- and lending-institution fraud. Variables pertaining to the characteristics of the offender include age, race, gender, family history, marital history, educational attainment, employment history, financial status, and standing in the community. Given this information, one is able to assess both offender- and offense-based characteristics that are integral to the study of white-collar crime.

Another data set that contains similar information on offenses and offenders was put together by Forst and Rhodes during the same period in which the Yale data were collected (Forst and Rhodes, 1987). This study is entitled *Sentencing in Eight Federal District Courts, 1973–1978*. The data were drawn from a different set of federal districts and included a large sample of both white-collar and non-white-collar offenders. Both data sets are available from the Inter-University Consortium for Political and Social Research, which is housed at the University of Michigan.

However, while both data sets are useful, neither is without limitation. As Benson and Simpson (2015) note, they are restricted in the sense that (1) they are not exhaustive, and only analyze eight federal offenses; (2) they contain information on only a small number of federal judicial districts; (3) like the UCR/NIBRS data, they only include convicted white-collar cases, excluding all others that were handled differently – for example, through civil court or regulatory hearings; and (4) they miss offenders who avoid detection by the criminal justice system in the first place. Additionally, unlike the UCR and NIBRS, these databases suffer from a lack of information regarding the victim's characteristics – for example, whether a victim was an individual or a business organization – and the nature of the victim's relationship to the offender. Finally, their data are based on cases that were prosecuted in the 1970s and therefore may not be representative of contemporary white-collar offenders.

However, data are available from the USSC that permit one to compare the people convicted for white-collar crimes today with those convicted in the 1970s (Benson and Simpson, 2015). The USSC collects data on the age, race, sex, and educational characteristics of individuals convicted of several white-collar offenses such as antitrust, tax, bribery, and embezzlement, as well as of crimes that fall under three other white-collar offense categories: fraud, environmental offenses, and food and drug offenses.

Prison data In addition to federal sentencing records, data sets from other sources may also be suitable in investigations of white-collar crime. In particular, there are prison databases that provide detailed information regarding the status and background of inmates, some of whom fit the criteria for white-collar offenders. For example, the DOJ's *Survey of Inmates in State and Federal Correctional Facilities 2004* – which is based on a nationally representative sample of over 18,000 inmates from 287 state and 39 federal correctional facilities – is useful because it includes a host of demographic variables such as age, race, education, employment history, level of income, family background, criminal history, and mental health history, among others. Such data facilitate comparisons between and among inmates of various social statuses on a host of prison outcomes. Of equal importance are the variables that are indicative of white-collar offending. While the term "white-collar crime" is not used as the name of an actual crime category or as the name of a variable in the data, the data nevertheless include questions pertaining to crimes of specialized access that, to our knowledge, are not available in other surveys. For example, inmates were asked the following questions:

- Before your conviction, did you have a job in which you were *entrusted* with money, property, or *opportunities* that could be turned into money?
- Were you able to commit the offense because you had some *special skills* you acquired from your *education* or *occupation*?
- Were you able to commit the offense because you had some *special knowledge* about business or government?

Questions pertaining to computer-assisted offenses are also included that assess whether the offender used a computer to (1) gain financial information; (2) steal identities; (3) gain access to other computer systems; (4) commit copyright infringement; (5) forge or alter documents; and (6) to steal intellectual property.

Such questions are particularly relevant because they can serve as proxies for opportunity structures within a given occupation, which are essential for understanding the nature of white-collar offending (Braithwaite, 1985; Benson and Simpson, 2015). Furthermore, the survey catalogues specific offense types, such as for-profit, nonviolent property crimes, as well as the victim's characteristics and the inmates' relationship to the victim. Unlike the UCR and NIBRS data, however, prison databases give information of this sort only insofar as the victim knew the offender at some individual level; they do not detail whether the offense was committed against governmental or financial institutions.

Limitations notwithstanding, databases such as these are useful for studying both offender- and offense-based definitions of white-collar crime. Moreover, through the proper use of statistical manipulation and filtering of cases, researchers can combine important elements of both offender and offense-based definitions of white-collar crime in relation to prison inmates. Put differently, these data allow for the examination of the prison experiences of inmates who are of high social status *and* who commit crimes that most would define as white-collar.

Unofficial sources

So far this section has examined the utility and limitations, for measuring white-collar crime, of data that are somehow derived from official sources. However, understanding white-collar crime and its measurement can be enhanced by consulting unofficial sources. Such sources include newspaper reports, studies of convicted offenders, and Internet searches. Some of these sources are qualitative in nature and are based on interviews with convicted white-collar offenders; others are based on more rigorous quantitative analyses from independent agencies.

Qualitative sources Newspaper reports and Internet articles – such as those published on the Web sites of large media corporations – may provide useful information regarding the characteristics of both white-collar offenders and their offenses. For instance, CNBC's official Web site has a section entitled "American Greed," which contains case files of and interviews with some of the most notorious white-collar offenders, such as Bernard Madoff. Examples of topics discussed in these interviews are the offenders' life story, the nature of and rationale for their offense, and the degree to which they have adjusted to prison life. Like the press releases given by the FBI and other official agencies, these cases often involve high-profile offenders and are not representative of the more typical white-collar offender in the justice system. However, such themes have also been mirrored in academic research and may be useful in creating an agenda for measuring various aspects of white-collar crime. Although it may be difficult to treat these data in a rigorously quantitative fashion, that is no reason to ignore them completely. These reports and interviews could be combed for themes that appear consistently and that may tell us something about these offenders and their offenses.

For example, Benson and Cullen (1988) conducted qualitative interviews with a small sample of incarcerated white-collar offenders regarding their prison experience (see also Benson, 1985; Stadler et al., 2013). On the basis of questions regarding fear, anxiety, and personal resources, the authors found that white-collar inmates – by virtue of their personal traits, social standing within the community, and deference to authority – may cope with the stress of incarceration better than other inmates. More importantly, Benson and Cullen proposed a research agenda for examining incarcerated white-collar offenders that includes operationalizing the following constructs: (1) psychological well-being and mental health; (2) personality type; and (3) level of discomfort, as evidenced by the experience of either verbal or physical abuse. Additionally, the authors asserted that the extent to which white-collar inmates adjust to prison life is a function of prison type and must be accounted for in subsequent studies. Put differently, one must control for the type of prison (e.g., state versus federal) when assessing the white-collar prison experience.

Quantitative sources While case studies and in-depth interviews comprise much of the unofficial information on white-collar crime, other Web sites take a more quantitative approach. For example, the National White-Collar Crime Center (NW3C) offers support, through its Web site, to both law enforcement and regulatory agencies in preventing, investigating, and prosecuting white-collar offenses. In addition to providing training on computer forensics, cybercrime and financial crime investigations, and intelligence analysis, the NW3C conducts its own original research on various features of white-collar crime. The results of this research are detailed in a report entitled *The National Public Survey on White-Collar Crime* and published every five years.

Included in this report is survey-based information regarding measures of the general public's experience with white-collar crime– for example measures of victimization, reporting behaviors, and perceptions of crime seriousness. Respondents' perceptions about the impact of white-collar crime on the current economic crisis and about the level of the resources allocated to the government to combat white-collar crime are also documented. For instance, descriptive statistics are presented for both complaint type (e.g., real estate fraud; auto fraud; intellectual property rights and trademark infringements) and complaint demographics (e.g., age; race; gender; estimated loss) – including whether the victimization was reported to the police or to some other entity. Similarly, perceptions of crime seriousness are assessed through 12 scenarios that present various white-collar and traditional crimes.

In conclusion, whether official or unofficial, qualitative or quantitative, the sources from which information on white-collar crime can be gleaned have both strengths and limitations. On the one hand, these sources offer information on the offender, the offense, and the victim that is valuable to the general public and scholars alike. On the other hand, the data are often gathered or created for other purposes, which are usually bureaucratic in nature, and this limits the ways in which the data can be used. For example, some data sets include relevant measures of white-collar crime (e.g., offense-based characteristics) at the exclusion of others (e.g., offender-based measures). Moreover, even when a host of relevant characteristics are taken in, the variables may be too vague in their description (e.g., victim demographics). Case studies and interviews may help to fill the void, but they are anecdotal and must be interpreted with caution.

Table 5.1 presents a summary of the characteristics of the data sources discussed so far, all of which are available from the data archives housed at the University of Michigan's Institute for Political and Social Research (ICPSR). As noted in the second column, headed "Offender-Based Measures," all of the data sets contain some information about the personal characteristics of offenders, such as race and age. However, the availability of additional information on matters such as income, marital status, or employment history varies substantially. Likewise, all of the data sets contain information about specific offense types (e.g., fraud, embezzlement), but the types of offenses covered and the availability of additional descriptive data about specific offenses vary substantially. Only the *Survey of Inmates in Federal and State Correctional Facilities* includes measures of opportunity, such as whether offenders were able to commit their crime by virtue of their job, education, or some other specialized form of knowledge. Lastly, data sets containing victim information record data on the characteristics of those who fall victim to white-collar crime—for example, age, sex, race, or ethnicity and whether the victim was an individual or an organization.

Table 5.1 Data sets available on white-collar crime and their characteristics.

Dataset Title	*Data Type*	*Variable Realms*			
		Offender-Based Measures	*Offense-Based Measures*	*Opportunity Measures*	*Victim Information*
Nature and sanctioning of white collar crime, 1976–1978	Event/transaction data	Yes	Yes	No	No
Psychological classification of adult male inmates in federal prison in Indiana, 1986–1988	Survey, administrative records, and clinical data	Yes	Yes	No	Yes
Fraud in the savings and loan industry: white-collar crime and government response, 1986–1993	Administrative records data	Yes	Yes	No	Yes
Sentencing in eight united states district courts, 1973–1978	Event/transaction data; survey data	Yes	Yes	No	No
Organizations convicted in federal criminal courts (series)	Case materials from united states probation offices	Yes	Yes	No	No
White-collar criminal careers, 1976–1978	Event/transaction data	Yes	Yes	No	No
Organized crime business activities and their implications for law enforcement, 1986–1987	Administrative records data	Yes	Yes	No	No
Controlling fraud in small business health benefits programs in the United States, 1990–1996	Administrative records data	Yes	Yes	No	Yes
Assessing identity theft offenders' strategies and perceptions of risk in the United States, 2006–2007	Survey data	Yes	Yes	No	No
Illegal corporate behavior, 1975–1975	Survey data	Yes	Yes	No	Yes
Six-year follow-up study on career criminals, 1970–1976	Event/transaction data	Yes	Yes	No	Yes
UCR: NIBRS (series)	Event/transaction data	Yes	Yes	No	Yes
Survey of inmates in state and federal correctional facilities (series)	Survey data	Yes	Yes	Yes	Yes

Measuring Corporate Crime

Definitions

Corporate crime is typically defined as an illegal act committed either by agents of an organization who are acting on behalf of and for the benefit of that organization or by the organization itself (Clinard and Quinney, 1973). The distinguishing feature of corporate crime is that the illegal act is committed in order to benefit an organization as opposed to an individual. Crimes committed in workplace settings that benefit individuals are called occupational crimes (Clinard and Quinney, 1973). For example, antitrust violations are regarded as corporate crimes, while bank embezzlement is an occupational crime.

Although the conceptual dichotomy of organizational versus individual interests appears straightforward, in the real world it can often be difficult to classify the interests involved in any given offense into one or the other of these mutually exclusive categories (Wheeler and Rothman, 1982). For example, consider the owner of a small business whose livelihood depends on the existence of the business. The interests of the individual owner seem virtually indistinguishable from the interests of the organization, that is, the small business. Crimes that benefit the latter automatically benefit the former as well. Even in large organizations where it is easier to distinguish between actions that benefit the organization and actions that benefit individuals, situations may arise in which criminal activity benefits both the organization and the individual. For example, a corporate executive who is willing to engage in criminal activity that improves profitability may be personally rewarded with a raise or promotion. Thus, while there is a substantial and informative body of research on the relationship between organizational characteristics and rates of corporate crime (Simpson, 2002; Simpson, 2013), it is important to recognize that organizations act through their employees and agents. The personal characteristics of these individuals mediate the relationship between the organization and crime, complicating the causal status of organizational characteristics (Braithwaite and Fisse, 1990; Cressey, 1989).

The overwhelming majority of corporate illegalities are not handled in criminal courts; rather they are handled either through administrative proceedings of regulatory agencies or via civil lawsuits (Clinard and Yeager, 2006; Simpson, 2013). This reality has obvious implications for counting and measuring corporate crime. If regulatory sanctions and civil lawsuits are included as indicators of corporate crime, the amount of "crime" to be tracked is considerably larger than if only criminal proceedings are counted. In addition, it is important to recognize that the underlying organizational behavior that provokes the regulatory enforcement action varies from minor paperwork infractions to serious violations that pose threats to health and safety. Efforts to correlate organizational characteristics with participation in corporate crime must be sensitive to these variations in the "seriousness" of corporate crimes.

Because no one agency is responsible for the policing and enforcement of criminal, administrative, and civil violations, multiple sources collect and maintain data on these violations. The agencies that regulate corporations collect a wide range of data on corporate violations, yet there is little overlap in the type of data that are collected. Nor are there any standards for reporting official or unofficial data on corporate violations. Data sets containing large amounts of systematically collected information about corporate violations are rare (but see the data on illegal corporate behavior in Clinard and Yeager, 1987 [1979] and 2006). This means that the study of corporate violations requires the integration of data from multiple sources. In the remainder of this section we identify and discuss official and unofficial data sources on corporate crime in relation to criminal, regulatory, and civil violations.

Official data sources

The majority of official data on corporate crimes come from the government agencies that regulate corporations. These data constitute the official record of the actions taken by the government against corporations that have violated criminal, civil, and administrative regulations. Sometimes more than one agency may be involved in a particular area. For example, both the Federal Trade Commission (FTC) and the DOJ are responsible for enforcing antitrust legislation. When a corporation is suspected of having violated antitrust laws, the FTC will investigate the case and will itself file a civil action, or it will work with the DOJ to bring criminal charges against that corporation. Because different government agencies are responsible for handling different responses to corporate violations, data on criminal violations may be produced by one agency while data on civil and administrative violations are reported by a separate agency.

Corporate crime data sources are, essentially, compilations of data from a variety of federal agencies and nongovernmental sources, each of which collects data according to its own standards. The diversity of the data collected, alongside the diversity of the styles in which they are collected, makes it difficult to find commonalities among the data obtained from different agencies. For example, many cases brought by the SEC, as found on this agency's Web site, have links to complaints filed in federal court against corporations or individuals. SEC complaints typically give explicit detail about the allegations brought by the agency, the specific laws that have been violated, the individuals involved, and the type of action being sought against the defendants. In contrast, the EPA Web site provides only a brief synopsis of the criminal actions brought against corporations and individuals, along with the specific statute that was violated and a summary of penalties.

In some cases two different regulatory agencies will handle a particular noncriminal case, and data about that case can be obtained from both agencies. For example, the Public Corporation Accounting Oversight Board (PCAOB), a nonprofit nongovernmental body that regulates the independent auditors of publicly traded corporations, has the authority to bring civil and administrative action when accounting rules or certain federal laws are violated. The PCAOB adjudicates or settles many of the cases it brings against independent auditors, yet it also turns some cases over to the SEC for resolution. Detailed information about adjudicated and settled cases can be found on the PCAOB's Web site; when a case is referred to the SEC, the PCAOB Web site lists a link to SEC documents. Linking information across regulatory agencies makes the collection of data about corporate violations easier. However, in the case of the PCAOB, data are publicly available only for cases where a violation is substantiated; all other investigations are off limits to outsiders.

With regard to corporate criminal violations, the data collected typically focus upon organizational characteristics, since it is the corporation that is usually charged with an offense. These data therefore ignore the characteristics of individual corporate agents, unless specific employees are charged with crimes alongside the company. This means that corporate crime data sources are usually rich in organization-level data, yet sparse when it comes to individual-level data; and this situation can lead to the debatable conclusion that organizational-level factors are all that matters in corporate violations, or at least the most important factors that lead to them.

For example, one of the best known studies of corporate violations was conducted by Clinard and Yeager (1987 [1979]), who collected and analyzed data on the 582 largest publicly traded corporations. (An updated version of the text detailing their findings was published in 2006; see Clinard and Yeager, 2006.) Using official government records and publicly available information about each corporation, Clinard and Yeager composed a record of each company's offending between 1975 and 1976. The data described the type of violation, the punishment imposed (if any), and many features of the offending corporation; yet no individual- or group-level data were reported, because the study focused upon the relationships among corporate metrics of profitability, liquidity, efficiency, size, and corporate violations.

Prior to the advent of electronic record-keeping and the Internet, the data available for the study of corporate violations required researchers to sift through thousands of pages of official records. This inevitably required a significant time investment, as researchers needed to gain access to official records by working directly with regulatory agencies. Today the task of combing official data on corporate violations has been made easier with the use of electronic files and with Internet access to official records. For example, the DOJ Web site provides a large amount of data on the antitrust violations the department has prosecuted. Data on antitrust violations are available in electronic format for cases brought by the DOJ since 1994; data on DOJ actions prior to 1994 still require the researcher to obtain hard-copy documents. As another example, the Commodities Futures Trading Commission (CFTC) supplies information about civil enforcement actions that are currently underway, and the use of electronic media allows the CFTC to make updates in situations where a disposition in a case has yet to be reached. The case update information gives a running record of the status of a case in the legal process until it is finally settled by the CFTC.

Electronic data available from many regulatory agencies, as well as from the DOJ, typically consist of federal court filings, official complaints, settlement agreements, and press releases. While the DOJ is responsible for prosecuting corporate criminal violations, regulatory agencies are responsible for conducting the investigations that build these cases, and they take the lead in administrative and civil cases. As a result, in addition to the data held by the DOJ, each regulatory agency collects useful information on corporate violations that can be used in the study of corporate crime together with what comes from the DOJ. For the most part, the type of data supplied by each regulatory agency on individual cases is consistent within that agency, but occasionally there are discrepancies and some cases may have more data available than others. Because regulatory agencies do not produce and distribute data sets containing the information they collect during their investigations, researchers must access data directly from an agency and compile their own database in order to obtain the most accurate information available.

Many of the data on corporate violations, criminal and noncriminal, are available from official Internet sources; yet data can still be obtained from each regulatory agency, in the manner in which Clinard and Yeager (1987 [1979]) collected theirs – by going directly to the agency to get hard-copy records. Official data on corporate violations can also be obtained from a publicly traded company itself, by reviewing its annual 10-K report. The 10-K will list any legal actions the company is currently involved in, or actions that have had, or may have, a material effect on corporate financial performance. Along with some data about offenses committed by the company, the 10-K is the best place to obtain end-of-year financial metrics, data on key corporate officers, and facilities and operations – as well as to get a small glimpse at the company's business strategy.

A corporation's disclosures of legal actions against it, while capturing official action by regulatory agencies, are likely to be colored in a way that downplays the seriousness of the charges. Nevertheless, the 10-K remains the best source for other forms of official data on the corporation, such as those mentioned above. Although 10-K reports provide a wealth of information about publicly traded companies, privately held corporations are exempt from the legal requirement of filing a 10-K report. According to the US Census Bureau, less than 1 percent of all companies in this country are publicly traded, meaning that over 99 percent of all companies do not have to provide public data on financial performance, organizational health, or legal issues, and there are no data sources reporting the corporate violations of nonpublic corporations.

As a result, most work on corporate crime has focused upon publicly traded corporations, as it is relatively easy to collect data on them. Yet focusing on publicly traded corporations means that our knowledge base rests on information from less than 1 percent of potential offenders. While it could be argued that this 1 percent is likely to be responsible for the most serious incidents of corporate crime, ignoring the remaining 99 percent of offenders means ignoring potential relationships that may be important to understanding the essence of corporate crime. Furthermore, this situation reinforces the impression that those with the "most power" are the ones whom we should fear most, when in reality the vast number of smaller, privately held corporations may also present a substantial threat in terms of the number and seriousness of their offenses.

Unofficial data sources

Unofficial data on corporate violations are available from different sources that collect, maintain, and distribute information about these violations and the companies responsible for them. Unofficial data are unique and important in the study of corporate violations because they can add richness and detail to the data that are gathered from official sources. For example, in the wake of the Enron scandal in the first decade of the twenty-first century, transcripts from congressional hearings and books written by insiders and by those close to the company (McLean and Elkind, 2003; Swartz and Watkins, 2003) became a source of useful unofficial data. In the case of Enron, as in that of many high-profile corporate violations, official data were unable to capture individual-, situational-, and organizational-level factors that are important to an understanding of how the violations occurred. Data from unofficial sources put together by investigative journalists (Eichenwald, 2005; Fox, 2003) shed light on the organizational dynamics within Enron, such as its culture of competition and the self-image employees were encouraged to assume. Furthermore, unofficial data sources give insight into the personal relationships that existed among the key offenders inside Enron, as well as into the way in which situational factors like government inquiries influenced decision-making and corporate strategy.

The transcripts of congressional hearings or regulatory agency hearings can provide a wealth of data about specific instances where a corporation has violated the law; yet hearings are not held every time a corporate violation occurs. Congressional and regulatory hearings are usually only held in cases where a small number of corporations has engaged in an alarming amount of corporate violations in a short period of time, or a larger number of corporations within a given industry have engaged in serious violations. In addition to books and transcripts from congressional hearings, newspaper articles and other journalistic accounts of corporate violations aid in understanding the details of corporate offending. These data are qualitative in nature, telling the story of a corporate violation in a manner that involves data that are inherently difficult to quantify. While there are examples, in the literature on corporate crime, of studies that take more of a qualitative approach to understanding how factors such as organizational culture influence corporate offending (Braithwaite, 2013; Clinard, 1983), such research is rare. It is difficult to obtain from offending corporations themselves quantitative data on the role that middle management or organizational ethics play in corporate violations. Yet unofficial data obtained from company insiders, investigative journalists, and researchers can offer very rich "inside" descriptions of corporate violations.

Another source of rich unofficial inside data on corporate violations can be the autobiographical works of corporate criminals. Because the stigma of being a corporate criminal is, typically, not as permanent as that of being a street criminal, some high-profile corporate offenders have written about their violations as a way to atone for their crimes (Minkow, 2005). Through these autobiographical accounts, white-collar offenders provide unofficial corporate crime data, as they describe patterns of illegal and unethical corporate behavior, while also detailing how the culture of the company may have contributed to illegal corporate acts. Unofficial data sources provide a wealth of information that is unavailable through official means; but there is no easy way to translate unofficial data into a format that can be merged with that of official data. Unofficial data are often found in the narratives of authors, journalists, and corporate insiders; and these narratives do not have a recognizable structure, as an SEC complaint would have. The researcher is therefore required to pull out of the data a form and structure that can be used alongside more official formats, such as a corporation's financial metrics or the amount of profit realized from a particular antitrust activity.

Looking Forward

Those who would study white-collar and corporate crime confront four main challenges or issues. These are (1) the problem of how to define these concepts; (2) the hidden nature of both white-collar and corporate crime; (3) the lack of consistent, readily available, centralized data sources; and (4) the technical complexity of many of the offenses. These problems are not all unique to white-collar crime. Researchers in other areas, such as sexual violence or violence between intimate partners, also face definitional issues, particularly with regard to comparative or transnational research, and lack reliable data on national trends (Gordon, 2000; Saltzman, 2004). And criminologists have long recognized that both official and unofficial statistical measures never completely capture the dark figure of street crime (Biderman and Reiss, 1967). Nevertheless, white-collar crime researchers are probably justified in feeling that their work is hampered by inadequate data to a higher degree than the work of those who study other forms of crime.

The situation, however, is not entirely hopeless. Indeed, in some ways, it is improving. For example, advances in electronic record-keeping and Internet connectivity have made it much easier for agencies to keep track of their activities and to post such data online – which, of course, makes it much easier for researchers to access and use official data. Furthermore, the whole idea that criminal justice and regulatory agencies have a responsibility to keep the data and to make them available to some degree to the public and to researchers seems to be a feature of modern governance that is now taken for granted. This development should no doubt be viewed with some scepticism, as agencies still control what they keep track of, what they release, to whom they release it, and how they release it. But the ready availability of official data online means that the shortcomings and inadequacies of the data that agencies post are now apparent and that interested parties can at least attempt to lobby for improvements. In addition, official data posted online can be accessed and put to unanticipated uses by researchers.

A recent example of researchers making innovative use of publicly available data can be found in Steffensmeier, Schwartz, and Roche (2013). Steffensmeier and colleagues used data from the DOJ's Corporate Fraud Task Force (CFTF). The CFTF was formed after the Enron and Worldcom scandals and focused on high-level corporate frauds. The CFTF compiled a database of indictments that contained rich data on 83 specific cases and on 436 offenders involved in them. The researchers supplemented the information on the indictments with other data, gathered from news sources, and with government reports and press releases. Besides being able to analyze the offenses in great detail, the researchers could gather extensive data on the sociodemographic and occupational characteristics of individual defendants and on their roles in the offenses. It is doubtful that such a project could have been conducted just 15 years ago.

There are other hopeful signs, too, that researchers may soon have access to better data on white-collar and corporate crime and to governmental responses to these offenses. In 2012, the Bureau of Justice Statistics (BJS) funded two research projects focused on improving data collection with regard to white-collar and corporate crime. As described in the request for proposals, one project calls for researchers to design a new statistical series that will integrate "criminal, civil, and regulatory enforcement data to comprehensively describe the federal response to white collar violations." The series will include "data collection on federal regulatory agency enforcement actions" and the "development of methods to integrate data from regulatory agencies with criminal and affirmative civil enforcement data that BJS receives from the Executive Office for US Attorneys and the Administrative Office of the US Courts" (US Department of Justice, 2012a). The other project focuses on state and local law enforcement efforts against white-collar crime. It calls upon applicants "to design and test strategies to field the State and Local White Collar Crime Program (SLWCCP)" – an effort by BJS "to focus on white collar crime investigated and sanctioned by state and local governments" (US Department of Justice, 2012b). Eventually it is hoped that the SLWCCP "will provide nationally representative case-level data on state and local governments' handling of white collar crime from criminal, civil and regulatory perspectives." Although neither of these ambitious projects has yet been completed, they represent important steps in the right direction and could at least mitigate, if not solve, the problem of the lack of a centralized data source on white-collar violations and enforcement actions at all levels of government.

References

Barnett, C. 2003. *The measurement of white-collar crime using Uniform Crime Reporting (UCR) data*. Washington, DC: US Department of Justice, Federal Bureau of Investigation, Criminal Justice Information Services Division.

Benson, M. L. 1985. Denying the guilty mind: Accounting for involvement in a white-collar crime. *Criminology*, 23: 583–608.

Benson, M. L. 1990. Emotions and adjudication: Status degradation among white-collar criminals. *Justice Quarterly*, 7: 515–528.

Benson, M. L., and Cullen, F. T. 1988. The special sensitivity of white-collar offenders to prison: A critique and a research agenda. *Journal of Criminal Justice*, 16: 207–215.

Benson, M. L., and Moore, E. 1992. Are white-collar and common offenders the same? An empirical and theoretical critique of a recently proposed general theory of crime. *Journal of Research in Crime and Delinquency*, 29: 251–272. doi: 10.1177/0022427892029003001.

Benson, M., and Simpson, S. S. 2015. *Understanding white-collar crime: An opportunity perspective*, 2nd edn. New York: Routledge.

Benson, M. L., and Walker, E. 1988. Sentencing the white-collar offender. *American Sociological Review*, 53: 294–302.

Biderman, A. D., and Reiss, A. J. 1967. On exploring the "dark figure" of crime. *Annals of the American Academy of Political and Social Sciences*, 374: 1–15.

Braithwaite, J. 1985. White collar crime. *Annual Review of Sociology*, 11: 1–25.

Braithwaite, J. 2013. *Corporate crime in the pharmaceutical industry*. New York: Routledge.

Braithwaite, J., and Fisse, B. 1990. On the plausibility of corporate crime control. *Advances in Criminological Theory*, 2: 15–37.

Clinard, M. B. 1983. *Corporate ethics and crime: The role of middle management*. Beverly Hills, CA: Sage.

Clinard, M. B., and Quinney, R. 1973. *Criminal behavior systems: A typology*. New York: Holt, Rinehart, and Winston.

Clinard, M. B., and Yeager, P. C. 1987 [1979]. *Illegal corporate behavior, 1975–1976*. ICPSR07855-v3. Ann Arbor, MI: Inter-University Consortium for Political and Social Research [distributor]. doi: 10.3886/ICPSR07855.v3.

Clinard, M. B., and Yeager, P. C. 2006. *Corporate crime*. New Brunswick, NJ: Transaction.

Cressey, D. R. 1989. The poverty of theory in corporate crime research. In *Advances in criminological theory*, edited by W. S. Laufer and F. Adler, 31–55. New Brunswick: Transaction.

Cullen, F. T., and Benson, M. L. 1993. White-collar crime: Holding a mirror to the core. *Journal of Criminal Justice Education*, 4: 325–348.

Edelhertz, H. 1970. *The nature, impact and prosecution of white-collar crime*. Washington, DC: US Department of Justice.

Eichenwald, K. 2005. *Conspiracy of fools: A true story*. New York: Random House.

Forst, B., and Rhodes, W. 1987. *Sentencing in eight federal district courts, 1973–1978*. Ann Arbor, MI: Inter-University Consortium for Political and Social Research.

Fox, L. 2003. *Enron: The rise and fall*. Hoboken, NJ: John Wiley & Sons, Inc.

Geis, G. 1996. Definition in white-collar crime scholarship: Sometimes it can matter. In *Definitional dilemma: Can and should there be a universal definition of white-collar crime. Proceedings of the academic workshop*, edited by J. Helmkamp, R. Ball, and K. Townsend, 159–211). Morgantown, WV: National White-Collar Crime Center.

Gordon, M. 2000. Definitional issues in violence against women: Surveillance and research from a violence research perspective. *Violence against Women*, 6: 747–783.

Hagan, J., Nagel (Bernstein), I. H., and Albonetti, C. 1980. The differential sentencing of white-collar offenders in ten federal district courts. *American Sociological Review*, 45: 802–820.

McLean, B., and Elkind, P. 2003. *The smartest guys in the room: The amazing rise and scandalous fall of Enron*. New York: Penguin Group.

Minkow, B. 2005. *Cleaning up: One man's redemptive journey through the seductive world of corporate crime*. Nashville, TN: Nelson Current.

Reiss, A. J., and Biderman, A. D. 1981. *Data sources on white-collar law-breaking*. Washington, DC: US Deptartment of Justice, National Institute of Justice.

Saltzman, L. E. 2004. Definitional and methodological issues related to transnational research on intimate partner violence. *Violence against Women*, 10: 812–830.

Shapiro, S. P. 1990. Collaring the crime, not the criminal: Reconsidering the concept of white-collar crime. *American Sociological Review*, 55: 346–365.

Simpson, S. S. 2002. *Corporate crime, law, and social control.* New York: Cambridge University Press.

Simpson, S. S. 2013. White-collar crime. *Annual Review of Sociology*, 39: 309–331.

Sparrow, M. K. 1996. *License to steal: Why fraud plagues America's health care system.* Boulder, CO: Westview.

Stadler, W. A., Benson, M. L., and Cullen, F. T. 2013. Revisiting the special sensitivity hypothesis: The prison experience of white-collar offenders. *Justice Quarterly*, 30: 1090–1114. doi: 10.1080/07418825.2011.649296.

Steffensmeier, D. J., Schwartz, J., and Roche, M. 2013. Gender and twenty-first-century corporate crime: Female involvement and the gender gap in Enron-era corporate frauds. *American Sociological Review*, 78: 448–476.

Sutherland, E. H. 1940. White-collar criminality. *American Sociological Review*, 5: 1–11.

Sutherland, E. H. 1945. Is "white-collar crime" crime? *American Sociological Review*, 10: 132–139.

Sutherland, E. H. 1949. *White-collar crime.* New York: Holt, Rinehart and Winston.

Swartz, M., and Watkins, S. 2003. *Power failure: The inside story of the collapse of Enron.* New York: Random House.

Tappan, P. W. 1947. Who is the criminal? *American Sociological Review*, 12: 96–102.

US Department of Justice, Office of Justice Programs, Bureau of Justice Statistics. 2012a. *Federal white-collar violations statistical series.* Grants.gov number BJS-2012-3352.

US Department of Justice, Office of Justice Programs, Bureau of Justice Statistics. 2012b. *State and local white-collar crime program.* Grants.gov number BJS-2012-3346.

Weisburd, D., and Waring, E. 2001. *White-collar crime and criminal careers.* New York: Cambridge University Press.

Weisburd, D., Wheeler, S., Waring, E., and Bode, N. 1991. *Crimes of the middle classes: White-collar offenders in the federal courts.* New Haven, CT: Yale University Press.

Wheeler, S., and Rothman, M. 1982. The organization as weapon. *Michigan Law Review*, 80: 1403–1426.

Wheeler, S., Weisburd, D., and Bode, N., producers. 2000 [1978]. *Nature and sanctioning of white collar crime, 1976–1978: Federal judicial districts*, 2nd ICPSR version. New Haven, CT/Ann Arbor, MI: Inter-University Consortium for Political and Social Research [distributor]. doi: ([0-9])0.3886/ICPSR08989.v2.

Wheeler, S., Weisburd, D., and Bode, N. 1982. Sentencing the white-collar offender: Rhetoric and reality. *American Sociological Review*, 47: 641–659.

6

Human Trafficking

Amy Farrell and Katherine Bright

Introduction

Over the past two decades, human trafficking has become recognized as a form of modern-day slavery. However, unlike in traditional forms of slavery, in the case of human trafficking the law does not require a person be physically bound into servitude. Human trafficking exists in many industries in the United States and involves the victimization of numerous populations, such as documented and undocumented workers who migrate to the United States to support their families financially, children who are exploited for sexual purposes after running away from abuse and family conflict, and disabled adults who labor for long hours without legitimate pay. Although the term "trafficking" suggests the movement of people or goods, federal and state laws do not require transportation of victims across state or country borders. Victims may be isolated from their support networks or from larger systems of care as a result of language or cultural barriers, and their experiences commonly include some type of initial vulnerability, such as poverty or gender discrimination, which puts them at greater risk for enslavement.

Although we do not know the true extent of victimization, human trafficking is perceived, both politically and publicly, as a serious problem. The International Labor Organization (ILO) estimates that, worldwide, 20.9 million people are victims of all forms of human trafficking, and roughly 1.5 million of these victims are exploited in the United States, Canada, and Western Europe (International Labor Organization, 2012). In addition, hundreds of thousands of children are estimated to be at risk for commercial sexual exploitation in the United States (Estes and Weiner, 2001).

The Handbook of Measurement Issues in Criminology and Criminal Justice, First Edition.
Edited by Beth M. Huebner and Timothy S. Bynum.

In response to a rise in public concern, the United Nations adopted a human trafficking protocol in November 2000 (United Nations, 2000). The *Protocol to prevent, suppress and punish trafficking in persons, especially women and children* defined human trafficking and outlined steps to foster international cooperation in prosecuting trafficking cases and in protecting the victims. In the same year, the United States passed the Victims of Trafficking and Violence Protection Act (TVPA) of 2000. The TVPA defined human trafficking (or, as the Act put it, "severe forms of trafficking in persons") as:

(a) sex trafficking in which a commercial sex act is induced by force, fraud, or coercion, or in which the person induced to perform such act has not attained 18 years of age; or
(b) the recruitment, harboring, transportation, provision, or obtaining of a person for labor or services, through the use of force, fraud, or coercion for the purpose of subjection to involuntary servitude, peonage, debt bondage, or slavery. (Victims of Trafficking and Violence Protection Act, 2000, Section 103, 8)[1]

Since that time, 164 countries have adopted antitrafficking laws (UN Global Report on Human Trafficking, 2014) and all 50 US states have passed state-specific laws that define and criminalize the practice of human trafficking.

Research on Human Trafficking

Despite numerous studies and reports published in the last 15 years, the human trafficking field has been slow to establish a systematic and generalizable research base. In large part, this challenge has been attributed to the lack of empirical research. An extensive review of the literature revealed that more than 700 research-based articles, reports, and books on human trafficking were published in the English language. However, only 12 percent of this research was subject to the traditional peer-review process, and over half (54 percent) was based on nonempirical research (Gozdziak and Bump, 2008). Prior to the twenty-first century, much of the writing on human trafficking was drawn from the experiences of advocates. In a recent issue of the *Annals of the Academy of Political and Social Science* devoted entirely to empirical research on human trafficking, Weitzer (2014) states that most writing about human trafficking is anecdotal, focuses on the problem of sexual exploitation, and conflates definitions of human trafficking with other social problems such as prostitution, smuggling, and debt bondage.

To some degree, the scarcity of empirical literature can be attributed to the field's relatively new status as a crime and social phenomenon. Like other fields that were once unrecognized or taboo (such as domestic violence or sexual assault), human trafficking has only recently garnered scholarly attention and therefore lacks research of the scope and breadth that would be necessary for establishing a comprehensive foundation. Whereas other fields have had decades in which to develop a robust research base, human trafficking is essentially still in its infancy.

Over the past decade, research on human trafficking has had three primary areas of focus: (1) estimating the scope or magnitude and the rate of change of human trafficking victimization; (2) understanding human trafficking operations and victimization experiences; and (3) assessing the effectiveness of the criminal justice response to human trafficking. In the following sections we briefly examine what is known about human trafficking and discuss the challenges of conducting research in each of these three areas.

Estimating the Scope of Human Trafficking

Substantial efforts have been made to estimate the prevalence of human trafficking, both in the United States and worldwide. This has been a challenging endeavor, since few victims have been officially identified and many of the elements of human trafficking needed in order to develop sound estimates are not known. In the United States alone, approximately 3,000 victims of human trafficking have received T-visa certification (US Department of Justice, 2014)[2] and over 1800 trafficking suspects have been prosecuted federally for trafficking-related crimes (US Department of Justice, 2007–2014; US Department of State, 2011); this figure does not include cases of prosecutions for the commercial sexual exploitation of children, which were not brought under the TVPA sex-trafficking provisions. Between 2007 and 2010, federally funded human trafficking task forces identified 3,744 potential human trafficking incidents (Banks and Kyckelhahn, 2011; Kyckelhahn, Beck, and Cohen, 2009). Given the illegal and hidden nature of human trafficking and the systematic barriers to its identification, the number of identified victims is likely to be much lower than the actual number of victims.

Open-Source Estimates

US estimates

The US government has utilized open-source information to provide a number of different estimates on the scope of human trafficking. The first US estimate, released in 1998, indicated that approximately 45,000 to 50,000 women and children were trafficked into the United States by loosely connected criminal networks each year (Richard, 1999). This estimate was developed from intelligence reports, law enforcement data, and news clippings about trafficking cases in the United States and internationally. In June 2003, the US government revised its estimate of trafficking from a figure of 18,000 to one of 20,000 people each year (US Department of State, 2003). Data for this new estimate were derived from counts of cross-border trafficking incidents that occurred between 2000 and 2002; and they came from a larger project undertaken by the federal government that estimated human trafficking worldwide. At this time an estimated 800,000 to 900,000 people were reported to be trafficked across borders globally each year (for a detailed description of the methodology, see Kutnick, Belser, and Danailova-Traino, 2007). After 2004, the US government relied upon a new estimate, which indicated that 14,500 to 17,500 people were trafficked into the United States annually (US Department of State, 2004; US Department of Justice, 2005).

However, numerous methodological problems and a lack of transparency about the way previous estimates were derived raised questions about the reliability of open-source estimates. These estimates have been limited to measuring women and children or to measuring the flow of foreign victims *into* the United States, and do not account for the number of US citizens or residents victimized within the country. In addition, these estimates neither account for the number of victims in the United States who escape trafficking each year nor provide a total number of victims in the United States at any one time. Perhaps signaling the unreliability of previous estimates, today the US government does not commonly provide estimates of the scope of human trafficking in official publications.

Other open-source estimates

In addition to the estimates provided by the US government, other organizations and scholars have developed global estimates of prevalence by using open-source information. Most recently the ILO estimated that 20.9 million people were in forced labor throughout the world. Of the total number of 20.9 million forced laborers, the ILO estimates that 18.7 million (90 percent) are exploited in the private economy, by individuals or enterprises, and 4.5 million people (22 percent total) are victims of forced sexual exploitation. An additional 14.2 million people (68 percent) are victims of forced labor exploitation, in economic activities such as agriculture, construction, domestic work, and manufacturing; and 2.2 million (10 percent) are in state-imposed forms of forced labor, for example in prison (under conditions that violate ILO standards on the subject), or in work imposed by the state military or by rebel armed forces (International Labour Organization, 2012).

The ILO used a capture–recapture methodology for identifying victims of human trafficking that appears in open-source information. Capture–recapture requires distinguishing trafficking flow (trafficked across time) versus stock (trafficking at one point in time). In this method, a portion of the population is captured through field survey and then marked, while a second sample is taken some time later. Individuals who are found in both the first and the second sample are then identified. In the 2012 ILO report, 5,491 reported cases of forced labor were found in the capture–recapture exercise; 4,069 were found only once; and 1,422 were found multiple times.

Walk Free, a nonprofit organization, estimated that there are 29.8 million people in some form of modern slavery worldwide. Data for the Walk Free estimate came from a review of secondary-source information in 162 countries and from data culled from representative sample surveys that provide information about potential victims of human trafficking available in a limited number of countries. Because representative sample data are not available for most countries, Walk Free researchers extrapolated the prevalence of human trafficking for countries without surveys (Walk Free Foundation, 2013).

The Walk Free estimate and others like it have been highly criticized for relying on open-source information, such as newspaper accounts or reports from agencies that have identified victims of trafficking. Instead of conducting ground-level research on trafficking within a country, researchers who seek to develop global estimates commonly rely on reports from other agencies, paying little attention to the quality of the data.

Additionally, definitional challenges continue to be the Achilles heel of efforts to estimate the scope of trafficking. Although legal definitions have existed since 2000, debates about what constitutes trafficking continue to exist within the field. While some scholars utilize a broad definition of human trafficking, which includes all situations in which a person is exploited, others argue that only a very specific and narrow type of force, fraud, and coercion should meet the criteria for trafficking. A good example of this discrepancy is found in the pro-sex work vs. sex-trafficking debate. For some scholars, all sex work should be considered harmful and exploitative, and therefore meets the conditions for human trafficking (Farley, 2006). Others argue that sex work is an individual's right. Although cases of human trafficking certainly exist within the larger sex-work context, these scholars argue that not all of sex work is defined by force, fraud, and coercion and that the two categories – sex work and human trafficking – should not be conflated (Weitzer, 2007). Definitional challenges are exacerbated when researchers attempt to use secondary data on identified victims, since the recognition of victims depends on the definitions applied by practitioners in the field.

County/region surveys or field observations

In light of these concerns, some scholars have used more direct methodological approaches for studying prevalence rates – such as field observations or country and region surveys. By working directly in the communities where trafficking or exploitation is occurring, researchers have been able to collect information from a broader sample of victims, extending beyond those who have sought out help or have been "freed" by a third party. In this way researchers have not only been able to tap into a victim's natural environment but often gained access to hidden populations. For instance, Steinfatt and Baker (2011) hired moto drivers to identify thousands of sex venues in Cambodia. By working with untraditional but deeply embedded informants, Steinfatt and Baker were able to gain access to participants who operated in less obvious and tourist-driven sex venues. From this study, Steinfatt and Baker estimated that sex trafficking numbers were closer to 3,000 – a number that was drastically lower than the one given by the previous reports, which claimed that between 80,000 and 100,000 people were victims of sex trafficking in Cambodia.

In addition, because traditional research often requires significant time and resources, some researchers have utilized a rapid assessment method, a process by which qualitative or quantitative data are captured in a discrete location over a very short time period, in an attempt to render the prevalence of trafficking. Although rapid assessment is usually only meant as a first step in estimating prevalence, it can play an important role in moving complex research forward or in gaining initial information about hard-to-reach populations. For example, in the early days of human trafficking research, a rapid assessment approach was used in order to explore the sex trafficking of children in Nepal. From this short, three-month data collection period, Kumar and colleagues (2001) declared that 12,000 children were trafficked from Nepal each year and that most of the girls who were trafficked were between the ages of 14 and 16. When little other information about trafficking was known or accessible, this early study served as a baseline for those working on the ground and set the stage for future studies.

Additionally, chain referral sampling methods have been used in defined geographic areas in order to identify labor-trafficking victims (Zhang et al., 2014) and minor sex trafficking victims (Curtis et al., 2008). These methods rely on identifying "seeds" within a hidden population – that is, people who can connect researchers to individuals who may have experienced a particular phenomenon. Respondents receive an incentive to participate in an interview and receive further incentives for each referral that successfully completes an interview. Referrals from each seed are limited and weights are applied to each respondent on the basis of the size and reach of his or her social network. Respondent-driven sampling methods have been successfully used to study other hidden populations, such as women and children in street prostitution (Tyldum and Brunovskis, 2005; Curtis et al., 2008), drug users (Heckathorn, 1997), and the homeless (Williams and Cheal, 2002). Utilizing chain referral methods, Zhang and colleagues (2014) surveyed over 800 undocumented migrant workers in San Diego, California and estimated that roughly 30 percent of the undocumented migrant workers in San Diego were victims of labor trafficking. This research also showed that the highest rates of labor trafficking occurred in construction and janitorial services and that immigration status was the most important variable in a person's risk for trafficking.

However, like all research methods, respondent-driven sampling and other chain referral approaches have also faced criticism. One obvious limitation is that, even when researchers are able to locate more hidden populations, participants may not be in a position to disclose victimization. For victims of human trafficking – who are, by definition, "working" for someone who has control over their daily decisions – admitting to exploitation and victimization could lead to retaliation from their trafficker. Fear, shame, or financial necessity may prevent participants from revealing victimization and may skew data toward a more conservative estimate. Furthermore, even with the support of "insider informants" (like moto drivers), it is likely that hidden populations continue to exist, being intentionally overlooked by informants or unknown to both the researchers and the community. For instance, given the social and political controversy around child exploitation, some informants may be reluctant to bring researchers to brothels where girls as young as six or seven are "working." In this way informants may selectively choose which sites they bring outsiders to. Lastly, data collected in this way have often been criticized for being too homogenous and cannot often be used for generalization. For instance, farmworkers might be able to provide researchers with valuable information about trafficking in agriculture or might connect researchers with victims of similar nationalities on other farms, but they will likely not be able connect researchers to other types of labor exploitation, such as trafficking in hotels, domestic service, or construction. By depending on a few community members to recruit all participants, researchers risk not being able to draw a diverse enough sample to permit them to generalize beyond the scope of their specific project.

Human Trafficking Victimization and Operations Research

The majority of data on human trafficking victimization have been collected from very small, homogenous samples and have largely focused on survivors who received assistance from state or social service agencies. In the absence of large-scale national or international databases, researchers have frequently relied on qualitative measurements as their primary method of data collection (Gozdziak and Bump, 2008). While qualitative approaches have traditionally been used to deepen the understanding of an *experience*, overemphasis on this type of data collection has often come at the expense of quantitative or statistical methods, which are used for capturing information across various backgrounds, characteristics, regions, and cultures. Dependence on qualitative measurements has also been criticized for their susceptibility to drawing from potentially biased information sources. Within the human trafficking field, scholars have questioned the legitimacy of using victim and stakeholder interviews as primary sources of data, since these sources have often been critiqued for skewing data toward a particular political stance or for reciting only the most appalling cases, so as to sensationalize a problem and promote future funding for particular services (Weitzer, 2014; Zhang, 2009; Schauer and Wheaton, 2006; Gozdziak and Collett, 2005). It could be argued that the prominence of certain types of stories in the past 20 years has led to the common notion that one must be chained to a bed to experience victimization (Haynes, 2006).

For the most part, despite acknowledging the limitations of current research, the field has continued to reproduce work within this narrow frame, utilizing case reviews and participant interviews as the only form of data collection. Zhang has called for researchers to move toward alternative methods, better suited for researching human trafficking victimization. For example, the layering of participant interviews with other, more quantitative methodological techniques can be used to balance out the defects of one method and to generalize information across a wide range of victims more accurately (Zhang, 2009).

Some experts have also suggested administering surveys as a way to explore hidden populations and garner large-scale information on the more private experiences of human trafficking victims (Tyldum and Brunovskis, 2005; Weitzer, 2014). While direct interviews provide researchers with the opportunity to explore certain subjects in depth, victims and key stakeholders may be more reluctant to admit to sensitive or personal details and may withhold valuable information when interviewed. In contrast, surveys provide anonymity and can, in principle, lead to higher rates of disclosure. For example, Lederer and Wetzel (2014) used a mixed methods approach in their study of 107 domestic sex-trafficking victims and survivors. While general information was collected through focus groups, a three-part survey was administered in order to collect detailed information about the victims' experiences with violence, reproductive health services, and the health conditions experienced during and after victimization. By layering traditional qualitative measures with a survey, Lederer and Wetzel collected information on approximately 200 health problems such as neurological symptoms, mental health issues, and the number of pregnancies and forced abortions that were part of a victim's trafficking experience. By reducing the amount of self-editing a participant engages in, a less invasive measurement such as a survey could lead to more accurate data and could give researchers better access to the most concealed parts of the human trafficking experience.

Like the broader field of human trafficking research, studies of victimization have disproportionally focused on the experiences of women engaged in the sex trade. Given the cultural and systematic propensity to prioritize the experiences of women and children, it is no surprise that researchers have been able to access this particular population more often than less recognized subgroups – such as men, labor trafficking victims, or child soldiers. Although researchers have often admitted to the gendered limitations of their samples, the field has traditionally pardoned this bias by claiming that other, harder-to-reach populations are too inaccessible for conventional research approaches.

However, in light of these criticisms, some scholars have dedicated their research to highlighting the needs and experiences of alternative populations. For instance, Budiani-Saberi and colleagues (2014) interviewed 103 victims of organ trafficking in India and discovered that 91 percent of victims were parents supporting an average of two children. Bayer, Klasen and Adam (2007) surveyed 163 former child soldiers and found that the average length of service was over three years; and Miller's (2011) study compared the experiences of men and boys working in Sri Lanka as "beach boys" to the dominant frames of commercial sexual exploitation of children. For these men and boys, recruitment into the sex industry occurred primarily through school-age peers; most had additional, nonsexual ways of earning money from tourists; and the average age of entry into the industry was 17.

The field has called for a new prioritization of labor trafficking. As a result, researchers have begun to expand what we know about labor trafficking victimization by specifically focusing their research on those who are exploited in industries such as agriculture, hospitality, and domestic servitude (Howard, 2014; Brennan,

2014; Owens et al., 2014). For example, Barrick and colleagues' (2013) study of migrant farmworkers highlighted the disparity between identified cases of labor trafficking and those reported by victims. While roughly a quarter of farmworker respondents reported instances of exploitation that met the requirements for labor trafficking, law enforcement was adamant that labor trafficking did not exist in their community. In addition, in a labor trafficking study, Owens and colleagues (2014) sampled closed service records for 122 victims and interviewed more than 80 labor-trafficking survivors, local and federal law enforcement agents, and social service providers. In contrast to the common stereotypes associated with labor-trafficking victims, this study showed that the vast majority of victims came into the United States legally and were from diverse educational backgrounds. Pier (2001) found that, even when migrants have legal documentation, as many domestic workers do, their status does not protect them from labor exploitation. Instead, Pier suggests that, because immigration status is most often tied to a specific employer for domestic workers, victims endure abusive working conditions in order to avoid deportation. Although rare, studies like the ones above help broaden our limited understanding of victimization and counteract the field's bias toward adult female victims of sex trafficking. By focusing on alternative populations, this recent shift in agenda has provided valuable information on less traditional subgroups and can be used to better inform policy, identification, and services for victims.

Victimization research has been further complicated by ethical concerns, as researchers are bound to report incidents in which study participants are being harmed or held against their will. Unlike other populations of study, where the risk of disclosure might be low, human trafficking victimization is ultimately defined by the connection to force, fraud, and coercion. Thus researchers who study human trafficking are inherently more likely to face situations in which they must break confidentiality and disclose cases of abuse or exploitation. To be able to ensure complete discretion to their research subjects, some researchers have purposefully chosen to include only postvictimization participants in their study. This preference has added to the research challenges, as data are only collected from victims who are in the final stages of their trafficking cycle.

Collecting post hoc data can be both beneficial and problematic. In one way, having completed an entire trafficking experience, victims can disclose information about recruitment as well as about escape and are able to reflect on each stage with varying degrees of critical analysis (Bélanger, 2014). However, without clearly designating which phase of trafficking study participants are in or acknowledging the limitations of that time-specific context, researchers often generalize a victim's experience from his or her past recollections of the crime – sometimes years after the original trafficking incident took place. As a result, research on human trafficking has depended more typically on a victim's *reflection* on his or her exploitation than on the true experience of it.

Some scholars have worked to bridge this gap by interviewing participants while an instance of exploitation was still active. For example, Chin and Finckenauer (2012) interviewed 164 women actively working in the sex industry. In this study, participants were recruited at the sex venues where they worked, on the streets of well-known prostitution areas, and through various referrals from the women's social network. By conducting research in this way, in "real time," Chin and Finckenauer were able to base their findings on the lived experiences of the women interviewed. Importantly, this research contradicted many of the commonly held beliefs about commercial sexual exploitation. For instance, though frequent narratives of commercial sexual exploitation and sex trafficking propose that women serve 15–20 men a night, Chin and Finckenauer (2012) found that 86 percent of women saw six clients or fewer.

Even when researchers are able to connect with victims directly or through a state or service agency, access to large sample sizes can be difficult to attain, as victims move, separate from assisted support, or are uninterested in talking about their experience with external entities (Brennan, 2005). For these reasons, even when research is drawn from easier-to-locate victim pools, the only point of access has often lied with key stakeholders, who are associated with an *identified* victim (Zhang, 2009). Though the victim–stakeholder relationship is the most commonly utilized resource for accessing information and collecting victim experience data (Brennan, 2014), gaining information through these channels can also lead to biased samples. By only examining those victims who seek out and receive services or who experience a third-party intervention (a police raid or an assisted-by-advocate escape), research can be limited to the experiences of only the most resilient victims. Victims with limited language skills, who don't have legal immigration status, who live in fear of their traffickers, or who might not be seen by the police or by the social service provider as "true" victims may not seek services or go to the police for help (Tyldum and Brunovskis, 2005). For most of the victims identified as such, the process of getting support means having to engage in the criminal justice, immigration, and social service systems – processes that can take months, or even years to be brought to completion. As a result, many victims choose to move on without services. Although many experts suggest that the percentage of victims connected to services is quite low, little research has been conducted to investigate the experiences of those who fall outside of these service parameters. Without research strategies that permit the inclusion of less resilient victims into the research, the field risks guiding support away from the most vulnerable victims – those who remain unconnected to interventions and who may experience exploitation several times before a systematic intervention. For example, Owens et al. (2014) found that the victims of labor trafficking, who are formally identified less often than the victims of sex trafficking, reported an average of seven forms of victimization before they escaped or were detected by police. Lastly, when providing access to victims, key stakeholders often take their role as safeguards very seriously and work diligently to protect their clients from exposure and further trauma (Brennan, 2005). This results in semi-selective sampling – whereby advocates point researchers toward victims who are "stable" enough to share their stories without being retraumatized. Though the reasons behind this practice are ethically important, it is important to recognize this bias, since many policy decisions and funding streams are based on studies of victimization.

As a result of the challenges of accessing victims, some of what we know about human trafficking has come directly from the key stakeholders – law enforcement, social service providers, legal advocates, shelter staff, and other community participants. In these cases, information about victimization is most often drawn from the stakeholder's perception of the victim's experience, from the agency's case records, or from the stakeholders' general knowledge as "experts." However, case record data can often be limited to the information routinely collected by an agency for professional purposes (Laczko and Gramegna, 2003). For example, law enforcement agencies might collect information about the criminal incident itself, as well as basic information about the victims – their citizenship status, age, gender – and about the suspects. Social service agencies, on the other hand, might collect more information about family ties, level of education, trauma history, and medical records. In some cases, stakeholder groups actively seek to avoid knowing and recording information about victims that might jeopardize their work. For example, law enforcement may not record information about a victim's mental health history, as such information would be discoverable at trial. As research on human trafficking and its victims is often collected from only one of these stakeholder groups at a time, this missing information makes it impossible to fully understand the experiences of human trafficking victims. Reliance on a small number of providers compromises the reliability of research by reducing an already limited sampling pool and by erroneously skewing victim and suspect characteristics.

To increase knowledge about a veiled population, Zhang (2009) suggests moving away from dependence on key stakeholders as access points and advises engaging the johns, facilitators, and community members (in addition to the victims themselves) who are connected to the victim's *hidden* world. Although his argument was originally purposed for sex trafficking, this logic could easily extend to other trafficking subgroups. In this way researchers can gain information about the realities of victimization in real time, through the victims themselves, or through their current "social networks" (Zhang, 2009, p. 188).

Research issues beyond sampling

Although human trafficking victims are subjected to extreme forms of force, fraud, and coercion, often for many months or years, research on human trafficking victimization has traditionally not incorporated a longitudinal perspective. While several studies explore the effects of trauma on such victims (Lederer and Wetzel, 2014; Hossain et al., 2010), very little research explores the long-term effects of human trafficking. Recognizing this void, Brennan focused her research on the aftermath of victimization by documenting the ways in which survivors reconstructed their lives and eventually reclaimed independence. Meeting with victims for approximately nine years after the initial interview, Brennan (2014) highlights how often victims continue to struggle, emotionally and financially, long after they stop being viewed as "victims" in need of saving. Without evidence to help guide long-term support, the resulting bias in research has inadvertently tilted the scaleoward immediate solutions.

By the same token, although several agencies have folded elements of human trafficking into their work since the induction of the TVPA, trafficking-only services are still rare in the United States and very little research has been done to explore the effectiveness of those that exist. Most scholarly work in this area has focused on such a specific subset of human trafficking victims that the data could not be generalized to broader groups. Additionally, solutions have often been proposed without accompanying evaluations designed to ensure that victim outcomes are successful (Macy and Johns, 2011), and very little research in this area has stemmed from those who are most affected by social services – the victims. For instance Clawson and colleagues' (2003) early needs assessment included data from roughly 124 sources; however, only 5 percent of those sources were the victims themselves. Aron, Zweig, and Newmark (2006) conducted an evaluation focusing largely on victim interviews; however, the sample size was incredibly small (34), there was gender bias (almost all participants were women), and the data were drawn from only three cities across the United States. Without studies capable of carrying out a rigorous evaluation, we continue to know very little about how to successfully move victims toward restoration. This represents a critical gap in our knowledge, especially when we consider the increase in political and public attention to human trafficking. To meet the victims' needs responsibly, representative, victim-based program evaluations are critical.

Assessing the Effectiveness of the Criminal Justice System and the Nongovernmental Response to the Problem of Human Trafficking

Other bodies of work have emerged that explore the history and impact of human trafficking laws and evaluate law enforcement responses to human trafficking. Since its induction in 2000, the Victims of Trafficking and Violence Protection Act (TVPA) has been the most widely used source of information in shaping national policy and in setting the human trafficking agenda in the United States. Researchers have examined the role of interest group politics in the design and passage of federal (DeStefano, 2007; McDonald, 2004; Stolz, 2005; Weitzer, 2007) and state antitrafficking laws (Bouché and Wittmer, 2014) and have used the TVPA as a case study in examining antitrafficking law as a form of symbolic politics (Stolz, 2007).

A separate body of scholarly work has focused on how the issue of human trafficking has been framed. For instance, Farrell and Fahy (2009) reviewed 2,462 newspaper articles to explore how the framing of human trafficking has changed over time. Their study revealed three dominant human trafficking frames: human trafficking as a human rights issue, as a crime and criminalization issue, and as a national security issue. While Farrell and Fahy argue that the changes in framing have been partly due to shifting political prioritizations, they also point to the roles media and other key stakeholders have played in the framing of human trafficking over time. For example, during the debate over the passage of the TVPA, interest groups focused on the abolition of prostitution attempted to broaden the definition of sex trafficking so as to make it include all forms of prostitution.

Despite the emergence of research on the process by which human trafficking laws were passed and on how the problem of human trafficking has been framed, there is little research that examines the effectiveness of federal or state human trafficking laws. The Center for Women Policy Studies and the Polaris Project publish yearly reports that summarize all human trafficking bills and the sponsors of those bills in every state (Center for Women Policy Studies, 2011; Polaris Project, 2014). These are helpful reference documents; but they do not analyze the laws or their effectiveness. Clawson and colleagues (2008) used surveys, interviews, and legal case reviews to determine what factors helped facilitate successful federal human trafficking prosecutions. Studies of this type, geared toward the effectiveness of state-level statutes, have not yet been undertaken.

Recently a body of research has emerged to assess the effectiveness of the criminal justice system's response to human trafficking. Farrell, McDevitt, and Fahy (2008) surveyed close to 2,000 law enforcement agencies in order to assess their knowledge of human trafficking and their readiness to enforce new antitrafficking laws. They discovered that, even eight years after the passing of the TVPA, 75 percent of police agency leaders viewed human trafficking as a rare or nonexistent problem. A smaller, state-specific survey of almost 100 law enforcement agencies discovered similar findings in Georgia, where approximately 75 percent of agencies reported that they had not received any human trafficking training and 88 percent indicated that they had no written policies to support their investigations (Grubb and Bennett, 2012). Similarly, research utilizing police surveys found that, although local law enforcement representatives are more likely to encounter victims and perpetrators of human trafficking in their daily operations, they commonly perceive human trafficking as a matter for federal law enforcement (Clawson, Dutch, and Cummings, 2006; Wilson, and Dalton, 2008). When law enforcement officers acquire knowledge about human trafficking through a sensationalist, media-informed lens, they are less likely to think that human trafficking is a problem in their community. (Wilson, Walsh, and Kleuber, 2006).

Research further suggests that the police are ill equipped to identify human trafficking cases. A 2008 study investigating law enforcement perceptions of human trafficking in sixty US counties found that, for the most part, law enforcement personnel was not able to properly define human trafficking and had little familiarity with state or federal human trafficking legislation (Newton, Mulcahy, and Martin, 2008). Mitchell, Finkelhor, and Wolak (2010) found that, even with the changes in federal and state laws – that is, even with laws that defined all juveniles involved in prostitution as sex-trafficking victims – law enforcement was slow to change its perceptions and continued to view roughly a third of the minors engaged in prostitution as delinquents, charging them with a crime. These skewed perceptions may explain why so few cases of human trafficking have been identified by the police.

Limited research focuses on how human trafficking cases are processed, once they have been identified. Using a multimethod approach based on case reviews and in-depth interviews with law enforcement officers, prosecutors, and victim services staff in 12 counties across the United States, Farrell and colleagues (2012) examined a sample of 140 human trafficking cases in order to determine whether certain types or features of this offense were more likely to be prosecuted under new human trafficking laws or other criminal offenses. In addition, Farrell and colleagues examined the organizational, structural, and cultural factors that inhibit or facilitate the prosecution of human trafficking. They found that the police did not proactively identify human trafficking cases and that the overwhelming majority of those identified by law enforcement were sex-trafficking cases (86 percent). Additionally, due to stereotypes about what a trafficking victim looks like, law enforcement often misclassified victims as offenders, blaming them for being undocumented, for being involved in prostitution, or for being otherwise complicit in their victimization.

In the Farrell et al. (2012) study approximately two thirds (67 percent) of the cases sampled went forward to prosecution; but, despite the existence of evidence of human trafficking elements in the majority of cases reviewed, few cases were actually classified, at either the state or the federal level, as human trafficking offenses. This suggests that, despite new state laws on human trafficking, state prosecutors continue to charge human trafficking offenders with crimes of other types. Defendants identified in this study were most commonly charged at the state level with compelling or promoting prostitution and at the federal level with transport of persons for the purposes of prostitution. Interviews with prosecutors revealed a striking lack of awareness about the problem of human trafficking in their local communities and a failure on the part of government officials, including the chief prosecutors, to prioritize the problem of human trafficking. State and local prosecutors commonly received referrals to human trafficking cases with little to no training or legal guidance on how to utilize the new laws. As a result, prosecutors were reluctant to peruse charges for human trafficking crimes and relied instead on previously existing offenses, with which they were more familiar.

Studies of the identification, investigation, and prosecution of human trafficking cases are severely limited by the lack of data. There are no mechanisms for gathering standardized data from all of the nongovernmental agencies that provide services to victims of human trafficking to compare them to data from police records or court records. It is difficult to find records of police investigations for human trafficking, and even more difficult to track those records through the courts. In 2013 the Uniform Crime Reporting program started to collect data from US law enforcement agencies about criminal incidents that involve sex trafficking and labor trafficking. As these data improve in the coming years, we will gain important new insight about where and under what conditions local police can identify human trafficking cases. These data will allow us to begin assessing the effectiveness of antitrafficking laws and measuring improvements in law enforcement responses to human trafficking in local communities.

Conclusions

Lacking rigorous measures to capture a wide range of victim experiences, the human trafficking field has often overgeneralized the accounts of identified victims. As opposed to unidentified victims, these victims are more likely to have been female, exploited in the sex industry, escaped their victimization and received services. Because we have very little reliable data on the mechanisms by which victims are recruited and transported, experience victimization, and leave situations of exploitation, we do not know what proportion of human trafficking victims get identified by the police or by victim service providers. Without this information we cannot effectively use police, court, or victim service records to accurately estimate the scope of human trafficking victimization. There are however, numerous sources of data about people who may be at risk for human trafficking victimization. For example, government officials routinely collect information on the number of foreign migrant workers who enter the United States annually. Research is needed to better understand what proportion of these workers experience exploitation rising to the level of human trafficking, in order to more effectively utilize existing data about at-risk populations.

As human trafficking continues to develop as a field of scholarly inquiry, numerous important areas present themselves for future research. We outline a few areas where empirical research is needed.

- More reliable information is required about how victims experience and recover from different types of trafficking. Are some forms of trafficking more harmful than others? How long does it take for trafficking victims to heal from their experience of victimization and what helps facilitate victim restoration?
- Significant research is needed on the perpetrators, including basic descriptive information – their characteristics, their level of involvement in trafficking, and their involvement in other criminal enterprises and networks. Research on businesses that engage in trafficking and utilize trafficked laborers (likely from contractors or third-party facilitators) is also needed. Some steps have been taken to hold businesses accountable for the instances of human trafficking in their supply chain, but we have very little information about this process.
- Research is also needed to monitor the effectiveness of antitrafficking campaigns and programs. As states quickly pass laws that criminalize human trafficking, increase the penalties for trafficking crimes, and allocate resources for antitrafficking programs, we need sound evaluation research about the effectiveness of programs such as demand reduction, prostitution diversion, survivor-led mentoring, public awareness campaigns, and targeted enforcement. In addition to evaluating the effectiveness of various antitrafficking programs to address trafficking, researchers should be attentive to possible unexpected consequences and costs of antitrafficking efforts.

Much remains to be learned about the phenomenon of human trafficking and the effectiveness of various antitrafficking strategies. It is critical to develop a stronger, more comprehensive research base, as access to services, funding, and the creation of new policies largely depend on information gained from human trafficking research.

Notes

1 Along with this more general definition of "severe forms of trafficking in persons" in Section 103, 8, the TVPA also gives a specific definition of sex trafficking as "the recruitment, harboring, transportation, provision, or obtaining of a person for the purpose of a commercial sex act" – in other words a definition that covers almost all forms of prostitution, regardless of the use of force, fraud, or coercion (Victims of Trafficking and Violence Protection Act, 2000, Section 103, 9). The use of two definitions represents the compromise that legislative leaders made in order to appease prostitution abolitionists, who wanted to see all forms of prostitution defined as trafficking. Instead, the TVPA recognizes the harms of prostitution but limits the delegation of resources and criminal penalties only to those cases where a severe form of trafficking is found.

2 A T visa is a special visa provided for human trafficking victims that are not US citizens. Victims must apply for certification and must receive support from law enforcement or other qualified legal authorities in order to prove their victim status. A T visa allows trafficking victims to access services and employment that traditionally would not be available to noncitizens.

References

Aron, L., Zweig, J., and Newmark, L. 2006. *Comprehensive services for survivors of human trafficking: Findings from clients in three communities*. Washington, DC: Urban Institute.

Banks, D., and Kyckelhahn, T. 2011. *Characteristics of suspected human trafficking incidents, 2008–2010*. Washington, DC: US Department of Justice, Office of Justice Programs, Bureau of Justice Statistics.

Barrick, K., Lattimore, P., Pitts, W., and Zhang, S. 2013. *Indicators of labor trafficking among North Carolina migrant farmworkers: Final report*. Washington, DC: National Institute of Justice.

Bayer, C. P., Klasen F., and Adam, H. 2007. Association of trauma and PTSD symptoms with openness to reconciliation and feelings of revenge among former Ugandan and Congolese child soldiers. *Journal of American Medicine Association*, 298 (5): 555–559.

Bélanger, D. 2014. Labor migration and trafficking among Vietnamese migrants in Asia. *The ANNALS of the American Academy of Political and Social Science*, 653 (1): 87–106.

Bouché, V., and Wittmer, D. 2014. Gendered diffusion on gendered issues: The case of human trafficking. *Journal of Public Policy*, 35: 1–33.

Brennan, D. 2005. Methodological challenges in research with trafficked persons: Tales from the field. *International Migration*, 43 (1–2): 35–54.

Brennan, D. 2014. *Life Interrupted trafficking into forced labor in the United States*. Durham, NC: Duke University Press.

Budiani-Saberi, D. A., Raja, K. R., Findley, K. C., Kerketta P., and Anand, V. 2014. Human trafficking for organ removal in India: A victim-centered, evidence-based report. *Transplantation*, 97 (4): 380–384.

Center for Women Policy Studies. 2011. *US policy to combat trafficking*. Accessed September 10, 2014. http://www.centerwomenpolicy.org/programs/trafficking/facts/default.asp.

Clawson, H., Dutch, N., and Cummings, M. 2006. *Law enforcement response to human trafficking and the implications for victims: Current practices and lessons learned*. Washington, DC: National Institute of Justice, US Department of Justice.

Clawson, H. J., Dutch, N., Lopez, S., and Tiapula, S. 2008. *Prosecuting human trafficking cases: Lessons learned and promising practices* (Grant No. 2006 -NIJ-1163). Washington, DC: ICF International.

Clawson, H. J., Small, K. M., Go, E. S., and Myles, B. W. 2003. *Needs assessment for service providers and trafficking victims*. Washington, DC: ICF International.

Chin, K. L., and Finckenauer, J. O. 2012. *Selling sex overseas: Chinese women and the realities of prostitution and global sex trafficking*. New York: NYU Press.

Curtis, R., Terry, K., Dank, M., Dombrowski, K., Khan, B., Muslim, A., Labriola, M., and Rempel, M. 2008. *The commercial sexual exploitation of children in New York City*. New York: Center for Court Innovation.

DeStefano, A. 2007. *The war on human trafficking: US policy assessed*. New Brunswick, NJ: Rutgers University Press.

Estes, R. J., and Weiner, N. A. 2001. *The commercial sexual exploitation of children in the US, Canada and Mexico*. Pennsylvania, PA: University of Pennsylvania School of Social Work, Center for the Study of Youth Policy.

Farley, M. 2006. Prostitution, trafficking, and cultural amnesia: What we must not know in order to keep the business of sexual exploitation running smoothly. *Yale Journal Law & Feminism*, 18: 109–143.

Farrell, A., and Fahy, S. 2009. The problem of human trafficking in the US: Public frames and policy responses. *Journal of Criminal Justice*, 37: 617–627.

Farrell, A., McDevitt, J., and Fahy, S. 2008. *Understanding and improving law enforcement responses to human trafficking* (Grant No. 2005-IJ-CX-0045). Washington, DC: National Institute of Justice, US Department of Justice.

Farrell, A., McDevitt, J., Pfeffer, R., Fahy, S., Owens, C., Dank, M., and Adams, W. 2012. *Final report: Identifying challenges to improve the investigation and prosecution of state and local human trafficking cases* (NCJ-238795). Washington, DC: US Department of Justice, National Institute of Justice.

Gozdziak, E. M., and Bump, M. N. 2008. *Data and research on human trafficking: Bibliography of research-based literature*. Washington, DC: Georgetown University, Institute for the Study of International Migration.

Gozdziak, E, M., and Collett, E. A. 2005. Research on human trafficking in North America: A review of literature. *International Migration*, 43 (1–2): 99–128.

Grubb, D., and Bennett, K. 2012. The readiness of local law enforcement to engage in US anti-trafficking efforts: An assessment of human trafficking training and awareness of local, county, and state law enforcement agencies in the state of Georgia. *Police Practice and Research*, 13 (6): 487–500.

Haynes, D. F. 2006. (Not) found chained to a bed in a brothel: Conceptual, legal, and procedural failures to fulfill the promise of the Trafficking Victims Protection Act. *Georgetown Immigration Law Journal*, 21: 337–381.

Heckathorn, D. D. 1997. Respondent-driven sampling: A new approach to the study of hidden populations. *Social Problems*, 44 (2): 174–199.

Hossain, M., Zimmerman, C., Abas, M., Light, M, and Watts, C. 2010. The relationship of trauma to mental disorders among trafficked and sexually exploited girls and women. *American Journal of Public Health*, 100 (12): 2442–2449.

Howard, N. 2014. Teenage labor migration and anti-trafficking policy in West Africa. *The ANNALS of the American Academy of Political and Social Science*, 653 (1): 124–140.

International Labour Organization. 2012. *ILO 2012 Global Estimate of Forced Labour*. Geneva: International Labour Organization.

Kumar, B., KC, Subedi, G., Gurung, Y. B., and Adhikari, K. P. 2001. *Trafficking in girls with special reference to prostitution: A rapid assessment*. Geneva: International Labour Organization.

Kutnick, B., Belser, P., and Danailova-Traino, G. 2007. *Methodologies for global and national estimation of human trafficking victims: Current and future approaches*. Geneva: International Labour Organization.

Kyckelhahn, T., Beck, A. J., and Cohen, T. H. 2009. *Characteristics of suspected human trafficking incidents, 2007–2008*. Washington, DC: US Department of Justice, Bureau of Justice Statistics.

Laczko, F., and Gramegna, M. A. 2003. Developing better indicators of human trafficking. *Brown Journal of World Affairs*, 10 (1): 179–194.

Lederer, L. J., and Wetzel, C. A. 2014. Health consequences of sex trafficking and their implications for identifying victims in healthcare facilities. *The Annals of Health Law*, 23 (1): 61–91.

Macy, R. J., and Johns, N. 2011. Aftercare services for international sex trafficking survivors: Informing US service and program development in an emerging practice area. *Trauma, Violence, & Abuse*, 12 (2): 87–98.

McDonald, W. F. 2004. Traffic counts, symbols and agendas: A critique of the campaign against trafficking of human beings. *International Review of Victimology*, 11 (1): 143–176.

Miller, J. 2011. Beach boys or sexually exploited children? Competing narratives of sex tourism and their impact on young men in Sri Lanka's informal tourist economy. *Crime, Law and Social Change*, 56 (5): 485–508.

Mitchell, K. J., Finkelhor, D., and Wolak, J. 2010. Conceptualizing juvenile prostitution as child maltreatment: Findings from the national juvenile prostitution study. *Child Maltreatment*, 15 (1): 18–36.

Newton, P., Mulcahy, T., and Martin, S. 2008. *Finding victims of human trafficking*. Bethesda, MD: National Opinion Research Center.

Owens, C., Dank, M., Breaux, J., Bañuelos, I., Farrell, A., Pfeffer, R., Bright, K., Heitsmith, R., and McDevitt, J. 2014. *Understanding the organization, operation, and victimization process of labor trafficking in the United States* (Award No. 2011-IJ-CX-0026). Washington, DC: National Institute of Justice, US Department of Justice.

Pier, C. 2001. *Hidden in the home: Abuse of domestic workers with special visas in the United States*. New York: Human Rights Watch.

Polaris Project. 2014. *2014 State ratings on human trafficking laws*. Accessed September 10, 2014.http://www.polarisproject.org/what-we-do/policy-advocacy/national-policy/state-ratings-on-human-trafficking-laws.

Richard, A. O. 1999. *International trafficking in women to the US: A contemporary manifestation of slavery and organized crime*. Washington, DC: Center for the Study of Intelligence.

Schauer, E. J., and Wheaton, E. M. 2006. Sex trafficking into the United States: A literature review. *Criminal Justice Review*, 31 (2): 146–169.

Steinfatt, T., and Baker, S. 2011. *Measuring the extent of sex trafficking in Cambodia, 2008.* Bangkok, Thailand: United Nations Interagency Project on Human Trafficking.

Stolz, B. A. 2005. Educating policymakers and setting the criminal justice policymaking agenda: Interest groups and the "Victims of Trafficking and Violence Act of 2000." *Criminology and Criminal Justice*, 5: 407–430.

Stolz, B. A. 2007. Interpreting the US human trafficking debate through the lens of symbolic politics. *Law and Politics*, 29: 311–338.

Tyldum, G., and Brunovskis, A. 2005. Describing the unobserved: Methodological challenges in empirical studies on human trafficking. *International Migration*, 43 (1–2): 17–34.

United Nations. 2000. *Protocol to prevent, suppress and punish trafficking in persons, especially women and children, supplementing the United Nations Convention against Transnational Organized Crime.* Washington, DC: General Assembly resolution 55/25.

UNODC. 2012. *Global report on trafficking in persons.* Vienna: United Nations.

US Department of Justice. 2005. *US Attorney General's report to Congress and assessment of US Activities to combat trafficking in persons.* Washington, DC: US Department of Justice, Attorney General's Office.

US Department of Justice. 2007. *Attorney General's report to Congress and assessment of US activities to combat trafficking in persons in fiscal year 2006.* Washington, DC: US Department of Justice, Attorney General's Office.

US Department of Justice. 2008. *Attorney General's report to Congress and assessment of US activities to combat trafficking in persons in fiscal year 2007.* Washington, DC: US Department of Justice, Attorney General's Office.

US Department of Justice. 2009. *Attorney General's report to Congress and assessment of US activities to combat trafficking in persons in fiscal year 2008.* Washington, DC: US Department of Justice, Attorney General's Office.

US Department of Justice. 2010. *Attorney General's Annual report to Congress and assessment of US government activities to combat trafficking in persons fiscal year 2009.* Washington, DC: US Department of Justice, Attorney General's Office.

US Department of Justice. 2011. *Attorney General's report to Congress and assessment of US activities to combat trafficking in persons in fiscal year 2010.* Washington, DC: US Department of Justice, Attorney General's Office.

US Department of Justice. 2012. *Attorney General's report to Congress and assessment of US activities to combat trafficking in persons in fiscal year 2011.* Washington, DC: US Department of Justice, Attorney General's Office.

US Department of Justice. 2013. *Attorney General's report to Congress and assessment of US activities to combat trafficking in persons in fiscal year 2012.* Washington, DC: US Department of Justice, Attorney General's Office.

US Department of Justice. 2014. *Attorney General's annual report to Congress and assessment of US government activities to combat trafficking in persons fiscal year 2012.* Washington, DC: US Department of Justice, Attorney General's Office.

US Department of State. 2003. *Trafficking in persons report, 2003.* Washington, DC: US Department of State.

US Department of State. 2004. *Trafficking in persons report, 2004.* Washington, DC: US Department of State.

US Department of State. 2011. *Trafficking in persons report, 2011.* Washington, DC: US Department of State.

Victims of Trafficking and Violence Protection Act. 2000. In *US laws of trafficking in persons.* US Department of State. Accessed December 17, 2015. http://www.state.gov/documents/organization/10492.pdf.

Walk Free Foundation. 2013. *Global slavery index, 2013.* Accessed December 14, 2015. www.globalslaveryindex.org.

Weitzer, R. 2007. The social construction of sex trafficking: Ideology and institutionalization of a moral crusade. *Politics & Society*, 35 (3): 447–475.

Weitzer, R. 2014. New directions in research on human trafficking. *The Annals of the American Academy of Political and Social Science*, 653 (1): 6–24.

Williams, M., and Cheal, B. 2002. Can we measure homelessness? A critical evaluation of the method of "capture-recapture." *International Journal of Social Research Methodology*, 5 (4): 313–331.

Wilson, D. G., Walsh, W. F. and Kleuber, S. 2006. Trafficking in human beings: Training and services among US law enforcement agencies. *Police Practice and Research*, 7 (2): 149–160.

Wilson, J. M., and Dalton, E. 2008. Human trafficking in the Heartland: Variation in law enforcement awareness and response. *Journal of Contemporary Criminal Justice*, 24 (3): 296–313.

Zhang, S. 2009. Beyond the "Natasha" story: A review and critique of current research on sex trafficking. *Global Crime*, 10 (3): 178–195.

Zhang, S., Spiller, M. W., Finch, B.K., and Qin, Y. 2014. Estimating labor trafficking among unauthorized migrant workers in San Diego. *The Annals of the American Academy of Political and Social Science*, 653 (1): 65–86.

Further Reading

Steinfatt, T. 2011. Sex trafficking in Cambodia: Fabricated numbers versus empirical evidence. *Crime, law, and Social Change*, 56: 443–462.

7

Challenges in Measuring and Understanding Hate Crime

Jack McDevitt and Janice A. Iwama

Since the Civil Rights Act of 1968, which gave the federal government permission to prosecute anyone who discriminates against any person because of his or her race, color, religion, or national origin in federally protected activities (18 USC § 245 [b] [2]; see https://www.law.cornell.edu/uscode/text/18/245), hate crime statutes have evolved by increasing the penalties for crimes motivated by bias and by adding other protected categories of individuals. Federal and state hate crime laws protect against discrimination because of race or other identifying characteristics, but differences across state laws present challenges for the measurement of hate crimes across different regions and targeted groups (Anti-Defamation League, 2012; Shively, 2005).

The passage of the Hate Crime Statistics Act (HCSA) of 1990 mandated that the attorney general collect hate crime reports from federal and state law enforcement agencies in order to provide a better understanding on the magnitude of hate crimes in the United States. For the purpose of data collection on this issue, Congress defined a hate crime as a "criminal offense against a person or property motivated in whole or in part by an offender's bias against a race, religion, disability, ethnic origin or sexual orientation" (Federal Bureau of Investigation, 2014). This information is published as a part of the Federal Bureau of Investigation's (FBI) annual Uniform Crime Reports (UCR) and constitutes the most promising source of national data for detecting significant trends in hate crime (Shively et al., 2013). However, a number of issues exist in terms of the quantity and quality of data being reported by law enforcement agencies, particularly issues of misclassification and underreporting. These issues raise questions on the UCR data as a reliable measure of hate motivated violence across the country (Haas et al., 2011).

The Handbook of Measurement Issues in Criminology and Criminal Justice, First Edition.
Edited by Beth M. Huebner and Timothy S. Bynum.

Most recently the New York City Police Department (NYPD) underwent an audit by the New York State Comptroller's Office, which discovered disparities between the number of individual incidents filed with the police department and the number of incidents found in the FBI UCR hate crime report (New York State Office of the State Comptroller, 2014). Although the audit was "unable to confirm that all reported bias incidents are properly captured, recorded, and reported," it did raise a number of questions on the credibility of the data published in the FBI UCR reports and on their capacity to accurately measure the level of hate crime in New York City (New York State Office of the State Comptroller, 2014, p. 1).[1] More importantly, the report brought up further questions about what other measurement issues exist and how to address them in order to gain a better understanding on the extent of hate crime in our communities.

To address these questions, we begin by providing background information on the origin of hate crime data collection in the United States. Next we define hate crime after the creation of hate crime legislation, describing the elements of the commonly used definition, and we discuss the evolution of this legislation. We provide an overview of national hate crime data from the three main national data collection programs: the UCR, the National Incident-Based Reporting System (NIBRS), and the National Crime Victimization Survey (NCVS). Each of these three data series is assessed for its utility in determining the extent and characteristics of hate crime. Although we describe the limitations of each hate crime data collection methodology, we also claim that it is possible to improve the capacity of the available data to measure the level and scope of hate crimes in the United States. We sketch out some possible ways of doing so and conclude by envisioning the next steps in measuring hate crime.

Background

Before 1990 national data on hate crimes committed in the United States were not available. The FBI undoubtedly received reports of hate crimes from law enforcement agencies in their annual reporting statistics. The problem was that these reports were coded as reports of crimes of other types, such as assault or vandalism. At the time there was no way of differentiating a bias-motivated assault from other assaults, and therefore the FBI could not provide any national estimate of the number of bias crimes reported to or investigated by local police. However, certain advocacy groups and law enforcement agencies collected data on hate crimes but focused on certain communities or groups that were being targeted.

Law enforcement agencies

Among the first police agencies to begin collecting data on hate crime were the Baltimore County Police Department, the Boston Police Department, and the NYPD. These agencies collected and, in some cases, published statistics about hate crime that were reported to and investigated by the police (e.g., New York City Commission on Human Rights, 1984, 1993). In these early attempts to collect hate crime data, the decision generally followed the establishment of a hate crime investigative unit in the agency that was designed to clarify certain events that had arisen. The purpose of collecting data on hate crimes was mainly to document the activities of these hate crime units and to identify the scope and trends of hate crime in the community.

In Boston, for example, the Boston Police Department created the Community Disorders Unit in April 1978, after a series of racially motivated attacks in the city (Finn and Hylton, 1994; Wexler and Marx, 1986). Following a ruling in 1974 by Judge W. Arthur Garrity, Jr., who had determined that Boston public schools were racially segregated, the residents of Boston were ordered to bus school children in the interest of achieving racial balance. This decision provoked a crisis. The order was met with fierce resistance from white residents in the city and resulted in heightened racial tensions and in an increasing number of racially motivated assaults. The unit was created as a means to control and prevent further violence in the city, as well as to act as a public relations tool and assure the residents of Boston that the police department was going to deal with this growing problem. The commander of the Community Disorder Unit, Superintendent William Johnston, decided to collect data as a way to justify the creation of the unit and to demonstrate that the unit required additional resources. Similar developments and data collection efforts took place in Baltimore County and New York City (Garofalo and Martin, 1991; Kelly, 1991; New York City Commission on Human Rights, 1993).

Advocacy groups

Just like law enforcement agencies, a number of national advocacy groups began to collect information on hate incidents that involved their constituents. The Anti-Defamation League (ADL), a leader in support of national data collection, began to collect data on hate incidents that came to its attention in hate crime annual Audit of Anti-Semitic Incidents in 1979 (Anti-Defamation League, 2014a). The ADL collects information about "vandalism, harassment and physical assault against Jewish individuals" and reports these data in an annual publication. In 1981 the Southern Poverty Law Center (SPLC) began to publish its Intelligence Report, which collected information on hate crimes committed by members of extremist organizations, and also began to count the number of these organizations in the United States. At the same time the Los Angeles County Human Relations Commission (LACHRC) began to publish its Annual Hate Crime Report, which reported on hate crimes brought to the attention of law enforcement agencies in Los Angeles County during the previous year, 1980 (e.g., Los Angeles County Human Relations Commission, 2014). The commission was created following the so-called "zoot suit" riots in Los Angeles County, when white sailors had attacked Latino youth, causing violence over several days. While the riots occurred and culminated in 1943, concerns expressed by residents led to the development of the commission, which later became an official agency of the county government and was charged with addressing these issues and with gathering information on how to prevent racially motivated violence.

Additionally, the National Gay and Lesbian Task Force, now called the National Lesbian, Gay, Bisexual, Transgender, and Queer (LGBTQ) Task Force, published its first annual report on homophobic violence and intimidation in 1984, following a national survey to capture acts of discrimination of this kind. The task force issued the first comprehensive report designed to bring antigay violence and victimization, as a national issue, to the attention of Department of Justice. It has continued to collect information on a number of other issues, including ones faced by the transgender community, through a national survey (e.g., National Gay and Lesbian Task Force, 2013).

It is interesting to note that this wide variety of groups – ranging from local police agencies to national advocacy organizations – saw the need for data collecting around the same period, the late 1970s to the mid-1980s, and began to collect such data on hate crimes. The problem with this decentralized and uncoordinated approach was that each group collected data of different types. Data were collected for an individual jurisdiction or for a single group of victims; and, more importantly, the definition of what qualified as a hate crime was similarly diverse, ranging from crimes reported to and investigated by the police to incidents reported via hotline. For example, the New York City Commission on Human Rights (CCHR) operated a hotline starting in August 1990 in order to understand the prevalence of hate crime in New York City and to act as an additional source of information for the NYPD's Bias Incident Investigations Unit. Unlike the police department, which in 1992 limited its investigations to racial, ethnic, religion, antisemitic, and antigay criminal acts, the Commission dealt with the above mentioned groups as well as with criminal acts that targeted the homeless, or people with low incomes. The Commission also collected information on noncriminal bias, in order to prevent tensions from escalating to criminal acts (New York City Commission on Human Rights, 1993). Therefore the hate crime data reported by CCHR diverged from the final figures handled and then reported by NYPD. Furthermore, another source of variation was the specific groups covered by each statute. In most states in the 1980s, for example, crimes motivated by race, ethnicity, or religion were counted in, but the treatment of crimes that targeted other groups (e.g., LGBTQ or women) varied widely from state to state.

Defining Hate Crime

In this chapter, we started by using the term "hate crime" to describe criminal behavior. As shown in the literature, this term is unfortunate, and probably a misnomer. A more accurate description of the phenomenon covered by this term is "bias crime" or "bias-motivated crime" (Berk, Boyd, and Hammer, 1992; Petrosino, 1999). Many crimes have hatred as a motivating factor, but they do not involve bias toward a group as a motivating factor. The homicide of an intimate partner is an example of a hate-motivated crime that has nothing to do with bias. Unfortunately the term "hate crime" has been codified into law by federal and state governments, for instance in the Hate Crime Statistics Act passed by Congress in 1990, and has become the primary description for these offenses. The crimes we are discussing in this chapter involve criminal incidents that are motivated, in whole or in part, by a person's perceived membership in a particular group – and not by the degree of animus the offender holds toward the victim. We will use here the terms "hate crime" and "bias crime" interchangeably, to describe such incidents; nevertheless, we do understand that the term "bias crime" describes more accurately the behavior we are referencing.

National legislation

While the federal government did not recognize hate crime as a protected category until 1990, the Civil Rights Act of 1968 prohibited harming individuals on the basis of their race, color, religion, or national origin and gave the federal government the authority to prosecute individuals who did so during a federally protected activity – which included attending school, serving as a jury member, or exercising your voting rights. It was not until 1988 that Representative John Conyers from Michigan introduced the Hate Crime Statistics Act. This act was supported by a large coalition of civil rights groups that consisted of the ADL, the National Association for Advancement of Colored People (NAACP), the National Gay and Lesbian Task Force (NGLTF), the National Organization of Black Law Enforcement officers (NOBLE), the American Jewish Congress, the American Psychological Association, and the Leadership Conference on Civil Rights (LCCR). Initially the Act was filed in 1988, then again in 1989, but Congress did not pass it until 1990.

The Act called for the collection of data on hate crime by the attorney general of the United States. While many advocates were looking for a much stronger piece of legislation, particularly one that would provide for an enhanced federal penalty against hate crimes, Representative Conyers and several other legislators believed that such an act would not be passed by Congress at the time. Therefore they pursued legislation that would collect data on these crimes, in order to provide support for future legislation that would enhance their penaltization.

Given the rising level of interest in understanding the nature and prevalence of hate crimes across the United States during the 1980s, the Hate Crime Statistics Act (HCSA) of 1990 (28 USC § 534 [1] [b] [1]: https://www2.fbi.gov/ucr/hc2009/hatecrimestatistics.html) ordered that a system be created to collect data on hate crimes in accordance with the following definition:

> crimes that manifest evidence of prejudice based on race, religion, disability, sexual orientation, or ethnicity, including where appropriate the crimes of murder, non-negligent manslaughter; forcible rape; aggravated assault, simple assault, intimidation; arson; and destruction, damage or vandalism of property.

In 1994 the Violent Crime Control and Law Enforcement Act (1994) was enacted (28 USC § 994), which required the United States Sentencing Commission to increase the penalties for hate crimes committed on the basis of the race, color, religion, national origin, ethnicity, or gender of any person – actual or perceived. Although the Act also expanded the scope of the HCSA of 1990 to include crimes based on disability, these enhanced penalties for targeted groups were only applicable to federal crimes. In the following year Congress permanently reauthorized the Act.

More recently, the federal government expanded federal hate crime law through the Matthew Shepard and James Byrd, Jr. Hate Crimes Prevention Act (HCPA), which was enacted in 2009 in response to a perceived gap in federal enforcement authority. The main purpose of the HCPA is to encourage partnerships between state and federal law enforcement officials to more effectively address hate violence, as well as to expand the authority of federal officials to investigate and prosecute hate crime cases where local authorities are unwilling or unable to act. The HCPA complements the HCSA of 1990 in that it stipulates collecting data on crimes directed against individuals by reason of their gender or gender identity and on hate crimes committed by or against juveniles. While these changes – which were designed to expand hate crime legislation so as to protect "new" categories of targeted groups – reflect a widespread belief that members of certain groups require protection against hate crimes, immigrants are not included as a protected category, despite anecdotal evidence showing that they are in need of protection (Anti-Defamation League, 2012; Lacayo, 2011, 2012; Leadership Conference on Civil Rights Education Fund, 2009; Southern Poverty Law Center, 2009). Although future legislation might provide immigrant populations with protection against hate crimes and might require officials to track such incidents, the current hate crime statutes do not require researchers to measure the prevalence of hate crimes against immigrants in the United States. Therefore this limits our understanding of hate crimes against this targeted group.

State hate crime statutes

As of September 2014, 45 states and the District of Columbia have enacted some form of hate crime legislation in order to address the sentencing of hate- or bias-motivated crime (Anti-Defamation League, 2014b; National Gay and Lesbian Task Force, 2013).[2] Each state has different penalties for these crimes, depending on the victim's particular status. For example, California hate crime statutes protect individuals against violence or threats of violence aimed at them or at their property because of their race, color, religion, ancestry, national origin, political affiliation, sex, sexual orientation, age, disability, or position in a labor dispute or because of a perceived characteristic based on one of these categories. In contrast to some states, California includes protection against crimes motivated by age and political affiliation (see Table 7.1). Also, as a part of the Bane Act in California's civil law (California

Table 7.1 States with penalty enhancement for protected groups.

States	*Race, Religion, Ethnicity*	*Sexual Orientation*	*Gender*	*Gender Identity*	*Disability*	*Other**
Alabama	✓				✓	
Alaska	✓		✓		✓	
Arizona	✓	✓	✓		✓	
Arkansas						
California	✓	✓	✓	✓	✓	✓
Colorado	✓	✓			✓	✓
Connecticut	✓	✓	✓	✓	✓	✓
Delaware	✓	✓			✓	
DC	✓	✓	✓	✓	✓	✓
Florida	✓	✓			✓	✓
Georgia						
Hawaii	✓	✓	✓	✓	✓	✓
Idaho	✓					
Illinois	✓	✓	✓		✓	
Indiana		✓				
Iowa	✓	✓	✓		✓	✓
Kansas	✓	✓				
Kentucky	✓	✓				
Louisiana	✓	✓	✓		✓	✓
Maine	✓	✓	✓		✓	✓
Maryland	✓	✓	✓		✓	✓
Massachusetts	✓	✓		✓	✓	
Michigan	✓		✓			
Minnesota	✓	✓	✓		✓	✓
Mississippi	✓		✓			
Missouri	✓	✓	✓	✓	✓	✓
Montana	✓					
Nebraska	✓	✓	✓		✓	✓
Nevada	✓	✓		✓	✓	
New Hampshire	✓	✓	✓		✓	✓
New Jersey	✓	✓	✓	✓	✓	
New Mexico	✓	✓	✓	✓	✓	✓
New York	✓	✓	✓		✓	✓
North Carolina	✓		✓			
North Dakota	✓		✓			
Ohio	✓					
Oklahoma	✓				✓	
Oregon	✓	✓		✓		✓
Pennsylvania	✓					
Rhode Island	✓	✓	✓		✓	
South Carolina						✓
South Dakota	✓					

(Continued)

Table 7.1 (*Continued*)

States	*Race, Religion, Ethnicity*	*Sexual Orientation*	*Gender*	*Gender Identity*	*Disability*	*Other*[*]
Tennessee	✓	✓	✓		✓	✓
Texas	✓	✓	✓		✓	✓
Utah						
Vermont	✓	✓	✓	✓	✓	✓
Virginia	✓					
Washington	✓	✓	✓		✓	
West Virginia	✓		✓			✓
Wisconsin	✓	✓			✓	
Wyoming	✓		✓			
Total	**46**	**32**	**29**	**11**	**31**	**22**

* This category covers political affiliation (CA, DC, IA, LA, SC, WV) and age (CA, DC, FL, IA, HI, KS, LA, ME, MN, NE, NH, NM, NY, TN, TX, VT).
Source: Anti-Defamation League, 2014b.

Penal Code § 422.75), California "provides for sentencing enhancements of one to three years for certain bias-motivated felonies" against targeted groups protected by hate crime laws.

On the other hand, Indiana is one of five states that do not have any hate crime penalty enhancement laws, and therefore it does not mandate police training on how to respond to hate crimes. Nevertheless, Indiana has bias crime-reporting legislation that defines a bias crime as

> an offense in which the person who commits the offense knowingly or intentionally: (a) selected the person who was injured; or (b) damaged or otherwise affected property by the offense because of the color, creed, disability, national origin, race, religion, or sexual orientation of the injured person or of the owner or occupant of the affected property was associated with any other recognizable group or affiliation. (Indiana Code, 2015: § 10.13.3.1)

While this legislation provides law enforcement agencies with a standard definition with which to collect hate crime data, they are unable to respond effectively to these crimes without any penalty enhancement laws. Many advocates argue that the lack of such laws leads in turn to the underreporting of hate crime by community members.

Overall, state hate crime legislation varies widely in terms of (1) the specific characteristics legally defined as targets of hate crime motivation; (2) whether and how they address criminal penalties and civil remedies; (3) the range of crimes covered; (4) whether the statutes require data collection, and for what crime types; and (5) whether training in hate crime is required for law enforcement personnel. Unfortunately these differences (see Table 7.1) make it difficult to analyze differences among crime types and victim groups across states; and such differences could help inform future responses and identify gaps in legislation. Most recently, a few state hate crime legislatures have amended their laws by including measures designed to protect against gender identity discrimination, but only ten states and the District of Columbia have actually issued protections for this targeted group. Therefore our understanding of hate crimes against this group is limited to the few states that have started to collect data against this group of victims.

Hate crime laws outside of the United States

Aside from the United States, other countries have started adopting similar measures to combat hate crimes: collecting data, educating communities, increasing public awareness, providing victims with protection and support, and training law enforcement personnel (Allen, 2012; Organization for Security and Cooperation in Europe, 2009; Walters, 2005). In 2004, participating states of the Organization for Security and Cooperation in Europe (OSCE) agreed to address hate crimes by "enacting or strengthening, where appropriate, legislation that prohibits discrimination based on or incitement to hate crimes" (Organization for Security and Cooperation in Europe, 2004). In order to gain a better understanding on the status of the participating states and of their efforts to combat hate crimes, OSCE Office for Democratic Institutions and Human Rights (ODIHR) began collecting information on hate crimes reported by participating states since 2006, which they disseminate to the public through an annual report (Organization for Security and Cooperation in Europe, 2004). In its most recent publication, ODIHR reported that, out of the 57 participating states, the number of those that report hate crime data increased from 27 in 2012 to 36 in 2013. Additionally, ODIHR also gathers information from non-governmental organizations (NGOs) and international organizations. Its aim is to obtain reliable data and statistics in sufficient detail on hate crimes.

Despite their efforts to collect accurate and reliable information on hate crime, the annual hate crime reports published by ODIHR demonstrate a number of challenges that confront collecting data of this type (Organization for Security and Cooperation in Europe, 2014). For example, fluctuations in the total number of hate crimes reported from year to year may reflect recording practices rather than the actual prevalence of hate crimes. On the one hand, areas where the data show a rise in the number of the reported hate crimes may simply mean that the respective countries are recording such crimes more diligently, or that victims are reporting these crimes to the authorities more often, perhaps due to an increase in educational awareness. As one of the member states, Canada collects and reports hate crime data through its Incident-Based Uniform Crime Reporting Survey, in addition to supplemental survey information, which covers about 99 percent of the Canadian population (Allen, 2012). While efforts by Canadian law enforcement agencies have continued to work on improving the identification and reporting of hate crime incidents, some of the changes in policies and practices may lead to a rise in the reporting of hate crime incidents over time; therefore trends in hate crime should be interpreted with caution. On the other hand, a decrease in the number of reported hate crimes in some areas might be an indication of underreporting rather than a sign that fewer hate crimes are being committed. Additionally, the absence of a common, simple, and comprehensive definition of the category of hate crime makes it difficult to track cases at all stages in the criminal justice system process, particularly if law enforcement agents and prosecutors are using different definitions to describe a particular case.

In order to improve the collection, analysis, and dissemination of hate crime data for the participating states, ODIHR has issued a number of recommendations and training programs intended to provide members of the community and criminal justice system with the necessary skills and tools to address some of these challenges (Organization for Security and Cooperation in Europe, 2014). These recommendations include adopting measures so as to encourage victims to report hate crimes and improve the identification of hate crimes by law enforcement officials through better training. In the next section we describe some of the challenges faced by hate crime data collection systems in the United States.

FBI UCR Hate Crime Statistics Program

Since 1996 the total number of hate crime incidents reported to the FBI by law enforcement agencies has been declining steadily, except for an anomalous peak in 2001 and a slight increase in 2006–2008 (see Figure 7.1) The total number of reported hate crimes dramatically dropped from 9,730 to 7,462 between 2001 and 2002 and has continued to decline – with a 40 percent overall decrease between 2001, when hate crimes reported were at their highest, and 2012, when the lowest number of reported hate crimes.

While the distribution of hate motivated crimes by bias have followed a consistent pattern over time, current events, new legislation, and changes in law enforcement policies and practices have a significant impact on their reporting (e.g., Disha, Cavendish, and King, 2011; Gan, Williams, and Wiseman, 2011; Grattet and Jenness, 2008; King and Sutton, 2013; Legewie, 2013; McDevitt et al., 2003; McVeigh, Welch, and Bjarnason, 2003; Rubenstein, 2003). For example, according to FBI hate crime statistics, 481 anti-Arab and anti-Muslim hate crimes were reported in 2001 and over half of these crimes, 58 percent, were perpetrated right after the 9/11 terrorist attacks. In a study investigating whether the attacks led to a rise in hate crimes, King and Sutton (2013) found that the attacks were significantly linked to an increase in hate crimes against Arabs and Muslims. In terms of the impact of new legislation, added protections, introduced in 2009, for crimes committed against individuals on the grounds of their gender or gender identity have been connected to an increase in the reporting of hate crimes motivated by sexual orientation. Since 1996 the percentage of the total number of single-bias hate crime incidents motivated by sexual orientation grew from a little over one tenth (11.6 percent) in 1996 to nearly

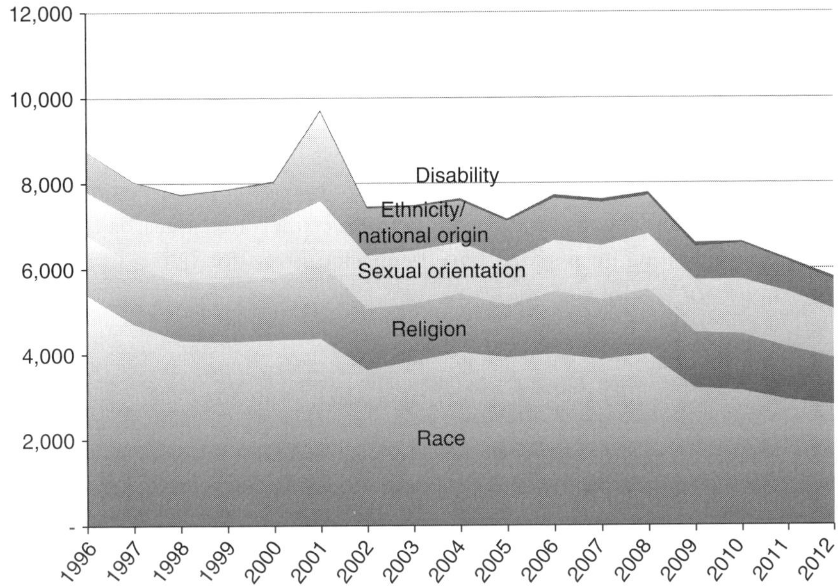

Figure 7.1 Bias-motivated hate crime incidents reported to FBI, 1996–2012. *Source*: Federal Bureau of Investigation, 2013.

one fifth (19.6 percent) in 2012. As indicated earlier, it is possible that these hate crimes were being reported to law enforcement agencies, yet data on them were not collected due to limitations in their classification and identification and in securing protections against them.

Furthermore, the number of law enforcement agencies submitting incident reports has increased from 1,834 agencies in 1996 to 3,223 agencies in 2012. Of the total number of participating agencies, the percentage of those that submit these reports has also risen from 16.2 to 22.2 percent, which indicates an increasing amount of attention being paid by agencies to the reporting of hate crime incidents. Although these changes in hate crime reporting are essential to improving our understanding of such incidents across the United States, a number of factors that are not easily identifiable do influence these numbers.

In 2012 nearly half (48.3 percent) of the hate crime incidents reported were motivated by race, and a smaller percentage were motivated by religion (19.0 percent), sexual orientation (19.6 percent), ethnicity and national origin (11.5 percent), and disability (1.6 percent). Of the 2,797 racially motivated hate crimes, about two thirds (65 percent) were committed against blacks and nearly a quarter (23 percent) were committed against whites. Despite public concerns that hate crimes offer "special protections" to minorities, it is useful to note that, over time, a significant number of reported hate crimes are the result of antiwhite bias (Bell, 2002). On the one hand, some criminologists have questioned the inclusion of "antiwhite" as a category of bias, since white victims are not a traditionally disadvantaged group (Perry, 2001, 2002). For example, Perry (2002) argues that there is reason to question these numbers, given the underreporting of crimes against minorities and the possibility that white victims are more likely to report what they perceive to be a hate crime. Yet others have argued that including in the definition white victims of bias-motivated attacks is important, because it sends the message that these laws protect everyone, that they are not special laws for special victims but are laws that protect anyone who is victimized by reason of his or her perceived membership in a particular group (Lyons, 2006). While these crimes are rare, it is true that, in some communities, white persons have been victimized for living in a nonwhite neighborhood, for example.

FBI UCR hate crime data limitations

Like many large-scale data collection systems, the UCR program has many known limitations, such as underreporting and misclassification. Consequently, official hate crime data are influenced by the number of crimes that are reported to police officials and by the number of crimes that are classified as hate crimes by police officials. If a victim does not report the crime to the police because s/he is afraid of retaliation from the offender, or because s/he does not trust the police, these crimes will never be included in the number of UCR cases. Even if a victim approaches the police to report a hate crime, often that crime is misclassified as a crime of another kind. For example, a racially motivated assault might be reported as an aggravated assault, and not a bias-motivated assault. There are a number of causes for this kind of misclassification. For example, a responding officer might not be trained in the matter of what factors help decide whether a crime is motivated by bias, and hence may not ask the appropriate questions. In some cases an officer may share the bias of the offender and not report the crime for that reason. Additionally, some police agencies fear that, if they report bias crimes, their community will be labeled as racist or homophobic; these agencies will fail to report hate crimes in order not to risk attracting such a label. For example, in their examination of bias crime-reporting practices across local law enforcement agencies, McDevitt and colleagues (2003) found that the departmental culture influenced the underreporting of hate crimes to the UCR program. The authors observed that some departments resisted identifying bias motivation in their reports – for various reasons, including fear of negative consequences for the department if bias were identified; lack of training; and individual biases of law enforcement officers (Cronin et al., 2007).

These failures to identify and properly classify hate crimes can raise serious questions about the accuracy of hate crime data. Additionally, in each year's UCR hate crime report, a large number of communities either do not report at all or they report zero hate crimes. While it is certainly true that many small jurisdictions may not experience any hate crime during one particular year, it is unlikely that major cities would not have a hate crime reported to them over a 12-month period. In 2012, for example, cities like Honolulu, Indianapolis, and

Oklahoma City did not report to the UCR hate crime program and, even more astonishingly, cities such as Atlanta, Raleigh, and Miami reported zero hate crimes.[3] The fact that Miami would report zero hate crimes in 2012 while a community such as Boston was reporting more than 200 cases does raise significant data-quality questions.

The NIBRS

Over the last two decades a growing number of law enforcement agencies have started participating in the FBI's NIBRS. The NIBRS represents an effort by the FBI to provide a more comprehensive and detailed crime-reporting system than the UCR and was developed in order to collect information on each reported crime incident. While the FBI continues to collect, through the UCR data, hate crime information that reflects aggregate counts of incidents, victims, suspected offenders, and categories of bias motivation, the NIBRS permits a wider range of information to be gathered on specific hate crime incidents. For example, the NIBRS includes all offenses involved in the incident, which are recorded and counted; by contrast, in the UCR the hierarchy rule dictates that only the most serious of all the crimes that took place during one event be recorded and counted. Yet, although the NIBRS is recognized for providing a better understanding of what occurred in the incident (and not just the number of events), there are several recognized limitations to the applicability of the data towards understanding the level of hate crime in the United States.

NIBRS limitations

Like many other large-scale data collection systems, the NIBRS suffers from the underreporting and misclassification of hate crimes. As of June 2013, as a result of the jurisdictions covered by law enforcement agencies that currently report incident-level information to the NIBRS, only about one third of the population (30 percent) is covered in these reports. This number has grown substantially in the past 10 years – whereas in 2004 only one fifth of the population was represented in the NIBRS data. The Justice Research and Statistics Association (2014) reports that seven states already have agencies testing the NIBRS (California, Indiana, Maryland, Nevada, New Jersey, New Mexico, and New York) and seven states and territories are in the process of developing capabilities to collect data for the NIBRS (Alabama, District of Columbia, Guam, Illinois, Maryland, Minnesota, and North Carolina). However, six states have not formalized any plans to participate in NIBRS (Alaska, Florida, Georgia, Hawaii, Nevada, and Wyoming), which makes it difficult to measure the level of hate crime at the national level or to conduct cross-state comparisons. Furthermore, only 15 states have all their law enforcement agencies submitting incident-based data, and therefore cover

100 percent of their population. Because not all agencies in each state are submitting NIBRS data, measuring hate crime across the state is only feasible for those states that are collecting NIBRS information from all their law enforcement agencies. Although NIBRS data may be useful in certain cases – particularly in states whose law enforcement agencies are submitting incident-based information[4] – they are limited in the scope of the information on hate crime that they make available at the national and state level.

Another limitation to using NIBRS data in examining hate crimes relates to classification error, which occurs when the facts of the crime incident are recorded, but the crime type is misidentified. For example, with the help of incident-level data reported by West Virginia law enforcement agencies to the NIBRS, Haas and colleagues (2011) examined the impact of the misclassification of hate crimes on the accuracy of reporting such crimes. On the basis of a sample of cases recorded as hate crimes by select law enforcement agencies in West Virginia, they found that misclassification of incidents does occur and that hate crimes are largely undercounted. Having made a systematic review of 1,308 incident reports where they looked for indicators of bias such as use of racial or ethnic slurs by the offender in cases that were not reported as motivated by bias, these researchers found that hate crime incidents were undercounted by about 67 percent in the incident-based reporting system. The majority of undercounted incidents stemmed from the failure of police officers to recognize bias indicators in a particular incident.

Hate crimes reported by the NIBRS

In 2008, the NIBRS reported a total number of 3,017 bias-motivated incidents, which made up less than one percent (0.06 percent) of the total number of reported incidents. With regard to hate crime incidents, the NIBRS requires law enforcement agencies to categorize according to the offender's perceived bias motivation. Sometimes more than one type of bias may arise in a single case (see Table 7.2). Due to the difficulty of determining an offender's motivations, law enforcement agencies record hate crimes only when the investigation reveals facts that are sufficient to conclude that the offender's actions were motivated by bias. Evidence used to support the existence of bias could include oral comments, written statements, gestures made by the offender at the time of the incident, or drawings or graffiti left at the crime scene. Additional factors, such as victim reporting and procedures followed by law enforcement agencies, might also impact the quality and accuracy of hate crime reporting. More recently, the FBI instituted a number of changes to the incident-based reporting system. These changes include (1) the addition of crimes motivated by gender or gender identity bias to the list of categories protected under the new federal hate crime statute and (2) the permission to report up to four additional bias motivations per offense type (Federal Bureau of Investigation, 2012).

Table 7.2 Total number of hate crimes by type of bias as reported by the NIBRS, 1996–2008.

Bias Type	*Total Number*	*Percent of Incidents*
Antiracial	14,402	59.0 percent
Antireligious	3,257	13.4 percent
Anti-ethnicity/national origin	2,767	11.3 percent
Antisexual	3,375	13.8 percent
Anti-physical/mental disability	610	2.5 percent
Total incidents*	**24,399**	

* A small number of incidents have multiple biases reported. Therefore the sum of individual biases is greater than the total number of incidents reported.

National Crime Victimization Survey

In addition to the data collected from law enforcement agencies, the Bureau of Justice Statistics' (BJS) National Crime Victimization Survey (NCVS) also collects information on hate crimes, in accordance with the definition provided in the Hate Crime Statistics Act of 1990 (28 USC § 534). The NCVS measures crimes perceived by victims or by households[5] to be motivated by an offender's bias against them on account of their belonging to, or being associated with, a group largely identified by characteristics based on race, ethnicity, gender or gender identity,[6] religion, disability, or sexual orientation. In order for a crime to be classified as a hate crime in the NCVS, the victim or the household must report at least one of these three types of evidence that the act was motivated by hate: the offenders used hate language; the offenders left behind hate symbols; or the police confirmed that a hate crime had taken place.

Since 2003 the BJS has been collecting information on hate crimes through the NCVS. According to the most recent report, the number of hate crime victimizations increased between 2004 and 2012 from 281,670 to 293,790, but the change was not found to be statistically significant (Wilson, 2014). In contrast to the FBI's UCR program, which collects data on hate crimes reported to the police, the NCVS allows the victim to define whether a hate crime occurred and asks whether it was reported to the police. Therefore it measures the number of hate crimes reported and unreported to the police (see Figure 7.2). For example, in 2012 only about one third (34 percent) of the hate crime victimizations were reported to police, whereas 60 percent were not reported. Another key strength of the NCVS data is that they include detailed information on the victim, such as victim–offender relationship and racial–ethnic background, which permits for an exploration of subgroup rates of victimization (Lauritsen and Heimer, 2010). For example, looking at the impact of the victim's race on the reporting of hate crimes to the police, Zaykowski (2010) found that minority victimizations were less likely to be reported than the victimizations of whites. This suggests that hate crime reporting may vary by racial or ethnic group.

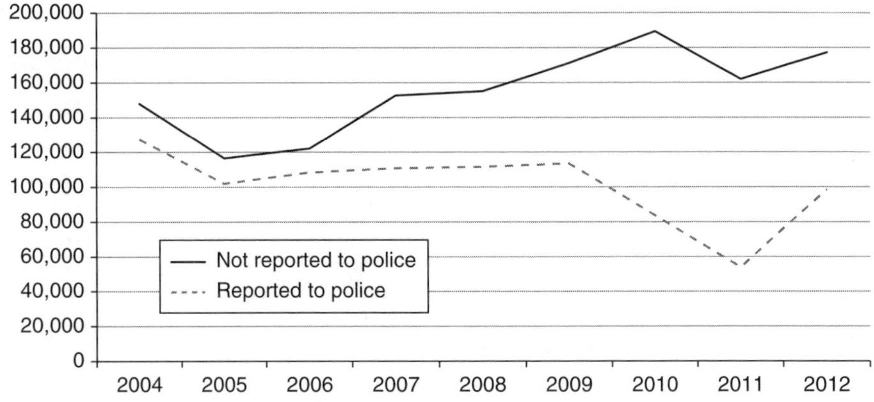

Figure 7.2 Hate crime victimizations reported and not reported to police, 2004–2012. *Source*: Wilson, 2014.

Limitations of the NCVS

Although the NCVS responds to the gap in the data by collecting information involving crimes not reported to law enforcement, there are certain limitations to the NCVS that prevent it from capturing crimes experienced by all victims. First, the NCVS only collects information from household members over the age of 12. As a result, incidents that involve the victimization of youth under the age of 12, such as serious bullying motivated by bias, are excluded from data collection. Second, the NCVS excludes those living in military barracks or in institutions like nursing homes and prisons, as well as the crew of vessels. The close proximity in which these individuals are often required to reside places them at a higher risk for becoming victims of a crime such as a hate crime – and repeated victims in situations where the individual is unable to leave by free will, as in the case of inmates. Finally, the NCVS did not originally track repeated incidents of victimization, also known as "series victimizations," which occurred to a victim within a short time frame and were similar in quality. This is fairly common in hate crimes such as bias-motivated harassment. However, one of the recent changes made to the NCVS (which are described below) has affected the way in which these incidents are counted. Additionally, in many hate crimes the victim may not realize why s/he is being targeted. If a rock is thrown through the window of a black family's home, members often do not know why the rock was thrown and thus might report the crime as vandalism, not as a hate crime.

While examining the NCVS as a tool for researchers, Addington (2008) highlights certain populations that should be addressed in the survey for the purpose of developing better measures of their victimization such as children under 12, immigrants, and the elderly. For example, Addington argues that, although the questions on the hate crime questionnaire of the survey might capture some understanding of crimes against immigrants, there is no direct measure on the number of hate crimes against immigrants in the survey, because an individual's immigrant status is not queried. On the other hand, victims of a hate crime who are under the age of 12 are by design excluded from the survey, due to considerations as to whether or not it is appropriate and feasible to question children as young as that on the subject of crime.

Recent changes to NCVS

Starting in 2010, two important changes were made to the way the BJS measures hate crime using NCVS data. First, as indicated above, the BJS modified its approach to counting repeated victimizations, or series victimizations. Series victimizations are "those that are similar in type but occur with such frequency that a victim is unable to recall each individual event or to describe each event in detail" (Sandholtz, Langton, and Planty, 2013). For example, victims who reported several victimization experiences with similar qualities were previously asked by NCVS interviewers to provide detailed information on only the most recent incident in the series. Following the modification, NCVS interviewers began to identify and classify each incident as a separate one and counted up to a maximum of 10 incidents experienced by the victim. While this new approach was applied in the 2010 NCVS data collection, the rate of violent hate crime victimization did not change in 2011 from the one 2004. Second, the passage of the Matthew Shepherd and James Byrd, Jr. Act of 2009 added crimes motivated by gender or gender identity bias to the list of categories protected under the federal hate crime statute (Langton and Planty, 2011). This inclusion was also made in the 2010 NCVS data collection to reflect the newly protected categories. However, the inclusion of these categories did not significantly change the number or rate of hate crime victimizations in 2010 or in 2011.

Hate crimes reported by the NCVS

According to the most recent estimates in NCVS, the BJS reported that 293,800 nonfatal violent and property hate crime victimizations occurred in 2012 (Wilson, 2014). From 2004 to 2012 no statistically significant change was observed in the total number of hate crimes or violent hate crimes and, except for a decline from 2004 to 2005, property hate crime victimization rate remained stable from 2005 to 2012. Although hate crime rates remained fairly stable since 2003, a few characteristics of hate crimes and hate crime victims have shifted. First, victims perceived that the offender was motivated by bias against the victim's ethnicity in 51 percent of hate crimes, which is a statistically significant increase from 30 percent and 22 percent in 2011 and 2004 respectively (see Table 7.3).

Additionally, whereas the violent hate crime victimization rates were similar among non-Hispanic white and non-Hispanic blacks – respectively 0.8 per 1,000 residents and 1.1 per 1,000 residents – Hispanics experienced a higher rate of

Table 7.3 Victims' perceptions of offender bias in hate crimes, 2004–2012.

Offender Bias	*2004*	*2011*	*2012*
Race	58 percent	58 percent	46 percent
Ethnicity	22	30	51
Association	23	40	34
Religion	10	25	28
Gender	12	25	26
Sexual orientation	22	19	13
Disability	11	22	11
Perceived characteristics	19	15	7

Source: Bureau of Justice Statistics, 2014.

2.0 per 1,000 residents in 2012. This rate had more than tripled from 2011, when 0.6 victimizations per 1,000 residents were reported among Hispanics. Given the recent speculation about the rise in hate crimes against immigrant groups, these findings are worth investigating through other measures and data collection methods in order to establish whether hate crimes against Hispanics or other immigrant groups are indeed rising and what might be causing this trend. Finally, an estimated 40 percent of total and violent hate crime victimizations were reported to police in 2012, which represents a slight increase from the 26 percent hate crime victimizations reported in 2011. This finding calls for further investigation into whether it reflects improvements in the relationship with law enforcement agencies, in the training of their members, and in the identification and reporting of hate crimes.

Before comparing the NCVS hate crime victimizations to those reported by the FBI's UCR, some significant differences should be noted between these two principal sources of annual information on hate crime in the United States. First, the NCVS collects information on incidents and victimizations whether or not these were reported to law enforcement agencies. In order to gain a better understanding of the number of incidents and victimizations that were reported to law enforcement agencies, the survey asks respondents whether the police were notified about the crime. Second, the NCVS hate-motivated incidents are defined by the victim and by the presence of crime scene evidence; therefore they include incidents that may not be recorded in police investigations as hate-motivated incidents. Third, the UCR captures hate crimes against all individuals, regardless of age, as well as hate crimes against organizations, institutions, schools, churches, and businesses. As mentioned earlier, children under the age of 12 and people living in institutions are excluded from the NCVS. Finally, the UCR includes hate crime homicides, which are excluded from the NCVS.

Given the major distinctions between the UCR and NCVS programs in relation to hate crime data collection, a number of differences emerge when we compare the overall trends in hate crime victimization across the two sources. First, hate crime victimizations reported to the police from 2008 to 2012 declined steadily according to the

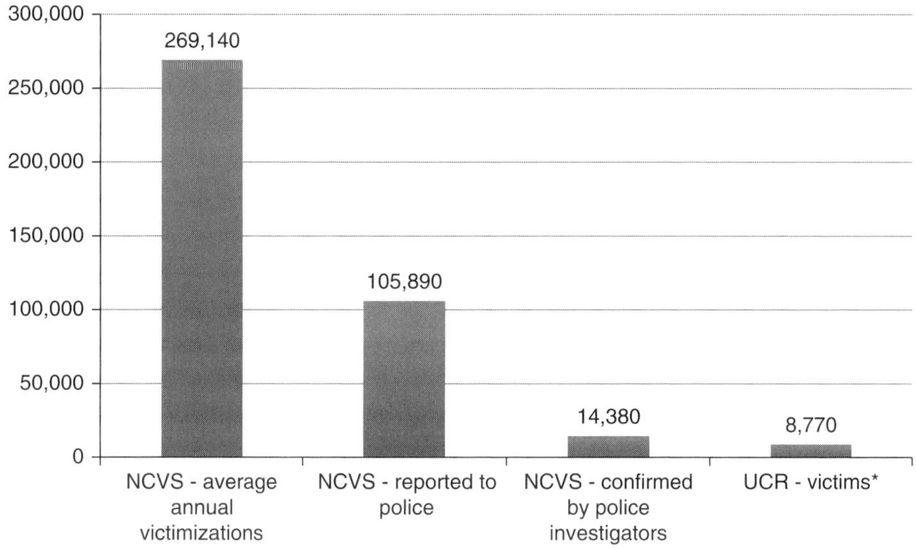

Figure 7.3 NCVS and UCR annual average hate crime victimizations, 2004–2012. *Source*: Wilson, 2014; based on data collected from the UCR Hate Crime Statistics Program of 2003–2012 and from the NCVS of 2003–2012.

UCR, whereas the NCVS found no statistically significant change during this period. Second, the UCR reported lower hate crime victimizations in 2012 than in 2004. The NCVS found no statistically significant difference in the number of hate crime victimizations reported to police in 2004 (127,390) and 2012 (98,460). Finally, the NCVS reported an annual average of 269,140 hate crime victimizations from 2004 to 2012, of which 105,890 were reported to police. However, of the 14,380 hate crime victimizations that were confirmed by police investigators from 2004 to 2012, FBI's UCR data reported an annual average number of 8,770 during the same period (Figure 7.3). While this number is not statistically different from the number of NCVS hate crime victimizations confirmed by police investigators, it is important to consider the need to continue improving both sources, given the gaps in data collection.

Recommendations

Improvements to hate crime data quality

There have been a number of recommendations on how to improve the quality and reliability of hate crime data in the United States. One area of improvement would be to increase the number of hate crimes reported to the police. Data from the NCVS indicate that the number of reported hate crimes has increased over the past decade but still remains at only 40 percent of the crimes that are reported. Increased reporting not only would improve the accuracy of hate crime statistics but, more importantly, would give more victims access to protection and services. If law enforcement wishes to improve reporting, it will have to improve its outreach, so as to target communities like Arab and Muslim or LBGTQ ones. When police employ methods to improve relations with those communities, and when these efforts include education about hate crimes and a commitment to respond to any hate crimes that occur, law enforcement agencies see an increase in the reported hate crimes. If law enforcement officers wait for victims to come to them, in many cases victims will not come forward.

Two-tier response

Initially, when the FBI organized the national training of law enforcement agencies after the passage of the 1990 Hate Crime Statistics Act, it recommended a two-tier strategy for law enforcement agencies when they receive and investigate hate crime reports. This approach involves asking all responding officers to refer any case that might involve bias to a trained investigator or unit. The approach recognizes that hate crimes are relatively rare events and that individual police officers will not see cases regularly. Additionally, many patrol officers do not have the training or the time to determine whether a crime was motivated by bias. The best that most patrol officers can do is to document the victim's statements, including any racial–ethnic slurs or other language that might have been used, and to refer the case to a hate crime unit or, in smaller agencies, to a trained hate crime investigator. Once a case has been referred, a trained investigator can look into whether the crime was in fact motivated by bias. Next, once the investigator has made a determination, the crime can be more accurately reported to the FBI. This approach has been recommended by the FBI, but many law enforcement agencies still do not adopt it.

Training

For either the outreach or the investigative recommendations presented above to be effective, law enforcement officers must be trained in how to determine whether a crime is motivated by hate and what to do if they find indicators of bias. This training should be done in the recruit academy, but also periodically, as a component of in-service training. It should include a component about the impact of hate crimes on the victim and on the broader community, as well as strategies for effective outreach to targeted communities.

Advancements in hate crime research

While the number of published studies of hate crime has declined for various reasons in recent years, some scholars have suggested that this is due to limitations in the quality of the data. Green and Spry (2014) suggest that researchers must adopt experimental models and new measurement techniques in order to improve our understanding of the underlying causes of hate crime. While some studies have examined hate crime and macroeconomic conditions or demographic transformation over a period of time (Green, Strolovitch, and Wong, 1998; Grattet, 2009), most studies have been limited by cross-sectional correlations (Green, McFalls, and Smith, 2001; Messner, McHugh, and Felson, 2004; Nolan and Akiyama, 1999). The adoption of new methods, such as interrupted time series analysis, has been relatively rare in hate crime research until recently. Using interrupted time series models, studies by King and Sutton (2013) and by Hanes and Machin (2014) tested whether particular types of hate crimes increased after events that might lead to a rise of those types of crimes. This type of approach could further inform hate crime research by examining a shift in hate crime over time following events that might spark an attack against particular groups.

Hate crimes are rare and go frequently unreported; but, because of their impact on victims and local communities, researchers and policymakers need to develop a deeper understanding of the causes, dynamics, and consequences of hate crimes. This will call for data of better quality and for a more rigorous analysis, so that researchers and policymakers may improve their efforts to prevent hate crimes from occurring and to help victims with recovery. We hope that this chapter has contributed to these efforts.

Notes

1 The disparity was discovered by comparing the NYPD's individual incident-level data to the data collected by the New York State Division of Criminal Justice Services, which submits the UCR reports to the FBI.
2 The five states that do not have hate crime penalty enhancement laws that include crimes based on any characteristics are Arkansas, Georgia, Indiana, South Carolina, and Wyoming (Anti-Defamation League, 2014b).
3 For more information, see the Anti-Defamation League's website at http://www.adl.org/combating-hate/hate-crimes-law.
4 As of June 2012, 15 states are submitting incident-based data alone. Examining NIBRS data for state-level trend analyses may be useful in these particular states.
5 Each household affected by a hate crime is counted as a single case of victimization.
6 While the passage of the Matthew Shepherd and James Byrd, Jr. Act of 2009 added crimes motivated by bias based on gender or gender identity, the BJS has been collecting information on these crimes since 2003.

References

Addington, L. 2008. *Current issues in victimization research and the NCVS's ability to study them*. Washington, DC: Bureau of Justice Statistics.

Allen, M. 2012. Police-reported hate crime in Canada. Canadian Centre for Justice Statistics. Accessed April 14, 2014. http://www.statcan.gc.ca/pub/85–002-x/2014001/article/14028-eng.htm.

Anti-Defamation League. 2012. Statement by Anti-Defamation League Senate Judiciary Subcommittee on Constitution, Civil Rights and Human Rights on Hate Crimes and the Threat of Domestic Extremism. Accessed October 14, 2014. http://archive.adl.org/combating_hate/Senate-Judiciary-Subcommittee-HCPA-statement.pdf.

Anti-Defamation League. (2014a). ADL audit: Anti-semitic incidents declined 19 percent across the United States in 2013. Accessed October 14, 2014. http://www.adl.org/press-center/press-releases/anti-semitism-usa/adl-audit-us-anti-semitic-incidents-declined-14-percent.html#.Ux2_JxjD99A.

Anti-Defamation League. (2014b). State hate crime statutory provisions (updated September 2014). Washington, DC. Accessed October 14, 2014. http://www.adl.org/combating-hate/hate-crimes-law.

Bell, J. 2002. *Policing hatred: Law enforcement, civil rights, and hate crime*. New York: NYU Press.

Berk, R. A., Boyd, E. A., and Hammer, K. M. 1992. Thinking more clearly about hate motivated crimes. In *Hate crimes: Confronting violence against lesbians and gay men*, edited by G. Herek and K. Berrill, 137–143. Thousand Oaks, CA: Sage.

Cronin, S. W., McDevitt, J., Farrell, A., and Nolan, J. J. 2007. Bias-crime reporting: Organizational Responses to ambiguity, uncertainty, and infrequency in eight police departments. *American Behavioral Scientist*, 51: 213–231.

Disha, I., Cavendish, J. C., and King, R. D. 2011. Historical events and spaces of hate: Hate crimes against Arabs and Muslims in post-9/11 America. *Social Problems*, 58 (1): 21–46.

Federal Bureau of Investigation. 2012. Recent changes to the NIBRS. Accessed July 8, 2014. http://www.fbi.gov/about-us/cjis/ucr/nibrs/2012/resources/recent-changes-to-the-nibrs.

Federal Bureau of Investigation. 2013. Table 1: Incidents, offenses, victims, and known offenders by bias motivation: Selected years 1996 through 2012. Accessed September 8, 2014. https://www.fbi.gov/about-us/cjis/ucr/hate-crime.

Federal Bureau of Investigation. 2014. Uniform Crime Reports: Hate crime reports. Accessed September 8, 2014. http://www.fbi.gov/about-us/cjis/ucr/hate-crime.

Finn, P., and Hylton, M. O. 1994. *Using civil remedies for criminal behavior: Rationale, case studies, and constitutional issues*. Washington, DC: National Institute of Justice.

Gan, L., Williams, R. C., and Wiseman, T. 2011. A simple model of optimal hate crime legislation. *Economic Inquiry*, 49 (3): 674–684.

Garofalo, J., and Martin, S. E. 1991. The law enforcement response to bias-motivated crimes. In *Bias crime: The law enforcement response*, edited by N. Taylor, 17–34. Chicago, IL: Office of International Criminal Justice.

Grattet, R. 2009. The urban ecology of bias crime: A study of disorganized and defended neighborhoods. *Social Problems*, 56 (1): 132–150.

Grattet, R., and Jenness, V. 2008. Transforming symbolic law into organizational action: Hate crime policy and law enforcement practice. *Social Forces*, 87 (1): 1–28.

Green, D. P., McFalls, L. H., and Smith, J. K. 2001. Hate crime: An emergent research agenda. *Annual Review of Sociology*, 27: 479–504.

Green, D. P., and Spry, A. D. 2014. Hate crime research: Design and measurement strategies for improving causal inference. *Journal of Contemporary Criminal Justice*, 30 (3): 228–246.

Green, D. P., Strolovitch, D. Z., and Wong, J. S. 1998. Defended neighborhoods, integration, and racially motivated crime. *American Journal of Sociology*, 104 (2): 372–403.

Haas, S. M., Nolan, J. J., Turley, E., and Stump, J. 2011. *Assessing the validity of hate crime reporting: An analysis of NIBRS data*. Charleston, WV: Criminal Justice Statistical Analysis Center.

Hanes, E., and Machin, S. 2014. Hate crime in the wake of terror attacks: Evidence from 7/7 and 9/11. *Journal of Contemporary Criminal Justice*, 30 (3): 247–267.

Indiana Code. 2015. Indiana General Assembly. Accessed January 16, 2015. http://iga.in.gov/static-documents/5/a/1/6/5a16ee24/TITLE10_AR13_ar13.pdf.

Justice Research and Statistics Association. 2014. Status of NIBRS in the states. Accessed September 8, 2014. http://jrsa.org/ibrrc/background-status/nibrs_states.shtml.

Kelly, R. J. 1991. Bias-motivated crime. In *Bias crime: The law enforcement response*, edited by N. Taylor, 135–142. Chicago, IL: Office of International Criminal Justice.

King, R. D., and Sutton, G. M. 2013. High times for hate crimes: Explaining the temporal clustering of hate-motivated offending. *Criminology*, 51 (4): 871–894.

Lacayo, E. 2011. One year later: A look at SB 1070 and copycat legislation. Washington, DC: National Council of La Raza. Accessed September 15, 2014. http://www.nclr.org/images/uploads/publications/AlookatSB1070v3.pdf.

Lacayo, E. 2012. The wrong approach: State anti-immigration legislation in 2011. Washington, DC: National Council of La Raza. Accessed September 15, 2014. http://issuu.com/nclr/docs/the_wrong_approach_anti-immigrationleg?e=1871004/3193857.

Langton, L., and Planty, M. 2011. Hate crimes, 2003–2009. Washington DC: Bureau of Justice Statistics, US Department of Justice. Accessed September 12, 2014. http://www.bjs.gov/content/pub/ascii/hc0309.txt.

Lauritsen, J. L., and Heimer, K. 2010. Violent victimization among males and economic conditions: The vulnerability of race and ethnic minorities. *Criminology & Public Policy*, 9 (4): 665–692.

Leadership Conference on Civil Rights Education Fund. 2009. Confronting the new faces of hate: Hate crimes in America. Accessed June 13, 2014. http://www.protectcivilrights.org/pdf/reports/hatecrimes/lccref_hate_crimes_report.pdf.

Legewie, J. 2013. Terrorist events and attitudes toward immigrants: A natural experiment. *American Journal of Sociology*, 118 (5): 1199–1245.

Los Angeles County Human Relations Commission. 2014. 2013 Hate Crime Report. Accessed September 15, 2014. http://www.lahumanrelations.org/hatecrime/reports/2013_hateCrimeReport.pdf.

Lyons, C. J. 2006. Stigma or sympathy? Attributions of fault to hate crime victims and offenders. *Social Psychology Quarterly*, 69 (1): 39–59.

McDevitt, J. Cronin, S. Balboni, J., Farrell, A., Nolan, J., and Weiss, J. 2003. *Bridging the information disconnect in bias crime reporting*. Washington, DC: Bureau of Justice Statistics, US Department of Justice.

McVeigh, R., Welch, M. R., and Bjarnason, T. 2003. Hate crime reporting as a successful social movement outcome. *American Sociological Review*, 68: 843–867.

Messner, S. F., McHugh, S., and Felson, R. 2004. Distinctive characteristics of assaults motivated by bias. *Criminology*, 42: 585–618.

National Gay and Lesbian Task Force. 2013. Nondiscrimination laws map. Washington, DC: National LGBTQ Task Force. Accessed July 8, 2014. http://www.thetaskforce.org/nondiscrimination-laws-map.

New York City Commission on Human Rights. 1984. Proposal for response to instances of racial and religious animosity. Accessed April 14, 2014. http://www.nyc.gov/html/cchr/

downloads/pdf/publications/selected-reports/proposal_for_response_to_instances_of_racial_and_relligious_animosity.pdf.

New York City Commission on Human Rights. 1993. Documenting the hate: A report on bias incidents in New York City from January 1992 to June 1993. Accessed April 14, 2014. www.nyc.gov/html/cchr/downloads/pdf/publications/selected-reports/documenting_the_hate-a_report_on_bias_incidents_in_new_york_city_from_january_1992_to_june_1993.pdf.

New York State Office of the State Comptroller. 2014. Reporting and utilization of bias incident datas. Accessed October 30, 2014. http://osc.state.ny.us/audits/allaudits/093014/14n2.pdf.

Nolan, J. J., and Akiyama, Y. 1999. An analysis of factors that affect law enforcement participation in hate crime reporting. *Journal of Contemporary Criminal Justice*, 15: 111–127.

Organization for Security and Cooperation in Europe. 2004. Decision no. 621, tolerance and the fight against racism, xenophobia and discrimination. Accessed April 14, 2014. http://www.osce.org/pc/35610.

Organization for Security and Cooperation in Europe. 2009. Hate crime laws: A practical guide. Accessed September 10, 2014. http://www.osce.org/odihr/36426.

Organization for Security and Cooperation in Europe. 2014. Hate crime data-collection and monitoring mechanisms: A practical guide. Accessed September 10, 2014. http://www.osce.org/odihr/datacollectionguide.

Perry, B. 2001. *In the name of hate: Understanding hate crime*. New York, NY: Routledge.

Perry, B. 2002. Defending the color line: Racially and ethnically motivated hate crime. *American Behavioral Scientist*, 46: 72–92.

Petrosino, C. 1999. Connecting the past to the future. *Journal of Contemporary Criminal Justice*, 15 (1): 22–47.

Rubenstein, W. B. 2003. The real story of US hate crime statistics: An empirical analysis. *Tulane Law Review*, 78: 1213–1246.

Sandholtz, N., Langton, L., and Planty, M. 2013. Hate crime victimization 2003–2011. Washington, DC: Bureau of Justice Statistics. Accessed May 10, 2014. http://www.bjs.gov/content/pub/pdf/hcv0311.pdf.

Shively, M. 2005. *Study of literature and legislation on hate crime in America*. Washington, DC: National Institute of Justice.

Southern Poverty Law Center. 2009. Climate of fear: Latino immigrants in Suffolk County, NY. Accessed April 14, 2014. http://www.splcenter.org/sites/default/files/downloads/publication/splc_suffolk_report.pdf.

Walters, M. 2005. Hate crimes in Australia: Introducing punishment enhances. *Criminal Law Journal*, 29: 201–216.

Wexler, C., and Marx, G. T. 1986. When law and order works: Boston's innovative approach to the problem of racial violence. *Crime and Delinquency*, 32 (2): 205–223.

Wilson, M. M. 2014. Hate crime victimization, 2004–2012: Statistical tables. Washington, DC: Bureau of Justice Statistics. Accessed September 14, 2014. http://www.bjs.gov/index.cfm?ty=pbdetail&iid=4883.

Zaykowski, H. 2010. Racial disparities in hate crime reporting. *Violence and Victims*, 25 (3): 378–394.

Further Reading

Balboni, J. M., and McDevitt, J. 2001. Hate crime reporting: Understanding police officer perceptions, department protocol and the role of the victim: Is there such a thing as a "love crime?" *Justice Research and Policy*, 3: 1–28.

Bashan, Y. 2014. NYPD improperly recorded some hate-crime data, audit found. Accessed September 8, 2014. http://online.wsj.com/articles/nypd-improperly-recorded-some-hate-crime-data-audit-found-1411701718.

Berk, R. A., Boyd, E. A., and Hammer, K. M. 2003. Thinking more clearly about hate motivated crimes. In *Hate and bias crime*, edited by B. Perry, 49–60. New York: Routledge.

Jenness, V., and Grattet, R. 2001. Making hate a crime: From social movement to law enforcement. New York: Russell Sage Foundation.

McDevitt, J., Balboni, J., and Bennett, S. 2000. *Improving the quality and accuracy of bias crime statistics nationally*. Washington, DC: Bureau of Justice Statistics, US Department of Justice.

National Archive of Criminal Justice Data. 2010. National Incident-Based Reporting System, 1996–2008. ICPSR02465-v3. Ann Arbor, MI: Inter-University Consortium for Political and Social Research [distributor], 2009–07–16. Accessed December 15 2015. http://doi.org/10.3886/ICPSR02465.v3.

Nolan, J. J., McDevitt, J., Cronin, S., and Farrell, A. 2004. Learning to see hate crimes: A framework for understanding and clarifying ambiguities in bias crime classification. *The Justice Professional*, 17 (1): 91–105.

Shively, M., McDevitt, J., Farrell, A., and Iwama, J. 2013. *Understanding trends in hate crimes against immigrants and Hispanic Americans*. Washington, DC: National Institute of Justice.

Smith, A. M., and Foley, C. L. 2010. *State statutes governing hate crimes*. Washington, DC: Congressional Research Service. Accessed April 14, 2014. https://www.fas.org/sgp/crs/misc/RL33099.pdf.

Southern Poverty Law Center. 2001. The hate crimes statistics act: Ten years later, the numbers don't add up. Intelligence Report, Issue No. 104. Accessed April 14, 2014. http://www.splcenter.org/get-informed/intelligence-report/browse-all-issues/2001/winter.

Part II

Offenders, Offending, and Victimization

8

Gangs and Gang Crime

Chris Melde

Street gangs and their members have been the focus of attention as a "special" population in the United States for over a century (Howell and Moore, 2010). While public attention to gangs ebbed and flowed over this time for myriad reasons (for reviews of the history of gangs, see Howell and Moore, 2010; Klein and Maxson, 2006; Decker and Van Winkle, 1996), the preoccupation with street gangs and their members, as displayed by police, policymakers, the media, and researchers, is not without merit. Members of street gangs are routinely associated with serious crime and violence in many communities and contribute disproportionately to overall rates of offending. For example, while gang members accounted for 23 percent of the sample in Fagan's (1990) three-city study, these individuals accounted for roughly two thirds of all felony assaults, robberies, and thefts reported across the entire sample. Similarly, while only 30 percent of the sample in the Rochester Youth Development Study (Thornberry, 1998) reported being members of a gang by the end of high school, these individuals accounted for 86 percent of all violent acts reported in the study and for 70 percent of all drug sales. Large-scale studies of youth in Seattle (Hill et al., 1999) and Denver (Huizinga, 1997) suggested similarly disproportionate rates of offending on the part of gang-involved youth. It is no wonder that over the last three decades significant resources have been devoted to understanding the causes, correlates, and consequences of gangs and gang membership, to developing gang prevention and intervention programs, and to controlling gang crime through antigang legislation and law enforcement initiatives. In the midst of all this certainty over the social problems that gangs cause for communities, and even for their own members, there remains a curious feature: there is yet no resolution on how best to define and measure gangs, gang membership, and gang crime.

The Handbook of Measurement Issues in Criminology and Criminal Justice, First Edition.
Edited by Beth M. Huebner and Timothy S. Bynum.

The inability to systematically define, identify, and reliably measure gangs, gang members, and gang crime is not simply an academic problem. This definitional ambiguity has very real consequences for organizations and individuals connected in some way to street gangs. For instance, a recent report from the United States Government Accountability Office (GAO, 2009) suggested that in 2008 alone the United States Department of Justice spent roughly $25 million on specialized anti-gang interventions located in a small fraction of communities across the country with a documented gang problem. This figure does not include the local- and state-level resources allocated to dealing with gangs and their members, which surely exceed this federal investment. The gist of the GAO (2009) report, unfortunately, was that we know little about our return on investments in these resources – too little to tell whether or not the money directed at gangs could be best spent elsewhere. The reason is that many of the communities in which these tax dollars are spent have little to no capacity to measure their own gang issues, for example the number of active gang members they have or the rate of gang crime amid them, let alone how their interventions may have altered local gang dynamics. The adage "you cannot manage what you cannot measure" is certainly applicable to the dilemma of defining gangs, given that all we "know" about gangs, gang members, and gang crime is shrouded in uncertainty due to our inability to know for sure whether the groups themselves (gang/nongang), their people (gang member/nongang member), and the actions we attribute to them (gang crime/nongang crime) are indeed what we have labeled them. As a consequence, we have yet to develop best practices for managing our efforts to prevent or control the serious consequences of the existence of gangs in our society.

The current chapter will review the most frequent sources of information we use to understand gangs, gang members, and gang crime, paying particular attention to the measurement issues that impact the reliability and validity of our understanding. As will be discussed, it is difficult to garner a complete understanding of the gang phenomenon through any single data source. In fact, if evidence on gangs from any single source were to be reviewed in isolation, this would likely lead to a distorted view of the entire phenomenon. Indeed, what we know about gangs is impacted by our methods of identifying the phenomenon and by our most frequently utilized data sources on the topic, which consist of police data, self-report surveys, ethnographic and interview-based studies, and – to a far lesser extent – victimization surveys. In the sections that follow we will discuss each of these data sources and their respective strengths and limitations. First, however, is a discussion of prior attempts to define gangs and gang members and of how such efforts have failed to adequately capture the phenomenon.

Defining Gangs, Gang Membership, and Gang Crime

Over a hundred years of journalistic, academic, and practitioner documentation suggest that we are quite confident that "gangs" exist and produce an inordinate amount of harm to communities through their frequent involvement in crime – especially violence – and disorder; moreover, this involvement also causes widespread anxiety and concern in areas recognized for their "gang problem." Indeed this is the intended effect of gangs, since public advertising – through graffiti, symbols, shared colors – of their dangerous and deviant propensities is precisely what makes them capable of fulfilling their goals: to intimidate other gangs and community members, protect their own members, and earn money through drug sales and other black market activities. It is gangs' frequent involvement in acts of crime and violence that makes them noteworthy; without these behaviors, they would not be the target of public concern. There is widespread disagreement on the necessary and sufficient[1] conditions that distinguish a gang from other peer groups, a gang member from a nongang-involved youth, or a gang crime from a nongang-related incident, each of which needs a unique definition that should articulate the group, personal, and behavioral boundaries between "gang" and "nongang." Common definitions of gangs, gang members, and gang crimes have been known to produce both type I errors – identifying a phenomenon as gang-related when it is not – and type II errors – identifying a phenomenon as nongang-related when it indeed is related to gangs – and such errors have led to large variations in the resulting estimates of the prevalence of these groups, members, and crimes.

So why has it been so difficult to define the necessary and sufficient conditions for discriminating gang from nongang groups, for example? First, research on the nature of street gangs suggests that the majority of individuals involved in them are between the ages of 12 and 24, which roughly coincide with the developmental period of adolescence. This is problematic because involvement in crime and delinquency peaks during this period of the life course more broadly, and deviance at this developmental stage is predominantly a group-based phenomenon. That is, youth regularly experiment with their own moral boundaries around deviant behaviors as they navigate adolescence; and they do so in the company of peers who make engaging in crime and deviance easier and provide the necessary feedback to encourage or discourage the behavior in future situations. The great majority of adolescents who engage in these criminal and delinquent behaviors do not, however, consider themselves gang members, nor do they consider their peer group a gang; neither do their educators, the police, or other concerned parties, for that matter. There is widespread agreement, therefore, that there is a distinction between "ordinary" delinquent peer groups and gangs, such that there is more to being a gang than committing crimes and delinquency in a group. Systematically documenting the nature of this difference for definitional purposes has been difficult, and most would agree that it has yet to be done successfully.

Klein (1971) provided one of the most influential definitions of street gangs, which was commonly used in the research literature for many years. Klein defined a gang as

> any denotable adolescent group of youngsters who (a) are generally perceived as a distinct aggregation by others in their neighborhood, (b) recognize themselves as a denotable group (almost invariably with a group name) and (c) have been involved

> in a sufficient number of delinquent incidents to call forth a consistent negative response from neighborhood residents and/or enforcement agencies. Klein (1971, p. 13)

This definition, like those suggested before and after, is limited in its ability to help discern gang from nongang groups. With respect to being exhaustive, it includes the characteristics of most, if not all, street gangs that are often thought of in discussions of the phenomenon by policymakers, researchers, and law enforcement. The problem is that this definition is not exclusive. As an example, many college campuses have numerous fraternities and sororities, each of which may have a notable reputation for some feature of its social life. As one might expect, you would not have to search far and wide to discover that certain Greek organizations have garnered a reputation for violence, loud parties with underage drinking, illegal drug use, and drug dealing – among other deviant activities. Fraternities or sororities with such a reputation fit all of Klein's (1971) criteria, but they do not likely fit our generalized conception of a street gang.

An earlier definition of a street gang, suggested by Frederick Thrasher (1927), is perhaps one of the best. Specifically, Thrasher (1927, p. 46) defined gangs as

> an interstitial group originally formed spontaneously and then integrated through conflict. It is characterized by the following types of behavior: meeting face to face, milling, movement through space as a unit, conflict, and planning. The result of this collective behavior is the development of tradition, unreflective internal structure, esprit de corps, solidarity, morale, group awareness, and attachment to a local territory.

This definition focuses primarily on the group processes that differentiate gang from nongang groups, and this strikes at the essence of the difference between the two types. Such a definition may be needed in order to avoid the overidentification or underidentification of gang groups in the population. This type of definition is, however, especially problematic for many stakeholders concerned with the identification of gangs, gang members, and gang crime. Specifically, how would one go about operationalizing this definition in practice? Take, for instance, the case of police officials interested in systematically identifying all of the gangs in their local jurisdiction, including identifying the membership roster of each respective gang. How useful is a definition based upon group processes inherent in a gang, even if it were to capture the primary factors differentiating gangs from nongang groups? The likely answer to this question is: not at all. The amount of intelligence needed to document this group history and evolution would be inordinate and impractical. Such intelligence would be difficult to substantiate in a court of law and would require constant surveillance, as groups of youth in the local jurisdiction transition into and out of adolescence. From an academic standpoint, Thrasher's (1927) definition is praiseworthy in that it attempts to capture how gangs differ from other peer groups; but such a definition is simply too cumbersome for most parties concerned with documenting and understanding gangs in a systematic and efficient manner.

Despite the difficulty of defining gangs, however, particular stakeholders continue to identify and document gang groups in a manner that serves their own purposes – which we now discuss.

The Use of Official Police Data

Given the robust association between gangs, gang members, and heightened levels of involvement in crime and violence, police departments across the country have a vested interest in finding out what the number of gangs in their communities is, who the members of these gangs are, and how these groups contribute to the crime problem. By necessity, however, identifying and documenting gangs, gang members, and gang crime cannot be accomplished using a single definition; each poses a unique challenge for law enforcement. In order for police departments to monitor the extent and nature of the gang issue in their local area and to control the effectiveness of gang prevention and intervention programs, they often develop gang databases to monitor these three dimensions of gang activity (i.e., gangs, gang members, gang crime). For all the strengths associated with having stable organizations such as the police collecting such data, the problems inherent in police data collection and management in general also plague the collection and monitoring of gang data.

Official police data offer some important advantages over other data sources with respect to the identification and tracking of gangs, gang members, and gang crime. For example, official data may be used to study gang violence at the city, county, state, or even national level on an ongoing basis, in a process similar to what is accomplished through the Uniform Crime Reports (UCR). The best example of this sort of ongoing monitoring of gangs across the United States is the National Gang Center's (n.d.-a) annual National Youth Gang Survey. This annual survey allows concerned parties to track trends in gang-related issues at the national and subnational levels, and thus can be used to monitor the relative threat posed by these groups across time and place. Given the stable and bureaucratic nature of police departments, standardized departmental, state, and federal guidelines for identifying gangs, gang members, and gang crime, including a system of checks and balances designed to strengthen the reliability and validity of the definitional process are also possible. As we discuss below, however, law enforcement agencies have yet to take full advantage of this potential strength.

The use of official police data for the identification of gangs and gang crime can be criticized on many fronts. Many of these criticisms are similar to those that plague official police crime data more generally. In general, police crime data are criticized on the grounds of the lack of objectivity in how police officials document criminal and delinquent events, which can lead to serious recording errors and can negatively impact the validity of crime data for calculating crime rates or for properly evaluating the effectiveness of criminal justice interventions (Black, 1980; Brownstein, 2000; Sherman and Glick, 1984). While recording errors that result from human error are understandable, some have blamed such errors on purposeful manipulation for political or financial gain (Brownstein, 2000).

Official gang crime databases suffer from similar limitations. Officer and administrative discretion, again, is at the heart of many of the limitations related to what is labeled as a gang, what is labeled a gang crime, who is labeled a gang member, and how gang members' files are updated across time. Take, for instance, the different possible definitions used across jurisdictions to identify a gang in relation to other known peer groups. Box 8.1 provides a few examples of different definitions of gangs that have been used across the federal, state, and local levels. As you can see when comparing these definitions, each law enforcement jurisdiction provides a unique definition of what constitutes a street gang, but each allows for ample discretion in deciding which group is actually labeled a street gang. The federal definition provides the most detailed description of particular qualifiers for street gangs, while the city of Chicago uses a broad definition, similar in many respects to that used by Klein (1971), which has the disadvantage of possibly including groups that many may not consider street gangs (e.g., fraternities). In this respect, by setting a low threshold for considering a group a gang, the city of Chicago relies more heavily on police discretion to identify gang from nongang groups. Other fundamental differences also exist across these definitions. For instance, in Iowa – and in the majority of other states that have codified a definition of street gang not listed in Box 8.1 – a group needs only to have three members in order to meet the criteria of a street gang, while Michigan set this threshold at five members. Michigan is also unique among these jurisdictions in that it requires there to be a hierarchical command structure in place in order to label a group a gang, while many other jurisdictions do not include such a factor in their respective definitions. As Howell (2007) discussed quite extensively, many (if not most) street gangs do not have a hierarchical structure, and thus Michigan's formal definition excludes many groups that other states would identify as gangs.

The use of official data to make cross-jurisdiction comparisons about the total number of gangs is therefore extremely problematic. The National Gang Center, recognizing that these discrepancies may impact its national survey of law enforcement, provides respondents with the following definition for jurisdictions that report their youth gang estimates: a youth gang is "a group of youths or young adults [the responding agency is] willing to identify as a 'gang'" (National Gang Center, n.d.-b). By using this broad definition, the National Gang Center recognizes and accepts that no singular definition is yet possible when drawing national estimates of the number of gangs, and therefore highlights the difficulties inherent in any attempt to do so. A similar issue also plagues official gang crime data, as is discussed next.

Defining gang crime: Membership or motivation?

There are a number of reasons why police agencies would desire to document whether crimes are gang related; tracking the level and nature of gang versus nongang crime across time and monitoring the effectiveness of special efforts to

Box 8.1 Examples of federal-, state-, and local-level definitions of street gangs.

Federal definition (United States Department of Justice, n.d.): The federal definition of "gang," as used by the Department of Justice and the Department of Homeland Security's Immigration and Customs Enforcement (ICE), is:

(a) an association of three or more individuals;
(b) whose members collectively identify themselves by adopting a group identity, which they use to create an atmosphere of fear or intimidation, frequently by employing one or more of the following: a common name, slogan, identifying sign, symbol, tattoo or other physical marking, style or color of clothing, hairstyle, hand sign or graffiti;
(c) whose purpose in part is to engage in criminal activity and which uses violence or intimidation to further its criminal objectives;
(d) whose members engage in criminal activity or acts of juvenile delinquency that, if committed by an adult would be crimes with the intent to enhance or preserve the association's power, reputation or economic resources.
(e) The association may also possess some of the following characteristics:
  1. The members may employ rules for joining and operating within the association.
  2. The members may meet on a recurring basis.
  3. The association may provide physical protection of its members from others.
  4. The association may seek to exercise control over a particular geographic location or region, or it may simply defend its perceived interests against rivals.
  5. The association may have an identifiable structure.

State of Iowa definition (State of Iowa, n.d.): *Criminal street gang* means any ongoing organization, association, or group of three or more persons, whether formal or informal, having as one of its primary activities the commission of one or more criminal acts, which has an identifiable name or identifying sign or symbol, and whose members individually or collectively engage in or have engaged in a pattern of criminal gang activity.

State of Michigan definition (State of Michigan, n.d.): "Gang" means an ongoing organization, association, or group of 5 or more people, other than a nonprofit organization, that identifies itself by all of the following:

(i) A unifying mark, manner, protocol, or method of expressing membership, including a common name, sign or symbol, means of recognition, geographical or territorial sites, or boundary or location.

(ii) An established leadership or command structure.
(iii) Defined membership criteria.

Chicago Police Department definition (Block and Block, 1993): The Chicago Police Department defines "street gang" as an association of individuals who exhibit the following characteristics in varying degrees:

1. A gang name and recognizable symbols.
2. A geographic territory.
3. An organized, continuous course of criminality.

reduce gang crime in particular neighborhoods in their city are among such reasons. An alternative function of monitoring gang crime is to compare one city's gang crime problem with other cities', in order to determine whether or not local offense patterns reflect broader changes that take place in other locations or are the product of more concentrated issues. As Maxson and Klein (1990) demonstrated, however, such between-jurisdiction comparisons are extremely difficult to make unless one is certain that police agencies define gang crime according to the same standards, which may not be the case. For example, over the past decades the cities of Los Angeles, California and Chicago, Illinois have made a concerted effort to document whether or not crimes are gang-related. To do so, however, they have utilized quite different definitional standards for what constitutes gang crime, which renders the comparison of gang crime rates between these cities difficult to achieve through official statistics. In particular, Los Angeles uses a member-based definition, while Chicago uses a motivation-based classification system. In fact municipalities throughout the United States have copied the tactics of either Chicago or Los Angeles, by picking one of these strategies to meet their own needs.

In order to officially label an incident as a gang crime, a member-based definition of gang crime, such as that used in Los Angeles, simply requires that either the offender or the victim is a documented gang member. A motivation-based definition, however, is far more stringent with respect to identifying a crime as gang-related. Motivation-based definitions require the presence of evidence that gang membership or gang activities were directly related to the motivation(s) for a given crime. For example, gang crimes identified on a motivation-based definition must be traced back to such activities as retaliation for previous crimes, recruitment of new members, or defense of a territory (Maxson and Klein, 1990). As one might surmise from these two types of definitional criteria, all else being equal, police departments that adopt membership-based definitions will evince higher gang crime rates than police departments that adopt motive-based strategies, because it is unlikely that all the crimes committed by or against gang members are in some way motivated by gang activities or gang membership. Indeed, in a comparison of gang homicide figures for Los Angeles under these two definitional standards, the total number of gang homicides dropped considerably when the motivation-based definition was applied instead of the city's regular membership-based criteria (Maxson and Klein, 1990).

As the above examples demonstrate, police officials have wide latitude in identifying gangs and gang crime. Beyond the definitional ambiguities associated with determining whether a group is a gang or whether particular crimes are gang-related, errors associated with identifying individuals as gang members can have serious and long-lasting consequences, given the advent of sentence enhancements for gang crimes across many states. Sentence enhancements are penalties that are added to a normal sentence; thus, if an individual is found guilty and convicted on a charge of felony robbery, and if the prosecution successfully demonstrates that the crime was gang-related, a number of extra years can be added to the prison sentence. Bjerregaard (2003) provided a nice overview of antigang legislation, which includes the use and potential misuse of sentence enhancements for gang members.

Some have questioned whether official procedures for documenting individuals as gang members – and, later, for updating these documents by removing those who are no longer gang-involved – are applied in practice (Katz, 2003; Klein and Maxson, 1989). After studying a gang task force unit that was responsible for verifying gang member lists and for updating the rosters so that they may reflect changing gang-member statuses, Katz (2003) suggested that official standards for documenting gang members were rarely applied in practice. He found that the method by which individuals in his study were most frequently identified as gang members was through individual patrol officers' crime reports. But the system of checks and balances put in place to eliminate the potential for misidentifying individuals as gang-involved was *never* utilized to override a patrol officer's judgment on an individual's gang membership status. So either the officers were 100 percent correct in their assessment or the rules and processes put in place were largely ignored. This led Katz to conclude that gang statistics were not "the product of the application of official definitions, or even informal definitions[,] but rather were the product of inadequate communication within the gang unit and between the gang unit and its operating environment" (Katz, 2003, p. 485).

After persons (typically, adults – to the exclusion of juveniles) are documented as a gang member by police officials, inefficient record-keeping practices may lead to the production of outdated gang member lists, which can be used for administrative and prosecutorial purposes. Given the high turnover rate in gang membership (Esbensen and Huizinga, 1993; Hill, Lui, and Hawkins, 2004; Peterson, Taylor, and Esbensen, 2004; Melde and Esbensen, 2011; Thornberry et al., 2003), if official gang member lists are not continuously updated according to standard practices, there is a high likelihood that such documents would soon contain names of inactive gang members (Spergel, 1995). Further, if names are added to the list at a faster rate than they are purged, these rosters will produce an inflated picture of the total number of individuals considered to be active gang members. The evidence produced by Katz (2003), as discussed above, confirmed this possibility, as police staff in the department he studied routinely failed to purge the files of inactive gang members, as they should have done according to the procedures put in place to ensure that the individuals listed were indeed still active participants in their groups. In fact, a 9th circuit court of appeals ruling in California made it mandatory that suspected gang members had the opportunity to challenge their official designation in a court of law before they could be included in a civil gang injunction[2] (Leal and Koerner, 2013). While errors are likely to be associated with any system designed to track the ebb and flow of gang-member status across individuals, when errors are systematic and pervasive, they can have serious consequences for our ability to understand the extent and nature of the gang population. Worse yet are the potential ramifications of the misidentification of individuals as gang-involved during civil proceedings and criminal trials, where sentence enhancements can cost persons years of freedom.

Beyond these problems, which are found in the process of documenting gang membership, some speculate that official gang statistics are compiled and reported in a manner that best suits the needs of the reporting agency. Bursik and Grasmick (2006) outlined the potential benefits of having a documented gang problem in certain jurisdictions, especially as it relates to the acquisition of federal funding for combating gang crime. That is, unless an organization can demonstrate a particular need for combating gangs and gang crime in its local jurisdiction, it is almost impossible to acquire competitive antigang grant dollars that can be used to purchase equipment, hire additional officers, and pay for the overtime hours necessary to carry out specialized police operations. Departments across the country that face budgetary challenges to offering services in an effective manner may feel pressure to overstate their local gang problem in order to procure competitive grant funding. Zatz (1987) suggested that such practices took place in the Phoenix police department in Arizona. In particular, Zatz suggested that the police overstated the number of active Chicano gangs, where official documents demonstrated an increase from five to *more than 100* gangs across a two year period. McCorkle and Miethe (1998) reported a similar phenomenon: Las Vegas police officials in Nevada reported a 400 percent increase in documented gang members over a one-year period, which coincided with requests for substantial increases in financial and staff resources.

A consequence of the improper documentation and maintenance of gang member lists is that they impact the validity and reliability of the official data used by researchers to investigate the role of gang members in crime and whether or not interventions targeting gang groups have had a desired effect. Inconsistent record-keeping has been blamed for a number of inconsistent findings related to gangs in the extant research literature. As an example, McCorkle and Miethe (1998) used official police data from Las Vegas to determine the extent to which gang members in the city contributed to the overall crime rate – in other words, whether gang members were disproportionately involved in crime and violence. On the basis of these data, they concluded that gang members were not disproportionately involved in acts of crime and violence in Las Vegas, which was inconsistent with the conclusions of similar studies in other locations across the United States. Specifically, those identified as gang members by the police were responsible for less than 5 percent of all drug offenses and for less than 15 percent of all violent crimes. So, while the police and public officials characterized the gang problem as a growing and serious concern in their community, McCorkle and Miethe concluded that "a 'ripple,' not a wave, may be a better characterization of the trend in gang activity during the period examined" (1998, pp. 59–60).

In what is hopefully a sign that police officials are becoming more capable of identifying and maintaining lists of active gangs and gang members, more recent literature suggests that police data are a valid and reliable source of information on local gang issues. Katz, Webb, and Schaefer (2000) found that officially documented youth gang members accounted for 16.9 percent of their sample but for 40 percent of all documented burglaries. In fact the gang-involved youth in the sample were disproportionately involved in every criminal offense examined in the study. In 2012 Katz led another team of researchers, in an examination of the reliability of National Youth Gang Survey data from 2005 through 2009 (Katz et al., 2012). Through the use of a number of measures of reliability, the team concluded that police reports of the number of gangs and gang members were highly reliable across jurisdictions and that gang homicide figures for cities of over 200,000 inhabitants also provided consistent estimates. Decker and Pyrooz (2010) offered further support for the idea that police data on gang homicide were indeed a reliable source of information.

While the documentation of gangs, gang members, and gang crime through official police data suffers from known limitations, recent evidence suggests that many jurisdictions have improved their capacity to collect information in reliable ways. Still, the duties associated with law enforcement agencies – to investigate crimes and to protect public safety – likely produce an incomplete picture of gang activity. That is, when dealing with gangs, police are likely to interact most frequently with those gang members they see as presenting the highest risk for engaging in crime and violence, while at the same time they ignore other facets of street gangs, which they may deem less worthy of their attention. Perhaps the best example of this incomplete view of street gangs taken by law enforcement officials was discussed extensively by Miller (2001) in her research on female gang members. As she argues, police departments, almost as a matter of policy, routinely failed to acknowledge the existence of female gang members in official reports and focused exclusively on males located in known gang areas. While police departments across the country now more readily identify females as gang members and as potentially serious criminals, this long-standing practice of ignoring upwards of half the actual gang population goes to show that the way law enforcement views gangs can seriously affect its resulting measures of the phenomenon. Given these limitations, many have advocated for a multimethod, triangulated approach to understanding gangs, gang membership, and gang crime (Bursik and Grasmick, 2006; Rennison and Melde, 2009).

The Use of Ethnographic Studies

Early, foundational criminological research on street gangs was based primarily on ethnographic methods. Researchers such as Thrasher (1927), Klein (1971), and Short and Strodtbeck (1965) spent years gathering ethnographic and interview data on gangs and their members in order to garner firsthand accounts on the lives and behaviors of group members and on how gangs were produced and interacted with their environment. The hallmark of ethnographic research is that it can illuminate the inner workings and dynamics of street gangs – a feature that is often lacking in studies that use official data or self-report survey methods, since with these methodologies it is difficult to tap into issues of group process, the meaning of gang membership for members themselves, and especially the more routine and noncriminal behaviors and activities engaged in by these individuals (Bursik and Grasmick, 2006). Unfortunately, the focused and intense attention needed to produce ethnographic data diminishes the capacity of such research to make these data generalizable. That is, what ethnographic studies gain in depth, through focused attention, they lose in breadth, because so few gangs or gang members can be studied at any one time. This means that the information collected through these methods has unknown applicability across time and place.

While the inability to draw broad conclusions from ethnographic research is a limitation of this methodology more generally, the way in which gangs are chosen for study can also lead to conclusions that are not applicable to gangs across place or time. As Bursik and Grasmick (2006) point out, gangs are not likely chosen at random, but for more practical reasons – such as notoriety or convenience – or through the work of social service agencies that provide access to particular members of street gangs, who act as gatekeepers for the group. And what are the processes that may lead a researcher to identify, seek out, and garner access to a gang for intense study? If the researcher became aware of a gang as a result of its notoriety in the community – be that due to its high levels of violent criminal activity, its high rate of female gang membership, or some other facet of the gang that made it stand out – then findings from an ethnographic study of this group are not likely to apply to the more typical gang, either in that location or elsewhere. If the researcher gained access to the group through a social service worker or agency that deals with that particular gang or gang members, then it becomes necessary to understand how the social service worker or agency identified the members of the group in question. Again, if there are particular reasons why social service was offered to one gang but not to others in the same local area, then this, too, would obviate the ability to draw general conclusions about gangs and their members from ethnographic methods. Thus it may be that the very existence of irregularities, which lead researchers to study particular gangs, is what limits the applicability of such research to other gangs across place and time.

Because ethnographic research is often focused on a limited number of subjects and because gang members may take great pride in deceiving outsiders through exaggerated or fully fictional accounts of gang life, it is particularly difficult for ethnographic researchers to discern fact from fiction. In his research, Klein (1971) provided a number of such examples, including gang members' tendency to embellish their story when recounting particular criminal and violent exploits. He referred to this practice as a "mythic system," as gang members in his study had a proclivity to "one-up" their fellow gang members through stories of violent crimes, even though such talk far outweighed the frequency with which they were actually involved in such behaviors (Klein, 1971, p. 85). While exaggerated rhetoric and storytelling are not unique to gangs, Bursik and Grasmick (2006) also reminded us that gang researchers are largely dealing with deviant persons, who just might take pleasure in fooling unsuspecting social workers or researchers into believing wildly inaccurate accounts of their actions. As Bursik recounted,

> during a conversation with a friend who formerly had been a central member of one of Chicago's most notorious fighting gangs ... He described with great pleasure how during times of boredom, members of his group would have an informal competition to see who could convincingly tell the most outrageous story to a social worker who had been assigned to the group. (Bursik and Grasmick, 2006, p. 8)

Decker and Van Winkle (1996) described ways in which they limited this practice, including by having their fieldworker introduce the respondents to the purpose of the study and explain how such storytelling was not acceptable. They also limited the number of respondents who could be interviewed from any one gang at any one time. This practice sought to limit the potential for group influence on their interviews, so that respondents would not feel compelled to one-up each other.

Second-hand reports from those (supposedly) involved in gang violence are usually what ethnographers are left to work with in their research, as they are rarely at the scene of gang violence. As Klein (1971, p. 123) described:

> Offhand, I can think of few categories of people who are less exciting to observe than gang members simply because, by and large, they just stand around and do nothing ... In studying gang delinquency, then, it is well to remember that one is studying a very minor sample of daily behavior, that this sample remains primarily undetected, and therefore that detected delinquent behavior is a lousy base from which to draw generalizations.

Last but not least, ethnographic research has also been criticized for the real possibility of its producing what is known as the Hawthorne effect. The Hawthorne effect is a situation where the simple presence of an outsider (i.e., someone not normally present in the setting under study, such as a researcher) changes the behavior of those being observed in their natural setting. Thus it is questionable whether or not gangs and their members behave naturally when they are being observed by a researcher. Both Klein (1971) and Short and Strodtbeck (1965), for instance, produced evidence that added attention from outside agencies such as law enforcement or social services may actually lead to increases in gang violence, if it is applied in a way that enhances group cohesion or is viewed as a threat to the group's status (or both). Thus, for all that ethnographic research can offer in the way of a more nuanced and complete understanding of particular gangs, such research is necessarily limited in other respects, including a broad-based understanding of the causes and consequences of gang membership. To overcome this limitation in particular and to better understand the epidemiology and etiology of gang membership, self-report survey methods have been utilized quite extensively over the past three decades.

The Use of Self-Report Methods

There are a number of advantages related to the use of self-report survey methods. One advantage is the ability to gather information on the "dark figure" of crime – that is, those cases that are not reported to the police – on so-called "victimless crimes" such as drug use and drug selling, and on minor delinquent behaviors that take place at school or in other formal institutions, are handled outside the formal legal system, and hence are not likely to come to the attention of authorities. In addition to these behaviors, survey methods also allow one to collect in-depth information on gang members themselves, for example on their beliefs and attitudes, on their involvement in nondelinquent activities (e.g., school activities, grade point average, legitimate employment, athletics), and on demographic (e.g., family information) and descriptive data. A second advantage is that self-report surveys enable researchers to collect systematic data from a wide array of gang members across space and time. For instance, unlike official statistics, which are based upon definitional standards that vary across jurisdictions (see above), self-report surveys can utilize a single standard for eliciting gang membership status. Third, self-report surveys allow researchers to gather systematic data across a large number of respondents in a relatively short period, and they allow for the analysis of change through the use of consistent measurements across time.

There are a number of well-known limitations associated with self-report methods as well. Perhaps the most important limitation is our inability to define a proper sampling frame (Bursik and Grasmick, 2006). After all, if a strength (and also a goal) of survey methods is to acquire more generalizable information than is possible with ethnographic studies or with official data, this strength is only truly realized if we are certain that our samples are representative of some known population. As in the case of self-report crime surveys in general, where it is particularly difficult to gain the cooperation of active criminals (Hindelang, Hirschi, and Weis, 1981), garnering the cooperation of gang members for the purposes of taking a survey may be especially difficult. Even if gaining the trust and cooperation of gang members could be accomplished, where would one find a location where a representative sample of gang members could be drawn? Options might include juvenile justice facilities, local jails, and prisons, but these places likely encompass only a small fraction of the entire gang population, and their use may lead to an overrepresentation of extremely crime-prone gang-involved persons. Locations such as schools and community centers suffer from the opposite problem, as they may not host the most violent or antisocial gang members who may have dropped out of school or might no longer be welcome at such institutions. This reality led Bursik and Grasmick (2006, p. 10) to conclude that, "in general, it is extremely difficult to draw a representative sample of gang members."

Another difficulty inherent in self-report research in general and that may be particularly problematic in criminological research concerns the veracity of the information collected from respondents. Can we be sure that gang members will be truthful when filling out a survey? Evidence exists that self-report surveys do produce valid data (Huizinga and Elliott, 1986). Such evidence is not straightforward, however, as it appears that the criminality of the respondents under study impacts the degree of truthfulness with which they report on their behaviors and other related phenomena. Hindelang and colleagues suggested: "Questionnaires and interviews appear to have differential validity depending on the criminality of the respondent. Thus the higher the level of criminality, the lower the validity of the crime measures" (Hindelang et al., 1981, p. 249). Given evidence that gang members are particularly deviant, there remains a concern that self-report data on gang membership and behavior may not be accurate.

Researchers have not yet agreed upon a standard definition of what constitutes a gang. How, then, do survey researchers identify such persons in self-report studies? While there is no single, unitary way in which researchers have operationalized gang membership across studies, the general practice of using such methods has received considerable support (see, e.g., Esbensen et al., 2001; Decker et al., 2014). For instance, researchers directing the International Self-Report Delinquency study (Junger-Tas et al., 2010; see also Melde and Esbensen, 2011) utilized a question that focused on the peer group. They asked, namely: "Do you consider your group of friends to be a gang?" This tactic was used so that individual respondents would not feel uncomfortable about reporting on their own gang membership status, which may produce underreports of the total number of gang-involved youth, even while providing a measure of gang involvement. The majority of self-report studies simply ask: "Are you a member of a street gang?" or "Are you now in a gang?" – with slight variations across projects. Some researchers prefer a more restrictive operationalization of gang membership; they will be more limiting in their questions by imposing additional restrictions. For example, the Add Health longitudinal study asked respondents whether they "had been *initiated* into a *named* gang in the past *12 months*" (DeLisi et al., 2009; emphasis added). Not all youth or young adults who consider themselves gang members could respond in the affirmative on this survey, because not all gang youth have had to be initiated. Although this is likely rare, there may be individuals who consider themselves gang members even though their gang does not have a name. Lastly, such a question also means that respondents who were initiated into a named gang more than a year before the survey would be free to respond "no" as well. At the opposite end of such a measurement tactic, other researchers prefer a more inclusive survey item; for instance the researchers who were part of the Montreal Longitudinal and Experimental study asked respondents: "During the past 12 months, were you part of a *group or gang* that did reprehensible acts?" (Tremblay et al., 2003; emphasis added). According to this question and how it has been used as a measure of gang membership, respondents need not even consider themselves gang members to respond in the affirmative, and thus to be treated as gang-involved.

There is certainly room for debate as to which measurement technique produces the most valid measure of gang membership. There is a growing body of research to suggest that self-report data from gang members are both valid and reliable. Webb, Katz, and Decker (2006), for example, examined this issue with a sample of self-reported gang members by comparing self-reports of drug use and urine samples collected as part of the Arrestee Drug Abuse Monitoring (ADAM) program. They concluded that respondents were generally truthful about their drug use and that gang members were no more likely to provide false answers than nongang respondents; of course they were also no less likely. Decker and colleagues (2014) also provide compelling evidence that self-reported gang members are truthful when reporting on their gang status and associated constructs. By using the relationship between self-reported gang membership and a scale of gang embededness as a measure of construct validity[3] (for this, see Maxfield and Babbie, 2014), they were able to determine that those who reported current and ongoing membership in a gang were more heavily immersed in their delinquent peer group than former gang members and those who were never involved. Decker and colleagues' (2014) results suggested that this was exactly the case; thus responses were consistent across groups in a manner that indicated that respondents were not simply answering at random. Esbensen and colleagues (2001) provided one of the strongest and most highly cited assessments of the robustness of the self-nomination technique by using a sample of roughly 6,000 students from across the United States. Through a comparison of a number of more and less restrictive definitional criteria for identifying gang youth, they concluded that "the self nomination technique is a particularly robust measure of gang membership capable of distinguishing gang from nongang youth" (Esbensen et al., 2001, p. 124), at least insofar as it relates to antisocial attitudes and behaviors.

Curry (2000) used a measure of criterion validity[4] in order to ascertain the validity of self-reported gang membership by comparing data from a self-report survey with official police data on gang youth in Chicago. His study demonstrated substantial overlap between the self-reported gang youth and those classified as such by the Chicago police department. In fact, the correlation measured by Curry (2000) was very similar to those of previous studies that have assessed the overlap between self-reported delinquency and official police crime data (Thornberry et al., 2003).

A limitation of the self-report method for identifying gang members often found in the literature is that all gang members from all types of gangs are treated similarly; gang members are lumped together even though they are a part of distinct groups. Klein and Maxson (2006) provided a framework for classifying gangs that has been successfully applied across the United States and globally. Their research suggests that a relatively small number of neighborhoods in a few major cities in the United States (e.g., Los Angeles, Chicago) have stereotypically large and well-organized gangs, which have survived through multiple generations. Active membership rosters for these "traditional" or "neo-traditional" gangs (Maxson and Klein, 1995) go easily over 100 persons, with possibly over 1,000 living former and inactive members. These stereotypical gangs, often depicted in movies and in the news media, include such groups as the founding sets of bloods and crips in Los Angeles and the vice lords, gangster disciples, and Latin kings in Chicago. The modal category of gangs that is found in cities throughout the world is, however, that of "compressed" gangs (Maxson and Klein, 1995). The membership roster for this type of gang ranges from roughly 10 to 50. Membership in these gangs last roughly for one to three years, if the gang itself lasts that long.[5] It would be difficult to confuse these groups with one another, but self-report methods often fail to distinguish between members of these unique groups unless additional questions are included in the survey and used during analysis – which is often not the case.

For developmental criminologists, who are often concerned with how gang membership changes the life-course trajectory of individuals across a number of relevant domains, drawing distinctions between types of gang members on the basis of group characteristics may not, however, be necessary. That is, if a respondent reports that s/he is in a gang, even though that gang does not live up to our preconceived notions of what a gang is (e.g., it has no leadership structure, no name, or no symbols), are we in a position to claim that the respondent is lying or naive? Should we ipso facto eliminate or de-identify such youth from our analyses? There is yet no research to support such a practice. For example, in a study of youth in Montreal, Le Blanc and Lanctot (1998) suggested that the structure of the gang was unrelated to the attitudinal and behavioral profiles of gang-involved youth. Rather they came to the conclusion that "participation in a group involved in illegal activities seems[,] in itself, more of an activator than the nature of the group" (Le Blanc and Lanctot, 1998, p. 24).

Conclusion

Each of the methods used to identify gangs, gang members, and gang crime discussed above is subject to a number of limitations. Official statistics on gangs, gang members, and gang crime have a tendency to overestimate the number of gang-involved persons at any one time and may produce an inaccurate portrayal of the characteristics of gang members. Police data have a tendency to undercount female gang members (Miller, 2001) as well as younger gang members (Curry, 2000). Ethnographic research has produced a wealth of knowledge on particular gangs and gang members in particular places at particular times, but such studies cannot be replicated across places or time, which leaves the generalizability of findings from such studies an unknown factor. Self-report survey methods are often plagued by the inability to identify a representative sample and to ensure that the data are valid and reliable. Findings derived from these methods, together, have produced a great deal of information on gangs, gang members, and gang crime, which has aided our understanding of the role of gangs in society. As with any scientific enterprise, however, when we consume information from any of these sources it is best to keep in mind the strengths and limitations associated with its collection. That said, as the study of gangs and their members continues, we should heed the advice of Egley and colleagues (2006, p. xiii), who encouraged the use of a "pluralistic approach" to the study of gangs.

Future gang research will have the opportunity to uncover many as yet misunderstood or unidentified facets of gang life. These opportunities stem directly from the foundation of knowledge provided by the numerous gang researchers who have left a lasting legacy in this area of study. For instance, the emergence of a number of longitudinal data sources in the 1980s, 1990s, and the first decade of the twenty-first century will permit long-term studies on the lives of gang-involved persons. In fact we are starting to see such research efforts, where respondents involved in scientific research as adolescents are now young adults with their own children. Data from the Rochester Youth Development Study, for instance, have been used to identify the consequences of adolescent gang membership on parenting practices (Augustyn, Thornberry, and Krohn, 2014), the socioeconomic implications of gang membership, and the likelihood of arrest in early adulthood (Krohn et al., 2011). Given other such data sources (e.g., the Denver Youth Survey, the Pittsburgh Youth Survey, the National Evaluations of the Gang Resistance Education and Training Surveys, the Seattle Social Development Project), the time is ripe for comparative research on the long-term impact of gang membership.

Researchers can also make use of new and emerging data analysis packages and sources of information to collect unique data on the lives of street gang members. For example, the emergence of user-friendly data analysis packages has made the use of social network analyses accessible to a growing body of researchers, which is reflected in recent scholarship on gang homicide (Papachristos, 2009). Geospatial modeling practices have allowed for the testing of theories related to the emergence and spread of gangs and gang crime (e.g., Zeoli et al., 2014). Similarly, big data sources – such as the Internet, cell phones, and social media – and associated methods for analyzing such data can be put to use in order to gather streaming, real-time information on the behaviors of gang-involved youth and adults in a way that will better test prominent theories of crime and deviance, while also informing policymakers and practitioners about the causes and consequences of gangs and gang membership. Perhaps most importantly, such sources of information create the capacity to collect information that integrates individual-level information on gang members and their behavior with microlevel group processes and macrolevel structural data, in conformity with the recommendations of Decker, Melde, and Pyrooz (2013).

Notes

1 There is a vast philosophical literature on the problem of necessary and sufficient conditions, but this is beyond our present concerns. Here we use these concepts in the ordinary sense, as defined in Merriam-Webster: a necessary condition is "a state of affairs that must prevail if another is to occur" and a sufficient condition is "a state of affairs whose existence assures the existence of another state of affairs" (Merriam-Webster Online Dictionary, 2013).

2 Civil gang injunctions are court orders that permit communities to call upon justice officials to regulate criminal and noncriminal behavior (e.g., associating in groups of

more than three individuals in a public place; wearing gang colors; being outside after midnight) deemed to be gang related and injurious to those communities' health and well-being.

3 Construct validity uses the relationship between two constructs in the same study in order to determine whether their association is consistent with expectations (Maxfield and Babbie, 2014).

4 Criterion validity uses the relationship between a measured construct and some outside source in order to determine whether the association between the study variable and the outside measure is consistent with expectations (Maxfield and Babbie, 2014).

5 Gangs are also different in many other respects, for example leadership hierarchy, organizational characteristics, and the nature of the offending behaviors.

References

Augustyn, M. B., Thornberry, T. P., and Krohn, M. D. 2014. Gang membership and pathways to maladaptive parenting. *Journal of Research on Adolescence*, 24 (2): 252–267.

Bjerregaard, B. 2003. Antigang legislation and its potential impact: The promises and the pitfalls. *Criminal Justice Policy Review*, 14 (2): 171–192.

Black, D. J. 1980. *The manners and customs of the police*. New York: Academic Press.

Block, C. R., and Block, R. 1993. Street gang crime in Chicago. *Research in Brief*. Washington, DC: US Department of Justice, Office of Justice Programs, National Institute of Justice. NCJ 144782.

Bursik, R. J. J., and Grasmick, H. G. 2006. Defining and researching gangs. In *The modern gang reader*, edited by A. J. Egley, C. L. Maxson, J. Miller, and M. W. Klein, 3rd edn., 2–14. Los Angeles, CA: Roxbury.

Brownstein, H. 2000. The social production of crime statistics. *Justice Research and Policy*, 2: 73–89.

Curry, G. D. 2000. Self-reported gang involvement and officially recorded delinquency. *Criminology*, 38 (4): 1252–1274.

Decker, S. H., Melde, C., and Pyrooz, D. C. 2013. What do we know about gangs and gang membership and where do we go from here? *Justice Quarterly*, 30 (3): 369–402.

Decker, S. H., and Pyrooz, D. C. 2010. On the validity and reliability of gang homicide: A comparison of disparate sources. *Homicide Studies*, 14: 359–376.

Decker, S. H., Pyrooz, D. C., Sweeten, G., and Moule Jr., R. K. 2014. Validating self-nomination in gang research: Assessing differences in gang embededness across non-, current, and former gang members. *Journal of Quantitative Criminology*, 30 (4): 577–598. doi: 10.1007/s10940-014-9215-8.

Decker, S. H., and Van Winkle, B. 1996. *Life in the gang: Family, friends, and violence*. New York: Cambridge University Press.

DeLisi, M., Barnes, J. C., Beaver, K. M., and Gibson, C. L. 2009. Delinquent gangs and adolescent victimization revisited: A propensity score matching approach. *Criminal Justice and Behavior*, 36: 808–823.

Egley, A. J., Maxson, C. L., Miller, J., and Klein, M. W., eds. 2006. *The modern gang reader*, 3rd edn. Los Angeles, CA: Roxbury.

Esbensen, F.-A., and Huizinga, D. 1993. Gangs, drugs, and delinquency in a survey of urban youth. *Criminology*, 31: 565–589.

Esbensen, F.-A., Winfree, L. T., Jr., He, N., and Taylor, T. J. 2001. Youth gangs and definitional issues: When is a gang a gang, and why does it matter? *Crime and Delinquency*, 47 (1): 105–130.

Fagan, J. 1990. Social processes of delinquency and drug use among urban gangs. In *Gangs in America*, edited by C. R. Huff, 183–219. Newbury Park, CA: Sage.

GAO. 2009. *Combating gangs: Better coordination and performance measurement would help clarify roles of federal agencies and strengthen assessment of efforts.* Report to the ranking member, Committee on Oversight and Government Reform, House of Representatives. Washington, DC: US Government Accountability Office.

Hill, K. G., Howell, J. C., Hawkins, J. D., and Battin-Pearson, S. R. 1999. Childhood risk factors for adolescent gang membership: Results from the Seattle social development projects. *Journal of Research in Crime and Delinquency*, 36: 300–322.

Hill, K. G., Lui, C., and Hawkins, J. D. 2004. Early precursors of gang membership: A study of seattle youth. In *American Youth Gangs at the Millennium*, edited by F.-A. Esbensen, S. G. Tibbetts, and L. Gaines, 191–199. Long Grove, IL: Waveland Press.

Hindelang, M. J., Hirschi, T., and Weis, J. G. 1981. *Measuring delinquency*. Beverly Hills, CA: Sage.

Howell, J. C. 2007. Menacing or mimicking? Realities of youth gangs. *Juvenile and Family Court Journal*, 58 (2): 39–50.

Howell, J. C., and Moore, J. P. 2010. History of street gangs in the United States. *National Gang Center Bulletin*, 5. Washington, DC, Bureau of Justice Assistance, Office of Juvenile Justice and Delinquency Prevention.

Huizinga, D. 1997. Gangs and the volume of crime. Paper presented at the Western Society of Criminology, Honolulu, Hawaii, February.

Huizinga, D., and Elliott, D. S. 1986. Reassessing the reliability and validity of self-report measures. *Journal of Quantitative Criminology*, 2: 293–327.

Junger-Tas, J., Marshall, I. H., Enzmann, D., Killias, M., Steketee, M., and Gruszczynska, B., eds. 2010. *Juvenile delinquency in Europe and beyond*. New York: Springer.

Katz, C. M. 2003. Issues in the production and dissemination of gang statistics: An ethnographic study of a large Midwestern police gang unit. *Crime and Delinquency*, 49 (3): 485–516.

Katz, C. M., Fox, A. M., Britt, C. L., and Stevenson, P. 2012. Understanding police gang data at the aggregate level: An examination of the reliability of National Youth Gang Survey data. *Justice Policy and Research*, 14 (2): 103–128.

Katz, C. M., Webb, V. J., and Schaefer, D. R. 2000. The validity of police gang intelligence lists: Examining differences in delinquency between documented gang members and non-documented delinquent youth. *Police Quarterly*, 3: 413–437.

Klein, M. W. 1971. *Street gangs and street workers*. Englewood Cliffs, NJ: Prentice Hall.

Klein, M. W. 2006. Street gangs: A cross-national perspective. In *The modern gang reader*, edited by A. J. Egley, C. L. Maxson, J. Miller, and M. W. Klein, 3rd edn., 104–116. Los Angeles, CA: Roxbury.

Klein, M. W., and Maxson, C. L. 2006. *Street gang patterns and policies*. New York: Oxford University Press.

Klein, M. W., and Maxson, C. L. 1989. Street gang violence. In *Violent crime, violent criminals*, edited by N. A. Weiner and M. E. Wolfgang, 198–234. Beverly Hills, CA: Sage.

Krohn, M. D., Ward, J. T., Thornberry, T. P., Lizotte, A. J., and Chu, R. 2011. The cascading effects of adolescent gang involvement across the life course. *Criminology*, 49: 991–1028.

Le Blanc, M. L., and Lanctot, N. 1998. Social and psychological characteristics of gang members. *Journal of Gang Research*, 5 (3): 15–28.

Leal, F., and Koerner, C. 2013. Court: Suspected gang members get to challenge claim. Accessed 30 July, 2014. http://www.ocregister.com/articles/gang-535021-injunction-orange.html.

Maxfield, M., and Babbie, E. 2014. *Research methods for criminal justice and criminology*, 7th edn. Boston: Cengage Learning.

Maxson, C. L., and Klein, M. W. 1990. Defining gang homicide: An updated look at member and motive approaches. In *Gangs in America*, edited by C. R. Huff, 2nd ed., 3–20. Thousand Oaks, CA: Sage.

Maxson, C. L., and Klein, M. W. 1995. Investigating gang structures. *Journal of Gang Research*, 3: 33–40.

McCorkle, R. C., and Miethe, T. D. 1998. The political and organizational response to gangs: An Examination of moral panic in Nevada. *Justice Quarterly*, 15: 41–64.

Melde, C., and Esbensen, F.-A. 2011. Gang membership as a turning point in the life course. *Criminology*, 49: 513–552.

Merriam-Webster Online Dictionary. 2013. Accessed December 15, 2015. http://www.merriam-webster.com.

Miller, J. 2001. *One of the guys: Girls, gangs, and gender*. New York: Oxford University Press.

National Gang Center. n.d.-a. National Youth Gang Survey. Accessed July 29, 2014. http://www.nationalgangcenter.gov/survey-analysis.

National Gang Center. n.d.-b. National Youth Gang Survey Analysis. Accessed December 2, 2010. http://www.nationalgangcenter.gov/Survey-Analysis/Methodology.

Papachristos, A. V. 2009. Murder by structure: Dominance relations and the social structure of gang homicide. *American Journal of Sociology*, 115 (1): 74–128.

Peterson, D., Taylor, T. J., and Esbensen, F.-A. 2004. Gang membership and violent victimization. *Justice Quarterly*, 21: 794–815.

Rennison, C. M., and Melde, C. 2009. The use of victim surveys to study gang crime: Prospects and possibilities. *Criminal Justice Review*, 34 (4): 489–514.

Sherman, L., and Glick, B. 1984. *The quality of police arrest statistics*. Washington, DC: Police Foundation.

Short, J. F., and Strodtbeck, F. L. 1965. *Group process and gang delinquency*. Chicago, IL: University of Chicago Press.

Spergel, I. A. 1995. *The youth gang problem: A community approach*. New York: Oxford University Press.

State of Iowa. n.d. Chapter 723A: Criminal street gangs. Accessed July 1, 2014. http://coolice.legis.iowa.gov/cool-ice/default.asp?category = billinfo&service = iowacode&ga = 83&input=723A.

State of Michigan. n.d. Section 750.411u. Accessed July 1, 2014. http://www.legislature.mi.gov/(S(0rkfhqfrossvafnidl1dvy45))/mileg.aspx?page=GetObject&objectname = mcl-750–411u.

Thornberry, T. P. 1998. Membership in youth gangs and involvement in serious and violent offending. In *Serious and violent juvenile offenders*, edited by R. Loeber and D. P. Farrington, 147–166. Thousand Oaks, CA: Sage.

Thornberry, T. P., Krohn, M. D., Lizotte, A. J., Smith, C. A., and Tobin, K. 2003. *Gangs and delinquency in developmental perspective*. New York: Cambridge University Press.

Thrasher, F. 1927. *The gang*. Chicago, IL: University of Chicago Press.

Tremblay, R. E., Vitaro, F., Nagin, D., Pagani, L., and Sequin, J. R. 2003. The Montreal longitudinal and experimental study: Rediscovering the power of descriptions.

In *Taking stock of delinquency: An overview of findings from contemporary longitudinal studies*, edited by T. P. Thornberry and M. D. Krohn, 205–254. New York: Kluwer.

United States Department of Justice. n.d. What is a gang? Definitions. Accessed July 1, 2014. http://www.nij.gov/topics/crime/gangs/Pages/definitions.aspx.

Webb, V. J., Katz, C. M., and Decker, S. H. 2006. Assessing the validity of self-reports by gang members: Results from the Arrestee Drug-Abuse Monitoring program. *Crime and Delinquency*, 52: 232–252.

Zatz, M. 1987. Chicano youth gangs and crime: The creation of a moral panic. *Contemporary Crises*, 11: 129–158.

Zeoli, A. M., Pizarro, J. M., Grady, S. C., and Melde, C. 2014. Homicide as infectious disease: Using public health methods to investigate the diffusion of homicide. *Justice Quarterly*, 31 (3): 609–632.

Further Reading

Decker, S. H., and Pyrooz, D. C. 2012. Contemporary gang ethnographies. In *Handbook on criminological theory*, edited by F. T. Cullen and P. Wilcox, 274–293. New York: Oxford University Press.

9

Gendered Pathways to Crime

Julie Yingling

Pathways Perspective

Research on the pathways perspectives concludes that gender is a key factor in shaping criminality (Belknap, 2007; Bloom et al., 2002). Men and women have different life experiences, and women's life experiences shape their patterns of offending (Bloom et al., 2002). Therefore the pathways perspective, when employed, seeks to uncover and understand the specific life events in women's lives that influence their future criminal behaviors (Belknap, 2007; Belknap and Holsinger, 2006; Bloom et al., 2002; Chesney-Lind and Shelden, 2004; Chesney-Lind and Irwin, 2007; Farr, 2000; Gavazzi, Yarcheck, and Chesney-Lind, 2006; Holsinger, 2000; Holtfreter and Morash, 2003; Salisbury and Van Voorhis, 2009).

Central to this perspective is examining "the broad life disadvantages and social circumstances that put women at risk of ongoing criminal involvement, many of which are fundamentally gendered experiences" (Bloom et al., 2003, p. 542). These experiences fall under three main categories: past abuse (Belknap, Holsinger, and Dunn, 1997; Browne, Miller, and Maguin, 1999; Daly, 1992; Dembo et al., 1992; Gaarder and Belknap, 2002; Gilfus, 1993; McClellan, Farabee, and Crouch, 1997), drug use (Daly 1994; McClellan et al., 1997; Chesney-Lind, 1997; Salisbury, Van Voorhis, and Spiropoulos, 2009), and male intimate partners (Salisbury and Van Voorhis, 2009; Belknap, 2007; Maher and Hudson, 2007; Maher, 1997; Sterk, 1999). These negative experiences typically occur with greater frequency – if not exclusively – in women's lives (Belknap and Holsinger, 2006; Chesney-Lind and Shelden, 2004; Farr, 2000; Funk, 1999; Holsinger, 2000; Holtfreter and Morash, 2003).

The Handbook of Measurement Issues in Criminology and Criminal Justice, First Edition.
Edited by Beth M. Huebner and Timothy S. Bynum.

When these factors do exist in men's lives, they impact men and women in very different ways. They tend to have a much greater negative impact, personal and social, in women's lives than in the lives of men (Belknap and Holsinger, 2006; Belknap, 2007; Chesney-Lind and Shelden, 2004; Holtfreter and Morash, 2003). It is not simply the *presence* of these issues that pushes an individual into engaging in illicit behavior, but also the *quantity* and *quality* of that individual's experiences – which, to repeat, impact women disproportionately more than men. It is well known that early-life trauma can alter brain chemistry and cognitive functioning, which can negatively impact academic success and the ability to appropriately interpret cues that may indicate risk or danger (van der Kolk, 1996). Further, women often self-harm and self-medicate with alcohol or drugs in order to numb themselves from the trauma of past abuse (Briere, 1996; Chu, 1998). For example, women who experience victimization at a younger age may engage in self-harm and heavy alcohol or drug use, do poorly in school due to a lack of concentration, and intensify their dependence on a partner to support them later in life, which exposes them to further abuse or to behavior that coerces them to engage in crime.

Throughout their lives, women offenders experience higher rates of victimization (Belknap, 2007) and higher rates of abuse (physical, verbal, and sexual) than men and boys (Belknap and Holsinger, 2006; Evans, Forsyth, and Gauthier, 2002). Prior to the pathways perspective, these life experiences were not used to describe why or how women became involved in criminal behavior. Daly's (1992, 1994) research greatly contributed to the pathways perspective by identifying four common themes among the different experiences of women offenders. By careful analysis of court documents and criminal justice records on female offenders, Daly (1992, 1994) identified a number of unique aspects of, pathways leading up to, or themes related to, women's criminality. The first theme was child abuse or neglect. These women, after experiencing abuse or neglect, developed behavioral or mental illness-related problems that they acted out frequently. They were also likely to suffer from substance abuse. The second pathway to criminal behavior was working as a prostitute. Women who ran away from abusive homes as children often resorted to prostitution and simultaneously became addicted to illicit substances as a way to deal with not only the past abuse, but their current situation as sex workers. The third pathway identified by Daly as unique to female offenders was their history of abuse by an intimate partner. Women often become involved in crime as a result of the abuse they sustained from their violent partners. They may use illicit substances to deal with the abuse, they may defend themselves by harming the violent partner, or they may make a calculated attack on that partner in order to get revenge or simply stop the abuse. The fourth female pathway to offending consists of being introduced to illicit substances by intimate or familial relationships. Women may begin using, selling, manufacturing, or trafficking drugs at the request of male partners or being forced by them to do so. The four pathways are highly interrelated, and the presence of several of these factors increases women's likelihood of engaging in criminal behavior (Belknap, 2007; Daly, 1992, 1994; Johansson and Kempf-Leonard, 2009).

Research on women's pathways into crime indicates that gender matters significantly in shaping criminality. Steffensmeier and Allan (1996) note that the "profound differences" between the lives of women and those of men shape their patterns of criminal offending. So far as women are concerned, these profound differences include high rates of victimization, substance use, and the influence of deviant or criminal intimate partners – often in combination. These unique factors will be discussed in detail below.

Common Pathways

Qualitative in-depth interviews and surveys with female offenders have greatly modified researchers' understanding of criminality (Belknap, 2007; Browne et al., 1999; Chesney-Lind and Shelden, 2004; Daly, 1992; Salisbury and Van Voorhis, 2009). Data have shown the magnitude of negative and often traumatic life experiences of women offenders since childhood (Belknap, 2007). Negative and traumatic life experiences significantly related to future offending include past abuse by family members (Belknap et al., 1997; Browne et al., 1999; Daly, 1992; Dembo et al., 1992; Gaarder and Belknap, 2002; Gilfus, 1993; McClellan et al., 1997), abuse by current or former male intimate partners (Salisbury and Van Voorhis, 2009; Belknap, 2007; Maher and Hudson, 2007; Maher, 1997; Sterk, 1999), and drug and substance abuse (Daly, 1992, 1994; Chesney-Lind, 1997; Salisbury et al., 2009).

Child and early adult experiences with physical and verbal abuse

Delinquent girls and criminal women have higher victimization rates than their non-offending counterparts (Belknap, 2007; Belknap and Holsinger, 2006). Specifically, delinquent girls report higher rates of abuse than delinquent boys on all forms of abuse: experiencing verbal abuse from family members or others, physical abuse from family members or others, and sexual abuse from family members or others – as well as witnessing any of these kinds of violence (Belknap and Holsinger, 2006; Evans et al., 2002). Girls are more likely than boys to experience neglect, and on average girls experience neglect at younger ages than boys. Girls also experience neglect for longer periods of time than boys (Dembo et al., 1992; McClellan et al., 1997; Widom and Maxfield, 2001).

While child abuse or neglect alone may not propel men or women into criminal behavior, it may simply lead to offending through its negative psychological and behavioral effects, such as mental health issues and substance use (Salisbury and Van Voorhis, 2009). Thus child abuse can be an indirect pathway to offending. Not only do girls experience more childhood abuse and neglect than boys, but female offenders have more negative life experiences than male offenders and female nonoffenders. Simply stated, women are more likely to have a constellation of disadvantages by comparison to men. When comparing the life histories of male and female offenders, McClellan and colleagues (1997) found that female offenders have significantly higher rates of child and adult victimization, mental health issues, and substance use than male offenders.

Girls are at a higher risk of experiencing sexual abuse than boys (Browne and Finkelhor, 1986; Homma et al., 2012; Stoltenborgh et al., 2011). When they are sexually abused, girls are more likely to be victimized by someone in their immediate family, such as a father or a stepfather (Browne and Finkelhor, 1986; Homma et al., 2012; Stoltenborgh et al., 2011). Female sexual abuse also occurs more often and extends over longer periods than the sexual abuse of boys, perhaps due to the easy access to the girl that the abusing relationship provides (Browne and Finkelhor, 1986; Homma et al., 2012; Stoltenborgh et al., 2011). Given the nature of the violation, which is committed by a previously trusted family member, and the length of time for which the abuse persists, girls experience many more negative effects of sexual abuse than boys: depression, anxiety, low self-esteem, shame, and substance abuse (Browne and Finkelhor, 1986; Homma et al., 2012; Stoltenborgh et al., 2011).

An immediate example of sexual abuse as a pathway to crime is that of running away. Running away and prostitution are the only two arrest categories where girls have a higher proportion of involvement than boys (Chesney-Lind and Irwin, 2007). In 2009, 51,370 girls were arrested for running away, while only 1,092 were arrested for prostitution (Puzzanchera and Adams, 2011). Many girls who flee their families are simply trying to escape a sexually abusive home life (Chesney-Lind and Irwin, 2007; Siegel and Williams, 2003). Girls are about three times more likely than boys to be victims of child sexual assault (Sedlak and Broadhurst, 1996) and victimized by family members (33 to 50 percent of girls versus 10 to 20 percent of boys) (Finkelhor, 1994). From the pathways perspective, victimization in the form of childhood sexual assault can directly and immediately result in criminal behavior and running away, as young girls and boys are simply trying to escape the abuse.

A great deal of research examines the connection between childhood abuse and future criminal offending (Belknap, 2007; Belknap and Holsinger, 2006; Dembo et al., 1992; Evans et al., 2002; McClellan et al., 1997; Widom and Maxfield, 2001). Girls and boys experience rather similar rates of (nonsexual) abuse and neglect (Evans et al., 2002; Widom and Maxfield, 2001). Both boys and girls who experience abuse and neglect as children are more likely to be arrested as juveniles, adults, and for a violent crime (Widom and Maxfield, 2001). However, the outcomes of these neglected boys and girls vary markedly. Girls who experienced abuse or neglect in childhood were 73 percent more likely to be arrested for property, alcohol, drug, and other misdemeanor offenses than similar girls who did not experience abuse or neglect. The former also have an increased risk of arrest for violent crime as juveniles and adults (Widom and Maxfield, 2001). Past physical abuse, sexual abuse, and neglect all act as pathways to additional criminal offenses for men and women.

Interestingly, girls overwhelmingly recognize the negative impact that victimization has on their life trajectories (Belknap and Holsinger, 2006). When Belknap and Holsinger (2006) asked girls to point to the events that led to, or caused, their criminal offenses, most identified these abusive and traumatic events as responsible factors. Conversely, Byrne and Trew (2008) found that male and female offenders who experienced childhood abuse and neglect do not point to those experiences as direct causes of their later offending, but merely as negative experiences that shaped their behavior toward other factors, which may in turn have acted as direct pathways to offending – such as substance abuse. It is interesting that men and women are aware of their own pushes and pulls toward criminal behavior and of their own past experiences as the source and foundation of such tendencies, but are unwilling or unable to counteract these negative effects.

Substance use

A large proportion of women offenders report experiencing physical, emotional, or sexual abuse, as established above (Belknap, 2007). Long-term effects of abuse include depression, anxiety, mental health problems, and post-traumatic stress disorder (Belknap, 2007; Chesney-Lind, 1997; Covington, 1998). Because of these elevated rates of experienced violence, illicit drug use is a highly gendered phenomenon. While exceptions exist, women often use and abuse illicit substances as a means to self-medicate negative life experiences such as abuse or trauma (Bloom et al., 2003; Chesney-Lind, 1997; Covington, 1998; Nelson-Zlupko, Kauffman, and Morrison Dore, 1995; Salisbury and Van Voorhis, 2009). Drugs may be a cheaper and more readily available treatment for depressive, stress-related, or mental health symptoms than conventional medication.

Regardless of women's reasons for using illicit substances, this habit is a strong causal factor in future delinquency (Nelson-Zlupko et al., 1995; Salisbury and Van Voorhis, 2009). Bloom and colleagues (2002) report that roughly 80 percent of incarcerated women have a substance abuse problem. Half of the women were under the influence of an illicit substance at the time of their offense (Bloom et al., 2003). For many women, regardless of their current intoxication status, the crime itself was motivated by the need for money to purchase drugs (Bloom et al., 2003). This process becomes a damaging cycle: women are victimized, seek out illicit substances in order to self-medicate and manage their resulting emotional or mental health problems, participate in criminal acts in order to obtain more drugs or property they can sell or trade for drugs, and get charged for a criminal offense. For many women, using or attempting to possess such substances is a pathway to additional criminal behavior.

For example, in their quantitative study on predictive factors of prison admission and recidivism, Salisbury and Van Voorhis (2009) find that substance use affects women's criminal choices and behaviors directly and significantly. There are several causal reasons. As Bloom and colleagues (2002) stated, while under the influence women may commit an offense that they would never have committed otherwise. Some offend to acquire money or goods that can be later traded for drugs. In most states in the United States, simply using illicit substances is a crime worthy of incarceration.

Male intimate partners

While past abuse or trauma and drug use are two types of experience that push women into criminal behavior differently from men, women's criminality is often connected to delinquent intimate partners. Women are typically introduced to illicit substances, criminal acts, and criminal networks through male intimate partners (Evans et al., 2002; Maher and Hudson, 2007; Dunlap, Johnson, and Maher, 1997; Maher, 1997; Sterk, 1999).

Similarly, when looking at how female offenders fare after incarceration, researchers find that these offenders' success is largely dependent upon their romantic relationships (Salisbury and Van Voorhis, 2009). Salisbury and Van Voorhis (2009) found that, in their sample of previously incarcerated women, those who were in relationships fraught with dysfunction or abuse could become depressed or experience other stress-related disorders and return to drug use. Dysfunctional relationships had a significantly negative impact on recidivism rates for female offenders. Women overwhelming offend through opportunities presented by their intimate partners and reoffend in response to poor treatment by their partners.

Specifically in drug-related offenses, women are overwhelmingly introduced to offending through their male intimate partners (Evans et al., 2002; Maher and Hudson, 2007; Dunlap et al., 1997; Maher, 1997; Sterk, 1999). Conversely, men are generally introduced to drug use and drug-related offenses through their male friendship networks (Evans et al., 2002; Maher and Hudson, 2007; Dunlap et al., 1997; Maher, 1997; Sterk, 1999). These findings apply regardless of the actual substance.

The bulk of research on drug markets finds that women primarily get access and become involved due to their links with men (Maher and Hudson, 2007). With regard to the crack cocaine market, research indicates that women enter the market and obtain a higher status within it through their male partners (Dunlap et al., 1997; Maher, 1997; Sterk, 1999). Maher's (1997) study of 211 women involved in the Brooklyn crack markets and Sterk's (1999) study of 149 women in the Atlanta crack markets showed that women obtained drug-dealing jobs through men in those markets. Maher's (1997) research specifically found that women obtained selling roles by having relationships with male dealers. Similarly, Sterk (1999) found that women not only gain access to the market through male partners, but still rely on the men for enforcement and protection even when they achieve higher status roles (such as selling or dealing narcotics). Women gain access and higher status roles in crack markets through their male partners, who often continue to vouch for the female sellers.

Morgan and Joe's (1996) study of 141 women using or selling methamphetamine shed some light on how women become involved in the drug market. The researchers describe women's experiences and advancement within the drug market, usually with or for a boyfriend or husband. Several dealers have experience in selling methamphetamine with former boyfriends and continue to sell with their current husbands (Morgan and Joe, 1996). Morgan and Joe (1996) detail two accounts, and refer to more, of women who are successfully running a methamphetamine manufacturing business but are only doing it because their partners were incarcerated, or in order to manage their partners' increasing substance abuse problems. These women were given the unique opportunity to run a manufacturing business only to replace their incapacitated partners.

Overview of Methodologies

The pathways perspective relies on an analysis of one's whole life, which is meant to explain crime causation (Bloom et al., 2002). There are three primary ways in which these data are collected: from official sources, through self-report methods, and throughethnographic studies.

Official data

One type of official data useful in ordering the life events relevant to men's and women's choices and behaviors consists of of pre-sentence investigation reports and other official records (Bloom et al., 2002). Pre-sentence reports are compiled by probation or pre-trial officers and are used to aid the judge in deciding an appropriate sentence:

> The elements of an offender-based report includes [*sic*] a summary of the offense, the offender's role, prior criminal justice involvement, and a social history with an emphasis on family history, employment, education, physical and mental health, financial condition and future prospects. (Macallair, 2008, p. 2)

Because of their comprehensiveness, pre-sentence reports contain a large amount of personal details about an individual that can help researchers understand offenders (Daly, 1996). In one example of pre-sentence reports used to study pathways to offending, Daly (1996) reduced pre-sentence investigation reports to criteria relevant to offending. She was surprised to find rich, detailed information about each offender in his or her pre-sentence report and wanted to determine what factors led or pushed a person into criminality. After combing through extensive records, Daly ultimately identified a number of categories relevant to offending, for example coming from a single-parent household, problems with drug or alcohol addiction, and finishing high school.

Similarly, Widom and Maxfield (2001) used official records to follow delinquent children through adolescence and adulthood. The researchers compared delinquent children with histories of sexual abuse, physical abuse, and neglect with delinquent children who did not have such histories. They found that the former were more likely to be arrested, both as juveniles and as adults – and for violent crimes. Essentially, abuse or neglect victimization in childhood acted as a pathway to additional and more violent criminal behavior for both boys and girls, but went at much higher rates for girls.

In a large study tracking male and female youth through official records between 1997 and 2003, Johansson and Kempf-Leonard (2009) examined the impact of child abuse victimization, mental health problems, running away, gang involvement, and juvenile justice involvement on adult male and female offending. The researchers used a variety of official records to capture the complete story of each juvenile, including juvenile court intake forms, law enforcement reports, processing information, self-report information from the youth, and reports from their parents. Child abuse was measured by indicating any suspected physical, emotional, or sexual abuse in the child's life or any involvement between the child's family and Child Protective Services. The existence of mental health problems was measured by intake forms administered to each individual when s/he entered the juvenile justice system. These forms use scales that reflect the many mental health needs that juveniles experience: alcohol and drug use, angrer and irritability, depression and anxiety, somatic complaints, and suicide ideation. Johansson and Kempf-Leonard were careful to note that the presence of these issues does not flag a mental health condition, but scoring above an established cutoff point does indicate mental health concerns. Running away was measured through the presence of the status offense in the juvenile's record. Gang involvement was measured by combing records that mentioned the juvenile's status as a former gang member, a current gang member, a hardcore gang member, or a wannabe gang member. Lastly, juvenile justice involvement measured the level of involvement with the system that a juvenile experienced. This allowed juveniles with no juvenile detention or with short stays in juvenile detention to be categorized differently from those with longer and frequent visits to detention centers.

Johansson and Kempf-Leonard (2009), uniquely, found gender similarities, in that mental health problems, running away, gang involvement, and secure detention rather equally predict serious, violent, and chronic offending in men and women. The gender differences they found are, however, quite interesting. Girls, but not boys, who spent time in foster care were more likely to be chronic offenders. Girls who spent time in a secure detention facility were more likely than boys to commit serious or violent offenses later on (Johansson and Kempf-Leonard, 2009). This study comprehensively documents adverse experiences in juveniles in order to determine their effect on future violent, serious, or chronic offending – in both boys and girls.

One publicly available data set that examines pathways to delinquency is the ICPSR data set *Pathways from Dependency and Neglect to Delinquency in a Mid-South County in the United States, 1984–1985 and 2000–2001* (Coleman-Davis and Forde, 2010). These data examine a set of children who are allegedly dependent and neglected and a set of children who are allegedly delinquent. This information was compiled from official court records between the two periods indicated in the title. In the report based on their collected data, Coleman-Davis and Forde (2007) find that most maltreated children do not offend. However, experienced physical or sexual abuse is the biggest predictor of delinquency. Further, out-of-home placements are positively correlated with later offending.

There are many advantages to using official data in order to measure criminal behavior and involvement. The primary advantage is the availability of data sets. Whether these are at a local or national level, they afford researchers the possibility to examine phenomena without the cost of administering surveys or conducting interviews (Piquero, Schubert, and Brame, 2014). Court documents, pre-sentence investigation reports, and other criminal justice system records can be exhaustive: they include specific charges, a chronological timeline of events, as well as social and family information about the offender that a participant may not be able to remember correctly or recall when questioned by researchers (Bloom et al., 2002; Daly, 1996). Lastly, to best determine the impact of gender on the independent variables, controlling for sex is not always the best strategy. A split-sample analysis can examine the direct effects of the independent variables separately for men and women (Wattanaporn and Holtfreter, 2014). The ability to maximize statistical predictability is crucial in quantitative analyses.

Despite these advantages, there are several drawbacks to using official data to study the pathways to crime phenomena. First, official records do not account for all the crimes committed by an individual, nor do they always provide the contextual "why" or "how" that would aid researchers in understanding the often gendered nuances of the offense (Piquero et al., 2014). Further, official records are a result of a great deal of contact between an offender and many actors in the criminal justice system. These records cannot control or account for the degree of discretion among the actors (Piquero et al., 2014). Pre-sentence reports contain a very large amount of information about defendants. Repeated arrests and charges require updates to be made in these documents. However, some fields of information – such as experienced abuse, gang involvement, and family information – may be overwritten with each new charge (Johansson and Kempf-Leonard, 2009). This can obviously cause relevant information about the individual to be lost. Lastly, official records are often not kept in a format that is easy to turn into data and may require a great deal of time to be organized and formatted in a usable way (Piquero et al., 2014).

Self-report methods

Self-report surveys collect a range of offending and victimization experiences (Cantor and Lynch, 2000). These surveys can corroborate police data; but they often reveal a great deal of information unknown to law enforcement. Further, these surveys can collect contextual information about offenses and victimizations that allow researchers to better understand the incident and the individual's role in it (Cantor and Lynch, 2000).

Because of these advantages, self-report surveys are effective in understanding men's and women's pathways to offending. Self-report surveys are useful in that they collect information about childhood abuse, families, school experiences, and mental health issues (Belknap and Holsinger, 2006). This information can then be used to connect negative experiences and victimizations to offending. These negative life experiences may be related to offending behaviors but may not be present in official records or fully known to the professionals who work with children, young adults, or adults (Belknap and Holsinger, 2006).

One example of the use of self-report data is a survey of incarcerated men and women about their experienced abuse, housing accommodations, mental illness, family contextual information, and other relevant issues (Van Voorhis et al., 2008). Assessment tools of this type measure challenges in women on probation, in incarcerated women, and in incarcerated women who are nearing institutional release. Assessment surveys are available to researchers, provided they register with the University of Cincinnati Division of Criminal Justice (see University of Cincinnati, 2014).

In their study of women probationers' pathways to incarceration, Salisbury and Van Voorhis (2009) used this kind of assessment tool to survey women in the Missouri Department of corrections. The researchers used a path-analytic approach to explain three statistically significant pathways to criminal involvement. The first, the childhood victimization model, found that childhood victimization is an indirect influence on later criminality. Childhood trauma is significantly associated with mental health problems and substance use, both of which are directly linked to offending. The second model, the relational model, finds that low self-esteem and low self-efficacy, current mental health issues, and ongoing substance abuse issues are all statistically significant pathways to women's criminal involvement. The last model, the social and human capital model, finds that, when structural challenges such as low education, family support, and self-efficacy are combined with dysfunctional intimate relationships, women are more likely to experience difficulties with employment and finances. This can ultimately lead to criminal behavior (Salisbury and Van Voorhis, 2009). Salisbury and Van Voorhis's (2009) quantitative models reiterate the findings of previous qualitative studies, but do so with significant causal power.

Causally linking gendered life experiences and victimization to future offending can be difficult in working with preexisting data sets where the data were not collected for that particular purpose (Hagan, 1997). However, there are many benefits to using self-report data in pathways research. Most importantly, individuals can indicate experiences that may not be reflected in official records because the offenses were not reported to police, or because they were simply entered without any information about duration, extent of abuse, source of abuse, and so on, which may be relevant to the participant's future criminal involvement (Hagan, 1997). Large-scale self-report surveys can also be representative of populations, whether these are communities, states, or countries (Hagan, 1997). Lastly, preexisting data sets that are publicly available make pathways research accessible to researchers who cannot afford to conduct a lengthy survey in a large population (Hagan, 1997).

But, as indicated above, there are also drawbacks to applying available data sets to pathways research. Surveys in general can be inaccurate in that are subject to the participant's memory and honesty during survey completion (Hagan, 1997). Also, not all surveys that collect information about childhood experiences can be used to test causality in cases of adult offending (Hagan, 1997). It can be difficult to find available data sets for use in pathways research.

Ethnographic studies

In extensive qualitative interviews with men and women, critical life events can be identified as explanations of criminal behavior (Bloom et al., 2003; Jacobs and Miller, 1998; Maher and Daly, 1996; Morgan and Joe, 1996; Sterk, 1999). Participants can explain their life events, how they happened, how these events impacted them and those around them, and what the collateral consequences were for the participants' criminal behavior.

Life events calendars are respondent-driven life histories marked by personal events, achievements, physical location, employment, school, or other such milestones of one's life (Glasner and van der Vaart, 2009; Hanks and Carr, 2008). Life events calendars improve the reliability and validity of self-report data by helping respondents gain access to long-term memories, place memories and events in chronological order, and use accessible memories to increase recall of other, related memories (Glasner and van der Vaart, 2009).

Kruttschnitt and Carbone-Lopez (2006) utilized life events calendars in their study of violent female offenders in order to contextualize incarcerated women's experiences with violent offending and victimization for the three years prior to their incarceration. Life events calendars help anchor the women's memories around memorable events. Kruttschnitt and Carbone-Lopez concluded that women use violence for a number of reasons, such as feeling jealousy, experiencing disrespect, acting in retaliation, and so on. However, rather than being introduced to violence and violent offending by their male partners, many women are enraged by their words or actions and use violence to physically attack their boyfriends or husbands. This is an interesting stretch of pathways theory in that it claims that women are engaging in criminal offending because of their male partners but use violence against, rather than with, the men (Kruttschnitt and Carbone-Lopez, 2006).

Life events calendars are relatively simple to use in data collection. The instrument's layout varies across disciplines but ultimately has a universal function: to give the respondent the ability to enter landmark events or behaviors and aid recall in the interest of obtaining additional details around that information (Glaser and van der Vaart, 2009). The appearance can be as simple as a straight horizontal line starting at a particular date or event of interest – or at birth (Hanks and Carr, 2008). Or the calendar can consist of two columns with unlimited rows; participants are to fill in dates or key events in the left column and contextual information in the right column (Morash, Stevens, Yingling, 2014). It is the visual layout itself that aids the recall and helps arrange events or behaviors in chronological order (Sutton, 2010).

In specifically investigating how women came to be involved in methamphetamine markets, researchers simply asked the women how they learned of the markets, how they gained access, what their experiences were in doing so, and who acted as their gatekeeper. Although the following examples all refer to methamphetamine markets, women – to repeat – overwhelmingly gain access to any kind of drug market through male friends and intimate partners (Carbone-Lopez and Miller, 2012; Herz, 2000; Jenkot, 2011; Kyle and Hansell, 2005; Morgan and Joe, 1996).

To understand how women methamphetamine users and sellers became involved in drug use and market roles, Morgan and Joe (1996) conducted a qualitative study spanning three cities and nearly 500 female participants. By using in-depth interviews, the researchers were able to rebuild the social reality of the participants and understand their motives and choices. Further, Morgan and Joe examine the lifestyle context of their participants – linking how the women view their lifestyle and how that intersects with their market entry, drug use, and market involvement. Women by and large entered methamphetamine markets through men; but unique to this study is the high number of women whose drug-dealing careers spanned decades and existed outside of men. This is one of the few studies where females hold high-level positions in a drug market and operate it freely.

In an ethnographic study on active female crack users, Sterk (1999) combines participant observation, informal conversations, group discussions, focus groups, and in-depth interviews with 150 women. Through all these data collection methods Sterk gains information about drug use in early life, negative experiences with teachers and parents, the influence of boyfriends and friends' boyfriends, and the women's experiences with violence throughout childhood, adolescence, and adulthood. By triangulating data through the various methods, Sterk identifies the numerous negative experiences of poor treatment, abuse, neglect, and peer influence and pressure that account for women's current use of crack cocaine.

In their study of methamphetamine-using women, Carbone-Lopez and Miller (2012) find that a few women link their past victimizations to their current drug use, regarding it as a cause. But what is a more predominant pathway to methamphetamine use is an early embodiment of adult roles. Specifically, women who became parents as teenagers, acted as caregivers to siblings, lived independently from their families, and by andlarge associated with older peers and partners were given opportunities to experiment with methamphetamine through these roles.

In another triangulated study of offending, Hutchings (2014) interviewed hackers in Australia in order to understand entry into computer crime networks. She first conducted a qualitative analysis of court documents and sentencing remarks for computer crime offenders in Australia, the United Kingdom, the United States, and New Zealand, in order to identify the size and scope of computer-based offending and its perpetrators' involvement in organized crime. Hutchings supplemented this information with in-depth interviews with Australian hackers in order to understand how they became involved in computer-based crimes and how they carried out their offenses. While this is largely a male-dominated field, Hutchings did not interview any females for the in-depth qualitative segment of her research. However, the male participants did report a few different methods of getting involved. Some got involved through other criminal acts. They had stolen some property with identity information on it and wanted to profit off it online; therefore they sought out mentors who could show them how to steal someone's identity. A second way to become involved in computer-hacking crime is to be recruited through online hacking or coding portals (Hutchings, 2004). Those with hacking skills would seek out online portals to talk about their abilities or to learn more. Of course simply having the ability to hack does not guarantee illicit activities. But criminally motivated hackers would actively recruit hackers from these sites in order to employ them on certain illicit missions (Hutchings, 2014).

The advantages to using ethnographic studies in examining pathways theory are relatively consistent with qualitative research in general and include the ability for researchers to present findings and patterns within the context of the participant's experiences (Opdenakker, 2006). This is necessary if one is to capture the complexities of offending and men's and women's movements in and out of illicit activities. Qualitative research also allows individuals to give their personal accounts of their actions, which may or may not be consistent with the official records (Opdenakker, 2006). Regardless of whether or not their accounts may match official records, how they perceive their victimization or treatment may drive their behaviors more than the actual experiences (Opdenakker, 2006). Lastly, qualitative research allows researchers to ask probing or follow-up questions so as to ensure that an understanding as near complete as possible is gathered about an event or a person's life (Opdenakker, 2006).

Disadvantages include problems commonly associated with qualitative research: it is time-consuming and not representative, it typically requires small sample sizes, and it can be expensive (Opdenakker, 2006). It also assumes a high level of honesty from the participant and is subject to his or her recall of personal experiences on the researcher's topics of interest (Opdenakker, 2006). Specifically related to conducting time-consuming interviews with victimized, criminally active, or impoverished women (or participants in general) is the burden of participating. Burgess-Proctor (2012) describes numerous problems she experienced while recruiting women in a particularly low-income area. Simply getting to the interview site could be an ordeal that requires the participant to learn public transportation routes, find transportation, and obtain money for transportation. A number of women could either not find childcare or not afford to pay for it, and thus could not participate (their children, if present, would have been too much of a distraction). Burgess-Proctor also documented women's inability to take time off work to participate in an interview despite receiving (moderate) compensation. Assisting women in making these preparations for the interview may be necessary for the sake of ensuring participation.

Suggestions for Future Development

Great strides have been made in the understanding of pathways theory and the various influences of childhood victimization and other negative experiences on male and female offending. The study of pathways theory is moving in several interesting directions. Burgess-Proctor (2012) extended the theory to determine whether the victims' actions related to victimization vary according to past victimizations. She conducted interviews with women who have sought help with intimate partner violence at a local shelter to determine whether the presence or type of childhood victimization affected their coping strategies (Burgess-Proctor, 2012). Ultimately, and not surprisingly, childhood victimizations reduce the effectiveness of one's coping strategies and the likelihood that the women will seek help regarding their abusive partner (Burgess-Proctor, 2012).

Using official records or self-report surveys can reveal a great deal of information; yet there are a number of shortcomings too (see above). To continue to advance pathways theory, there is a move toward utilizing multiple data sources or mixed methods research designs (Brennan et al., 2012; Burgess-Proctor, 2006; Chesney-Lind, 2006; Daly and Chesney-Lind, 1988). Mixed method approaches offer researchers a more complete understanding of past and current victimizations, past and current criminal offending, and nuanced gender differences (Wattanaporn and Holtfreter, 2014).

Lastly, pathways theory can be further expanded by examining within-gender rather than between-gender differences (Wattanaporn and Holtfreter, 2014). Male and female gender differences have been well documented, but pathways theory can truly advance by further exploring their nuances among girls and women (Wattanaporn and Holtfreter, 2014).

Intersectionality

While examining gender differences and similarities is important to feminist and pathways research, it does not capture the nuances of the participants' experiences or social inequality (Andersen, 2005, 2008; Collins, 1990; Crenshaw, 1991). Intersectionality is a perspective that understands that people have multiple roles and identities – such as race, ethnicity, gender, class, ability, religion, language, income, occupation, and sexuality, among others (Andersen, 2005, 2008; Collins, 1990; Crenshaw, 1991). It is impossible to discuss one's role as a woman without taking into consideration her identity as white, disabled, and heterosexual, for example. Therefore grouping individuals into categories of male or female often excludes the other complex factors operating in their lives. This is particularly relevant in research involving the criminal justice system, as inequities exist at each stage of the system (Cole, 1999).

This approach is related to pathways research in that race, ethnicity, and class, among other factors, may influence a child's experiences of entering the juvenile justice system, of being placed in foster care, of receiving community sanctions, and of facing detention. Johansson and Kempf-Leonard (2009) examined racial differences (categorized under "white," "African American," and "Hispanic") in their study of court records and of how childhood experiences predict adult offending. They found that, within their sample of juveniles with substance abuse problems and who spent time in foster care or in an institutional group home, African American and

Hispanic boys were more likely to offend than white boys. However, when controlling for socioeconomic status at the neighborhood level, the race effects are minimized, which suggests that what might really be linking these negative childhood experiences to later offenses is poverty (Johansson and Kempf-Leonard, 2009).

While these social factors are largely representative of individuals in the western context, other factors, such as poverty, contribute to individuals' pathways to offending (Erez and Berko, 2010). When examining such pathways in a larger context, it is important to consider the influence of culture and caste at intersections. The unique ways in which these factors exist within strict patriarchal societies and lead to criminal behavior through poverty and arranged marriages are examined in the next section (see Cherukuri, Britton, and Subramaniam, 2009; Erez and Berko, 2010; Khalid and Khan, 2013; Sadeghi-Fassaei and Kendall, 2001).

International research

International research provides a unique context to pathways theory, as culture shapes the different ways in which women are exposed to crime and offending. One such study examines the different pathways to crime for Arab and Palestinian women who are serving time in an Israeli prison (Erez and Berko, 2010). Arab and Palestinian women divulge vastly different reasons and pathways to offending from those of women in western countries. Erez and Berko conducted in-depth interviews with women incarcerated in Israeli prisons, law enforcement and correctional staff, and Arab and Palestinian community leaders in order to capture the context of cultural and patriarchal constraints.

Erez and Berko identify three pathways that lead Arab and Palestinian women to crime and imprisonment. The first is abusive homes and the women's attempts to resist gender oppression. Most of the incarcerated women had histories of domestic abuse, which was often used to enforce harsh patriarchal gender roles. For example, girls were often forced to marry men they did not want to, and at young ages. Additionally, parents would ignore their young daughters' claims of molestation by a brother or abuse by fiancé. Acknowledging this or altering the engagement plans would bring shame to the family. The incarcerated women discuss their acts of rebellion, running away, attacking, or having others attack their abuser by way of explaining their criminal actions. The second pathway to crime and imprisonment is association with criminal men or forbidden potential mates. Girls or women who broke gender norms in their behavior or actions, particularly norms involving sexuality, were punished. If it was discovered that women were not "pure" – that is, virgins – upon their wedding night (which was often due to past molestation or rape), those women could be subjected to abuse, forced prostitution, or abandonment by their husbands or families. When presented with this situation, many girls then left home and forged their own way, often with older men, and engaged in crime to survive. Common offenses included stealing cars, robberies, and drug use. The last pathway to crime revealed by incarcerated Arab and Palestinian women is managing family honor expectations, as they reflect the cultural and patriarchal demands. Two women, a mother and a daughter, describe the difficult situation in which they found themselves. The mother was instructed by her incarcerated husband to honor-kill their 17-year-old daughter with the help of their 30-year-old daughter, on the grounds that the former's actions were continually inconsistent with family expectations. The father planned the killing from prison and received a small punishment for his role. The mother and her older daughter, however, received a lengthy sentence for their actions (Erez and Berko, 2010).

Research examining pathways to crime in other countries, like Iran (Sadeghi-Fassaei and Kendall, 2001), Pakistan (Khalid and Khan, 2013), and India (Cherukuri et al., 2009), reveals different stressors plaguing women: poverty. In India, nearly all of the women incarcerated in the women's prison in Tehran were from the lower caste and had been arrested for survival offenses, such as drug smuggling, prostitution, fraud, and forgery (Sadeghi-Fassaei and Kendall, 2001). Similarly, women interviewed in Indian and Pakistani prisons link their criminal behavior to their economic marginalization (Cherukuri et al., 2009; Khalid and Khan, 2013). Women were separated or divorced, often as a result of husband abuse, and engaged in a number of offenses to support themselves and their children (Cherukuri et al., 2009; Khalid and Khan, 2013).

Women in Israel (Erez and Berko, 2010), Iran (Sadeghi-Fassaei and Kendall, 2001), and India (Cherukuri et al., 2009) trace their pathways to crime back to lashing out at an abusive husband. Without their husbands abusing them to breaking point, these women may not have offended. However, women in India also attribute their involvement in criminal activity to the enforcement of strict gender roles and patriarchy, to which the Israeli women in Erez and Berko's (2010) study also found themselves victims (Cherukuri et al., 2009). Women incarcerated in India, acting in their role as mothers-in-law or sisters-in-law, killed a bride or harassed her family as a result of the imposed demand for a dowry (Cherukuri et al., 2009). They overwhelmingly denied the homicide with which they were charged, claiming that the bride died due to an accident, an illness, or suicide (Cherukuri et al., 2009). It is important to understand the cultural nuances that caste systems, arranged marriages, early marriages, and dowries can have on how women become involved in criminal offending. When such women are asked about the factors that led them to offending, these matters take precedence in their minds over childhood victimization, substance use, and other factors found in western research.

Policy implications

The often gendered results of pathways theory studies have clear policy implications. Because juveniles who are peripherally involved in the system, and especially those who are detained, incur an increased risk of subsequent criminal behavior (Johansson and Kempf-Leonard, 2009), the juvenile justice system could reform to better meet the needs of youth involved in it. Transitioning to probation only or restorative justice practices may reduce future offending. A second natural implication stemming from pathways research is the updating and revising of standardized intake forms. These forms can better meet the needs of the individuals in a particular treatment or detention facility when they ask appropriately about proven factors that influence later offending behaviors (Daly, 1992, 1994; Johansson and Kempf-Leonard, 2009).

Lastly, Burgess-Proctor (2012) conducted a study on how past victimization experience influences whether (and how) women who are in abusive relationships seek help. After finding a few mechanisms (e.g., learned silence, lowered self-worth, learned withdrawal) through which childhood victimization causes a decrease in women's attempts to seek help, she calls for service care providers, shelters, counselors, and therapists to understand this link, so that past and current victimization may be treated (Burgess-Proctor, 2012). Further, counselors and therapists with young patients who have experienced victimization can discuss the increased likelihood of victimization and offending later in life, in order to try and counteract that trend (Burgess-Proctor, 2012).

References

Andersen, M. L. 2005. Thinking about women: A quarter century's view. *Gender & Society*, 19: 437–455.

Andersen, M. L. 2008. Thinking about women some more: A new century's view. *Gender & Society*, 22: 120–125.

Belknap, J. 2007. *Invisible woman: Gender, crime and justice*, 3rd edn. Belmont, CA: Thompson Wadsworth.

Belknap, J., and Holsinger, K. 2006. The gendered nature of risk factors for delinquency. *Feminist Criminology*, 1 (1): 4 8–71. doi: 10.1177/1557085105282897.

Belknap, J., Holsinger, K., and Dunn, M. 1997. Understanding incarcerated girls: The results of a focus group study. *The Prison Journal*, 77 (4): 381–404. doi: 10.1177/0032855597077004003.

Bloom, B., Owen, B., Covington, S., and Raeder, M. 2002. Gender-responsive strategies: Research, practice, and guiding principles for women offenders. National Institute of Corrections, October. Accessed December 15, 2015. https://s3.amazonaws.com/static.nicic.gov/Library/018017.pdf.

Bloom, B., Owen, B., Covington, S., and Raeder, M. 2003. Gender responsive strategies: Research, practice, and guiding principles for women offenders. Washington, DC: US Department of Justice, National Institute of Corrections.

Brennan, T., Breitennach, M., Dieterich, W., Salisbury, E. J., and Van Voorhis, P. 2012. Women's pathways to serious and habitual crime: A person-centered analysis incorporating gender responsive factors. *Criminal Justice and Behavior*, 39: 1481–1508.

Briere, J. 1996. *Therapy for adults molested as children*, 2nd edn. New York: Springer.

Browne, A., and Finkelhor, D. 1986. Impact of child sexual abuse: A review of the research. *Psychological Bulletin*, 99 (1): 66–77. doi: 10.1037/0033–2909.99.1.66.

Browne, A., Miller, B., and Maguin, E. 1999. Prevalence and severity of lifetime physical and sexual victimization among incarcerated women. *International Journal of Law and Psychiatry*, 22 (3–4): 301–322. doi: 10.1016/S0160–2527(99)00011–4.

Burgess-Proctor, A. 2006. Intersections of race, class, gender, and crime: Future directions for feminist criminology. *Feminist Criminology*, 1: 27–47.

Burgess-Proctor, A. 2012. Pathways of victimization and resistance: Toward a feminist theory of battered women's help-seeking. *Justice Quarterly*, 29 (3): 309–346.

Byrne, C. F., and Trew, K. J. 2008. Pathways through crime: The development of crime and desistance in the accounts of men and women offenders. *The Howard Journal of Criminal Justice*, 47 (3): 238–258. doi: 10.1111/j.1468–2311.2008.00520.x.

Cantor, D., and Lynch, J. P. 2000. Self-report surveys as measures of crime and criminal victimization. *Criminal Justice*, 4: 85–138.

Carbone-Lopez, K., and Miller, J. 2012. Precocious role entry as a mediating factor in women's methamphetamine use: Implications for life-course and pathways research. *Criminology*, 50 (1): 187–220.

Cherukuri, S, Britton, D. M., and Subramaniam, M. 2009. Between life and death: Women in an Indian state prison. *Feminist Criminology*, 4: 252–274.

Chesney-Lind, M. 1997. *The female offender: Girls, women, and crime*. Thousand Oaks, CA: Sage.

Chesney-Lind, M. 2006. Patriarchy, crime, and justice: Feminist criminology in an era of backlash. *Feminist Criminology*, 1: 6–26.

Chesney-Lind, M., and Irwin, K. 2007. *Beyond bad girls: Gender, violence and hype*. New York: Routledge.

Chesney-Lind, M., and Shelden, R. G. 2004. *Girls, delinquency, and juvenile justice*, 3rd edn. Belmont, CA: Wadsworth/Thomson Learning.

Chu, J. A. 1998. *Rebuilding shattered lives: The responsible treatment of complex post-traumatic and dissociative disorders*. New York: John Wiley & Sons.

Cole, D. 1999. *No equal justice: Race and class in the American criminal justice system*. New York: New Press.

Coleman-Davis, V. F., and Forde, D. R. 2007. *Pathways from dependency and neglect to delinquency. Part II: Final report*. NCJ 220288. Washington, DC: United States Department of Justice, National Institute of Justice.

Coleman-Davis, V. F., and Forde, D. R. 2010. *Pathways from dependency and neglect to delinquency in a mid-south county in the United States, 1984–1985 and 2000–2001*. January 29, ICPSR21185-v1. Ann Arbor, MI: Inter-University Consortium for Political and Social Research [distributor]. http://doi.org/10.3886/ICPSR21185.v1.

Collins, P. H. 1990. *Black feminist thought: Knowledge, consciousness, and the politics of empowerment*. New York: Routledge.

Covington, S. 1998. The relational theory of women's psychological development: Implications for the criminal justice system. In *Female offenders: Critical perspectives and effective interventions*, edited by R. Zaplin, 113–128. Gaithersburg, MD: Aspen.

Crenshaw, K. 1991. Mapping the margins: Intersectionality, identity politics, and violence against women of color. *Stanford Law Review*, 43: 1241–1299.

Daly, K. 1992. Women's pathways to felony court: Feminist theories of lawbreaking and problems of representation. *Southern California Review of Law and Women's Studies*, 2: 11–52.

Daly, K. 1994. *Gender, crime, and punishment*. New Haven, CT: Yale University Press.

Daly, K. 1996. *Gender, crime, and punishment: Is justice gender-blind, or are men and women offenders treated differently by the courts?* New Haven, CT: Yale University Press.

Daly, K., and Chesney-Lind, M. 1988. Feminism and criminology. *Justice Quarterly*, 5: 497–538.

Dembo, R., Williams, L., Wothke, W., Schmeidler, J., and Brown, C. H. 1992. The role of family factors, physical abuse, and sexual victimization experiences in high-risk youths' alcohol and other drug use and delinquency: A longitudinal model. *Violence and Victims*, 7 (3): 245–266.

Dunlap, E., Johnson, B. D., and Maher, L. 1997. Female crack sellers in New York City. *Women & Criminal Justice*, 8 (4): 25–55. doi: 10.1300/J012v08n04_02.

Erez, E., and Berko, A. 2010. Pathways of Arab/Palestininan women in Israel to crime and imprisonment: An intersectional approach. *Feminist Criminology*, 5 (2): 156–194.

Evans, R. D., Forsyth, C. J., and Gauthier, D. K. 2002. Gendered pathways into and experiences within crack cultures outside of the inner city. *Deviant Behavior*, 23 (6): 483–510. doi: 10.1080/01639620290086468.

Farr, K. A. 2000. Classification for female inmates: Moving forward. *Crime & Delinquency*, 46: 3–15.

Finkelhor, D. 1994. Current information on the scope and nature of child sexual abuse. *The Future of Children*, 4 (2): 31–53.

Funk, S. J. 1999. Risk assessment for juveniles on probation: A focus on gender. *Criminal Justice and Behavior*, 26 (1): 44–68. doi: 10.1177/0093854899026001003.

Gaarder, E., and Belknap, J. 2002. Tenuous borders: Girls transferred to adult court. *Criminology*, 40 (3): 481–517. doi: 10.1111/j.1745-9125.2002.tb00964.x.

Gavazzi, S. M., Yarcheck, C. M., and Chesney-Lind, M. 2006. Global risk indicators and the role of gender in a juvenile detention sample. *Criminal Justice and Behavior*, 33 (5): 597–612. doi: 10.1177/0093854806288184.

Gilfus, M. E. 1993. From victims to survivors to offenders: Women's routes of entry and immersion into street crime. *Women & Criminal Justice*, 4 (1): 63–89. doi: 10.1300/J012v04n01_04.

Glasner, T., and van der Vaart, W. 2009. Applications of calendar instruments in social surveys: A review. *Quality & Quantity*, 43 (3): 333–349. doi: 10.1007/s11135-007-9129-8.

Hagan, F. E. 1997. *Research methods in criminal justice and criminology*. Needham Heights, MA: Allyn and Bacon.

Hanks, R. S., and Carr, N. T. 2008. Lifelines of women in jail as self-constructed visual probes for life history research. *Marriage & Family Review*, 42: 105–116.

Herz, D. C. 2000. Drugs in the heartland: Methamphetamine use in rural Nebraska. National Institute of Justice. Accessed December 15, 2015. http://www.ncjrs.gov/pdffiles1/nij/180986.pdf.

Holsinger, K. 2000. Feminist perspectives on female offending: Examining real girls' lives. *Women & Criminal Justice*, 12 (1): 23–51. doi: 10.1300/J012v12n01_03.

Holtfreter, K., and Morash, M. 2003. The needs of women offenders. *Women & Criminal Justice*, 14 (2–3): 137–160. doi: 10.1300/J012v14n02_07.

Homma, Y., Wang, N., Saewyc, E., and Kishor, N. 2012. The relationship between sexual abuse and risky sexual behavior among adolescent boys: A meta-analysis. *Journal of Adolescent Health*, 51: 18–24.

Hutchings, A. 2014. Crime from the keyboard: Organised cybercrime, co-offending, initiation and knowledge transmission. *Crime, Law, and Social Change*, 62: 1–20.

Jacobs, B. A., and Miller, J. 1998. Crack dealing, gender, and arrest avoidance. *Social Problems*, 45 (4): 550–569. doi: 10.2307/3097212.

Jenkot, R. 2011. "Cooks are like gods": Hierarchies in methamphetamine-producing groups. *Deviant Behavior*, 29 (8): 667–689.

Johansson, P., and Kempf-Leonard, K. 2009. A gender-specific pathway to serious, violent, and chronic offending? Exploring Howell's risk factors for serious delinquency. *Crime & Delinquency*, 55 (2): 216–240.

Khalid, A., and Khan, N. 2013. Pathways of women prisoners to jail in Pakistan. *Health Promotion Perspectives*, 3 (1): 31–35.

Kruttschnitt, C., and Carbone-Lopez, K. 2006. Moving beyond the stereotypes: Women's subjective accounts of their violent crime. *Criminology*, 44 (2): 321–351.

Kyle, M. D., and Hansell, B. 2005. The meth epidemic in America. National Association of Counties. Accessed December 15, 2015. http://www.csdp.org/news/news/naco_meth_2005.pdf.

Macallair, D. 2008. The history of the pre-sentence investigation report. Center on Juvenile and Criminal Justice. Accessed December 15, 2015. http://www.cjcj.org/uploads/cjcj/documents/the_history.pdf.

Maher, L. 1997. *Sexed work: Gender, race, and resistance in a Brooklyn drug market*. New York: Oxford.

Maher, L., and Daly, K. 1996. Women in the street-level drug economy: Continuity or change? *Criminology*, 34 (4): 465–491.

Maher, L., and Hudson, S. L. 2007. Women in the drug economy: A metasynthesis of the qualitative literature. *Journal of Drug Issues*, 37 (4): 805–826.

McClellan, D. S., Farabee, D., and Crouch, B. M. 1997. Early victimization, drug use, and criminality: A comparison of male and female prisoners. *Criminal Justice and Behavior*, 24 (4): 455–476. doi: 10.1177/0093854897024004004.

Morash, M., Stevens, T., and Yingling, J. 2014. Focus on the family: Juvenile court responses to girls and their caretakers. *Feminist Criminology*, 9 (4): 298–322.

Morgan, P., and Joe, K. A. 1996. Citizens and outlaws: The private lives and public lifestyles of women in the illicit drug economy. *Journal of Drug Issues*, 26: 125–142.

Nelson-Zlupko, L., Kauffman, E., and Morrison Dore, M. 1995. Gender differences in drug addiction and treatment: Implications for social work intervention with substance-abusing women. *Social Work*, 40 (1): 45–54.

Opdenakker, R. 2006. Advantages and disadvantages of four interview techniques in qualitative research. *Forum: Qualitative Social Research*, 7 (4). Accessed December 15, 2015. http://www.qualitative-research.net/index.php/fqs/article/view/175/391.

Piquero, A. R., Schubert, C. A., and Brame, R. 2014. Comparing official and self-report records of offending across gender and race/ethnicity in a longitudinal study of serious youthful offenders. *Journal of Research in Crime and Delinquency*, 51 (4): 526–556.

Puzzanchera, C., and Adams, B. 2011. Juvenile arrests 2009. Washington, DC: Office of Juvenile Justice and Delinquency Prevention. Accessed December 15, 2015. http://www.ojjdp.gov/pubs/236477.pdf.

Sadeghi-Fassaei, S., and Kendall, K. 2001. Iranian women's pathways to imprisonment. *Women's Studies International Forum*, 24: 701–710.

Salisbury, E. J., and Van Voorhis, P. 2009. Gendered pathways: A quantitative investigation of women probationers' paths to incarceration. *Criminal Justice and Behavior*, 36 (6): 541–566. doi: 10.1177/0093854809334076.

Salisbury, E. J., Van Voorhis, P., and Spiropoulos, G. V. 2009. The predictive validity of a gender-responsive needs assessment: An exploratory study. *Crime & Delinquency*, 55 (4): 550–585. doi: 10.1177/0011128707308102.

Sedlak, A., and Broadhurst, D. 1996. *Executive summary of the third national incidence study of child abuse and neglect*. Washington, DC: US Department of Health and Human Services.

Siegel, J. A., and Williams, L. M. 2003. The relationship between child sexual abuse and female delinquency and crime: A prospective study. *Journal of Research in Crime and Delinquency*, 40 (1): 71–94. doi: 10.1177/0022427802239254.

Steffensmeier, D, and Allan, E. 1996. Gender and crime: Toward a gendered theory of female offending. *Annual Review of Sociology*, 22: 459–487.

Sterk, C. E. 1999. *Fast lives: Women who use crack cocaine*. Philadelphia, PA: Temple University Press.

Stoltenborgh, M., van Ijzendoorn, M. H., Euser, E, M., and Bakermans-Kranenburg, M. J. 2011. A global perspective on child sexual abuse: Meta-analysis of prevalence around the world. *Child Maltreatment*, 16 (2): 79–101.

Sutton, J. E. 2010. A review of the life-events calendar method for criminology research. *Journal of Criminal Justice*, 38: 1038–1044.

University of Cincinnati. 2014. Women's risk needs assessment: About. Accessed December 15, 2015. http://www.uc.edu/womenoffenders/about.html.

van der Kolk, B. A. 1996. The complexity of adaptation to trauma: Self-regulation, stimulus discrimination, and characterological development. In *Traumatic stress: The effects of overwhelming experience on mind, body, and society*, edited by B. A. van der Kolk, A. C. McFarlane, and L. Weisaeth, 182–213. New York: Guilford.

Van Voorhis, P., Salisbury, E., Wright, E., and Bauman, A. 2008. Achieving accurate picture of risk and identifying gender-responsive needs: Two new assessments for women offenders. Washington, DC: National Institute of Corrections, US Department of Justice.

Wattanaporn, K. A., and Holtfreter, K. 2014. The impact of feminist pathways research on gender-responsive policy. *Feminist Criminology*, 9 (3): 191–207.

Widom, C. S., and Maxfield, M. G. 2001. An update on he "cycle of violence": National Institute of Justice Research in brief. US Department of Justice. Accessed December 15, 2015. http://files.eric.ed.gov/fulltext/ED451313.pdf.

Further Reading

Brecht, M.-L., O'Brien, A., von Mayrhauser, C., and Anglin, M. D. 2004. Methamphetamine use behaviors and gender differences. *Addictive Behaviors*, 29 (1): 89–106.

Roberts, J., and Horney, J. 2010. The life event calendar method in criminological research. In *Handbook of Quantitative Criminology*, edited by A. R. Piquero and D. Weisburd, 289–312. New York: Springer.

Yingling, J. 2013. *Qualitative study of pathways to involvement and law enforcement avoidance strategies in methamphetamine markets*. PhD thesis, Michigan State University, Michigan.

10

Mental Health and Physical Studies

Daryl G. Kroner and Maranda Quillen

Mental health issues and physical illness occur at substantially higher rates among those who are involved in criminal justice than among the general population. The detection of mental and physical health concerns is not a preference of optimal practice; it is required. This goal of detection is accomplished by conducting assessments of those who are criminal justice-involved. The combination of setting (i.e., confinement, security emphasis) and personal characteristics (i.e., psychosis, being confined to wheelchair) lead to unique measurement issues for mental health and physical illness. For the mental health issues, this chapter addresses the benefits of diagnostic versus dimensional measurement, the co-occurrence of mental illnesses, and methods of gathering mental health information. Studies relating to three basic types of research – classification, prevalence rates, and prediction for negative outcomes – are covered.

The section on physical illnesses will cover the difficulties in conducting measurement research, focusing on standardized data recording, screening accuracy, reduced measurement validity, and difficulties in the management of databases.

The overall goal of the chapter is to cover the current assessment practices and the shortcomings of continuing with these practices. Alternative ways of conducting assessments for mental and physical illness are suggested. The application of these recently developed methods and assessment tools will assist with basic assessment issues, but also in the evaluation of intervention and in the understanding of potential mechanisms of change. The chapter provides practical suggestions on assessment methods and instruments, and also discusses future directions that will facilitate a higher level of validity in mental health and physical assessments.

The Handbook of Measurement Issues in Criminology and Criminal Justice, First Edition.
Edited by Beth M. Huebner and Timothy S. Bynum.

Mental Health Measurement Issues

This section covers four measurement issues of diagnostic (e.g., the client "has" schizophrenia) versus dimensional models of assessing mental health, categories of offenders with mental illness, the co-occurrence of disorders (i.e., the presence of two mental health disorders), and how mental health information is recorded. The use of either diagnostic or dimensional models has direct implications for measuring intervention change and understanding causal mechanisms. Basic categories of mental illness, ranging from two to six, will be covered. Next, the measurement difficulties in using a co-occurrence framework will be reviewed. The strengths and weaknesses of using charts, ratings and self-report to gather mental health information will also be covered.

Diagnostic versus dimensional models

In the measurement of mental health, considerable debate has occurred over whether a diagnostic (present, not present) or a continuous (weak to strong indicators) method of measurement is optimal for representing a mental illness. The debate involves conceptual, statistical, and financial issues. A basic assumption of a diagnostic measurement model is to have mental illness conceptualized as being dichotomous (i.e., the prototype of a disorder) rather than along a continuum. A dimensional model recognizes that the underlying structure falls along a continuum, representing exemplars that are important facets of a homogeneous construct (Blackburn and Coid, 1999). A dichotomous model has benefits for communicating mental health issues (e.g., the presence of mental illness: Engel and Silver, 2001). The use of diagnoses allows for a simple, shorthand way of communicating potentially complex phenomena. This can simplify the presentation of research, which results in an easier understanding of the results (Farrington and Loeber, 2000). Some diagnoses, such as schizophrenia, have been well researched, which can help indicate behavioral actions and reactions in multiple contexts. Also, communication with diagnoses allows for determining the rates of mental illness. This brings organization to a criminal justice population that could have many possible permutations of psychopathology with cumbersome criteria (Hersen, 1988).

Statistically, one of the arguments levied against a diagnostic measurement model is the potential reduction of the relationship strength. Dichotomizing variables or a variable in a relationship of normally distributed variables will reduce the maximum potential Pearson correlation to about 0.81 (MacLennan, 1988). This observed relationship is restricted (maximum potential ~0.81), even though the underlying relationship is potentially perfect. Not only will the underlying relationship be underestimated; if the occurrence of the rate of the dichotomous variable is low (e.g., has few of "one" in a variable made up only of zeros and ones), the relationship will be even more restricted. In this case, the entire range of correlations will be compressed. An assumption of correlation is that the two variables involved have the same variance. With a dichotomous variable (with its restrictive variance) and a continuous variance (which can have a variance of any value), the assumption of equal variances is always violated. Hence the correlation is also restricted. The reporting of zero-ordered relationships may better occur through a tetrachoric correlation (Farrington and Loeber, 2000). The tetrachoric correlation assumes that there is an underlying continuous variable in the dichotomous observed variable. The tetrachoric correlation estimates the correlation between the assumed underlying continuous variables. Thus the potential reduction of strength is not necessarily a valid criticism against using diagnostic categories.

Even with these potential benefits of using a diagnostic measurement model, the gains of using a dimensional model are greater, at least from a measurement perspective (Livesley, Jackson, and Schroeder, 1992). A potential benefit of dimensional measures is having the full continuum of a phenomenon available for analyses (Beal, Kroner, and Weekes, 2003). Even with this potential strength, it is possible to have the continuous distribution not representing a normal or near normal distribution. This would limit the number of statistical techniques available for analysis. But, given the proliferation of mental illness measures that have multiple stages of development with various norming procedures, the number of measures that, for psychometric reasons, do not have a normal distribution (limited low and high scores) has been greatly reduced. In addition, the area of behavioral assessment on mental illness has emphasized observable, precise measurement of symptoms (Lachar et al., 2001). The benefits of a dimensional model are its assessment of severity, its potential for greater scope of information, and its ability to measure change over time – all of which are described below.

Assessment of severity Measuring psychopathology along a continuum recognizes that mental illness varies according to severity. Mental illness characteristics can range from occurrence in a "normal" offender to very severe expression (Coolidge et al., 2011; Persons, 1986). Among offenders with mental illness, measurement along a continuum has been done for the personality disorders of psychopathy (Blackburn, 2007) and antisocial personality (Blackburn, 2007), and for avoidant and schizoid conditions (Blackburn et al., 2004). The diagnostic measurement model cannot account for those offenders who are just below the criteria for a diagnosis. Cases that do not meet the formal diagnostic criteria are referred to as "subclinical," yet many of them will still present the clinical features of those with a diagnosis. For example, antisocial traits will be present in many who have personality disorder symptoms but do not meet all of the criteria for antisocial personality disorder (Blackburn et al., 1990). Thus a main benefit of measuring mental illness along a continuum is that the severity of dysfunction (i.e., the degree of symptomatology: Silver, 2000) can be assessed – rather than solely its presence or absence.

Potential for greater scope of information A diagnostic measurement model will limit its potential to research phenomena that are relevant to mental illness. There are four reasons for this limitation. First, there is considerable overlap among the diagnostic categories, which reduces the independent precision of a diagnostic category. Second, apart from definitional concerns, there is little substantive evidence that mental illness categories are natural, discrete entities. Third, multiple aetiological forces occur in a single diagnostic category (biological versus social cause of depression), which suggests that what is causal for one person may not be causal for another, even though the same categorial label is being used. Fourth, the emphasis in the development of diagnostic measurement models has been on temporal reliability rather than on validity. These four limiting characteristics of diagnostic categories reduce the precision and potential of intervention research on understanding new mechanisms of change among offenders with mental illness. An additional benefit of using a dimensional measurement model is that scales can be dichotomized. The setting of the cutscores can be changed according to tolerances and policies and then evaluated (Edens and Ruiz, 2008).

Intervention research A major contribution of examining mental health within the criminal justice system is to provide future guidance, ranging from the delivery of individual services to public policy. Given the negative consequences of mental illness and the legal requirements to intervene, most criminal justice systems will make efforts at intervention. The use of diagnostic categories poorly informs intervention efforts, which typically treat specific behaviors rather than broad diagnoses. As a consequence of the four limitations of diagnoses noted above, there is no one-to-one congruence between a diagnostic category and effective interventions. Additional information beyond diagnosis is needed for determining interventions (Hersen, 1988; Wulff, 1986).

In intervention research, dimensional measures allow for the detection of treatment change. An intervention that appropriately addresses mental health concerns can expect to find reductions in the putative measures. For example, an area of impulsiveness, as measured on the Eysenck Personality Scales, has been found to show reductions among British offenders (Shuker and Newton, 2008).

In addition to the use of dimension measures, one advancement in measuring intervention effectiveness has been the use of reliable change indexes. Typically pre-treatment measures are compared to post-treatment measures, which may capture multiple sources of a change, including measurement error. A Reliable Change Index (RCI) indicates what percentage of the group demonstrates meaningful change between pre- and post-testing, the change being higher than what could be attributed to measurement error. A modified RCI was developed by Christensen and Mendoza (1986). The calculations are as follows. First, the standard error of measurement for the pre-testing scores, S_E, was computed with the standardized coefficient alpha (the test–retest coefficient can be used), r_{xx}, and s_1, the standard deviation:

$$S_E = s_1\sqrt{1 - r_{xx}}$$

The standard error of measurement (S_E) was then used to calculate the standard error of the difference (S_{diff}).

$$S_{diff} = \sqrt{2(S_E)^2}$$

The S_{diff} was the denominator for the difference between the pre-testing (x_1) and the post-testing (x_2) scores.

$$RCI = \frac{x_2 - x_1}{S_{diff}}$$

When the RCI is 1.96 or greater, the difference between pre- and post-scores is statistically significant (95 percent confidence interval) and indicative of meaningful change (Wise, 2004). It is the instrument's reliability that is integrated into the statistic, and hence the less reliable the instrument, the greater the pre- and post-differences that are necessary to obtain statistically reliable change. Offenders with RCI scores of greater than 1.96 are considered to be "recovered" by Wise (2004), and have been incorporated in intervention studies among offenders with mental illness (Newton, 1998; Shuker and Newton, 2008; Tapp et al., 2009: British studies). The reported matrix commonly is the percentage of the sample that obtained reliable change index scores above 1.96. For mental health symptom measures, the percentage over 1.96 has ranged from 4.0 percent to 54.5 percent (Morgan et al., 2014: USA study). For social skills, the percentage over 1.96 has ranged from 4.0 percent to 42.6 percent (Chakhssi, de Ruiter, and Bernstein, 2010; Tapp et al., 2009: British studies).

Although the use of RCI is an advancement, there are two potential limitations to routinely incorporating it into studies. First, there is a lack of usage of standardized instruments. In a review of intervention studies in forensic mental health, it appeared that only 13 percent of the studies used a standardized instrument (Chambers et al., 2009). Second, incarceration can result in the decrease of mental illness (Hassan et al., 2012). Thus there is a downward trend of mental illness without specific interventions.

Understanding new mechanisms The use of causal mechanisms is essential to understanding the role of mental illness among offenders, and specifically the relationship between violence and mental illness (Harris and Lurigio, 2007). Solely using a broad measure of serious mental illness, or even specific diagnostic categories, may have limited contributions to the understanding of an illness or its relationship with an outcome such as violence. For example, delusion-related hallucinations have been shown to be related to violent outcomes, but this crime-based motivation is not captured in a diagnosis (Arboleda-Flórez, 1998; Junginger and McGuire, 2004). In a Norway study, a broad measure of serious mental illness was not related to past crime (Friestad and Hansen, 2005). Focusing on context-specific symptoms such as motivation allows for an easier approach to formulating hypotheses about underlying mechanisms and for a tighter link between measurement and potential mechanisms (Persons, 1986). Without information beyond the diagnosis, relationships with criminal justice outcomes are minimal.

Among offenders, the type of diagnosis has no significant relationship with the types of crimes (Ferguson, Ogloff, and Thomson, 2009). More specifically, among schizophrenic homicide offenders, the type of delusions or hallucinations did not predict the use of excessive violence (Laajasalo and Häkkänen, 2006). Among offenders with mental illness, higher rates of violence are not associated with specific interpersonal styles (Blackburn, 1998). These findings reinforce the position of research as being offender-focused, and not solely offense-focused (Blackburn, 2004).

Categories of mental illness among offenders

The categories of mental illness encountered among offenders have ranged from two to five. A traditional division into two categories – psychiatric mental disorders and personality disorders – has some support, as it reflects differences in quality of life (Bouman et al., 2008). But most of the measurement research among offenders and offenders with mental illness suggests that this is a false dichotomy. Only a small minority of offenders with a mental illness will not have personality disorders, and only a small minority of offenders with personality disorders will not have a mental illness. In other words, the overlap is so strong that the distinction between these two categories is almost meaningless. These results are obtained with multiple instruments and with both interview and self-report methods of measurement (Blackburn et al., 2003). A prominent two-category conceptualization has placed mental illness along internalizing (anxiety, depression) and externalizing (conduct problems, substance abuse) dimensions. Among offenders, evidence for the internalizing and externalizing categories has been gathered through a variety of methodological studies. Methods have included factor analysis (Ruiz and Edens, 2008), structured equation modeling (Blonigen et al., 2010), and relationships with similar variables (internalizing having a strong inverse relationship with warmth: see Edens, 2009).

Other conceptual categories have been proposed within the criminal justice system. Rationally derived categories, coming from nonoffender literature, have been suggested for the offender population. Categories of mood, psychotic spectrum, and substance use have been proposed (Edens and Riuz, 2008). These categories had adequate convergent and divergent validity with corresponding self-report measures. Hodgins and Gaston (1989) proposed the existence of five groups among a sample of offenders with mental illness: (1) career criminals, who had one acute disorder episode; (2) violent psychotics, who committed crimes only during a psychotic episode; (3) chronic schizophrenics, who committed predominantly minor crimes; (4) crimes of passion, committed by middle-class men with no history of mental disorder; and (5) intellectually handicapped patients. These five groups differed on the three criminal justice outcomes of length of sentences, number of violent crimes, and severity of violent crimes. Career criminals and intellectually handicapped people had longer sentences than chronic schizophrenics, violent psychotics, and people in the crimes of passion group. The intellectually handicapped group registered the greatest number of violent crimes. The intellectually handicapped, the violent psychotics, and those in the crimes of passion group committed the greatest damage on their victims. Blackburn and colleagues (2004) have examined personality disorders among offenders with mental illness. They found four factors, which they labeled "internalizing/externalizing," "acting out," "dependency," and "negative beliefs about others." Overall, the literature tends to support between two and five clusters or groups among offenders with mental illness. Notably, very few of these empirically based clusters or groups correspond to diagnostic categories in the *Diagnostic and Statistical Manual of Mental Disorders* (DSM). A challenge is to develop typologies that incorporate standardized instruments of mental illness and crime-related variables.

Co-occurrence

Measuring mental illness within a diagnostic measurement model allows for an assessment of the co-occurrence of mental disorders. By definition, co-occurrence refers to two discrete diagnoses for the same person, the corresponding conditions occurring either at a single point in time or across the life span (Hayward and Moran, 2008). The most common form of co-occurrence is that of a mental illness and a substance use disorder (Ogloff, Lemphers, and Dwyer, 2004). Offenders with a mental illness and substance use disorders offend more than offenders with mental illness alone (Abram, 1990; Baillargeon et al., 2010; Ferguson et al., 2009). Among offenders with antisocial personality disorder, 36 percent and 34 percent will have avoidant and paranoid personality disorders respectively (Coolidge et al., 2011). Although common, the use of co-occurrence to measure mental illness has several difficulties. These difficulties include unreliable measurement, unwarranted increase in complexity, lack of aetiology, and reduced access to causal mechanisms.

Reliable measurement Issues of reliable measurement with co-occurring disorders can take three forms. First, the assessment process of gathering information could be difficult due to the client's experience of an acute mental illness. For example, a psychotic offender may not be able to accurately disclose the nature of his or her social interactions, which are essential for deriving personality disorders. Second, co-occurrence can be indicated solely because of the covariation of the error variance associated with two diagnostic categories (Lilienfeld, Waldman, and Israel, 1994). The measurement of a disorder will be associated with error components (e.g., fuzzy criteria, rater bias) that are not directly due to the diagnostic construct. At times this error may have a shared influence on the criteria – a tension that leads to the diagnosis of two or more disorders. Third, within a prison environment a tension in making personality diagnosis over psychiatric diagnosis may be rooted in systemic prison issues. Thus certain types of information will not be routinely assessed or downplayed. The identification of personality disorders, notably antisocial personality disorder, may take precedence because this identification may help prevent injury to staff and the victimization of vulnerable offenders (Rhodes, 2000).

An unwarranted increase in complexity occurs when co-occurrence is used to measure mental illness. In the area of classification research, the measurement of mental illness through co-occurrence can unduly complicate the understanding of the individual offender. One way this happens is by claiming that more than one disorder is present, when in fact the disorders have been artificially separated. This results in more illness being reportedly measured than is actually the case.

Another difficulty with using co-occurrence to measure mental illness is restrictiveness in examining the aetiology of mental illness. With regard to developing explanations associated with mental illness, co-occurrence is based on an assumption that may be difficult to make – namely the assumption of two independent and equally severe conditions. It is commonly thought that co-occurrence indicates greater severity. But this may not be the case. For example, anxiety may have a protective role for those with conduct disorder. In the medial field, co-occurrence incorporates both the symptoms and the aetiology of a disorder. Thus co-occurrence will be unified by what causes the disorder. With mental health diagnosis, only symptoms are used for a diagnosis. Consequently co-occurrence can only reference descriptive information and not directly address etiology (Lilienfeld et al., 1994).

Yet another difficulty of using co-occurrence in the measurement of mental illness is the reduced access it gives to causal mechanisms in examining the aetiology of mental illness. If an additional goal is to understand the causal mechanisms of mental illness, moving the construct further away from the person will be counterproductive. For example, a group of offenders with psychosis and substance abuse disorder may have multiple sources for the occurrence of their condition, yet fall within the same category.

The high rate of co-occurrence among criminal justice samples suggests that a distinct construct is not being measured. In fact, a portion of the co-occurrence rate can be directly attributed to overlapping diagnostic criteria (Hayward and Moran, 2008). Thus, if one intended to isolate a causal mechanism among other variables, the use of a diagnostic system would not advance that effort. Also, the overlapping of diagnostic criteria may create an illusion of co-occurrence, arbitrary separating two disorders that are not naturally distinct.

Chart records, ratings, and self-report

Research that relies solely on a review of chart records – that is, on the routine recording of clinical information – will likely have underrecorded rates of mental illness. In clinical practice the efforts put into a comprehensive diagnosis can be limited and reduced, often because of a lack of resources. Also, once a diagnosis has been made, the efforts put into developing a secondary diagnosis can be greatly reduced. In some studies the difference can be substantial – such as in Ogloff et al.'s

(2004) Australian study, where the chart indicated 8 percent with a diagnosis of substance abuse and the research diagnosis indicated 74 percent. Past research has indicated that only one third of the offenders with personality disorder who had a mental illness (assessed via a research project) had a mental illness recorded in their charts. Similarly, only a half of the offenders with mental illness who had a personality disorder had a personality disorder recorded in their charts (Blackburn et al., 2003). In a study of jail offenders, the chart recording of mental health problems was not related to standardized measures of mental health, whereas the current diagnosis on the chart showed a moderate relationship with such measures (Corrado et al., 2000). Other prison research has shown the benefit of using more than just chart information.

Mental Health Measurement in Applied Studies

There are three basic types of research that highlight mental health measurement issues in the criminal justice system. These are classification studies, assessment of prevalence rates studies, and prediction of negative outcomes studies.

Classification

Criminal justice systems spend considerable effort in classifying offenders. For offenders with mental illness, screening assists in triage decision-making. A screen is not meant to develop a definite course of action for an offender with mental disorder, but rather to identify offenders who need a more in-depth assessment (Ogloff, Roesch, and Hart, 1993). Even though screening instruments have been unduly criticized for not having the same predictive validity as a full assessment instrument, total accuracy is not expected, as a second phase is an in-depth assessment from the screening referrals. This second phase is necessary because of high rates of false positives (Martin et al., 2013) and the system's costs, which result in an inappropriate delivery of limited mental health resources (Hassan et al., 2012). Some authors, though, argue for a high rate of false positives in the screening of offenders with mental illness (Ogloff et al., 1993). Poor screening procedures can underestimate the level of mental illness by 50 percent (McKinnon and Grubin, 2010).

A recent systematic review of mental health-screening instruments found 22 screening instruments from 24 studies, but only six had been cross-validated on subsequent samples (five recommended for further use) (Martin et al., 2013). The overall accuracy of these five scales ranged from 60 percent to 79 percent. Most standardized mental health instruments used in the criminal justice system have been imported from the mental health literature. In a structured review of 450 instruments used in forensic mental health studies, very little evidence was found to support the psychometric properties of the reviewed instruments (Chambers et al., 2009).

In a systematic review of screening for depression in offender samples, 13 studies were found to meet the requirements of using a brief screening instrument and a standardized diagnostic interview. The predominant screening instrument was self-report and took between three and 15 minutes to complete. At the depression measures' optimum cut point, solid values for sensitivity (0.88; identify depression) and specificity (0.84; exclude those without depression) (Hewitt et al., 2011) occur. For female offenders the same depression measure as for male offenders can be used, but the norms and interpretation guidelines should be unique for female offenders (Kroner, Kang, et al., 2011). Thus the measurement of depression among various offender samples appears to have solid validity.

The screening instruments listed below have shown some validity within criminal justice settings:

1. The Holden Psychological Screening Inventory (HPSI) (Holden, 1996) is a self-report instrument that contains 36 items (Book, Knap, and Holden, 2001; Mills and Kroner, 2005: Canadian studies).
2. The Prison Screening Questionnaire (PriSnQuest) (Shaw, Tomenson, and Creed, 2003) is a self-report instrument that contains eight items (originally 7 items) (Brooker et al., 2012; Hassan et al., 2012; Senior et al., 2013: British studies).
3. The Brief Jail Mental Health Screen (BJMHS) (Steadman et al., 2005) is a rated measure with eight items (Baksheev, Ogloff, and Thomas, 2012; Eno Louden, Skeem, and Blevins, 2013: USA studies).
4. The Correctional Mental Health Screen (CMHS) has two versions, one for women (CMHS-F), the other for men (CMHS-M) (Ford et al., 2009). From the 56-item CMHS yes/no items, an eight-item rated instrument for women (CMHS-F) and a 12-item rated instrument for men (CMHS-M) were developed (USA study).
5. The K6 (Kessler et al., 2002) is a self-report measure with six items and is designed to distinguish between general distress and mental illness (Eno Louden et al., 2013: USA studies).

In criminal justice settings difficulties in conducting adequate screening assessments can occur, which will impact the quality of the data (Kroner, Mills, et al., 2011). Birmingham et al. (2000) examined the intake screening process and found that mental health staff identified only 21 percent of those with psychiatric history and health staff identified only 8 percent. The comparison standard consisted of independent research ratings. Other research has shown that 42 percent of intake offenders did not disclose past psychiatric involvement (Mitchison et al., 1994). These two studies demonstrate that the screening information gathered was far below what could be expected. Birmingham et al. (2000) concluded that lack of training, inadequate interviewing space, low staffing ratios, and the lack of rapport were major contributors to the underreporting of mental illness.

The need to use structured instruments was highlighted in a structured review conducted by Chambers et al. (2009) on studies between 1990 and 2006. The review included all forensic mental health research whose instruments were used in five or more studies. For the prediction of nonviolent and violent recidivism (394 studies), only 65 studies (6.1 percent) used a standardized instrument. The increased use of standardized instruments would allow for the assessment of instrument reliability, would increase generalizability conclusions, and would facilitate meta-analyses.

Prevalence rates of mental illness

The measurement of prevalence rates of mental illness will be influenced by definitions of mental illness (narrow vs. broad) and by settings (e.g., prison, community), which highlights sampling differences. Notably, regardless of the definition or the setting, prevalence rates for all mental illness among offenders are greater (typically 3 to 5 times greater) than prevalence rates for the general public (Diamond et al., 2001).

Narrow versus broad definition Obtaining lower prevalence rates when using a narrow definition of mental illness and higher prevalence rates when using a broad definition is a straightforward and reasonable result. A narrow definition usually encompasses major mental illness like schizophrenia and psychotic disorders, major depression, and bipolar disorder (Senior et al., 2013). A broad definition will include other conditions (i.e., anxiety) or will measure a general category of "mental illness." In terms of method of measurement, narrow definitions usually involve DSM diagnoses (or rating measures that can be scored for diagnosis). Current DSM interviews will result in slightly lower prevalence rates (i.e., Baillargeon, Binswanger, et al., 2009). Broader definitions typically use screening measures and historical psychiatric involvement. Using historical psychiatric involvement (clinical intervention) to measure mental illness is limited in its precision of measurement. Contributing to past psychiatric involvement could be limited by the available resources, the personal and system's costs of admittance for intervention, and inadequacies in screening for mental illness (Birmingham et al., 2000).

A narrow versus broad definition of mental illness will impact the reliability of the data. Corrado et al. (2000) compared narrow and broad definitions in the case of jail offenders. Both kinds of definitions were applied to three measures of mental illness. There was greater congruence among the three measures for the narrow definition (11 percent–16 percent discordance) than among the three measures for the broad definition (14 percent–80 percent discordance).

Prison rates Studies that use a diagnosis and a narrow definition of mental illness typically find prevalence rates between 3.1 percent and 8.7 percent (Baillargeon et al., 2010; Walters et al., 1988). Using diagnosis from the prison clinical chart and a narrow definition for mental illness, the prevalence rates are 14.7 percent (Walters, 2011). Using a diagnosis and a broad definition for mental illness, the prevalence rates are between 23 percent and 29 percent (Hodgins and Côté, 1991: Canada;

Senior et al., 2013: United Kingdom). For incarcerated segregated offenders, the prevalence rates are above 50 percent (Haney, 2003). After reviewing the literature among offenders with mental illness in the US federal system, Magaletta et al. (2006) used mental health service utilization rates to indicate mental illness prevalence rates. They found that, for prison outpatient service, the rate was 12 percent, and for inpatient services the rate was between 5 and 8 percent.

Community rates Rates of mental illness for offenders in the community are typically higher than rates for offenders in prisons. Eno Lounden, Skeemm, and Blevins (2013) found community rates of mental illness at 20.4 percent. Among offenders who have served their sentences, rates of 19.8 percent for major depression, 9.3 percent for anxiety, and 47.0 percent for alcohol abuse were found (Schnittker, Massoglia, and Uggen, 2012). If a general screening measure (broad definition of mental illness) is used, a prevalence rate of 48.6 percent can be found (Brooker et al., 2012). If the sample parameters are community participants who have had an arrest in the past year, rates are considerably lower. Rates of 6.0 percent for major depression, 2.5 percent for anxiety, and 34.4 percent were found for alcohol abuse (Swartz and Lurigio, 2007).

Negative outcome prediction/explanation

Further caution in using diagnostic categories is warranted when, in addition to the issues stated above, certain disorders – antisocial personality disorder, borderline personality disorder, intermittent explosive disorder – are used to predict violence or criminal justice outcomes. Certain disorder criteria include a reference to violence or criminal justice outcomes (e.g., arrests). The defining criteria for these disorders are a part of the criminal justice outcomes, which makes the use of such criteria meaningless through circularity. Thus a spurious relationship between a disorder and its outcome can occur solely with overlapping criteria and consequently confounding definitions (Arboleda-Flórez, Holley, and Crisanti, 1998). Such results would preclude any predictive or explanatory conclusions. Problems with overlapping of criteria also apply to personality disorder instruments. This overemphasis on crime in the measurement of psychopathy may obscure the role of personality disorders and their relationships with outcomes. Institutional adjustment is better predicted by dimensional measures of mental illness than by diagnosis and by a narrow definition of mental illness (i.e., by a major mental illness) than by a broad definition (Corrado et al., 2000).

Within criminal justice settings, a measurement of mental health without accounting for the client's criminality will be incomplete. At a minimum, measuring criminality helps provide context to mental health issues. There is a systemic tension between what is represented in a mental health approach and in a criminal justice approach. A mental health approach emphasizes treatment and criminal justice control (Rhodes, 2000). Without accounting for antisocial or risk measures, mental health variables will often be predictive of criminal justice outcomes (Baillargeon et al., 2010; Messina et al., 2004); Steinert, 2002; Swartz and Lurigio, 2007). Once antisocial or risk measures are incorporated, the predictive ability of mental health variables is eliminated or greatly reduced (Bonta, Blais, and Wilson, 2014; Bonta, Law, and Hanson, 1998). Some recent research, though, has shown mental health variables to be related with recidivism, even after using a standardized risk assessment instrument (Ostermann and Matejkoski, 2014).

Conducting Physical Health Research

The difficulties of conducting physical health research can be highlighted by two comparisons. First, there are unique characteristics to criminal justice settings, in contrast to the characteristics of the general population that impact physical health studies. Criminal justice settings such as jails have high turnover rates, prisons have disproportionately many young adults, males, and ethnic–racial minorities (Baillargeon, Binswanger, et al., 2009). Thus general population research designs cannot be easily applied to criminal justice settings. Second, by comparison to the mental health research with offender samples, the research on physical health is less developed. There are two factors that contribute to the dearth of literature: approvals for research and data recording. Approval for health-related research is more difficult to obtain, as over a half of the states refuse permission to conduct biomedical or drug-testing research. Within the Federal Bureau of Prisons offenders are not allowed to participate in biomedical or drug-testing areas of research. However, researchers have argued that many correctional health-care issues can be safely collected, analyzed, and published, since they pose minimal or no risks to offenders (Boutwell, Allen, and Rich, 2005). These concerns specific to criminal justice populations are further compounded by typical limitations found in general health research (e.g., administrative barriers, paper medical charts, ethics, privacy concerns, approval processes, and lack of coordination across health systems). All this makes research in this area a difficult task (Binswanger et al., 2012).

Standardized data recording in national health surveys (e.g., the National Health Interview Survey and the Behavioral Risk Factor Surveillance Survey) often exclude criminal justice populations, which reduces the amount of data available. In many large epidemiological studies, offenders who are overrepresented in the criminal justice system (e.g., African American and Latino men) are not adequately represented in the data set, which leads to an underestimation of health conditions such as HIV, commonly found in this population. This methodological error generates inaccurate data regarding health disparities and health statistics in the offender population (Binswanger et al., 2012).

Screening accuracy is also a major issue for data recording. By comparison to offenders supervised in the community, individuals serving time in jail and prison are less likely to be screened and diagnosed for many health conditions such as diabetes, which results in the underreporting of these conditions (Binswanger,

Krueger, and Steiner, 2009). National regulations require that, within 14 days of arrival to jail, all detainees be screened for sexually transmitted diseases (STDs) (Wolfe et al., 2001); however, "fewer than one half of all jails (47 percent) routinely screen their populations for syphilis" and, in the jails that do deliver routine screenings, "fewer than one half of the detainees actually receive screening" (Wolfe et al., 2001, p. 1223). While this is attributed to the short stay of many inmates, which is on average under 48 hours, jail screening misses the population that poses the greatest risk for syphilis infections: drug users and commercial sex workers (Wolfe et al., 2001). Similarly, there is a lack of screening for women, who are unlikely to receive gynecologic examinations. As a result, many sexually transmitted diseases within prisons and jails are not identified (Binswanger et al., 2011).

A significant data-recording issue is the gathering of information via self-report. In other crime-related content areas, self-report can be a valid method of data collection (Kroner, Mills, and Morgan, 2007; Walters, 2006). But many scholars have concerns about physical health measurement (Binswanger et al., 2009; Binswanger et al., 2011; Binswanger et al., 2012; Fox et al., 2005; Weir et al., 2009; Wish, O'Neil, Baldau, 1988; Wolfe et al., 2001). The validity of self-report data could be increased by addressing five key factors identified in past research. The first is the language barrier, or the lack of appropriate languages being used in the interview (Binswanger et al., 2010). Second, many offenders are unaware of their conditions and are therefore more likely to underreport (e.g., incarcerated females are less likely to report high cholesterol than nonincarcerated females (Binswanger et al., 2009). Third, some offenders simply do not like to reveal detailed information about their personal lives and activities to a seemingly impersonal system. Self-reports of Pap testing for cervical cancer among women may not always be accurate, as women may not be as forthcoming about their individual medical history as they should, unless they give it anonymously (Binswanger et al., 2011). Fourth, there is a reluctance to report on illicit behaviors. These behaviors, such as drugs and needle sharing, are common among offenders who often have positive test results for drug use but do not admit to having them (Fox et al., 2005; Wish et al., 1988). Not only do inmates hesitate to report their drug activities, but Weir and his colleagues (2009) suggest that they are also unwilling to divulge information on partner violence and sexually risky behavior, because doing so may jeopardize their security level or terms of supervision. Research has suggested that using partner notification is not a useful method for identifying sexually transmitted diseases, since many offenders do not want to divulge the names or their partners or simply cannot recall their past sexual encounters (Wolfe et al., 2001).

Summary

The measurement of mental health and physical illness does present unique challenges due to offender characteristics and criminal justice settings. The traditional measurement of offenders with mental illness has used DSM diagnostic categories.

Very few empirically based psychiatric clusters or groups correspond to DSM diagnostic categories. The use of dimensional models, when compared to that of diagnostic categories, improves the measurement of associated features of mental illness and the predictability of psychiatric and criminal justice outcomes and provides information for interventions. The challenge of future measurement endeavors is not only to use dimensional models, but to incorporate crime-causing variables. This would acknowledge that offenders with mental illness have both mental health and crime-causing characteristics, and that principles of correctional intervention (see Cullen, 2007) also apply to these offenders. Such an incorporation of these two areas would give greater ecological validity to the measurement of mental health.

Advancements have been made in the screening of illnesses, in the recording of data, and in the measurement of change. Building on these advancements, the criminal justice system can expect greater reliability and validity in the measurement of mental health and physical illnesses.

References

Abram, K. M. 1990. The problem of co-occurring disorders among jail detainees: Antisocial disorder, alcoholism, drug abuse, and depression. *Law and Human Behavior*, 14: 333– 345. doi: 10.1007/BF01068160.

Arboleda-Flórez, J. 1998. Mental illness and violence: An epidemiological appraisal of the evidence. *Canadian Journal of Psychiatry. Revue Canadienne de Psychiatrie*, 43 (10): 989–996.

Arboleda-Flórez, J., Holley, H., and Crisanti, A. 1998. Understanding causal paths between mental illness and violence. *Social Psychiatry and Psychiatric Epidemiology*, 33: S38–S46. doi: 10.1007/s001270050208.

Baillargeon, J., Binswanger, I., Penn, J., Williams, B., and Murray, O. 2009. Psychiatric disorders and repeat incarcerations: The revolving prison door. *American Journal of Psychiatry*, 166: 103–109. doi: 10.1176/appi.ajp.2008.08030416.

Baillargeon, J., Penn, J. V., Knight, K., Harzke, A. J., Baillargeon, G., and Becker, E. A. 2010. Risk of reincarceration among prisoners with co-occurring severe mental illness and substance use disorders. *Administration and Policy in Mental Health and Mental Health Services Research*, 37: 367–374. doi: 10.1007/s10488-009-0252-9.

Baillargeon, J., Penn, J., Thomas, C., Temple, J., Baillargeon, G., and Murray, O. 2009. Psychiatric disorders and suicide in the nation's largest state prison system. *Journal of the American Academy of Psychiatry and the Law Online*, 37: 188–193.

Baksheev, G. N., Ogloff, J., and Thomas, S. 2012. Identification of mental illness in police cells: A comparison of police processes, the Brief Jail Mental Health Screen and the Jail Screening Assessment Tool. *Psychology, Crime and Law*, 18: 529–542. doi: 10.1080/1068316X.2010.510118.

Beal, C. A., Kroner, D. G., and Weekes, J. R. 2003. Persecutory ideation and depression in mild violence among incarcerated adult males. *International Journal of Offender Therapy and Comparative Criminology*, 47: 159–170. doi: 10.1177/0306624X03252173.

Binswanger, I., Krueger, P., and Steiner, J. 2009. Prevalence of chronic medical conditions among jail and prison inmates in the United States compared with the general population. *Journal of Epidemiology and Community Health*, 63: 912–919.

Binswanger, I., Merrill, J., Krueger, P., White, M., Booth, R., and Elmore, J. 2010. Gender differences in chronic medical, psychiatric, and substance-dependence disorders among jail inmates. *American Journal of Public Health*, 100: 476–482. doi: 10.2105/AJPH.2008.149591.

Binswanger, I., Mueller, S., Clark, C., and Cropsey, K. 2011. Risk factors for cervical cancer in criminal justice settings. *Journal of Women's Health*, 20: 1839–1845.

Binswanger, I., Redmond, N., Steiner, J., and Hicks, L. 2012. Health disparities and the criminal justice system: An agenda for further research and action. *Journal of Urban Health*, 89: 98–107.

Birmingham, L., Gray, J., Mason, D., and Grubin, D. 2000. Mental illness at reception into prison. *Criminal Behaviour and Mental Health*, 10: 77–87. doi: 10.1002/cbm.347.

Blackburn, R. 1998. Criminality and the interpersonal circle in mentally disordered offenders. *Criminal Justice and Behavior*, 25: 155–176. doi: 10.1177/0093854898025002001.

Blackburn, R. 2004. "What works" with mentally disordered offenders. *Psychology, Crime and Law*, 10: 297–308. doi: 10.1080/10683160410001662780.

Blackburn, R. 2007. Personality disorder and psychopathy: Conceptual and empirical integration. *Psychology, Crime and Law*, 13: 7–18. doi: 10.1080/10683160600869585.

Blackburn, R., and Coid, J. W. 1999. Empirical clusters of DSM-III personality disorders in violent offenders. *Journal of Personality Disorders*, 13: 18–34. doi: 10.1521/pedi.1999.13.1.18.

Blackburn, R., Crellin, M. C., Morgan, E. M., and Tulloch, R. M. B. 1990. Prevalence of personality disorders in a special hospital population. *The Journal of Forensic Psychiatry*, 1: 43–52. doi: 10.1080/09585189008408453.

Blackburn, R., Donnelly, J. P., Logan, C., and Renwick, S. J. D. 2004. Convergent and discriminative validity of interview and questionnaire measures of personality disorder in mentally disordered offenders: A multitrait-multimethod analysis using confirmatory factor analysis. *Journal of Personality Disorders*, 18: 129–150. doi: 10.1521/pedi.18.2.129.32779.

Blackburn, R., Logan, C., Donnelly, J., and Renwick, S. 2003. Personality disorders, psychopathy and other mental disorders: Co-morbidity among patients at English and Scottish high-security hospitals. *Journal of Forensic Psychiatry & Psychology*, 14: 111–137. doi: 10.1080/1478994031000077925.

Blonigen, D. M., Patrick, C. J., Douglas, K. S., Poythress, N. G., Skeem, J. L., Lilienfeld, S. O., ... Krueger, R. F. 2010. Multimethod assessment of psychopathy in relation to factors of internalizing and externalizing from the Personality Assessment Inventory: The impact of method variance and suppressor effects. *Psychological Assessment*, 22: 96–107. doi: 10.1037/a0017240.

Book, A. S., Knap, M. A., and Holden, R. R. 2001. Criterion validity of the Holden Psychological Screening Scale in a prison sample. *Psychological Assessment*, 13: 249–253.

Bonta, J., Blais, J., and Wilson, H. A. 2014. A theoretically informed meta-analysis of the risk for general and violent recidivism for mentally disordered offenders. *Aggression and Violent Behavior*, 19: 278–287. doi: 10.1016/j.avb.2014.04.014.

Bonta, J., Law, M., and Hanson, K. 1998. The prediction of criminal and violent recidivism among mentally disordered offenders: A meta-analysis. *Psychological Bulletin*, 123: 123–142. doi: 10.1037/0033-2909.123.2.123.

Bouman, Y. H., Van Nieuwenhuizen, C., Schene, A. H., and De Ruiter, C. 2008. Quality of life of male outpatients with personality disorders or psychotic disorders: A comparison. *Criminal Behaviour and Mental Health*, 18: 279–291. doi: 10.1002/cbm.703.

Boutwell, A., Allen, S., and Rich, J. 2005. Opportunities to address the hepatitis C epidemic in the correctional setting. *Clinical Infectious Diseases*, 40 (Supplement 5): S367–S372.

Brooker, C., Sirdifield, C., Blizard, R., Denney, D., and Pluck, G. 2012. Probation and mental illness. *Journal of Forensic Psychiatry & Psychology*, 23: 522–537. doi: 10.1080/14789949.2012.704640.

Chakhssi, F., de Ruiter, C., and Bernstein, D. 2010. Change during forensic treatment in psychopathic versus nonpsychopathic offenders. *Journal of Forensic Psychiatry and Psychology*, 21: 660–682. doi: 10.1080/14789949.2010.483283.

Chambers, J. C., Yiend, J., Barrett, B., Burns, T., Doll, H., Fazel, S., … Fitzpatrick, R. 2009. Outcome measures used in forensic mental health research: A structured review. *Criminal Behaviour and Mental Health*, 19: 9–27. doi: 10.1002/cbm.724.

Christensen, L., and Mendoza, J. L. 1986. A method of assessing change in a single subject: An alteration of the RC index. *Behavior Therapy*, 17: 305–308.

Coolidge, F. L., Marle, P. D., Van Horn, S. A., and Segal, D. L. 2011. Clinical syndromes, personality disorders, and neurocognitive differences in male and female inmates. *Behavioral Sciences & the Law*, 29: 741–751. doi: 10.1002/bsl.997.

Corrado, R. R., Cohen, I. M., Hart, S. D., and Roesch, R. 2000. Diagnosing mental disorders in offenders: Conceptual and methodological issues. *Criminal Behaviour and Mental Health*, 10: 29–39. doi: 10.1002/cbm.341.

Cullen, F. T. 2007. Make rehabilitation corrections' guiding paradigm. *Criminology & Public Policy*, 6: 717–727. doi: 10.1111/j.1745-9133.2007.00469.x.

Diamond, P. M., Wang, E. W.,III, C. E. H., Thomas, C., and Cruser, des A. 2001. The prevalence of mental illness in prison. *Administration and Policy in Mental Health and Mental Health Services Research*, 29: 21–40. doi: 10.1023/A:1013164814732.

Edens, J. F. 2009. Interpersonal characteristics of male criminal offenders: Personality, psychopathological, and behavioral correlates. *Psychological Assessment*, 21: 89–98. doi: 10.1037/a0014856.

Edens, J. F., and Ruiz, M. A. 2008. Identification of mental disorders in an in-patient prison psychiatric unit: Examining the criterion-related validity of the Personality Assessment Inventory. *Psychological Services*, 5: 108–117. doi: 10.1037/1541-1559.5.2.108.

Engel, R. S., and Silver, E. 2001. Policing mentally disordered suspects: A reexamination of the criminalization hypothesis. *Criminology*, 39: 225–252. doi: 10.1111/j.1745-9125.2001.tb00922.x.

Eno Louden, J., Skeem, J. L., and Blevins, A. 2013. Comparing the predictive utility of two screening tools for mental disorder among probationers. *Psychological Assessment*, 25: 405–415. doi: 10.1037/a0031213.

Farrington, D. P., and Loeber, R. 2000. Some benefits of dichotomization in psychiatric and criminological research. *Criminal Behaviour and Mental Health*, 10: 100–122. doi: 10.1002/cbm.349.

Ferguson, A. M., Ogloff, J. R. P., and Thomson, L. 2009. Predicting recidivism by mentally disordered offenders using the LSI-R:SV. *Criminal Justice and Behavior*, 36: 5–20. doi: 10.1177/0093854808326525.

Ford, J. D., Trestman, R. L., Wiesbrock, V. H., and Zhang, W. 2009. Validation of a brief screening instrument for identifying psychiatric disorders among newly incarcerated adults. *Psychiatric Services*, 60: 842–846. doi: 10.1176/appi.ps.60.6.842.

Fox, R., Currie, S., Evans, J., Wright, T., Tobler, L., Phelps, B., Busch, M., and Page-Shafer, K. 2005. Hepatitis C virus infection among prisoners in the California state correctional system. *Clinical Infectious Diseases*, 41: 177–186.

Friestad, C., and Hansen, I. L. S. 2005. Mental health problems among prison inmates: The effect of welfare deficiencies, drug use and self-efficacy. *Journal of Scandinavian Studies in Criminology & Crime Prevention*, 6: 183–196. doi: 10.1080/14043850510035100.

Haney, C. 2003. Mental health issues in long-term solitary and "supermax" confinement. *Crime & Delinquency*, 49: 124–156. doi: 10.1177/0011128702239239.

Harris, A., and Lurigio, A. J. 2007. Mental illness and violence: A brief review of research and assessment strategies. *Aggression and Violent Behavior*, 12: 542–551. doi: 10.1016/j.avb.2007.02.008.

Hassan, L., Rahman, M. S., King, C., Senior, J., and Shaw, J. 2012. Level of mental health intervention and clinical need among inmates with mental illness in five English jails. *Psychiatric Services*, 63: 1218–1224. doi: 10.1176/appi.ps.201100344.

Hayward, M., and Moran, P. 2008. Comorbidity of personality disorders and mental illnesses. *Psychiatry*, 7: 102–104. doi: 10.1016/j.mppsy.2008.01.010.

Hersen, M. 1988. Behavioral assessment and psychiatric diagnosis. *Behavioral Assessment*, 10: 107–121.

Hewitt, C. E., Perry, A. E., Adams, B., and Gilbody, S. M. 2011. Screening and case finding for depression in offender populations: A systematic review of diagnostic properties. *Journal of Affective Disorders*, 128: 72–82. doi: 10.1016/j.jad.2010.06.029.

Hodgins, S., and Côté, G. 1991. The mental health of penitentiary inmates in isolation. *Canadian Journal of Criminology*, 33: 175–182.

Hodgins, S., and Gaston, L. 1989. Patterns of recidivism and relapse among groups of mentally disordered offenders. *Behavioral Sciences & the Law*, 7: 551–558. doi: 10.1002/bsl.2370070409.

Holden, R. R. 1996. *The Holden Psychological Screening Inventory manual*. North Tonawanda, NY: Multi-Health Systems.

Junginger, J., and McGuire, L. 2004. Psychotic motivation and the paradox of current research on serious mental illness and rates of violence. *Schizophrenia Bulletin*, 30: 21–30.

Kessler, R. C., Andrews, G., Colpe, L. J., Hiripi, E., Mroczek, D. K., Normand, S.-L. T., … Zaslavsky, A. M. 2002. Short screening scales to monitor population prevalences and trends in non-specific psychological distress. *Psychological Medicine*, 32: 959–976. doi: 10.1017/S0033291702006074.

Kroner, D. G., Kang, T., Mills, J. F., Harris, A. J. R., and Green, M. M. 2011. Reliabilities, validities, and cutoff scores of the Depression Hopelessness Suicide Screening Form among women offenders. *Criminal Justice and Behavior*, 38: 779–795. doi: 10.1177/0093854811409004.

Kroner, D. G., Mills, J. F., Gray, A., and Talbert, K. O. N. 2011. Clinical assessment in correctional settings. In *Correctional mental health: From theory to best practice*, edited by T. Fagan J. and R. K. Ax, 79–102. Thousand Oaks: Sage.

Kroner, D. G., Mills, J. F., and Morgan, R. D. 2007. Underreporting of crime-related content and the prediction of criminal recidivism among violent offenders. *Psychological Services*, 4: 85–95. doi: 10.1037/1541–1559.4.2.85.

Laajasalo, T., and Häkkänen, H. 2006. Excessive violence and psychotic symptomatology among homicide offenders with schizophrenia. *Criminal Behaviour and Mental Health*, 16: 242–253. doi: 10.1002/cbm.635.

Lachar, D., Bailley, S. E., Rhoades, H. M., Espadas, A., Aponte, M., Cowan, K. A., … Wassef, A. 2001. New subscales for an anchored version of the Brief Psychiatric Rating Scale: Construction, reliability, and validity in acute psychiatric admissions. *Psychological Assessment*, 13: 384–395. doi: 10.1037/1040–3590.13.3.384.

Lilienfeld, S. O., Waldman, I. D., and Israel, A. C. 1994. A critical examination of the use of the term and concept of comorbidity in psychopathology research. *Clinical Psychology: Science and Practice*, 1: 71–83. doi: 10.1111/j.1468-2850.1994.tb00007.x.

Livesley, W. J., Jackson, D. N., and Schroeder, M. L. 1992. Factorial structure of traits delineating personality disorders in clinical and general population samples. *Journal of Abnormal Psychology*, 101: 432–440. doi: 10.1037/0021-843X.101.3.432.

MacLennan, R. N. 1988. Correlation, base-rates, and the predictability of behaviour. *Personality and Individual Differences*, 9: 675–684. doi: 10.1016/0191-8869(88)90165-1.

Magaletta, P., Diamond, P., Dietz, E., and Jahnke, S. 2006. The mental health of federal offenders: A summative review of the prevalence literature. *Administration and Policy in Mental Health and Mental Health Services Research*, 33: 253–263. doi: 10.1007/s10488-005-0022-2.

Martin, M. S., Wamboldt, A. D., O'Connor, S. L., Fortier, J., and Simpson, A. I. F. 2013. A comparison of scoring models for computerised mental health screening for federal prison inmates. *Criminal Behaviour and Mental Health*, 23: 6–17. doi: 10.1002/cbm.1853.

McKinnon, I., and Grubin, D. 2010. Health screening in police custody. *Journal of Forensic and Legal Medicine*, 17: 209–212. doi: 10.1016/j.jflm.2010.02.004.

Messina, N., Burdon, W., Hagopian, G., and Prendergast, M. 2004. One year return to custody rates among co-disordered offenders. *Behavioral Sciences & the Law*, 22: 503–518. doi: 10.1002/bsl.600.

Mills, J. F., and Kroner, D. G. 2005. Screening for suicide risk factors in prison inmates: Evaluating the efficiency of the Depression, Hopelessness and Suicide Screening Form (DHS). *Legal & Criminological Psychology*, 10: 1–12. doi: 10.1348/135532504X15295.

Mitchison, S., Rix, K. J. B., Renvoize, E. B., and Schweiger, M. 1994. Recorded psychiatric morbidity in a large prison for male remanded and sentenced prisoners. *Medicine, Science and the Law*, 34: 324–330. doi: 10.1177/002580249403400410.

Morgan, R. D., Kroner, D. G., Mills, J. F., Bauer, R. L., and Serna, C. 2014. Treating justice-involved persons with mental illness: Preliminary evaluation of a comprehensive treatment program. *Criminal Justice and Behavior*, 41: 902–916. doi: 10.1177/0093854813508553.

Newton, M. 1998. Changes in measures of personality, hostility and locus of control during residence in a prison therapeutic community. *Legal and Criminological Psychology*, 3: 209–223. doi: 10.1111/j.2044-8333.1998.tb00362.x.

Ogloff, J. R. P., Lemphers, A., and Dwyer, C. 2004. Dual diagnosis in an Australian forensic psychiatric hospital: Prevalence and implications for services. *Behavioral Sciences & the Law*, 22: 543–562. doi: 10.1002/bsl.604.

Olgoff, J. R. P., Roesch, R., and Hart, S. D. 1993. Screening, assessment, and identification of services for mentally ill offenders. In *Mental illness in America's prisons*, edited by H. J. Steadman and J. J. Cocozza, 61–90. [Seattle, WA]: National Coalition for the Mentally Ill in the Criminal Justice System.

Ostermann, M., and Matejkowski, J. 2014. Exploring the intersection of mental health and release status with recidivism. *Justice Quarterly*, 31: 746–766. doi: 10.1080/07418825.2012.677465.

Persons, J. B. 1986. The advantages of studying psychological phenomena rather than psychiatric diagnoses. *American Psychologist*, 41: 1252–1260. doi: 10.1037/0003- 066X.41.11.1252.

Rhodes, L. A. 2000. Taxonomic anxieties: Axis I and Axis II in prison. *Medical Anthropology Quarterly*, 14: 346–373. doi: 10.1525/maq.2000.14.3.346.

Ruiz, M. A., and Edens, J. F. 2008. Recovery and replication of internalizing and externalizing dimensions within the Personality Assessment Inventory. *Journal of Personality Assessment*, 90: 585–592. doi: 10.1080/00223890802388574.

Schnittker, J., Massoglia, M., and Uggen, C. 2012. Out and down: Incarceration and psychiatric disorders. *Journal of Health & Social Behavior*, 53: 448–464. doi: 10.1177/0022146512453928.

Senior, J., Birmingham, L., Harty, M. A., Hassan, L., Hayes, A. J., Kendall, K., … Shaw, J. 2013. Identification and management of prisoners with severe psychiatric illness by specialist mental health services. *Psychological Medicine*, 43: 1511–1520. doi: 10.1017/S0033291712002073.

Shaw, J., Tomenson, B., and Creed, F. 2003. A screening questionnaire for the detection of serious mental illness in the criminal justice system. *Journal of Forensic Psychiatry & Psychology*, 14 (1): 138–150. doi: 10.1080/1478994031000077943.

Shuker, R., and Newton, M. 2008. Treatment outcome following intervention in a prison-based therapeutic community: A study of the relationship between reduction in criminogenic risk and improved psychological well-being. *The British Journal of Forensic Practice*, 10: 33–44. doi: 10.1108/14636646200800018.

Silver, E. 2000. Extending social disorganization theory: A multilevel approach to the study of violence among persons with mental illnesses. *Criminology*, 38: 1043–1074. doi: 10.1111/j.1745-9125.2000.tb01414.x.

Steadman, H. J., Scott, J. E., Osher, F., Agnese, T. K., and Robbins, P. C. 2005. Validation of the Brief Jail Mental Health Screen. *Psychiatric Services*, 56: 816–822. doi: 10.1176/appi.ps.56.7.816.

Steinert, T. 2002. Prediction of inpatient violence. *Acta Psychiatrica Scandinavica*, 106: 133- 141. doi: 10.1034/j.1600-0447.106.s412.29.x.

Swartz, J. A., and Lurigio, A. J. 2007. Serious mental illness and arrest the generalized mediating effect of substance use. *Crime & Delinquency*, 53: 581–604. doi: 10.1177/0011128706288054.

Tapp, J., Fellowes, E., Wallis, N., Blud, L., and Moore, E. 2009. An evaluation of the Enhanced Thinking Skills (ETS) programme with mentally disordered offenders in a high security hospital. *Legal & Criminological Psychology*, 14: 201–212. doi: 10.1348/135532508X336178.

Walters, G. D. 2006. Risk-appraisal versus self-report in the prediction of criminal justice outcomes: A meta-analysis. *Criminal Justice and Behavior*, 33: 279–304. doi: 10.1177/0093854805284409.

Walters, G. D. 2011. Criminal thinking as a mediator of the mental illness–prison violence relationship: A path analytic study and causal mediation analysis. *Psychological Services*, 8: 189–199. doi: 10.1037/a0024684.

Walters, G. D., Mann, M. F., Miller, M. P., Hemphill, L. L., and Chlumsky, M. L. 1988. Emotional disorder among offenders inter- and intrasetting comparisons. *Criminal Justice and Behavior*, 15: 433–453. doi: 10.1177/0093854888015004002.

Weir, B., O'Brien, K., Bard, R., Casciato, C., Maher, J., Dent, C., Dougherty, J., and Stark, M. 2009. Reducing HIV and partner violence risk among women with criminal justice system involvement: A randomized controlled trial of two motivational interviewing-based interventions. *AIDS and Behavior*, 13: 509–522.

Wise, E. A. 2004. Methods for analyzing psychotherapy outcomes: A review of clinical significance, reliable change, and recommendations for future directions. *Journal of Personality Assessment*, 82: 50–59. doi: 10.1207/s15327752jpa8201_10.

Wish, E., O'Neil, J., and Baldau, V. 1988. *Lost opportunity to combat AIDS: Drug abusers in the criminal justice system*. Washington, DC: US Department of Justice.

Wolfe, M., Xu, F., Patel, P., O'Cain, M., Schillinger, J., St. Louis, M., and Finelli, L. 2001. An outbreak of syphilis in Alabama prisons: Correctional health policy and communicable disease control. *American Journal of Public Health*, 91: 1220–1225.

Wulff, H. R. 1986. Rational diagnosis and treatment. *Journal of Medicine and Philosophy*, 11: 123–134. doi: 10.1093/jmp/11.2.123.

Further Reading

Akers, T., and Lanier, M. 2009. "Epidemiological criminology": Coming full circle. *American Journal of Public Health*, 99 (3): 397–402.

Baillargeon, J., Kelley, M., Leach, C., Baillargeon, G., and Pollock, B. 2004. Methicillin-resistant Staphylococcus aureus infection in the Texas prison system. *Clinical Infectious Diseases*, 38: e92–e95.

Silver, E., Arseneault, L., Langley, J., Caspi, A., and Moffitt, T. E. 2005. Mental disorder and violent victimization in a total birth cohort. *American Journal of Public Health*, 95: 2015–2021. doi: 10.2105/AJPH.2003.021436.

Snowden, R. J., Gray, N. S., Taylor, J., and MacCulloch, M. J. 2007. Actuarial prediction of violent recidivism in mentally disordered offenders. *Psychological Medicine*, 37: 1539- 1549. doi: 10.1017/S0033291707000876.

11

Rehabilitation and Treatment Programming

Faye S. Taxman and Brandy L. Blasko

The concept of rehabilitation assumes that criminal behavior is caused by some factor(s). In other words, crime is influenced by a person's social surroundings, psychological or developmental factors, or biological make-up (Cullen and Johnson, 2012). Traditionally, individuals who commit crime participate in treatment programs and services directed at altering their behavior, attitudes, or values in order to reduce the odds of criminal justice involvement in the future. A myriad of topics and themes that affect the health and well-being of an individual can be addressed in the course of rehabilitation and treatment – such as mental health symptoms, interpersonal and social skills, life skills, educational needs, vocational needs, religious–spiritual aspects, parenting. Some of these topics and themes have a direct relationship to criminal behavior on the basis of existing theories or empirical literature (or both). For example, some programs are aimed at changing antisocial cognitions, peer or social networks, or values, all of which have a direct relationship to criminal behavior. Programs that target other areas, such as life skills, parenting, and financial management, can moderate changes in criminal conduct. The nature of the program affects the likely outcomes.

Measuring any aspect of a treatment program is not a simple venture. The complicated nature of psychosocial programs has led to a call for better documentation and description of such programs in the scientific literature (Michie et al., 2009; Taxman and Friedmann, 2009). Michie and colleagues (2009) contend that this documentation will advance our understanding of the key program components and client characteristics, which in turn will facilitate positive outcomes. Programs have a number of components that can affect the production of outcomes. These components can be categorized as (1) structure, or the way the program is set up;

The Handbook of Measurement Issues in Criminology and Criminal Justice, First Edition.
Edited by Beth M. Huebner and Timothy S. Bynum.

(2) content and core features of each programmatic component, including ancillary or wrap-around services; (3) the setting where services are delivered; (4) the organization involved in the delivery of the program, be it as a direct service provider, as a host for the program, or as some hybrid model; and (5) the staffing for the program. All these components have to do with the program (or intervention) itself and with the environment in which it is implemented. The type of clients can also affect the production of outcomes – for example whether the clients' psychosocial needs are compatible with the underlying theory of a program.

In justice settings, the existing research on the core components of a program that are linked to positive outcomes is limited. Overall, the research literature has established that cognitive behavioral orientations outdo other approaches (employment, restorative justice, talk therapy, etc.) to produce positive outcomes (Andrews and Bonta, 2010; Landenberger and Lipsey, 2005; Aos et al., 2001). But knowing what is the most effective theoretical orientation does not necessarily help us understand other features of a program that impact effective outcomes. In fact only Landenberger and Lipsey (2005) have explored the program features and clientele characteristics that affect effective programming. Finding a community-based treatment, serving higher risk clients, making room for sessions on anger management, and increasing the length of treatment are most effective at producing positive outcomes in cognitive behavioral programming.

Given the complex nature of treatment programming, intervention science points to the following factors that should be considered when measuring whether a treatment program is effective (see Figure 11.1):

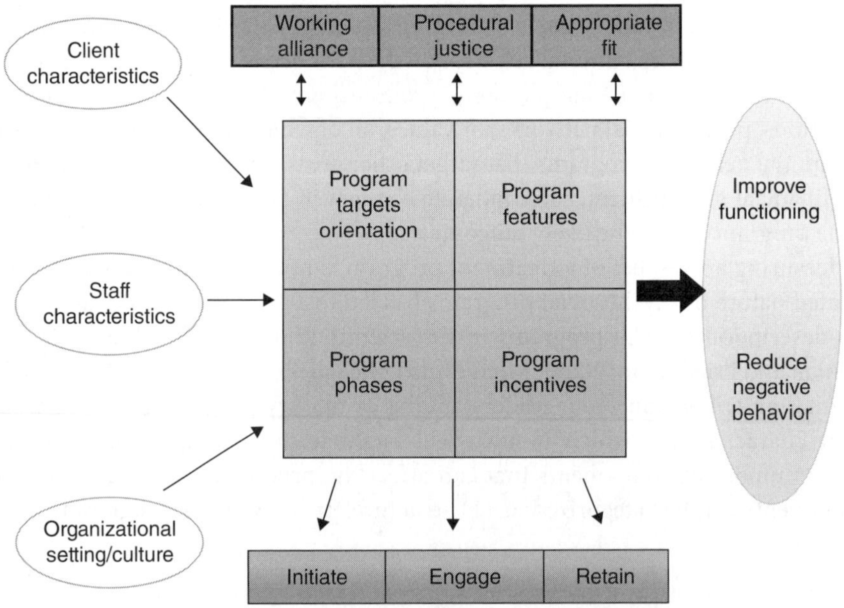

Figure 11.1 Components of rehabilitation and treatment programs.

1. program orientation (e.g., 12-step, cognitive behavioral, multisystemic);
2. core services and features;
3. program goals and objectives;
4. the organizational context in which the services are delivered;
5. staffing; and
6. sequencing of programmatic components.

These factors also affect two sets of proximal outcomes: the client's initiation and engagement in treatment; and the client's assessment of a program's support, alliance, and fairness. In this chapter we specifically tackle some of the issues inherent in measuring each of these six areas.

Factors Influencing (Predicting) Program Outcomes

In any treatment program, regardless of the topic, there are three major factors that can affect the outcomes. These three factors are: (1) characteristics of the clients, including those related to demographics and criminal history; (2) characteristics of the staff; and (3) characteristics of the organization and setting. That is, the nature of a treatment program is affected by these "inputs" or factors that contribute to the delivery of services within that program. Below we summarize the three factors and the findings that are key to determining how these factors affect outcomes.

Clients

An *implicit* component of an effective program is that the target population – the clients (offenders) involved in the program – is appropriate for the program. Essentially there are three major components of a program related to client characteristics that should be measured and documented: general demographics; criminal justice risks and needs factors; and psychosocial functioning.

Demographics Demographics covers factors such as age, gender, race and ethnicity, education level, and socioeconomic status. These factors often affect program components and outcomes – including reaction and commitment to change – in different ways. For example, the gender match between a client and his or her group facilitator or individual counselor is shown to influence how that client perceives the treatment process (Kiesler and Watkins, 1989; Norcross, 2010; Persons, Persons, and Newmark, 1974; Wintersteen, Mensinger, and Diamond, 2005). Educational levels and educational needs may also affect the ability to comprehend treatment materials, especially those that affect cognitive processing or executive decision-making.

Criminal justice history and criminogenic factors Criminal justice history and criminogenic factors describe both a client's justice history and factors that affect that client's involvement in the justice system. There are four important factors in this category of client factors. The first is the nature of the criminal justice charges (or conviction) for the current offense. This refers to both the type of crime committed (e.g., assault, theft) and how the crime is classified (e.g., a misdemeanor or a felony offense). Since in the United States the categories of misdemeanor and felony vary according to the state, it is often useful to have both the actual charge (or conviction) and the legal ranking, particularly for studies or evaluations that involve more than one jurisdiction.

A second client factor of interest is the criminal justice risk presented by an individual. A person's risk level refers to the probability that that person would commit a new crime. Assessing risk is important for determining treatment intensity; higher risk offenders tend to have better outcomes with more intensive programming.

Assessing risk is also important for determining the factors to be targeted (Lowenkamp, Latessa, and Holsinger, 2006; Taxman and Marlowe, 2006) during the course of treatment. Criminogenic need refers to a cadre of factors that are known to be related to involvement in criminal behavior. The most common factors are those identified by Andrews and Bonta (2010): criminal personality, antisocial values and attitudes, antisocial peers, substance abuse, dysfunctional family, employment and education, and leisure time activities. Many of these factors are included in current, commonly used risk assessment instruments such as the Ohio Risk Assessment System (ORAS) (see Latessa et al., 2010), the Correctional Offender Management Profiling for Alternative Sanctions (COMPAS) (see Brennan, Dieterich, and Ehret, 2009), the Level of Service Inventory-Revisited (LSI-R) (see Andrews and Bonta, 1995), and the Wisconsin Risk and Need Assessment (WRN) (see Wright, Clear, and Dickson, 1984).

It is important to note that many risk instruments do not rely upon psychometrically sound subscales for the measurement of psychosocial functioning or factors related to criminal conduct such as antisocial cognitions, antisocial peers, and antisocial family. Many also measure the lifetime presence of some conditions, such as substance use. For example, an individual who abused substances many years ago would be considered a current risk for substance use. This means that the instruments do not adequately measure the intended construct. They could address this pitfall by specifying whether substance use occurred within the past six months or one year rather than in the client's lifetime. As a result, clients who used in their lifetimes, but not recently, would be considered a lower risk than clients who used in the past six months or one year. Similarly, many risk measures do not consider the severity of a substance use disorder (i.e., use, abuse, dependence) and do not differentiate between primary drug of choice. Drug of choice in particular is known to be an important factor related to progress in treatment and the type of treatment program an individual may benefit from. Recent reviews of the literature by Wooditch, Tang, and Taxman (2014) and Taxman (2014) address some of these measurement concerns by specifying the features that should be captured when measuring criminal risk factors. Table 11.1 offers a list of the factors and components.

Table 11.1 Overview of major criminogenic needs and measurement factors.

Risk Factor	*Description*
Criminal personality	Antisocial personality disorder, mood disorder, or psychopathy
Antisocial values and attitudes	Criminal thinking errors including anti-authority attitudes. tolerance for antisocial behavior, personal irresponsibility
Antisocial peers	Number of antisocial peer networks, involvement in co-offending behaviors, and frequency and nature of contacts
Substance abuse	Type of substance use disorder (i.e., addiction, abuse, recreational use within the past 12 months), primary drug of choice (e.g., heroin, cocaine, marijuana, alcohol, poly-substance abuser)
Family	Family involvement in the justice system, family dysfunction and conflict
Employment/education	Lack of high school diploma, failure to retain employment for at least 90 days
Leisure time activities	Lack of constructive leisure time activities

Researchers should be aware of the quality of measures when assessing risk factors. An emphasis should be placed on using instruments that provide accurate, reliable, and valid measures for these constructs. (For a well-documented tool identifying psychometrically sound and well-validated tools, see PhenX Toolkit at https:// www.phenxtoolkit.org.)

Psychosocial functioning Beyond demographic and risk factors, a number of other psychosocial factors related to the client are important to measure in order to assist in assessing the efficacy of treatment. These are typically referred to as "tailoring factors" and can affect the delivery of the treatment program. Psychosocial functioning includes factors such as mental health or housing status, which may impact daily decisions and choices. For example, client-based factors such as attachment style (Beech and Mitchell, 2009; Eames and Roth, 2000; Horvath, 2001; Norcross, 2010) and symptom severity are often related to program responses and outcomes. Some studies found that clients with lower global functioning, more interpersonal problems, and more symptoms of depression were more likely to demonstrate poor outcomes (Castonguay, Constantino, and Gross Holtforth, 2006; Constantino et al., 2005; Hersoug et al., 2009). The physical location of a client's residence, particularly in communities with concentrated disadvantage or with a concentration of individuals involved in the justice system, may also affect response to programming and services (Hipp, Petersilia, and Turner, 2010).

Essentially, knowledge of the three categories discussed in the subsections above can be helpful with treatment matching or with placement decision-making: it strengthens programs and their ability to facilitate change. This requires that we turn our attention to client factors that affect, advance, accelerate, or facilitate individual-level change. If we do so, the process is more about *how* the programming or the environment can be adapted to address these individual factors and hence to achieve long-term outcomes. Achieving long-term change is unlikely to happen without first achieving these short-term treatment goals.

Staffing and resources

Several resources and staff-related factors are needed to carry out an effective program. While the process is complex, it is important to measure several key indicators such as program financing, staff credentials, staff training, and quality assurance. The financing of programs is complex, and it is important to understand how a given program is funded and what resources are available to run it. Funding can involve contributions from justice organizations such as the Office of Justice Program's Justice Assistance Grant (JAG) Program and contributions from other agencies or private donors. Another important resource-related issue is that of staffing a program. Staff can include administrators, medical or psychological staff, counseling or therapeutic staff, security staff, and other kinds (e.g., nurses). Understanding staff-related factors can help understand openness to innovation and the organization's flexibility or capacity to offer a wider variety of programming. Studies have typically found that staff with college or graduate degrees tend to embrace new ideas easier than staff with high school credentials (Murphy, Rhodes and Taxman, 2012). In substance abuse treatment programs, programs that do not include medical staff are unlikely to offer medication-assisted treatments (e.g., methadone, naltrexone, burphorine; Knudsen et al., 2009) or to provide infectious disease services for HIV/AIDS and hepatitis C. A key way to measure staff resources is to determine the ratio of clinical staff to security staff. A small ratio of clinical to security staff is often an indicator of more limited resources and of an inability to offer a fuller range of services.

The remaining two resource- and staff-related factors are (1) staff training and professional development; and (2) quality assurance procedures. Training and preparing staff to administer the program is critical. Training can include observations, courses that train in the program, and credentialing or clinical training in a particular treatment modality (e.g., cognitive behavioral therapy, motivational interviewing). That is, training can range from the minimal training needed to deliver a program to full professional clinical training. Whether staff is clinical, security, or volunteer is also important. Establishing this involves assessing the degree to which members of staff have a formalized role in the program – as in therapeutic communities where correctional officers may assist in facilitating group sessions. Items from the National Criminal Justice Treatment Practices (NCJTP) survey (Taxman et al., 2007), available at ICPSR (see http://www.icpsr.umich.edu/icpsrweb/ICPSR/studies/27382), provide a selection of validated scales to measure the desired topics – such as the mission and goals of correctional and treatment programs and the opinions of their administrators and staff regarding rehabilitation, punishment, and services, cynicism about change, culture of the organization, and other key facets. Finally, quality assurance procedures are needed in order to monitor the quality of programming. These procedures can include receiving accreditation from outside agencies (e.g., from the American Correctional Association, from the Therapeutic Communities of America, from the Joint Commission on Health Accreditation); having internal staff that observes and grades the programming through audiotapes, videotapes, or in-person reviews; and having external staff that provides feedback to staff members on their use of the adherence to the treatment programming. The type of quality assurance procedures, along with the staffing and frequency of the procedures, provides other critical resource-related information. Good quality training programs improve program outcomes, particularly those that focus on skill enhancement among staff (Bonta et al., 2013).

Setting and organizational culture

Programs are generally not self-enclosed entities. They exist within an organizational environment, both in terms of the support agencies that host them and in terms of the external organizations that reinforce their goals and importance. Many well-designed programs falter, generally not because of the design, but rather due to the degree to which the organization, either internal to the program or external, provides a ready environment. This is an area of emerging research, but later in the chapter we list the core factors that are important to measure in order to discern the organizational support for a program. One useful tool is the National Criminal Justice Treatment Practices Survey (NCJTP) (see Taxman, et al., 2007; Taxman, Henderson, and Belenko, 2009). This survey covers five domains: organizational structure and leadership; organizational culture and climate; training and resources (e.g., funding, staff, physical plant); administrators' attitudes; and network connectedness.

Organizational structure There are a number of organizational factors that can help explain how treatment programs are administered:

1. Where is the treatment program delivered: in an institution, a private residence, a halfway house, a probation or parole office, or some other location?
2. Who is responsible for the delivery of the treatment program: correctional staff, correctional counseling or social work staff, contractual staff, staff in a coordinated relationship with other justice or health agency, or volunteers?
3. Is the same staff responsible for treatment program delivery *and* for continuum of care (e.g., aftercare, supplemental services)? And
4. Who selected the components of the treatment program: the leadership, the leadership and the staff, or an interagency team of corrections and health or treatment agencies?

Answers to these questions will provide detailed information about how the organizational structure contributes to the treatment's efficacy.

Culture and climate Given the inherent security focus of correctional agencies, a major component of assessing the environment is concerned with whether the culture and climate of the correctional agency (e.g., prison, jail, halfway house, residential treatment, probation/parole) supports rehabilitation. The culture clash between treatment and punishment – and especially the degree to which the priorities placed on security and control undermine or minimize the goals of rehabilitation – is a long-standing topic in many studies of treatment programming in justice settings. Contemporary studies continue to find that the security-driven culture of an agency negatively alters the treatment programming in untold ways, for example through reductions in the number of sessions allowed, lack of support from the correctional officers for the offenders' participation in programming, limitations in the degree to which individuals have autonomy to express their feelings and experiences, and negative impacts on the structure of the program (Dahlen and Johnson, 2010).

Farabee and colleagues (1999) outline some threats to quality programming that center on whether the correctional environment supports treatment programming. Correctional staff is more likely to support treatment programming when the leadership and the culture endorse it as a priority (a scenario referred to as "goal cohesion"). Using a competing values framework, Cameron and Quinn (1999) offer four types of cultures that exist in an organization in relation to support for change: cohesive, hierarchical, performance achievement, and innovative–adaptive. The description "cohesive" indicates the degree to which there is a consensus around goals and priorities in the organization. A "hierarchical" culture is one where decision-making is top-down. A "performance achievement" culture describes an organization with clear goals and priorities and where organizational activities center on achieving these goals. The label "innovative–adaptive" captures the openness of the environment to new ideas and approaches. Finally, there is a related construct, rendered by the notion of "organizational learning"; this characterizes an organization or environment that promotes new learning. Organizational learning is found to be supportive of more treatment adoption (Friedmann, Taxman, and Henderson, 2007).

Measuring organizational culture and context requires surveys of administrators and staff. While it is possible to use the lens of one type of staff, a richer and more detailed understanding of culture issues results from an examination of the degree to which there is agreement among staff and administrators on the importance of goals, priorities, and treatment programming. The use of multilevel modeling, either nesting the data within facilities and administrators or examining the degree of concurrence between administrators and staff, is a more appropriate measurement strategy. Another issue that can be measured by using multilevel modeling concerns interagency support for treatment programming; staff and administrator perspectives can be integrated (see Grella et al., 2007 or Visher et al., 2014).

Administrators' attitudes The administrators' attitude and knowledge are important for facilitating good programming. In a study of the adoption of evidence-based practices in correctional agencies, Friedmann and colleagues (2007) found that uptake of evidence-based practices and innovations occurred for agencies that had administrators with a human service background, for agencies that had a strong personal belief in rehabilitation, for agencies that created a learning culture, and for agencies that identified performance standards. Since leaders are an important resource, the following measures are relevant: educational and other credentialed background; length of time in the position, experience in administering programs, and tenure in the field; perspective on rehabilitation and correctional programming; management techniques, including the use of team work; and organizational priorities.

External relationships and networks As a whole, the criminal justice system depends on external support and collaborative relationships with many organizations such as the judiciary or health services – particularly regarding the provision of treatment programs. Endorsement or support from justice organizations (e.g., prosecutors, judiciary, defenders, correctional agencies), other treatment agencies, and policymakers (e.g., legislators, executive government staff) are often needed if treatment programming is to be successfully implemented and sustained. The nature and type of external relationships among these organizations are important. Several models are available that describe and conceptualize the levels and intensity of efforts present in cross-agency collaborations (e.g., Himmelman, 1996, 2001; Konrad, 1996). Fletcher and colleagues (2009) specifically developed an instrument designed to measure the working relationships among justice actors around treatment programming; it identifies whether the relationships range from informal information sharing to integrated service delivery. This 12-item tool is useful for measuring how treatment programs network with other justice organizations.

The Program: Structure, Components, and Features

Orientation and program targets

Programs are not merely a collection of activities but are usually built on a theory of how to facilitate change. A theoretically driven program has a theory that relates to addressing some mechanism (e.g., behavioral, cognition, support systems) that needs to be activated if the chain reaction that culminates in assisting a person to make changes is to be created. For example, in their seminal work, Andrews and Bonta (2010) identified eight theoretically relevant factors that have a direct relationship with offending: criminal personality, antisocial values, antisocial cognitions, antisocial peers, dysfunctional families, substance abuse, employment and educational deficits, and poor leisure time activities. Using this framework, a program would target one or more of these factors in order to affect criminal behavior. Other factors – such as mental illness, place of residence, housing, food insecurity, trauma, post-traumatic stress disorder, parenting, and factors related to other areas of a person's life (referred to as "noncriminogenic," since they have an indirect relationship to offending) – may be included in the program for the benefit of achieving other objectives – for example stability, functionality, or motivation, which may ultimately impact criminal behavior. These components may not be considered among the theoretically relevant features that could interrupt patterns of offending; they are ancillary or secondary program components that do not affect offending behavior directly. Yet they form a gateway to affecting or impacting offending. Many programs combine the core and the secondary program components in order to be holistic or to ensure that sufficient services are provided; in some programs, the secondary factors are used to stabilize the person or to motivate him or her to invest in addressing the criminogenic factors.

Table 11.2 outlines some core program areas (grouping) and the related area in which change might occur in order to facilitate different outcomes. To improve client-level outcomes, it is important to understand the client's mechanism of action (MOA). The MOA is a specific target; a treatment is effective at reducing criminal justice outcomes (e.g., crime, substance use, parole violations) by targeting successfully (or breaking) the client's MOA. For example, in a cognitive behavioral program such as the National Institute of Correction's Thinking for a Change (Bush, Glick, and Taymans, 2011), the MOA consists of criminal thinking errors and illustrates how individuals distort their thinking to rationalize, justify, or mollify their behavior. For the treatment to prove effective at reducing subsequent offending, the program must target and effectively reduce thinking errors of this kind and increase prosocial

Table 11.2 Theoretical approaches to programming.

Program Group	*Mechanism of Action*	*Research Evidence*
Severe substance use/dependence	Treatments to reduce use of heroin, cocaine, amphetamines, and methamphetamine	Holloway, Bennett, and Farrington, 2006; Prendergast, Huang, and Hser, 2008; Prendergast et al., 2002; Lipton et al., 2002; Mitchell, Wilson, and MacKenzie, 2007
Criminal thinking	Cognitive restructuring to change maladaptive thinking and behavior patterns	Andrews and Bonta, 2010; Lipsey, Landenberger, and Wilson, 2007; Tong and Farrington, 2006, 2008
Self-improvement and management	Developing social and problem solving skills to address MH, SA, and self-control.	Botvin and Wills, 1984; Griffin, Botvin, and Nichols, 2006; Martin et al., 2011
Social and interpersonal skills	Structured counseling and modeling of behavior to reduce interpersonal conflict and develop more positive interactions.	Botvin and Wills, 1984; Visher, Winterfield, and Coggeshall, 2005
Life skills	Stabilize education, housing, employment, and financial concerns; focus on daily skills to manage life.	Andrews and Bonta, 2010

attitudes and beliefs among program participants. Often in programs that offer some services that cover a broad range of topics (the so-called "bundled programs"), the program's primary target area is unclear. Specifying the primary target and ensuring that the program components feed into it is the signal of a theoretically sound program. A major issue in justice programs is that many interventions have a number of components, and it is often unclear which features are the core ones.

Program structure

The program structure, or the various treatment stages or phases within a program, will also impact outcomes in different ways. Simpson (2004) describes a model of substance abuse treatment programs designed to reduce substance use in three phases with three eponymous goals: early engagement, early recovery, stabilized recovery. There are many components within each phase. Behavioral and cognitive interventions are provided; and the interventions are designed to improve the client's skills in recovery. This conceptual model also recognizes the importance of client attributes and program attributes. The general goal is to reduce or eradicate substance abuse, on the assumption that the services are linear and hosted within a single organization or network of services that shares this goal.

Criminal justice interventions vary considerably as to how programs are structured or who is responsible for the administration and delivery of services. Programs can be offered by a correctional or justice agency in a justice-related setting, by a contractual or volunteer service provider within a correctional or justice agency, through referral to a network of services in a community, or by a separate organization, in a setting outside of the justice agency. Since individuals may be incarcerated while receiving services, there is often a demand to continue the services after release, so as to prevent relapse; in fact research studies demonstrate the importance of aftercare or continuing treatment after incarceration (Mitchell, Wilson, and MacKenzie, 2007). Understanding the administration and the service providers is important in justice programs because it can signal which goals or which MOAs are being pursued. For example, most substance abuse treatment providers may structure their services so as to educate the person about substance abuse, address cravings, provide skills for managing use and abuse behaviors, assist the person in using self-help groups to manage sobriety, and provide relapse prevention skills. Religious groups may focus on spirituality, while vocational and educational providers may focus on job skills. The relationship to the offending behavior may not be direct, and service providers may not view their services as being part of a recidivism reduction plan. And, if there are bundled programs, then the message of the desired outcomes may be murky to the program, to the service providers, and, most importantly, to the clients.

Programs are complicated as a result of variation in how program components are nested or combined. These variations present challenges to measuring the desired outcomes and how each service component is directly or indirectly related.

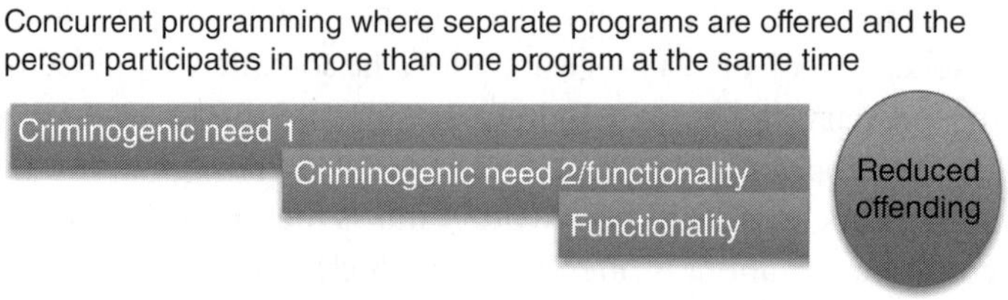

Figure 11.2 Conceptual models of treatment service delivery.

For example, in studies of therapeutic communities for prisoners, researchers assess how and where the client participated in the program – in prison, in aftercare, or in both components – in order to illustrate the impact on recidivism (Simpson, Wexler, and Inciardi, 1999). The studies have not examined whether the treatment providers were the same in all three parts, or whether the curricula were similar in each component. Nor do the studies assess what area of change the program is designed to achieve (e.g., substance abuse, antisocial values). To advance an understanding of program structures and features, it is important to identify the mechanisms of action tied to different program components and the structure for the service delivery.

Figure 11.2 presents conceptual arrangements for the delivery of programs and services to justice-involved clients. The central issue is how criminogenic or noncriminogenic programmatic components are offered. In other words, does the program focus on more than one target need at a time (single emphasis or concurrent), treat each target need as part of phases (sequential), or integrate several target needs or functionality issues into one program (integrated)? In assessing how substance abuse and mental health services are provided within treatment programs, Muesser, Noordsy, and Drake (2003) describe the sequential, the parallel, and the integrated model. The sequential model treats comorbid disorders; in this model one program ends before the other one begins. Parallel models treat co-occurring conditions consecutively, often with different providers (working for different agencies), who may create coordination issues as well as secure the consistency of messages delivered to clients. The integrated care model offers services concurrently, from the same provider or team – which is more likely to ensure integration. Two major concerns with integrated models are whether sufficient programming time is available to address one factor, and whether the staff is capable of addressing the comorbid conditions. Sequential models generally suffer from a lack of the evidence that should guide the order or timing in order to achieve optimal care. Parallel models all too often suffer from a lack of communication or coordination between providers and from the distraction of having competing providers and potentially different therapeutic messages. Gaps in our knowledge about service delivery models concern the ordering of treatments and whether treating one type of condition (e.g., a criminogenic need, or psychosocial functioning) has better outcomes than treating another in terms of various goals and objectives. The structure is important because it dictates a number of issues that affect the basic understanding of the program and the desired goal. In multiple-goal programs there are high demands on client performance, given the programmatic expectations to master one or more clinical disorders or conditions.

The conceptual models assist researchers in considering the full range of places where there is a need to measure aspects of the treatment program: structure, relationship of justice and service provider (e.g., staff, contractual, brokerage), degree of integrated services, and desired client outcomes. Each of these areas is important to consider in fully documenting the program structure.

There are a number of target areas within a program. It is important to distinguish the behaviors that a program is designed to target before assessing that program's components and outcomes. For example, in a program that targets antisocial cognitions, the question is: What aspects of a client's behavior is this type of program targeting? If a program consists of ballroom dancing, cooking, basketball, counseling, and vocational training, the question is: Which of these components is going to create a change in antisocial cognitions? Essentially, in bundled programs where multiple services and activities are occurring (either concurrently or consecutively), there is a need to identify the primary program's targets and features. This can be done by rank-ordering the services or by examining the amount of program time (e.g., hours, sessions) devoted to any particular area.

Program orientation

Services can be delivered through a myriad of theoretical orientations. Each orientation offenders a different understanding of how an individual's problems develop and how they can be solved. Common orientations relied on in offender rehabilitation programs are:

1. educative or reeducative – where the goal is to educate the person about a particular issue, for instance by providing new information or by increasing the person's awareness of a particular topic; the material is usually presented in a didactic or classroom style, where the focus is on instruction or on the presentation of material;
2. normative – where the goal is to help the person understand societal norms either through didactic lessons or through role-playing and case studies;
3. cognitive – where the emphasis is on thinking patterns and on how information is processed;
4. behavioral – where the emphasis is on an individual's actions and behaviors;
5. situational analysis – with an emphasis on helping the person understand how s/he is responding to her or his environment;
6. "talk" therapy-type – with an emphasis on allowing the individual to discuss freely any issues; and
7. a social milieu-type– with an emphasis on creating a new environment that allows the person to have new experiences.

Each change process frames the issues differently and offers varying views or theories of how an individual will change. It is important to know the specific way in which the material is presented to the clients and whether the emphasis is on increasing their awareness of the issue, on improving their interpersonal, cognitive, or behavioral skills, on providing social support for change, or on other factors.

Another related issue is whether the emphasis is on the individual's deficits, strengths, hopes, or redirection. Most criminal justice interventions focus on deficits or look at the individual's past behaviors. Increasingly there is a focus on a strengths-based approach that emerges from positive psychology. Strengths-based approaches emphasize the positive assets of a person. Akin to positive psychology, which is based on the assumption that individuals desire to lead fulfilling lives acquired from love, play, work, and survival, this approach assists individuals in obtaining a new identity and perception of themselves by changing their narratives (Wilson, 2011). There is no easy method for measuring how the individual or the presentation of self occurs, except through the observation of the setting or the review of tapes from the sessions. As discussed by Prendergast and colleagues (2009), even when programs acknowledge a strength-based approach, measuring how the counselors interact with the offenders can be very revealing regarding the tendency to focus on deficits or past behaviors. In a series of systematic observational techniques of programs, Taxman and Bouffard (2003) found similar discrepancies between stated programmatic features and delivery among treatment services provided to drug court clients. In this case, where the programs stated a cognitive approach, almost all program time was devoted to educational or didactic approaches (and administrative activities).

Another major issue regarding programming is how the services are offered. Delivery techniques have three components: their curriculum basis; their format; and their techniques. A major advancement over the past 30 years has been the formulation of standardized manuals for the delivery of programming. The manuals present the material as a guidebook for facilitators. A noted advantage of the manualized curriculum is that it standardizes the material delivered, provides training tools for counselors, and offers an easier mechanism for assessing whether the treatment programming is consistent with the curriculum. Many programs are now encouraged to use standardized curricula and many are available in the public domain, which increases the widespread availability of the approach.

The delivery technique of a program is also important. Many programs are delivered via group counseling models where there are eight to 10 clients and one or more group facilitators. In the group format, one advantage is that the clients learn through their own reaction and those of other group members. Some group sessions are classified as closed groups, which means that members must begin and experience the program together. The advantage of the closed-group model is that it builds trust among members, which facilitates greater and deeper discussion. Open-group models allow new members to join at any time. In assessing the delivery technique, it is important to examine whether the group is open or closed, the size of the group, and who facilitates the group. Another form of program delivery is individual counseling, which is a one-to-one session between an individual and a staff member, clinician, or therapist. A third form of treatment delivery, which is not frequently used for adult offenders but is more likely to be used for youth, is family therapy. This form usually involves the offender and his or her major support system. Often this treatment is provided in the home. The goal of family sessions is to address issues within that environment, which may be contributing to negative (offending) behavior. Finally, another type of delivery is peer counseling or support. This is generally a situation where someone who has been involved in the justice system acts as a former offender responsible for mentoring, guiding, or assisting the client. The peer-support model typically supplements individual, group, or family clinical approaches, but it is possible for programs to rely upon peers to facilitate groups, augment group sessions, or provide individual sessions (Lifers Public Safety Steering Committee, 2004; Welsh, 2007).

Duration: Frequency and length of sessions

The length and duration of a treatment programming is important to measure. Exposure to and duration of treatment programming can be captured as: (1) the length of the program in terms of weeks or months; (2) the number of sessions per week and the number of minutes per session; and (3) the components of the program that are required and those that are mandatory. The weeks of the program, the number of sessions, and the hours of treatment will indicate the intensity of the services. The typical outpatient program is about four months in duration. In the substance abuse treatment literature, programs that are at least 90 days in duration (with one session per week) are considered to be more effective than shorter programs (Simpson, Joe, and Rowan-Szal, 1997), but this type of research has not been conducted for a broader range of programs offered to justice-involved clients. The number of sessions per week describes the intensity of the program. For example, in the substance abuse treatment literature there is a distinction between outpatient and intensive outpatient programming on the basis of the number of program hours a week: intensive outpatient programming is generally two to three sessions a week (approximately four to nine hours).

A recent focus is on the concept of dosage, or the number of hours of services provided (Bourgon and Armstrong, 2005; Sperber, Latessa, and Makarios, 2013a, 2013b; Crites and Taxman, 2013). Much of the existing research has been conducted in halfway houses or in residential treatment centers for offenders. The dosage rates articulated in this small literature are: under 100 hours for low-risk offenders, 100–200 hours for moderate-risk offenders, and over 200 hours (200 to 300 hours) for high-risk offenders. The unresolved question is what these hours refer to: In other words, how are they measuring dosage? Some contend that dosage should refer to clinical or therapeutic hours in terms of time spent in group or individual counseling sessions. Others indicate that direct clinical care and ancillary services such as self-help groups, vocational or educational programming, and aftercare are also relevant because the individual is involved in prosocial and change-related activities. This is an area for future research. But, more importantly, the dosage debate illustrates how important it is to measure the hours spent in certain activities instead of relying upon mere program labels.

Treatment Progress Measures

In the first years of the twenty-first century, the Washington Circle, a group of scholars and practitioners, outlined a series of treatment progress measures that have subsequently been found to facilitate better treatment outcomes (e.g., reduced drug use, reduced recidivism). Garnick and colleagues (2009) have examined the impact of these treatment progress measures and have generally found that they have moderately positive outcomes: clients who initiate treatment, engage in it, and remain in care are more likely to demonstrate less recidivism than those who do not.

Four key treatment progress measures (Garnick et al., 2009) are: treatment initiation; treatment engagement; treatment retention; and treatment program completion.

Treatment initiation

Initiation is generally considered the length of time from assessment to first appearance at a program. Initiation length is considered appropriate when treatment begins within 14 days after the assessment.

Treatment engagement

Following the Washington Circle measures of treatment engagement, engagement is considered to be the completion of at least two treatment sessions within 30 days after the date of initiation of the treatment program.

Treatment retention

Following the measures of the Washington Circle and the National Treatment Improvement Network (NIATx), retention is considered appropriate when a client has participated in at least four treatment services within 30 days of initiating treatment.

Treatment program completion

Treatment program completion refers to successfully completing the treatment program by a positive discharge status. Completion occurs when the offender has met the agreed-upon plan (or any modifications thereof), or has completed the duration of the course of treatment without dropping out or failing to attend more than 30 percent of the sessions. Many studies focus solely on treatment completion as a measure of treatment success, but this measure captures the fact of simply making it through the program, without clear behavioral markers of whether the client has made progress on the target behaviors – which are the reason why the person is involved in a treatment program. Therefore, when assessing the treatment process, treatment completion should not be the sole factor measured.

Client-Level Proximal Measures

At the client level there are key proximal areas that have been paid less attention in the literature: measuring change, the client–facilitator relationship, and procedural justice.

Measuring change

Programs should operate with an underlying theory in mind. In doing so, the program will target a factor (or series of factors) that is empirically proven to impact criminal behavior – that is, a dynamic risk factor. Essentially, when this factor is targeted, clients should show changes in it. For example, to assess whether a program that targets antisocial peer involvement is effective, a baseline measure of the number of antisocial peers in clients' networks should be taken at the start of treatment and then periodically throughout; this will indicate whether the network has increased, decreased, or stayed the same. If the number of antisocial peers has increased or stayed the same, one must assume that the treatment has made little progress and that therefore any change in distal outcomes is random error instead of true change. It is, then, possible to use different statistical techniques to examine incremental change, for example, by calculating change scores (also referred to as simple difference scores), raw gain score, or raw change, which is the difference between baseline and follow-up measures (see Fitzmaurice, 2001 for a more in-depth discussion); and it is possible to use generalized estimating equations (GEE) models that control for baseline scores and examine the impact of change scores (e.g., Wooditch et al., 2014), This is why it is important to measure dynamic factors at baseline and periodically throughout the treatment period.

Client–facilitator relationship

The client–therapist relationship encompasses the feelings and attitudes that a treatment facilitator and a client have toward each other and how they are expressed (Bordin, 1979; Horvath and Greenberg, 1989; Norcross, 2010). Findings from the general psychotherapy literature have long demonstrated that the client–therapist relationship positively correlates with client outcomes, even beyond the specific treatment intervention utilized (Horvath and Bedi, 2002; Horvath and Symonds, 1991; Lambert and Barley, 2001; Murphy, Cramer, and Lillie, 1984; Norcross and Lambert, 2005). It is estimated that up to 30 percent of patient improvement in psychotherapy can be attributed to a positive therapeutic relationship between the client and the therapist (Lambert and Barley, 2001) and that correlations between the client–therapist relationship and outcomes range from 0.22 to 0.26, the client–therapist relationship explaining about 5 percent of the outcome variance (Baldwin, Wampold, and Imel, 2007; Horvath and Bedi, 2002).

The working alliance reflects the degree to which the client and the therapist have "a mutual understanding and agreement about change goals and the necessary tasks to move toward these goals along with the establishment of bonds to maintain the partners' work" (Bordin, 1979, p. 130). He quantified the working alliance (also referred to by others as the helping alliance or the therapeutic alliance) by identifying three main dimensions of the collaboration between client and facilitator or helper: goals, tasks, and bond. The goals dimension refers to the agreement between the therapist and the client regarding the goals for treatment; the tasks dimension refers to the specific therapeutic interventions utilized in treatment; and the bond dimension refers to the mutual trust, acceptance, and confidence between the client and therapist (Bordin, 1979).

A growing body of work is measuring the practitioner–client relationship within justice settings and finding that the nature of the relationship affects outcomes either directly or as a mediating factor. For example, a strong client–facilitator relationship (therapeutic alliance, working alliance, or helping relationship) is associated with program retention (Beyko and Wong, 2005; Brocato and Wagner, 2008) and with reduced odds of recidivism (Holmqvist, Hill, and Lang, 2007; Skeem et al., 2007). Our ability to better understand those aspects of the criminal justice practitioner–offender relationship that are associated with positive treatment outcomes lies in our measuring the construct consistently.

The Working Alliance Inventory (WAI) (Horvath and Greenberg, 1989) was designed to measure the quality of the therapeutic alliance and has been heavily grounded in empirical research over the past 30 years, including among offender populations (Blasko and Jeglic, 2014; Tatman and Love, 2010; Taxman and Ainsworth, 2009). This measure has demonstrated good convergent and discriminant validity, as shown by high correlations with other alliance measures, overlap with other measures of the therapeutic relationships, and little overlap with unrelated concepts (see Horvath, 1994 for a review).

Given the client–therapist relationship as measured by the WAI, its importance for positive treatment outcomes with general psychotherapy clients (e.g., Lambert and Barley, 2001; Westen, Novotny, and Thompson-Brenner, 2004), and growing evidence that this is also the case with offender populations, it seems logical for researchers examining practitioner–client relationships within the criminal justice system to use the WAI. At a minimum, this would help us understand whether the aspects of the client–practitioner relationship that are so important in general psychotherapy parallel the aspects of the criminal justice practitioner–offender relationship that are important for positive outcomes. Intuitively, it seems illogical to reinvent the wheel. After all, if we continue to report that a "relationship" is important to offender outcomes without parceling out its specific dynamics, research will tell us little about which aspects of the relationship (e.g., agreement on goals, agreement on tasks, formation of a bond) are important for different outcomes. In fact Tatman and Love (2010) recently adapted the short form of the WAI by substituting roles where appropriate (e.g., "therapist" was changed to "parole officer"), for use with individuals under probation and parole supervision. This approach can be used in other settings where appropriate.

Focusing on the mandated nature of the relationship between treatment on the one hand, supervision staff and justice clients on the other, Skeem and her colleagues (2007) have recently developed a relationship measure, the Dual Relationships Inventory-Revised (DRI-R), which captures three dimensions: caring and fairness; trust; and toughness. In a recent article, however, Kennealy and colleagues (2012) used the DRI-R to assess whether the relationship, as perceived by 109 general probationers, was associated with rearrest. They found that the caring and fairness dimension was negatively associated with rearrest. Although the other two dimensions (trust and toughness) also predicted rearrest, neither did after controlling for shared variance with the caring and fairness dimension. These recent findings suggest that, before we stop using the WAI, a measure heavily grounded in theoretical and empirical literature, more research is needed on the psychometric properties of the DRI-R.

Procedural justice

Another emerging construct is the perceived procedural justice of the program from the viewpoint of the client – the notion that internalized attitudes and judgments about institutions and procedures drive behavior. Procedural justice broadly relies on measuring perceptions of fairness – specifically, it is the perceived fairness of the program or agency that matters rather than the favorability or fairness of the outcomes of the procedures themselves (e.g., successful treatment completion) (Bottoms and Tankebe, 2012). Therefore, to measure procedural justice, surveying the client questions should be centered on *processes*. For example, surveys might contain questions about whether the procedures the staff uses to determine offender treatment placement are fair, rather than about whether the offenders are successfully placed into treatment programming. Fair processes for placing offenders into treatment programs would improve procedural justice and would be more important for it than placing a large number of offenders into treatment programs.

Skeem and her colleagues (2007), in their relationship measure (DRI-R), focus on the mandated nature of the relationship, referring to the DRI-R dimensions as potentially "an interpersonal form of procedural justice" (p. 399). Yet no studies have measured whether procedural justice in the traditional sense – as measured in the form deemed important for outcomes at other stages of the criminal justice system (Tyler, 2006) – is important in mandated supervision settings. While this traditional form may not measure interpersonal relationship dynamics, it seems likely that many of the facets of procedural justice outlined by Tyler and his colleagues (e.g., fairness, consistency; see Jackson et al., 2010) could have implications for the long-term behavior of individuals enrolled in treatment programs.

Conclusion: Principles of Effective Programs and Services to Measure

An ever-expanding list of programmatic components outlines key features that should be measured in order to determine the efficacy of programs. This list applies not only to criminology but also to medicine, social work, education, child welfare, and other human service areas. In general, the principles address the nature of the program, the characteristics of the clients, the nature of the organization hosting or providing the services, and the systems that support the program. The following list summarizes the different components that should be measured in assessing the efficacy of a rehabilitation or treatment program: organizational culture; program implementation and maintenance; management and staff characteristics; client characteristics; program characteristics; core correctional practices designed to reinforce learned behavior; interagency communication; and outcomes. Others have added to this list the following items: integrated programs; multiple program goals; certification and quality assurance processes; use of standardized assessment and responsivity tools; degree of restrictiveness of the program; and program capacity (Crites and Taxman, 2013). Many of these components are part of checklists, program inventories, or quality assessment instruments that are meant to aid practitioners and scholars in measuring the features of a program in order to determine their efficacy. In correctional research, the Correctional Program Assessment Inventory (CPAI) (Gendreau, Goggin, and Smith, 1999), the Standardized Program Evaluation Protocol (SPEP) (Lipsey, 2008), and the Risks–Needs–Responsivity (RNR) Program Tool (Crites and Taxman, 2013; Taxman, Pattavina, and Caudy, 2014) are available. Using these structured instruments is a step in the right direction in terms of effectively measuring components of rehabilitation and treatment programs.

References

Andrews, D. A., and Bonta, J. 1995. *LSI-R: The Level of Service Inventory – Revised.* Toronto: Multi-Health Systems.

Andrews, D. A., and Bonta, J. 2010. *The psychology of criminal conduct.* Newark, NJ: Anderson.

Aos, S., Phipps, P., Barnoski, R., and Lieb, R. 2001. *The comparative costs and benefits of programs to reduce crime.* Washington, DC: United States Department of Education, Washington State Institute for Public Policy.

Baldwin, S. A., Wampold, B. E., and Imel, Z. E. 2007. Untangling the alliance–outcome correlation: Exploring the relative importance of therapist and patient variability in the alliance. *Journal of Consulting and Clinical Psychology*, 75: 842–852.
Beech, A. R., and Mitchell, I. J. 2009. Attachment difficulties. In *Personality, personality disorder and violence: An evidence-based approach*, edited by M. McMurran and R. Howard, 213–228. Chichester, UK: John Wiley & Sons, Ltd.
Beyko, M. J., and Wong, S. C. 2005. Predictors of treatment attrition as indicators for program improvement not offender shortcomings: A study of sex offender treatment attrition. *Sexual Abuse: A Journal of Research and Treatment*, 17: 375–389.
Blasko, B. L., and Jeglic, E. L. 2014. Sexual offenders' perceptions of the client–therapist relationship: The role of risk. *Sexual Abuse: A Journal of Research and Treatment*. doi: 10.1177/1079063214529802.
Bonta, J., Bourgon, G., Rugge, T., Gress, C., and Gutierrez, L. 2013. Taking the leap. *Justice Research and Policy*, 15: 17–36.
Bordin, E. S. 1979. The generalizability of the psychoanalytic concept of the working alliance. *Psychotherapy: Theory, Research & Practice*, 16: 252–260.
Bottoms, A., and Tankebe, J. 2012. Beyond procedural justice: A dialogic approach to legitimacy in criminal justice. *Journal of Criminal Law & Criminology*, 102: 119–169.
Botvin, G. J., and Wills, T. A. 1984. Personal and social skills training: Cognitive–behavioral approaches to substance abuse prevention. In *Prevention research: Deterring drug abuse among children and adolescents* (NIDA Research Monograph), edited by C. S. Bell and R. Battjes, 8–49. Rockville, MD: Department of Health and Human Services.
Bourgon, G., and Armstrong, B. 2005. Transferring the principles of effective treatment into a "real world" prison setting. *Criminal Justice and Behavior*, 32: 3–25.
Brennan, T., Dieterich, W., and Ehret, B. 2009. Evaluating the predictive validity of the COMPAS risk and needs assessment system. *Criminal Justice and Behavior*, 36: 21–40.
Brocato, J. O., and Wagner, E. F. 2008. Predictors of retention in an alternative-to-prison substance abuse treatment program. *Criminal Justice and Behavior*, 35: 99–119.
Bush, J., Glick, B., and Taymans, J. 2011. *Thinking for a change: Integrated cognitive behavior change program*. Washington, DC: National Institute of Corrections.
Cameron, K. S., and Quinn, R. E. (1999). *Diagnosing and changing organizational culture*. Reading: Addison-Wesley.
Castonguay, L., Constantino, M. J., and Grosse Holtforth, M. 2006. The working alliance: Where are we and where should we go? *Psychotherapy: Theory, Research, Practice, Training*, 43: 271–279.
Constantino, M. J., Arnow, B. A. Blasey, C., and Agras, W. S. 2005. The association between patient characteristics and therapeutic alliance in cognitive–behavioral and interpersonal therapy for bulimia nervosa. *Journal of Consulting and Clinical Psychology*, 73: 203–211.
Crites, E. and Taxman, F. S. 2013. The responsivity principle: Determining the appropriate program and dosage to match risk and needs. In *Simulation strategies to reduce recidivism: Risk need responsivity (RNR) modeling in the criminal justice system*, edited by F. S. Taxman and A. Pattavina, 43–166. New York: Springer.
Cullen, F., and Jonson, C. 2012. *Correctional theory: Context and consequences*. Thousand Oaks, CA: Sage.
Dahlen, K., and Johnson, R. 2010. The humanism is in the details: An insider's account of humanistic modifications to a cognitive-behavioral treatment program in a maximum-security prison. *The Prison Journal*, 90: 115–135.

Eames, V., and Roth, A. 2000. Patient attachment orientation and the early working alliance: A study of patient and therapist reports of alliance quality and ruptures. *Psychotherapy Research*, 10: 421–434.

Farabee, D. Prendergast, M, Cartier, J, Wexler, H., Knight, K., and Anglin, M. D. 1999. Barriers to implementing effective correctional drug treatment programs. *The Prison Journal*, 90: 150–162.

Fitzmaurice, G. 2001. The conundrum in the analysis of change. *Nutrition*, 17: 360–361.

Fletcher, B. W., Lehman, W. E., Wexler, H. K., Melnick, G., Taxman, F. S., and Young, D. W. 2009. Measuring collaboration and integration activities in criminal justice and substance abuse treatment agencies. *Drug and Alcohol Dependence*, 103: S54–S64.

Friedmann, P. D., Taxman, F. S., and Henderson, C. E. 2007. Evidence-based treatment practices for drug-involved adults in the criminal justice system. *Journal of Substance Abuse Treatment*, 32: 267–277.

Garnick, D. W., Lee, M. T., Horgan, C. M., and Acevedo, A. 2009. Adapting Washington Circle performance measures for public sector substance abuse treatment systems. *Journal of Substance Abuse Treatment*, 36: 265–277.

Gendreau, P., Goggin, C., and Smith, P. 1999. The forgotten issue in effective correctional treatment: Program implementation. *International Journal of Offender Therapy and Comparative Criminology*, 43: 180–187.

Grella, C. E., Greenwell, L., Prendergast, M., Farabee, D., Hall, E., Cartier, J., and Burdon, W. 2007. Organizational characteristics of drug abuse treatment programs for offenders. *Journal of Substance Abuse Treatment*, 32: 291–300.

Griffin, K. W., Botvin, G. J., and Nichols, T. R. 2006. Effects of a school-based drug abuse prevention program for adolescents on HIV risk behaviors in young adulthood. *Prevention Science*, 7: 103–112.

Hersoug, A. G., Hoglend, P., Havik, O. E., Von der Lippe, A., and Monsen, J. T. 2009. Pretreatment patient characterisitics related to the level and development of working alliance in long-term psychotherapy. *Psychotherapy Research*, 19: 172–180.

Himmelman, A. T. 1996. On the theory and practice of transformational collaboration: From social service to social justice. In *Creating collaborative advantage*, edited by C. Huxham, 19–43. London: Sage.

Himmelman, A.T., 2001. On coalitions and the transformation of power relations: Collaborative betterment and collaborative empowerment. *American Journal of Community Psychology*, 29: 277–284.

Hipp, J. R., Petersilia, J., and Turner, S. 2010. Parolee recidivism in California: The effect of neighborhood context and social service agency characteristics. *Criminology*, 48 (4): 947–979.

Holloway, K. R., Bennett, T. H., and Farrington, D. P. 2006. The effectiveness of drug treatment programs in reducing criminal behavior: A meta-analysis. *Psicothema*, 16: 620–629.

Holmqvist, R., Hill, T., and Lang, A. 2007. Treatment alliance in residential treatment of criminal adolescents. *Child and Youth Care Forum*, 36: 163–178.

Horvath, A. O. 1994. Empirical validation of Bordin's pantheoretical model of the alliance: The Working Alliance Inventory perspective. In *The working alliance: Theory, research, and practice*, edited by A. O. Horvath and L. S. Greenberg, 109–128. New York: Wiley.

Horvath, A. O. 2001. The alliance. *Psychotherapy*, 38: 365–372.

Horvath, A. O., and Bedi, R. P. 2002. The alliance. In *Psychotherapy relationships that work: Therapists contributions and responsiveness to patients*, edited by J. C. Norcross, 37–69. London: Oxford.

Horvath, A. O., and Greenberg, L. S. 1989. Development and validation of the Working Alliance Inventory. *Journal of Counseling Psychology*, 36: 223–233.

Horvath, A. O., and Symonds, B. D. 1991. Relation between working alliance and outcome in psychotherapy: A meta-analysis. *Journal of Counseling Psychology*, 38: 139–149.

Jackson, J., Tyler, T. R., Bradford, B., Taylor, D., and Shiner, M. 2010. Legitimacy and procedural justice in prisons. *Prison Service Journal*, 191: 4–10.

Kennealy, P. J., Skeem, J. L., Manchak, S. M., and Eno Louden, J. 2012. Firm, fair, and caring officer-offender relationships protect against supervision failure. *Law and Human Behavior*, 36: 496–505.

Kiesler, D. J., and Watkins, L. M. 1989. Interpersonal complementarity and the therapeutic alliance: A study of relationship in psychotherapy. *Psychotherapy: Theory, Research, Practice, Training*, 26: 183–194.

Knudsen, H. K., Abraham, H. J., Johnson, J. A., and Roman, P. M. 2009. Buprenorphine adoption in the National Drug Abuse Treatment Clinical Trials Network. *Journal of Substance Abuse Treatment*, 37: 307–312.

Konrad, E. L. 1996. A multidimensional framework for conceptualizing human services integration initiatives. *New Directions for Evaluation*, 69: 5–19.

Lambert, M. J., and Barley, D. E. 2001. Research summary on the therapeutic relationship and psychotherapy outcome. *Psychotherapy: Theory, Research, Practice, Training*, 38: 357–361.

Landenberger, N. A., and Lipsey, M. W. 2005. The positive effects of cognitive–behavioral programs for offenders: A meta-analysis of factors associated with effective treatment. *Journal of Experimental Criminology*, 1: 451–476.

Latessa, E. J., Lemke, R., Makarios, M., and Smith, P. 2010. Creation and validation of the Ohio Risk Assessment System (ORAS). *Federal Probation*, 74 (1): 16–22.

Lifers Public Safety Steering Committee. 2004. Ending the culture of street crime. *Prison Journal*, 84: 48S–68S.

Lipsey, M. W. 2008. *The Arizona Standardized Program Evaluation Protocol (SPEP) for assessing the effectiveness of programs for juvenile probationers: SPEP ratings and relative recidivism reduction for the initial SPEP sample* (A report to the Juvenile Justice Services Division, Administrative Office of the Courts, State of Arizona). Nashville, TN: Center for Evaluation Research and Methodology, Vanderbilt Institute for Public Policy Studies.

Lipsey, M. W., Landenberger, N. A., and Wilson, S. J. 2007. *Effects of cognitive–behavioral programs for criminal offenders*. Campbell Systematic Reviews. doi: 10.4073/csr.2007.6.

Lipton, D., Pearson, F., Cleland, C., and Yee, D. 2002. The effectiveness of cognitive–behavioral treatment methods on offender recidivism: Meta-analytic outcomes from the CDATE project. In *Offender rehabilitation and treatment: Effective programmes and policies to reduce re-offending*, edited by J. McGuire, 79–112. Chichester: John Wiley & Sons, Ltd.

Lowenkamp, C. T., Latessa, E. J., and Holsinger, A. M. 2006. The risk principle in action: What have we learned from 13,676 offenders and 97 correctional programs? *Crime & Delinquency*, 52: 77–93.

Martin, M. S., Dorken, S. K., Wamboldt, A. D., Wootten, S. E. 2011. Stopping the revolving door: A meta-analysis on the effectiveness of interventions for criminally involved individuals with major mental disorders. *Law and Human Behavior*, 36: 1–12.

Michie, S., Fixsen, D., Grimshaw, J. W., and Eccles, M. P. 2009. Specifying and reporting complex behaviour change interventions: The need for a scientific method. *Implementation Science*, 4: 40–45.

Mitchell, O. J., Wilson, D. B., and MacKenzie, D. L. 2007. Does incarceration-based treatment reduce recidivism? A meta-analytic synthesis of the research. *Journal of Experimental Criminology*, 3: 353–375.

Mueser, K. T. Noordsy, D. L., and Drake, R. E. 2003. *Integrated treatment for dual disorders: A guide to effective practice*. New York: Guilford.

Murphy, A., Rhodes, A. G., and Taxman, F. S. 2012. Adaptability of contingency management in justice settings: Survey findings on attitudes toward using rewards. *Journal of Substance Abuse Treatment*, 43: 168–177.

Murphy, P. M., Cramer, D., and Lillie, F. J. 1984. The relationship between curative factors perceived by patients in their psychotherapy and treatment outcome: An exploratory study. *British Journal of Medical Psychology*, 57: 187–192.

Norcross, J. 2010. The therapeutic relationship. In *The heart and soul of change: Delivering what works*, edited by B. L. Duncan, S. D. Miller, B. E. Wampold, and M. A. Hubble, 2nd ed., 113–141. Washington, DC: American Psychological Association.

Norcross J. C., and Lambert, M. J. 2005. The therapy relationship. In *Evidence-based practices in mental health: Debate and dialogue on the fundamental questions*, edited by J. C. Norcross, L. E. Beutler, and R. F. Levant, 208–218. Washington, DC: American Psychological Association.

Persons, R. W., Persons, M. K., and Newmark, I. 1974. Perceived helpful therapists' characteristics, client improvements, and sex of therapist and client. *Psychotherapy: Theory, Research & Practice*, 11: 63–65.

Prendergast, M., Greenwell, L., Cartier, L., Sacks, J., Frisman, J., Rodis, E., and Havens, J. R. 2009. Adherence to scheduled sessions in a randomized field trial of case management: The CJ-DATS Transitional Case Management Study. *Journal of Experimental Criminology*, 5: 273–279.

Prendergast, M., Huang, D., and Hser, Y. 2008. Patterns of crime and drug use trajectories in relation to treatment initiation and 5-year outcomes: An application of growth mixture modeling across three data sets. *Evaluation Review*, 32: 59–83.

Prendergast, M. L., Podus, D., Chang, E., and Urada, D. 2002. The effectiveness of drug abuse treatment: A meta-analysis of comparison group studies. *Drug and Alcohol Dependence*, 67: 53–72.

Simpson, D. D. 2004. A conceptual framework for drug treatment process and outcomes. *Journal of Substance Abuse Treatment*, 27: 99–121.

Simpson, D. D., Joe, G. W., and Rowan-Szal, G. A. 1997. Drug abuse treatment retention and process effects on follow-up outcomes. *Drug and Alcohol Dependence*, 47: 227–235.

Simpson, D. D., Wexler, H. K., and Inciardi, J. A. 1999. Drug treatment outcomes for correctional settings. *Prison Journal*, 79: 291–293.

Skeem, J. L., Louden, J. E., Polaschek, D., and Camp, J. 2007. Assessing relationship quality in mandated community treatment: Blending care with control. *Psychological Assessment*, 19: 397–410.

Sperber, K. G., Latessa, E. J., and Makarios, M. D. 2013a. Establishing a risk–dosage research agenda. *Justice Research and Policy*, 15: 123–142.

Sperber, K. G., Latessa, E. J., and Makarios, M. D. 2013b. Examining the interaction between level of risk and dosage of treatment. *Criminal Justice and Behavior*, 40: 338–348.

Tatman, A. W., and Love, K. M. 2010. An offender version of the Working Alliance Inventory–Short Revised. *Journal of Offender Rehabilitation*, 49: 165–179.

Taxman, F. S. 2014. Substance abuse is sometimes a primary criminogenic need and sometimes a secondary criminogenic need. *Perspectives*, 38: 48–56.

Taxman, F. S., and Ainsworth, S. 2009. Correctional milieu: The key to quality outcomes. *Victims and Offenders*, 4: 334–340.

Taxman, F. S., and Bouffard, J. A. 2003. Substance abuse counselors' treatment philosophy and the content of treatment services provided to offenders in drug court programs. *Journal of Substance Abuse Treatment*, 25: 75–84.

Taxman, F. S., and Friedmann, P. D. 2009. Fidelity and adherence at the transition point: Theoretically driven experiments. *Journal of Experimental Criminology*, 5: 219–226.

Taxman, F. S., Henderson, C. E., and Belenko, S. 2009. Organizational context, systems change, and adopting treatment delivery systems in the criminal justice system. *Drug and Alcohol Dependence*, 103 (Suppl. 1): S1–S94.

Taxman, F. S., and Marlowe, D. 2006. Risk, needs, responsivity: In action or inaction? *Crime & Delinquency*, 52: 3–6.

Taxman, F. S., Pattavina, A., and Caudy, M. 2014. Justice reinvestment in the United States: An empirical assessment of the potential impact of increased correctional programming on recidivism. *Victims & Offenders*, 9: 50–75.

Taxman, F. S., Young, D. W., Wiersema, B., Rhodes, A., and Mitchell, S. 2007. The national criminal justice treatment practices survey: Multilevel survey methods and procedures. *Journal of substance abuse treatment*, 32: 225–238.

Tong, L. S., and Farrington, D. P. 2006. How effective is the "reasoning and rehabilitation" programme in reducing reoffending? A meta-analysis of evaluations in four countries. *Psychology, Crime & Law*, 12: 3–24.

Tong, L. S., and Farrington, D. P. 2008. Effectiveness of reasoning and rehabilitation in reducing reoffending. *Psicothema*, 20: 20–28.

Tyler, T. R. 2006. Restorative justice and procedural justice: Dealing with rule breaking. *Journal of Social Issues*, 62: 307–326.

Visher, C. A., Hiller, M., Belenko, S., Pankow J, Dembo, R., Frisman, L. K., ...Wiley, T. R. 2014. The effect of a local change team intervention on staff attitudes towards HIV service delivery in correctional settings: A randomized trial. *AIDS Education Prevention*, 26: 411–428.

Visher, C., Winterfield, L., and Coggeshall, M. 2005. Ex-offender employment programs and recidivism: A meta-analysis. *Journal of Experimental Criminology*, 1: 295–316.

Welsh, W. N. 2007. A multisite evaluation of prison-based therapeutic community drug treatment. *Criminal Justice and Behavior*, 34: 1481–1498.

Westen, D., Novotny, C. M., and Thompson-Brenner, H. 2004. The empirical status of empirically supported psychotherapies: Assumptions, findings, and reporting in controlled clinical trials. *Psychological Bulletin*, 130: 631–663.

Wilson, T. D. 2011. *Redirect: The surprising new science of psychological change*. New York: Little, Brown.

Wintersteen, M. B., Mensinger, J. L., and Diamond, G. S. 2005. Do gender and racial differences between patient and therapist affect therapeutic alliance and treatment retention in adolescents? *Professional Psychology: Research and Practice*, 36: 400–408.

Wooditch, A., Tang, L. L., and Taxman, F. S. 2014. Which criminogenic need changes are most important in promoting desistance from crime and substance use? *Criminal Justice and Behavior*, 41 (3): 276–299. doi: 0093854813503543.

Wright, K. N., Clear, T. R., and Dickson, P. 1984. Universal applicability of probation risk-assessment instruments. *Criminology*, 22: 113–134.

Further Reading

Bordin, E. S. 1994. Theory and research on the therapeutic working alliance: New directions. In *The working alliance: Theory, research, and practice*, edited by A. O. Horvath and L. S. Greenburg, 13–37. New York: John Wiley.

Hamilton, C. M., Strader., L. C., Pratt, J. G., Maiese, D., Hendershot, T., Kwok., R. K., ... Neffles, D. S. 2011. The PhenX toolkit: Get the most from your measures. *American Journal of Epidemiology*, 174: 253–260.

Himmelman, A. T. 1996. On the theory and practice of transformational collaboration: From social service to social justice. In *Creating collaborative advantage*, edited by C. Huxham 19–43. London: Sage.

Himmelman, A.T. 2001. On coalitions and the transformation of power relations: Collaborative betterment and collaborative empowerment. *American Journal of Community Psychology*, 29: 277–284.

Horvath, A. O. 1991. Relation between working alliance and outcome in psychotherapy: A meta-analysis. *Journal of Counseling Psychology*, 38: 139–149.

Lipsey, M. W. 2009. The primary factors that characterize effective interventions with juvenile offenders: A meta-analytic overview. *Victims and Offenders*, 4: 124–147.

Makarios, M., Sperber, K. G., and Latessa, E. J. 2014. Treatment dosage and the risk principle: A refinement and extension. *Journal of Offender Rehabilitation*, 53: 334–350.

12

Measuring Victimization: Issues and New Directions

Leah E. Daigle, Jamie A. Snyder, and Bonnie S. Fisher

When persons first began to study crime victims, it was with the realization that victims may play a role in their own victimization. Those at the forefront of the process that generated the field of victimology were primarily concerned with the role of victim precipitation and with creating victim typologies; they were much less concerned with measuring or estimating the extent of criminal victimization (Schafer, 1968; von Hentig, 1948). That is, early work in the field of victimology was centered on identifying the extent to which victims contributed to their own victimization and with classifying victims into groups on the basis of their level of contribution or responsibility. When researchers began identifying and counting the number of different types of crime victims and collecting information about the characteristics of these incidents, they quickly found themselves challenged by the complexity of what, on the surface, appears to be a deceivingly simple measurement tasks. It is important that victimization is measured effectively, so that the true extent of this phenomenon is known. Moreover, who is most likely to be victimized needs to be appropriately identified so that prevention resources can be directed at those most at risk.

Measuring criminal victimization, as it turns out, is surprisingly difficult. Estimates derived are highly contingent upon how victimization is measured and upon a host of methodological choices. In this chapter we describe how some of the issues surrounding measurement influence the estimates and the characteristics of victimization that are produced. In addition, we present new developments in measurement, as well as potential new strategies for reducing measurement error and for analyzing survey data.

The Handbook of Measurement Issues in Criminology and Criminal Justice, First Edition.
Edited by Beth M. Huebner and Timothy S. Bynum.

How Is Victimization Typically Measured?

When we want to know the extent to which people are victimized, one source of information is official reports of crime. Most commonly in the United States, this source of data is the Uniform Crime Reports (UCR), which provides an account of the amount of crime known to law enforcement in a given year, along with information about the offense and offender (if known) (FBI, 2013a). To provide this information, police departments throughout the United States voluntarily submit monthly reports to the Federal Bureau of Investigation (FBI) about each offense of which they are aware. These reports meet specific criteria. To be included in the annual report, *Crime in the United States*, an offense reported to the police must be one of eight Part I index offenses (murder, rape, robbery, aggravated assault, burglary, arson, motor vehicle theft, larceny). Information about Part II offenses is broken into 21 offense categories: other assaults; forgery and counterfeiting, fraud; embezzlement; stolen property (buying, receiving, possessing); vandalism; weapons (carrying, possessing, etc.); prostitution and commercialized vice; sex offenses; drug abuse violations; gambling; offenses against the family and children; driving under the influence; liquor laws; drunkenness; disorderly conduct; vagrancy; suspicion; curfew and loitering laws (for persons under age 18); runaways (for persons under age 18); and all other offenses (except traffic violations) for which an arrest has been made (FBI, 2012). In 2013 in the United States, the violent crime rate was 367.9 offenses per 100,000 people and the property crime rate was 2,730.7 per 100,000 people. Both rates declined – which made that year the 11th in a period during which property crime had declined continuously (FBI, 2013b). Although violent crime increased slightly in 2012 by comparison with 2011, overall violent crime has been decreasing since 2006 (FBI, 2013c).

Although beneficial for tracking crime trends across the years, the UCR provides limited information about crime victims and only contains information about crimes known to the police. Producing estimates of crime on the basis of crimes known to police – and known mainly through reporting – is problematic, given that many crime victims do not report their victimization to the police. For instance, in 2012 less than half of all victimizations were reported to the police – namely about one third of all property crimes and less than 50 percent of all violent crimes (Truman, Langton, and Planty, 2013). Because of this gap in reporting, other ways of measuring the extent to which people and their property are victimized are necessary.

It was during the mid-1960s that self-report victimization surveys were first developed, in response to recommendations put forth from the DC Crime Commission and the President's Commission on Law Enforcement and Administration of Justice (Cantor and Lynch, 2000). These original exploratory studies were designed with two primary objectives in mind: (1) to determine the extent of victimization that was not reliant upon reporting to law enforcement yet occurred in the nation; and (2) to learn about the methodological issues underlining the administration of self-report victimization surveys. One of the most illuminating findings from these early surveys was that crime victims had difficulty in recalling incidents. For example, from the early studies it was discovered that individuals were more likely to recall events near the end and the beginning of a reference period – a phenomenon called "recency bias" (Cantor and Lynch, 2000).

Recalling a criminal incident's details speaks to methodological issues, which are the focus of this chapter. As noted just above, results from early pilot studies revealed that victimizations, even quite serious ones, were not easily recalled by people. Taking this difficulty into account, researchers have to create survey instruments and interview protocols that are best able to cue respondents about these specific events with the least amount of measurement error. Measurement error can be produced from a variety of sources, not all of which will be discussed in this chapter; however, we will consider kinds of measurement error that are derived from sampling and from other sources (e.g., measuring concepts; who is included in study; question-wording or ordering; measurement strategies; bounding or telescoping; and mode of data collection). Whatever the source of measurement error, one of the goals of designing research is to minimize or prevent systematic measurement error, which creates bias in our findings by making us over- or underestimate key parameters. For example, in estimating the extent of victimization through a survey, we should watch whether the question used to measure victimization is vague, worded poorly, or too broad: persons responding to "bad" questions may not know how to answer. When answering "bad" questions, true estimates of victimization may not be able to be estimated.

What Is the Phenomenon Being Measured?

One of the key criteria in evaluating victimization research is considering the context of the survey. When doing this, one should examine the cover letter or the introduction to the survey, which is read or sent out to respondents. This context cues the respondents as to the topic or focus of the survey, and hence indicates what is important for the respondents to consider when answering the questions. In this way respondents are being told what they should be paying attention to, what they should be considering, and what they should be recalling. Other events in their life may get dismissed, then, as they attend to what they think researchers are interested in. For example, individuals who participate in the National Crime Victimization Survey (NCVS) are specifically told that they are going to be asked questions about crime. The name of the survey is the National *Crime* Victimization Survey, the survey is sponsored by the federal government, and the persons conducting the face-to-face interview wear identification badges (Tourangeau and McNeeley, 2002; see National Criminal Justice, 2014). These features of the NCVS are likely to cue respondents that the purpose of the study is to measure crimes rather than events that may be victimizing but not rise to the level of crimes (e.g., coercion). Contrast this context to that presented in other surveys that measure victimization – such as the National Intimate Partner and Sexual Violence Survey, whose name does not denote official crime, but rather violence (Black et al., 2011). Similarly, the National Violence

Against Women survey is described as a survey about personal safety rather than as a survey explicitly designed to measure violence within interpersonal relationships (Tjaden and Thoennes, 2000). As part of examining the effect of a survey's name and how it may cue a respondent to think in certain ways, the National Survey of Drug Abuse changed its name to the National Survey of Drug Use and Health. After it did so, drug use reports increased (Office of Applied Studies, 2003). It is possible that introducing a study in terms related to health and well-being rather than crime may create a context in which respondents are cued to recall a greater variety of victimization events in their life; thus mentions of victimization would increase. In a recent report on the measurement of rape and sexual assault in the NCVS, researchers concluded that the context of the NCVS likely contributes to an underestimation of rape and sexual assault (Panel on Measuring Rape and Sexual Assault in Bureau of Justice Statistics Household Surveys, 2014).

Who Is Administered the Survey, and Who Is Not?

A main consideration when designing and administering victimization surveys is identifying the population of interest and then creating a sampling frame from which the sample will be chosen. Ideally, probability samples would be generated and victimization surveys would be administered to the largest sample possible, but doing so is not often practical – or even possible – given financial, time, and other resource constraints. As an example, if the aim is to study elder abuse, the population of interest is older adults; so a sampling frame of older adults would have to be identified, and then a sample would have to be drawn from that frame. Although this process may seem simple, identifying a population of interest and developing a sampling frame may be quite difficult when one preforms victimization research on older adults (and on children). Older adults may live in long-term care facilities, nursing homes, or other forms of residence that would not allow ready access to researchers.

Not only could it be difficult to generate a representative sample; it is also important to consider the developmental and cognitive capabilities of individuals when deciding whom to include in a sample. First, researchers should consider the age of the sample they wish to study and the abilities that go along with it. Although researchers may be interested in finding out about childhood victimization, very young children do not have the ability to comprehend and cognitively process or navigate complex survey questions, especially ones about victimization. Children may often not be able to understand what is being asked of them. To ensure that they do understand, a simple vocabulary, syntax, and grammar and examples of explicit behaviors should be used in questionnaires (Hamby and Finkelhor, 2000). For example, in the Juvenile Victimization Questionnaire, persons are asked: "In the last year, did anyone break or ruin any of your things on purpose?" This question is intended to measure vandalism (Finkelhor et al., 2005).

Research on children's ability to answer questions about their victimizations indicates that children can be good self-reporters (Hamby and Finkelhor, 2000).

Seven-year-olds have been included in research about domestic violence, eight-year-olds have been interviewed about child abuse experiences, six- and seven-year-olds have been interviewed about exposure to community violence (as cited in Hamby and Finkelhor, 2000).

A further consideration is that, when children are included, the permission of a legal guardian, parent, or caretaker must first be secured. This person may not want the child to participate in research. Moreover, this person may be present when the child is completing home-based surveys, which could reduce the likelihood that the child would disclose abuse (Hamby and Finkelhor, 2000). Lack of disclosure is particularly problematic, given that children are most likely to be abused and neglected by their biological parents (Department of Health and Human Services, 2012).

Similar issues arise when attempting to study elders. Older persons may not be able to cognitively assess their own victimization experiences due to decline in mental acuity. In addition, older people may be difficult to include in general population samples, since they might be in long-term care or live in residential facilities that are difficult to access, such as nursing homes. Americans aged 65 and over are also less likely than younger adults to use the Internet (the proportion of those who use it is 59 percent, by comparison with 85 percent for younger adults: see Smith, 2014). This makes them less accessible for online surveys. For these reasons, when attempting to compare findings from surveys, it is important to examine who constitutes the sample in terms of age. The NCVS, for instance, only includes in its study individuals who are aged 12 and over (see Table 12.1). Any year's estimates of victimization produced from the NCVS are, then, restricted to such individuals and leave out children younger than 12. The Crime Survey in England and Wales (CSEW) only includes individuals aged 16 and over. To measure the victimization of younger children (specifically, 10- to 15-year-olds), the CSEW offers a supplement with questions about bullying and cyberbullying, crime, alcohol and drug use; behaviors that children may engage in to keep their belongings safe, and carrying knives (see http://www.crimesurvey.co.uk/10–15-Surveys.html).

Similar issues arise when attempting to examine other populations in victimization research. For example, certain groups such as prisoners or people with intellectual disabilities or severe mental illness may not be able to comprehend survey questions written at an advanced reading level. When writing questions for such groups of people, one should make sure that they are able to understand the content and meaning of the survey. Doing so is especially important, because these populations are at particular risk of being victimized (Daigle, 2013); thus they are ripe for inclusion in victimization research.

Second, it is important to consider other factors and components in the sampling design that may lead to the systematic exclusion of certain individuals from victimization surveys. Many of the national-level studies using self-report surveys are community-based surveys that exclude individuals who reside in institutions (e.g., mental health facilities, group homes, dormitories), are homeless, and are imprisoned. For example, the NCVS excludes homeless and institutionalized persons (e.g., people in jail). Importantly, these persons, who are often excluded

Table 12.1 Description of common surveys used to measure victimization.

Study	*Year Began*	*When Administered*	*Recall Period*	*Types of Victimization Measured*	*Sample*	*Measurement Process*
BCS[a] CSEW	1982 2012	Every two years until 2001, every year thereafter	Previous 12 months	Violence with and without injury, robbery, personal theft, burglary, vehicle theft, bicycle theft, other household theft and criminal damage	About 35,000 persons aged 16 and older; and 3,000 children between the ages 10 and 15 in supplement	Face to face survey, CAPI
				Sexual violence, domestic partner violence, stalking		Self-completion module on intimate violence
National Study of Drug- or Alcohol-Facilitated, Incapacitated, and Forcible Rape	2007		Previous 12 months; Lifetime	Forcible rape, Drug or alcohol facilitated rape, Incapacitated rape	2,000 adult female college students and 3,001 adult women (2,000 between the ages of 18 and 34 and 1,000 of 35 and older)	Random digit dial for community sample; College students selected from American Student List. CATI
NCS/NCVS[b]	1973	Every 6 months, rotating panel design with households in sample for 7 survey administrations	Previous 6 months	Rape, sexual assault, robbery, aggravated assault, simple assault, personal theft, household burglary, motor vehicle theft, theft	92,390 households, 162,940 (in 2012) people aged 12 and older	In-person interview, telephone survey, CATI
NCWSVS[c]	1996		Since school began in fall 1996	Rape, sexual coercion, nonforceful unwanted sexual contact, forceful unwanted sexual contact, stalking, threats	4,446 college females	Telephone survey, CATI

NISVS[d]	2010		Previous 12 months; Lifetime	Intimate partner violence; stalking; sexual victimization (rape, noncontact unwanted sexual experience, unwanted sexual contact, sexual coercion, for males being forced to penetrate)	9,086 females, 7,421 males	Random digit dialing telephone survey, CATI
NVAWS[e]	1998		Previous 12 months; Lifetime	Sexual assault, physical assault, stalking	8,000 females 18 years old and older, 8,000 males 18 years old and older	Random digit dialing telephone survey, CATI
NVACWS[f]	1996		Since school began in fall 1996	Rape, sexual assault, robbery, aggravated assault, simple assault, unwanted sexual contact	4,432 College females	Telephone survey, CATI
NWS[g]	1990	3-year longitudinal study	Previous 12 months; Lifetime	Forcible rape	4,008 women 18 years old and older	Telephone interviews

[a] British Crime Survey; Crime in England and South Wales, at https://www.gov.uk/government/statistics/crime-outcomes-in-england-and-wales-2013-to-2014.
[b] National Crime Survey/National Crime Victimization Survey, at http://www.bjs.gov/index.cfm?ty=dcdetail&iid=245.
[c] National College Women Sexual Victimization Survey, at https://www.ncjrs.gov/pdffiles1/nij/grants/179977.pdf.
[d] National Intimate Partner and Sexual Violence Survey, at http://www.cdc.gov/violenceprevention/nisvs/index.html.
[e] National Violence against Women Survey, at https://www.ncjrs.gov/pdffiles1/nij/183781.pdf.
[f] National Violence against College Women Survey.
[g] National Women's Study.

from general, large-scale victimization surveys, present a high risk of being victimized; so leaving them out could bias the magnitude of the estimates of victimization downward. In addition, their exclusion is problematic for research on the risk factors for victimization, because the characteristics of such people cannot be examined as potential risk factors. Research on employment has demonstrated the effects of not accounting for the differential rates of incarceration among subpopulations. This research is instructive in that it shows that standard labor force data that do not account for the rates at which black and white persons are incarcerated influence the estimates of employment inequality among black and white persons: among young people who have dropped out of high school, employment inequality is underestimated by 45 percent (Western and Pettit, 2000). Although not specific to victimization, this finding may be relevant for victimization research, insofar as it shows that not accounting for incarceration, for the rates at which incarcerated people are victimized, and for differences across groups can influence both the estimates of victimization and the identification of its risk factors.

Another issue raised by the exclusion of persons who live in shelters and receive care in hospitals is related to measuring intimate partner violence. There is a debate surrounding gender symmetry – namely a debate as to whether males and females perpetrate (and are victims of) intimate partner violence at similar levels. Some research has found that females and males experience intimate partner violence (IPV) at similar rates (Archer, 2000). One major criticism of the research that leads to this view has been that, as a result of using mainly community-based samples, it most likely does not include in its estimates victims of very serious forms of IPV, because these individuals are likely to reside in shelters, be hospitalized, and overall not participate in survey research (Johnson, 1995). This is particularly important, because research shows that women in shelters or who have left their home are likely to have experienced abuse at higher rates than women (or men) surveyed in general, community-based national samples (Johnson, 1995).

Also to consider is whether both males and females are covered in the sample of persons surveyed. Although most national-level, community-based surveys include both males and females, not all research is conducted on both sexes. Initially the elimination of males was done when examining types of victimization for which women were thought to be at particular risk, such as sexual victimization. Even national-level studies of sexual victimization often either only took females in the sample (see, for example, the National Study of Drug- or Alcohol-Facilitated, Incapacitated, and Forcible Rape in Table 12.1) or allowed males, but asked about their perpetration of this type of violence rather than about their experiences of being victimized (see for example the Sexual Experiences Survey developed by Koss and Oros, 1982). As a result of the fact that only females' experiences of sexual victimization were taken into account, the extent to which males, especially college males, suffered experiences of the same kind could not be determined. Moreover, the omission of males erroneously sends the message that they are not affected by this type of victimization. Research from the NISVS shows, however, that males do experience sexual victimization too, and at high rates. In that study, 3 percent of women reported having had unwanted noncontact sexual experiences during the previous 12 months – by comparison with 2.7 percent of men. Over the same period, slightly less than 3 percent (2.2 percent) of women experienced unwanted sexual contact, by comparison with 2.3 percent of men (Black et al., 2011). These results indicate that men and women actually suffer this type of sexual victimization at similar rates.

Although this is not tied directly to the omission of particular groups of individuals from surveys, it is also important to consider that it may be difficult to provide estimates of victimization for subpopulations, given the rarity of occurrence of some victimization types. Even when one works with large, national-level surveys like the NCVS, the victimization rate estimates produced for subpopulations (e.g., rape and sexual assault of American Indians and Alaska Natives) may have corresponding large sampling errors, which render conclusions about risk difficult to make (Panel on Measuring Rape and Sexual Assault in Bureau of Justice Statistics Household Surveys, 2014). Instead, researchers may want to oversample for specific subpopulations when conducting their own research, or be mindful of the challenges of working with estimates calculated from small samples. One way to combat this problem is by using estimates produced by pooling data from sources such as the NCVS across years, so that the numbers for subpopulations are large enough to produce reliable estimates (Lauritsen, 2012).

Two-Stage versus One-Stage Measurement Strategies

Researchers must be concerned not only about who is included in the sample, but also about how various events are classified as "victimizations" and then "counted." One of the major differences across victimization surveys is the use of either a one-stage or a two-stage measurement strategy. In a one-stage measurement strategy, respondents are asked about their victimization experiences via a single question (or series of single questions) designed to assess victimization incidence. In the NISVS, a one-stage measurement process is used. For example, to measure attempted rape, researchers ask: "How many people have ever used physical force or threats of physical harm to try to have vaginal, oral, or anal sex with you, but sex did not happen?" (Black et al., 2011). On the other hand, in a two-stage measurement strategy that resembles the one used in the NCVS, respondents are asked about victimization experiences via questions similar to those used in the one-stage process. If any of the questions are answered affirmatively, or if respondents indicate that they experienced victimization at least once, they then complete the second stage of the measurement process.

An important consideration when developing surveys and when examining estimates of victimization produced by surveys is how responses to victimization questions are "counted" with the help of a two-stage versus an one-stage measurement strategy. A seeming advantage to using a two-stage measurement strategy is that the second stage can be used to verify (1) that a victimization did in fact occur; and

Box 12.1 Example of NCVS Screen Question Designed to Measure Theft.

I'm going to read some examples that will give you an idea of the kinds of crimes this study covers. As I go through them, tell me if any of these happened to you in the last six months, that is since _____, 20___:

Was something belonging to YOU stolen, such as:

a. Things that you carry, like luggage, a wallet, purse, briefcase, book	b. Clothing, jewelry, or cellphone	c. Bicycle or sports equipment
d. Things in your home-like a TB, stereo, or tools	e. Things outside your home such as a garden hose or lawn furniture	f. Things belonging to children in the household
g. Things from a vehicle, such as a package, groceries, camera, or CDs	h. Did anyone ATTEMPT to steal anything belonging to you?	

(2) the type of victimization that occurred. In this way, using a two-stage measurement strategy can be a conservative and a more valid way to measure victimization. How is this verification process carried out? As noted, only individuals who answer affirmatively to a victimization screen question will continue to the second stage. This second stage, though, often has a variety questions that can be used to verify that a victimization did, in fact, occur. For example, a screen question may ask whether a person had been attacked or threatened (see Box 12.1 for an example of a screen question from the NCVS). If a person answers "yes" to this question, he or she would then complete questions (in an incident report in the NCVS) about that specific incident. In this second stage, additional questions are asked about the incident that can be used to verify that a person was in fact attacked or threatened. In the NCVS, for instance, in the incident report, a person is asked: "Did the offender hit you, knock you down, or actually attack you in any way?" "Did the offender try to attack you?" and "Did the offender threaten you with harm in any way?" If a person answers "no" to these questions and to every other victimization question in the incident report, then there would be a mismatch between the screen question answer and the incident report verification. The screening questionnaire indicates that the respondent was a victim, but, when more probing questions are asked, it appears that no victimization occurred (for an evaluation of the NCVS screen questions, see Peytchev et al., 2012).

Along these same lines, the incident report can also be used to verify that a specific type of victimization occurred. In the screen questions in the National College Women Sexual Victimization (NCWSV) study (see Box 12.2), college women were

Box 12.2 Example of NCWSV Study Screen Questions to Measure Completed Rape.

1. Since school began in the fall of 1996, has anyone *made* you have *sexual intercourse* by using *force or threatening to harm* you or someone close to you? Just so there is no mistake, by intercourse I mean putting a penis in your vagina.
2. Since school began in the fall of 1996, has anyone *made* you have *oral sex by force or threat of harm*? By oral sex, I mean did someone's mouth or tongue make contact with your vagina or anus or did your mouth or tongue make contact with someone else's genitals or anus.
3. Since school began in the fall of 1996, has anyone *made* you have *anal sex by force or threat of harm*? By anal sex, I mean putting a penis in your anus or rectum.
4. Since school began in the fall of 1996, has anyone ever used *force or threat of harm to sexually penetrate you with a foreign object*? By this, I mean, for example, placing a bottle or finger in your vagina or anus.

asked about 10 types of sexual victimization they could have experienced. If a woman responded "yes" to any of these questions, she then completed an incident report for each incident she experienced. The incident report included detailed questions designed to measure the elements of sexual victimization (the questions were based on type of force used, means of coercion, and whether the incident was attempted or completed), so that the incidents could be appropriately classified. The incident was then classified according to the answers given in the incident report, so that the classification matched the type of sexual victimization (criteria matched a legal definition). Thus incidents were classified not according to the affirmative response given on a victimization screen question, but through a confirmation process that used responses to questions in the incident report.

One seemingly simple question arises from this discussion of the two-stage process: Is this confirmation step necessary for reducing measurement error? As noted by Fisher and Cullen (2000), in the NCWSV study there were 314 incidents that initially screened into the second stage, which is called the incident report. Of these 314 incidents, 157 were ultimately classified as rapes and 155 were classified as incidents other than rape. Eighty incidents could not be classified on the basis of responses to the incident report, the respondent could not recall sufficiently many details for the incident to be classified, or the incident fell outside of the recall period. In these 80 cases, it is not clear whether the incident was in fact a rape, as not enough information was provided by the respondent in the incident report for the second-stage classification procedure to be conducted. On the other hand, 78 incidents that initially screened in through other nonrape screen questions were ultimately classified as rape incidents, because the details of the incident report met the legal definition of rape (i.e., penetration, force or threat of force, lack of consent). If the screen question responses alone had been used to determine the rape victimization rate, the rate would have been 1.6 times greater than the rate that was calculated using the incident report (Fisher and Cullen, 2000). What these findings show is that using an incident report helps identify the specific details of an incident, so that there is a greater likelihood that incidents are being classified correctly.

Bounding and Telescoping

The measurement of victimization is also affected by bounding, a process that provides a reference point for subsequent interviews in a panel study. This technique uses information collected from prior interviews to inform later interviews within the same study. For instance, information about victimization incidents is collected in the first interview, and then used in future interviews to prevent the duplication of incidents that have already been reported, as well as to increase recall. The first interview is referred to as "bounded" and provides a temporal point of reference or a time frame for respondents.

Bounding has been utilized in several victimization studies. For example, the NCVS originally used its first interview for bounding purposes, although since 2007 it has been using the first interview in its annual estimates (National Criminal Justice, 2014). In each subsequent wave of the survey, the interviewer may reference the first interview to help prevent the replication of a victimization that has already been recorded. Common errors could include reporting an incident that occurred outside the reference period (which, for the NCVS, is six months) or reporting an incident such as a burglary, which was already reported by another member of the household. To "jog" a participant's memory, interviewers may include details from prior incidents that were reported.

Bounding can significantly reduce measurement error in the form of overestimating incidents of victimization. On the other hand, unbounded surveys could inflate estimates of victimization. Planty (2003) reported 30 percent fewer victimizations in surveys that were bounded than in surveys that were unbounded. Biderman and Cantor (1984) asserted that unbounded surveys can increase estimations by up to 50 percent. It must also be noted that estimates from unbounded and from bounded surveys should not be compared with each other. Further, surveys that utilize different bounding procedures should not be compared. For example, Kilpatrick and colleagues' (1992) report (see the material from the National Women's Study [NWS] in Table 12.1, note g) used its first wave of interviews with a reference period of 12 months, and also asked about experiences over the lifetime. The NCVS also uses its first interview for bounding purposes, but has a reference period of six months. In contrast, in both the NVAWS and the NCWSV study, participants were only interviewed on one occasion, so neither is able to bound its interviews.

Bounding can also help prevent telescoping, which is the movement of victimizations either forward or backward in time. Survey participants often cannot remember exactly when a victimization incident has occurred, so the incident may fall outside the reference period. For example, the incident actually occurred nine months ago, but the respondent reports it as having occurred in the past six months. The reporting of incidents that fall outside of the reference period is a common source of measurement error in surveys that do not bound their interviews (Addington, 2005). The bounded interview can provide helpful information about a time line of events. Biderman and Lynch (1991) suggest that property victimizations are more likely to be telescoped, since these incidents tend to be reported in the most distant month of the reference period (as opposed to the most recent). Bounding surveys can serve to signal to participants the importance of determining correctly when an incident occurred. In other words, bounding lets participants know that precision and reporting incidents in the correct reference period is essential to increasing the accuracy of measurement (Biderman and Cantor, 1984).

Although bounding can considerably reduce measurement error, it is not without its problems. First, bounding can be expensive and time-consuming. Bounding requires multiple interviews to be conducted, and each wave could cost thousands of dollars. Cantor and Lynch (2000) not only note this concern, but also suggest that bounding may result in other types of measurement error and issues for data collection. Specifically, in the NCVS, when new members of a household are added into the sample, they are unbounded, because they were not in the sample at the time of the first interview. The combination of bounded and unbounded data may result in an increase in the number of incidents that are reported (Cantor and Lynch, 2000). Second, bounding requires that multiple interviews be conducted. Thus, questionnaires that are cross-sectional and only report incidents for one point in time cannot be bounded. Finally, data collected in the first interview are not usually included in the final calculations for the survey. For example, only incidents recorded in the second wave of the National Women's Study (NWS) were used to compute estimates of victimization (see Fisher and Cullen, 2000). Between wave 1 and wave 2, about 19 percent of participants were lost (Kilpatrick et al., 1992). Overall, when developing and administering victimization surveys, the advantages and disadvantages of bounding should be considered in terms of measurement error, cost, and the accuracy of categorizing incidents into the appropriate type of crime.

Question-Wording and Question Order

Another consideration that must be made when studying victimization relates to how questions are worded and ordered on the survey. Since there are several types of victimization, it is not surprising that there is wide variation in how questions are worded on victimization surveys. Past surveys have relied on simply asking about a behavior (e.g., "Have you ever been stalked?"), giving legal definitions (e.g., "the willful, malicious, and repeated following and harassing of another person"), and asking behaviorally specific questions (e.g., "Have you been repeatedly called, spied on, sent gifts or letters, or has someone shown up at your home so that this resulted in fear or concern for your safety?"). The NVACW study describes the behavior of interest in detail to the participant (e.g., "Have you experienced forced kissing, touching of private parts, grabbing, and fondling even if it is over your clothes?"). Other surveys, such as the NCVS, rely on victimization screen questions with short cues (e.g., "Has anyone attacked or threated you in any of these ways?") designed to help respondents recall incidents, and then ask for more details about the experience to be added in the incident report, in order to categorize the victimization.

Several advancements related to question-wording have been made in the measurement of victimization. In the past, victimization surveys relied heavily on nondescriptive questions (e.g., vague or without a definition) about crimes, especially in cases of sexual assault. These surveys were criticized for underestimating the prevalence of sexual victimization. Arguably one of the most important changes from these measures is the use of behaviorally specific questions and definitions. Questions of this type describe the behavior of interest in graphic detail to the respondent (Fisher and Cullen, 2000). The Sexual Experiences Survey (Koss and Oros, 1982) was one of the first instruments to measure sexual aggression and victimization in this fashion. The original survey contained 10 behaviorally specific questions designed to measure different types of unwanted sexual experiences and rape. Another example is the detailed descriptions of sexual victimization used in the NCWSV study. One question used for rape is:

> Since school began in fall 1996, has anyone made you have sexual intercourse by using force or threatening to harm you or someone close to you? Just so there is no mistake, by intercourse I mean putting a penis in your vagina. (Fisher, Cullen, and Turner, 2000, p. 6)

Not only does this definition cover behaviors that are considered rape, but it provides the participant with descriptions that aim to increase understanding of which behaviors constitute this type of victimization. The use of behaviorally specific questions typically results in significantly higher estimates of victimization. For example, by comparison with estimates from the NCVS, those found in the NCWSV study were 11 times higher for rape, six times higher for attempted rape, and four times higher for the threat of rape (Fisher et al., 2000).

Other surveys rely on the wording of screen questions to "cue" respondents. The NCVS uses the words "rape, attempted rape, and types of sexual attack" to prompt respondents. Simply asking a respondent, however, whether he or she has experienced a type of victimization raises several problems. First, the respondent may not know how to accurately categorize his or her victimization (e.g., robbery versus theft). Second, the respondent may not consider what happened to him or her to be a case of victimization. Many women do not see their experience of rape as "rape," even though it meets the definition for this type of victimization. Koss (1988) found that only 27 percent of women perceived their experience as rape, even though what happened to them qualified as a victimization of this type. Consequently, not providing the participant with definitions of different types of victimization in detail may underestimate prevalence. This point is further highlighted in the Panel on Measuring Rape and Sexual Assault in Bureau of Justice Statistics Household Surveys (2014, p. 142), as the panel concludes that the wording used by the NCVS may not be "consistently understood by survey respondents." Providing behaviorally specific language helps respondents to more precisely understand what constitutes different types of victimizations. It may also "prompt" women to report behaviors that they may not have reported without the detailed descriptions (Fisher, 2009). In other words, in the absence of a descriptive definition, a participant may not realize that he or she was victimized. Further, victims may feel more comfortable with descriptions that do not "label" their experiences. This comfort is most apparent in the case of victims of sexual offenses, who may feel uneasy about labeling their victimization as rape. Overall, using behaviorally specific questions can increase the accuracy of categorizing incidents (e.g., rape versus unwanted sexual contact) and can reduce measurement error, because respondents are more likely to comprehend which types of behaviors the survey question is asking about.

Other factors should also be considered when deciding on question-wording. First, whom the survey is being administered to may impact on the type of vocabulary utilized (e.g., older versus younger participants). For example, studies that target college-age participants often use much more descriptive and graphic language than studies that target older populations. If the participants are older, a different stylistic register or alternative methods may be more appropriate (Jobe and Mingay, 1990). Piloting the survey with a small group chosen from the target population may help in this respect. Second, a recall or reference period must be selected. Reference periods for victimization surveys vary from weeks to months, or even to lifetime periods. A lifetime "ever happen to you" reference period can be dramatically impacted by its length. Commonly used reference periods are of six months or one year. For example, the NCVS and the Conflict Tactics Scale (CTS) both ask participants about their experiences in the last six months. The NCWSV and the National Violence against College Women (NVACW) studies did not use set reference periods, but asked respondents about their experiences since school began. Surveys were administered in the spring semester of the current academic year and were designed to capture events that had occurred during the fall semester of that same year. This reference period, which averaged to seven months, was used in order to provide participants with an exact time frame and hopefully increase recall (Fisher et al., 2000). The NVACW study estimated both lifetime and 12-month rates of victimization. When selecting a reference period, one should be aware that shorter periods may result in more accurate measurement. Longer reference periods may result in increased measurement error. Victims may forget details, events, and the timing of their victimization. Whenever feasable, reference periods that are shorter and give respondents more concrete limits (e.g., since the spring of 2013) are optimal. Skogan (1981) argues that a reference period of three months is ideal. Nearly 90 percent of victims were able to correctly place their victimization in time when the interview happened three or fewer months after the incident. However, this method may not be as cost-effective as using a longer reference period. Considering these factors together, Cantor and Lynch (2000) recommend that reference periods should be no longer than six months, to provide the best chance for accuracy in recall.

Once the wording has been decided upon and the reference period selected, decisions need to be made about the ordering of the questions. The ordering of questions on victimization surveys – for example, which type of victimization is asked about first, second – could have an effect on several dimensions. First, it may lead participants one way or another. Grouping "similar" victimizations together can provide a substantive context for a participant. For example, asking participants about theft, then about burglary may orient the respondent to thinking about property crimes. Once they do so, participants are cued to a type of questioning and do not have to "switch gears" mentally between types of victimization. It may be best to start with less sensitive types of victimization and progress to more serious ones. This progression gives the participant enough time to build a rapport with the interviewer, so that the former feels more comfortable with answering sensitive questions. Second, question ordering can alter the responses. Ramirez and Straus (2006) found that changing the order of questions on the Conflict Tactics Scale (CTS) resulted in different estimates for some types of victimizations. Order may influence a participant's thought processes, and thus it may affect reporting. For example, when the questions were asked in random order, they elicited higher rates of reporting for physical assault, injury, and sexual coercion than when they were asked in sequential order (e.g., along a scale of seriousness of the incident; see Ramirez and Straus, 2006). Finally, question order may impact the labeling of an experience as a criminal incident. If all types of victimization are asked about together, respondents may be more likely to view all behaviors as belonging in that category. Many women do not name their sexual victimization experiences for what they are, and asking about these incidents in the context of other types of criminal behaviors, such as assault, may alter their perception. Recall that Koss (1988) found that only 27 percent of women labeled their experience as "rape," even though that experience met the criteria for this definition. Thus respondents may be more likely to regard their experience as criminal if they are asked about it in the context of other, more traditional names of criminal experiences (e.g., assault). The NCVS screen question used to measure rape asks respondents whether they have been attacked or threatened in several ways, including through rape and other sexual attacks. It is possible that grouping rape in with other behaviors defined as criminal would prompt individuals to view their experience as criminal too. And they may be more likely to report the incident, because they now perceive it as a victimization and not just as an unpleasant experience. On the other hand, the Panel on Measuring Rape and Sexual Assault in Bureau of Justice Statistics Household Surveys (2014) argues that this strategy could also prompt respondents to focus on the weapons (e.g., gun or knife), which are also asked about in this question, with the result that they would answer "no," when in reality they had experienced a form of victimization. Examining the context and framing are important considerations when deciding on question-wording and question order.

Modes of Data Collection

Not only question selection and ordering are important; the way in which the survey will be delivered is important too, and should also be considered. Victimization surveys use a wide variety of methods to collect their data. Developments in technology have further influenced the different types of data collection modes available. Common methods of data collection are phone conversations (landline or mobile), face-to-face interviews, and computer assistance. All of these data collection modes have their advantages and disadvantages, which need to be considered when collecting data on victimization.

Phone interviews

Many victimization surveys, such as the NCVS, utilize the phone interview as a way to collect data. A typical phone interview involves an interviewer contacting a participant over the phone and administering the survey by reading the questions aloud to the participant. Phone interviews can remove interviewer bias, which may be present in face-to-face interviews, and can put the participant more at ease with talking about sensitive issues. Participants may also be more likely to respond to phone interviews than to other methods of data collection. For example, Skogan (1999) reported that individuals who reside in highly populated urban areas are generally more inclined to complete a telephone survey than a face-to-face interview. Participants are typically more comfortable with a phone call than with an interviewer's visit to their home. Phone interviews also allow for the interviewer to clear up confusions about questions and address concerns that the participant may have. This ability to clarify is extremely important when it comes to defining types of victimization and accurately coding experiences. Further, phone interviews can reach a wide range of people and can benefit from techniques like random digit dialing to achieve a more representative sample. For example, the NVAWS used random digit dialing to obtain a nationally representative sample of 8,000 men and 8,000 women. More recently, the NISVS utilized a dual-sampling frame that was designed to reach both landlines and cell phones. Random digit dialing was used to select individuals from both landline and mobile phone lists, which increased the chances that individuals without landlines would also be included in the sample.

However, phone interviews can also add measurement error into victimization surveys. First, it is difficult to tell whether another person is in the room when the participant is taking the survey, and this presence may alter his or her responses. To address this difficulty, Schwartz (2000) suggests invoking an alternative reason for the participant to be on the phone (e.g., the interviewer pretends to be selling something). Second, even though the survey is over the phone, interviewer bias may still be a problem. This possibility is especially strong when more severe types of victimization are discussed. Participants may simply not feel comfortable discussing these experiences without having some rapport with the interviewer. One suggestion is to give participants vignettes that describe the targeted behavior. Then participants are asked a question about a victimization type that corresponds to the vignette and asked whether they have experienced anything of the kind. Data on victimization can then be collected without having the participant discuss in detail what he or she may have experienced (Schwartz, 2000). Third, in many surveys it is difficult to keep track of who took the survey (as opposed to who was actually called when random digit dialing is used). This issue can lead to sampling bias through the over- or underrepresentation of some groups (Schwartz, 2000). Finally, telephone surveys omit anyone who does not have a phone, including the homeless, lower socioeconomic status (SES) people, transient people, incarcerated persons, or persons who do not have a landline anymore. Many of these individuals may also be at high risk for victimization, so it is important to try and capture a diverse population. Recent changes in technology have resulted in many people's cancelling their home phones in favor of mobile phones. The Centers for Disease Control (CDC) reported that in 2013 over 39 percent of households only have wireless mobile phones for communication. In addition, about 2 percent of homes had no telephone service, either wireless or landline (Blumberg and Luke, 2013). While an increasing number of households are going wireless, nonlandline numbers such as those of mobile phones are more difficult to access, and this possibly results in sampling bias. The use of a dual sampling frame such as the one utilized by the NISVS, which includes both mobile phones and landlines, is one possible solution to this issue.

Face-to-face interviews

Many researchers choose to interview their participants face to face. Generally the first interviews conducted by the NCVS are face to face. There are several advantages to this type of interviewing. First, face-to-face surveying may allow the interviewer to build rapport with the participant. The participant and the interviewer have personal contact, since they are normally sitting in the same room together. This close proximity may result in the participant feeling more comfortable to answer questions. Second, face-to-face interviewing allows for the clarification of any confusion; it also permits the participant to ask questions. Being able to ask questions may increase both the quality and the accuracy of responses. Third, the participant may be more likely to take the survey if it is face to face. The NCVS reported a response rate of 89 percent for interviews conducted in the respondents' households, by comparison with an average response rate of 70 percent for interviews conducted over the telephone by the NVAWS (Rand and Rennison, 2005).

On the other hand, face-to-face interviews are both time-consuming and costly. Interviewers must be located, trained, and paid for their time. If the desired sample is large, several interviewers may be needed, which increases costs still further. Additionally, while face-to-face surveying allows the interviewer to build a rapport, participants may still feel uneasy about answering sensitive questions. It may be very difficult for some victims to talk about their experiences with an interviewer sitting across the table from them. This discomfort may result in omissions or the nonreporting of victimizations. Other individuals may also be present for the interview, adding to the participant's discomfort. For example, if the interviews take place in a room full of other people who are also being interviewed, this may affect the overall comfort of the participant, possibly reducing the reporting of victimization experiences. The presence of others during an interview is particularly likely to influence a respondent when he or she is being asked about sexual or intimate partner violence. Research by Coker and Stasny (1995) revealed that, when a person's spouse was present, persons were less likely to make disclosures about these two types of victimizations. Several suggestions have been offered to reduce this problem; for example, the interviewer may offer the participant the possibility of invoking an alternative explanation for the interview (say, to give an opinion on a new household product), or the interview could take place in an alternative location (say, a doctor's office) if the victim is too fearful to discuss his or her experiences (Schwartz, 2000).

Online surveys

Web or online surveys are another option that can reduce the costs associated with conducting interviews. Web surveys give access to a large population, possibly resulting in larger sample sizes. It is estimated that 70 percent of adult Americans now have access to the Internet at home (Pew Research Center, 2013). Participants can also fill out the survey in a location chosen by them, and do it in their own time. This may increase response rates and make the participant more comfortable with answering sensitive questions. This may be particularly advantageous for victimization surveys. With the advent of survey tools such as Survey Monkey and other online survey design websites, constructing and administering online surveys can be quick and easy. For example, the Campus Sexual Assault (CSA) study used a web survey that was specifically designed to be "user friendly" for participants by reducing the amount of scrolling they had to do, by using common and straightforward language, and by adopting large fonts in order to encourage completion of the survey (Krebs et al., 2007). The study collected responses from nearly 7,000 male and female college students – including detailed information on various forms of sexual victimization such as physically forced and incapacitated sexual assault.

Like telephone interviewing, online surveys can miss significant populations of interest. Individuals who are elderly, of lower SES, and disabled may not have access to the Internet. Further, homeless individuals and individuals who are living in transient locations such as shelters would also be left out. Given that these populations are found to be at high risk of victimization, their exclusion may underestimate victimization prevalence rates and may influence risk factors found to be associated with predicting victimization. If online surveys are utilized, the target population should be carefully considered. For example, this method of administering a survey may give good results with a college population, but not with individuals over the age of 65. Online surveys can also produce lower response rates (e.g., 38 percent for the CSA), pushing up the costs of this type of survey when follow-ups and other efforts to increase responses are employed.

Computer-assisted interviewing

A further development in the area of victimization measurement is the use of computer-assisted interviewing. This type of interviewing comes in various forms. Computer-assisted telephone interviews (CATI) provides the interviewer with a systematic procedure for conducting interviews. Instead of the interviewer' handing a piece of paper and a pencil to the participant, or having the participant read off a document that the interviewer then has to transcribe, the computer displays each question and the responses are then read by the interviewer and selected for the participant. Having the survey read from and data entered via a computer can eliminate the skipping of questions, errors in recording, coding, and changes to question-wording. In can also increase the accuracy of responses through enhanced supervision of the interviewers, since this technique is often used in a centralized facility (Lynch, 2006). Response rates may also increase with this type of interviewing. The NCWSV study used CATI and reported a response rate of over 84 percent (Fisher and Cullen, 2000), by comparison with an average response rate of 34 percent for the NWS.

Other types of computer-assisted interviewing are also available. Computer-assisted self-interviews (CASI) allow the participant to read and select responses off a screen, removing the interviewer all together. This type of interviewing may be very helpful for sensitive topics such as victimization. Originally developed for self-report drug surveys, this method of surveying removes the concern of reporting victimization to a person and secures extra privacy for the participant (Cantor and Lynch, 2000). A modified version of this method, audio computer-assisted self-interviews (ACASI), provides assistance for those who may have trouble reading and comprehending questions. In this type of interviewing the questions are read to the participant through headphones. Tourangeau and Smith (1996) found that men and women who used ACASI were more likely to report that they had used illegal drugs than men and women who were given other types of surveys. These findings suggest that the type of interviewing may have an effect on the likelihood of reporting. The major disadvantage of this type of data collection is that it can be very costly. Also, while measurement error may be reduced, participants or interviewers may select the incorrect responses, or other errors can still be made – which generates other types of measurement issues.

Considerations for the Future

Much work has been done to reduce measurement error in victimization surveys. Methodological issues remain, however, and the measurement of victimization can still be improved. To develop the best measures and measurement strategies possible, most critically, more experiments and quasi-experiments need to be conducted to determine the features of surveys that influence both comprehension of the question and recall of any events of interest. Several studies have contributed to the existing knowledge base. For example, Fisher (2009) reported results of a quasi-experimental design study in which she investigated the effects of different question-wording on the production of rape estimates, using two nationally representative studies of college women. She found that, depending on the questions used, there were significant differences in the estimates produced, with the behaviorally specific questions producing higher estimates than the short-cue, direct, broad-net questions. Similar studies, which manipulate one variable at a time, would allow for the examination of how study design features play a role in influencing recall and response.

In addition to this approach, more research is needed on other features of surveys, such as question ordering. Recent experimental research has shown that question-wording and question order influence responses to questions on fear of crime. In a study that examines question-wording and question order, respondent characteristics, and fear, Yang and Wyckoff (2010) found that general and vague questions about safety produced a question-order effect for females. Similarly, a question-order effect was found for general and vague safety questions for persons who had experienced a previous victimization. That is, when these types of safety questions were asked in a telephone survey before victimization questions, victims reported lower levels of perceived safety. When victimization questions were asked before safety questions, the victims' and the nonvictims' perceived safety levels were almost identical. This study highlights the importance of considering question order, question-wording, and also respondent characteristics (e.g., age) when developing surveys to measure victimization and concepts germane to it, such as personal safety.

Beyond experimental and quasi-experimental research to examine survey design features, more work is needed that should incorporate both quantitative and qualitative designs in single studies in order to better understand the extent and nature of victimization. As previously discussed, one of the debates in victimization literature concerns whether males or females are more likely to be victimized in certain types of crimes (especially intimate partner violence). The sample used, the context of the survey, and the types of questions asked all influence estimates. Gender symmetry has been found in some instances and marked gender differences have been produced in others. One explanation for this divergence in estimates is that, even when females are aggressively attacking their partners, they do so in response to aggression from them. Others argue that females may engage in aggressive and violent behaviors, but the tools of their aggression are less serious: if serious, battering forms of violence were measured, then males would be shown to be the primary abusers. To uncover the true extent of victimization and the motivations underlying it – for example by answering questions like: Is it that males are more victimized in retaliation to violence? – one needs to use qualitative as well as quantitative research, namely in the form of mixed methods research. Such designs incorporate numeric and text information, allowing us to understand research problems better

(Maruna, 2010). In this manner the strengths of both qualitative and quantitative research methods would inform research simultaneously (Maruna, 2010), enabling a researcher to produce rich, holistic data about victimization – data concerning its steps, motivations, and related beliefs. Generalizable findings that allow for the statistical control of confounding variables associated with the risk for and the consequences of victimization can also be produced. Estimates of victimization could be produced, who is likely to be victimized could be determined with some confidence, and events could be dissected for precise patterns.

Using such methods could be particularly beneficial for victimologists as they continue to work on finding the reasons why it is that some persons are at an increased risk for being victimized. Since the development of routine activities theory (Cohen and Felson, 1979) and lifestyles exposure theory (Hindelang, Gottfredson, and Garofalo, 1978), the creation of theories meant to specifically explain victimization has stalled. Instead, criminological theories originally designed to explain criminal perpetration have largely been employed in studies that attempt to explain victimization. Although useful, the development of victimization theories to explain specific types of victimization, the processes leading up to victimization, and the responses to being victimized should be a priority in the future, and mixed methods research can be a powerful tool in this regard, as qualitative research allows for the exploration of new patterns to produce theory with testable hypotheses (Maruna, 2010).

A final consideration for victimologists comes from work on the construction of key dependent variables in criminology. Victimologists should bear in mind not only the wording and order of their key constructs (as explained above), but also the construction of dependent variables. Much attention has been paid to how key constructs such as delinquency and deviance are measured and then used in analysis in the criminology literature. Specifically, research has been conducted on whether researchers should create measures of frequency – that is, should researchers measure how many times a person has engaged in delinquent activity (see Elliott and Ageton, 1980; Huizinga and Elliott, 1986) – or should create measures of variety – that is, should researchers measure how many types of delinquent activities a person has engaged in (see Hindelang, Hirschi, and Weiss, 1979, 1981). These studies produced a debate surrounding the appropriate construction of the dependent variable in delinquency research, particularly as it pertains to the explanation of offending (Osgood, McMorris, and Potenza, 2002). Although a similar debate has not been formally carried out in victimization literature, attention should be paid to the construction of dependent variables there too.

The types of items grouped together should also be taken into account. That is, should fairly "nonserious" forms of victimization be taken together with more "serious" ones? For example, should items designed to measure a car's being broken into and items designed to measure someone's being shot be part of the same analysis? Most commonly, researchers use multiple indicators of victimization to determine whether someone in their sample is a crime victim. Often they will then code a person as a victim dichotomously, if he or she responds affirmatively to any of those items. Doing this type of coding may mask differences between those who have experienced less serious, moderate, and serious types of victimization. Another strategy would be to count the number of times a person has been victimized and to create a frequency measure. Employing this type of measurement strategy may also be problematic, in that it is "easier" to endorse less serious forms of victimization and it is more common for these types of victimizations to occur. The "easier" items, then, make a greater contribution to the measure than the serious items. When attempting to explain victimization, this strategy may be misleading, as there may be inherent qualitative differences between a person who experiences serious forms of victimization (even once) and a person who experiences two minor types of victimization. A final strategy to be used would be to create a variety score that indicates the number of different types of victimization a person has experienced (i.e., poly-victimization). This type of measurement strategy has been used in the child victimization literature as a special case of recurring victimization, but it has not been readily used otherwise (for exceptions, see Listwan et al., 2014; Snyder et al., 2012). A variety score limits very high scores, like those that may be produced via frequency measures; it also limits the contribution of minor forms of victimization (Osgood et al., 2002).

Even after considering the measure itself, its analysis remains important. The majority of victimization studies, when using scales, have created summative scales. In the criminological literature, however, recent studies have used item response theory to demonstrate that items in the scales may be related to individual characteristics and that measurement should account for this relationship (for example see Osgood et al., 2002; Ousey and Lee, 2010; Piquero, MacIntosh, and Hickman, 2000). Item response models relate responses to a set of items to positions on a latent dimension of a hypothetical variable of interest – in this case, victimization. This latent trait is measured on a scale that is continuous on an interval level and free of measurement error. In item response models, both item difficulty and the participant's ability are important. Item difficulty is assessed by knowing how many people endorsed that particular item, while the participant's ability is assessed by the number of items endorsed by a person. Items are rated in accordance with the likelihood of their being endorsed (rather than items from another category), and this endorsement depends on a person's ability and on item difficulty. Item response models are advantageous in that the item difficulty parameter is "sample-free" – its value is not sample-specific – and item difficulty estimates are expected to be the same across samples from the same population, unlike scores and item difficulties in factor analysis (Piquero et al., 2000). These types of models also allow for the identification of certain groups, for which the items may be functioning differently. That is, it is possible that, for persons with the same abilities, items are more or less difficult to endorse (Piquero et al., 2000).

Research using item response models to measure delinquency has shown how some items are easier to endorse than others (e.g., the theft of less than $50, by comparison with robbery) and how some items contribute more information toward distinguishing delinquents in terms of "moderate" and "serious" offending (e.g., robbery contributes more than the theft of less than $50; see Osgood et al., 2002). Further, these models indicated that the biggest difference was between persons who committed one offense and persons who committed no offense – so distinguishing between high-frequency offenders and moderately high-frequency offenders is not worth worrying about. At the same time, the items used did little to differentiate between low-level offenders and nonoffenders (Osgood et al., 2002). A traditional approach to measurement is unable to capture these distinctions. As mentioned, these types of analyses have not yet been conducted with victimization data, but they may prove fruitful. They may help inform victimologists as to whether serious forms of victimization are related to the same latent trait as more minor forms (Osgood et al, 2002). Further, they could help victimologists understand if certain types of victimization mean the same thing for different groups of people (i.e., if there are differential item functions). For example, it is possible that rape items in surveys do not mean the same thing for males and for females. Recent research has shown the utility of item response models in assessing whether victims specialize in victimization (violent versus nonviolent victimization; see Schreck et al., 2012). Future research employing item response models could be used to investigate these other possibilities.

Conclusion

Nevertheless, much is known about how to measure victimization most effectively. Specifically, work has been conducted to try to identify the ways in which the most reliable estimates of victimization can be generated. Whether it be through survey design, question-wording, question ordering, mode of administration, choice of who is included in the sample, or recall periods, ways in which to reduce measurement error are known. Future research is still needed, however, that continues to build on this knowledge so that the best estimates of particular types of victimization may continue to be developed and then analyzed in a manner that capitalizes on advancements in measurement theory.

References

Addington, L. A. 2005. Disentangling the effects of bounding and mobility on reports of criminal victimization. *Journal of Quantitative Criminology*, 21: 321–343.

Archer, J. 2000. Sex differences in aggression between heterosexual partners: A meta-analytic review. *Psychological Bulletin*, 126: 651–680.

Biderman, A. D., and Cantor, D. 1984. A longitudinal analysis of bounding, respondent, conditioning and mobility as sources of panel bias in the National Crime Survey (invited paper). *Proceedings of the American Statistical Association: The survey methodology section*, 708–713. Washington, DC: American Statistical Association. Accessed December 12, 2015. http://www.amstat.org/sections/srms/Proceedings.

Biderman, A. D., and Lynch, J. P. 1991. *Understanding Crime Incidence Statistics: Why the UCR Diverges from the NCS*. New York: Springer.

Black, M. C., Basile, K. C., Breiding, M. J., Smith, S. G., Walters, M. L., Merrick, M. T., Chen, J., and Stevens, M. R. 2011. *The National Intimate Partner and Sexual Violence Survey (NISVS): 2010 Summary report*. Atlanta, GA: National Center for Injury Prevention and Control, Centers for Disease Control and Prevention.

Blumberg, S. J., and Luke, J. V. 2013. Wireless substitution: Early release of estimates from the National Health Interview Survey, January–June 2013. National Center for Health Statistics. Accessed December 12, 2015. http://www.cdc.gov/nchs/data/nhis/earlyrelease/wireless201312.pdf.

Cantor, D., and Lynch, J. P. 2000. Self-report surveys as measures of crime and criminal victimization. In Criminal justice 2000: Measurement and analysis of crime and justice, edited by D. Duffee, vol. 4, 85–138. Washington, DC: US Department of Justice.

Cohen, L. E., and M. Felson. 1979. Social change and crime rate trends: A routine activity approach. *American Sociological Review*, 44: 588–608.

Coker, A. L., and Stasny, E. A. 1995. *Adjusting the National Crime Victimization Survey's estimates of rape and domestic violence for "gag" factors*. Washington, DC: US Department of Justice, National Institute of Justice.

Daigle, L. E. 2013. *Victimology: The essentials*. Thousand Oaks, CA: Sage.

Department of Health and Human Services 2012. *Child Maltreatment 2012*. Washington, DC: US Department of Health and Human Services, Administration for Children and Families, Youth and Families, Children's Bureau. Accessed December 12, 2015. http://www.acf.hhs.gov/sites/default/files/cb/cm2012.pdf#page=16.

Elliott, D. S., and Ageton, S. S. 1980. Reconciling race and class differences in self-reported and official estimates of delinquency. *American Sociological Review*, 45: 95–110.

Federal Bureau of Investigation. 2012. Crime in the United States, 2012. Accessed December 12, 2015. http://www.fbi.gov/about-us/cjis/ucr/crime-in-the-u.s/2012/crime-in-the-u.s.-2012/resource-pages/about-cius/about-cius.

Federal Bureau of Investigation. 2013a. Crime in the United States, 2013: About UCR. Accessed December 12, 2015. http://www.fbi.gov/about-us/cjis/ucr/crime-in-the-u.s/2013/crime-in-the-u.s.-2013/about-ucr.

Federal Bureau of Investigation. 2013b. Crime in the United States, 2013: FBI releases, 2013 crime statistics. Accessed December 12, 2015. http://www.fbi.gov/about-us/cjis/ucr/crime-in-the-u.s/2013/crime-in-the-u.s.-2013/summary-2013/2013-cius-summary-_final.

Federal Bureau of Investigation. 2013c. Crime in the United States, 2013: Table 1. Accessed January 1, 2016. https://www.fbi.gov/about-us/cjis/ucr/crime-in-the-u.s/2013/crime-in-the-u.s.-2013/tables/1tabledatadecoverviewpdf/table_1_crime_in_the_united_states_by_volume_and_rate_per_100000_inhabitants_1994-2013.xls.

Finkelhor, D. Hamby, S. L., Ormrod, R., and Turner, H. 2005. Juvenile Victimization Questionnaire. Accessed December 12, 2015. http://www.unh.edu/ccrc/pdf/jvq/JVQ_Self-reportScreeners_6_8_05.pdf.

Fisher, B. S. 2009. The effects of survey question-wording on rape estimates: Evidence from a quasi-experimental design. *Violence against Women*, 15: 133–147.

Fisher, B. S., and Cullen, F. T. 2000. Measuring the sexual victimization of women: Evolution, current controversies, and future research. In *Criminal justice 2000: Measurement and analysis of crime and justice*, edited by D. Duffee, vol. 4, 317–390). Washington, DC: US Department of Justice.

Fisher, B. S., Cullen, F. T., and Turner, M. G. 2000. *The sexual victimization of college women*. Washington, DC: US Department of Justice, Bureau of Justice Statistics.

Hamby, S., and Finkelhor, D. 2000. The victimization of children: Recommendations for assessment and instrument development. *Journal of the American Academy of Child and Adolescent Psychiatry*, 39 (7): 829–840.

Hindelang, M., Gottfredson, M., and Garofalo, J. 1978. *Victims of personal crime: An empirical foundation for a theory of personal victimization*. Cambridge, MA: Ballinger.

Hindelang, M. J. Hirschi, T., and Weis, J. G. 1979. Correlates of delinquency: The illusion of discrepancy between self-report and official measures. *American Sociological Review*, 44 (6): 995–1014.

Hindelang, M. J. Hirschi, T., and Weis, J. G. 1981. *Measuring delinquency*. Thousand Oaks, CA: Sage Publications.

Huizinga, D., and Elliott, D. S. 1986. Reassessing the reliability and validity of self-report delinquency measures. *Journal of Quantitative Criminology*, 2: 293–327.

Jobe, J. B., and Mingay, D. J. 1990. Cognitive laboratory approach to designing questionnaires for surveys of the elderly. *Public Health Reports*, 105 (5): 518–524.

Johnson, M. P. 1995. Patriarchal terrorism and common couple violence: Two forms of violence against women. *Journal of Marriage and Family*, 57: 283–294.

Kilpatrick, D. G., Edmunds, C. N., and Seymour, A. K. 1992. *Rape in America: A report to the nation*. Arlington, VA: National Victim Center.

Koss, M. P. 1988. Hidden rape: Sexual aggression and victimization in a national sample of college students in higher education. In *Rape and sexual assault*, edited by Ann W. Burgess, 3–25. New York: Garland.

Koss, M. P., and Oros, C. J. 1982. Sexual experiences survey: A research instrument investigating sexual aggression and victimization. *Journal of Consulting and Clinical Psychology*, 50: 455–457.

Krebs, C. R., Lindquist, C. H., Warner, T. D., Fisher, B. S., and Martin, S. T. 2007. The differential risk factors of physically forced and alcohol or other drug enabled sexual assault among university women. *Violence and Victims*, 24 (3): 302–322.

Lauritsen, J. L. 2012. *Subpopulations at high risk for rape and sexual assault: What does the NCVS tell us?* Paper commissioned by the National Research Council Panel on Measuring Rape and Sexual Assault in the Bureau of Justice Statistics Household Surveys, Washington, DC. Accessed January 3, 2016. http://sites.nationalacademies.org/cs/groups/dbassesite/documents/webpage/dbasse_080065.pdf.

Listwan, S. J., Daigle, L. E., Hartman, J. L., and Guastaferro, W. P. 2014. Poly-victimization risk in prison: The influence of individual and institutional factors. *Journal of Interpersonal Violence*, 29: 2458–2481.

Lynch, J. P. 2006. Problems and promise of victimization surveys for cross-national research. *Crime and Justice*, 34 (1): 229–287.

Maruna, S. 2010. Mixed method research in criminology: Why not go both ways? In *Handbook of quantitative criminology*, edited by A. R. Piquero and D. Weisburd, 123–139. New York: Springer.

National Criminal Justice. 2014. National Crime Victimization Survey: Technical documentation. NCJ 247252. Bureau of Justice Statistics, US Department of Justice, Washington, DC. Accessed December 12, 2015. http://www.bjs.gov/content/pub/pdf/ncvstd13.pdf.

Office of Applied Studies. 2003. NSDUH changes and their impact on trend measurement. In *Results from the 2002 National Survey on Drug Use and Health: National findings,*

Appendix C, pp. 107–137. Washington, DC: US Department of Health and Human Services.
Osgood, D. W., McMorris, B. J., and Potenza, M. T. 2002. Analyzing multiple-item measures of crime and deviance I: Item response theory scaling. *Journal of Quantitative Criminology*, 18: 267–296.
Ousey, G. C., and Lee, M. R. 2010. The southern culture of violence and homicide-type differentiation: An analysis across cities and time points. *Homicide Studies*, 14: 268–295.
Panel on Measuring Rape and Sexual Assault in Bureau of Justice Statistics Household Surveys. 2014. Comparison of rape and sexual assault across data sources. In *Estimating the incidence of rape and sexual assault*, edited by C. Kruttschnitt, W. D. Kalsbeek, and C. C. House, 91–108. Washington, DC: National Academies Press. Accessed December 12, 2015. http://www.ncbi.nlm.nih.gov/books/NBK202264.
Pew Research Center. 2013. Broadband technology factsheet. Pew Research Center, Washington, DC. Accessed December 12, 2015. http://www.pewinternet.org/fact-sheets/broadband-technology-fact-sheet.
Peytchev, A., Caspar, R., Neely, B., and Moore, A. 2012. NCVS screening questions evaluation: Final report. Research Triangle Park, NC: RTI International.
Piquero, A. R., MacIntosh, R., and Hickman, M. 2000. Does self-control affect survey response? Applying exploratory, confirmatory, and item response theory analysis to Grasmick et al.'s self-control scale. *Criminology*, 38: 897–930.
Planty, M. 2003. An examination of adolescent telescoping: Evidence from the national crime victimization survey. Unpublished paper presented at the 58th Annual AAPOR Conference in Nashville, Tennessee, May 15–18.
Ramirez, I. L., and Straus, M. A. 2006. The effect of question order on disclosure of intimate partner violence: An experimental test using the conflict tactics scales. *Journal of Family Violence*, 21 (1): 1–9.
Rand, M. R., and Rennison, C. M. 2005. Bigger is not necessarily better: An analysis of violence against women estimates from the National Crime Victimization Survey and the National Violence against Women Survey. *Journal of Quantitative Criminology*, 21 (3): 267–291.
Schafer, S. 1968. *The victim and his criminal: A study in functional responsibility*. New York: Random House.
Schreck, C. J., Ousey, G. C., Fisher, B. S., and Wilcox, P. 2012. Examining what makes violent crime victims unique: Extending statistical methods for studying specialization to the analysis of crime victims. *Journal of Quantitative Criminology*, 28: 651–671.
Schwartz, M. D. 2000. Methodological issues in the use of survey data for measuring and characterizing violence against women. *Violence against Women*, 6: 815–838.
Skogan, W. G. 1981. *Issues in the measurement of victimization*. Washington, DC: US Department of Justice.
Skogan, W. G. 1999. Measuring what matters: Crime, disorder, and fear. In *Measuring what matters: Proceedings from the Policing Research Institute meetings*, edited by R. Langworthy, 37–53. Washington, DC: National Institute of Justice.
Smith, A. 2014. Older adults and technology use. Pew Research Center's Internet Project, July 18–September 20, 2013.
Snyder, J. A., Fisher, B. S., Scherer, H. L., and Daigle, L. E. 2012. Unsafe in the camouflage tower: Sexual victimization and perceptions of military academy leadership. *Journal of Interpersonal Violence*, 27: 3171–3194.

Tjaden, P., and Thoennes, N. 2000. *Full report of the prevalence, incidence, and consequences of violence against women.* Washington, DC: Department of Justice, National Institute of Justice and US Department of Health and Human Services, Centers for Disease Control and Prevention.

Tourangeau, R., and McNeeley, M. E. 2002. Measuring crime and crime victimization: Methodological issues. In J. V. Pepper and C. V. Petrie, eds., *Measurement problems in criminal justice research: Workshop summary*, 10–42. Washington, DC: National Academies Press.

Tourangeau, R., and Smith, T. W. 1996. Asking sensitive questions: The impact of data collection mode, question format, and question context. *Public Opinion Quarterly*, 60 (2): 275–304.

Truman, J., Langton, L., and Planty, M. 2013. Criminal victimization, 2012. Washington, DC: US Department of Justice, Bureau of Justice Statistics. Accessed December 12, 2015. http://www.bjs.gov/content/pub/pdf/cv12.pdf.

von Hentig, H. 1948. *The criminal and his victim: Studies in the sociobiology of crime.* New Haven, CT: Yale University Press.

Western, B., and Pettit, B. 2000. Incarceration and racial inequality in men's employment. *Industrial and Labor Relations Review*, 54: 3–16.

Yang, S., and Wyckoff, L. A. 2010. Perceptions of safety and victimization: Does survey construction affect perceptions? *Journal of Experimental Criminology*, 6: 293–323.

Further Reading

Tjaden, P., and Thoennes, N. 1998. *Prevalence, incidence, and consequences of violence against women: Findings from the National Violence against Women Survey.* Research in Brief, NCJ 172837. Washington, DC: US Department of Justice, National Institute of Justice and US Department of Health and Human Services, Centers for Disease Control and Prevention.

Part III

Criminal Justice Organizations and Outcomes

13

Community Policing and Police Interventions

Michael J. Kyle and Joseph A. Schafer

Introduction

Measurement of community policing and of other police interventions is inherently problematic due to a number of factors. This chapter considers the measurement and research design challenges associated with more clearly establishing the extent to which various police interventions achieve desired outcomes, such as reductions in crime and disorder, diminished fear of crime, improved community conditions, and enhanced police–community relations. The challenges are more than just complications researchers must confront; they mean that consolidating what is known about a given form of police intervention is inherently problematic because of validity, reliability, and generalizability concerns. These major issues that researchers must confront stem from a number of complications of definition, measurement, and research design associated with studying police interventions, police organizations, and the nexus between the police and the communities they serve.

First, many police interventions are defined in vague and ambiguous ways, and this complicates the ability to define and measure expected outcomes. For example, even now, more than three decades after the idea reached the mainstream of policing, exactly what constitutes community policing remains a subject of debate and disagreement, among law enforcement practitioners and academics alike (Eck and Rosenbaum, 1994; Flynn, 1998; Gill et al., 2014; Greene, 2004; Maguire and Katz, 2002; Mastrofski, 2006; Moore, 1992; Roth, Roehl, and Johnson, 2004; Skogan, 2006a; Skogan and Hartnett, 1997). Other police intervention strategies replicate this state of uncertainty. These flexible definitions provide the advantage of allowing agencies and officers to customize interventions in different communities

The Handbook of Measurement Issues in Criminology and Criminal Justice, First Edition.
Edited by Beth M. Huebner and Timothy S. Bynum.

and across unique circumstances, but they work to obstruct the ability to define, measure, and test the effects of strategies in ways that produce valid and reliable results (Gill et al., 2014; Trojanowicz, Kappeler, and Gaines, 2002). The variability also means that, even when researchers overcome measurement and methodological challenges, consideration of a given innovation implemented in two jurisdictions might actually create a comparison between two fundamentally different strategies.

Second, even when a researcher adequately conceptualizes an element believed to be indicative of community policing or a specific police intervention, operationalization is often equally problematic (Moore, 1992). Community policing and most police intervention strategies simply do not lend themselves easily to measurement, regardless of research design or method. It can be difficult for researchers to craft measurement approaches and research designs that lead to valid and reliable conclusions about whether purposive police interventions yielded the desired outcome, while controlling for all the variables that might also contribute to changes in the dependent variables. For example, if a community implements an intervention and the crime rate remains static, how does a researcher rule out that under normal circumstances crime might otherwise have increased – which suggests that an apparently neutral program actually "worked" in reducing crime?

This chapter uses examples from the extant research literature to review the ways in which the definition, measurement, and design challenges have been addressed. The review begins with a consideration of how community policing and police interventions have been conceptualized and operationalized. Next, research design, methodology, and limitations in research approaches that seek to assess community policing and other police interventions are considered. In addition, emerging research is examined for the double purpose of highlighting the complexities of assessing police interventions and of illustrating the "best practices" that might be associated with managing these research nuances.

Defining Community Policing, Police Interventions, and Expected Outcomes

A universal definition of community policing has long been elusive, which immediately complicates any efforts to study this form of policing intervention. Robert Trojanowicz, one of the fathers of this police innovation, maintained that the definition of its object required by its philosophy has to remain vague, in order to allow agencies and officers to apply the approach to local conditions and contexts (Trojanowicz et al., 2002). However, while vague definitions of community policing may serve a purpose for many agencies, they pose a serious problem for researchers.

An ambiguous and vague definition of community policing makes conceptualization the first problem that the researcher must address (Eck and Rosenbaum, 1994; Flynn, 1998; Greene, 2004; Maguire and Katz, 2002; Mastrofski, 2006; Moore, 1992; Roth et al., 2004; Skogan, 2006a; Skogan and Hartnett, 1997). The vague nature of the definition also means that agencies often undertake community policing without a clear consideration of expected outcomes; this creates serious complications for researchers, who have to determine what dependent variable(s) are expected to change (and in which direction) when community-policing efforts are implemented. Prior to examining how researchers have conceptualized elements of community policing in the extant literature, a brief description of the conflicting views as to what exactly community policing entails is in order.

The concept of community policing (often also referred to as "community-oriented policing") stands in stark contrast to the professional policing model, with its focus on crime control through internal mechanisms such as centralized command, specialization, education and training of personnel, intelligence gathering, and use of technology (Cordner, 1988; Greene, 2004; Kelling and Moore, 1988; Moore, 1992). The professional model of policing calls for police to determine both what crime problems exist in their respective jurisdictions and how best to deal with them; it emphasizes addressing crime through legalistic responses and is reactionary in nature, as strategies are formulated in response to crime as it occurs. Conversely, the community-policing model is preventative in nature, as it calls for an external focus: as part of that focus, law enforcement agencies form partnerships with the communities they serve in order to identify problems and formulate solutions, the primary goal being quality-of-life improvement (Eck and Rosenbaum, 1994; Skogan, 2006a; Trojanowicz et al., 2002).

Assessments of the overall idea of community policing have varied widely. It has been asserted that community policing is nothing more than an ambiguous buzzword for some trendy token programs intended to obscure or veil the same business-as-usual practices of the police (Klockars, 1988; Manning, 1997). Others contend that, while the idea has merit, the implementation is likely "more rhetoric than reality" (Bayley, 1988, p. 225; see also Greene and Mastrofski, 1988). Community policing has been characterized as a philosophy that is adopted at the executive and command level but must also be embraced at the line level in order for actual community-policing practices to be employed (Chappell, 2009). Yet compelling arguments can be made that community policing has largely been deployed as a tactic and remains untested and unproved as a philosophy or strategy (Cordner, 2010). John Eck and Dennis Rosenbaum (1994) contend that "community policing is a plastic concept, meaning different things to different people" (p. 3), yet many scholars and practitioners have seen community policing as an organizational strategy (Kelling and Moore, 1988; Moore, 1992; Skogan, 2006a) that lends itself to empirical research and testing.

While there are different ways in which researchers have defined community policing by utilizing an organizational strategy approach, the concepts tend to be similar. Wesley Skogan (2006a) has conducted extensive research on the topic; this research includes one of the first in-depth studies of community-policing implementation on a large scale, beginning in 1992 in Chicago. The framework he developed to define community policing by using the organizational strategy approach is representative of this notion in general. According to Skogan,

> Community policing is not a set of specific projects; rather, it involves changing decision-making processes and creating new cultures within police departments. It is an organizational strategy that leaves setting priorities and the means of achieving them largely to residents and the police who serve in their neighborhoods. Community policing is a process rather than a product. (Skogan, 2006a, p. 5)

Skogan identified "three core strategic components" of community policing: "decentralization, citizen involvement, and problem solving" (p. 6).

The first of the three foundational components, decentralization, involves empowering the line-level police officer with decision-making authority that, in the traditional hierarchical paramilitary structure of police agencies, is centralized in command and supervisory ranks. Under the traditional structure of the professional policing model, the line officer typically receives orders as to where, when, and how to address a particular crime problem. However, a major tenet of community policing – the police–community partnership – requires a great deal of autonomy and decision-making authority at the line patrol officer level (Greene, 2004; Skogan, 2006a; Skogan and Hartnett, 1997). Moreover, the holistic nature of community policing requires each officer to be a generalist, which departs from the compartmentalized specializations (detectives, vice officers, crime prevention officers, etc.) common to the traditional structure (Greene, 2004). In some instances this is accomplished through some form of flattening of the organization – for example, through the elimination of some layers of supervisory and management ranks and specializations; another method has been to shift greater decision-making authority from the command level to mid-level managers at neighborhood precincts or substations (Greene, 2004; Skogan, 2006a; Skogan and Hartnett, 1997).

Citizen involvement, the second of the three foundational components identified by Skogan (2006a), refers to listening to community members about the problems they would like the police to address. This involvement often extends to the provision of venues for the exchange of information, and also to taking systemic steps to repeatedly encourage citizen participation in solving problems identified as such. Some examples of citizen engagement are community meetings and focus groups, community surveys, and citizen police academies (Skogan, 2006a; Skogan and Hartnett, 1997). In effect, community policing is an intervention that is to be done *with* the community rather than *to* the community.

The third component, problem-solving, is a key element of community policing. It overlaps the first two components in that, for the line-level officer who has daily contact with the citizens, decentralization must take place in order for him or her to engage in problem-solving, and the citizens must be engaged for the two to arrive at innovative solutions. Problem-solving in a community-policing context draws upon foundational ideas, such as James Q. Wilson and George L. Kelling's (1982) "broken windows" concept, and requires training line-level patrol officers to identify the source of problems and work with citizens to find long-term solutions (Skogan, 2006b). Problem-solving, however, should not be confused with problem-oriented policing. The latter, introduced by Herman Goldstein (1979), is a method of developing strategies to address particular crime problems through analysis of the available intelligence and can be engaged in entirely separately, apart from community policing (Skogan, 2006b). However, problem-oriented policing is often employed along with community policing and shall be addressed later in the chapter, in the discussion of police interventions.

Having defined community policing as a strategy, Skogan (2006b) points out that programs such as foot, bicycle, and mounted patrol, neighborhood police substations, and collaboration with social service agencies are all activities that many police agencies engage in and are the basis for claims that they are "doing" community policing. Skogan (2006b) asserts, however, that these are but tactics (see also Trojanowicz et al., 2002). While they are certainly interventions that an agency would consider and most likely engage in if it implemented the community-policing strategy, "community policing is not defined by these kinds of activities" (Skogan, 2006b, p. 27).

Other police interventions have sought to address a wide range of police, public, and community conditions by using myriad strategies, tactics, and techniques. Though the umbrella of "police interventions" encompasses a very broad range of initiatives, this chapter primarily focuses on those categorized as place-based or offender- and offense-based. In addition, problem-oriented policing must be addressed, as it is widely utilized as an approach to determine where and what type of intervention may be required, both as a stand-alone form of police intervention and as a component of other intervention strategies. It should be noted that, while the terms "community policing" and "problem-oriented policing" are often used together, some interventions produced by a problem-oriented approach can be considered at odds with community-policing principles. As previously mentioned, problem-oriented policing can be, and often is, engaged in separately from community policing.

Unlike community policing, problem-oriented policing does not suffer from ambiguity in its definition. Problem-oriented policing is an approach utilized by police agencies to identify problems and to craft suitable responses in order to solve them. According to Herman Goldstein, the father of problem-oriented policing,

> Problem-oriented policing is an approach to policing in which discrete pieces of police business (each consisting of a cluster of similar incidents, whether crime or acts of disorder, that the police are expected to handle) are subject to microscopic examination (drawing on the especially honed skills of crime analysts and the accumulated experience of operating field personnel) in hopes that what is freshly learned about each problem will lead to discovering a new and more effective strategy for dealing with it. Problem-oriented policing places a high value on new responses that are preventive in nature, that are not dependent on the use of the criminal justice system, and that engage other public agencies, the community and the private sector when their involvement has the potential for significantly contributing to the reduction of the problem. Problem-oriented policing carries a commitment to implementing the new strategy, rigorously evaluating its effectiveness, and, subsequently, reporting the results in ways that will benefit other police agencies and that will ultimately contribute to building a body of knowledge that supports the further professionalization of the police. (Goldstein, 2001)

Thus problem-oriented policing views the police as having the capacity to recognize issues (problematic people, places, or circumstances) within an area. Through analysis of those issues, the police can deploy strategies to disrupt or eliminate the problem, using assessment to determine the efficacy of the intended solutions.

Problem-oriented policing is linked with Compstat, an innovative police performance measurement system first developed and implemented by the New York City Police Department (NYPD) in the 1990s. Police performance measures typically emphasized crime rates, arrest rates, and response times (among other metrics; see Moore and Braga, 2003). Historically, such systems have failed to hold organizations and leaders strongly accountable for crime, disorder, and community conditions. Compstat was developed to create internal and external accountability for police organizations, while also helping agencies identify problems and implement solutions in a more timely fashion. According to James Willis, Stephen Mastrofski, and David Weisburd (2007), as it originally operated in the NYPD, Compstat involved two crime control strategy meetings per week, in which

> Precinct commanders appear before the department's top echelon to report on crime in their districts and what they are doing about it. This occurs in a data-saturated environment. Crime analysts collect, analyze, and map crime statistics to spot trends and help precinct commanders identify underlying factors that explain crime incidents. Top administrators use this information to quiz precinct commanders on the crime in their beats and to hold them responsible for solving the problems. Failure to provide satisfactory responses to these inquiries may lead to stern criticism or removal from command. (Willis et al., 2007, p. 148)

Compstat has been adopted in some form by many police agencies across the United States. While it may be given different names, according to Willis and colleagues (2007) the system is generally comprised of four principles:

> (1) Accurate, timely information made available at all levels in the organization; (2) the most effective tactics for specific problems; (3) rapid, focused deployment of resources to implement those tactics; and (4) relentless follow-up and assessment to learn what happened and make adjustments. (Willis et al., 2007, p. 148)

The conceptualization of place-based and offender-based interventions, like that of problem-oriented policing and Compstat (notwithstanding some criticism), has generally not been subject to the kind of debate that surrounds that of community policing. Place-based interventions are predicated on the concept of "hot spots." Hot spots are specific geographic areas in which a certain type of crime or disorder problem is concentrated. The hot spots are normally identified through the examination of intelligence information and data, such as call for service records, arrest and incident reports, citizen complaints, and officer observations and self-initiated contacts (Braga, 2001; Sherman and Weisburd, 1995). In larger jurisdictions this information is often statistically analyzed and utilized to construct crime maps in order to identify hot spots (National Institute of Justice, 2010). The specific interventions that are implemented once a hot spot is identified range from directed and saturation patrols to the demolition of abandoned buildings and other types of collaboration with non-law enforcement agencies. These interventions are often simply referred to as "hotspot policing."

Offender- and offense-based interventions are based on empirical evidence generated from numerous studies that indicate that small portions of offenders commit a large portion of crime (Spelman and Eck, 1989). These interventions can be initiated in response to a broad or less focused concern with a specific offense or set of offenses (e.g., gangs, drug markets, or prostitution) in an area. According to David Kennedy (2006), pulling levers strategies, also referred to as focused deterrence strategies, involve enforcement actions, specific services, and direct communication targeting specific groups, individuals, and behaviors. Kennedy describes a six-step process for the implementation of these interventions: (1) choosing a specific crime problem; (2) forming an "interagency enforcement group, typically including police, probation, parole, state and federal prosecutors, and sometimes federal enforcement agencies"; (3) collecting information regarding individual offenders, groups of offenders, and the situational aspects of their offending; (4) developing an operational plan to target the identified offenders and groups for enforcement action; (5) focusing community attention and appropriate services on targeted offenders; and (6) communicating

> directly and repeatedly with offenders and groups to let them know that they are under particular scrutiny, what acts (such as shootings) will get special attention, when that has in fact happened to particular offenders and groups, and what they can do to avoid enforcement action. (Kennedy, 2006, pp. 156–157)

Equally important and often just as problematic as defining and operationalizing community policing or the particular intervention to be studied is the identification, definition, and operationalization of the expected outcomes to be measured. While the expected outcomes of place-based and offender- or offense-based interventions are, by nature, focused on the reduction of a specific crime problem (e.g., illicit drug sales, prostitution, or gun violence), those of community policing are much broader and can be as difficult to define as the community-policing concept itself. Although the ultimate goal of community policing is still the reduction and prevention of crime, community policing is thought to achieve this goal through intermediate outcomes, which include reduction of community disorder, reduction of fear of crime, and increase of citizen satisfaction with the police, thereby improving quality of life and increasing community collective efficacy (Gill et al., 2014; Kochel, 2012). But what exactly constitutes disorder? How are fear of crime and citizen satisfaction with the police conceptualized and operationalized? Like community policing itself, these expected outcomes can be difficult to define and a challenge to measure.

First, what exactly does disorder mean in the context of the community and as it relates to crime? According to Douglas Perkins and Ralph Taylor:

> Community disorder is a broad and elusive concept, difficult to define or measure in a way that all would understand and agree with. It refers to social and physical conditions and events in a locale beyond the serious crimes that may be occurring there. These conditions and events may relate to any or all of the following: residents who are no longer able to maintain a satisfactory quality of community life; unregulated, uncivil or rowdy behaviors observed on the street that may be associated with social conflict; a lack of investment in or supervision over a locale on the part of residents or external public and private institutions, or both; and a degeneration over time in neighborhood-based physical capital, reflected in diminishing quality and/or maintenance of both public and private property. (Perkins and Taylor, 1996, p. 64)

Disorder in this context has been defined in terms of incivilities (Taylor, 1999; Wilson and Kelling, 1982). According to Zhao and colleagues, "traditionally, disorder or incivilities have been conceptualized in two distinct dimensions: social disorder/incivilities (e.g. public drinking, drug sales, and vandalism) and physical disorder/incivilities (e.g. rundown buildings, empty lots, and abandoned cars)" (Zhao et al., 2014, p. 397). While these concepts may appear to be rather straightforward, as Perkins and Taylor (1996) assert, determining what degree of such "incivilities" constitutes disorder is complicated.

For example, is the public consumption of alcoholic beverages under any circumstances indicative of disorder (e.g., street fairs or other public events where alcoholic beverages may be served)? How many instances of vandalism, rundown buildings, or abandoned cars are indicative of disorder? There may be several vacant lots in a residential subdivision development, but is that indicative of disorder? Obviously the mere occurrence or manifestation of these factors, in any form whatsoever, does not rise to the level of disorder. Thus, as in the case of community policing, a universal definition is elusive in the case of disorder too. Despite this difficulty in conceptualization, researchers have measured disorder through surveys of citizen perceptions, direct observation, and review of local media sources concerning incivilities (see Perkins and Taylor, 1996 for a review). Citizen perceptions of incivilities, which are both the most common and the most useful measurement for the community-policing researcher, have been shown to be linked to fear of crime (Gau, Corsaro, and Brunson, 2014; Perkins and Taylor, 1996; Roccato, Russo, and Vieno, 2011), although this relationship has raised questions as to the discriminant validity of such measures (see Armstrong and Katz, 2010; Taylor, 1999; Worrall, 2006).

The reduction of citizens' fear of crime is another important expected outcome as, along with the associated level of disorder, it is considered a key quality-of-life factor (Reisig and Parks, 2004). While fear of crime may appear to be a rather straightforward concept, it has been defined and measured in various ways. Fear of crime has been defined both in terms of a "negative emotional reaction" and in terms of a "psychological assessment of perceived risk," and these definitions have been seen as conflicting with one another (see Ferraro and LaGrange, 1987; Stein, 2014). The measurement of fear of crime through a single indicator on a survey (typically a question regarding how safe the subject feels walking alone in his or her neighborhood at night) versus multiple survey indicators has been a subject of debate (see Abdullah et al., 2014; Stein, 2014). Fear of crime has been shown to be positively related with disorder and incivilities – as the level of disorder increases, fear of crime increases (Perkins and Taylor, 1996; Skogan, 1990; Stein, 2014; Wyant, 2008) – and both contribute to the level of the citizens' satisfaction with the police (Cao, Frank, and Cullen, 1996; Merry et al., 2012).

Citizen satisfaction with the police is a multidimensional concept; it consists of (1) confidence in the competence of the police to protect the citizens they serve, to prevent crime, and to address crime when it does occur; and (2) legitimacy, which is rooted in the citizens' perception that the police enforce the law consistently and treat people fairly (procedural justice). Worrall (1999) demonstrated that citizen satisfaction is indeed made up of these two distinct dimensions, which he called efficacy and image, respectively. Put another way, efficacy is the dimension of citizen satisfaction that relates to perceptions of the ability of the police to protect lives, property, prevent and address crime; and image is the dimension that relates to legitimacy and the citizens' perception that the police enforce the law consistently and treat people fairly. Of the expected outcomes of community policing and other police interventions, citizen satisfaction is perhaps the most difficult to measure. Key in the measurement of both dimensions of citizen satisfaction is the term "perception." As with fear of crime, regardless of what true crime trends exist or how officers are actually interacting with community members, the citizens' perceptions are the basis of their satisfaction or dissatisfaction with the police. This presents a considerable measurement challenge. Carefully constructed survey items and interview questions have been utilized to measure both of these dimensions (see Hough, Jackson, and Bradford, 2013; Mazerolle, Antrobus, et al., 2013; and Schafer, Huebner, and Bynum, 2003 for a review).

Across the spectrum of policing strategies, researchers confront a host of very basic challenges and obstacles. Though it is advantageous for agencies to have some license to implement strategies in ways that make sense given local context, resources, constraints, and opportunities, this renders ambiguous the umbrella terms often used to categories types of interventions. Two agencies deploying hotspots policing might actually be using differing tactics, and this complicates scholars' task to look across a range of studies and assess the efficacy of a given policing intervention. Key independent variables themselves (e.g., are all interventions enacted in the same way, with similar resources, orientations, and vigor?) cannot be presumed to be analogous. Within the context of a given intervention, the concepts comprising common dependent variables (crime, disorder, satisfaction, fear, etc.) are often difficult to measure in reliable and valid ways, especially given finite research resources and access. Researchers often find themselves conducting assessments of intervention strategies under conditions that trigger additional concerns about the external validity and generalizability of research design and findings.

Research Designs and Methodologies: The Challenges and Best Practices

Researchers have employed a variety of research designs and methodologies to study police interventions. These include experimental, quasi-experimental, longitudinal, and cross-sectional designs that utilize both quantitative and qualitative methods – such as surveys, interviews, observation, and the analysis of various types of data. Studies often make use of multiple designs and methods in order to enhance the content validity and the understanding of the nuanced outcomes associated with crime reduction efforts. While the challenges and limitations associated with research designs and methods are common to the study of both community policing and other interventions, there are unique factors related to each that require consideration in selecting an approach.

Community policing

There are two basic approaches to studying community policing. The first is examining cultural, operational, and structural changes in law enforcement organizations that claim to have engaged in a community-policing initiative, including the implementation of specific elements of community policing (e.g., programs and practices). The second is the examination of citizens' perceptions and level of satisfaction with the police in specific jurisdictions that ostensibly engage in community policing. Depending on the purpose of the research, neither of these approaches may be sufficient without the other (Cordner, 2010; Skogan and Hartnett, 1997; Skolnick and Bayley, 1986). For instance, if one is seeking to determine how effective a specific community-policing approach has been in a particular jurisdiction, it must first be determined that the corresponding law enforcement agency has in fact established community policing and it must be specified to what extent (e.g., specifically where, when, how often, for how long, etc.) the approach has been employed. Utilizing the first of the two approaches, a researcher may discover evidence that the agency has indeed established community policing by determining that the agency has engaged in at least some of the specified elements associated with community policing. Such evidence, however, says nothing about effectiveness. Conversely, one cannot conclude that results of a survey of citizens that indicate a high level of satisfaction with local law enforcement, overall favorable perceptions, and a relatively low level of fear of crime are due to a particular community-policing initiative lacking the information provided through the first approach. Although the study of community policing is problematic by nature, creative and carefully crafted research designs and methods have been utilized to conduct such research.

Other interventions

Place-based and offender- or offense-based interventions are somewhat less problematic for the researcher than community policing; however, problem-oriented policing requires special attention. As addressed earlier, problem-oriented policing is a stand-alone type of police intervention, although it relates closely to community-oriented policing. Both interventions rely on problem-solving, as both generally make use of the scanning, analysis, response, and evaluation SARA model (Goldstein, 2001). The subtle distinction between the two approaches is important at a number of levels. While community policing necessitates the use of problem-solving approaches, problem-oriented policing does not necessitate the use of citizen engagement, input, or involvement. From a research perspective, this means that the indicators, measures, and outcomes used to assess problem-oriented policing may overlap with those used in studying community policing, but the subtle distinction holds important implications. For example, researchers assessing problem-oriented approaches might not be concerned with gauging citizen involvement in this process, nor might researchers be as concerned with citizen perceptions of the propriety and efficacy of the strategy.

Experimental and quasi experimental research designs

While an experimental research design is the gold standard in terms of rigorous empirical hypothesis-testing, such opportunities are infrequent in criminological and criminal justice research in general, and particularly rare for police scholars. Some factors that may contribute to this are the fact that most studies are conducted after the implementation of an intervention has already occurred; the fact that oftentimes the random assignment of police agency personnel or subjects of police contact is operationally infeasible; and; the fact that such random assignment may pose insurmountable ethical issues (e.g., one group receiving a more desirable treatment than another, which produces a more favorable outcome). Nevertheless, some studies of community policing, place-based, and offender- or offense-based interventions have been conducted utilizing experimental or quasi-experimental research designs – but, as will be demonstrated in the examples that follow, not without challenges.

One such unique opportunity was an evaluative study of the implementation and impact of community policing in the Madison Police Department (MPD) in Wisconsin; the study was conducted by Wycoff and Skogan over the course of three years (1987–1990). Wycoff and Skogan (1994) utilized a quasi-experimental design and a combination of methods: direct observation, interviews, and surveys of both personnel and citizens. The study involved the establishment of an experimental policing district (EPD) that was housed in its own facility, apart from other MPD districts (Wycoff and Skogan, 1994). However, random assignment was not possible, as the EPD was selected by the MPD and was staffed by a combination of volunteers and officers assigned on the basis of seniority, which thus prohibited a true experimental research design. While the rest of the MPD maintained its traditional structure and operation, the EPD was decentralized and restructured through a participatory management approach, which emphasized employee involvement in decision-making, problem-solving, and community-policing practices (Wycoff and Skogan, 1994).

The challenges noted by Wycoff and Skogan (1994) were that the outcome measures for the external impact (i.e., those derived from the citizen survey) may have suffered from some validity issues, that the relatively short time frame of the study was probably not sufficient to measure the impact of community policing, and that the results were not necessarily generalizable, as every community is unique. Additional limitations and cautions can be added to measuring the outcome of community policing in such a case-study fashion. These include cautions when weighing evidence based on interviews and surveys of police administrators, line personnel, and citizens, all of which shall be addressed later, in the section on surveys.

Generally community policing is implemented in a department-wide fashion that prohibits an experimental approach, which makes the Madison study especially unique; however, the nature of place-based interventions in particular allows for experimental research designs when a researcher is able to partner with a police agency prior to the implementation of an intervention. Several such studies have been conducted with a variety of methods (see Braga, 2005; and Braga, Papachristos, and Hureau, 2012 for review); two examples of studies that utilized experimental designs follow.

One study of place-based interventions was conducted over a 90-day period in 2009. Taylor, Koper, and Woods (2011) employed an experimental design in a study of hotspot interventions in Jacksonville, Florida, in which the researchers compared the impact of problem-oriented policing solutions and directed-saturation patrol treatments to that of a control condition in 83 hot spots that had been identified as having particularly high incidences of violent crimes. The 83 hot spots were randomly assigned to either one of the two treatments or to the control group (Taylor et al., 2011). The problem-oriented approach treatment included such interventions as crime prevention through environmental design (CPTED) assessments and related improvements (e.g., lighting, barriers, fencing), repairs and cleanup of properties (e.g., graffiti removal), collaboration with social service agencies, working with area businesses to improve security measures, nuisance abatement, and so on. The research methods employed included direct observation on ride-alongs and the collection and analysis of Uniform Crime Report (UCR) data, arrest reports, call for service data, and field interview or self-initiated activity data (Taylor et al., 2011). The results showed no change in arrests for violent crimes during the treatment period, but they did show a significant reduction in violent crime (33 percent) 90 days after the conclusion of the treatment period in the hot spots that received the problem-oriented treatment. However, through the collection and examination of data during the follow-up period, the researchers discovered evidence of displacement of that violent crime to adjacent areas (Taylor et al., 2011).

The challenges encountered by these researchers included problems associated with the direct observation of police officers in a ride-along setting (these are discussed later in the chapter) and concerns with displacement, though the researchers were able to measure the latter, at least geographically. In addition, these researchers identified the limitations of the use of UCR and call for service data for outcome measures (this topic, too, is discussed later in the chapter). In particular, Taylor and colleagues (2011) point out that, as citizens became aware of the program, their reporting of crimes to the police may have increased. The broad nature of the interventions in this study further highlights the tension between the need for agencies and officials to have flexibility in the specific tactics they use (e.g., directed patrol versus CPTED) and the desire that researchers control as much as they can during natural experiments, which trigger validity and reliability concerns. Do modest or null findings suggest that place-based interventions do not work, or simply that a specific tactic did not work? Even if the latter can be established, researchers can struggle to determine whether that reflects a fundamental flaw with that tactic or simply the fact that the tactic was not the appropriate solution for a given problem in a given area at a given point in time.

The second example chosen here is the nine-month randomized controlled study of hotspot policing to reduce nondomestic assaults and robberies involving firearms in St. Louis, Missouri. Rosenfeld, Deckard, and Blackburn (2014) identified 32 hotspots among eight police districts in St. Louis and randomly assigned them to one of three groups: two different treatment conditions or a control group. According to this study, "directed patrols were increased in both treatment conditions, whereas the experimental protocol limited other enforcement activity in one of the treatment conditions and increased it in the other" (p. 432). The results indicated that the number of nondomestic assaults involving firearms was significantly reduced while the intervention appeared to have no impact on the number of robberies involving firearms (Rosenfeld et al., 2014).

The challenges that Rosenfeld and colleagues related were about fidelity and monitoring for displacement. With regard to fidelity, they state:

> Poor fidelity to experimental procedures is the downfall of many otherwise promising field experiments. Fidelity refers to whether the experiment was carried out the way it was supposed to be carried out. Recall that officers in the two treatment conditions were to engage in directed patrol in the hot spots and call out their presence at predesignated locations at least three times during a duty shift. In addition, officers assigned to treatment 1 were to limit self-initiated enforcement activity, whereas those assigned to treatment 2 were encouraged to engage in self-initiated activity. We should therefore observe roughly equal frequencies of directed patrol in the hot spots assigned to the two treatment conditions, more directed patrols in the treatment conditions than in the control condition, and more self-initiated activity in treatment 2 than in treatment 1. Also, we should observe more self-initiated activity in the control condition than in the treatment 1 hotspots where officers were told to limit self-initiated activity. (Rosenfeld and colleagues, 2014, p. 435)

Rosenfeld and colleagues (2014) report that their results "indicate appreciable, but not complete, fidelity with experimental procedures" (p. 435). With regard to the second challenge, they report that they found no indication of displacement.

Evaluation research

Due to the factors limiting the opportunities for experimental research designs, more often than not the community-policing and police intervention researcher is limited to evaluation research that utilizes cross-sectional designs or secondary data analysis for comparison. While the literature made up of these types of studies is vast, a prime example is that of a study of three interventions – Boston's Operation Ceasefire, New York City's Compstat, and Richmond City's Project Exile – and of their impact on homicide rates. This study was conducted by Rosenfeld, Fornango, and Baumer (2005a). Compstat has been described earlier, but a brief description of both Operation Ceasefire and Project Exile is in order.

Operation Ceasefire was a "pulling levers" strategy (offender-/offense-based intervention) that was developed and implemented in Boston as a result of a problem-oriented approach to an alarmingly high rate of youth homicides involving gang activity and guns (National Institute of Justice, 2008). In a unique approach, researchers David Kennedy, Anthony Braga, and Anne Piehl teamed with criminal justice practitioners (the Boston Police Department, the Massachusetts Departments of Probation and Parole, the Suffolk County District Attorney's Office, the US Attorney's Office, the Bureau of Alcohol, Tobacco, and Firearms, the Massachusetts Department of Youth Services, the Boston School Police, and Boston Community Center gang outreach and prevention street workers) in order to develop a violence-reduction intervention (Braga et al., 2001). With the help of an evaluation design, these researchers assessed the impact of this intervention. The study utilized outcome measures that consisted of comparisons of homicide and violent crime rates before and after May 15, 1996 – when the intervention commenced with the first contact of target individuals (Braga et al., 2001). According to Braga and colleagues:

> The well-known large reduction in yearly Boston youth homicide numbers certainly suggests that something noteworthy happened after Operation Ceasefire was implemented in mid-1996 ... Boston averaged 44 youth homicides per year between 1991 and 1995. In 1996, the number of Boston youth homicides decreased to 26 and then further decreased to 15 youth homicides in 1997. (Braga et al., 2001, p. 204)

The challenges faced by the researchers in this study were somewhat unique, and Braga and colleagues related them as follows:

> Unfortunately we were not able to collect the necessary pretest and posttest data to shed light on any shifts in street-level dynamics that could be associated with the

> pulling-levers deterrence strategy. Our research efforts during the pretest phase were focused on problem analysis and program development. A priori, we did not know what form the intervention would take and who our target audience would be. In this regard, our assessment is very much a "black box" evaluation. Additional research on the deterrence mechanisms of the pulling-levers approach to controlling offenders is necessary. (Braga et al., 2001, p. 219)

As a result, while the authors can clearly note the reduction in youth homicides and it is reasonable to attribute at least some of the decline to the intervention, just how much credit the latter deserves is difficult to determine. Likewise, given the complex set of partners and interventions involved, it is impossible to conclusively determine what elements of the intervention are necessary to ensure success when replicating this approach in other communities. These are more than ivory tower considerations; the inclusion of irrelevant elements in any intervention approach inflates costs and complexity, while depriving viable elements of the resources and focus they need.

Project Exile in Richmond, Virginia was a very similar offender- and offense-based intervention that also targeted gun violence. In this case the US Attorney's Office for the Eastern District of Virginia initiated the intervention in collaboration with the Bureau of Alcohol, Tobacco, and Firearms, the Federal Bureau of Investigation, the Richmond Commonwealth's Attorney's Office, the Richmond Police Department, the Virginia Attorney General's Office, and the Virginia State Police, as well as in collaboration with members of the community (Comey and Miller, 2002). However, as a federal prosecutor-developed intervention (and as its name implies), Project Exile was more focused than Ceasefire on specific deterrence through federal prosecution and imprisonment. Those who researched through its implementation did not evaluate Project Exile as they did Operation Ceasefire; however, claims have been made that the program played a significant role in the reduction of homicides in Richmond (Comey and Miller, 2002).

Rosenfeld and colleagues (2005a) sought to evaluate all three of these interventions – Boston's Operation Ceasefire, New York's Compstat, and Richmond's Project Exile – in the light of claims that the interventions had a significant impact on the reduction of homicides in their respective jurisdictions. According to Rosenfeld and colleagues:

> To assess the effects of the three interventions, we apply growth-curve models to homicide trends in Boston, New York, and Richmond. We estimate each city's homicide trend as a function of a baseline model of covariates fit to data for the 95 largest US cities. An intervention's effectiveness is indicated by a reduction in homicide during the intervention period that is significantly greater than the average reduction for the sample. Our strategy cannot conclusively rule out other possible explanations for observed differences in homicide trends between cities with and without the interventions. However, the absence of such differences would place a particularly strong onus on program defenders to demonstrate that an observed homicide reduction resulted from a particular intervention. (Rosenfeld et al., 2005a, p. 428)

The results of this study indicated that Richmond's intervention contributed to a significant reduction in homicides, while no such impact was found in either Boston or New York. However, Rosenfeld and colleagues' (2005a) study posed some considerable challenges. According to these authors:

> Few commonly accepted standards exist for undertaking statistical evaluations of crime-control interventions using observational data and econometric methods, even though these are the data and methods we are stuck with for evaluating large-scale initiatives such as those addressed in this study. (Rosenfeld and colleagues, 2005a, p. 440)

The use of observational data and the statistical methods employed by Rosenfeld and colleagues in this study attracted a critical response, to which the authors in turn responded and provided further details concerning these methodological challenges (see Berk, 2005; Rosenfeld, Fornango, and Baumer, 2005b).

The previous examples demonstrate the research design challenges confronting researchers who assess community policing and police interventions. These examples also provide some insight into the methodological issues and challenges that are ever present in this type of research. The sections that follow review the issues and challenges most often encountered in community policing and in police intervention research with specific methodologies.

Surveys and interviews

Surveys and interviews are among the methods most readily available to the police scholar who studies community policing and other interventions, and the sole methods for assessing some expected outcomes, in particular fear of crime and citizen satisfaction. Surveys and interviews of both police personnel and citizens present challenges that the policing scholar must understand and mitigate inasmuch as possible.

First, one must exercise caution when weighing evidence based on interviews and surveys of police administrators with regard to popular innovations, particularly those subject to funding opportunities. Interview participants may give socially desirable responses, and the perceptions of command officers may differ appreciably from those of line personnel (Maguire and Katz, 2002; Mastrofski, 2006). For example, community policing has been a very popular concept since the 1980s, and government officials at every level have been motivated to see their respective jurisdictions implement community-policing principles based on the potential to improve relations between the police and the community, along with the political capital that such improvements muster (Maguire and Katz, 2002; Mastrofski, 2006). Institutional theory suggests that law enforcement executives may implement some token programs and may claim to have adopted community policing in order to improve their public image and perceptions of legitimacy, while largely maintaining business as usual (Maguire and Katz, 2002; Phillips and Gayadeen, 2014). The Crime

Act of 1994 created additional incentives in the form of financial assistance that might have further contributed to the token engagement in community policing. Resource-dependence theory would predict that, in the environment of tight budgets in which public agencies operate, such financial incentives might lead to some level of exaggeration concerning community-policing involvement (Maguire and Katz, 2002). Parallel conditions repeatedly emerge that might incentivize the symbolic adoption of various interventions in order to secure financial resources.

This does not suggest that many law enforcement executives have been blatantly dishonest. An executive's vision may not always mirror what actually occurs at the line level in the field. Surveys and interviews of law enforcement executives alone will capture that executive's perception of his or her agency's level of commitment to community policing and to other innovations. Field studies and surveys of line personnel are necessary to confirm that a core of innovations are practiced and that the prescribed tactics are carried out (Maguire and Katz, 2002).

Surveys and interviews of line officers are not completely challenge-free. Line officers may provide answers that are based on the agency's expectations of them rather than on their actual practices, regardless of anonymity assurances. Officers might be reluctant to express views or report behaviors that run against the paradigm dominant in their agency at that point in time. In either case, researchers should endeavor to minimize these potential problems by paying careful attention to the development of the survey instrument. Lastly, equal caution must be exercised with surveys of the public regarding satisfaction with police services, due to challenges in generating quality samples, especially when the research design calls for repeated surveys or interviews with the same panel of residents.

Direct observation

Direct observation has been utilized extensively in community policing and police intervention research, often in conjunction with other methods, as this is sometimes the sole means by which a researcher can confirm intervention fidelity. As mentioned above, surveys of law enforcement personnel can be particularly problematic; the information obtained from police administrators concerning the implementation of an intervention such as community policing might not be reflected in field operations at the line level. The information gathered from surveys of line personnel might not reveal this either, for the reasons stated earlier. Thus the researcher may only be able to confirm intervention fidelity through direct observation (see Hassell and Lovell, 2014). However, there are significant challenges with this methodology – challenges that can create serious validity concerns and limitations of the data collected. These include the potential for reactivity or the reactive effect, and reliability issues when multiple observers are employed.

A reactive effect is "the changes in individual or group behavior that are due to being observed or otherwise studied" (Bachman and Schutt, 2014, p. 242). The potential for a reactive effect is a salient concern when observing police officers, and this is due to three primary reasons. First, the very nature of police work, which is frequently criticized by the public and in the media, makes it likely that the officer being observed will be on his or her "best behavior" and may not exhibit the same attitudes and behaviors that s/he normally would in the absence of the observer. Second, for the same reason (and also given the paramilitary structure, which promotes loyalty, duty, and discipline), the officer under observation might refrain from certain behaviors while engaging in activities like community policing duties, which s/he may not perform in normal circumstances. Third, the officer may feel compelled to impress the observer by engaging in more exciting activities rather than in more mundane duties.

The second challenge that presents itself in direct observation is that of reliability issues when multiple observers are involved. Of first concern for the researcher is that detailed and accurate observations are made and that those observations are recorded adequately in fieldnotes that can be coded. Reliability issues arise with multiple observers when they are not observing and noting the same things, or simply when they are noting them differently. Both of these challenges are evident in the following example.

In a study of community policing that utilized student observers, Chappell (2009) notes several threats to validity: the data were generated by undergraduate observers who each conducted a single ride-along; students may have "misinterpreted" what they observed due to limited training; the shifts chosen may have not been the norm; and officers may have reacted to the presence of a student observer. While reactivity effects are a challenge in any form of direct observation, they can be magnified in this case, due to both the limited period of observation and the age of the observer. The latter could have the most significant effect, as officers may view community-policing tasks – such as simply getting out of the patrol car and speaking with citizens – as quite mundane and boring for a younger person, especially one presumably aspiring for a career in criminal justice. The officer might feel compelled to "show off" instead and might seek to show the student something more exciting, such as an arrest.

Both of the aforementioned challenges were also present in the Project on Policing Neighborhoods (POPN), a study of community policing practices at the line officer level in Indianapolis and St. Petersburg. Using systematic social observations, POPN deployed "carefully trained project staff members, who accompanied police officers assigned to one of 24 neighborhoods that were matched across the two cities (12 neighborhoods in each city)" (Parks et al., 1999, p. 491). These participant observers documented approximately 360 shifts in each city, recording observations of roughly 6,500 police–citizen contacts in Indianapolis and 5,500 in St. Petersburg. The observers were trained to take systematic fieldnotes during their observations; those notes were transformed into prepared narrative reports and coded data after each shift observed. Although participant observers were not always assigned to the same officer, they were permanently assigned to specific beats and undoubtedly became known to the officers. The combination between the length of the study, the well-trained participant observers, and their assignment to the same beat likely served to minimize the reactive effect and multiple-observer reliability issues in this particular study.

Use of internal police and official data

The use of both internally generated police data and official data presents challenges for the community-policing and police intervention researcher. While police agencies engaged in problem-oriented policing (such as some form of Compstat) produce internal data that a researcher may be able to access in order to evaluate interventions, the primary challenge is that these data were not generated with the researcher's purpose in mind. Police agencies often identify a problem and develop and implement an intervention without giving consideration to a rigorous evaluation of the results. The problem may not have been adequately defined, concepts associated with the intervention may not have been appropriately or adequately conceptualized and operationalized, and pretest data may be lacking, which makes it highly unlikely that any kind of causal determination could be made (Braga, Hureau, and Papachristos, 2011).

The use of official data can be a challenge for the researcher of community policing (and of other interventions as well). The primary difficulty with official data is that they may not accurately reflect what the researcher is attempting to measure. UCR data fail to capture many types of crime – many of those indicative of disorder or unreported crimes, for instance; or it might not be possible to disaggregate the data for the geographical area to be studied. As indicated in an earlier example, Taylor and colleagues (2011) point out issues with both internal and official data utilized in their study. These researchers recognized that, as citizens became aware of the program, their reports of crime to the police may have increased, which rendered reliance on UCR and call-for-service data for outcome measures problematic.

Moving Forward

While research related to community policing has slowed down in recent years, some innovative research has been emerging. Community-policing research in the 1980s and 1990s tended to addressed implementation, line officer buy-in, and citizen perceptions. More recently, scholars have begun to ask deeper questions about community-policing processes and outcomes. The impact of community policing on crime and disorder has been called into question (Gill et al., 2014). Researchers have utilized institutional theory in order to examine factors associated with the adoption of community policing (Burruss and Giblin, 2009; Phillips and Gayadeen, 2014). Evaluations have sought to assess the effectiveness of the Chicago Police Department's web-based system for engaging citizens in community-policing problem-solving (Graziano, Rosenbaum, and Schuck, 2014). Researchers have sought to link the use of websites by municipal police departments to relationships with community policing and legitimacy (Rosenbaum et al., 2011).

Notable research on the subject is emerging in Europe as well. Two recent studies have examined citizen attitudes to and perceptions of the police. One utilized survey data to compare such citizen attitudes and perceptions across 26 European nations (Schaap and Scheepers, 2014). The other developed a survey for comparisons between countries and contrasted the level of citizens' trust in police in the United Kingdom and in Bulgaria (Jackson et al., 2011). Each of these studies indicates the need for future international comparative studies.

The relationship between police interventions and resulting procedural justice and police legitimacy appears to be a likely future avenue for policing scholars. While there has been a marked decline in the amount of attention that community policing has received since the September 11, 2001 terrorist attacks, procedural justice and police legitimacy have emerged as significant concerns, and community policing is thought to be a catalyst for achieving them (Gill et al., 2014; Mazerolle, Bennett, et al., 2013). This, combined with the scrutiny that police have received in 2013, 2014 with regard to possible racial bias, will probably call for research regarding their impact. However, Gill and colleagues (2014) point out that currently there is no theoretical framework to explain the mechanism by which community policing promotes procedural justice and increases police legitimacy, or to explain how community policing reduces crime, disorder, or fear of crime. Therefore research will likely be undertaken to address these needs as well.

This chapter has demonstrated that the measurement of community policing and police interventions is inherently problematic. Police interventions of all types are frequently ill defined and their anticipated outcomes tend to be implicitly, rather than explicitly, identified and stated. Researchers often find themselves studying a singular case, typically in a purposive venue. Data about pre-intervention conditions are often altogether absent. Many interventions are not introduced with the use of control groups and some approaches (e.g., Compstat) essentially have to be implemented agency-wide. Researchers can find themselves charged with studying an initiative without fully knowing whether the results (positive, negative, or neutral) are specific to the overall policing intervention (e.g., problem-oriented policing approaches) or to the exact tactics used in the study venue (e.g., directed patrol targeting open-air drug markets). As a result, studies may suffer from validity problems due to a lack of clarity about whether findings can be generalized to other times, places, or problems. Negative results might reflect that a given strategy or tactic is fundamentally flawed, but might also mean that the intervention was not properly implemented within the study jurisdiction.

These difficulties are compounded by additional measurement and research design challenges that researchers must struggle to overcome. There may be status, financial, and professional incentives that drive police executives to characterize intervention efforts in a particular fashion. Observing police officers in the actual performance of their duties can provide the richest understanding of how an intervention is actually being brought to life, but it can also trigger reactivity considerations.

Citizen perceptions can give key insights into how the police and their efforts are perceived, but those perceptions can be based on distorted, limited, or inaccurate understandings of crime and justice. The unfortunate reality is that our ability to understand the capacity of the police to influence crime and associated community conditions remains quite limited on the basis of the existing literature. An understanding of how research has addressed these measurement challenges can, however, open pathways to grow and expand more systematically our knowledge of police interventions.

References

Abdullah, A., Marzbali, M. H., Woolley, H., Bahauddin, A., and Maliki, N. Z. 2014. Testing for individual factors for the fear of crime using a multiple indicator: Multiple cause model. *European Journal on Criminal Policy and Research*, 20 (1): 1–22.

Armstrong, T., and Katz, C. 2010. Further evidence on the discriminant validity of perceptual incivilities measures. *Justice Quarterly*, 27 (2): 280–304.

Bachman, R., and Schutt, R. K. 2014. *The practice of research in criminology and criminal justice*, 5th edn. Thousand Oaks, CA: Sage.

Bayley, D. H. 1988. Community policing: A report from the devil's advocate. In *Community policing: Rhetoric or reality*, edited by J. R. Greene and S. D. Mastrofski, 224–237. New York: Praeger.

Berk, R. A. 2005. Knowing when to fold'em: An essay on evaluating the impact of Ceasefire, Compstat, and Exile. *Criminology & Public Policy*, 4 (3): 451–466.

Braga, A. A. 2001. The effects of hot spots policing on crime. *The Annals of the American Academy of Political and Social Science*, 578 (1): 104–125.

Braga, A. A. 2005. Hot spots policing and crime prevention: A systematic review of randomized controlled trials. *Journal of Experimental Criminology*, 1 (3): 317–342.

Braga, A. A., Hureau, D. M., and Papachristos, A. V. 2011. An ex post facto evaluation framework for place-based police interventions. *Evaluation Review*, 35 (6): 592–626.

Braga, A. A., Kennedy, D. M., Waring, E. J., and Piehl, A. M. 2001. Problem-oriented policing, deterrence, and youth violence: An evaluation of Boston's Operation Ceasefire. *Journal of Research in Crime and Delinquency*, 38 (3): 195–225.

Braga, A. A., Papachristos, A. V., and Hureau, D. M. 2012. The effects of hot spots policing on crime: An updated systematic review and meta-analysis. *Justice Quarterly*, 31 (4): 633–663.

Burruss, G. W., and Giblin, M. J. 2014. Modeling isomorphism on policing innovation: The role of institutional pressures in adopting community-oriented policing. *Crime & Delinquency*, 60 (3): 331–355.

Cao, L., Frank, J., and Cullen, F. T. 1996. Race, community context and confidence in the police. *American Journal of Police*, 15 (1): 3–22.

Chappell, A. T. 2009. The philosophical versus actual adoption of community policing: A case study. *Criminal Justice Review*, 34 (1): 5–28.

Comey, J., and Miller, S. 2002. Project exile. In *Project Safe Neighborhoods: America's Network against Gun Violence*, 11–15. Special issue of *United States Attorneys' Bulletin*, 50 (1).

Cordner, G. W. 1988. A problem-oriented approach to community-oriented policing. In *Community policing: Rhetoric or reality*, edited by J. R., Greene and S. D. Mastrofski, 135–152. New York: Praeger.

Cordner, G. W. 2010. Community policing: Elements and effects. In *Critical issues in policing: Contemporary readings*, edited by R. G. Dunham and G. P. Alpert, 6th edn., 432–449. Long Grove, IL: Waveland.

Eck, J. E., and Rosenbaum, D. P. 1994. The new police order: Effectiveness, equity, and efficiency in community policing. In *The challenge of community policing: Testing the promises*, edited by D. P. Rosenbaum, 3–23. Thousand Oaks, CA: Sage.

Ferraro, K. F., and LaGrange, R. 1987. The measurement of fear of crime. *Sociological Inquiry*, 57 (1): 70–101.

Flynn, D. W. 1998. *Defining the "community" in community policing*. Washington, DC: Police Executive Research Forum.

Gau, J. M., Corsaro, N., and Brunson, R. K. 2014. Revisiting broken windows theory: A test of the mediation impact of social mechanisms on the disorder–fear relationship. *Journal of Criminal Justice*, 42 (6): 579–588.

Gill, C., Weisburd, D., Telep, C. W., Vitter, Z., and Bennett, T. 2014. Community-oriented policing to reduce crime, disorder and fear and increase satisfaction and legitimacy among citizens: A systematic review. *Journal of Experimental Criminology*, 10 (4): 399–428.

Goldstein, H. 1979. Improving policing: A problem-oriented approach. *Crime & Delinquency*, 25 (2): 236–258.

Goldstein, H. 2001. What is POP? Center for Problem-Oriented Policing. Accessed September 21, 2014. http://www.popcenter.org/about/?p=whatiscpop.

Graziano, L. M., Rosenbaum, D. P., and Schuck, A. M. 2014. Building group capacity for problem solving and police–community partnerships through survey feedback and training: A randomized control trial within Chicago's community policing program. *Journal of Experimental Criminology*, 10 (1): 79–103.

Greene, J. R. 2004. Community policing and organizational change. In *Community policing: Can it work?* edited by W. G. Skogan, 30–53. Belmont, CA: Wadsworth.

Greene, J. R., and Mastrofski, S. D., eds. 1988. *Community policing: Rhetoric or reality?* New York: Praeger.

Hassell, K. D., and Lovell, R. D. 2014. Fidelity of implementation: Important considerations for policing scholars. *Policing and Society*, 25 (5): 504–520. doi: 10.1080/10439463.2014.881811.

Hough, M., Jackson, J., and Bradford, B. 2013. The drivers of police legitimacy: Some European research. *Journal of Policing, Intelligence and Counter Terrorism*, 8 (2): 144–165.

Jackson, J., Bradford, B., Hough, M., Kuha, J., Stares, S., Widdop, S., Fitzgerald, R., Yordanova, M., and Galev, T. 2011. Developing European indicators of trust in justice. *European Journal of Criminology*, 8 (4): 267–285.

Kelling, G. L., and Moore, M. H. 1988. From political reform to community: The evolving strategy of police. In *Community policing: Rhetoric or reality*, edited by J. R. Greene and S. D. Mastrofski, 3–25. New York: Praeger.

Kennedy, D. M. 2006. Old wine in new bottles: Policing and the lessons of pulling levers. In *Police innovation: Contrasting perspectives*, edited by D. Weisburd and A. A. Braga, 155–170. New York: Cambridge University Press.

Klockars, C. B. 1988. The rhetoric of community policing. In *Community policing: Rhetoric or reality*, edited by J. R. Greene and S. D. Mastrofski, 239–258. New York: Praeger.

Kochel, T. R. 2012. Can police legitimacy promote collective efficacy? *Justice Quarterly*, 29 (3): 384–419.

Maguire, E. R., and Katz, C. M. 2002. Community policing, loose coupling, and sensemaking in American police agencies. *Justice Quarterly*, 19 (3): 503–536.

Manning, P. K. 1997. *Police work: The social organization of policing*, 2nd edn. Prospect Heights, IL: Waveland.

Mastrofski, S. 2006. Community policing: A skeptical view. In *Police innovation: Contrasting perspectives*, edited by D. Weisburd and A. A. Braga, 44–73. New York: Cambridge University Press.

Mazerolle, L., Antrobus, E., Bennett, S., and Tyler, T. R. 2013. Shaping citizen perceptions of police legitimacy: A randomized field trial of procedural justice. *Criminology*, 51 (1): 33–63.

Mazerolle, L., Bennett, S., Davis, J., Sargeant, E., and Manning, M. 2013. Procedural justice and police legitimacy: A systematic review of the research evidence. *Journal of Experimental Criminology*, 9 (3): 245–274.

Merry, S., Power, N., McManus, M., and Alison, L. 2012. Drivers of public trust and confidence in police in the UK. *International Journal of Police Science & Management*, 14 (2): 118–135.

Moore, M. H. 1992. Problem-solving and community policing. *Crime and Justice*, 15: 99–158.

Moore, M. H., and Braga, A. A. 2003. Measuring and improving police performance: The lessons of Compstat and its progeny. *Policing: An International Journal of Police Strategies & Management*, 26 (3): 439–453.

National Institute of Justice. 2008. Gun violence programs: Operation Ceasefire. Accessed October 21, 2014. http://nij.gov/topics/crime/gun-violence/prevention/pages/ceasefire.aspx.

National Institute of Justice. 2010. How to identify hot spots. Accessed October 5, 2014. http://www.popcenter.org/about/?p=whatiscpop.

Parks, R. B., Mastrofski, S. D., De Jong, C., and Gray, M. K. 1999. How officers spend their time with the community. *Justice Quarterly*, 16 (3): 483–518.

Perkins, D. D., and Taylor, R. B. 1996. Ecological assessments of community disorder: Their relationship to fear of crime and theoretical implications. *American Journal of Community Psychology*, 24 (1): 63–107.

Phillips, S. W., and Gayadeen, S. M. 2014. The coercive impact of federal grants: COPS grants and the diffusion of the community policing philosophy. *The Police Journal*, 87 (1): 49–60.

Reisig, M. D., and Parks, R. B. 2004. Community policing and quality of life. In *Community policing: Can it work?* edited by W. G. Skogan, 207–227. Belmont, CA: Wadsworth.

Roccato, M., Russo, S., and Vieno, A. 2011. Perceived community disorder moderates the relation between victimization and fear of crime. *Journal of Community Psychology*, 39 (7): 884–888.

Rosenbaum, D. P., Graziano, L. M., Stephens, C. D., and Schuck, A. M. 2011. Understanding community policing and legitimacy-seeking behavior in virtual reality: A national study of municipal police websites. *Police Quarterly*, 14 (1): 25–47.

Rosenfeld, R., Deckard, M. J., and Blackburn, E. 2014. The effects of directed patrol and self-initiated enforcement on firearm violence: A randomized controlled study of hot spot policing. *Criminology*, 52 (3): 428–449.

Rosenfeld, R., Fornango, R., and Baumer, E. (2005a). Did Ceasefire, Compstat, and Exile reduce homicide? *Criminology & Public Policy*, 4 (3): 419–449.

Rosenfeld, R., Fornango, R., and Baumer, E. (2005b). The straw man bluff: Reply to Berk. *Criminology & Public Policy*, 4 (3): 467–470.

Roth, J. A., Roehl, J. and Johnson, C. C. 2004. Trends in the adoption of community policing. In *Community policing: Can it work?* edited by W. G. Skogan, 3–29. Belmont, CA: Wadsworth.

Schaap, D., and Scheepers, P. 2014. Comparing citizen's trust in the police across European countries: An assessment of cross-country measurement equivalence. *International Criminal Justice Review*, 24: 82–98.

Schafer, J. A., Huebner, B. M., and Bynum, T. S. 2003. Citizen perceptions of police services: Race, neighborhood context, and community policing. *Police Quarterly*, 6 (4): 440–468.

Sherman, L. W., and Weisburd, D. 1995. General deterrent effects of police patrol in crime "hot spots": A randomized, controlled trial. *Justice Quarterly*, 12 (4): 625–648.

Skogan, W. G. 1990. *Disorder and decline: Crime and the spiral of decay in American neighborhoods*. Berkley: University of California Press.

Skogan, W. G. 2006a. *Police and community in Chicago*. New York: Oxford University Press.

Skogan, W. G. 2006b. The promise of community policing. In *Police innovation: Contrasting perspectives*, edited by D, Weisburd and A. A. Braga, 27–43. New York: Cambridge University Press.

Skogan, W. G., and Hartnett, S. M. 1997. *Community policing, Chicago style*. New York: Oxford University Press.

Skolnick, J. H., and Bayley, D. H. 1986. *The new blue line: Police innovation in six American cities*. New York: Free Press.

Spelman, W., and Eck, J. E. 1989. Sitting ducks, ravenous wolves and helping hands: New approaches to urban policing. *Public Affairs Comment*, 35 (2): 1–9.

Stein, R. E. 2014. Neighborhood residents' fear of crime: A tale of three cities. *Sociological Focus*, 47 (2): 121–139.

Taylor, B., Koper, C. S., and Woods, D. J. 2011. A randomized controlled trial of different policing strategies at hot spots of violent crime. *Journal of Experimental Criminology*, 7 (2): 149–181.

Taylor, R. B. 1999. The incivilities thesis: Theory, measurement, and policy. In *Measuring what matters: Proceedings from the police research institute meetings*, edited by R. Langworthy, 65–88. Washington, DC: National Institute of Justice.

Trojanowicz, R., Kappeler, V. E., and Gaines, L. K. 2002. *Community policing: A contemporary perspective*, 3rd edn. Cincinnati, OH: Anderson.

Willis, J. J., Mastrofski, S. D., and Weisburd, D. 2007. Making sense of COMPSTAT: A theory-based analysis of organizational change in three police departments. *Law & Society Review*, 41 (1): 147–188.

Wilson, J. Q., and Kelling, G. L. 1982. Broken windows. *Atlantic Monthly*, 249: 29–38.

Worrall, J. L. 1999. Public perceptions of police efficacy and image: The "fuzziness" of support for the police. *American Journal of Criminal Justice*, 24 (1): 47–66.

Worrall, J. L. 2006. The discriminant validity of perceptual incivility measures. *Justice Quarterly*, 23 (3): 360–383.

Wyant, B. R. 2008. Multilevel impacts of perceived incivilities and perceptions of crime and risk on fear of crime: Isolating endogenous impacts. *Journal of Research in Crime and Delinquency*, 45 (1): 39–64.

Wycoff, M. A., and Skogan, W. G. 1994. Community policing in Madison: An analysis of implementation and impact. In *The challenge of community policing: Testing the promises*, edited by D. P. Rosenbaum, 75–91. Thousand Oaks, CA: Sage.

Zhao, J. S., Tsai, C. F., Ren, L., and Lai, Y. L. 2014. Public satisfaction with police control of disorder crime: Does the public hold police accountable? *Justice Quarterly*, 31 (2): 394–420.

14

Measurement Issues in Criminal Case-Processing and Court Decision-Making Research

Brian D. Johnson and Christina D. Stewart

Concern over measurement is a pervasive theme running through contemporary research on criminal case-processing and court actor decision-making. In part this stems from the fact that case-processing involves a legion of complex, interconnected discretionary decisions made by multiple actors, often across diverse legal environments. Understood in this way, punishment decisions are the "end result of a decision-making process that involves offenders moving through a series of potentially important stages in a complex criminal justice system" (Hagan and Bumiller, 1983, p. 3). Members of the courtroom workgroup occupy dynamic positions within the structures of their local environments, and therefore capturing the full complexity of influences on the various outcomes decided by different justice agents is inherently difficult. The task is further complicated by the disconnected nature of the justice system. Data on court-processing are typically collected by multiple agencies that are only "loosely coupled" (Hagan, Hewitt, and Alwin, 1979). This not only introduces logistical difficulties in obtaining usable data, but also results in a number of potentially problematic measurement concerns for research: limited conceptualization of both dependent and independent variables, weak or indirect measures of key theoretical constructs believed to affect court-processing, and important analytical and statistical challenges that can jeopardize the validity of findings.

This chapter provides an overview of the various challenges associated with conducting empirical research on case-processing and decision-making in criminal courts. It discusses common methodological concerns and pitfalls encountered, describes recent research advances and contemporary data collection efforts, and provides an overview of promising new developments and future directions for improving our understanding of the crucial role of the criminal courts in American punishment.

The Handbook of Measurement Issues in Criminology and Criminal Justice, First Edition.
Edited by Beth M. Huebner and Timothy S. Bynum.

The (Mis)measure of Criminal Punishment

The very nature of criminal case-processing presents significant measurement issues for research. Numerous decisions comprise the sequential process of criminal punishment, from initial arrest and charging decisions to final sentencing, appeal, and parole outcomes. Because multiple actors and diverse agencies exercise discretion across decision-making stages, adequately measuring all that enters into case-processing outcomes represents a mammoth challenge. Seldom is the broader punishment process measured in its full complexity; as Thomson and Zingraff (1981) long ago noted, "the majority of disparity research has not analyzed the processual nature of criminal justice decision making" (p. 871). Instead, much research has examined only a single stage of case-processing, which has often been restricted to the final sentencing decision (Spohn, 2000). Even within this narrow area, prior work has relied on limited measures of the sentencing outcome. Moreover, research often suffers from the omission of important independent variables, for example certain offender characteristics, case-processing factors, decision-maker characteristics, structural and cultural influences, and appropriate measures of essential theoretical constructs such as punishment rationales. The following section explores these measurement issues in greater detail.

Measurement of dependent variables

The way in which dependent variables have been measured thus far involves a relatively narrow conceptualization of criminal punishment, as prior research on court-processing and decision-making has focused heavily on final sentencing outcomes. This was at least partially the result of historical accident. In the late 1970s and early 1980s, public concern over unbridled judicial discretion led to fervent scrutinizing of sentencing decisions. This culminated in the establishment of sentencing commissions, which began collecting systematic data on judges' sentences. The result was several decades of research focused primarily on final sentencing decisions, and relatively little attention paid to other case-processing outcomes. Understudied outcomes include initial charging and plea-bargaining decisions, pretrial detention and bail outcomes, and the application of discretionary sentencing enhancements such as mandatory minimum penalties. The importance of these intermediate processes is difficult to overstate: not only do they allow for greater insight into the discretion of different court actors, but they also have significant consequences for later court outcomes.

A small group of studies has examined these outcomes, but with a near exclusive focus on individual defendant characteristics. For example, Shermer and Johnson (2010) examined charge reductions by federal prosecutors and found that male defendants were less likely to receive charge reductions, as were black and Hispanic defendants for firearms offenses. Underscoring the implications of these decisions for subsequent sentencing outcomes, the researchers also determined that much of the disparity in sentence lengths was accounted for by charge reductions. Several other studies have similarly found racial–ethnic and gender differences in pre-trial release (Demuth, 2003; Demuth and Steffensmeier, 2004; Spohn, 2009). White and female defendants are typically less likely to be detained, though a recent study by Freiburger and Hilinski (2010) suggests that socioeconomic factors may be responsible for these differences. Rarely have researchers examined other discretionary decisions that precede sentencing. For instance, Crawford, Chiricos, and Kleck (1998) analyzed prosecutors' decisions to apply habitual offender enhancements to eligible defendants in Florida and found stark disparities in their application. More recent work investigated the imposition of mandatory minimum and three strikes penalties in Pennsylvania and found notable differences by race or ethnicity and gender (Ulmer, Kurlychek, and Kramer, 2007). Given the variation in these types of laws across states, together with the fact that existing studies often find evidence of their disproportionate application, future work would benefit substantially from expanding this body of research.

Future work on early-case outcomes would also benefit from incorporating recent advances in sentencing research that recognize the importance of accounting for multiple, overlapping influences. Research that investigates case-processing outcomes in a multilevel context remains rare. D'Alessio and Stolzenberg (2002) examined pre-trial detention decisions in a sample of urban courts and found that unemployed defendants were more likely to be detained in areas with higher unemployment rates. In addition to finding evidence of racial–ethnic disparity in the application of mandatory minimum penalties in Pennsylvania (as mentioned above), Ulmer et al. (2007) found that such disparity was conditioned by the racial composition of the county. Recent work by Johnson (2012) used cross-classified models to investigate early-case outcomes in federal terrorism cases. He found significant variation in the likelihood of case dismissal and conviction across both terrorist groups and federal district courts. Finally, Franklin (2010) examined case dismissal decisions in a sample of large urban counties and found mixed evidence for the importance of social contexts. Expanding this research on multilevel influences on early case-processing outcomes has the potential to provide new and valuable insights into the ways in which criminal case outcomes vary across social contexts.

A far more extensive corpus of research has focused on final sentencing decisions (Ulmer, 2013). Although much has been learned from this work, a number of important measurement issues continue to be of concern. Over 30 years ago, the Panel on Sentencing Research critiqued that "a methodological concern affecting most research on the determinants of sentences is the treatment of the outcome variable – sentence imposed" (Blumstein et al., 1983, p. 81). To a large degree, the same issue persists today, as the dependent variables employed in most of the contemporary sentencing research are typically restricted to incarceration and sentence length. Yet reducing the sentencing decision to these two simple components obscures and ignores meaningful distinctions within each. A sentence to incarceration can mean jail or prison, but these represent qualitatively different punishments, given that prison sentences often bring greater collateral consequences for offenders (Holleran and Spohn, 2004). Collapsing these two types of sentence into a "total incarceration variable" runs the risk of distorting the effects of important predictors of sentencing. For example, Steffensmeier, Kramer, and Streifel (1993) found an effect of gender on the probability of receiving jail or prison versus probation, but not on the probability of receiving prison versus jail, or probation or prison versus jail. Researchers are only beginning to incorporate the complete range of sentencing options available to judges. Schanzenbach and Yaeger (2006), for instance, found that fines are often used to offset prison time in the sentencing of federal white-collar offenders. Few other studies, however, adequately consider the role that financial penalties play in final punishment decisions. Studies examining judicial decisions to impose intermediate punishments are also scarce, despite the explicit incorporation of these sentencing alternatives into many state sentencing guidelines (Engen et al., 2003; Gainey, Steen, and Engen, 2005; Johnson and DiPietro, 2012; Wooldredge and Gordon, 1997). As Engen et al. (2003) noted, the use of intermediate sanctions represents a locus of judicial discretion where unwarranted disparity may be reintroduced into the sentencing process. In line with this assertion, recent work by Johnson and DiPietro (2012) reported that individual offender characteristics, such as race or ethnicity and gender, were significantly related to the likelihood of being diverted to intermediate punishments. Significant gains would be made for the benefit of future research through the development and incorporation of more dynamic measures of sentence type, which should go beyond the traditional dichotomy between prison and probation.

A related measurement concern surrounds the proper estimation of imprisonment lengths in sentencing research. Judges often impose full or partially suspended sentences and give credit for time served, yet the optimal way of capturing these important facets of the sentencing decision remains unresolved. A sentence of suspended incarceration represents a substantively different punishment from a sentence to probation, but in typical analyses the two are routinely combined. Credit given for time served in pre-trial detention can also substantially impact the determination of sentence lengths, and is entirely dependent on the pre-trial status of the defendant. Rarely are these issues explicitly acknowledged in sentencing research. As a first step, greater transparency is required in how sentence length variables are calculated. Beyond this, expanding the conceptualization of the sentencing decision to adequately capture the intricacies of punishment outcomes is a crucial direction for advancing knowledge in the field.

Measurement of independent variables

The largest part of prior research on criminal punishment has focused explicitly on unwarranted disparity, specifically on racial–ethnic or gender inequities in court outcomes (for reviews, see Spohn, 2000; Zatz, 2000; Ulmer, 2012). Notable improvements have been made over time in the measurement of offender demographic characteristics; in particular, research on race or ethnicity has moved beyond the traditional black–white dichotomy, to examine the influence of other racial–ethnic backgrounds on case-processing outcomes. Early work that failed to separate Hispanic populations may have led to misestimated black–white differences (Steffensmeier and Demuth, 2000), though it is now common practice in court-processing research to examine white, black, and Hispanic offenders. Research is also beginning, in small part, to focus on the case-processing and sanctioning experiences of American Indians and Asian Americans. Alvarez and Bachman (1996), for example, compared Native American sentencing outcomes to those for white offenders in Arizona and found longer sentences for Native Americans for some crime types, but not for others. Similarly, Johnson and Betsinger (2009) incorporated Asian Americans in their examination of sentencing disparities in the federal district courts. They found that, while black and Hispanic offenders tended to receive more severe outcomes, Asian Americans were treated similarly as, or even more leniently than, white offenders. Some recent work has begun to move beyond discrete racial–ethnic categories, by arguing that more dynamic measures like skin tone and Afrocentric facial features can provide unique leverage for investigating racial bias in sentencing (King and Johnson, 2013). This line of inquiry holds considerable promise, but is currently only in its infancy.

An overarching concern with research on sentencing disparity is that analyses often suffer from the potential for omitted variable bias. One pervasive example is the lack of quality measures of the defendant's social class. The socioeconomic status (SES) of defendants is notoriously difficult to capture, noted scholars calling the existing measures "abysmal" (Zatz, 2000, p. 515). Most studies fail to include measures of SES, and those that do typically rely on crude proxies, such as education or employment. Importantly, offenders with similar employment status or educational attainment may have very different life circumstances (Zatz, 2000). Offender populations are also often characterized by limited variation in SES, a situation that makes it difficult to estimate these influences reliably (Blumstein et al., 1983; Zatz, 2000). A number of other potentially important variables are frequently absent from case-processing research. Relatively little work includes measures of citizenship status, though this factor is increasingly being incorporated in recent research on federal sentencing practices, particularly in the context of immigration crimes (Hartley and Tillyer, 2012). With the growth of the noncitizen population in America, this factor will be even more important for future research. One complication, however, is that citizenship status is closely tied to ethnic background, so researchers will need to pay special attention to disentangling the effects of each. Finally, the influence of a defendant's demeanor, behavior, and appearance is all but ignored in studies of criminal case-processing. This omission is important, given that, from a symbolic interactionist perspective, court outcomes can be viewed as joint social acts – which, Ulmer (2012) explains, "are produced by actors who define situations, interpret the communications and actions of other participants, and processes" (p. 7). By failing to include these measures, researchers miss accounting for some element of defendant agency in shaping case-processing outcomes.

The emphasis of prior work on unwarranted disparity has resulted in an almost exclusive focus on individual defendant characteristics. The role of case-processing factors in court outcomes has received significantly less attention, these variables being typically included in analyses as controls, if at all. One case-processing measure that is seldom incorporated into court research is the type of defense representation. While a limited literature exists that compares the effectiveness of private attorneys and public defenders in securing favorable outcomes for defendants, few research efforts examine the impact of court-appointed counsel vis-à-vis public defenders or compare private attorneys, public defenders, and court-appointed counsel simultaneously (Cohen, 2014). Additionally important are measures of evidentiary strength and case complexity, since these factors are likely to account for a large part of earlier case-processing outcomes, such as initial case acceptance and subsequent charging decisions. Albonetti (1998), for instance, examined the sentencing of white-collar offenders and found that complex cases involving an overarching plan of illegal acts or a high level of criminal organization were more likely to result in a plea of guilty, which in turn decreased the length of the imprisonment received. Measuring case complexity and strength of evidence represents an essential but monumental task for researchers. Most of the publicly available data lack the level of information necessary to capture these important theoretical constructs. The result is that studies examining them are rare and typically limited to small samples of independently collected cases. Victim characteristics also constitute an important omitted variable in much of the extant case-processing literature. Some research on prosecutorial decision-making has examined victim effects. For instance, Spears and Spohn (1997) found that victim characteristics were the most important predictors of charging decisions in sexual assault cases. Similarly, Spohn and Holleran (2001) demonstrate that charging decisions in sexual assault cases can be contingent on whether the victim and the offender were strangers or acquaintances. Considerable research finds evidence of the influence of victim characteristics in death penalty cases as well. Baldus, Woodworth, and Pulaski (1990), for example, reported that death sentences were over four times more likely when the victim was white than when the victim was black. Despite these persuasive findings, most of the case-processing research contains no information on victim characteristics, either because such information is not available in official data sources or because crimes involving victims (e.g., robbery) are routinely aggregated with "victimless" crimes (e.g., drug offenses).

In addition to commonly omitted defendant, case, and victim characteristics, there is a need for improved measurement of the social contexts of punishment. While early work on decision-maker characteristics found limited evidence for the effects of judge characteristics (Spohn, 1990), more recent research has uncovered some important influences. Johnson (2006), for instance, found that minority judges were significantly less likely to imprison minority defendants in Pennsylvania. The vast majority of sentencing studies, however, provide no information on judge characteristics, in part because obtaining official court records that contain judge identifiers can be difficult. Perhaps even more importantly, virtually no research examines the impact of prosecutor and defense counsel characteristics on case-processing outcomes (e.g., Spohn and Fornango, 2009). There is clearly a need to collect and analyze this information in future work. One recent development in sentencing research has been the widespread incorporation of measures that capture the broader influences of the surrounding court environment (e.g., Britt, 2000; Johnson, Ulmer, and Kramer, 2008; Ulmer and Johnson, 2004). Typically this work is framed in terms of court community perspectives, which argue that structural characteristics of the court environment shape localized cultural norms that guide case-processing and punishment decisions (Eisenstein, Flemming, and Nardulli, 1988). Commonly examined structural influences include the relative size of the court, its caseload, and characteristics of the surrounding community, such as racial–ethnic demographics and crime rates. Ulmer and Johnson (2004), for instance, found that the size of the court, its caseload pressure, and the availability of local jail space affected the probability of incarceration across courts. Other measures that have been frequently examined are guideline departure rates, trial rates, and the surrounding political environment (Franklin, 2010; Helms and Jacobs, 2002; Johnson, 2005; Kautt, 2002). Beyond these, though, conceptualizations of relevant contextual factors remain fairly limited. Of particular importance is the ability to measure the social networks of court actors and their perceptions of local cultural norms. In one innovative study, Haynes, Ruback, and Cusick (2010) examined the effects of similarity, proximity, and stability of the courtroom workgroup on incarceration decisions and financial penalties. They found mixed results for these influences; but, to date, there has been no work replicating this approach. It is important for researchers to begin collecting information on local cultural norms toward punishment, court actor perceptions of their working relationships, and local financial resources and expenditures on the criminal justice system. Development of new and refined measures in these areas offers valuable opportunities to significantly advance our understanding of criminal case-processing.

Research on criminal case-processing has also struggled to develop and to include valid measures of core theoretical constructs hypothesized to influence court decision-making. The problem is twofold. First, extant theorizing lacks sufficient specification for identifying clear testable propositions. For instance, focal concerns theory argues that "practical constraints" can affect punishment decisions, but the specific factors and the ways in which they alter the punishment calculus are not formally elaborated (Hartley, Maddan, and Spohn, 2007). Increased efforts by researchers to translate broad theoretical principles into specific and testable hypotheses are necessary in order to measure these types of inchoate theoretical concepts. Second, new and creative research approaches are needed in order to develop better measures of theoretical constructs in case-processing research. Multiple perspectives, for example, suggest that court actor concerns with community protection and offender blameworthiness drive punishment decisions (Albonetti, 1991; Steffensmeier, Ulmer, and Kramer, 1998; Ulmer and Johnson, 2004). Prior research, though, fails to include direct measures of court actor concern over community protection or blame, as offense severity and the offender's prior record are typically relied upon as proxies, with little theoretical circumspection. This is in part the product of an overreliance on official data sources (Wellford, 2007). Contemporary theoretical frameworks emphasize the local, interpretive, and subjective value assessments of court actors, yet the almost exclusive use of official data restricts analyses to variables provided by justice agencies. In order to more directly tap court actors' interpretations of and relative emphasis on different focal concerns of punishment, it will be important that researchers begin thinking outside the methodological box, exploring the use of qualitative interviews, surveys, and similar approaches in addition to official data.

Analytical Challenges and Methodological Advances

Apart from measurement concerns regarding key dependent and independent variables, there are a number of critical analytical challenges involved in conducting empirical research on criminal courts. These include long-standing issues of case attrition across agencies, difficulties with capturing the full range of relevant influences on criminal court processes, and concerns regarding causal inferences made using cross-sectional data (Blumstein et al., 1983). Recent advances have been made in addressing many of these issues, and several promising approaches are available that may improve contemporary estimates of the determinants of court-processing outcomes.

Analytical challenges in court-processing and decision-making research

The multistage nature of the criminal justice system introduces unique complexities into the analysis of criminal case-processing. First and foremost is the availability of appropriate data. Publicly available data on criminal case-processing can be difficult to obtain and are often limited in terms of the breadth and scope of information that it includes. Because multiple agencies collect their own distinct information, often for internal purposes, official case-processing data are imperfect. Few large-scale, systematic databases exist that track offenders across concurrent stages of adjudication. There are important exceptions – cases where researchers have expended considerable effort to collect data across multiple stages of the criminal justice system (e.g., Kingsnorth, MacIntosh, and Wentworth, 1999; Spohn and Tellis, 2014; Wooldredge, Griffin, and Rauschenberg, 2005), but these examples are relatively rare and often have other limitations, such as small sample sizes, limited offense types, and narrow geographical coverage.

When data are available across multiple stages of case-processing, important concerns emerge over sample attrition and potential selection effects. The inherent filtering process involved in criminal case-processing means that a select subsample of offenders advances across decision-making points. Only some reported crimes result in arrests, only some arrests are prosecuted, and only some prosecuted cases are convicted and sentenced. The result is that estimates derived from any one stage may suffer from selection bias. A common approach to addressing selection bias is Heckman's (1976) selection model. Berk (1983) describes its application to sentencing research and notes the potential for both internal and external validity to be compromised when nonrandom subsamples are analyzed. Although the Heckman model can be a useful way of addressing selection bias, Bushway, Johnson, and Slocum (2007) note potential concerns over its widespread application in criminal case-processing research and suggest that it is not a "magic" solution to the ubiquitous problem of selectivity. Ideally, the correction should be implemented with an exclusion restriction or with a theoretical predictor that is related to the underlying selection process but not to the substantive outcome of interest, in order to avoid problems of multicollinearity. One example of an exclusion restriction offered by Bushway et al. (2007) is strength of evidence, which is likely to affect the probability of conviction but not the severity of the sentence after conviction. Yet the difficulty of identifying quality exclusion restrictions means that in practice they are seldom, if ever, applied.

An alternative method for dealing with dependency across decision-making stages of the criminal justice system was developed by Tobin (1958). His model, the Tobit model, applies to situations in which values of the dependent variable that fall above or below some threshold are systematically censored. For these cases, the Tobit model treats the censored values as part of an underlying latent variable, the same process determining the censored values as the observed continuous values. In practice the model can be conceptualized as combining a probit model for the censoring of values with an ordinary least squares regression model for the observed values, where the same explanatory variables are used to predict both the probability of censoring and the uncensored outcome. Increasingly, the Tobit model has been used in predicting sentence severity, where sentences of zero incarceration are treated as censored values. Applied in this manner, the Tobit model captures the effects of the explanatory variables on both the probability of receiving a sentence of incarceration and the length of confinement for those incarcerated (Kurlychek and Johnson, 2004). Like the Heckman model, however, the Tobit model is limited in important ways. While the model can be useful when there is a strong a priori rationale for believing that the factors that determine selection have consistent relationships with the outcome of interest (Osgood, Finken, and McMorris, 2002), this is a restrictive assumption that is difficult to formally test (Wooldridge, 2005). The application of the Tobit model to research questions involving multiple stages of concurrent selection is also far from straightforward, and it has yet to be done in order to model selection across multiple stages of the criminal justice system.

Recent work has begun to move beyond these approaches by formally incorporating selection processes into estimates of the cumulative effects of explanatory factors in punishment. For instance, Stolzenberg, D'Alessio, and Eitle (2013), in examining racial disparity in felony cases, obtained estimates of the effects of race from eight different decision-making points in the system and combined them into overall effect sizes by using meta-analytical techniques. In addition, Sutton (2013) used a sample of male defendants from large urban counties in multiple states in order to examine cumulative disparity across pre-trial detention, plea-bargaining, and sentencing. He calculated probabilities of various sentence outcomes for defendants that were conditional on pre-trial status and mode of conviction, in effect combining common categories of sequential processing outcomes to investigate their joint probabilities for different racial–ethnic groups. Using a similar approach, Kutateladze, Andiloro, Johnson, et al. (2014) examined cumulative effects across prosecution and sentencing outcomes for a sample of defendants of various racial–ethnic backgrounds in New York City by focusing on the joint probabilities of commonly occurring punishment constellations. The researchers found evidence of cumulative disadvantage for black and Latino defendants by comparison with white defendants. Black defendants were 5 percent more likely and Latino defendants were 2 percent more likely to receive the most severe combination of outcomes (i.e., being detained, being not dismissed, and being incarcerated). Although this type of work remains relatively rare, it offers examples of important ways in which to advance research on criminal case-processing. First, these studies examine multiple interrelated punishment decisions rather than single, discrete outcomes. Second, they estimate cumulative effects across consecutive stages of case-processing instead of reporting independent effects for separate outcomes. Future studies that build on and advance this type of work hold tremendous potential to enhance our understanding of not only the key correlates of sentencing, but also the interrelated outcomes that collectively constitute the punishment process.

Another analytical challenge characterizing contemporary research on criminal case-processing is the intrinsic overlap of multiple units of explanatory analysis. Several defendants are sentenced by the same judge and several judges share the same organizational context, which introduces unique statistical and analytical difficulties. The dominant approach to court research is to estimate regression equations that predict punishment outcomes, but one of the basic assumptions of standard regression models is that error terms are uncorrelated, and this assumption is likely to be violated in the context of multiple levels of analysis. This is because cases prosecuted by the same district attorney or sentenced by the same judge, for example, are likely to share unaccounted-for similarities. Furthermore, because multiple court actors can influence outcomes, isolating the discretionary influence of single actors can be difficult to accomplish. For instance, both judges and prosecutors can initiate mitigating guidelines departures in the federal court system (Johnson et al., 2008). Additional complexity arises from the fact that several different units of analysis may be jointly salient. Cases may involve complex arrangements of offender–victim dyads; they may be simultaneously nested within multiple and overlapping contexts, and these relationships may vary over time. Increasingly, researchers have been developing more sophisticated methodological approaches for dealing with these analytical challenges in the study of criminal case-processing (Johnson, 2010, 2012), and these approaches are discussed in the following section.

Methodological advances in research on court-processing and decision-making

Recently a number of innovative methodological approaches have been developed that have the potential to significantly improve empirical research on criminal case-processing. One development has been the increased use of statistical matching techniques to ensure more equivalent comparisons. As noted above, much research is focused on estimating unwarranted disparity across different groups of offenders. For example, punishment outcomes for male defendants are often compared to those for female defendants, and outcomes for white defendants are routinely compared to those for black and Hispanic defendants (Spohn, 2000). The problem is that different offenders may systematically commit different types of crimes, for example. Official arrest statistics indicate that both male and minority defendants tend to be overrepresented in certain violent crime categories, such as homicide and robbery (Federal Bureau of Investigation, 2010). Differences such as this, in case characteristics, may not be sufficiently accounted for through traditional regression techniques (Smith and Paternoster, 1990). An approach for dealing with them involves using statistical matching designs, which can help create more comparable samples of offenders. One such method, propensity score matching (Rosenbaum and Rubin, 1983), uses observed covariates to estimate the likelihood of experiencing a "treatment effect," in an attempt to approximate random assignment in an experiment. First a propensity score is calculated, and then individuals are matched on the propensity score so as to create groups that are as comparable as possible. The goal is to investigate what the punishment outcome would have been (i.e., the counterfactual) if the defendant had been female instead of male, black instead of white, juvenile instead of adult, and so on.

While several different matching types are available (Apel and Sweeten, 2010), each seeks to create a pool of defendants who are conditionally independent across a range of observable factors. Kurlychek and Johnson (2010), for instance, used propensity score matching to compare sentencing outcomes for young adults and juveniles transferred to adult court in Maryland, and found evidence that transferred juveniles were consistently sentenced more harshly. Similarly, Bales and Piquero (2012) used both precision-matching methods and traditional regression techniques to compare sentencing outcomes for black, Hispanic, and white defendants in Florida. Regardless of the approach, the authors reported that black defendants were at an increased risk of incarceration, although they suggested that researchers can "derive more precise comparison groups using precision matching" (Bales and Piquero, 2012, p. 767). Franklin (2013) conducted a similar comparison of standard regression analysis and propensity score matching in examining racial–ethnic disparity in federal sentencing and found that, while the two methods produced similar results, the magnitude of estimates varied across analytic approaches.

A variation on statistical matching techniques that has recently been applied to the analysis of sentence lengths is quantile regression. Britt (2014) details the various applications of quantile regression models to the study of criminological data.

The utility of these models stems from their ability to overcome common violations of the assumptions of ordinary least squares regression. Specifically, ordinary least squares regression assumes normal and homoscedastic error terms; that is, it assumes that observations are normally distributed and that the variance of the dependent variable is constant across all values. With case-processing data, these assumptions are often violated. As an alternative, quantile regression allows the effects of independent variables to be examined separately across different slices of the distribution of the dependent variable. Defendant race or ethnicity, for instance, might have a significant effect on sentence length for very long, but not for very short sentences. In his analysis of Pennsylvania sentencing data, Britt (2009) found evidence that certain predictors of sentencing had varying effects at different parts of the sentence length distribution. Although quantile regression is in its infancy in criminology, it may offer new and interesting ways of examining the varying effects of key covariates on case-processing outcomes.

Another recent methodological advance has been the proliferation of multilevel models, sometimes referred to as hierarchical linear models (HLM), which are designed to account for the nesting of individual cases within higher order units (for a discussion of multilevel modeling in criminology and criminal justice, see Johnson, 2010). As mentioned previously, the nesting of cases within court actors and court contexts introduces certain statistical problems. If researchers are only interested in addressing the statistical dependencies that arise in these instances, they can correct standard errors for clustering or employ fixed effects models. However, if researchers are interested in examining variation across multiple units of analysis, or if they have substantive questions relating to characteristics of higher order units, then multilevel modeling offers a useful approach. These models provide several advantages, such as properly adjusted standard errors, corrected statistical significance tests, and the ability to separate variance in the outcome among levels of analysis (Johnson, 2010). Spohn and Fornango (2009), for instance, utilized multilevel modeling to demonstrate that the likelihood of receiving a federal departure for providing substantial assistance varied significantly across US attorneys in three federal district courts. Multilevel models also provide an opportunity to examine variation in the effects of individual-level predictors across higher order units. Research by Ulmer and Johnson (2004) demonstrated that many individual offense and offender characteristics have varying effects on punishment outcomes across different social contexts. Similarly, these models facilitate the examination of interactive and conditional relationships across levels of analysis. Johnson (2006), for example, found that the effect of a defendant's race or ethnicity on incarceration depended upon the race or ethnicity of the sentencing judge; specifically, minority judges were less likely to imprison black and Hispanic defendants. Thus multilevel models not only provide a statistical solution to common violations of the ordinary least squares regression, they also represent a conceptual tool for developing and testing more nuanced theoretical relationships across interrelated units of analysis. In the context of criminal case-processing, such models allow for the integration of individual and contextual predictors of court decision-making outcomes.

An approach that has been underutilized but is becoming increasingly popular in court-processing research is path-analytic modeling (Heise, 1969; Land, 1969). Path analysis is well suited to the study of criminal case-processing because it allows for intermediate outcomes of interest to be incorporated into a single statistical model. This approach is particularly useful for examining both the direct and the indirect influences of various factors in punishment. Long ago, early research on criminal punishment argued for the use of path analysis. Hagan (1974), for instance, analyzed the effect of race and SES on case-processing outcomes by specifying a path model that incorporated initial charging and plea-bargaining outcomes along with final sentencing dispositions. He demonstrated that much of the influence of the offender's background on punishment operated indirectly, by charging decisions controlled by prosecutors. In his later work, Hagan (1975) used path models to examine the intermediary influence of probation officer recommendations on sentencing outcomes, and found additional evidence that part of the effects of the offender's sociodemographic characteristics were mediated by intermediate stages of case-processing. Specifically, race and SES directly influenced the probation officer's recommendations, which were subsequently related to sentencing decisions.

After Hagan's (1974, 1975) work, regression largely replaced path analysis as the paradigm regnant in sentencing research. Recently, though, researchers (e.g., Baumer, 2013) have begun to call for more attention to the consequential case-processing decisions of other court actors, especially prosecutors. With this renewed interest in the indirect effects of earlier case-processing decisions, path analysis has again risen to the vanguard. Brennan (2006), for example, examined case-processing outcomes in a sample of female misdemeanants in New York City. Her study found no direct effects for race or ethnicity on the use of jail sentences, but suggested that racial–ethnic disparity operated indirectly, through a number of other factors such as community ties, socioeconomic background, and prior record. Similarly, Spohn and Belenko (2013) found both direct and indirect effects of drug use on federal sentencing outcomes by using path analysis. Jeffries, Fletcher, and Newbold (2003) combined a matched sampling approach with regression and path analysis to examine gender disparity in a New Zealand sample of offenders. They found that judges were less likely to imprison female offenders, and that part of this effect was due to earlier processes involving prior records and the pre-sentence recommendations of probation officers.

Some research has applied traditional regression techniques to examine indirect effects of earlier case-processing decisions on punishment. Spohn (2009), for instance, showed that pre-trial detention is an essential determinant of both the likelihood of a sentencing guidelines departure and sentence length in the federal courts. Similarly, Shermer and Johnson (2010) demonstrated the importance of early charging decisions in federal sentencing, finding that defendants who received a charge reduction earned sentences that were almost 20 percent shorter than defendants who did not. Regression approaches, however, are somewhat limited in that they require multiple models for the examination of indirect effects and they do not provide other analytic advantages of path models, such as the ability to easily calculate indirect, direct, and total effects, or the flexibility to specify and examine correlations among error terms for predictors in the model. Given the burgeoning interest in conceptualizing punishment as a dynamic process that involves multiple interrelated outcomes, path models hold special promise for advancing the study of criminal case-processing. Moreover, as these models become further integrated into existing software packages, they may be ultimately combined with other methodological approaches, such as hierarchical linear models, in order to examine multilevel influences across multiple stages of case-processing.

A number of experimental methods that are designed to improve causal inferences also hold promise for advancing the scientific study of court decision-making. Although criminologists continue to debate the extent to which experiments represent the "gold standard" in research (Sampson, 2010), well-designed and well-implemented experiments provide the surest method for assessing causal influences. Research on criminal case-processing has relied almost exclusively on cross-sectional data for examining associations between variables. This work provides a wealth of valuable information about the correlates of punishment, but it requires the obligatory caveat that observed relationships may be spurious, or due to other, unmeasured factors. Without random assignment, it is extremely difficult to ensure that unmeasured factors are not influencing observed relationships in the data. In court-processing research, true random assignment is often unrealistic, because arbitrary assignment of different punishments to offenders raises obvious ethical issues. This does not mean, however, that experimental approaches are irrelevant. In fact, decision-making research in other disciplines frequently employs experimental designs to study court processes. For instance, a considerable literature exists on jury decision-making that uses experimental methods with mock jurors (e.g., Devine et al., 2001; Golding et al., 2007; Warling and Peterson-Badali, 2003). Related work has examined defendant decision-making by using the experimental manipulation of case vignettes. Research by Dervan and Edkins (2013), for example, examined false confessions in the context of plea-bargaining and found that more than half of innocent participants were willing to admit guilt in exchange for plea benefits. Reliance on mock juries and hypothetical case vignettes clearly has its limitations (Wiener, Krauss, and Lieberman, 2011), but it also offers important advantages, allowing the researcher to systematically manipulate key variables of interest. In one example, Freiburger (2010) manipulated variables such as gender, race, and employment status using a factorial survey of Pennsylvania judges and found that gender remained a significant predictor of incarceration even after controlling for family variables. Similar work has also been done with juvenile offenders (Applegate et al., 2000). Ideally, such experimental techniques could be combined with real data on criminal cases. One possibility is for research to begin with actual criminal cases and then to experimentally manipulate specific case dimensions in order to more systematically examine the impact of specific factors on court decision-making processes.

Experimental methods have particular potential for policy evaluation in criminal court-processing. Unlike randomly assigning punishments, randomly assigning new programming may be more feasible. For instance, recent work has employed the random assignment of eligible offenders to drug treatment courts in Baltimore, Maryland, finding sustained differences in recidivism for offenders who received the treatment (Gottfredson et al., 2006). Researchers interested in the effects of new and innovative approaches to criminal court-processing may well be able to utilize random assignment in such instances. A related approach is the use of natural experiments created by policy changes to study criminal case-processing. Blackwell, Holleran, and Finn (2008), for instance, made use of a temporary suspension of the Pennsylvania sentencing guidelines in order to evaluate their impact on gender disparities in sentencing. Similarly, as the Supreme Court's decision in *United States v. Booker* (2005) transformed the federal sentencing guidelines from mandatory to advisory, a number of studies have exploited this to evaluate the impact of shifting guidelines structures on punishment (e.g., Ulmer, Light, and Kramer, 2011). Analytical leverage can often be gleaned from temporal shifts in punishment policy, though relatively little work takes advantage of such changes.

Some research has utilized more creative approaches to approximating experimental designs. To estimate the causal effect of imprisonment on recidivism, Green and Winik (2010) capitalized on the fact that in certain jurisdictions cases are randomly assigned to judges with varying sentencing tendencies. Although the researchers could not randomly assign punishments, the fact that cases were randomly assigned to judges allowed them to simulate an experimental design. Other econometric approaches offer similar opportunities. For instance, Hjalmarsson (2009) employed a regression discontinuity design to identify the effect of incarceration on the post-release criminal behavior of juveniles. She argued that defendants who were very close to one another on the Washington State sentencing guidelines grid but fell on different sides of the incarceration cutoff were substantively equivalent. Opportunities to take advantage of these types of methodological approaches are more prevalent than most scholars realize. They can serve as very useful alternatives to traditional experimental techniques and hold considerable promise for improving estimates of the causal effects of key variables of interest on court outcomes.

Research on criminal case-processing can also benefit greatly from mixed methods approaches. Early work conducted by political scientists arguably represents the best example of this type of research. Eisenstein and Jacob (1977), for instance, conducted a comprehensive study of case-processing outcomes in three cities in the 1970s. Integrating information across levels of analysis, including defendant characteristics, judge and courtroom workgroup characteristics, and characteristics of the surrounding community, the researchers employed quantitative analysis of case details in addition to systematic observation of courtroom workgroups and informal conversations with court actors. Subsequent work utilized a similar approach in different locations (Eisenstein et al., 1988; Flemming, Nardulli, and Eisenstein, 1992). Even today, these studies represent some of the most widely cited and influential research ever conducted on criminal courts. Relatively little work has attempted to replicate this comprehensive approach to understanding case-processing, despite dramatic changes that have occurred since that time in the American courts.

A number of more recent, mixed methods studies that have been conducted on a smaller scale demonstrate the unique and valuable insights provided by this approach. Kramer and Ulmer (2002) conducted judge interviews in order to better understand their analysis of sentencing guidelines departures in Pennsylvania. Similarly, Johnson et al.'s (2008) investigation of departures under the federal sentencing guidelines included interviews with judges and prosecutors. Spohn and Tellis's (2014) recent study of case-processing outcomes in sexual assault cases also combined quantitative analysis with interviews. Notably, the researchers found that the primary locus of attrition in sexual assault cases was the arrest decision, but this decision was actually a product of discretion jointly exercised by both police and prosecutors. An important consequence of this overlap was a failure to arrest in cases deemed to be "problematic." In each of these studies, qualitative data proved to be essential in interpreting quantitative results. One of the best recent examples of the utility of mixed methods research is Frederick and Stemen's (2012) study of prosecutorial discretion. The researchers examined a variety of decision-making outcomes by using a broad range of methodological approaches, including statistical analysis of case outcomes, hypothetical vignettes given to court actors, survey questions, and two waves of interviews and focus groups with prosecutors. Although their study was limited to two counties, it stands apart from much of the extant work on court-processing through its comprehensive coverage and through the impressive array of techniques employed. What emerges from Frederick and Stemen's study is a unique portrait of the interrelated factors that affect the exercise of prosecutorial discretion – factors that include not only individual case characteristics but also the broader contextual constraints that shape prosecutorial decision-making. This type of research is far too rare in the field and should set a model for future work that examines decision-making processes in the criminal courts.

Data advances in research on court-processing

One of the main challenges to addressing measurement issues in court-processing and decision-making research is the availability of data. Unfortunately, some of the most widely used sources of data have been discontinued. Early research on prosecutorial discretion used detailed case-processing data from the Prosecutor Management Information System (PROMIS) (e.g., Albonetti, 1986, 1987), but that data source was abandoned in the early 1980s, amid legal disputes (*United States v. Inslaw, Inc.*, 1991). Considerable research on sentencing also relied upon the State Court Processing Statistics (SCPS), a biennial data collection by the Bureau of Justice Statistics that contained case-processing information from a sample of 40 of the largest 75 counties in the United States. These data collections were discontinued in 2006 and, although the Bureau of Justice Statistics plans to redesign the SCPS, currently no timetable has been established. Since the creation of sentencing commissions in the 1980s, the vast majority of research has used sentencing guidelines data, which are based on samples of convicted offenders. Much information has been gained from these sources (Ulmer, 2012), but they also have important drawbacks, such as being restricted to a minority of states and containing limited information on case-processing decisions that precede final punishment. Several relatively recent data advances, however, offer promising new directions for empirical research on the criminal courts.

A few researchers have systematically collected detailed data on multiple case-processing outcomes from the criminal courts (e.g., Kingsnorth and MacIntosh, 2007; Spohn and Tellis, 2014; Wooldredge and Thistlethwaite, 2004). These types of studies allow for a more nuanced and detailed analysis of the full range of relevant factors that affect decision-making across stages of the criminal justice system, but they tend to be time- and resource-intensive. Because much of this work was conducted prior to recent improvements in case management technology, it required researchers to comb through paper files in order to record relevant information. As a result, these studies were generally limited to small samples of cases drawn from single jurisdictions and focused on single offense types, often sexual or domestic assaults. New technological advances, however, may help facilitate future research efforts toward data collection. Electronic case management systems are increasingly being implemented across jurisdictions, providing opportunities for researchers to collect and analyze difficult-to-obtain information on earlier case-processing decisions. Recent work by Kutateladze, Andiloro, and Johnson (2014), for example, combined independent data collection with official case management data from New York City to examine the effect of race on plea-bargaining among misdemeanor marijuana offenders.

Recent efforts by the Bureau of Justice Statistics constitute one of the most promising new sources of case-processing data. These data, known as the Federal Justice Statistics Resource Center (FJSRC) data, allow researchers to link information from different federal agencies in order to track offenders across stages of the criminal justice system. The FJSRC data represent an important breakthrough in the study of criminal case-processing, as they include information on federal arrests, prosecutions, sentencings, and prison populations that can be matched to individual defendant cases with the help of unique identifiers. Like any data source, the FJSRC data have important limitations. Data breadth and quality vary considerably across individual data sets, and the linking processes are not perfect. Nevertheless, these data offer an immense opportunity to study case-processing as a complex whole with interrelated parts. Early research using these data linked information on federal charging decisions to federal sentencing data in order to study the impact of charge reductions on punishment (Shermer and Johnson, 2010). More recent research has extended this work by examining jurisdictional variation in federal charging practices (Johnson, 2014), as well as racial and gender disparity in prosecution and sentencing (Rehavi and Starr, 2012; Starr, 2012). Another benefit of the FJSRC data is that they date back to the 1990s, which allows researchers to study temporal changes in federal case-processing (Starr and Rehavi, 2013). Although relatively few studies to date have utilized the FJSRC data, in the future these data will likely become a key source of information for research that seeks to advance understanding of the interrelated nature of case-processing decisions in the federal courts.

One largely untapped resource for data on criminal case-processing is survey research with court actors. Although the limitations of survey research are well documented (Krosnick, 1999), this kind of research holds tremendous potential for expanding the scope of the samples used in research and for improving the measurement of key variables. Unlike official records, which are nearly always limited to a small number of jurisdictions, survey research offers the opportunity to use large and nationally representative samples. By conducting a nationally representative survey of US adults, Johnson and colleagues (2011) were able to examine the influence of more proximate measures of social threat on the support for ethnic disparity in punishment. They found geographic variation in punitive attitudes toward minority defendants – variation that was influenced by both subjective perceptions and objective indicators of minority threat. Survey research like this also has the capacity to better capture elusive theoretical constructs such as local court culture, because scholars are able to craft data collection instruments according to their specific research interests. In particular, surveys may provide a way of tapping into the attitudes and opinions of different court actors to their local environments. Johnson and Ulmer (2012), for instance, utilized this approach and found that local organizational characteristics of the federal courts, such as the coercive power of the circuit courts, were related to judicial departures from the federal sentencing guidelines. In view of this, survey research represents an underutilized yet promising approach to accessing more complete information on court-processing and decision-making.

Summary and Conclusion

Measurement represents an ongoing challenge to empirical research on court-processing and decision-making. The life courses of criminal cases traverse multiple agencies, involve decisions made by multiple court actors, and are influenced by a myriad of factors across dynamic contexts. Although punishment is often conceptualized simply as imprisonment, it in fact involves a series of interrelated decision-making processes, which range from initial case acceptance and plea-bargaining decisions to intermediate bail and detention judgments to final sentencing determinations that include a host of alternative and financial sanctions in addition to incarceration.

Capturing this complexity in its entirety is a Sisyphean task, but a number of important advances can provide ways of improving future research on criminal case-processing. First, researchers can strive to develop more dynamic operationalizations of case-processing outcomes – operationalizations that incorporate information from preceding decision-making stages and more fully capture the complete range of available punishment options. Second, they can work to incorporate new and innovative measures of oft-omitted variables. This will likely require secondary data collection designed to supplement official data sources, but such investments are likely to bring long-term benefits to research. Third, scholars need to devote additional energy to the development, elaboration, and measurement of key theoretical constructs. Empirical advances are only useful to the extent that they contribute to a deeper understanding of the decision-making processes that shape criminal punishment, and this will inevitably require improved theories of criminal justice. Fourth, researchers can take advantage of recent methodological and statistical advances that open new possibilities for better capturing the effects of key factors in case-processing. Experimental and quasi-experimental methods that are designed to better identify the causal impacts of key policy innovations can be instrumental in improving the future development of evidence-based policy. Finally, it is essential that efforts continue to be made to bridge the significant gap between researchers, practitioners, and policymakers. The recent evidence-based movement in criminal justice offers an opportunity to further this important task. Practitioners and policy-makers are beginning to realize the gains in efficiency and effectiveness to the criminal court system provided by academic studies, and researchers should realize that their scholarship can only be improved through court actors' local knowledge and expertise, which are made available from these actors' direct involvement in the research process.

References

Albonetti, C. A. 1986. Criminality, prosecutorial screening, and uncertainty: Toward a theory of discretionary decision making in felony case-processings. *Criminology*, 24: 623–644. doi: 10.1111/j.1745-9125.1986.tb01505.x.

Albonetti, C. A. 1987. Prosecutorial discretion: The effects of uncertainty. *Law & Society Review*, 21: 291–313. doi: 10.2307/3053523.

Albonetti, C. A. 1991. An integration of theories to explain judicial discretion. *Social Problems*, 38: 247–266. doi: 10.2307/800532.

Albonetti, C. A. 1998. Direct and indirect effects of case complexity, guilty pleas, and offender characteristics on sentencing for offenders convicted of a white-collar offense prior to sentencing guidelines. *Journal of Quantitative Criminology*, 14: 353–378. doi: 10.1023/A:1023077704546.

Alvarez, A., and Bachman, R. B. 1996. American Indians and sentencing disparity: An Arizona test. *Journal of Criminal Justice*, 24: 549–561. doi: 10.1016/S0047-2352(96)00039-6.

Apel, R., and Sweeten, G. 2010. Propensity score matching in criminology and criminal justice. In *Handbook of quantitative criminology*, edited by A. R. Piquero and D. Weisburd, 595–612. New York: Springer. doi: 10.1007/978-0-387-77650-7_26.

Applegate, B. K., Turner, M. G., Sanborn, J. B., Jr., Latessa, E. J., and Moon, M. M. 2000. Individualization, criminalization, or problem resolution: A factorial survey of juvenile court judges' decisions to incarcerate youthful felony offenders. *Justice Quarterly*, 17: 309–331. doi 10.1080/07418820000096341.

Baldus, D. C., Woodworth, G. G., and Pulaski, C. A., Jr. 1990. *Equal justice and the death penalty: A legal and empirical analysis*. Boston, MA: Northeastern University Press.

Bales, W. D., and Piquero, A. R. 2012. Racial/ethnic differentials in sentencing to incarceration. *Justice Quarterly*, 29: 742–773. doi: 10.1080/07418825.2012.659674.

Baumer, E. P. 2013. Reassessing and redirecting research on race and sentencing. *Justice Quarterly*, 30: 231–261. doi: 10.1080/07418825.2012.682602.

Berk, R. A. 1983. An introduction to sample selection bias in sociological data. *American Sociological Review*, 48: 386–398. doi: 10.2307/2095230.

Blackwell, B. S., Holleran, D., and Finn, M. A. 2008. The impact of the Pennsylvania sentencing guidelines on sex differences in sentencing. *Journal of Contemporary Criminal Justice*, 24: 399–418. doi: 10.1177/1043986208319453.

Blumstein, A., Cohen, J., Martin, S. E., and Tonry, M. H., eds. 1983. *Research on sentencing: The search for reform*. Washington, DC: National Academy Press.

Brennan, P. K. 2006. Sentencing female misdemeanants: An examination of the direct and indirect effects of race/ethnicity. *Justice Quarterly*, 23: 60–95. doi: 10.1080/07418820600552477.

Britt, C. L. 2000. Social context and racial disparities in punishment decisions. *Justice Quarterly*, 17: 707–732. doi: 10.1080/07418820000094731.

Britt, C. L. 2009. Modeling the distribution of sentence length decisions under a guidelines system: An application of quantile regression models. *Journal of Quantitative Criminology*, 25: 341–370. doi: 10.1007/s10940-009-9066-x.

Britt, C. L. 2014. Quantile regression models to analyze experimental data. In *Encyclopedia of criminology and criminal justice*, edited by G. Bruinsma and D. Weisburd, 4207–4221. New York: Springer. doi: 10.1007/978-1-4614-5690-2_183.

Bushway, S., Johnson, B. D., and Slocum, L. A. 2007. Is the magic still there? The use of the Heckman two-step correction for selection bias in criminology. *Journal of Quantitative Criminology*, 23: 151–178. doi: 10.1007/s10940-007-9024-4.

Cohen, T. H. 2014. Who is better at defending criminals? Does type of defense attorney matter in terms of producing favorable case outcomes? *Criminal Justice Policy Review*, 25: 29–58. doi: 10.1177/0887403412461149.

Crawford, C., Chiricos, T., and Kleck, G. 1998. Race, racial threat, and sentencing of habitual offenders. *Criminology*, 36: 481–512. doi: 10.1111/j.1745-9125.1998.tb01256.x.

D'Alessio, S. J., and Stolzenberg, L. 2002. A multilevel analysis of the relationship between labor surplus and pretrial incarceration. *Social Problems*, 49: 178–193. doi: 10.1525/sp.2002.49.2.178.

Demuth, S. 2003. Racial and ethnic differences in pretrial release decisions and outcomes: A comparison of Hispanic, black, and white felony arrestees. *Criminology*, 41: 873–908. doi: 10.1111/j.1745-9125.2003.tb01007.

Demuth, S., and Steffensmeier, D. 2004. The impact of gender and race–ethnicity in the pretrial release process. *Social Problems*, 51: 222–242. doi: 0.1525/sp.2004.51.2.222.

Dervan, L. E., and Edkins, V. A. 2013. The innocent defendant's dilemma: An innovative empirical study of plea bargaining's innocence problem. *The Journal of Criminal Law & Criminology*, 103: 1–48.

Devine, D. J., Clayton, L. D., Dunford, B. B., Seying, R., and Pryce, J. 2001. Jury decision making: 45 years of empirical research on deliberating groups. *Psychology, Public Policy, and the Law*, 7: 622–727. doi: 10.1037//1076-8971.7.3.622.

Eisenstein, J., Flemming, R. B., and Nardulli, P. F. 1988. *The contours of justice: Communities and their courts*. Boston, MA: Little, Brown.

Eisenstein, J., and Jacob, H. 1977. *Felony justice: An organizational analysis of criminal courts*. Boston, MA: Little, Brown.

Engen, R. L., Gainey, R. R., Crutchfield, R. D., and Weis, J. G. 2003. Discretion and disparity under sentencing guidelines: The role of departures and structured sentencing alternatives. *Criminology*, 41: 99–130. doi: 10.1111/j.1745-9125.2003.tb00983.x.

Federal Bureau of Investigation. 2010. *Crime in the United States, 2009*. Washington, DC: US Government Printing Office.

Flemming, R. B., Nardulli, P. F., and Eisenstein, J. 1992. *The craft of justice: Politics and work in criminal court communities*. Philadelphia, PA: University of Pennsylvania Press.

Franklin, T. W. 2010. Community influence on prosecutorial dismissals: A multi-level analysis of case- and county-level factors. *Journal of Criminal Justice*, 38: 693–701. doi: 10.1016/j.jcrimjus.2010.04.043.

Franklin, T. W. 2013. Race and ethnicity effects in federal sentencing: A propensity score analysis. *Justice Quarterly*. doi: 10.1080/07418825.2013.790990.

Frederick, B., and Stemen, D. 2012. *The anatomy of discretion: An analysis of prosecutorial decision making: Technical report* (NCJ 240334). New York: Vera Institute of Justice. Accessed December 22, 2015. https://www.ncjrs.gov/pdffiles1/nij/grants/240334.pdf.

Freiburger, T. L. 2010. The effects of gender, family status, and race on sentencing decisions. *Behavioral Sciences and the Law*, 28: 378–395. doi: 10.1002/bsl.901.

Freiburger, T. L., and Hilinski, C. M. 2010. The impact of race, gender, and age on the pretrial decision. *Criminal Justice Review*, 35: 318–334. doi: 10.1177/0734016809360332.

Gainey, R. R., Steen, S., and Engen, R. L. 2005. Exercising options: An assessment of the use of alternative sanctions for drug offenders. *Justice Quarterly*, 22: 488–520. doi: 10.1080/07418820500219219.

Golding, J. M., Bradshaw, G. S., Dunlap, E. E., and Hodell, E. C. 2007. The impact of mock jury gender composition on deliberations and conviction rates in a child sexual assault trial. *Child Maltreatment*, 12: 182–190. doi: 10.1177/1077559506298995.

Gottfredson, D. C., Najaka, S. S., Kearley, B. W., and Rocha, C. M. 2006. Long-term effects of participation in the Baltimore City drug treatment court: Results from an experimental study. *Journal of Experimental Criminology*, 2: 67–98. doi: 10.1007/s11292-005-5128-8.

Green, D. P., and Winik, D. 2010. Using random judge assignments to estimate the effects of incarceration and probation on recidivism among drug offenders. *Criminology*, 48: 357–387. doi: 10.1111/j.1745-9125.2010.00189.x.

Hagan, J. 1974. Parameters of criminal prosecution: An application of path analysis to a problem of criminal justice. *The Journal of Criminal Law & Criminology*, 65: 536–544. doi: 10.2307/1142527.

Hagan, J. 1975. The social and legal construction of criminal justice: A study of the presentencing process. *Social Problems*, 22: 620–637. doi: 10.2307/799695.

Hagan, J., and Bumiller, K. 1983. Making sense of sentencing: A review and critique of sentencing research. In *Research on sentencing: The search for reform*, edited by A. Blumstein, J. Cohen, S. E. Martin, and M. H. Tonry, 1–54. Washington, DC: National Academy Press.

Hagan, J., Hewitt, J. D., and Alwin, D. F. 1979. Ceremonial justice: Crime and punishment in a loosely coupled system. *Social Forces*, 58: 506–527. doi: 10.1093/sf/58.2.506.

Hartley, R. D., Maddan, S., and Spohn, C. C. 2007. Concerning conceptualization and operationalization: Sentencing data and the focal concerns perspective: A research note. *The Southwest Journal of Criminal Justice*, 4: 58–78.

Hartley, R. D., and Tillyer, R. 2012. Defending the homeland: Judicial sentencing practices for federal immigration offenses. *Justice Quarterly*, 29: 76–104. doi: 10.1080/07418825.2011.585140.

Haynes, S. H., Ruback, B., and Cusick, C. R. 2010. Courtroom workgroups and sentencing: The effects of similarity, proximity, and stability. *Crime & Delinquency*, 56: 126–161. doi: 10.1177/0011128707313787.

Heckman, J. J. 1976. The common structure of statistical models of truncation, sample selection and limited dependent variables and a simple estimator for such models. *Annals of Economic and Social Measurement*, 5: 475–492.

Heise, D. R. 1969. Problems in path analysis and causal inference. *Sociological Methodology*, 1: 38–73. doi: 10.2307/270880.

Helms, R., and Jacobs, D. 2002. The political context of sentencing: An analysis of community and individual determinants. *Social Forces*, 81: 577–604. doi: 10.1353/sof.2003.0012.

Hjalmarsson, R. 2009. Juvenile jails: A path to the straight and narrow or to hardened criminality? *Journal of Law and Economics*, 52: 779–809. doi: 10.1086/596039.

Holleran, D., and Spohn, C. 2004. On the use of the total incarceration variable in sentencing research. *Criminology*, 42: 211–240. doi: 10.1111/j.1745–9125.2004.tb00518.x.

Jeffries, S., Fletcher, G. J. O., and Newbold, G. 2003. Pathways to sex-based differentiation in criminal court sentencing. *Criminology*, 41: 329–354. doi: 10.1111/j.1745–9125.2003.tb00990.x.

Johnson, B. D. 2005. Contextual disparities in guidelines departures: Courtroom social contexts, guidelines compliance, and extralegal disparities in criminal sentencing. *Criminology*, 43: 761–796. doi: 10.1111/j.0011–1348.2005.00023.x.

Johnson, B. D. 2006. The multilevel context of criminal sentencing: Integrating judge- and county-level influences. *Criminology*, 44: 259–298. doi: 10.1111/j.1745–9125.2006.00049.x.

Johnson, B. D. 2010. Multilevel analysis in the study of crime and punishment. In *Handbook of quantitative criminology*, edited by A. R. Piquero and D. Weisburd, 615–648. New York: Springer. doi: 10.1007/978–0-387–77650–7_30.

Johnson, B. D. 2012. Cross-classified multilevel models: An application to the criminal case-processing of indicted terrorists. *Journal of Quantitative Criminology*, 28: 163–189. doi: 10.1007/s10940–011–9157–3.

Johnson, B. D. 2014. The missing link: Examining prosecutorial decision-making across federal district courts (NCJ 245351). Washington, DC: US Department of Justice, National Institute of Justice. Accessed December 22, 2015. https://www.ncjrs.gov/pdffiles1/nij/grants/245351.pdf.

Johnson, B. D., and Betsinger, S. 2009. Punishing the "model minority": Asian American criminal sentencing outcomes in federal district courts. *Criminology*, 47: 1045–1090. doi: 10.1111/j.1745–9125.2009.00169.

Johnson, B. D., and DiPietro, S. M. 2012. The power of diversion: Intermediate sanctions and sentencing disparity under presumptive guidelines. *Criminology*, 50: 811–850. doi: 10.1111/j.1745–9125.2012.00279.x.

Johnson, B. D., Stewart, E. A., Pickett, J., and Gertz, M. 2011. Ethnic threat and social control: Examining public support for judicial use of ethnicity in punishment. *Criminology*, 49: 401–441. doi: 10.1111/j.1745–9125.2011.00225.x.

Johnson, B. D., and Ulmer, J. T. 2012. Court communities in context: Variations in criminal case processing across US district courts. Paper presented at the Annual Meetings of the Law and Society Association, Honolulu, Hawaii.

Johnson, B. D., Ulmer, J. T., and Kramer, J. H. 2008. The social context of guidelines circumvention: The case of the federal district courts. *Criminology*, 46: 737–783. doi: 10.1111/j.1745–9125.2008.00125.x.

Kautt, P. M. 2002. Location, location, location: Interdistrict and intercircuit variation in sentencing outcomes for federal drug-trafficking offenses. *Justice Quarterly*, 19: 633–671. doi: 10.1080/07418820200095381.

King, R. D., and Johnson, B. D. 2013. *A punishing look?* Paper presented at the annual meetings of the American Society of Criminology, Atlanta, Georgia, November.

Kingsnorth, R. F., and MacIntosh, R. C. 2007. Intimate partner violence: The role of suspect gender in prosecutorial decision-making. *Justice Quarterly*, 24: 460–495. doi: 10.1080/07418820701485395.

Kingsnorth, R. F., MacIntosh, R. C., and Wentworth, J. 1999. Sexual assault: The role of prior relationship and victim characteristics in case-processing. *Justice Quarterly*, 16: 275–302. doi: 10.1080/07418829900094141.

Kramer, J. H., and Ulmer, J. T. 2002. Downward departures for serious violent offenders: Local court "corrections" to Pennsylvania's sentencing guidelines. *Criminology*, 40: 897–932. doi: 10.1111/j.1745-9125.2002.tb00977.x.

Krosnick, J. A. 1999. Survey research. *Annual Review of Psychology*, 50: 537–567. doi: 10.1146/annurev.psych.50.1.537.

Kurlychek, M. C., and Johnson, B. D. 2004. The juvenile penalty: A comparison of juvenile and young adult sentencing outcomes in criminal court. *Criminology*, 42 (2): 485–517. doi: 10.1111/j.1745-9125.2004.tb00527.x.

Kurlychek, M. C., and Johnson, B. D. 2010. Juvenility and punishment: Sentencing juveniles in adult criminal court. *Criminology*, 48: 725–758. doi: 10.1111/j.1745-9125.2010.00200.x.

Kutateladze, B. L., Andiloro, N. R., and Johnson, B. D. 2014. Opening Pandora's box: How does defendant race influence plea bargaining?" *Justice Quarterly*. doi: 10.1080/07418825.2014.915340.

Kutateladze, B. L., Andiloro, N. R., Johnson, B. D., and Spohn, C. C. 2014. Cumulative disadvantage: Examining racial and ethnic disparity in prosecution and sentencing. *Criminology*, 52: 514–551. doi: 10.1111/1745-9125.12047.

Land, K. C. 1969. Principles of path analysis. *Sociological Methodology*, 1: 3–37. doi: 10.2307/270879.

Osgood, D. W., Finken, L. L., and McMorris, B. J. 2002. Analyzing multiple-item measures of crime and deviance, II: Tobit regression analysis of transformed scores. *Journal of Quantitative Criminology*, 18: 319–347. doi: 10.1023/A:1021198509929.

Rehavi, M. M., and Starr, S. B. 2012. *Racial disparity in federal criminal charging and its sentencing consequences*. Working Paper No. 12-002. Ann Arbor, MI: University of Michigan Law School. Accessed December 22, 2015. Downloaded from http://papers.ssrn.com/sol3/papers.cfm?abstract_id=1985377 (abstracts site).

Rosenbaum, P. R., and Rubin, D. B. 1983. The central role of the propensity score in observational studies for causal effects. *Biometrika*, 70: 41–55. doi: 10.2307/2335942.

Sampson, R. J. 2010. Gold standard myths: Observations on the experimental turn in quantitative criminology. *Journal of Quantitative Criminology*, 25: 489–500. doi: 10.1007/s10940-010-9117-3.

Schanzenbach, M., and Yaeger, M. L. 2006. Prison time, fines, and federal white-collar criminals: The anatomy of a racial disparity. *Journal of Criminal Law & Criminology*, 96: 757–793.

Shermer, L. O., and Johnson, B. D. 2010. Criminal prosecutions: Examining prosecutorial discretion and charge reductions in US federal district courts. *Justice Quarterly*, 27: 394–430. doi: 10.1080/07418820902856972.

Smith, D. A., and Paternoster, R. 1990. Formal processing and future delinquency: Deviance amplification as selection artifact. *Law & Society Review*, 24: 1109–1132. doi: 10.2307/3053663.

Spears, J., and Spohn, C. 1997. The effect of evidence factors and victim characteristics on prosecutors' charging decisions in sexual assault cases. *Justice Quarterly*, 14 (3): 501–524.

Spohn, C. 1990. Decision making in sexual assault cases: Do Black and female judges make a difference? *Women & Criminal Justice*, 2: 83–105. doi: 10.1300/J012v02n01_06.

Spohn, C. 2000. Thirty years of sentencing reform: The question for a racially neutral sentencing process. In *Criminal justice 2000: Policies, processes, and decisions of the criminal justice system*, edited by J. Horney, vol. 3, 427–501. Washington, DC: US Department of Justice, Office of Justice Programs, National Institute of Justice.

Spohn, C. 2009. Race, sex, and pretrial detention in federal court: Indirect effects and cumulative disadvantage. *Kansas Law Review*, 57: 879–901.

Spohn, C., and Belenko, S. 2013. Do the drugs, do the time? The effect of drug abuse on sentences imposed on drug offenders in three US district courts. *Criminal Justice and Behavior*, 40: 646–670. doi: 10.1177/0093854812468433.

Spohn, C., and Fornango, R. 2009. US attorneys and substantial assistance departures: Testing for interprosecutor disparity. *Criminology*, 47: 813–846. doi: 10.1111/j.1745-9125.2009.00163.x.

Spohn, C., and Holleran, D. 2001. Prosecuting sexual assault: A comparison of charging decisions in sexual assault cases involving strangers, acquaintances, and intimate partners. *Justice Quarterly*, 18: 651–688. doi: 10.1080/07418820100095051.

Spohn, C., and Tellis, K. 2014. *Policing and prosecuting sexual assault: Inside the criminal justice system*. Boulder, CO: Lynne Rienner.

Starr, S. B. 2012. *Estimating gender disparities in federal criminal cases.* Law And Economics Research Paper Series, Paper No. 12-018. Ann Arbor, MI: University of Michigan Law School. Accessed December 22, 2015. Downloaded from http://papers.ssrn.com/sol3/papers.cfm?abstract_id=2144002 (abstracts site).

Starr, S. B., and Rehavi, M. M. 2013. Mandatory sentencing and racial disparity: Assessing the role of prosecutors and the effects of *Booker*. *Yale Law Journal*, 123: 2–80.

Steffensmeier, D., and Demuth, S. 2000. Ethnicity and sentencing outcomes in US federal courts: Who is punished more harshly? *American Sociological Review*, 65: 705–729. doi: 10.2307/2657543.

Steffensmeier, D., Kramer, J., and Streifel, C. 1993. Gender and imprisonment decisions. *Criminology*, 31: 411–446. doi: 10.1111/j.1745-9125.1993.tb01136.x.

Steffensmeier, D., Ulmer, J., and Kramer, J. 1998. The interaction of race, gender and age in criminal sentencing: The punishment cost of being young, black, and male. *Criminology*, 36: 763–798. doi: 10.1111/j.1745-9125.1998.tb01265.x.

Stolzenberg, L., D'Alessio, S. J., and Eitle, D. 2013. Race and cumulative discrimination in the prosecution of criminal defendants. *Race and Justice*, 3: 275–299. doi: 10.1177/2153368713500317.

Sutton, J. R. 2013. Structural bias in the sentencing of felony defendants. *Social Science Research*, 42: 1207–1221. doi: 10.1016/j.ssresearch.2013.04.003.

Thomson, R. J., and Zingraff, M. T. 1981. Detecting sentencing disparity: Some problems and evidence. *American Journal of Sociology*, 86: 869–880. doi: 10.1086/227320.

Tobin, J. 1958. Estimation of relationships for limited dependent variables. *Econometrica*, 26: 24–36. doi: 10.2307/1907382.

Ulmer, J. T. 2012. Recent developments and new directions in sentencing research. *Justice Quarterly*, 29: 1–40. doi: 10.1080/07418825.2011.624115.

Ulmer, J. T. 2013. Sentencing research. In *Encyclopedia of criminology and criminal justice*, edited by G. Bruinsma and D. Weisburd, 4759–4769. New York: Springer.

Ulmer, J. T., and Johnson, B. D. 2004. Sentencing in context: A multilevel analysis. *Criminology*, 42: 137–177. doi: 10.1111/j.1745-9125.2004.tb00516.x.

Ulmer, J. T., Kurlychek, M. C., and Kramer, J. H. 2007. Prosecutorial discretion and the imposition of mandatory minimum sentences. *Journal of Research in Crime and Delinquency*, 44: 427–458. doi: 10.1177/002242780730585.

Ulmer, J., Light, M. T., and Kramer, J. 2011. The "liberation" of federal judges' discretion in the wake of the Booker/Fanfan decision: Is there increased disparity and divergence between courts? *Justice Quarterly*, 28: 799–837. doi: 10.1080/07418825.2011.553726.

United States v. Booker, 543 US 220 (2005).

United States v. Inslaw, Inc., 932 F.2d 1467 (D.C. Cir. 1991).

Warling, D., and Peterson-Badali, M. 2003. The verdict on jury trials for juveniles: The effects of defendant's age on trial outcomes. *Behavioral Sciences and the Law*, 21: 63–82. doi: 10.1002/bsl.517.

Wellford, C. F. 2007. Sentencing research for sentencing reform. *Criminology & Public Policy*, 6: 399–402. doi: 10.1111/j.1745-9133.2007.00444.x.

Wiener, R. L., Krauss, D. A., and Lieberman, J. D. 2011. Mock jury research: Where do we go from here? *Behavioral Sciences and the Law*, 29: 467–479. doi: 10.1002/bsl.989.

Wooldredge, J., and Gordon, J. 1997. Predicting the estimated use of alternatives to incarceration. *Journal of Quantitative Criminology*, 13: 121–142. doi: 10.1007/BF02221305.

Wooldredge, J., Griffin, T., and Rauschenberg, F. 2005. (Un)anticipated effects of sentencing reform on the disparate treatment of defendants. *Law & Society Review*, 39: 835–873. doi: 10.1111/j.1540-5893.2005.00246.x.

Wooldredge, J., and Thistlethwaite, A. 2004. Bilevel disparities in court disposition for intimate assault. *Criminology*, 42: 417–456. doi: 10.1111/j.1745-9125.2004.tb00525.x.

Wooldridge, J. M. 2005. *Introductory econometrics: A modern approach*, 3rd edn. Mason, OH: South-Western College Publishing.

Zatz, M. S. 2000. The convergence of race, ethnicity, gender, and class on court decisionmaking: Looking toward the 21st century. In *Criminal justice 2000: Policies, processes, and decisions of the criminal justice system*, edited by J. Horney, vol. 3, 503–552. Washington, DC: US Department of Justice, Office of Justice Programs, National Institute of Justice.

15

Sentencing Outcomes and Disparity

Jared M. Ellison and Pauline K. Brennan

Ideally, court processing decisions should be based on legally relevant characteristics that surround a case (e.g., the criminal history of the offender, offense severity, evidentiary strength) rather than on an offender's personal characteristics (e.g., race, gender, socioeconomic status). In reality, however, researchers have discovered that both legal *and* extralegal factors are related to sentencing outcomes (Baumer, 2013; Blumstein et al., 1983; Spohn, 2009; Ulmer, 2012). But relationships between independent and dependent variables are sometimes difficult to detect, may vary in magnitude or significance due to differences in variable measurement and in the analytic techniques employed across studies, and may not always lend themselves to straightforward interpretation.

Scholars have long been aware of the complexity involved in detecting and explaining sentencing disparity. In two of the earliest reviews of the literature, Blumstein and colleagues (1983) and Kleck (1981) highlighted the need for researchers to consider both prior record and offense seriousness in studies of racially disparate outcomes, and researchers now routinely include measures of these concepts in their multivariate examinations of sentencing outcomes. Moreover, most data sets now contain multiple measures of criminal history, charge type, and charge severity as well as an array of defendant demographic characteristics (e.g., age, race or ethnicity, gender). With improved data from varied jurisdictions, scholars have employed advanced statistical methods in their investigations of sentencing disparity. And, in so doing, they now generally agree that examinations of merely direct (or main) effects of extralegal variables are insufficient; studies of sentencing disparity also require analyses of conditioning (moderating) and of

The Handbook of Measurement Issues in Criminology and Criminal Justice, First Edition.
Edited by Beth M. Huebner and Timothy S. Bynum.

indirect (mediating) effects of legal and extralegal variables (Brennan, 2006; Spohn, 2009; Steffensmeier, Ulmer, and Kramer, 1998; Ulmer, 2012).

Overall, despite numerous reforms that were intended to equalize punishment severity (e.g., mandatory minimums, habitual offender statutes, guideline sentencing), outcomes differ for minorities versus whites and for males versus females (Spohn and Brennan, 2013; Wang et al., 2013). These extralegal variables have been found to influence the likelihood of incarceration, prison sentence length, imposition of mandatory minimums, receipt of intermediate sanctions, and departures from sentencing guidelines. And, to explain the punishment disparities found, scholars have developed and tested several theoretical perspectives over time (Ulmer, 2012).

The purpose of this chapter is to summarize research findings from examinations of sentencing disparity since the late 1980s (both before and after sentencing reform) and to discuss the methodological challenges that scholars have faced when conducting research in this area. Gaps in the existing research are also identified, and recommendations for future studies are offered.

An Overview of Sentencing Reform and of the Available Data

Prior to the 1970s and 1980s, judges exercised considerable discretion when deciding what punishments to impose on convicted offenders. They were free to impose punishments that comported with broad limits stipulated by legislators; community-based punishments (e.g., probation) could be given to most offenders, and, for the most part, prison or jail sentences were not mandatory (Spohn, 2009). Critics argued that the punishments imposed by judges were wildly disproportionate with the type of offense committed, highly disparate from one offender to the next (Frankel, 1972; von Hirsch, 1976), and often related to a defendant's extralegal characteristics (Zatz, 1987).

Evidence of disparate treatment concerned both liberals and conservatives during the 1970s and 1980s, albeit for different reasons. Due process advocates (i.e., liberals) stressed that courts should punish criminals equitably; a defendant's extralegal characteristics (e.g., race) should have no bearing on the imposed punishment (Packer, 1968). Any evidence of possible discriminatory treatment undermined notions of fair treatment and threatened the legitimacy of the criminal justice system. Advocates of the crime control perspective (i.e., conservatives), on the other hand, took issue with disparate sentencing because inconsistent treatment undermined the deterrent and retributive values of punishment (Packer, 1968). As bipartisan concern over the criminal justice system swept the American nation in what we now refer to as the "crime control era," many states – for instance Minnesota, Pennsylvania, Oregon – and the federal government drafted sentencing reforms that constrained judicial discretion.

In 1984, for example, Congress passed the Sentencing Reform Act (SRA), which mandated that federal judges impose prescribed punishments for convicted offenders (Nagel and Schulhofer, 1992). To be more specific, the SRA stipulated that judges were to use a predetermined grid of presumptive sentences when imposing punishments, and the point on it at which an offender's criminal history and the seriousness of the offense intersected determined the intended punishment. If incarceration was the designated punishment (which was the case for over 90 percent of all convicted federal offenders), a judge was required to impose the length specified in the guidelines. Currently sentencing guidelines are used in some form by 19 states and by the federal government (Harmon, 2014).

Mandatory minimum-sentencing laws, such as Oregon's Measure 11, which stipulated mandatory prison terms for offenders convicted of certain violent and sex offenses, also appeared during the 1980s and 1990s (Merritt, Fain, and Turner, 2006). Much like sentencing guidelines, mandatory minima were intended to result in equitable and sufficient punishment for similar offenses. With mandatory minimum laws, those found guilty of the stipulated crimes must be sent to prison regardless of their criminal history. Thus judges cannot use their discretion to impose other punishments, even when mitigating circumstances may warrant alternatives to incarceration.

Although laws were passed to restrict judicial discretion, legislators did very little to limit prosecutorial discretion at the front end of the process; for the most part, prosecutors remained free to make discretionary charging and plea-bargaining decisions. In fact the US Sentencing Commission, which created federal sentencing guidelines, stipulated no firm standards regarding prosecutorial decision-making (Nagel and Schulhofer, 1992). For example, a federal prosecutor's recommendation for a substantial assistance departure, which lessens sentence severity for offenders who provide assistance with a criminal investigation, remains a critical decision with very little oversight. Researchers have found that substantial assistance departures are filed irregularly across federal jurisdictions (Nagel and Schulhofer, 1992), and that an offender's race or ethnicity (Spohn and Brennan, 2011) and gender (Shermer and Johnson, 2010) affect the likelihood of having such a motion filed.

Mandatory minimum laws may also be circumvented by prosecutors. Merritt and colleagues (2006), for example, found that offenders avoided mandatory prison sentences when prosecutors filed charges for alternative (albeit similar) offenses that did not require a specified amount of prison time. In effect, legislative constraints on allowable sentences have shifted discretionary authority from the judge to the prosecutor. Miethe (1987) argued that this "hydraulic displacement of discretion" has a profound influence on the types of sentences judges may ultimately impose.

While upstream decisions made by prosecutors are certainly relevant to downstream decisions made by judges, most of the research on sentencing disparity has focused on whether judges impose incarceration (i.e., the in–out decision) and on how much prison time they impose, rather than on decisions made by prosecutors or on the effects of those decisions on punishment severity. Indeed, the US Sentencing Commission is tasked with providing routine analyses of sentencing outcomes under federal guidelines. Its database, however, does not contain information on upstream outcomes, including the types of charging decisions made by prosecutors. Rather, US Sentencing Commission data are limited in that they provide only post-conviction information through the sentencing phase. Databases at the state level, such as the one used by the Pennsylvania Sentencing Commission, do not contain information on upstream court outcomes either (e.g., the number and types of charges initially filed by prosecutors). Thus researchers interested in studying the decisions made prior to the sentencing stage must generally review paper files (if allowed access by court administrators) in order to construct data files suitable for quantitative analyses (see, e.g., Brennan, 2006, 2009b; Brennan and Spohn, 2008; Sorensen and Wallace, 1999; Spohn and Holleran, 2001). In short, data sets that include pre-conviction information are rare and difficult to create or obtain (Ulmer, 2012).

Theoretical Perspectives on Judicial Decision-Making

With regard to theoretical explanations related to the imposition of punishment, most scholars postulate that disparate or unequal sentencing outcomes are not necessarily a consequence of overt prejudice toward the defendant (Spohn, 2009). In other words, judges do not intentionally sentence males more harshly than females, or whites more leniently than blacks. Rather, racial–ethnic and gender disparities in punishment are likely to materialize because race, ethnicity, and gender are related to other variables that judges deem important when making their sentencing decisions (Spohn, 2009).

Some judges, for example, consider whether offenders are employed or whether they have community ties, because such characteristics may be indicative of an offender's potential for rehabilitation and presumed desistence from crime in the future (Brennan, 2002, 2006; Spohn, 2009). Judicial consideration of such factors may, unintentionally and indirectly, result in harsher sentences for blacks and Hispanics; if blacks and Hispanics are less likely to be employed than whites, for example, punishment outcomes may be more severe (Brennan, 2002, 2006; Spohn, 2009). Subtle forms of discrimination are difficult to detect with standard methods of analysis (Baumer, 2013; Brennan, 2002, 2006).

Turning now to some specific explanations of why sentencing disparity arises, Albonetti (1991) argued that judges rely on stereotypes that help them reduce the uncertainty of the decisions they must render. Because judges have limited information on the basis of which to make predictions, they cannot arrive at punishment decisions with complete certainty. To compensate for their lack of certainty, judges rely on attributions (or stereotypes) linked to a defendant's characteristics (e.g., blacks are likely to commit crime) and to the circumstances of the crime (e.g., violent offenders are dangerous) when they have to assess whether a given offender is inclined to pose a continued threat to society. By relying on stereotypes, judges achieve a "bounded rationality," which allows them to feel reasonably certain about their sentencing decisions (Albonetti, 1991, p. 250).

Steffensmeier and colleagues (1998) offered a related explanation for differential offender treatment. According to their focal concerns theory, judges' sentencing decisions are a reflection of how culpable they perceive a given offender to be (e.g., on the basis of offense seriousness, prior record, and role played in the commission of the offense), how much they wish to protect the community from further harm, and how concerned they are over the practical constraints or societal costs of punishment (e.g., overcrowding of prisons, issues related to an offender's health, concerns over removing a primary caretaker from the home). Like Albonetti (1991), Steffensmeier and colleagues (1998) claimed that judges do not possess all of the necessary information to accurately determine offender blame, risk to society, or punishment cost. Consequently judges develop a "perceptual shorthand" that is based on stereotypes linked to an offender's age, race, and gender (and other characteristics). In other words, stereotypical attributions shape judicial attitudes about, say, an offender's potential for rehabilitation or the threat s/he poses to society, and consequently about the appropriate sanction (Steffensmeier et al., 1998, p. 767). Within this framework, young black males are especially likely to receive more severe treatment because they are seen as posing a considerable threat to the community. Such perceptions are fueled by negative images of minority men that are perpetuated by the media and by the high numbers of black men in prison (Brennan and Vandenberg, 2009). And, given the extent of disproportionate minority confinement, black men are viewed as better equipped to handle incarceration. Their confinement is also believed to have fewer societal consequences (Steffensmeier et al., 1998).

Racial threat theorists (Blalock, 1967; Blumer, 1958) also highlight the influence of negative stereotypes on decisions made by criminal justice actors. Such theorists argue that the need to take punitive action against racial and ethnic minorities materializes only in places where a given minority population is notable in size, which would allow it to compete for power, economic resources, and political influence (Blalock, 1967). Consequently the threatened white majority may feel compelled to suppress the growing minority group through social control (Blumer, 1958; Ulmer, 2012). In the context of sentencing, the predominantly white legislature and judiciary may strive to protect their dominance by creating and imposing more punitive sanctions that affect minorities disproportionately (e.g., mandatory minimums for drug offenses).

Women, on the other hand, might receive sentence discounts because they are perceived as less culpable, less dangerous, more amenable to treatment, and more strongly tied to others in the community (Spohn and Beichner, 2000; Spohn and Brennan, 2013; Steffensmeier et al., 1998). Judges may believe that women are more likely than men to have childcare responsibilities and other seminal familial obligations; for this reason judges may be disinclined to sentence women to prison (Spohn and Beichner, 2000; Spohn and Brennan, 2013; Steffensmeier et al., 1998). Moreover, women are seemingly less blameworthy because female offenders tend to have mental health or substance abuse problems and are often abused or coerced by men (Steffensmeier et al., 1998).

It is also possible that women receive more lenient sentences than men due to chivalrous or paternalistic attitudes held by judges (Spohn, 2009; Spohn and Brennan, 2011). Judges with chivalrous attitudes perceive women as gentle and weak and believe that women must not be subjected to the harsh realities of prison life (Spohn, 2009; Spohn and Brennan, 2011). If, however, women do not conform to traditional gender stereotypes (e.g., if they are single, self-sufficient, promiscuous), it is possible that they will receive harsher sentences as a result (Brennan, 2006; Koons-Witt, 2002; Spohn and Brennan, 2011). This might be particularly true for black and Hispanic women who are likely to violate traditional gender role expectations (Brennan, 2002, 2006).

In sum, most would argue that judges are unlikely to consciously or intentionally discriminate against members of certain groups, but their preconceived notions may lead to unintentional disparate treatment. Similar processes are likely at work when prosecutors make decisions, as Albonetti (1987) and others (Shermer and Johnson, 2010; Spohn, Beichner, and Davis-Frenzel, 2001) have argued. The following section summarizes the empirical findings from studies of sentencing disparity. Areas that remain at issue are also identified.

Summary of Empirical Findings of Sentencing Disparity

In 2009, over 1.6 million inmates were held in state and federal prisons – 38 percent were black, 34.2 percent were white, and 20.7 percent were Hispanic (Glaze, 2010). Around that time, blacks and Hispanics comprised only 13 and 16 percent, respectively, of the United States population (Spohn, 2009). In terms of male–female differences in punishment, women were less likely to be sentenced to prison (e.g., 42 percent of the men vs. 27 percent of the women were sent to prison), were more likely to receive shorter prison sentences (e.g., average terms were 61 months for men vs. 42 months for women), and were less likely to be sentenced to death (e.g., 51 of 3,228 prisoners on death row were female) (Durose, 2007; Spohn, 2009, p. 143).

While the evidence appears to be compelling, it is important to remember that findings of disparity do not necessarily constitute proof of discriminatory treatment. If black men have longer criminal histories and commit more serious offenses than white men, for example, disparate sentences may be justified. Unfortunately, a large portion of the studies before 1990 utilized data that lacked adequate statistical controls for important legally relevant case characteristics (Hagan, 1974; Kleck, 1981). Given that controls for legally relevant variables are crucial to examinations of punishment severity, databases were created, largely by state and federal sentencing commissions, in order to provide adequate measures of charge severity and offender criminal history, along with information on offender demographics (Ulmer, 2012). As a consequence, most of the research on racial–ethnic and gender differences in sentencing has been conducted with data from only a few states (primarily in Florida, Pennsylvania, and Washington) and from the federal government (Spohn, 2000).

Scholars have made important contributions by analyzing data from jurisdictions with sentencing guidelines, but have not fully responded to the directives provided decades ago by Kleck (1981), Blumstein and colleagues (1983), and Zatz (1987) for the advancement of sentencing research. Researchers have certainly incorporated data from multiple jurisdictions (e.g., federal districts or state counties), examined more diverse pools of defendants (e.g., black, white, and Hispanic), studied how racial–ethnic and gender effects may differ by jurisdiction, and have explored how an array of variables may moderate the effects of race, ethnicity, and gender. But most researchers have examined racial and ethnic disparities for only one of two outcomes: the decision to incarcerate (i.e., the "in" or "out" outcome: placement in prison or jail versus in the community) and the length of confinement (Baumer, 2013; Mitchell, 2005; Spohn, 2000). Thus they have largely ignored extralegal disparities in the use of alterative sanctions.

Some additional limitations were recently outlined by Baumer (2013) and deserve being mentioned here. For one, most of those who examine the effect of a defendant's race and ethnicity on sentencing severity discount the possibility that the race and ethnicity of victims, judges, jurors, attorneys, and community members (among other participants) may also matter. Moreover, the effect of race, ethnicity, and gender likely affect a wide array of criminal justice decisions that occur prior to the sentencing stage (e.g., arrest, charge-filing, plea-bargaining, pre-trial detention), and these pre-sentencing decisions are likely pivotal to punishment outcomes. That is, exclusive focus on sentencing – the final stage in the criminal justice process – ignores other areas where race, ethnicity, or gender are likely to have some influence, either directly, through discriminatory practices, or more subtly, through factors such as prior record, pre-trial incarceration, or legal representation. Put another way, Baumer (2013) suggested that we focus not solely on the main or interactive effects of race and ethnicity, but also on the indirect pathways through which a defendant's race and ethnicity may affect sentencing outcomes.

The sections that follow provide a discussion of findings from studies of racial–ethnic and gender disparity in punishment and highlight the complexity of the research conducted to date. Areas where scholars may move sentencing research forward are also identified.

Direct Effects of Race–Ethnicity

Scholars typically find that a defendant's race or ethnicity exerts a small but significant direct effect on the incarceration decision; in general, blacks and Hispanics are more likely than whites to receive prison or jail time instead of community-based punishments (Baumer, 2013; Mitchell, 2005; Spohn, 2000; Ulmer, 2012). Some estimates reveal that blacks have an imprisonment rate about six times higher than whites and about two and a half times higher than Hispanics (Bales and Piquero, 2012). In terms of the odds of avoiding imprisonment, on the other hand, Brennan and Spohn (2008) found that whites were eight times more likely than Hispanics and five times more likely than blacks to receive punishments that allowed them to remain in the community. In sum, examinations of the in–out decision generally suggest that minorities are more likely to be sent to prison or jail than whites, even after the effects of legally relevant variables are considered.

Some scholars have also found that minorities receive longer prison terms than whites (Bushway and Piehl, 2001; Feldmeyer and Ulmer, 2011), and most conclude that the direct effect of race and ethnicity is weaker in examinations of sentence length than in investigations of the decision to incarcerate (Baumer, 2013; Mitchell, 2005; Spohn, 2000). In a comprehensive review of 40 state-level and 22 federal-level studies published during the 1980s and 1990s, Spohn (2000) found that in a little less than half (43.5 percent) of the state studies and in nearly three quarters (68.2 percent) of the federal studies blacks received more severe sentences than whites, and these disparities were especially pronounced when the in–out decision was considered. In line with this conclusion, in a meta-analysis of 71 studies, Mitchell (2005) found that blacks had a greater likelihood of incarceration than whites. However, the influence of defendant race on sentence length was generally weak and not statistically significant. Mitchell also found that race effects were highly variable; larger estimates of racial disparity were found in studies of drug offenders and in studies conducted with data gathered from a single city or county than in studies with data from a single state (e.g., data pooled from several counties within a single state). While informative, Mitchell's analyses, it must be noted, were limited to the examination of black–white differences. Others have acknowledged that Hispanics, and especially Hispanic drug offenders, also receive more punitive sentences than whites (Brennan and Spohn, 2008; Feldmeyer and Ulmer, 2011; Steffensmeier and Demuth, 2000). We discuss the moderating effects of charge type (and other variables) below.

Direct Effects of Gender

As with findings of racial and ethnic disparity, differences that favor women are more pronounced in examinations of the in–out decision than in examinations of the sentence length decision and do not disappear once legally relevant case characteristics are taken into consideration (Spohn, 2009; Spohn and Brennan, 2013). In one widely cited study, for example, Steffensmeier, Kramer, and Streifel (1993) used data provided by the Pennsylvania Sentencing Commission and found that female offenders faced significantly lower odds of incarceration than male offenders, but that gender did not affect prison sentence length. In a more recent study of sentencing outcomes under Pennsylvania's guidelines, Steffensmeier and Demuth (2006) also found that female offenders were significantly less likely to be incarcerated; the odds of incarceration for males were 71 percent higher than the odds for females. In contrast to findings from the earlier study, however, male offenders also received sentences that were about 20 percent longer than the terms imposed on females. Blackwell, Holleran, and Finn (2008) also examined outcomes using Pennsylvania data. Like Steffensmeier and Demuth (2006), they found that females were less likely than males to be incarcerated in jail or prison and also received shorter sentences.

Other scholars have examined the direct effects of gender on sentencing decisions in jurisdictions other than Pennsylvania. Stacey and Spohn (2006), for example, found that in three separate federal districts – Minnesota, Nebraska, and Southern

Iowa – females received an average sentence discount of 9.93 months. In a more recent study of data from the United States Sentencing Commission, Doerner and Demuth (2014) found that female defendants were 39 percent less likely to be incarcerated than males and, when incarcerated, females received sentences that were 23 percent shorter. Koons-Witt and colleagues (2012) found that females were consistently given more lenient sentences in South Carolina. Overall, they found that females received average prison sentences that were 12.8 months shorter than the terms given to males. Findings of gender disparity, therefore, appear to be more consistent across studies than findings of racial–ethnic disparity.

Moderating (Contextual) Effects

While a number of researchers have focused their attention on assessing the direct (or main) effects of race, ethnicity, and gender on sentencing outcomes, others have examined how race, ethnicity, and gender effects are moderated (or conditioned) by one another or by other variables. These researchers caution that race, ethnicity, and gender are likely to exert subtle effects rather than direct (or main) effects. Evidence of moderating effects, even in the absence of direct effects, would still mean that criminal sentences are not free of extralegal bias.

A fair amount of past research is largely premised on the assumption that most women are likely to be treated more leniently than most men and that most minority offenders are likely to receive harsher punishment than most white offenders. But findings of leniency for female offenders may be conditioned by race or ethnicity, and findings of preferential treatment for white offenders (or more punitive treatment for minorities) may be conditioned by gender. Thus, as other researchers have warned, a failure to consider the intersection of gender on the one hand and race and ethnicity on the other may result in inaccurate conclusions about the effects of these variables on sentencing outcomes (Brennan, 2009a; Daly and Tonry, 1997; Spohn and Beichner, 2000; Steffensmeier and Demuth, 2006; Steffensmeier et al., 1998).

Along this line of research, scholars have found that black females are less likely to be incarcerated than black males (Albonetti, 1997; Gruhl and Welch, 1984; Steen, Engen, and Gainey, 2005; Steffensmeier and Demuth, 2006). Among whites, the likelihood of receiving a prison or a jail sentence is higher for males (Albonetti, 1997; Gruhl and Welch, 1984; Steen et al., 2005; Steffensmeier and Demuth, 2006). And, among Hispanics, females are less likely to be put behind bars than males (Gruhl and Welch, 1984; Steffensmeier and Demuth, 2006). Studies of the length of incarceration generally support these findings (Albonetti, 1997; Steen et al., 2005; Steffensmeier and Demuth, 2006).

With regard to cross-race comparisons, researchers have also found that white women are treated more leniently than white men, black men, and Hispanic men (Spohn and Beichner, 2000; Spohn and Spears, 1997; Steffensmeier and Demuth, 2006). In relation to men of the same (or different) race or ethnicity, black and

Hispanic women appear, just like white women, to "benefit more from their female status than would be expected all else [being] equal (i.e., given their racial/ethnic status)" (Steffensmeier and Demuth, 2006, p. 257). Black men, by contrast, are likely to be treated more punitively than females of varying races or ethnicities (Hartley, Maddan, and Spohn, 2007; Spohn and Beichner, 2000; Spohn and Spears, 1997) and than white males (Crew, 1991; Hartley et al., 2007; Kruttschnitt, 1984; Spohn and Beichner, 2000; Spohn and Holleran, 2000; Steffensmeier and Demuth, 2006; Steffensmeier et al., 1993, 1998). This may be the case especially for young black males (Spohn and Holleran, 2000; Steffensmeier et al., 1998). For example, when studying outcomes in Pennsylvania, Steffensmeier and colleagues (1998) found that black males aged between 18 and 29 were the most likely of all offenders – young and old white or black females, young and old white males, and older black men – to be incarcerated and to receive the longest sentences. But the odds of incarceration were very similar among black and white males aged 50 and over (Steffensmeier et al., 1998, p. 780). In short, the influence of race on the sentencing of males depended on the age of the defendant.

Overall, findings from the extant literature indicate that, by comparison to males, females of all races and ethnicities seem to benefit as a result of their gender. And, by comparison to whites, black males (young ones in particular) seem to be penalized as a result of their race. In terms of how women are treated in relation to one another, however, there is little evidence to suggest that white women receive more lenient sentences than minority women. In fact, in two separate studies of sentencing outcomes that occurred before and after guidelines implementation, researchers found either no differences between black and white females or differences that favored black females (Griffin and Wooldredge, 2006; Koons-Witt, 2002). Others have observed that minority and white women receive similar sentences (Bickle and Peterson, 1991; Crew, 1991; Farnworth and Teske, 1995; Kruttschnitt 1984; Spohn and Beichner, 2000; Spohn and Spears, 1997; Steffensmeier and Demuth, 2006).

While most scholars have failed to find evidence of preferential treatment for white women in relation to minority women, some of them caution that differences are likely to exist if focus is placed on specific types of offenders. To elaborate, Crawford (2000) found that minority women were more likely to receive harsher sentences than white women if convicted of drug offenses. In line with these findings, Kautt and Spohn (2002) and Steen and colleagues (2005) observed that preferential treatment for white women (as opposed to white men) convicted of drug offenses was more likely than preferential treatment for black women (as opposed to black men) convicted of drug offenses. Future researchers would be wise to consider the joint effects of the offender's race or ethnicity and sex on sentencing outcomes, especially among drug offenders.

Many have argued that sentencing outcomes are likely to be particularly severe for minority drug offenders (Brennan and Spohn, 2008; Demuth and Steffensmeier, 2004; Mitchell, 2005; Steffensmeier and Demuth, 2001). This may be because judges' "punitive impulses" are linked to their perceptions of "racial threat," which are in turn linked to "urban underclass blacks and drugs" (Crawford, Chiricos, and Kleck,

1998, p. 506). Such an argument is based, in part, on theoretical discussions of the "moral panic" surrounding drug use and the war on drugs (Tonry, 1995). Moral panic theorists (Jenkins, 1994) argue that society is characterized by a variety of commonsense perceptions about crime and drugs that result in community intolerance for such behaviors and in increased pressure for punitive action. Sentencing scholars have similarly argued that the moral panic surrounding drug use and drug-related crime, coupled with stereotypes linking racial minorities to a drug-involved lifestyle, have resulted in more severe sentences for black and Hispanic drug offenders (Brennan and Spohn, 2008; Steen et al., 2005).

Although there is now a number of studies that focus on the issue of racial and ethnic disparities in the sentencing of drug offenders (for a review, see Brennan and Spohn, 2008), most of these studies do not allow for comparisons to be made between black, white, and Hispanic females. This is unfortunate because, as Steen and colleagues (2005) have suggested, stereotypes about drug offending are likely to be influenced by stereotypes about gender *and* race or ethnicity. Recall, moreover, that most researchers have considered only the in–out or sentence length decisions; "research[ers] ha[ve] virtually ignored factors affecting the application of qualitatively different kinds of sentences like alternative or intermediate sanctions" (Gainey, Steen, and Engen, 2005, p. 489).

In Washington State, for example, "structured alternatives" may be granted to legally eligible offenders – that is, offenders charged with certain offenses and offenders with less severe criminal histories. These structured alternatives differ from standard probation or total confinement. Thus Gainey and colleagues (2005) focused on a sample of drug offenders sentenced in fiscal years 1996–1999 and looked at three alternatives: (1) incarceration combined with chemical dependency treatment; (2) up to 90 days of confinement, combined with up to two years of community supervision; and (3) placement in a work-ethic camp (i.e., correctional boot camp). They found that "males, racial and ethnic minorities, and offenders who [took] their cases to trial [were] less likely than their counterparts to receive alternative sanctions" (Gainey et al., 2005, p. 513). Hispanics were the least likely to receive any of the alternative punishments.

To help explain their findings, Gainey and colleagues (2005) conducted interviews with judges, prosecutors, and defense attorneys who had experience in dealing with drug offenders. Information gleaned from their interviews indicated that Hispanic defendants were less likely to receive alternative sanctions due to concerns about their citizenship status – there was no incentive to offer an alternative to someone who was going to be deported – and due to notions that such defendants would be reluctant to go into treatment. A few also believed that "some court actors [were] more sympathetic to offenders more like themselves" (Gainey et al., 2005, p. 508). These qualitative findings suggested that perceptions of defendants and of the appropriateness of sanctions were shaped by the ethnicity of defendants. Gainey and colleagues directed future scholars to explore the use of intermediate punishments and judicial discretion. However, few have done so. In short, future researchers are encouraged to consider how race or ethnicity, gender, and crime intersect to influence the severity of punishment. Ideally, scholars should examine an array of sentencing outcomes rather than merely focus their attention on in–out decision or on the sentence length decision.

Researchers would also do well to consider how extralegal disparities may be conditioned by the characteristics of courtroom actors (e.g., by the characteristics of judges) (Ulmer, 2012). Steffensmeier and Britt's (2001) analysis of judge-specific sentencing outcomes in Pennsylvania from 1991 to 1994 provides an example. Black judges were more likely to sentence drug offenders (both black and white) to prison than white judges. Violent and property offenders, on the other hand, were sentenced similarly by black and white judges. Other researchers, however, have found that more lenient punishments are imposed by minority judges. When Johnson (2006) examined court and judge variation in sentencing outcomes across Pennsylvania, for example, he found that black and Hispanic judges sentenced all offenders, and especially minority offenders, more leniently than white judges. In addition, he concluded that male judges sentenced female offenders more leniently than female judges.

Jurisdictional and court-level social contexts may also influence the effects of race, ethnicity, and gender on sentencing outcomes (Hagan and Bumiller, 1983; Peterson and Hagan, 1984; Thompson and Zingraff, 1981; Ulmer, 2012). Researchers, for example, have examined how the racial–ethnic composition of the population where a given courthouse is located and the racial–ethnic composition of those who work in a given courthouse contextualize extralegal sentencing disparities. Regarding the former, researchers have found that the percentage of blacks and Hispanics in a given jurisdiction predicts whether racial disparities in imprisonment and sentence length are likely (Kramer and Ulmer, 2009; Ulmer and Johnson, 2004), as well as the likelihood that a given defendant will receive upward or downward departures (Johnson, 2006; Johnson, Ulmer and Kramer, 2008). In one study, for example, blacks and Hispanics were given more severe sentences in Pennsylvania counties that had higher concentrations of minorities (Ulmer and Johnson, 2004). Johnson and colleagues (2008) came to a similar conclusion in their analysis of federal guideline departures. Specifically, they found that, although minorities received fewer downward departures and slightly shorter sentencing discounts, these "individual-level racial and ethnic effects were exacerbated in socioeconomically disadvantaged districts and in districts with larger minority populations" (p. 769). Others, however, conclude that the racial–ethnic composition of a jurisdiction's population has very little bearing on sentencing outcomes (Britt, 2000) or, at the very least, affects racial–ethnic disparities in ways not predicted by the racial threat hypothesis (e.g., districts with few Hispanics give out the most severe sentences to Hispanics) (Feldmeyer and Ulmer, 2011). In terms of the contextualizing effects of the characteristics of courtroom actors, Farrell, Ward, and Rousseau (2009) found that black–white incarceration disparities were smaller in federal districts with larger proportions of black district attorneys. Racial disparities in punishment have also been found to be less pronounced in jurisdictions with more black attorneys at the county level (King, Johnson, and McGeever, 2010).

Mediating (Indirect) Effects and Important Considerations

Researchers should also consider how (and the extent to which) earlier case-processing decisions (e.g., pre-trial release) affect sentencing outcomes, and whether the effects of legal and extralegal variables on sentencing outcomes are mediated by pre-conviction outcomes. Scholars identified these research gaps in the 1980s and 1990s (Blumstein et al., 1983; Smith, 1986; Spohn, 2000; Thompson and Zingraff, 1981), and the need for such research has also been documented in more recent reviews (Baumer, 2013; Frase, 2013; Ulmer, 2012). Baumer, for example, pointed out that

> the vast majority of studies in the modal research tradition on race and sentencing forge ahead with a focus on estimating either main or interactive effects, neither of which address the many indirect pathways through which race may influence sentencing outcomes. (Baumer, 2013, p. 249)

One of the few exceptions, and one that was noted in Baumer's (2013) review, is Brennan's (2006) study of female misdemeanants sentenced in New York City. Upon analyzing outcomes for a sample of persons arrested in 1989, she found indirect, but not direct effects between the defendant's race or ethnicity and the sentencing outcome. Black and Hispanic females were more likely than white females to receive jail sentences due to differences in socioeconomic status, community ties, prior record, earlier case-processing, and charge severity (Brennan, 2006). These differences would have been masked if Brennan controlled merely for the effects of important mediators.

Brennan's study illustrates the complexity of examining sentencing outcomes, and researchers are strongly encouraged to focus more on the possible role that pertinent mediators may play in the process. In doing so, scholars should approach the task of accurately quantifying the direct and indirect effects of variables of interest via structural equation modeling (see Spohn et al., 2014 for a recent example). Likewise, more would be learned about sentencing disparity if researchers paid more attention to upstream outcomes, especially the pre-conviction decisions made by prosecutors. The need for this type of research was stressed by attendees and speakers who participated in a "Symposium on the Past and Future of Empirical Sentencing Research," sponsored by the National Science Foundation and hosted by the University at Albany in 2010; and it also resurfaced in three recent publications where scholars provided commentaries and reviews linked to the symposium (Bushway, 2013; Bushway and Forst, 2013; Ulmer, 2012). One should not interpret this as meaning that scholars have completely ignored prosecutorial decision-making in their studies, because a substantial amount of research does exist on the actions taken by prosecutors (see, for example, Hartley et al., 2007; Shermer and Johnson, 2010; Sorensen and Wallace, 1999; Spohn and Holleran, 2001). However, most researchers have not empirically linked prosecution outcomes to imposed punishments.

Charge-filing decisions are crucial, and prosecutors have virtually unlimited discretion when deciding what charges to file. For example, when pursuing prosecution for a murder charge, a prosecutor may choose to file a capital charge or may decide instead to seek prosecution for a noncapital offense. Sorensen and Wallace (1999) found that black offenders who killed white victims were significantly more likely than others to have capital charges filed against them. In contrast, black offenders who killed black victims were less likely to be prosecuted for capital murder, which provided evidence of racial disparity in the pre-trial stages of decision-making.

Prosecutors may also use their discretion to impact sentencing in other ways. For example, federal prosecutors may reduce the harshness of punishment by filing motions for substantial assistance guideline departures. A motion for such a departure may only be filed by a US attorney; the decision to do so is highly discretionary and generally unreviewable. Hartley and colleagues (2007) sought to identify the variables that affected an offender's likelihood of receiving a substantial assistance departure in federal court. Using the focal concerns theory and the bounded rationality perspective, they predicted that prosecutors filed motions for substantial assistance to mitigate the sentences of offenders perceived to be sympathetic and nondangerous. They found that offenders charged with more serious crimes and offenders who had more extensive criminal histories were more likely to receive departures, as were females, whites, and more educated offenders. In other words, prosecutors filed motions for substantial assistance to reduce the harshness of punishment only for some offenders – for females and whites. Overall, Hartley and colleagues' (2007) findings suggested that "prosecutors' discretionary decisions regarding departures for substantial assistance [were] reintroducing unwarranted disparity into the federal sentencing process" (p. 404).

Sentencing outcomes may also be affected by prosecutors' decisions about whether to drop or reduce charges prior to case disposition. Shermer and Johnson (2010) examined whether prosecutors reduced charges, and the effect of charge reductions on sentence length outcomes. Data from the US Office of the Administrative Courts (e.g., for the number of counts and initial and final charge dispositions) were linked with data from the US Sentencing Commission (e.g., for offender characteristics and final sentencing outcomes) to allow an analysis of both charging and sentencing outcomes.

Charge reductions were more likely for offenders with more serious offenses and more charges. Moreover, females, those who accepted responsibility for their crimes, and offenders released before trial were more likely to be granted charge reductions. An offender's race or ethnicity, however, did not affect the odds of his or her receiving a charge reduction. In terms of the sentencing outcome, shorter sentences were given to offenders granted charge reductions, substantial assistance departures, and pre-trial release. Females and whites also received shorter sentences, as did those with less serious offenses and less extensive criminal histories. On the basis of these findings, Shermer and Johnson (2010) concluded that "prosecutorial charging discretion plays an important role in the determination of final punishment outcomes in US District Courts. Although not surprising, this conclusion confirms a little-tested but often discussed empirical research question" (p. 424).

The Impact of Sentencing Legislation

More research is also needed on whether the exercise of discretion is affected by changes in policy, including changes to guidelines-based sentencing structures, passage of mandatory minimum and three strike laws, and modifications to time-served requirements (Bushway and Forst, 2013). Federal sentencing policy, in particular, has undergone major changes over time. As we mentioned earlier in this chapter, the SRA of 1987 mandated that federal judges sentence offenders under prescribed guidelines. However, the US Supreme Court rendered the federal sentencing guidelines merely advisory and no longer mandatory in its *Booker* and *Fanfan* rulings of 2005 (the two cases were consolidated as *United States v. Booker*, 2005). In addition, *Rita v. United States* (2007) and *Gall v. United States* (2007) made the review standards more relaxed and deferent toward judicial authority. As a joint result of these cases, the Supreme Court has removed much of the binding nature of the federal sentencing guidelines on judges.

Given that federal judges were authorized to use a greater degree of discretion following *Booker*, some predicted that sentencing outcomes would become more disparate (Paternoster, 2011). But few have found evidence in support of that prediction. A study by Ulmer, Light, and Kramer (2011) of whether unwarranted disparity increased after *Booker* offers one of the best examples of such research. Data were gathered from the US Sentencing Commission for all cases sentenced in 89 federal districts during five distinct time periods. A series of multivariate hierarchical analyses revealed that "extralegal disparity and between-district variation in the effects of extralegal factors on sentencing have not increased post-*Booker*" (Ulmer et al., 2011, p. 800), which suggested that "judges still regard the Guidelines as useful normative tools for reaching sentencing decisions" – that is, judges sentenced in ways similar to those of the pre-*Booker* period (p. 831).

Other researchers have examined whether the implementation of sentencing guidelines (where none had existed previously) reduced punishment disparity. Koons-Witt's (2002) and Griffin and Wooldredge's (2006) studies are among the few examinations of the impact of sentencing guidelines at the state level. Koons-Witt (2002) examined the in–out sentencing decision for a sample of pre-guidelines cases (1977–1978), early guidelines cases (1980–1984), and later guidelines cases (1994) in Minnesota. The effect of gender was insignificant in all three periods. In terms of the main effect of race, nonwhite offenders were less likely to be incarcerated during the pre-guidelines period, but there were no differences by race after guidelines were implemented. Thus it appeared that Minnesota's guidelines reduced racial disparity in punishment but did not decrease (or increase) gender disparity.

In their analysis of sentencing outcomes for offenders in Ohio, Griffin and Wooldredge (2006) reached different conclusions. They examined the likelihood and the length of incarceration for offenders sentenced during a pre-guidelines period (1995–1996) and a during a post-guidelines period (1997). They found that females were less likely than males to be incarcerated both before and after guidelines went into effect, but that the offender's gender did not affect the length of incarceration during either period. With regard to the effect of the offender's race, there were no differences between blacks and whites in the likelihood of incarceration or in sentence length before the guidelines were implemented. Blacks were more likely to be incarcerated after guidelines were in place, but they received shorter sentences. In short, Ohio's sentencing guidelines did not reduce gender disparity and appeared to increase racial disparity in punishment.

Summary and Suggestions for Future Research

To summarize, sentencing research has come a long way since the late 1980s. Over time, scholars have generally responded to research directives, and their efforts have been reflected in various publications. Notable progress has been made by sentencing scholars due in large part to post-conviction data that became available in the late 1980s and early 1990s for cases at the federal level and for cases in many states with guidelines-based sentencing structures (e.g., Pennsylvania, Washington State). These data have allowed researchers to assess punishment disparities while examining (and statistically controlling for) the effects of legally relevant variables, analyze contextual effects across jurisdictions, and consider different sentencing outcomes. In doing all these things, sentencing scholars have created new theoretical frameworks (e.g., the focal concerns perspective) designed to aid in our understanding of why punishment disparities exist. With the availability of large data sets, scholars have employed advanced statistical techniques in examining outcomes in different jurisdictions. In most studies, female offenders are found to receive more lenient sentences than male offenders. And in many studies minority offenders are more likely to be incarcerated than whites. This appears to be especially true for young male minority offenders and for offenders charged with drug offenses. Sentencing disparity exists in places with sentencing guidelines (e.g., at the federal level, in North Carolina, Pennsylvania, and Washington) and in places without guidelines (e.g., in New York State).

While notable advancements have been made in the study of sentencing disparity, much work still needs to be done. For example, researchers are encouraged to examine whether intermediate or alternative punishments are disparately imposed (for the few who have examined this issue, see Brennan, 2009b; Brennan and Spohn, 2008; Gainey et al., 2005). Other understudied outcomes are the use of suspended sentences, rehabilitative diversions, and sentencing waivers (Ulmer, 2012). Researchers are also encouraged to continue to investigate how the exercise of discretion is affected by changes in policy directives. Ulmer and colleagues' (2011) study regarding sentencing outcomes in the federal system after *Booker*, Koons-Witt's (2002) examination of sentences in Minnesota, and Griffin and Wooldredge's (2006) study of pre- and post-guidelines sentences in Ohio are notable in this regard and may serve as examples for other researchers. Researchers should also consider how and to what extent earlier case-processing decisions (e.g., pre-trial release, prosecutorial charging decisions) affect sentencing outcomes; and, while they are at it, they should also look at the many indirect pathways through which race, ethnicity, and gender may influence sentencing outcomes (for an example, see Brennan, 2006). More work of this sort is needed, because the punishment decision does not happen in isolation.

In particular, decisions made by prosecutors affect sentencing outcomes; prosecutors yield considerable power and exercise it across multiple stages of court-processing. For cases that move forward, possible punishments often depend on (1) whether a prosecutor files specific charges – for example, death may only be imposed for defendants charged and convicted of capital murder; (2) whether a prosecutor files a motion for a substantial assistance departure (which permits a federal judge to sentence outside of the guidelines); or (3) whether a prosecutor reduces the severity or the number of charges from initial filing to case disposition (which allows for a less severe penalty).

While researchers have examined prosecutorial decision-making, most have not examined the extent to which prosecutorial outcomes mediate the effects of race or ethnicity and gender on sentencing. This is probably because scholars have a difficult time obtaining data on decisions that occur prior to case disposition; many of the data that are routinely available include only information for post-conviction outcomes, which means that information is generally missing on pre-conviction outcomes related to case screening, the number and types of charges initially filed by a prosecutor, pre-trial detention, characteristics of guilty pleas, and case dismissal or acquittal. Thus scholars who are interested in assessing decisions made by prosecutors must often collect their own data by manually going through case files, extracting relevant information, and then entering that information into a database. This was the method employed by Brennan and Spohn (2008) in their study of sentencing outcomes for drug offenders in North Carolina. Some have also engaged in the painstaking task of combining data from different agency databases (which sometimes contain different case identifiers). Sorensen and Wallace (1999), for example, merged data from four different databases – the State Department of Corrections, the State Supreme Court, the Midwest County Court, and the Midwest County Coroner – in order to investigate filings for capital murder. While these data challenges exist, it is worth noting that the Urban Institute (through the Federal Justice Statistics Program) has recently linked federal data from the Administrative Office of the US Courts to data from the US Sentencing Commission to create a database with information that ranges from initial prosecution to sentencing. Shermer and Johnson (2010) recently used these linked databases to study the effects of charge reduction on sentencing outcomes for federal offenders. Over time, we anticipate that state-level databases will improve in ways that will link case-processing outcomes from the arrest stage through sentencing; this would allow for more comprehensive examinations of punishment disparity. Until such databases become available, however, we encourage researchers to gather data from any available sources, even if this entails a manual extraction of pertinent information from paper case files.

The substantial literature that addresses disparities in court-processing would also be enhanced by additional qualitative examinations. In a recent review, Brennan, Ellison, and Britt (2013) noted that less than 10 percent of all the research on courts published in *Justice Quarterly* (a leading journal in the field of criminology and criminal justice) over a period of 30 years had an ethnographic focus. The focus on quantitative measurement and statistical analysis is not a problem per se, but "if we do not match that focus on modeling with a parallel focus on the *in situ* decisions and activities of courtroom workgroup participants ... our understanding of sentencing will be truncated" (Ulmer, 2012, p. 33). To put it another way, quantitative studies provide merely a sketch of the sentencing process rather than a more detailed picture; while quantitative findings may give evidence of disparity, the reasons for findings of disparity cannot be fully discerned from numerical data alone. We therefore encourage future researchers to use a mixed methodological approach in their investigations of sentencing disparity. Such an approach typically involves quantitative analyses of the data, followed by interviews with courtroom decision-makers who may be asked questions about court-processing, the handling of minorities and of females, and whether and why disparate outcomes may materialize. As we discussed earlier, Gainey and colleagues (2005) employed such an approach in their study of the use of alternative sanctions in Washington State. One may recall that they began their study with a quantitative analysis of punishment outcomes for felony drug offenders. Then, to impart meaning to their quantitative findings, they conducted interviews with prosecutors, defense attorneys, and judges who had experience in dealing with drug offenders. Those interviewed were asked for their thoughts about racial and ethnic disparities in the criminal justice system and the use of alternative sanctions. According to the researchers, the answers given shed

> a great deal of light on the ways these court actors view[ed] alternative sanctions ... [and] also help[ed] us understand the strong effect of ethnicity, the fact that Hispanic offenders are much less likely than White[s] or Blacks to receive alternative sanctions. (Gainey et al., 2005, p. 507)

In other words, those interviewed explained why race and ethnicity played a role in the sentences given, which provided the researchers with a richer understanding of their quantitative findings. Overall, mixed methodological approaches (e.g., quantitative analyses of data sets combined with interviews with key court actors, quantitative analyses combined with reviews of plea-bargaining narratives or other court documents) allow researchers to more completely examine *how* and *why* sentencing outcomes may be related to extralegal variables. Future researchers would be wise to consider employing such an approach in their studies, if at all possible.

References

Albonetti, C. A. 1987. Prosecutorial discretion: The effects of uncertainty. *Law & Society Review*, 21: 291–313. doi: 10.2307/3053523.

Albonetti, C. A. 1991. An integration of theories to explain judicial discretion. *Social Problems*, 38: 247–266. doi: 10.2307/800532.

Albonetti, C. A. 1997. Sentencing under the federal sentencing guidelines: Effects of defendant characteristics, guilty pleas, and departures on sentence outcomes for drug offenses, 1991–1992. *Law & Society Review*, 31: 789–822. doi: 10.2307/3053987.

Bales, W. D., and Piquero, A. R. 2012. Racial/ethnic differentials in sentencing to incarceration. *Justice Quarterly*, 29: 742–773. doi: 10.1080/07418825.2012.659674.

Baumer, E. P. 2013. Reassessing and redirecting research on race and sentencing. *Justice Quarterly*, 30: 231–261. doi: 10.1080/07418825.2012.682602.

Bickle, G. S., and Peterson, R. D. 1991. The impact of gender-based family roles on criminal sentencing. *Social Problems*, 38: 372–394. doi: 10.2307/800605.

Blackwell, B. S., Holleran, D., and Finn, M. A. 2008. The impact of the Pennsylvania sentencing guidelines on sex differences in sentencing. *Journal of Contemporary Criminal Justice*, 24: 399–418. doi: 10.1177/1043986208319453.

Blalock, H. M. 1967. *Toward a theory of minority-group relations*. New York: John Wiley & Sons.

Blumer, H. 1958. Race prejudice as a sense of group position. *Pacific Sociological Review*, 1: 3–7. doi: 10.2307/1388607.

Blumstein, A., Cohen, J., Martin, S. E., and Tonry, M. H. 1983. *Research on sentencing: The search for reform*, vol. 1. Washington, DC: National Academy Press.

Brennan, P. K. 2002. *Women sentenced to jail in New York City*. New York: LFB Scholarly Publishing.

Brennan, P. K. 2006. Sentencing female misdemeanants: An examination of the direct and indirect effects of race/ethnicity. *Justice Quarterly*, 23: 60–95. doi: 10.1080/07418820600552477.

Brennan, P. K. 2009a. The joint effects of offender race/ethnicity and sex on sentencing outcomes. In *Handbook of crime and deviance*, edited by M. D. Krohn, A. Lizotte, and G. Hall, 319–347. New York: Springer.

Brennan, P. K. 2009b. Race and sentencing outcomes among female drug offenders in North Carolina: An exploratory consideration of earlier case processing outcomes. *Journal of Crime and Justice*, 32: 77–115. doi: 10.1080/0735648X.2009.9721271.

Brennan, P. K., Ellison, J. M., and Britt, C. L. 2013. 30 years of research on court processing. Special online issue of *Justice Quarterly*. Accessed July 15, 2014. http://explore.tandfonline.com/page/bes/justice-quarterly-vsi/jq-court-processing/rjqyvsi-30-years-of-research-on-court-processing-in-justice-quarterly.

Brennan, P. K., and Spohn, C. 2008. Race/ethnicity and sentencing outcomes among drug offenders in North Carolina. *Journal of Contemporary Criminal Justice*, 24: 371–398. doi: 10.1177/1043986208322712.

Brennan, P. K. and Vandenberg, A. L. 2009. Depictions of female offenders in front-page newspaper stories: The importance of race/ethnicity. *International Journal of Social Inquiry*, 2: 141–175.

Britt, C. L. 2000. Social context and racial disparities in punishment decisions. *Justice Quarterly*, 17: 707–732. doi: 10.1080/07418820000094731.

Bushway, S. D. 2013. Editorial introduction. *Justice Quarterly*, 30 (2): 195–198.

Bushway, S. D., and Forst, B. 2013. Studying discretion in the processes that generate criminal justice sanctions. *Justice Quarterly*, 30 (2): 199–222. doi: 10.1080/07418825.2012.682604.

Bushway, S. D., and Piehl, A. M. 2001. Judging judicial discretion: Legal factors and racial discrimination in sentencing. *Law & Society Review*, 35: 733–764. doi: 10.2307/3185415.

Crawford, C. 2000. Gender, race, and habitual offender sentencing in Florida. *Criminology*, 38: 263–280. doi: 10.1111/j.1745–9125.2000.tb00890.

Crawford, C., Chiricos, T., and Kleck, G. 1998. Race racial threat, and sentencing of habitual offenders. *Criminology*, 36: 481–512. doi: 10.1111/j.1745-9125.1998.tb01256.x.

Crew, B. K. 1991. Sex differences in criminal sentencing: Chivalry or patriarchy? *Justice Quarterly*, 6: 59–83. doi: 10.1080/07418829100090911.

Daly, K., and Tonry, M. 1997. Gender, race, and sentencing. *Crime and Justice*, 22: 201–252.

Demuth, S., and Steffensmeier, D. 2004. Ethnicity effects on sentence outcomes in large urban courts: Comparisons among white, black, and Hispanic defendants. *Social Science Quarterly*, 85: 994–1011. doi: 10.1111/j.0038-4941.2004.00255.

Doerner, J. K., and Demuth, S. 2014. Gender and sentencing in the federal courts: Are women treated more leniently? *Criminal Justice Policy Review*, 25: 242–269. doi: 10.1177/0887403412466877.

Durose, M. R. 2007. State court sentencing of convicted felons, 2004: Statistical tables. Washington, DC: US Department of Justice, Bureau of Justice Statistics. Accessed July 15, 2014. http://www.bjs.gov/index.cfm?ty=pbdetail&iid=1533.

Farnworth, M., and Teske, R. H. 1995. Gender differences in felony court processing: Three hypotheses of disparity. *Women & Criminal Justice*, 6: 23–44. doi: 10.1300/J012v06n02_02.

Farrell, A., Ward, G., and Rousseau, D. 2009. Race effects of representation among federal court workers: Does black workforce representation reduce sentencing disparities? *The Annals of the American Academy of Political and Social Science*, 623: 121–133. doi: 10.1177/0002716208331128.

Feldmeyer, B., and Ulmer, J. T. 2011. Racial/ethnic threat and federal sentencing. *Journal of Research in Crime and Delinquency*, 48: 238–270. doi: 10.1111/j.1745-9133.2011.00761.

Frankel, M. E. 1972. Lawlessness in sentencing. *University of Cincinnati Law Review*, 41: 1–54.

Frase, R. S. 2013. *Just sentencing: Principles and procedures for a workable system*. New York: Oxford University Press.

Gainey, R. R., Steen, S, and Engen, R. L. 2005. Exercising options: An assessment of the use of alternative sanctions for drug offenders. *Justice Quarterly*, 22: 488–520. doi: 10.1080/07418820500219219.

Gall v. United States, 552 US 38 (2007).

Glaze, L. E. 2010. *Correctional populations in the United States, 2009*. Washington, DC: US Department of Justice, Bureau of Justice Statistics.

Griffin, T., and Wooldredge, J. 2006. Sex-based disparities in felony dispositions before versus after reform in Ohio. *Criminology*, 44: 893–923. doi: 10.1111/j.1745-9125.2006.00067.

Gruhl, J., and Welch, S. 1984. Women as criminal defendants: A test for paternalism. *The Western Political Quarterly*, 37: 456–467. doi: 10.2307/448446.

Hagan, J. 1974. Extra-legal attributes and criminal sentencing: An assessment of a sociological viewpoint. *Law & Society Review*, 8: 357–384. doi: 10.2307/3053080.

Hagan, J., and Bumiller, K. 1983. Making sense of sentencing: A review and critique of sentencing research. *Research on sentencing: The search for reform*, 2: 1–54.

Harmon, M. G. 2014. Sentencing guidelines. In *Encyclopedia of criminology and criminal justice*, edited by J. S. Albanese, 1–5. Oxford: Wiley Blackwell. doi: 10.1002/9781118517383.wbeccj352.

Hartley, R. D., Maddan, S., and Spohn, C. C. 2007. Prosecutorial discretion: An examination of substantial assistance departures in federal crack-cocaine and powder-cocaine cases. *Justice Quarterly*, 24: 382–407. doi: 10.1080/07418820701485379.

Jenkins, R. 1994. Rethinking ethnicity: Identity, categorization and power. *Ethnic and Racial Studies*, 17: 197–223. doi: 10.1080/01419870.1994.9993821.

Johnson, B. D. 2006. The multilevel context of criminal sentencing: Integrating judge and county level influences. *Criminology*, 44: 259–298. doi: 10.1111/j.1745-9125.2006.00049.

Johnson, B., Ulmer, J. L., and Kramer, J. H. 2008. The social context of guidelines circumvention: The case of federal district courts. *Criminology*, 46: 735–783. doi: 10.1111/j.1745-9125.2008.00125.

Kautt, P., and Spohn, C. 2002. Cracking down on black drug offenders? Testing for interactions among offenders' race, drug type, and sentencing strategy in federal drug sentences. *Justice Quarterly*, 19: 1–35. doi: 10.1080/07418820200095151.

King, R. D., Johnson, K. R., and McGeever, K. 2010. Demography of the legal profession and racial disparities in sentencing. *Law & Society Review*, 44: 1–32. doi: 10.1111/j.1540-5893.2010.00394.

Kleck, G. 1981. Racial discrimination in criminal sentencing: A critical evaluation of the evidence with additional evidence on the death penalty. *American Sociological Review*, 46: 783–805.

Koons-Witt, B. A. 2002. The effect of gender on the decision to incarcerate before and after theintroduction of sentencing guidelines. *Criminology*, 40: 297–328. doi: 1111/j.1745-9125.2002.tb00958.

Koons-Witt, B. A., Sevigny, E. L., Burrow, J. D., and Hester, R. 2012. Gender and sentencing outcomes in South Carolina: Examining the interactions with race, age, and offense type. *Criminal Justice Policy Review*, 25: 299–324. doi: 10.1177/0887403412468884.

Kramer, J., and Ulmer, J. T. 2009. *Sentencing guidelines: Lessons from Pennsylvania*. Boulder, CO: Lynn Rienner.

Kruttschnitt, C. 1984. Sex and criminal court dispositions: The unresolved controversy. *Journal of Research in Crime and Delinquency*, 21: 213–232. doi: 10.1177/0022427884021003003.

Merritt, N., Fain, T., and Turner, S. 2006. Oregon's get tough sentencing reform: A lesson injustice system adaptation. *Criminology & Public Policy*, 5: 5–36. doi: 10.1111/j.1745-9133.2006.00110.

Miethe, T. D. 1987. Charging and plea bargaining practices under determinate sentencing: An investigation of the hydraulic displacement of discretion. *Journal of Criminal Law and Criminology*, 78: 155–176. doi: 10.2307/1143578.

Mitchell, O. 2005. A meta-analysis of race and sentencing research: Explaining the inconsistencies. *Journal of Quantitative Criminology*, 21: 439–466. doi: 10.1007/s10940-005-7362-7.

Nagel, I., and Schulhofer, S. 1992. A tale of three cities: An empirical study of charging and bargaining practices under the federal sentencing guidelines. *California Law Review*, 66: 501–561.

Packer, H. L. 1968. *The limits of the criminal sanction*. Stanford, CA: Stanford University Press.

Paternoster, R. 2011. Racial disparity under the federal sentencing guidelines pre- and post-Booker. *Criminology & Public Policy*, 10: 1063–1072. doi: 10.1111/j.1745-9133.2011.00778.

Peterson, R. D., and Hagan, J. 1984. Changing conceptions of race: Towards an account of anomalous findings of sentencing research. *American Sociological Review*, 49: 56–70.

Rita v. United States, 551 US 338 (2007).

Sentencing Reform Act 18 USC § 3551 (1984).

Shermer, L. O., and Johnson, B. D. 2010. Criminal prosecutions: Examining prosecutorial discretion and charge reductions in US federal district courts. *Justice Quarterly*, 27: 394–430. doi: 10.1080/07418820902856972.

Smith, D. A. 1986. The plea bargaining controversy. *Journal of Criminal Law and Criminology*, 7: 949–968. doi: 10.2307/1143445.

Sorensen, J., and Wallace, D. H. 1999. Prosecutorial discretion in seeking death: An analysis of racial disparity in the pretrial stages of case processing in a Midwestern county. *Justice Quarterly*, 16: 559–578. doi: 10.1080/07418829900094261.

Spohn, C. 2000. Thirty years of sentencing reform: The quest for a racially neutral sentencing process. In *Policies, processes, and decisions of the criminal justice system*, edited by J. Horney, vol. 3: 427–501. Washington, DC: National Institute of Justice.

Spohn, C. 2009. *How do judges decide? The search for fairness and justice in punishment.* New York: Sage.

Spohn, C., and Beichner, D. 2000. Is preferential treatment of female offenders a thing of the past? A multisite study of gender, race, and imprisonment. *Criminal Justice Policy Review*, 11: 149–184.

Spohn, C., Beichner, D., and Davis-Frenzel, E. 2001. Prosecutorial justifications for sexual assault case rejection: Guarding the "gateway to justice." *Social Problems*, 48: 206–235. doi: 10.1525/sp.2001.48.2.206.

Spohn, C., and Brennan, P. K. 2011. The joint effects of offender race/ethnicity and gender on substantial assistance departures in federal courts. *Race and Justice*, 1: 49–78. doi: 10.1177/2153368710396228.

Spohn, C. and Brennan, P. K. 2013. Sentencing and punishment. In *The Routledge international handbook of crime and gender studies*, edited by C. M. Renzetti, S. L. Miller, and A. R. Gover, 213–230. New York: Routledge.

Spohn, C., and Holleran, D. 2000. The imprisonment penalty paid by young, unemployed black and Hispanic male offenders. *Criminology*, 38: 281–306. doi: 10.1111/j.1745-9125.2000.tb00891.

Spohn, C., and Holleran, D. 2001. Prosecuting sexual assault: A comparison of charging decisions in sexual assault cases involving strangers, acquaintances, and intimate partners. *Justice Quarterly*, 18: 651–688. doi: 10.1080/07418820100095051.

Spohn, C. C., Kim, B., Belenko, S., and Brennan, P. K. 2014. The direct and indirect effects of offender drug use on federal sentencing outcomes. *Journal of Quantitative Criminology*, 30: 549–576. doi: 10.1007/s10940-014-9214-9.

Spohn, C. C., and Spears, J. W. 1997. Gender and case processing decisions: A comparison of case outcomes for male and female defendants charged with violent felonies. *Women & Criminal Justice*, 8: 29–59. doi: 10.1300/J012v08n03_02.

Stacey, A. M., and Spohn, C. 2006. Gender and the social costs of sentencing: An analysis of sentences imposed on male and female offenders in three US district courts. *Berkeley Journal of Criminal Law*, 11: 43–76.

Steen, S., Engen, R. L., and Gainey, R. R. 2005. Images of danger and culpability: Racial stereotyping, case processing, and criminal sentencing. *Criminology*, 43: 435–468. doi: 10.1111/j.0011-1348.2005.00013.

Steffensmeier, D., and Britt, C. L. 2001. Judges' race and judicial decision making: Do black judges sentence differently? *Social Science Quarterly*, 82: 749–764. doi: 10.1111/0038-4941.00057.

Steffensmeier, D., and Demuth, S. 2000. Ethnicity and sentencing outcomes in US federal courts: Who is punished more harshly? *American Sociological Review*, 65: 705–729.

Steffensmeier, D., and Demuth, S. 2001. Ethnicity and judge's sentencing decisions: Hispanic–black–white comparisons. *Criminology*, 39: 145–178. doi: 10.1111/j.1745-9125.2001.tb00919.

Steffensmeier, D., and Demuth, S. 2006. Does gender modify the effects of race–ethnicity on criminal sanctioning? Sentences for male and female white, black, and Hispanic defendants. *Journal of Quantitative Criminology*, 22: 241–261. doi: 10.1007/s10940-006-9010-2.

Steffensmeier, D., Kramer, J., and Streifel, C. 1993. Gender and imprisonment decisions. *Criminology*, 31: 411–446. doi: 10.1111/j.1745-9125.1993.tb01136.

Steffensmeier, D., Ulmer, J., and Kramer, J. 1998. The interaction of race, gender, and age in criminal sentencing: The punishment cost of being young, black, and male. *Criminology*, 36: 763–798. doi: 10.1111/j.1745-9125.1998.tb01265.

Thompson, R. J., and Zingraff, M. T. 1981. Detecting sentencing disparity: Some problems and evidence. *American Journal of Sociology*, 86: 869–880.

Tonry, M. 1995. *Malign neglect: Race, crime, and punishment in America*. New York: Oxford University Press.

Ulmer, J. 2012. Recent developments and new directions in sentencing research. *Justice Quarterly*, 29: 1–40. doi: 10.1080/07418825.2011.624115.

Ulmer, J. and Johnson, B. 2004. Sentencing inn context: A multilevel analysis. *Criminology*, 42: 137–178. doi: 10.1111/j.1745-9125.2004.tb00516.

Ulmer, J., Light, M. T., and Kramer, J. 2011. The "liberation" of federal judges' discretion in the wake of the Booker/Fanfan decision: Is there increased disparity and divergence between courts? *Justice Quarterly*, 28: 799–837. doi: 10.1080/07418825.2011.553726.

United States v. Booker, 543 US 220 (2005).

von Hirsch, A. 1976. *Doing justice: The choice of punishments*. New York: Hill and Wang.

Wang, X., Mears, D. P., Spohn, C., and Dario, L. 2013. Assessing the differential effects of race and ethnicity on sentence outcomes under different sentencing systems. *Crime & Delinquency*, 59: 87–114. doi: 10.1177/0011128709352234.

Zatz, M. S. 1987. The changing forms of racial/ethnic biases in sentencing. *Journal of Research in Crime and Delinquency*, 24: 69–92. doi: 10.1177/002242788702400100.

16

Correctional Interventions and Outcomes

Eric Grommon and Jason Rydberg

Correctional Interventions and Outcomes

At the end of 2012, 6.9 million adults or 1 out of every 35 residents of the United States were supervised by the correctional system (Glaze and Herberman, 2013). According to the most recent data available for juveniles, an additional 541,000 youth were on probation (Livsey, 2012) and 79,000 in residential placement (Hockenberry, 2013). With the dramatic increase in correctional populations over the past 30 years, many states and local jurisdictions are experimenting with a variety of interventions designed to reduce correctional populations, assist individuals returning to the community, decrease recidivism, and maintain public safety. Correctional interventions are informed by an expansive body of theoretical perspectives and models, encompass a variety of elements, and are delivered in an assortment of contexts that consist of institutional settings, the community, or a combination of both. Acknowledging the wide range of interventions used in the correctional field, this chapter provides insights on common research challenges that will need to be contended with while working in the trenches of primary-data collection in order to determine the efficacy of correctional interventions (see Hepburn, 2013). The focus is purposely broad, in an effort to provide a framework of fundamental considerations that can be adjusted to specific interventions.

The Handbook of Measurement Issues in Criminology and Criminal Justice, First Edition.
Edited by Beth M. Huebner and Timothy S. Bynum.

Brief background

Correctional interventions use a combination of treatment and control strategies that affects one's attitudes, emotions, character, skills, and ultimately behavior (Palmer, 1992). Contemporary scholarship continues to validate past research that indicates the effectiveness of correctional interventions in reducing recidivism. Effect sizes from a variety of meta-analyses estimate that rehabilitative interventions reduce recidivism by 10 percent on average (Lipsey and Cullen, 2007; Lösel, 1995). However, results of outcome evaluations are not uniformly distributed. In some instances, interventions do not have any effects on recidivism and may unintentionally *increase* it. For instance, meta-analyses of sanction or supervision-based correctional interventions tend to produce null or unanticipated effects when compared to rehabilitative interventions (Lipsey and Cullen, 2007). This variability in intervention effects has triggered research that aims to determine why some interventions are more effective than others and to identify characteristics of effective interventions. These characteristics include attention to assessment and identification of who will receive an intervention, what individual needs should be targeted, and how interventions are to be delivered to suit participants best (Andrews and Bonta, 2010; Gendreau, 1996).

Despite the solid framework provided by this growing literature, practical questions remain about pathways that must be taken in order to achieve positive results. Effort must be put into understanding the intervention, its various components, and the processes that occur before and during implementation. In the sections that follow insights are provided into the measurement of the intervention itself, the measurement of recidivism outcomes, and the emerging trends in program evaluation stemming from prisoner reentry research.

First Things First: Understanding the Intervention

Know thy logic

When evaluating the efficacy of a correctional intervention, one of the first components to consider is the underlying theory and logic of *why* an intervention should produce beneficial outcomes. This is often a difficult question to answer. Interventions often involve multiple stakeholders with an array of missions and organizational objectives, which may or may not be consistent. Ongoing collaborative discussions involving stakeholders in the intervention can formulate explicit and observable linkages that connect thoughts on *why* an intervention should work to thoughts on *how* the intervention will be carried out.

To facilitate conversations and to achieve stakeholder agreement on the underlying theory of a specific correctional intervention, logic models can be created. Logic models can come in a variety of forms and are more or less complex depending upon the intervention. In general these models provide a feasible representation of how an intervention will operate so as to fulfill a specific need or solve an identified problem (Bickman, 1987). The model contains the following structure and information:

- NEEDS–PROBLEMS STATEMENT Identifies the current nature and scope of the problem an intervention could reasonably address. Ideally such statements are informed by needs assessments, where a variety of data sources are reviewed and quantified in order to generate profiles of participant needs or problems (or both).
- GOALS STATEMENT Specifies the ultimate goals and objectives of the intervention. This statement is logically deduced from the needs–problems statement and symbolizes the shared understanding of what the intervention seeks to accomplish.
- INPUTS Interventions require significant investment from a variety of agencies and organizations. This section lists stakeholders who play and active role or are committed to meeting participant needs, solving participant problems, and achieving intervention objectives.
- APPROACH Details the various intervention actions and activities expected to take place. Many interventions are multimodal by design. This portion of a logic model captures the various services being delivered. Planned activities are made explicit, so they can be measured and monitored.
- OUTPUTS Forms the anticipated, direct products of intervention activities that are to be expected if the intervention was consistently delivered. As the first form of results about an intervention, outputs provide evidence about implementation and enable the identification of strengths and shortcomings in service delivery. These conclusions can only be determined with data collection on intervention actions and activities.
- OUTCOMES Like outputs, outcomes concern the anticipated results. Rather than being measures of monitored service delivery, outcomes differ from outputs by placing emphasis on relevant, theoretically informed, and measurable future benefits the intervention is intended to achieve. Outcomes are time-ordered and sequential. It is common to identify short-term outcomes (i.e., outcomes that become visible immediately after the intervention), intermediate outcomes (i.e., outcomes that become visible in one to three years after the intervention), and long-term outcomes (i.e., outcomes that become visible in three or more years after the intervention).

Logic models are interpreted as a series of interconnected "if, then" statements. For instance, *if* the intervention approach is fully operational and delivered to specification, *then* a specific amount of products or "dosage" of service delivery will be provided. Process evaluations are used to measure such outputs and assess the level of disconnect between initial intentions and how the intervention operates in practice. Further, *if* sufficient intervention outputs are produced, *then* specific outcomes should follow. Outcome evaluations are used to measure and determine whether the intervention has met the desired benefits it aimed to achieve.

Figure 16.1 provides an applied example of a logic model for the evaluation of a multimodal community-based prisoner reentry program. As is readily apparent, the program approach and outputs were comprised of a number of moving parts, which in combination were supposed to decrease rates of substance relapse and recidivism for program participants in relation to a control group whose members were randomly assigned to traditional parole supervision. Process and outcome evaluation components were included in the overall assessment of the program (see Grommon, Davidson, and Bynum, 2013). The coupling of these two components provided important insights. With regard to the process portion, program participants were found to have received fewer hours of direct services in either of the two phases than originally prescribed by the program approach. Additional deviations from the program model were observed with the frequency of drug-testing, as the two groups were subjected to different rates. In essence, the program delivered a different model than the one originally conceived. This appeared to influence outcome evaluation results. The program did not meet long-term objectives of decreasing relapse or recidivism.

The creation of a logic model serves a number of valuable purposes for understanding the rationale and components of an intervention. First, all stakeholders will be informed of the anticipated outcomes and roles of all parties involved in the intervention. This process can reinforce commitments and accountability while also enhancing resource and data-sharing. Second, the casual model of hypothesized relationships between intervention approach, outputs, and outcomes can be measured and subjected to empirical evaluation. As observed from the multimodal community-based community reentry program, if only some output goals were achieved, but not others, this could in principle explain the variation in short-term and long-term outcomes. Finally, the possession of a detailed understanding of the underlying mechanisms and pathways of an intervention can inform future policy and practice about how interventions operate and for whom they are most effective (Duwe, 2013; Sampson, Winship, and Knight, 2013). Context is an important feature of interventions; some may be more effective within specific locations, with specific staff and specific activities. Capturing this is important when the evaluation could ultimately result in the intervention being implemented in other locations.

Know thy target population and participants

Outcomes are a function of an intervention and its affiliated context and approaches, but they are also influenced by the individuals who participate. Recognizing the importance of individual participants and of the variation in behavior that exists within and between individuals, the risk–need–responsivity model of offender rehabilitation has emerged as a dominant explanatory framework and intervention paradigm in corrections (Andrews and Bonta, 2010; Andrews, Bonta, and Hoge, 1990). While not without criticism (Ward, Melser, and Yates, 2007), the model is rooted in general personality and cognitive social learning psychological perspectives and

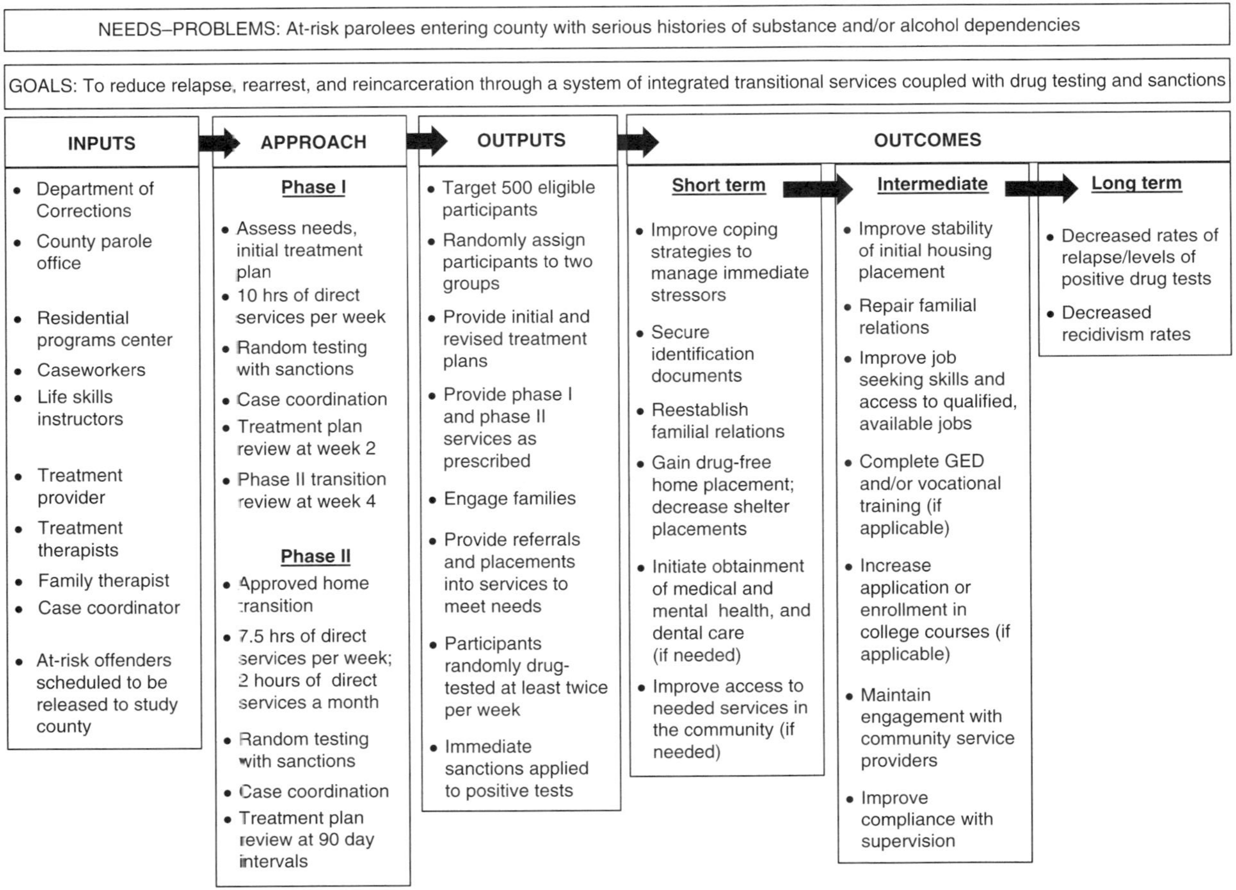
NEEDS–PROBLEMS: At-risk parolees entering county with serious histories of substance and/or alcohol dependencies
GOALS: To reduce relapse, rearrest, and reincarceration through a system of integrated transitional services coupled with drug testing and sanctions
INPUTS
Department of Corrections
County parole office
Residential programs center
Caseworkers
Life skills instructors
Treatment provider
Treatment therapists
Family therapist
Case coordinator
At-risk offenders scheduled to be released to study county
APPROACH
Phase I
Assess needs, initial treatment plan
10 hrs of direct services per week
Random testing with sanctions
Case coordination
Treatment plan review at week 2
Phase II transition review at week 4
Phase II
Approved home transition
7.5 hrs of direct services per week; 2 hours of direct services a month
Random testing with sanctions
Case coordination
Treatment plan review at 90 day intervals
OUTPUTS
Target 500 eligible participants
Randomly assign participants to two groups
Provide initial and revised treatment plans
Provide phase I and phase II services as prescribed
Engage families
Provide referrals and placements into services to meet needs
Participants randomly drug-tested at least twice per week
Immediate sanctions applied to positive tests
OUTCOMES
Short term
Improve coping strategies to manage immediate stressors
Secure identification documents
Reestablish familial relations
Gain drug-free home placement; decrease shelter placements
Initiate obtainment of medical and mental health, and dental care (if needed)
Improve access to needed services in the community (if needed)
Intermediate
Improve stability of initial housing placement
Repair familial relations
Improve job seeking skills and access to qualified, available jobs
Complete GED and/or vocational training (if applicable)
Increase application or enrollment in college courses (if applicable)
Maintain engagement with community service providers
Improve compliance with supervision
Long term
Decreased rates of relapse/levels of positive drug tests
Decreased recidivism rates

Figure 16.1 Multimodal community-based prisoner reentry program.

assumes that criminal behavior can be reliably predicted. Using available empirical knowledge on primarily psychological individual-level factors found to indirectly or directly contribute to criminal behavior, one can determine the intensity of services to be delivered and the identification of intermediate service targets. That is, the participant–intervention interaction should be acknowledged as one of the most important aspects that shape correctional intervention outcomes. At its core, the model offers three key principles that can be used to link specific groups of individuals to particular types of services, in an effort to maximize the effectiveness of correctional interventions. Each of the three principles will be elaborated upon below.

Risk The risk principle holds that interventions should be targeted to higher risk individuals. Risk generally refers to an assortment of factors representing characteristics of individuals and their immediate circumstances or environment that tend to be associated with a higher likelihood of criminal activity or behavior. According to the best available evidence, these factors include a history of antisocial behavior, antisocial cognition, antisocial peers or associates, and antisocial personality traits (Andrews and Bonta, 2010). It is important to note that, while there is some focus on static factors (e.g., history of antisocial behavior), most of the risk factors offered in the risk–need–responsivity model are dynamic and thus more amenable to change. Addressing these risks will then lower criminal behavior.

The challenge is how to measure and determine which participants are higher risks than others. To determine risk, participants need to be systematically assessed by clinicians through tools that capture information on static and dynamic factors determined to predict future criminal activity or behavior. Risk assessment instruments continue to evolve, and a number of instruments are available for correctional administrators and practitioners (see Andrews, Bonta, and Wormith, 2006; Duwe, 2014). For instance, the Level of Service Inventory-Revised (LSI-R) is one of the most common risk assessment tools used in corrections (Andrews and Bonta, 1995). It is comprised of 54 items covering 10 risk-factor domains: criminal history, education and employment background, financial status, family and marital relationships, living accommodations, leisure and recreational activities, peer companions and associates, alcohol and drug problems, emotional and personal distresses, and attitudes and belief systems. Responses are tallied to create a summary risk score. Score ranges are specified to classify participants into low, low–moderate, moderate, moderate–high, and high-risk designations. The LSI-R, like many available risk assessment instruments, therefore captures information on available risk factors that is then used to direct participants to interventions with suitable levels of intensity. With a variety of assessment instruments available and new tools continuing to emerge, it is important to use assessments that have been validated and to possess a working understanding of what the assessments do and do not measure.

At first take, the focus on providing correctional interventions to high-risk individuals seems counterproductive. It would be easier to include lower risk individuals who possess less entrenched behaviors and may be more amenable to change (see Lipsey, 2014). However, the problem with including low-risk participants is that these individuals are likely to change of their own accord, which biases outcomes (see Rossi, Lipsey, and Freeman, 2004). Moreover, interventions with higher risk participants tend to produce larger and more consistent effects than interventions with lower risk populations (Lipsey and Cullen, 2007). Thus a second, but equally relevant, contribution of the risk principle is the suggestion that individual risk should be matched to the intensity of an intervention. High-risk individuals should be placed in more intensive, structured, and controlled interventions, while low-risk individuals should be placed in low-intensity interventions (if they are placed in interventions at all).

Need The need principle contends that interventions should target factors known to be closely associated with criminality and to be amenable to intervention. These factors include a history and continuance of antisocial behavior, antisocial personality patterns affiliated with impulsiveness, low self-control, risk-seeking, egocentrism, antisocial cognitive patterns linked to attitudes, values, beliefs, and rationalizations that support criminal behavior, and close association with criminal peers accompanied by isolation from conventional peers. These dynamic factors related to individual cognition and social support form the core elements interventions should seek to address. Expanding from the core are additional factors that hold promise for effecting change. These include prioritized points of focus that seek to improve dysfunctional family, marital, and close social relationships, performance in and satisfaction with educational endeavors and employment, opportunities to participate in noncriminal leisure or recreational activities, and alternatives to substance use and abuse.

Interventions that assess participant needs and target core and promising factors outperform interventions that do not actively target criminogenic needs or address noncriminogenic needs (Smith, Gendreau, and Swartz, 2009). Additionally, there appear to be differential effects whereby the more factors an intervention targets, the higher the likelihood of beneficial outcomes is. In the examination of residential interventions, Latessa and Lowenkamp (2006) noted that the targeting of one to three of the core and promising factors was significantly less effective than interventions that target at least four needs. The most effective interventions targeted seven or more factors. Unfortunately Latessa and Lowenkamp were unable to specify combinations of factors that contribute to the overall findings. Difference scores tallying the number of criminogenic and noncriminogenic needs targeted by correctional interventions are a common measurement strategy used to examine the effect of the need principle (see Dowden and Andrews, 2004). A meta-analysis from Andrews and Dowden (2006) suggests that interventions for high-risk participants targeting self-control deficits, familial relations, and peer associations or networks tend to produce larger recidivism reductions.

Assessments of individual need are not as prominent as risk assessments, but the available measurement tools continue to be developed and assessed for reliability and validity (see Andrews et al., 2006). Since the central feature of the need principle is the dynamic nature of core and promising factors, it is critical to understand that needs change. Assessments should therefore be administered repeatedly across intervals in order to generate data on intra-individual change. These data can be integrated to refer participants to additional services, self-assess intervention activities, and contextualize outcomes. Beyond the focus on individuals, a simple form of measurement can be used to assess the adherence of interventions to the needs principle. The creation of a matrix of core and promising factors can be tallied with descriptions of how an intervention affects these factors (see Bourgon et al., 2013 for a similarly structured matrix approach). Ideally, the number of needs targeted by the intervention should exceed the number of less promising factors or other factors not associated with principle.

Responsivity The responsivity principle notes that interventions should utilize active social learning and cognitive behavioral techniques that are consistent with participants' personalities, motivation, ability, and style of learning. In essence, the responsivity principle states that the three-way interaction between participant, intervention approach, and intervention staff is instrumental to shaping outcomes. Indeed, the responsivity principle has been found to be the most important principle of effective intervention, even though it is one of the most difficult to measure and examine empirically (Smith et al., 2009).

At the participant level, the responsivity principle reinforces notions of understanding the social background and life circumstances that have shaped one's cognitive and intellectual aptitude. This requires measurement of the participant's intelligence, motivation, personality, and background. Effort must be made to match a participant to an intervention approach that is consistent with one's level of learning and to staff members who can motivate, relate, and challenge participants. For instance, an intervention that relies upon an instructor to develop role-playing scenarios and to critically examine simulations may not be best suited for participants with high anxiety (see Spiropoulos, Salisbury, and Van Voorhis, 2014).

At the intervention level, a few heuristics have been developed around the dosage that is required to overcome motivation challenges and affect behavioral change. Bourgon and Armstrong (2005) inform that 300 or more direct contact hours are needed for high-risk participants with multiple needs defined by the need principle. Moderate-risk participants are most likely to benefit from interventions with more than 200 hours of direct contact. Participants with at least one need and assessed as low risk require no more than 100 direct contact hours.

Finally, responsivity at the staff level concerns the credentials, training, therapeutic and interpersonal skill, and supervision of those responsible for carrying out the day-to-day tasks of the intervention approach. In the process of delivering interventions, individual program staff must have the ability to integrate operant conditioning techniques of reinforcement and punishment as well as the capacity to model and demonstrate alternatives to criminogenic attitudes and values. Meta-analytic research has suggested that correctional treatment programs utilizing these staff characteristics were associated with positive effects on recidivism, but only among programs already consistent with the broader risk, need, and responsivity principles (Dowden and Andrews, 2004).

The most effective interventions will adopt and abide by all three principles of effective intervention. Given the importance of these prevailing principles in shaping intervention outcomes, assessment tools have been developed to help local jurisdictions translate and transfer the principles into practice. George Mason University's Center for Advancing Correctional Excellence recently recreated a web-based Risk, Need, Responsivity Simulation Tool that assesses available programming, individual clients, and jurisdictional service delivery capacity domains (see Center for Advancing Correctional Excellence, 2013). The tool is based in part on meta-analyses of correctional interventions, as well as on recidivism outcomes forecasted by risk and need profiles for over 20,000 individuals. The program domain uses 46 primary items with numerous subitem contingencies to inventory and assess existing interventions according to their content, quality, implementation, dosage, and assessment protocols. Responses result in the classification of an intervention by its level of intensity, a determination of the risk and need profiles of participants who would best be served by the intervention, and insight on how well the intervention is operating. The individual domain consists of 17 items concerning risk, need, and lifestyle factors, which are used to support programming and case management decision-making. Finally, the jurisdictional capacity domain examines the prevalence of risks and needs among clients, served according to existing interventions. The gap between available programming and the type of programming that should be in place within a specific jurisdiction is examined with 18 items.

The Correctional Program Assessment Inventory is another standardized tool that can be used to assess the adherence of correctional interventions to the risk–need–responsivity model principles (Gendreau and Andrews, 1996; Gendreau and Andrews, 2001; Gendreau, Andrews, and Thériault, 2010). While also informed by meta-analyses of correctional interventions, the tool is based on the architects' clinical experience and knowledge of intervention implementation and operations. With the help of semi-structured site visit interviews with select program staff and case file and program material reviews, eight domains are examined across a total of 133 items. Domains include organizational culture, program implementation and maintenance, management and staff characteristics, client risk and need practices, program characteristics, core correctional practices, interagency communication, and research evaluation activities. Each domain is scored as "very satisfactory," "satisfactory," "satisfactory but needs improvement," or "unsatisfactory" and then totaled across domains to create an overall assessment score. Intervention strengths, areas in need of improvement, and recommendations are documented in a report that accompanies the scores.

Know thy bane: Implementation

Although there is a solid foundation to the design and planning of correctional interventions, goals on paper must be actualized by those responsible for delivering the intervention. Implementation reflects this leap into real-world practice.

Implementation is a stage where even the best intentions are met with practical constraints – such as of time, resources, and competency. Unfortunately this can mean that interventions designed to adhere to evidence-based practices may be pressured to make compromises that ultimately reduce the effectiveness of the program (Rhine, Mawhorr, and Parks, 2006). For instance, Project Greenlight was a prison-based reentry program implemented in New York City in the first years of the twenty-first century and designed to adhere to the principles above (Wilson and Davis, 2006). In the course of implementation several adjustments had to be made. Among these changes, the risk–needs assessment instrument was considered by program staff to be too time-consuming and was discontinued. The changes resulted in divergences from the principles of effective correctional programs and contributed to explaining why the parolees receiving the intervention performed *worse* than the control group.

On the other hand, variation in the implementation of the program can impact the ability of researchers to draw conclusions about whether the intervention was ultimately responsible for the observed outcomes. Even if the intervention was associated with positive results, the internal validity of any claims about the intervention's effectiveness becomes suspect if it is apparent that the intervention was never properly implemented. Fortunately researchers can operationalize and measure the implementation of the program so as to track its process over time and ultimately characterize what exactly the participants received. There are several templates available for defining and measuring the dosage and fidelity of the intervention (see Dane and Schneider, 1998; Gearing et al., 2011). By creating these measures, researchers can come to a better understanding of the delivery of the program and how it would potentially influence the results of an evaluation. Moreover, the collection of these data can improve the certainty that any observed effects were actually due to the intervention.

Recidivism: The Bottom Line

Recidivism is the outcome measure most often utilized in evaluating the effectiveness of correctional programs (Petersilia, 2004). As noted by Latessa (2012), even though there is a variety of outcomes on which correctional interventions can have an impact, historically recidivism has been used as the primary indicator of whether a program "works." This section of the chapter will outline some general concepts and trends in the measurement of recidivism, before moving on to more innovative models that have been utilized in recent research.

Recidivism: The basics

When we think specifically about correctional interventions, recidivism refers to instances where participants or individuals being compared to the participants engage in a violation behavior following their release into the community. Recidivism measures capture reversions to criminal behavior that the intervention was presumably designed to correct (Maltz, 1984). As it is generally used in correctional research, the definition of recidivism has two primary elements: a reoffense or violation event; and a follow-up period during which the reoffense of interest can occur. Utilizing a desired indicator of reoffending as the criterion for recidivism, if a program participant (or a person being compared to a participant) is recorded engaging in the defined reoffense behavior within a given amount of follow-up time, that person is considered as recidivating. The recidivism definitions deployed in corrections evaluation research tend to vary across each of these elements, utilizing a variety of reoffense definitions and variable follow-up times.

Definitions of reoffense or violation events There is a multitude of ways in which correctional researchers have defined or could define recidivism events. Frequently used definitions invoke rearrest, technical violation, reconviction, and return to prison – either for a supervision revocation or for conviction on a new criminal sentence. Scholars also differentiate between serious and less serious forms of these measures, for instance, by defining recidivism only as a reconviction for a felony (e.g., Cochran, Mears and Bales, 2014), or as a reconviction for a sex offense (e.g., Olver, Wong, and Nicholaichuk, 2009). Important to note is that these measures do not simply reflect criminal behavior, but rather capture a combination of reoffending behavior on the part of the program participant and processing by the criminal justice system (Lin, Grattet, and Petersilia, 2012). The amount of processing by the criminal justice system varies across these events. For instance, technical violations and rearrests involve significantly less processing than does a reconviction. For recidivism measures that require the highest relative degree of processing by the criminal justice system – reconvictions to jail or prison, or supervision revocation on a technical violation – the outcomes will be subject to administrative discretion to a much higher degree, having resulted from a series of decisions by criminal justice actors (Lin, 2010). This degree of discretion will further distance the recidivism indicator from the actual reoffending behavior. For instance, Lin and colleagues (2012) observed that decisions on whether reoffending parolees in California should be processed in criminal court or brought before a parole board was only partially a function of the seriousness of the parolees' offense. Instead, factors such as the perceived risk posed by the parolee and demographic characteristics drove these decisions.

In general, as the level of processing increases, the recidivism definition becomes more exclusive (Sellin, 1931). Recidivism measures using events that require little processing by the criminal justice system will capture a larger number of reoffending incidents, but with increased potential for false positives. As an example, consider the observed recidivism rates for a sample of parolees from Lansing, Michigan in Table 16.1 (see Grommon, Rydberg, and Bynum, 2012; Rydberg, Grommon, and Bynum, 2013). Using the least exclusive recidivism measure, incurring a parole violation, the recidivism rate was 94.9 percent. Using the most exclusive measure, a return to prison, the rate was only 20.5 percent. In these circumstances, the choice of a reoffending event can have strong implications for observed recidivism rates.

Table 16.1 Variation in recidivism rates by reoffending event definitions.

Reoffending Event	*Percent Recidivating*
Technical violation	94.9 percent
Rearrest	87.2 percent
Rearrest and prosecution	64.1 percent
Rearrest and reconviction	61.5 percent
Reconviction to jail	23.1 percent
Return to prison	20.5 percent

Source: Adapted with modification from Rydberg et al., 2013.

The decision as to which event is most appropriate for the evaluation of an intervention should consider the behavior that the program was designed to address. If the goal was to reduce noncompliance among parolees, the use of technical violations as a reoffending event would be appropriate. On the other hand, if the program was designed to address serious violent offending, the use of technical violations would likely overestimate recidivism, but rearrests and other events requiring greater processing would produce more accurate estimates. Maltz (1984) suggests that, if false positives are a concern, using arrests combined with deeper points of processing can help vet recidivism rates. For instance, for the sample described in Table 16.1, 87.2 percent were rearrested, but only 64.1 percent had their arrest followed by a prosecution. A similar concern, when considering the goals of the intervention, is the inclusion of information on offense type into definitions of recidivism. As noted, previous evaluations have restricted recidivism definitions to types of offense that the respective interventions were designed to affect – sex offenses or violent offenses, for instance. If possible, program evaluators can differentiate between recidivism offense types in order to compare the effect of the intervention on its intended outcomes and other recidivism indicators (e.g., Marques et al., 2005). If the program was operating as intended, it should presumably have a larger effect on its intended recidivism indicators, as opposed to the nonequivalent dependent variables (Shadish, Cook, and Campbell, 2002).

Defining a follow-up period The second component of a recidivism definition in correctional research is the follow-up period. The follow-up period corresponds to the duration of time during which a researcher could observe a program participant reoffend. For instance, a Bureau of Justice Statistics recidivism study defined recidivists as those former prisoners who were rearrested, reconvicted, or resentenced to prison within three years of being released (Langan and Levin, 2002). Common follow-up times used in the literature range from six months to over a decade. Shorter or longer follow-up periods can be used on the basis of the goals of the evaluation and the nature of the data available. For example, if the parole technical violations are being used as the reoffending event, individuals can only commit a technical violation while they are on active parole supervision (Ostermann, 2013).

In this case, the researcher would want to restrict the follow-up time to make it correspond to the length of the parole supervision term.

This point raises the broader issue of *censoring*. No study can follow program participants indefinitely, and data collection must end at some point. As indicated by Rhodes (2011), there are three primary ways data can be censored in the context of community supervision and of related evaluations. First, the data collection or the follow-up period ends. The end of the follow-up period is a censoring point because afterward any recidivism that the study sample engaged in would not be observed by the researchers. All that would be known was that there were individuals who "failed" (i.e., recidivated) during the follow-up period, and individuals who "survived" to the end of the follow-up period. Of those who survived, it would not be known whether they would recidivate in the future. The length of the follow-up time set by the researcher has implications for censoring and for the observed recidivism rate. In general, shorter follow-up periods will result in high rates of censoring and lower rates of recidivism (Kurlychek, Bushway, and Brame, 2012). On the other hand, longer follow-up periods will result in lower rates of censoring and higher recidivism rates, the reason being that the sample is given more time to recidivate.

Second, the individual's supervision is completed (Rhodes, 2011). Considering the evaluation of interventions delivered in the context of community corrections, parole or probation discharge can represent a censoring point if the outcome measures are associated with receiving technical violations, or if the individual's supervision represents the primary mechanism through which data are collected. In either case, the completion of supervision will result in the inability to determine whether any recidivism events occur beyond that point in time.

Third, an individual sample member can be censored for particular outcomes if he or she experiences a competing recidivism event (Rhodes, 2011; see Hamilton and Campbell, 2014 for an empirical application). For instance, consider the evaluation of an intervention where the primary recidivism event of interest is a felony rearrest. Consider the possibility that, prior to being rearrested in such a manner, the individual is returned to prison for a technical violation. At this point, it is not possible for that individual to be rearrested for a felony, given that he or she is no longer under supervision in the community. In this sense, the possibility of supervision revocation is a competing event that censors the observation of the recidivism event of interest. As Rhodes (2011) indicates, such problems will not occur if technical violations are considered as equivalent to other indicators of a new offense.

Within the context of correctional interventions comparing outcomes between groups, censoring necessitates that each group be followed for an equitable duration. Consider the following example from Nicholaichuk and colleagues (2000). The authors evaluated the effect of a treatment program for sex offenders by comparing program participants to a matched sample of untreated sex offenders. The sample was followed for an average of six years, and sex offense reconviction rates of 14.5 percent and 33.2 percent were observed for the treatment group and the comparison group respectively. However, Hanson and Nicholaichuk (2000) later observed that the follow-up periods for the two groups differed significantly.

Table 16.2 Example of unbalanced follow-up time: Sex offense recidivism rates by year of release for treatment and control groups.

Year of release	*Treatment Group Recidivism rate*	*Comparison Group Recidivism rate*
<1983	[None released]	82%
1983–1984	23%	67%
1985–1986	21%	52%
1987–1988	17%	30%
1989–1990	22%	35%
1991–1992	16%	21%
1993–1994	10%	13%
1995–1996	0%	7%
Proportion released prior to 1990	44.9%	61.8%

Source: Adapted with modification and permission from Hanson and Nicholaichuk, 2000.

Table 16.2 demonstrates that recidivism rates were the highest for the sample members who had been at risk for the longest period and the lowest for those who had been released more recently, due to censoring. Further, no member of the treatment group had been released prior to 1983. While these differences did not entirely negate the effectiveness of the treatment, they did indicate that at least some of the observed difference between the groups was due to unbalanced follow-up times.

Trends in measurement There are some commonalities in the measurement of recidivism that stem from defining recidivism as a reoffense or violation within a specified follow-up period. With almost no exceptions, an individual's recidivism is measured as a dichotomous variable. That is, a given recidivism measure will capture whether a program participant recidivated during the follow-up period (e.g., rearrest = 1), or did not (e.g., rearrest = 0). In these instances, a common statistical modeling strategy is to use logistic regression (i.e., a binomial generalized linear model with a logit link function: see Long, 1997) in order to estimate the conditional probability of an individual's being a recidivist, given the values of a set of regressors (e.g., demographic characteristics, criminal history, or participation in a given program).

More recently there have been attempts to incorporate into statistical modeling the time until the initial recidivism events. This is an important consideration; whether an individual recidivates after 18 months or 18 days, logistic regression modeling treats all recidivism events as equivalent. Additionally, logistic regression is unable to incorporate information on censoring, which means that the estimates from the model do not reflect that censored cases contribute only partial information about the relationship between the regressors and recidivism (Tableman and Kim, 2004). As a result, criminologists have used various forms of survival regression to incorporate information about censoring and time to recidivism. In particular, the semi-parametric Cox proportional hazards model (Cox, 1972) has been used to estimate the relationship between the distribution of survival times (i.e., the time an individual survives before recidivating) and covariates of interest (e.g., participation in an intervention). Yet, even when this approach is utilized, correctional researchers have focused almost exclusively on the first instance of recidivism which occurs for each participant during the follow-up period. A sample member's time to recidivism is measured as the amount of time until the first recidivism event occurs.

The implication of these trends is that, even in the instances where time to event is incorporated into the analysis, correctional research on recidivism has typically only differentiated between program participants who recidivate and those who do not. More recently, research in the area of prisoner reentry has suggested that, as parolees transition to the community, they encounter peaks and valleys of psychosocial stress (Garland, Wodahl, and Mayfield, 2011) and substance use (Grommon and Rydberg, 2013). As a result, reentry scholarship has suggested that measuring individual recidivism incidents as terminal events fails to capture actual trajectories of noncompliance, recidivism, and desistance in the context of community corrections. The following section will outline how correctional program evaluations can recalibrate recidivism measures to better reflect participant behavioral trajectories during the reentry process.

Recidivism: Beyond the basics

Frequency and timing of subsequent recidivism Although most of the previous research has treated recidivism as if it were a terminal event in the reentry process, not all individuals who receive a technical violation, are rearrested, or are even reconvicted fully exit the community. Rather parolees can experience a variety of intermediate sanctions that result from technical violations and arrests – sanctions such as verbal warnings, short stays in local jails, and temporary placement in residential substance abuse treatment (Harding, Morenoff, and Herbert, 2013). Simply stopping data collection for a program participant at the first instance of recidivism, particularly a less serious one, has the potential to miss a great deal of information if that program participant remains in the community. This is to say that important program effects may not be detected when only initial recidivism events are considered, but have the potential to emerge when subsequent recidivism is brought under examination.

Consider the following examples from a small cohort of Lansing, Michigan parolees followed for approximately three years after release from prison. For this cohort there were three possible outcomes at the conclusion of data analysis – when they were still on active supervision: the parolee could be successfully discharged from supervision, returned to prison, or censored. Table 16.3 displays nonmutually exclusive recidivism information for the cohort across these possible outcomes. Recidivism was common, even among those who were successfully discharged from

Table 16.3 Parole outcomes and recidivism for a Lansing cohort (N = 38).

Supervision Outcomes → *Recidivism Measures ↓*	*Successful Discharge (n = 19)*	*Returned to Prison (n = 8)*	*Censored (n = 11)*
	N (%)	*N (%)*	*N (%)*
Parole violation	17 (89.5%)	8 (100%)	11 (100%)
Rearrest	14 (73.7%)	8 (100%)	11 (100%)
Rearrest and reconviction	7 (36.8%)	6 (75%)	11 (100%)
Extended jail sentence[a]	0 (0%)	0 (0%)	9 (81.1%)
Return to prison	0 (0%)	8 (100%)	0 (0%)
	Mean (SD)	Mean (SD)	Mean (SD)
Total parole violations	2.8 (2.8)	3.1 (2.8)	7.3 (4.2)
Technical violations	2.3 (2.7)	2.5 (3.2)	5.2 (3.3)
Criminal violations[b]	0.5 (0.7)	0.6 (0.7)	2.1 (1.5)

[a] Extended jail sentence refers to being sentenced to 180–365 days in a local jail – distinct from returns to prison.

[b] Criminal violations refer to parole violations received for criminal behavior.

Source: Adapted from Rydberg et al., 2013.

supervision. Using only returns to prison as a recidivism measure would miss all of the information appearing above that row in Table 16.3. Additionally, the frequency of technical and criminal violations was similar between successful discharges and returns to prison, but was significantly higher for those who were censored, which indicated that their extended time on parole was related to chronic violation behavior.

Recidivism scholars and program evaluators may find it useful to systematically analyze the timing of subsequent recidivism events through the concept of intermittency. Intermittency refers to the fact that individuals do not engage in crime at a constant rate, but rather have periods of heightened and periods of reduced offending, which vary in the relative frequency and seriousness of offending (Piquero, 2004). Figure 16.2 plots intermittency patterns for a cohort of Lansing parolees under high and low levels of supervision intensity.[1] Each point represents the average duration (in days, adjusted for time spent in jail) between each parole violation. With respect to low supervision intensity, parolees with a high degree of supervision contact demonstrated shorter intermittency periods between violations – potentially a reflection of the increased capacity of parole agents to detect noncompliance.

It is possible for evaluators to compare the intermittency patterns of program participants and to examine differences in the frequency and seriousness of recidivism, with the expectation that, even if program participants still recidivate, they do so less often and through less serious offenses. Incorporating subsequent recidivism measures and intermittency into community corrections evaluations provides a more accurate reflection of the process-based nature of reentry, which is particularly

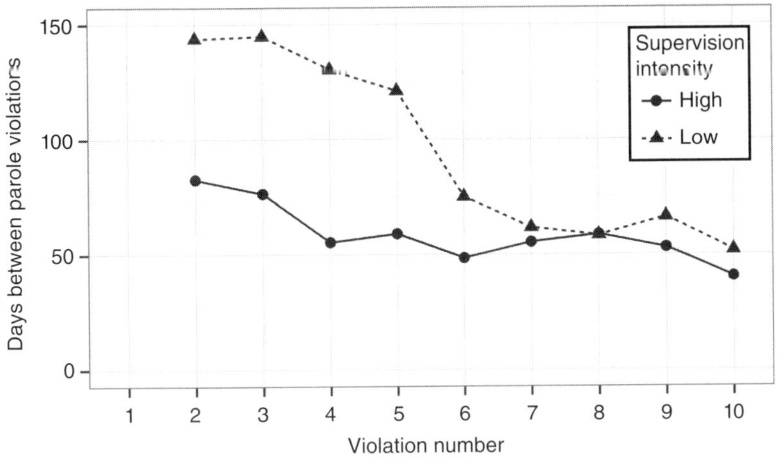

Figure 16.2 Parole violation intermittency by supervision intensity.

important, given that this process reflects the context in which correctional programming participants transition to society. Indeed, qualitative research on reentry has suggested that returning prisoners initially carry out violations and receive a sanction before they fully commit to "going straight." For example, parolees have noted the role of salient experiences of relapse and positive substance abuse tests in their motivation to maintain sobriety (Grommon et al., 2012; Grommon and Rydberg, 2013), and initial sanctions have been influential on parolees' eventual willingness to comply with supervision (Werth, 2012).

The preceding discussion provided guidance in the measurement of recidivism, which is the primary outcome of interest for the majority of correctional interventions. The next section will explore the contribution of prisoner reentry research to highlighting the importance of other measures of intervention outcomes.

Relevant and Collateral Outcomes: Contributions from the Contemporary Reentry Focus

Within the past two decades criminologists and policymakers alike have taken an increased interest in examining the process by which individuals reenter society, and particularly in documenting the challenges that returning prisoners face during this transition. This research has suggested that the period following release from prison can be characterized by more than whether or not the individual ended up committing a new crime. A lot can happen to individuals within the follow-up periods specified by recidivism outcome studies. Indeed this research has observed that, even within the first month of reentry, an individual can experience variation in numerous intermediate outcomes, such as finding stable housing, avoiding criminogenic environments, obtaining accessible transportation, and securing access to necessary treatment and services (Nelson, Deess, and Allen, 1999). One of the main contributions of reentry discussions and research is forwarding the need to move beyond recidivism as the sole measure of correctional effectiveness. In particular, reentry research has suggested the salience of three relevant and interconnected reentry dimensions: housing, employment, and substance use. Within the risk–need–responsivity framework, these factors have been highlighted as stabilizers or destabilizers, because their presence or absence increases or decreases an individual's receptivity to services and supervision (Ainsworth and Taxman, 2013).

Salient reentry dimensions

Housing Upon release from prison, securing housing is often one of the most immediate concerns that face returning prisoners (Nelson et al., 1999). Scholars have indicated that housing forms the bedrock of a successful transition from prison, as it allows parolees to focus efforts on other reentry dimensions, such as employment and treatment (Grommon, 2013). Yet research has consistently demonstrated that securing stable housing is a challenge for returning prisoners, given that their available options tend to be temporary arrangements relying on informal social networks (Visher and Travis, 2003). When these options are unavailable, the private housing market is often out of financial reach for an initial placement, and homeless shelters expose returning prisoners to noxious environments, making it difficult for them to abstain from substance use (Nelson et al., 1999). At a practical level, unstable living arrangements are associated with the likelihood of unsuccessful program completion, which in turn disrupt the delivery of an intervention to a community-based target population (Broner, Lang, and Behler, 2009).

Employment Returning prisoners identify employment as key to a successful transition (Visher, Baer, and Naser, 2006). This is occasionally necessitated, as failure to hold a job may be met with supervision sanctions. Reentry populations face numerous barriers to securing gainful employment: formal rules that prevent those with felony records from receiving particular benefits or from working in particular occupations; lack of viable skills; and informal discrimination against those with criminal records (Pager, 2007; Travis, 2005). Employment has been found to shape the reentry process by providing economic security, which in turn enables individuals to actualize intentions to change (Harding et al., 2014). Concerning the delivery of correctional interventions, full-time employment has been found to increase participant contacts with treatment providers (Rossman and Roman, 2003) by increasing the likelihood of successful outcomes.

Substance use Substance use, abuse, and dependence are frequent among institutionalized populations (Mumola and Karberg, 2006). These issues often remain unresolved as individuals transition into the community, presenting an important challenge to successful reintegration. Indeed returning prisoners have identified abstaining from substance use as important for staying out of prison (Visher et al.,

2006); and substance abuse and dependency are associated with higher risk of recidivism, although the precise causal mechanism is unclear (Ainsworth and Taxman, 2013).

Housing, employment, and substance use constitute several reentry dimensions that shape the context in which interventions are often delivered and in which recidivism takes place. Reentry scholarship contends that events in these dimensions can be considered important events or outcomes themselves. Recent research has examined how these reentry dimensions can shape outcomes through relationships with one another and with recidivism. For instance, employment shares a reciprocal relationship with housing as a reentry dimension: obtaining housing opens employment opportunities, while securing employment allows access to more stable housing options (Grommon, 2013). Further, these factors can influence the delivery of community-based interventions. Grommon (2013) found that housing instability negatively influenced length of employment and rate of participation in substance abuse treatment. These patterns contributed to rates of relapse and recidivism. These findings suggest that capturing additional dimensions of the reentry process may be fruitful for understanding the effects of correctional interventions.

Incorporating reentry dimensions into correctional intervention evaluations

Incorporating reentry dimensions into the evaluation of correctional interventions holds great potential for understanding how these interventions affect and are affected by broader reentry processes. Yet there remains the practical question of how such evaluations can actualize these suggestions. These issues can be fruitfully approached through two primary considerations: what to capture and sources for capturing it.

What to capture In line with the needs principle, it has been suggested that effective reentry programs use a multimodal or "wraparound" intervention strategy (Roman and Visher, 2009). These interventions facilitate the participant's contact with a variety of service providers who can address his or her specific needs. To the extent that treatment plans can vary according to individual risks and needs, it is important for any community-based intervention to capture the breadth of services provided. This suggestion is consistent with the "exposure" dimension of measuring program implementation – who received what services and in what level of dosage. This will allow a more precise measurement of the effect of specific aspects of the intervention on specific outcomes.

The next step is to incorporate measures of reentry dimensions that are hypothesized to be affected by the intervention, to affect the delivery of the intervention, or both. In this chapter the focus has been on the relevant dimensions of housing, employment, and substance abuse. Because the reentry process is best conceptualized as a dynamic one, marked by periods of progress and by setbacks (Grommon et al., 2012; Rydberg et al., 2013), the evaluation should attempt to capture the stability and instability of these dimensions over time. This entails utilizing measures of reentry dimensions that reflect varying levels, rather than the simple presence or absence of these dimensions over the entire observation period. For instance, employment could be measured as the number of hours of work during a specified period, the proportion of time at risk spent unemployed, or whether an individual was unemployed within a given time period. Multiple prospective data collection points will allow for the depiction of potentially reciprocal relationships between intervention dosage and reentry dimensions, and vice versa.

Data sources for reentry dimensions Although there is a solid base of literature to inform the measurement of recidivism, there is substantially less guidance on how to best measure reentry dimensions in correctional evaluations. An intervention may be interested in a variety of collateral outcomes that may not be systematically kept across jurisdictions – for instance, there may be no equivalent to examining arrest records that could measure recidivism. This being the case, utilizing multiple data sources is the safest approach. A variety of quantitative and qualitative data sources can be deployed to triangulate measures of reentry dimension stability and instability. Although reentry stability and instability measures have been relatively rare in the correctional program evaluation literature, the use of triangulating data sources is a common practice. For instance, Rudes, Lerch, and Taxman (2011) used surveys, observation, and in-depth interviews in order to measure organizational culture, and Geis and colleagues (2012) used official records and surveys in order to measure the implementation and effectiveness of a Global Positioning System (GPS) monitoring program for high-risk sex offenders.

Just like official and self-report measures of offending behavior, measures of reentry dimensions will each have benefits and drawbacks. As administrative records, parole agent case notes are a reflection of the attentiveness of the agent and only contain information on reentry events that the agent is aware of. Parolee self-reports can capture reentry dimensions that do not appear in any official records; but such measures are subject to typical errors, such as telescoping and recall bias. As a result, official and self-report measures of reentry dimensions are likely to produce correlated, but slightly different estimates. Consider the following example from a cohort of Lansing, Michigan parolees. As parolees were interviewed several times over their first year on parole, they were asked about the places they had lived in since being released, and whether they were currently employed. Similarly, parole agent case notes can be used to capture these measures over the same time period. The comparison between these two sources is in Table 16.4. The records contained information on a larger number of housing moves than did the interviews. This appeared to be driven by the fact that agents systematically recorded addresses that parolees were staying at as they bounced between friends' residences, while in the interviews parolees did not consider such moves to be changes of address. There was a uniform distribution of instances where the records indicated fewer moves than, more moves than, or an equal number of moves as, the interviews. Concerning

Table 16.4 Comparison of housing moves and jail stays between parolee interviews and correctional records (N = 39)

	Interviews	*Records*
Average number of housing moves	1.3	1.9
Employed at time 1[a]	12.8%	5.0%
Employed at time 2	53.3%	40.0%
Employed at time 3	41.7%	50.0%
Employed at time 4	28.5%	42.8%

Housing moves comparison	N (percent)
Records > interviews	14 (35.9)
Records = interviews	15 (38.5)
Records < interviews	10 (25.6)

Employment comparison[b]	Records	
Interviews ↓	Unemployed	Employed
Unemployed	65.9%	2.3%
Employed	8.0%	23.9%

[a] "Time" refers to the date of their interview (see Grommon et al., 2012).
[b] The unit of analysis is the parolee interview time.

employment, the extent and nature of the disagreement between the sources shifted over time – from early interviews that captured more employment spells than the records, to later interviews that indicated the opposite situation. Overall, when comparing whether the interviews and the records were consistent with each other at a given time point, they disagreed only 10.3 percent of the time.

With these caveats in mind, building checks into the data collection can be informative. Using multiple data sources to triangulate measures can help evaluators to quantify the validity and reliability of reentry dimension indicators. By pairing these measures with recidivism outcomes, it will be possible for evaluators to determine whether reentry instability affects program delivery and outcomes, while also examining whether positive recidivism outcomes come at the expense of reentry stability.

Conclusion

In this chapter a wide variety of measurement concerns in the evaluation of correctional interventions – including measuring program processes and capturing traditional and nontraditional outcomes – have been discussed. However, determining the effect of a given intervention on recidivism and reentry indicators requires additional considerations, which could not be given a full discussion here. Most importantly among these, to improve knowledge regarding the intervention's impact, program evaluators should make efforts to utilize experimental and quasi-experimental research designs (see Shadish et al., 2002). Deploying these designs will aid in addressing the policy-relevant question "Compared to what?" and will reduce the possibility that observed intervention effects were due to spurious factors.

Note

1 Supervision intensity was measured as the sum of the number of contacts between the parolee and his or her parole agent that took place at the parolee's home, in the parole office, or via telephone and the number of substance abuse tests administered, divided by the time at risk in the community. Parolees above the median supervision intensity score were coded as "high intensity"; those falling below the median were coded as "low intensity."

References

Ainsworth, S. A., and Taxman, F. S. 2013. Creating simulation parameter inputs with existing data sources: Estimating offender risks, needs, and recidivism. In *Simulation strategies to reduce recidivism: Risk need responsivity (RNR) modeling for the criminal justice system*, edited by F. S. Taxman and A. Pattavina, 115–142. New York: Springer.

Andrews, D. A., and Bonta, J. 1995. *The level of service inventory-revised*. Toronto, Canada: Multi-Health Systems.

Andrews, D. A., and Bonta, J. 2010. *The psychology of criminal conduct*, 5th edn. New Providence, NJ: Matthew Bender.

Andrews, D. A., Bonta, J., and Hoge, R. D. 1990. Classification for effective rehabilitation: Rediscovering psychology. *Criminal Justice and Behavior*, 17: 19–52.

Andrews, D. A., Bonta, J., and Wormith, J. S. 2006. The recent past and near future of risk and/or need assessment. *Crime & Delinquency*, 52: 7–27.

Andrews, D. A., and Dowden, C. 2006. Risk principle of case classification in correctional treatment: A meta-analytic investigation. *International Journal of Offender Therapy and Comparative Criminology*, 50: 88–100.

Bickman, L. 1987. The functions of program theory. In *Using program theory in evaluation: New directions for program evaluation*, edited by L. Bickman, 5–18. San Francisco, CA: Jossey-Bass.

Bourgon, G., and Armstrong, B. 2005. Transferring the principles of effective treatment into a "real world" prison setting. *Criminal Justice and Behavior*, 32: 3–25.

Bourgon, G., Bonta, J., Rugge, T., Scott, T., and Yessine, A. K. 2013. Program design, implementation, and evaluation in "real world" community supervision. *Federal Probation*, 74: 2–15.

Broner, N., Lang, M., and Behler, S. A. 2009. The effect of homelessness, housing type, functioning, and community reintegration supports on mental health court completion and recidivism. *Journal of Dual Diagnosis*, 5: 323–356.

Center for Advancing Correctional Excellence. 2013. *The risk–need–responsivty simulation tool*. Fairfax, VA: George Mason University, Center for Advancing Correctional Excellence.

Cochran, J. C., Mears, D. P., and Bales, W. D. 2014. Assessing the effectiveness of correctional sanctions. *Journal of Quantitative Criminology*, 30: 317–347.

Cox, D. R. 1972. Regression models and life tables. *Journal of the Royal Statistical Society, B*, 34: 187–220.

Dane, A. V., and Schneider, B. H. 1998. Program integrity in primary and early secondary prevention: Are program effects out of control? *Clinical Psychology Review*, 18: 23–45.

Dowden, C., and Andrews, D. A. 2004. The importance of staff practice in delivering effective correctional treatment: A meta-analytic review of core correctional practice. *International Journal of Offender Therapy and Comparative Criminology*, 48: 203–214.

Duwe, G. 2013. What's inside the "black box"? The importance of "gray box" evaluations for the "what works" movement. *Criminology & Public Policy*, 12: 145–152.

Duwe, G. 2014. The development, validity, and reliability of the Minnesota screening tool assessing recidivism risk (MnSTARR). *Criminal Justice Policy Review*, 25: 579–613.

Garland, B., Wodahl, E. J., and Mayfield, J. 2011. Prisoner reentry in a small metropolitan community: Obstacles and policy recommendations. *Criminal Justice Policy Review*, 22: 90–110.

Gearing, R. E., El-Bassel, N., Chesquiere, A., Baldwin, S., Gillies, J., and Ngeow, E. 2011. Major ingredients of fidelity: A review and scientific guide to improving the quality of intervention research implementation. *Clinical Psychology Review*, 31: 79–88.

Geis, S. V., Gainey, R., Cohen, M. I., Healy, E., Duplantier, D., Yeide, M., ... Hopps, M. 2012. *Monitoring high-risk sex offenders with GPS technology: An evaluation of the California supervision program: Final report*. Bethesda, MD: Development Services Group.

Gendreau, P. 1996. Offender rehabilitation: What we know and what needs to be done. *Criminal Justice and Behavior*, 23: 144–161.

Gendreau, P., and Andrews, D. A. 1996. *Correctional program assessment inventory* (CPAI), 6th edn. New Brunswick, Canada: University of New Brunswick.

Gendreau, P., and Andrews, D. 2001. *Correctional program assessment inventory* (CPAI-2000). New Brunswick, Canada: University of New Brunswick.

Gendreau, P., Andrews, D. A., and Thériault, Y. L. 2010. *Correctional program assessment inventory* (CPAI-2010). New Brunswick, Canada: University of New Brunswick.

Glaze, L. E., and Herberman, E. J. 2013. *Correctional populations in the United States, 2012*. Washington, DC: US Department of Justice, Office of Justice Programs, Bureau of Justice Statistics.

Grommon, E. 2013. *Prisoner reentry programs: Penetrating the black box for better theory and practice*. El Paso, TX: LFB Scholarly Publishing.

Grommon, E., Davidson, W. S., and Bynum, T. S. 2013. A randomized trial of a multimodal community-based prisoner reentry program emphasizing substance abuse treatment. *Journal of Offender Rehabilitation*, 52: 287–309.

Grommon, E., and Rydberg, J. 2013. Managing the reentry transition with substance use propensities: Insights from a sample of parolees in a small, industrialized midwestern city. In *Offender reentry in the 21st century: Rethinking criminology and criminal justice*, edited by J. Smykla and M. Crow, 271–298. Sudbury, MA: Jones and Bartlett Learning.

Grommon, E., Rydberg, J., and Bynum, T. S. 2012. *Understanding the challenges facing offenders upon their return to the community: Final report*. East Lansing, MI: Michigan Justice Statistics Center.

Hamilton, Z., and Campbell, C. 2014. Uncommonly observed: Evaluation of the New Jersey halfway house system. *Criminal Justice and Behavior*, 41: 1354–1375.

Hanson, R. K., and Nicholaichuk, T. 2000. A cautionary note regarding Nicholaichuck et al. 2000. *Sexual Abuse: A Journal of Research and Treatment*, 12: 289–293.

Harding, D. J., Morenoff, J. D., and Herbert, C. W. 2013. Home is hard to find: Neighborhoods, institutions, and residential trajectories of returning prisoners. *Annals of the American Academy of Political and Social Science*, 647: 214–236.

Harding, D. J., Wyse, J. B., Dobson, C., and Morenoff, J. D. 2014. Making ends meet after prison. *Journal of Policy Analysis and Management*, 33: 440–470.

Hepburn, J. R. 2013. Get dirty. *Western Criminology Review*, 14: 1–5.

Hockenberry, S. 2013. *Juveniles in residential placement*. Washington, DC: US Department of Justice, Office of Justice Programs, Office of Juvenile Justice and Delinquency Prevention.

Kurlychek, M., Bushway, S. D., and Brame, R. 2012. Long-term crime desistance and recidivism patterns – Evidence from the Essex County convicted felon study. *Criminology*, 50: 71–103.

Langan, P. A., and Levin, D. J. 2002. Recidivism of prisoners released in 1994. *Federal Sentencing Reporter*, 15: 58–65.

Latessa, E. 2012. Why work is important, and how to improve the effectiveness of correctional reentry programs that target employment. *Criminology & Public Policy*, 11: 87–91.

Latessa, E. J., and Lowenkamp, C. 2006. What works in reducing recidivism. *University of St. Thomas Law Journal*, 3: 521–535.

Lin, J. 2010. Parole revocation in the era of mass incarceration. *Sociology Compass*, 4: 999–1010.

Lin, J., Gratted, R., and Petersilia, J. 2012. Justice by other means: Venue sorting in parole revocation. *Law & Policy*, 34: 349–372.

Lipsey, M. W. 2014. Interventions for juvenile offenders: A serendipitous journey. *Criminology & Public Policy*, 13: 1–14.

Lipsey, M. W., and Cullen, F. T. 2007. The effectiveness of correctional rehabilitation: A review of systematic reviews. *Annual Review of Law and Social Science*, 3: 297–320.

Livsey, S. 2012. *Juvenile delinquency probation caseload, 2009*. Washington, DC: US Department of Justice, Office of Justice Programs, Office of Juvenile Justice and Delinquency Prevention.

Lösel, F. 1995. The efficacy of correctional treatment: A review and synthesis of meta-evaluations. In *What works: Reducing reoffending: Guidelines from practice and research*, edited by J. McGuire, 79–111. Chichester, UK: John Wiley & Sons, Ltd.

Long, J. S. 1997. *Regression models for categorical and limited dependent variables*. Thousand Oaks, CA: Sage.

Maltz, M. D. 1984. *Recidivism*. Orlando, FL: Academic Press.

Marques, J. K., Wiederanders, M., Day, D. M., Nelson, C., and van Ommeren, A. 2005. Effects of a relapse prevention program on sexual recidivism: Final results from California's sex offender treatment and evaluation project (SOTEP). *Sexual Abuse: A Journal of Research and Treatment*, 17: 79–107.

Mumola, C. J., and Karberg, J. 2006. *Drug use and dependence, state and federal prisoners, 2004*. Washington, DC: US Department of Justice, Office of Justice Programs, Bureau of Justice Statistics.

Nelson, M., Deess, P., and Allen, C. 1999. *The first month out: Post-incarceration experiences in New York City*. New York: Vera Institute of Justice.

Nicholaichuk, T., Gordon, A., Gu, D., and Wong, S. 2000. Outcome of an institutional sex offender treatment program: A comparison between treated and matched untreated offenders. *Sexual Abuse: A Journal of Research and Treatment*, 12: 139–153.

Olver, M. E., Wong, S. C. P., and Nicholaichuk, T. P. 2009. Outcome evaluation of a high-intensity inpatient sex offender treatment program. *Journal of Interpersonal Violence*, 24: 522–536.

Ostermann, M. 2013. Active supervision and its impact upon parolee recidivism rates. *Crime & Delinquency*, 59: 487–509.

Pager, D. 2007. *Marked: Race, crime, and finding work in an era of mass incarceration*. Chicago, IL: University of Chicago Press.

Palmer, T. 1992. *The re-emergence of correctional intervention*. Newbury Park, CA: Sage.

Petersilia, J. 2004. What works in prisoner reentry? Reviewing and questioning the evidence. *Federal Probation*, 68: 4–8.

Piquero, A. R. 2004. Somewhere between persistence and desistance: The intermittency of criminal careers. In *After crime and punishment: Pathways to offender reintegration*, edited by S. Maruna and R. Immarigeon, 102–125. Cullompton, UK: Willan.

Rhine, E. E., Mawhorr, T. L., and Parks, E. C. 2006. Implementation: The bane of effective correctional programs. *Criminology & Public Policy*, 5: 347–357.

Rhodes, W. 2011. Predicting criminal recidivism: A research note. *Journal of Experimental Criminology*, 7: 57–71.

Roman, J. K., and Visher, C. 2009. Prisoner reentry programming. In *Investing in the disadvantaged: Assessing the benefits and costs of social polices*, edited by D. L. Weimer and A. R. Vining, 127–150. Washington, DC: Georgetown University Press.

Rossi, P., Lipsey, M. W., and Freeman, H. E. 2004. *Evaluation: A systematic approach*, 7th edn. Thousand Oaks, CA: Sage.

Rossman, S. B., and Roman, C. G. 2003. Case managed reentry and employment: Lessons from the opportunity to succeed program. *Justice Research and Policy*, 5: 75–100.

Rudes, D. S., Lerch, J., and Taxman, F. S. 2011. Implementing a reentry framework at a correctional facility: Challenges to the culture. *Journal of Offender Rehabilitation*, 50: 467–491.

Rydberg, J., Grommon, E., and Bynum, T. S. 2013. *Risk of recidivism facing offenders upon their return to the community*. East Lansing, MI: Michigan Justice Statistics Center.

Sampson, R. J., Winship, C., and Knight, C. 2013. Translating causal claims: Principles and strategies for policy-relevant criminology. *Criminology & Public Policy*, 12: 587–616.

Sellin, T. 1931. The basis of a crime index. *Journal of Criminal Law and Criminology*, 22: 335–356.

Shadish, W., R., Cook, T. D., and Campbell, D. T. 2002. *Experimental and quasi-experimental designs for generalized causal inference*. Boston, MA: Houghton Mifflin.

Smith, P., Gendreau, P., and Swartz, K. 2009. Validating the principles of effective intervention: A systematic review of the contribution of meta-analysis in the field of corrections. *Victims & Offenders*, 4: 148–169.

Spiropoulos, G. V., Salisbury, E. J., and Van Voorhis, P. 2014. Moderators of correctional treatment success: An exploratory study of racial differences. *International Journal of Offender Therapy and Comparative Criminology*, 58: 835–860.

Tableman, M., and Kim, J. S. 2004. *Survival analysis using S: Analysis of time-to-event data*. Boca Raton, FL: Chapman and Hall.

Travis, J. 2005. *But they all come back: Facing the challenges of prisoner reentry*. Washington, DC: Urban Institute Press.

Visher, C. A., Baer, D., and Naser, R. 2006. *Ohio prisoner's reflections on returning home*. Washington, DC: Urban Institute.

Visher, C. A., and Travis, J. 2003. Transitions from prison to community: Understanding individual pathways. *Annual Review of Sociology*, 29: 89–113.

Ward, T., Melser, J., and Yates, P. M. 2007. Reconstructing the risk–need–responsivity model: A theoretical elaboration and evaluation. *Aggression and Violent Behavior*, 12: 208–228.

Werth, R. J. 2012. I do what I'm told, sort of: Reformed subjects, unruly citizens, and parole. *Theoretical Criminology*, 16: 329–346.

Wilson, J. A., and Davis, R. C. 2006. Good intentions meet hard realities: An evaluation of the Project Greenlight reentry program. *Criminology & Public Policy*, 5: 303–338.

Further Reading

Bernfeld, G. A., Farrington, D. P., and Leschied, A. W., eds. 2001. *Offender rehabilitation in practice: Implementing and evaluating effective programs*. New York: John Wiley & Sons.

Gendreau, P., Goggin, C., and Smith, P. 1999. The forgotten issue in effective correctional treatment: Program implementation. *International Journal of Offender Therapy and Comparative Criminology*, 43: 180–187.

Mallik-Kane, K., and Visher, C. A. 2008. *Health and prisoner reentry: How physical, mental, and substance abuse conditions shape the process of reintegration*. Washington, DC: The Urban Institute, Justice Policy Center.

Matthews, B., Hubbard, D. J., and Latessa, E. 2001. Making the next step: Using evaluability assessment to improve correctional programming. *The Prison Journal*, 81: 454–472.

Petrosino, A., and Soydan, H. 2005. The impact of program developers as evaluators on criminal recidivism: Results from meta-analyses of experimental and quasi-experimental research. *Journal of Experimental Criminology*, 1: 435–450.

Smith, P., and Schweitzer, M. 2012. The therapeutic prison. *Journal of Contemporary Criminal Justice*, 28: 7–22.

17

How Theory Guides Measurement: Public Attitudes toward Crime and Policing

Jonathan Jackson and Jouni Kuha

The fact that many of the concepts in the social sciences are unobservable creates a number of problems for researchers. How do we know that something exists if we cannot observe it directly? If a concept is defined in different ways, how do you know which one is somehow "correct," and whether our measurement tools adequately reflect (or form) the particular definition at hand?

In this chapter we discuss some fundamental links between theory and measurement. Our overarching goal is to illustrate how conceptual and theoretical positions guide measurement. Moving, section by section, from an account of a central construct to an account of plausible predictors, then to a fully overarching theoretical framework, we consider how theory shapes the operationalization process. We use fear of crime and public attitudes toward the police as two substantive examples.

We also discuss the use of formative and reflective approaches to measurement (see also Spearman, 1904; Moustaki and Knott, 2000; Edwards and Bagozzi, 2000; Borsboom, Mellenbergh, and Van Heerden, 2003, 2004; Howell, Breivik, and Wilcox, 2007). Our empirical applications demonstrate not only some pragmatic considerations related to forming indices, but also how latent variable modeling can provide insight into the underlying structure of the data. We finish with the observation that latent variable modeling cannot bridge the fundamental gap between an unobservable construct and its empirical referents.

The Handbook of Measurement Issues in Criminology and Criminal Justice, First Edition.
Edited by Beth M. Huebner and Timothy S. Bynum.

Organization of the Chapter

The chapter falls into four sections. By way of scene-setting, the first section summarizes some trends and trajectories in public attitudes from 1980 to the present day. Précising three *Public Opinion Quarterly* papers (Shaw et al., 1998; Shaw and Brannan, 2009; Ramirez, 2013), we discuss (1) trends in public opinion over the past 30 or so years in the United States and (2) how attitudes toward crime and policing have been measured in national US polls.

The next section then turns to the first substantive example, fear of crime, using data from the European Social Survey (ESS). We discuss how theory about the central construct guided the design of new measures and we demonstrate two different strategies for scaling the resulting data. One is a formative or pragmatic approach based on local rules and judgments; the other is a reflective or representational approach that uses latent variable modeling. Generating a categorial index of worry about crime through a combination of these two different approaches to measurement, we show that theoretically informed measures produce lower national estimates of fear of crime in many of the countries of Round 3 of the ESS – at least by comparison with the sort of single indicator that is popular in national opinion polls.

In the third section we stay with the example of fear of crime, but this time we illustrate the utility of theory in a slightly different way. Using data from another multicountry European survey, we "tweak" an existing categorial index of fear of crime (Gray, Jackson, and Farrall, 2011) in order to better identify a qualitative "type" of fear of crime that theory would predict. Extending the measurement scheme to include a type of chronic and persistent worry about future victimization, we show that the perception of risk and the need for cognitive closure are strong predictors of this particular category of emotional experience.

In the final section we turn to public attitudes toward the police. We consider how an integrative theoretical framework makes key conceptual distinctions; how the theoretical framework broadens the explanatory focus of the research; and how it posits specific empirical relationships between constructs. Applying Tyler's procedural justice theory (Tyler and Huo, 2002; Sunshine and Tyler, 2003; Tyler, 2006a, 2006b) to data from a national probability survey of England and Wales, we link prior contact with the police to trust in the police, to perceptions of police legitimacy, and finally to people's willingness to cooperate with legal authorities. Of specific methodological interest are the conceptual and operational distinction between trust and legitimacy, the use of confirmatory factor analysis to assess the dimensionality of the data, and what latent variable modeling can and cannot do when addressing concepts and measures.

Trends and Trajectories in US Public Opinion

National opinion polls highlight not only how public attitudes have changed over time, but also how they have been variously defined and measured over the years. In a review of national opinion polls, Shaw et al. (1998) examined whether public attitudes toward crime, police, and civil liberties changed between 1980 and 1997. Stable majority support for "get tough" approaches to crime was evident. Gallup polls between 1984 and 1996 asked respondents whether the overall level of public funding for law enforcement is "too little," "about right," or "too much." In each of the 11 polls, somewhere between 50 percent and 60 percent of respondents said "too little" (note: all percentages given in this section are weighted to reflect the national adult population of the United States).

When asked how much confidence they have in the police, more than half of respondents in polls between 1981 and 1997 said "a great deal" or "quite a lot," with a small positive upward trend in public opinion over time. Interestingly, polls also suggested that people distinguish between (1) fighting crime when evaluating the police and (2) what Shaw et al. (1998, p. 407) rather dismissively call "the by-products of competent policing: officers being friendly, responding quickly to calls for help, and not using excessive force." Polls also asked citizens about the potential trade-off between security and freedom, and the picture that emerged was both complex and sensitive to question-wording. When asked: "How concerned are you that new measures enacted to fight terrorism in this country may end up restricting some of our civil liberties?" 70 percent reported being "concerned" and 28 percent reported being "not concerned." In the same poll 57 percent said they were "willing" in response to the question: "Would you be willing to give up some civil liberties if that were necessary to curb terrorism in this country, or not?"

In a later review paper, Shaw and Brannan (2009) considered trends in public confidence in law enhancement between the late 1990s and 2007. They reviewed opinion polls in which people were asked about their confidence in the ability of the police to protect "them" from violent crime, to prevent crime in their community, to solve crime in their community, to be helpful and friendly, to treat people fairly, to not use excessive force, to tell the truth, and so forth. Respondents were also asked whether they thought of the police as friends or enemies, whether they were afraid that the police would stop and arrest them when they were completely innocent, whether the police used brutality against blacks and Hispanics in their community, and whether racial profiling was widespread.

On some indicators public opinion improved slightly during this period. Between 2000 and 2005 the proportion of people who thought that different minority groups received equally fair treatment as whites increased somewhat. On other indicators public opinion stayed relatively stable. When asked in 1999 whether the local police department was doing an excellent job, a good job, or a fair job, 23 percent said "excellent" and 51 percent said "good"; in 2006, 22 percent said "excellent" and 46 percent said "good."

In Ramirez's (2013) review of polls between 1994 and 2013, the focus was on public attitudes toward crime and punishment. A complex picture emerged regarding attitudes toward crime. When asked: "Is there more crime in the United States than there was a year ago, or less?" 71 percent said "more" in 1996, by comparison to 41 percent in 2001. After that the figures went up again (62 percent in 2002 and 68 percent in 2011), possibly because of what Ramirez (2013, p. 1007) calls a potential "spillover from the terrorist attacks on November 11, 2001." A similar pattern was found in perceptions of local crime, although the four respective figures were lower, namely 46 percent (1996), 26 percent (2001), 37 percent (2002), and 48 percent (2011).

Trends in public attitudes toward punishment indicated a clear and consistent decrease, over time, in levels of public punitiveness. When asked: "Are you in favor of the death penalty for a person convicted of murder?" 80 percent said "favor" in 1994 and 63 percent said "favor" in 2012. When asked: "In general, do you think that the courts in this area deal too harshly or not harshly enough with criminals?" 85 percent said "not harshly enough" in 1994 and 62 percent said "not harshly enough" in 2012. Interestingly, the author concludes: "Overall, these data illustrate that leaders now have the opportunity to move policy in a less punitive direction" (Ramirez, 2013, p. 1006).

How Theory Guides Measurement: The Value of Concept Clarification

The opinion polls reviewed by Shaw et al. (1998), Shaw and Brannan (2009), and Ramirez (2013) provide important time-series data. They also give us some useful insights into how public attitudes have been defined and measured over time. But, looking across the various opinion polls, one is left with the impression that the measures are rather vague and unstructured.

This is understandable; polls are there to get headline figures. In the rest of the chapter we consider how theory can help to produce more precise and comprehensive measurement schemes. We start with fear of crime.

Defining and measuring fear of crime

The study of fear of crime has produced a rich and interdisciplinary literature on the nature, antecedents, and consequences of people's feelings, thoughts, and behaviors regarding victimization risk (for reviews, see Hale, 1996; Farrall, Jackson, and Gray, 2009; Lorenc et al., 2012). Important contributions have come from criminology (e.g., Fisher and Sloan, 2003; Cops and Pleysier, 2011; Cook and Fox, 2012), sociology (e.g., Innes, 2004; Hawdon et al., 2013), geography (e.g., Bromley and Stacey, 2012), public health (e.g., Stafford, Chandola, and Marmot, 2007; Shinew et al., 2013), feminism (e.g., Rader and Cossman, 2011; Hollander, 2001) and urban studies (e.g., Pain, 2001).

Yet debate continues on how best to measure the central emotional aspect of "fear of crime." One concern is whether standard measures adequately capture everyday emotional experience (e.g., Farrall et al., 1997; Gray, Jackson, and Farrall, 2008; Yang and Hinkle, 2012; Hinkle, 2014). Consider two of the measures reported by Ramirez (2013). One is: "I'm going to read a list of problems facing the country. For each one, please tell me if you personally worry about this problem a great deal, a fair amount, only a little, or not at all. How much do you personally worry about crime and violence?" The other is: "Is there any area near where you live – that is, within a mile – where you would be afraid to walk alone at night?" What exactly are these measures measuring?

How might you answer the first question? If you were to answer, for example, that you worried "a great deal" about crime and violence, would this be because you worried about becoming a victim yourself? Are you worried about the state of society? Is it a bit of both? If you do worry about yourself falling victim, what does "a great deal" mean in terms of frequency, intensity, or impact of your emotional responses to the environment and risk? Do you worry frequently? Is the intensity of the emotion high when you do worry? Does the worry have a serious effect on your well-being?

These questions are important. There is value in precision: we want answers to survey questions to be readily interpretable, and we want respondents to interpret the wording in comparable ways. But there is also prior criminological work that suggests (1) that fear of crime comprises both the lived, affective experience of crime threat and a more diffuse and value-expressive phenomenon (Girling, Loader, and Sparks, 2000; Farrall et al., 2009); and (2) that measures of fear of crime struggle to differentiate between these two aspects (Gray et al., 2011).

In an exploration of these two issues, Farrall et al. (2009) found that a good proportion of respondents of the British Crime Survey who said they were "very" or "fairly" worried also reported that they had not worried even once over the past 12 months. Actual and recallable moments of fear or worry were rare, and a good proportion of those individuals who reported some overall intensity of worry were not being able to recall a single instance when their emotions surfaced. Yet these people (who said they were worried about crime but could not recall having worried recently) perceived a lack of order and cohesion in their neighborhood and were concerned about the pace and direction of social change in society. In such instances, diffuse anxiety and a set of value-expressive attitudes regarding the state of society may be better descriptors than worry about falling victim of crime, if by "worry" we mean what Berenbaum (2010, p. 963) defines as "repetitive thoughts that also have all three of the following characteristics: (1) the repetitive thoughts concern an uncertain future outcome; (2) the uncertain outcome about which the person is thinking is considered undesirable; and (3) the subjective experience of having such thoughts is unpleasant."

Concerns about the precision of many criminological indicators partly drove the development of new measures of worry about victimization in the ESS. First fielded in Round 3 of the ESS, these four new measures allow us to assess the link between the frequency and impact of worry about burglary and violent crime:

1. "How often, if at all, do you worry about your home being burgled?" with the response options "All or most of the time," "Some of the time," "Just occasionally," and "Never."

2. (If the answer to the first question was other than "Never":) "Does this worry about your home being burgled have:
   - a serious effect on the quality of your life;
   - some effect;
   - or no real effect on the quality of your life?

3–4. Two more questions with similar wording, but with "your home being burgled" replaced by "becoming a victim of violent crime."

Why might it be helpful to ask survey respondents about the frequency and impact of their worries? One reason is that worry can have both positive and negative effects. Psychological research shows that it can motivate behavior that has positive consequences in the eyes of individuals (Gladstone and Parker, 2003). In a study of the phenomenology of "normal" worry, for instance, Tallis, Davey, and Capuzzo (1994) found that, when thinking about their general life concerns, many individuals considered worry to be a routine and mostly acceptable activity, which occurred more or less daily, was addressed to various issues, and transpired mostly in the form of thoughts with a narrative course. Worry was typically associated with real-life triggers, was both present and future-orientated, and was focused upon problems that were real or plausible rather than imaginary or remote. Worry was also seen by research participants to have clear benefits as an incentive, by stimulating them into action. That the majority of participants in that study perceived worrying as a problem-solving activity suggests that the worrying process helps some people cope with an uncertain future by making them avoid negative possible events.

Functional properties of fear of crime have been highlighted in the criminological literature. In agreement with the ways in which worry can positively motivate, Jackson and Gray (2010) found that a significant minority of individuals who claimed to be worried about crime also reported that they took precautions, which made them feel safer, and that neither their precautions nor their worries about crime affected their quality of life. In such circumstances worry might be best viewed as a functional defense against crime, because it motivates socially beneficial behavior – something that allows individuals to exert control over perceived risks and stimulates them into action – rather than being an inherently negative feeling that erodes quality of life.

Yet worry is not always functional. Frequent worry can damage well-being, and Tallis et al.'s (1994) study shows a range of deleterious cognitive (e.g., pessimism, problem exaggeration) and affective (e.g., emotional discomfort, depression) consequences to worry. Here are some of the features displayed by "high" worriers: more frequent (at least daily) episodes of worry; greater difficulty to stop worrying; rebounding worries; and mood disturbance and perceived impairment in everyday functioning. "High" worriers also reported greater indecision and doubt when worrying, and they were more likely to perceive worry as having a negative effect on their health. Indeed, in Jackson and Gray's (2010) study, 20 percent of the sample fell into the dysfunctional category (compared to 8 percent in the functional category). Having been a victim of crime in the past 12 months was a strong predictor of dysfunctional worry, but not of functional worry.

The ESS measures were designed in part to avoid prior ambiguities in measurement schemes. By asking people how often they worry about being burgled or about being a victim of violent crime and whether their worry (if they worry at all) has an impact on their quality of life, one can for instance isolate those people who worry occasionally but do not believe that this has any real effect on their well-being from those people who worry occasionally but do believe that their well-being is thereby reduced.

Creating a single categorial measure by exploring the structure of the data

What do we find when these measures are fielded? Weighted percentages using each of the single survey questions in the total sample of 43,000 respondents from 23 countries can be found in Jackson and Kuha (2014, pp. 112–113). One can also scale the four items into a single index. Combining the four measures into a single index is convenient for subsequent analysis, of course, but in the process of assessing the scaling properties one can also gain insight into the links between frequency and impact of worry.

One approach to index construction is to do it "by hand," using pragmatic considerations. One might decide a priori on the number of different categories of worry about victimization, and then use logic and reasoning to assign which cell in the four-way cross-tabulation in Table 17.1 translates into which category. In this example we have decided, for the sake of illustration, that there are four categories, where 1 indicates people who never worry about burglary and violence, 2 indicates relatively infrequent worry that does not have a particular serious impact on quality of life, 3 indicates more frequent worry that has a moderate impact, and 4 indicates frequent worry that has a serious impact.

We have done this via logical rules regarding the sensible combination of these measures. This is a formative approach to measurement. We do not assume that the unobservable psychological construct is causally related to the measures. We assume instead that the measures constitute the phenomenon. In this instance our scoring dimensions are, in essence, defining key aspects of the construct. The researcher is guided by the data, of course, but the researcher is the one who ultimately makes the decision about how to combine the items to construct the index.

A second approach would be to fit a statistical model – typically, some variant of latent variable modeling – to guide the scoring. One models the intercorrelations among the items in order to draw some empirically founded conclusions about the underlying structure of the data, and thus about how the items can be combined. The statistical technique also allows one to assess the relative fit of models that specify different numbers of categories. To analyze the current data, we used latent class analysis, which specifies a categorial latent variable; we calculated predicted values of the latent variable in order to assign scores to individuals; and, after deriving model-based classifications from the latent class model, we adjusted some

Table 17.1 Classifying responses to four questions on worry about crime into six classes.

Worry about violent crime		*Worry about burglary (Frequency / Effect on quality of life)*									
		Never	*Just occasionally*			*Some of the time*			*All or most of the time*		
Frequency	*Effect*	*None*	*None*	*Some*	*Serious*	*None*	*Some*	*Serious*	*None*	*Some*	*Serious*
Never	*None*	1	1	2	2	2	2	2	2	3	3
Just	*None*	1	1	2	2	2	2	2	2	3	3
occasionally	*Some*	2	2	3	3	3	3	3	3	3	3
	Serious	2	2	3	3	4	4	4	4	4	4
Some of	*None*	2	2	3	3	3	4	4	3	4	4
the time	*Some*	2	2	3	3	3	4	4	3	4	4
	Serious	2	2	4	4	3	4	4	4	4	4
All or most	*None*	2	2	3	3	3	4	4	3	4	4
of the time	*Some*	2	2	4	4	3	4	4	4	4	4
	Serious	2	2	4	4	4	4	4	4	4	4

of the initial classifications "by hand," so as to produce a more logical scoring pattern (for full details, see Jackson and Kuha, 2014).

In the formative example given in Table 17.1 we chose four categories "by hand." But what emerged from our latent class-modeling (Table 6 in Jackson and Kuha, 2014, p. 119) was a solution with six latent classes that had the best balance of model fit and the interpretability of the classifications derived from the model. Importantly, the latent variable model placed constraints; it guided the classification scheme that we produced on the basis of the empirical relationships between the individual items.

We then assigned each cell in the four-way cross-tabulation (Figure 17.1) to one of the six categories. Class 1 corresponds to those who are not worried about crime or worry only occasionally and do not believe that these worries affect their quality of life. Class 2 corresponds to those who worry only about burglary, and class 3 to

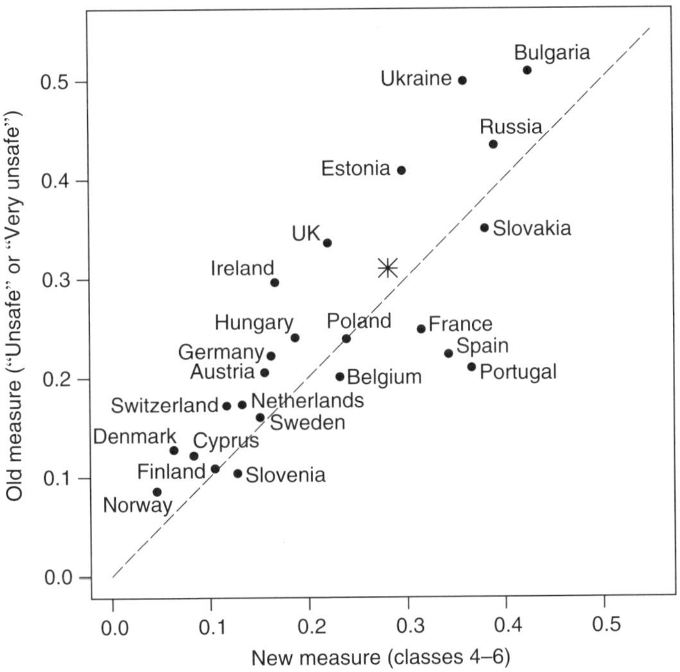

Figure 17.1 Estimated proportions of levels of fear of crime in each of 23 European countries. *Source*: ESS Round 3, 2006. The figure is based on four new survey questions, assigned as shown in Table 6 in Jackson and Kuha (2014, p. 119) and on a question related to perceived safety: "How safe do you feel walking alone in this area after dark?"

The estimates are for the combined proportions of classes 4–6 of the new measures and the two highest levels of the perceived safety measure. The star shows these proportions estimated for the combined populations of the countries. Country-level proportions have been estimated using both sampling weights and population size weights. The straight line in the plot shows where the two proportions are equal.

those who worry only about violent crime. Classes 4–6 correspond to increasing frequency and impact of worry about both types of crime. Each individual with that scoring pattern gets that score on the single index. Note that substantive insight into the phenomenon emerged from the latent class-modeling. It seems that there is a strong link between frequency and impact, and small proportions of various populations worry only occasionally about one crime or the other, without its having much impact on quality of life.

Using the new measures to estimate levels of fear of crime

One can then use the new index to estimate appropriate cross-national variation. Pooling data from the 23 countries, we estimated levels of worry about crime across Europe (for full details, see Jackson and Kuha, 2014). We found that 59 percent of citizens were unworried, 13 percent worried occasionally, only about burglary or only about violent crime, 20 percent had some moderate level of worry, 3 percent a fairly high level of worry, and 5 percent a very high level of worry. There were, however, clear differences in levels of worry between countries. Small Northern European countries had the lowest levels of worry about crime. Southern and Eastern European countries had the highest levels of worry about crime, and countries like Germany, the United Kingdom, and the Netherlands were in the middle of the tables. The range of the differences was quite dramatic. For example, the proportion of individuals with moderate to very high levels of worry was 4 percent in Norway but 43 percent in Bulgaria.

Recall, however, that the measures were designed to be more precise about capturing the lived experience of fear of crime. An interesting comparison can thus be made with the help of the single question about perceived personal safety that was fielded in Round 3 of the ESS in the form (a question similar to the one from Gallop polls, mentioned earlier): "How safe do you – or would you – feel walking alone in this area after dark?" One might hypothesize that the new measures would produce lower estimates of fear of crime, partly because they focus more precisely on negative emotional experience (for critiques of perceived safety questions, see Hale, 1996).

Figure 17.1 plots country-level estimates of the proportion of individuals in classes 4–6, derived from the new measures, against the proportion of those who feel unsafe or very unsafe walking alone after dark. Each of these proportions might be used as a measure of how many individuals are substantially worried about crime. We can see from Figure 17.1 that the two questions give a broadly similar but not identical picture of cross-national differences, in that the ordering of countries is roughly similar according to both measures. But there are also some clear differences. For example, the level of worry in France, Spain and Portugal is substantially higher than in the United Kingdom (and higher than the European average) according to the new measures, but clearly lower according to the perceived safety measure. There are also differences in the magnitude of the estimated proportions:

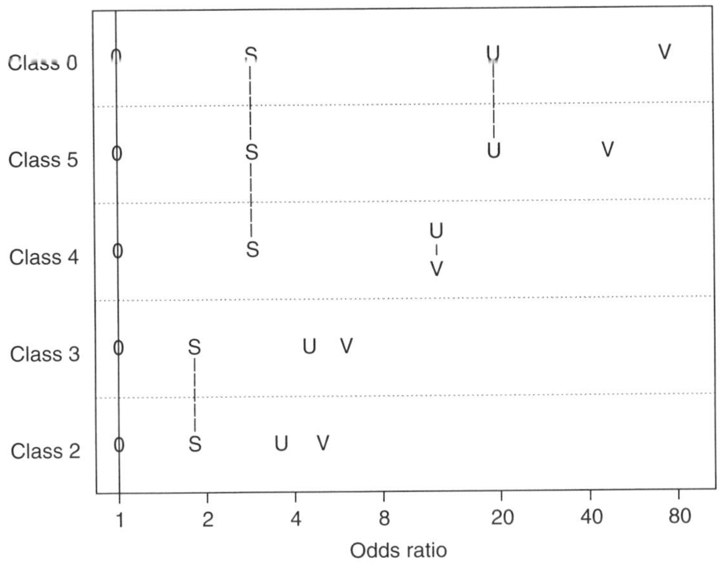

Figure 17.2 Estimated coefficients in the multinomial logistic model for responses to a perceived-safety question on fear of crime ("How safe do you feel walking alone in this area after dark?"), given six classes of fear of crime. *Source*: ESS Round 3, 2006, pooled data for 23 countries. The figure is based on four survey questions assigned as shown in Table 6 in Jackson and Kuha (2014, p. 119).

The symbols in the plot show the coefficients of dummy variables for classes 2–6 of the standard perceived safety measure in this model, for different levels of the perceived safety measure (V = very unsafe, U = unsafe, S = safe) by comparison to the reference level (O = very safe). The fitted model includes the respondent's country as an explanatory variable.

in most cases these are substantially higher for the perceived safety question, the clearest exception being the Mediterranean countries.

A second way of comparing the measures is to consider the odds of falling into each of the perceived safety categories, which is conditional upon the category into which one's worry about crime falls. Figure 17.2 examines the individual-level association between the two measures in more detail. This is a version of the odds ratio plot proposed by Long (1997; see also Long and Freese, 2006). First we fitted a multinomial logistic regression model (see, e.g., Agresti, 2002) where the perceived safety question was the response variable and the new measure (and the country of respondent) was a categorial explanatory variable. The symbols in Figure 17.3 show the values, in this model, of the estimated exponentiated coefficients of the dummy variables of classes 2–6 of the new measure (thus class 1 is used as a reference class). For example, the S in the bottom row corresponds to the coefficient of the dummy variable for class 2 in the model for feeling "safe" (rather than "very safe"). It is thus the log odds ratio of "safe" versus "very safe" when we compare new classes 2 and 1 against each other. Its estimated value is 0.599, which corresponds to an odds ratio of 1.82.

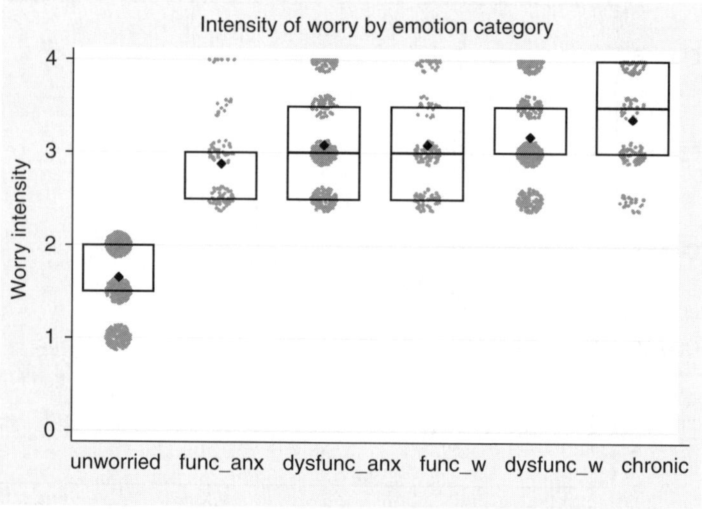

Figure 17.3 Jittered boxplot showing average of intensity of worry about street robbery and burglary (mean of two items ranging from 1 to 4) plotted against membership of the new categorial measure. *Source*: National probability sample survey of adults in Italy, Bulgaria, and Lithuania.

n = 2,490 (n = 502, 1,007 and 981 respectively). The new measure takes six categories (see Table 17.2), where "unworried" means just that, "func_anx" means functionally anxious, "dysfunc_anx" means dysfunctionally anxious, "func_w" means functionally worried, "dysfunc_w" means dysfunctional worry, and "chronic" means persistent and chronic worry. The boxes provide 25%, 50%, and 75 % interquartile points for the intensity of worry scale (when there are only two lines, this means that there were only two unique values for the 25%, 50%, and 75% interquartile points). The large dot indicates the mean. Analysis was conducted on the pooled sample.

In the model summarized in Figure 17.2, some parameters are actually constrained to be equal to each other. These constraints, indicated by the vertical dashed lines in the plot, were arrived at after the initial examination of an unconstrained model, the difference between the constrained and the unconstrained model being statistically not significant. The constrained results help to provide a parsimonious description of the associations between the new and the perceived safety measures of fear of crime. First, all of the odds ratios are greater than 1, which means that, when compared to class 1, members of all other classes are more likely to give "more worried" responses than "very safe." Second, classes 2 (burglary only) and 3 (violence only) do not differ from each other in the chances of responding "safe" (rather than "very safe"), but the more worried responses "unsafe," and "very unsafe" are more likely to occur in class 3 – which suggests, unsurprisingly, that feeling unsafe in the streets is more strongly associated with worrying about violence than with worrying about burglary. Then, by comparison to classes 1–3, class 4 has higher odds of all the responses other than "very safe," but it does not distinguish between the two most worried responses. Moreover, classes 5 and 6 do not differ from class 4 in the odds of "safe," but individuals in them are more likely to respond "unsafe" and "very unsafe" than those in class 4. Finally, classes 5 and 6 differ from each other only in the probability of the most worried response, "very unsafe," which is highest in class 6.

The picture, overall, is one where the probabilities of worried responses to the perceived safety question generally increase toward new classes that are more highly numbered, but where some contrasts between pairs of new classes are predictive of distinctions between only some levels of the perceived safety measure. Therefore it may be that the new index allows us to identify more finely tuned gradations in the everyday experience of worry about crime. Theory regarding the nature of the central construct may have helped to generate more precise measures of everyday negative emotional experience.

How Theory Guides Measurement: The Role of Process Clarification

In the present section we turn to a categorial index of fear of crime that is also based on qualitative distinctions between different types of emotional experience. We show how theory about the construct and its plausible predictors can guide measurement.

We build upon Gray et al.'s (2011) formative categorization scheme, which turned on two key distinctions. The first is between worry and anxiety. The second is between productive and counterproductive effects of worry on behavior and well-being. Residents of seven London neighborhoods were asked (1) about the frequency and intensity of their worry, (2) whether they took precautions against crime, and (3) whether their quality of life was reduced as a result of their worries or precautions. Answers to these questions were then combined through simple rules (see the paper for full detail), and this operation created five categories of emotional experience:

1. unworried (not worried about crime);
2. functional anxiety (the participant reports being worried according to intensity measures, but cannot recall having worried over the past year; the participant also reports that worries and precautions do not reduce his or her quality of life);
3. dysfunctional anxiety (the participant reports being worried according to intensity measures, but cannot recall having worried over the past year; the participant also reports that worries or precautions, or both, reduce his or her quality of life);
4. functional worry (the participant reports being worried according to intensity measures and has worried at least once over the past year; the participant also reports that worries and precautions do not reduce his or her quality of life);
5. dysfunctional worry (the participant reports being worried according to intensity measures and has worried at least once over the past year; the participant also reports that worries or precautions, or both, reduce his or her quality of life).

In the current analysis we attempt to extend this formative categorization scheme in the light of prior theory about plausible predictors of emotional experience. Our data come from a nationally representative survey of adults in Italy, Bulgaria, and Lithuania, conducted between October and November 2010 as part of a project funded by the European Commission under the 7th Framework Programme entitled Euro-Justis.

We focus on risk perception and on the need for cognitive closure as plausible predictors. Following prior research, we define risk perception as perceptions of the likelihood and controllability of the event, as well as perceptions of the impact of the event, if it were to occur (Acuña-Rivera, Brown, and Uzzell, 2014; Custers and Van den Bulck, 2013; Ireland, 2011; Jackson, 2011). Importantly for the current context, we posit that this sense of threat and vulnerability may differentially predict different "types" of emotional experience. In particular, there may be a kind of dysfunctional worry that is chronic and persistent and is strongly correlated with believing that the likelihood and impact of victimization are high and that it is difficult to control whether one becomes a victim. To test this, we extend the fifth category of Gray et al. (2011) to more cleanly capture a more serious category of fear of crime.

We also add the category "need for cognitive closure" as a predictor. Need for cognitive closure refers to individual differences in the need for certainty and definite knowledge. Psychological research has shown that people vary in their basic need to believe that things are stable, certain, and predictable (Kruglanski and Webster, 1996). When this notion is applied to fear of crime, it is plausible to suggest that people with a high need for cognitive closure will be motivated to achieve closure about crime risk by gaining knowledge about how to manage and avoid threat. But if they cannot do so – if subjective risk remains high – they will experience further negative affect, because they are averse to uncertainty (Jackson, 2015b). We thus posit that the need for cognitive closure will have an additive statistical effect on top of the perceived risk, both of these categories being especially strongly correlated with the most "serious" type of emotional experience that involves frequent, chronic, and persistent worry.

In short, we predict that a strong sense of subjective risk and an aversion to uncertainty will be related to a pattern of worry (negative affect) that is frequent and damaging in its impact on well-being. To do this, we replicate the measures of Gray et al. (2011), but we make a small "tweak." In their study, in order to be put in the "dysfunctionally worried" group, a respondent had to say (among other things) that he or she was worried about becoming a victim of crime and had worried at least once in the past year.

To identify persistent and chronic worry, we split the dysfunctionally worried group (n = 745) into two. Members of the "persistent and chronic" group said that they worried "some of the time" or "most or all of the time"; they also said that their quality of life was reduced by their worry about crime "quite a bit" or "very much." A number of 176 people fell into this category (24 percent of the dysfunctionally worried group, or 8 percent of the total sample). Table 17.2 presents the breakdown

Table 17.2 Levels of fear of burglary and violence in Italy, Bulgaria, Lithuania, and the pooled sample (unweighted data)

Category of emotional experience	*Pooled sample* %	*Italy* %	*Bulgaria* %	*Lithuania* %
Unworried	40	60	39	29
Functionally anxious	5	2	7	4
Dysfunctionally anxious	19	11	19	24
Functionally worried	6	3	10	8
Dysfunctionally worried	23	22	21	26
Persistent and chronic worry	8	4	6	10
Total	**100**	**100**	**100**	**100**

Source: National probability sample survey of adults in Italy, Bulgaria, and Lithuania.
n = 2,490 (n = 502, 1,007 and 981 respectively).

for the pooled sample and for each individual country. Note that, instead of focusing solely on street robbery – as in Gray and colleagues' work – we asked respondents about stranger violence in the street and burglary.

How does this extended categorial scale relate to standard-intensity measures of worry?

To facilitate comparison, respondents were also asked: "Overall, how worried (if at all) are you about having your home broken into and having things stolen?" and "Overall, how worried (if at all) are you about being physically attacked in the street by strangers?" Responses ran from "not at all worried" (1) to "not very worried" (2), "fairly worried" (3), and "very worried" (4). The mean was calculated for each respondent. Figure 17.3 presents a box plot with jittered data (25 percent, 50 percent and 75 percent interquartile points are presented, and the large dot indicates the mean): it plots the new categorial variable against this standard intensity index. We can see that the unworried group tends to have low levels of worry intensity; the functionally anxious, the functionally worried, and the dysfunctionally anxious have relatively similar distributions of worry intensity; and the dysfunctionally worried and chronic or persistent groups have relatively high levels of worry intensity (unsurprisingly, the chronic or persistent group has the highest).

Having done some descriptive analysis, we can now examine the theoretically relevant predictors of membership of the six categories. Table 17.3 presents the findings from three multinomial logistic regression models. Comparisons are made to the reference category of "unworried." Model 1 includes gender, age, crime experience, and the two dummy variables differentiating between individuals in Italy, Bulgaria, and Lithuania. Model 2 adds the need for cognitive closure. Model 3 adds perceptions of risk and threat (for details on how perceived risk and need for cognitive closure were measured, see Jackson, 2015b). Control variables were gender,

Table 17.3 Multinomial logistic regression predicting membership of six fear of crime groups.

	Model 1 OR	*[95% CI]*	*Model 2 OR*	*[95% CI]*	*Model 3 OR*	*[95% CI]*
COMPARING "UNWORRIED" AND "FUNCTIONAL ANXIETY"						
Female (0 = male)	1.45	[0.96, 2.20]	1.42	[0.94, 2.16]	1.23	[0.80, 1.91]
Age (in years)	0.98**	[0.97, 0.99]	0.98***	[0.97, 0.99]	0.98***	[0.97, 0.99]
Direct experience of crime (0 = no experience in past 12 months, 1 = experienced 1 crime, 2 = experienced 2 crimes)	1.24	[0.61, 2.54]	1.27	[0.62, 2.59]	1.24	[0.60, 2.56]
Indirect experience of crime (0 = friends and family had no experience in past 12 months, 1 = experienced 1 crime, 2 = experienced 2 crimes)	1.04	[0.75, 1.43]	1.03	[0.75, 1.42]	0.99	[0.72, 1.37]
Bulgaria dummy variable	6.28***	[3.04, 12.97]	5.87***	[2.83, 12.18]	5.45***	[2.58, 11.51]
Lithuania dummy variable	4.14***	[1.93, 8.88]	4.38***	[2.03, 9.45]	3.71**	[1.69, 8.15]
Need for cognitive closure			1.23	[0.95, 1.61]	1.20	[0.92, 1.58]
Perceptions of the likelihood of victimization					1.40*	[1.08, 1.83]
Perceptions of the consequences of victimization					1.21	[0.99, 1.48]
Perceptions of control over victimization					0.89	[0.73, 1.09]
COMPARING "UNWORRIED AND "DYSFUNCTIONAL ANXIETY"						
Female (0 = male)	1.63***	[1.28,2.08]	1.62***	[1.27,2.06]	1.37*	[1.06,1.77]
Age (in years)	1.00	[0.99,1.00]	1.00	[0.99,1.00]	0.99*	[0.99,1.00]
Direct experience of crime (0 = no experience in past 12 months, 1 = experienced 1 crime, 2=experienced 2 crimes)	0.77	[0.47,1.27]	0.78	[0.47,1.29]	0.71	[0.43,1.19]
Indirect experience of crime (0 = friends and family had no experience in past 12 months, 1=experienced 1 crime, 2=experienced 2 crimes)	0.87	[0.72,1.05]	0.87	[0.72,1.05]	0.82*	[0.67,0.99]
Bulgaria dummy variable	2.38***	[1.68,3.39]	2.30***	[1.61,3.28]	2.02***	[1.39,2.93]
Lithuania dummy variable	3.97***	[2.80,5.64]	4.09***	[2.87,5.83]	3.13***	[2.16,4.54]
Need for cognitive closure			1.11	[0.96,1.30]	1.09	[0.92,1.28]
Perceptions of the likelihood of victimization					2.13***	[1.81,2.50]

Perceptions of the consequences of victimization					1.13*	[1.01,1.27]
Perceptions of control over victimization					0.84**	[0.74,0.95]
COMPARING "UNWORRIED" AND "FUNCTIONALLY WORRY"						
Female (0 = male)	2.14***	[1.50,3.08]	2.18***	[1.52,3.13]	1.72**	[1.17,2.51]
Age (in years)	0.99	[0.98,1.00]	0.99	[0.98,1.00]	0.99*	[0.98,1.00]
Direct experience of crime (0 = no experience in past 12 months, 1 = experienced 1 crime, 2=experienced 2 crimes)	3.32***	[2.14,5.15]	3.33***	[2.14,5.17]	3.16***	[2.00,4.98]
Indirect experience of crime (0 = friends and family had no experience in past 12 months, 1=experienced 1 crime, 2=experienced 2 crimes)	1.51**	[1.18,1.93]	1.51**	[1.18,1.93]	1.41**	[1.10,1.82]
Bulgaria dummy variable	4.64***	[2.53,8.49]	4.91***	[2.66,9.06]	4.25***	[2.27,7.97]
Lithuania dummy variable	5.01***	[2.73,9.19]	4.97***	[2.70,9.12]	3.78***	[2.02,7.07]
Need for cognitive closure			0.90	[0.73,1.11]	0.84	[0.68,1.05]
Perceptions of the likelihood of victimization					2.07***	[1.65,2.50]
Perceptions of the consequences of victimization					1.31**	[1.10,1.56]
Perceptions of control over victimization					0.77**	[0.64,0.92]
COMPARING "UNWORRIED" AND "DYSFUNCTIONALLY WORRY"						
Female (0 = male)	2.63***	[2.07,3.34]	2.59***	[2.04,3.29]	2.02***	[1.56,2.52]
Age (in years)	1.00	[0.99,1.01]	1.00	[0.99,1.01]	0.99	[0.99,1.00]
Direct experience of crime (0 = no experience in past 12 months, 1 = experienced 1 crime, 2=experienced 2 crimes)	2.66***	[1.90,3.72]	2.73***	[1.94,3.82]	2.53***	[1.77,3.52]
Indirect experience of crime (0 = friends and family had no experience in past 12 months, 1=experienced 1 crime, 2=experienced 2 crimes)	2.03***	[1.72,2.38]	2.01***	[1.71,2.36]	1.87***	[1.57,2.21]
Bulgaria dummy variable	1.74***	[1.28,2.36]	1.58**	[1.16,2.16]	1.27	[0.91,1.77]
Lithuania dummy variable	2.09***	[1.54,2.84]	2.22***	[1.63,3.03]	1.58**	[1.13,2.20]
Need for cognitive closure			1.28**	[1.10,1.48]	1.19*	[1.01,1.39]
Perceptions of the likelihood of victimization					2.43***	[2.08,2.85]
Perceptions of the consequences of victimization					1.36***	[1.21,1.53]
Perceptions of control over victimization					0.77***	[0.69,0.88]

(*continued*)

Table 17.3 (*Continued*)

	Model 1 OR	*[95% CI]*	*Model 2 OR*	*[95% CI]*	*Model 3 OR*	*[95% CI]*
COMPARING "UNWORRIED" AND "CHRONIC AND PERSISTENT WORRY"						
Female (0 = male)	3.14***	[2.14,4.59]	3.07***	[2.10,4.50]	2.41***	[1.60,3.63]
Age (in years)	1.01**	[1.00,1.02]	1.01*	[1.00,1.02]	1.01	[0.99,1.02]
Direct experience of crime (0 = no experience in past 12 months, 1 = experienced 1 crime, 2=experienced 2 crimes)	4.62***	[3.06,6.98]	4.78***	[3.16,7.25]	4.11***	[2.63,6.42]
Indirect experience of crime (0 = friends and family had no experience in past 12 months, 1=experienced 1 crime, 2=experienced 2 crimes)	1.98***	[1.55,2.52]	1.95***	[1.52,2.48]	1.83***	[1.42,2.36]
Bulgaria dummy variable	2.25**	[1.29,3.93]	1.88*	[1.07,3.32]	1.31	[0.72,2.40]
Lithuania dummy variable	3.78***	[2.22,6.44]	4.21***	[2.46,7.22]	2.51**	[1.42,4.44]
Need for cognitive closure			1.53***	[1.20,1.95]	1.38*	[1.07,1.78]
Perceptions of the likelihood of victimization					3.79***	[2.98,4.81]
Perceptions of the consequences of victimization					1.69***	[1.38,2.07]
Perceptions of control over victimization					0.91	[0.75,1.10]

Source: National probability sample survey of adults in Italy, Bulgaria, and Lithuania.

n = 2,490 (n = 502, 1,007 and 981 respectively); N = 2,221 for all models; *OR* = adjusted odds ratio; *CI* = confidence interval for the adjusted odds radio; *p < 0.05; **p < 0.01' ***p<0.001. Response variable took six levels: "unworried," "functional anxiety," "dysfunctional anxiety," "functional worry," "dysfunctional worry," and "chronic and persistent worry"; the reference category is "unworried."

age (in years), country (two dummy variables: Italy and Bulgaria), direct victimization experience ("Have you been a victim of burglary in the past five years?" "Have you been physically attacked in the street by a stranger in the past five years?"), and indirect victimization experience ("Do you know someone who has been a victim of burglary in the past five years?" "Do you know someone who has been physically attacked in the street by a stranger in the past five years?").

Figure 17.4 provides fitted probabilities for the four key variables, fixing the values of the other predictors to the mean. On the *y* axis is the fitted probability of an individual falling into the particular "fear group," plotted as a function of varying

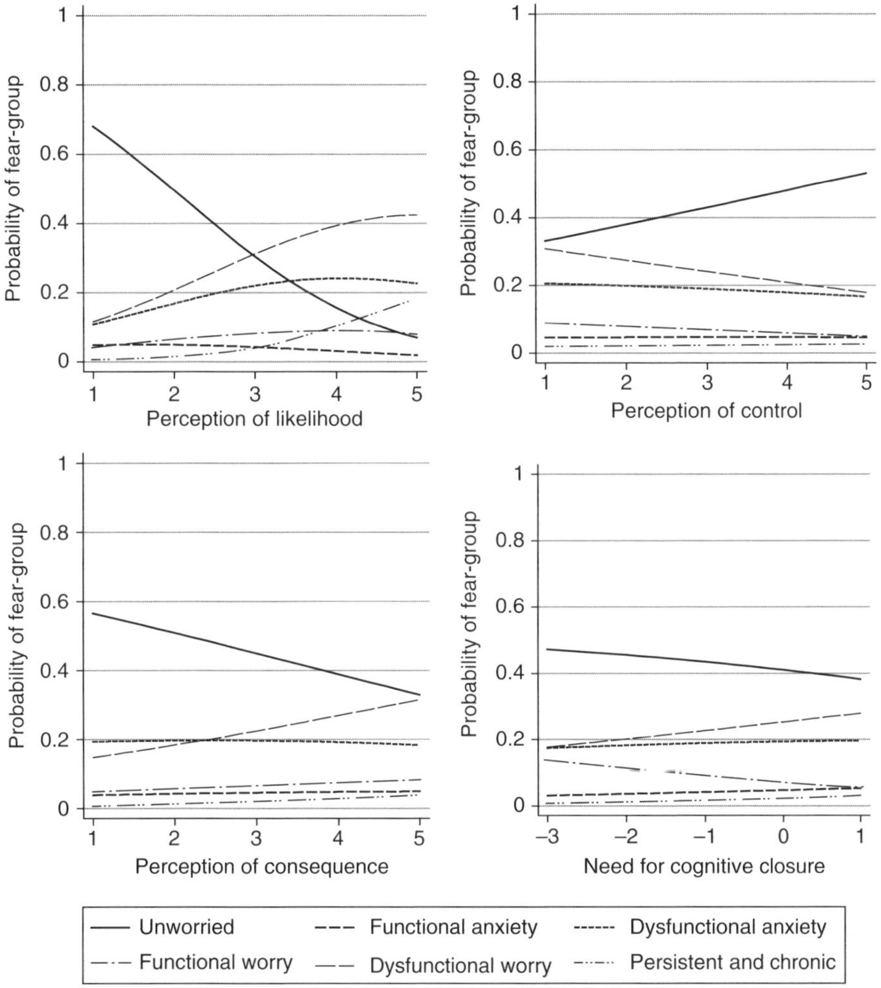

Figure 17.4 Fitted probabilities for risk perception and need for cognitive closure, predicting membership of six "fear of crime" groups. *Source*: National probability sample survey of adults in Italy, Bulgaria, and Lithuania.

n = 2,490 (n = 502, 1,007 and 981 respectively); fitted probabilities are calculated from fitted multinomial logistic regression (see Table 17.3).

levels of the specific variable on the x axis. The six lines trace fitted probabilities for each of the six "fear groups." A number of findings are of note. First, one sees that perceived likelihood of victimization is a strong predictor: the higher the perceived likelihood, the greater the chance that an individual falls into one of the higher groups. Consider how quickly the fitted probability of being "unworried" falls as perceived likelihood increases, and how the fitted probability of being in the "persistent and chronic" group increases quite steeply above 4 (5 is the maximum). Second, perceptions of the controllability and of the consequences of criminal victimization are relatively weak predictors (controllability is a negative predictor of being in one of the higher groups, consequences are a weak positive predictor). Finally, the need for cognitive closure is only a predictor of membership of the "dysfunctional worry" and the "persistent and chronic" groups (Table 17.3 and Figure 17.3). This finding is consistent with the idea that people with a high need for closure have difficulty accepting the prospect of threatening harm in the future: they have an aversion to uncertainty and are more likely to have a negative affect in response to a sense of threat they find it difficult to come to terms with.

How Theory Guides Measurement: The Role of an Organizing Framework

In the previous section we used a formative index to show how theory about both the constructs and their potential predictors can guide measurement. In the final section we consider how an ambitious organizing framework – in this case, procedural justice theory (Sunshine and Tyler, 2003; Tyler, 2003, 2006a, 2006b; Tyler and Jackson, 2013) – helps us schematize measures, refine concepts and indicators, and more generally broaden out the focus of empirical inquiry. We show the utility of such an overarching framework; we illustrate the use of latent variable modeling; and we finish with a cautionary tale about what latent variable modeling can and cannot do in the current context.

According to procedural justice theory, people place great store by the justice or fairness of the behavior of authority figures. People are less interested in the effectiveness of the authority or in the outcomes it provides than in the processes by which it makes decisions and in the motivations behind its actions. What looms most prominently in people's minds is the fairness of the processes by which power holders wield their power. Importantly, when officers treat people with respect and dignity, utilize neutral and fair decision-making processes, and allow the individual concerned a voice in the interaction, those officers communicate messages of status and worth to that individual (that he or she is a valued and respected member of the social group the police represent) and demonstrate to citizens that their power is balanced by due process and that they are acting in accordance with values of legality and propriety.

In these circumstances, when officers act in procedurally fair ways, the people they police are more likely to regard them as legitimate, to defer to their authority, and to feel that the power they wield is justified (Geller et al., 2014; Tyler, Fagan, and

Geller, 2014; Trinkner and Cohn, 2014; Tyler, Jackson, and Mentovich, 2015). Procedural justice promotes legitimacy, in other words the belief that (1) one has a duty to allow the police to dictate appropriate behavior (Murphy, Tyler, and Curtis, 2009; Papachristos, Meares, and Fagan, 2012; Mazerolle et al., 2013; Wolfe et al., 2015) and (2) the police wield their power in normatively appropriate ways (Jackson, Bradford, Hough, et al., 2012; Jackson, Bradford, Stanko, et al., 2012; Jackson, 2015a; Cheng, 2015). Finally, studies have found that legitimacy predicts self-reported offending behavior (Sunshine and Tyler, 2003; Fagan and Tyler, 2005; Tyler, 2006a; Fagan and Piquero, 2007; Cohn et al., 2012; Jackson, Bradford, Hough, et al., 2012; Trinkner and Cohn, 2014; Tyler and Jackson, 2014; Murphy, Bradford, and Jackson, forthcoming) and willingness to cooperate with the police (Tyler, Schulhofer, and Huq, 2010; Huq, Tyler, and Schulhofer, 2011a, 2011b; Jackson, Bradford, Stanko, et al., 2012; Dirikx and van den Bulck, 2014; Murphy, Sargeant, and Cherney, 2015; White, Mulvery, and Dario, 2015).

Measuring public trust and institutional legitimacy

To illustrate how attitudes toward the police can be organized within this more ambitious framework, we draw upon data from a national probability sample survey of adults in England and Wales that was conducted in June–August of 2009. The analytical sample size is 937 (for more details on the methodology, see Quinton, 2010 and Jackson, Bradford, Hough, et al., 2012).

The first thing that procedural justice theory does in the current context is conceptual. Recall that the national opinion polls that Shaw and Brannan (2009) reviewed included measures of confidence in the ability of the police to protect "you" from violent crime, to prevent crime in the community, to solve crime in the community, to be helpful and friendly, to treat people fairly, to not use excessive force, to tell the truth, and so on. Procedural justice helps us organize the concepts by making key distinctions between (1) people's experience with the police; (2) assessments of the trustworthiness of the police in the matter of being effective and fair; (3) assessments of the legitimacy of the police; and (4) various law-related behaviors that may be shaped by trust and legitimacy. These conceptual distinctions can then guide the measurement and modeling process.

To measure prior experience with the police, respondents were asked about their experience of (and satisfaction with) public-initiated contact and police-initiated contact. The question about self-initiated contact referred to satisfaction or dissatisfaction with "the way the police handled this matter." The question about police-initiated contact referred to satisfaction or dissatisfaction with "the conduct of the officers." For the purpose of analysis, four dichotomous variables were constructed (the reference category being "no recent contact with the police"), indicating whether individuals had experienced:

(a) positive public-initiated contact (18 percent of the sample);
(b) negative public-initiated contact (8 percent of the sample);

(c) positive police-initiated contact (8 percent of the sample);
(d) negative police-initiated contact (2 percent of the sample).

Did respondents in our survey believe that the police are fair in their interpersonal treatment and decision-making? Trustworthiness judgments regarding procedural fairness were measured by asking (1) whether people believed that the police would treat them with respect if they had contact with them and (2) whether people believed that the police generally make decisions on the basis of the facts and generally explain these decisions to the people they deal with (for a discussion on the nature of trust, see, among others, Stoutland, 2001; Tyler and Huo, 2002; Hawdon, 2008; Jackson and Gau, 2015). Response options were "strongly agree," "agree," "disagree," and "strongly disagree."

Did respondents believe that the police are effective? Trustworthiness judgments regarding effectiveness were measured using a four-item scale that asked people how effective they thought their local police were at solving crime, at preventing crime, at keeping order on the streets, and at responding to emergencies. Response options were "very effective," "fairly effective," "not very effective," and "not at all effective."

What about legitimacy? On the one hand, legitimacy is a response to an institution's claim to rightful authority. Legitimacy exists in the eyes of citizens partly when those citizens believe that the institution has a positive right to dictate appropriate behavior and when they feel that they have a corresponding duty to obey (Tyler, 2006a, 2006b). To measure people's felt obligation to obey, a two-item scale was used: "You should do what the police tell you, even if you disagree" and "You should accept decisions made by the police, even if you think they are wrong."

On the other hand, legitimacy is also a response to the claim that power is rightfully held and exercised. Legitimacy exists in the eyes of citizens partly when they believe that the institution acts in ways that accord with prevailing notions of appropriate moral conduct. People judge the normative appropriateness of an institution on the basis of the normative appropriateness of the officers who embody that institution and wield institutional power (Jackson, Bradford, Hough, et al., 2012; Jackson, Bradford, Stanko, et al., 2012; Jackson, 2015a). This aspect of legitimacy was captured by two questions: "The police in this area usually act in ways that are consistent with my own ideas about what is right and wrong" and "The police in this area can be trusted to make decisions that are right for the people in this neighborhood." For all legitimacy questions, response options were "strongly agree," "agree," "disagree," and "strongly disagree."

In order to measure people's willingness to cooperate with the police, respondents were asked how likely it was that they would "call the police to report a crime they had witnessed," "report suspicious activity near their house," and "provide information to the police to help find a suspected criminal." Response alternatives were "very likely," "fairly likely," "fairly unlikely," and "very unlikely."

Assessing the dimensionality of trust, legitimacy and willingness to cooperate

To assess the empirical distinctiveness of trust, legitimacy, and willingness to cooperate, we fit a series of confirmatory factor analysis models. Taking a reflective approach to measurement, we assume that these are unobservable psychological constructs. Using imperfect behavioral indicators of the underlying concept (indicators that are subject to measurement error), we assume that (1) the correlations between the measures occur by virtue of their measuring the same underlying concept of interest; and (2) the variance that is not shared represents measurement error.

Results from a series of confirmatory factor analysis (CFA) models using Mplus 7.2 are shown in Table 17.4 (indicators were set as categorial). The exact and approximate fit statistics suggest that models 1, 2, and 3 fit the data poorly. Models 4a and 4b also have an unsatisfactory fit. Only models 4c and 5 fit the data well (at least according to the approximate fit statistics, where one typically looks for CFI > 0.95; TLI > 0.95; RMSEA < 0.06; see Hu and Bentler, 1999). From this perspective, trust in police effectiveness, the felt obligation to obey the police, and willingness to cooperate with the police seem to be separate judgments, strongly correlated (see Table 17.5) but nevertheless empirically distinct. However, trust in police fairness and normative alignment with the police overlap significantly. On the basis of Table 17.4 at least, it is a judgment call whether to treat them as separate (although one would need to be careful of multicollinearity in subsequent analysis if one were to treat them as separate).

We should also note that, in the five-factor model, factor loadings and R^2s are all relatively high. For perceptions of police effectiveness, the standardized factor loadings range from 0.70 to 0.86, and the R^2s range from 0.49 to 0.74. For perceptions of police procedural fairness, the standardized factor loadings range from 0.82 to 0.95, and the R^2s range from 0.67 to 0.90. For normative alignment, the standardized factor loadings range from 0.50 to 0.93, and the R^2s range from 0.25 to 0.86. For obligation to obey, the standardized factor loadings range from 0.82 to 0.88, and the R^2s range from 0.67 to 0.78. For willingness to cooperate, the standardized factor loadings range from 0.73 to 0.83, and the R^2s range from 0.53 to 0.69. In the four-factor model (model 4c in Table 17.4) the standardized factor loadings for the combined fairness and normative alignment indicators range from 0.70 to 0.91 and the R^2s range from 0.49 to 0.83.

Table 17.5 presents correlations, means, and variances of latent variables estimated within the five-factor confirmatory factor analysis model. In the five-factor model we can see especially strong bivariate associations between each pair of (1) trust in police effectiveness and procedural fairness ($r = 0.66$); (2) normative alignment and trust in police effectiveness ($r = 0.69$); and (3) normative alignment and trust in police procedural fairness ($r = 0.89$). This last association is of concern, as it suggests a lack of discriminant validity between normative alignment and procedural fairness.

Table 17.4 Fit statistics for a series of fitted confirmatory factor analysis models.

Model		*Chi-Square*	*df*	p	*RMSEA*	*RMSEA 90% CI*	*CFI*	*TLI*
M1	One factor	2,408	77	<0.0005	0.180	0.174–0.186	0.798	0.762
M2	Two factors (trust and legitimacy, and cooperation)	1,623	76	<0.0005	0.147	0.141–0.154	0.866	0.840
M3	Three factors (trust, legitimacy and cooperation)	1,344	74	<0.0005	0.135	0.129–0.142	0.890	0.865
M4a	Four factors (combining effectiveness and fairness)	551	71	<0.0005	0.085	0.078–0.092	0.958	0.947
M4b	Four factors (combining felt obligation and normative alignment)	985	71	<0.0005	0.117	0.111–0.124	0.921	0.899
M4c	Four factors (combining procedural justice and normative alignment)	198	71	<0.0005	0.044	0.037–0.051	0.989	0.986
M5	Five factors	129	67	<0.0005	0.031	0.023–0.040	0.995	0.993

Source: Compiled by the authors from various internal government documents.

Table 17.5 Correlations between elements of trust, legitimacy, and cooperation.

	1	*2*	*3*	*4*	*5*
1. Trust in police effectiveness	–				
2. Trust in police procedural fairness	0.66***	–			
3. Felt obligation to obey the police	0.25***	0.33***	–		
4. Normative alignment with the police	0.69***	0.89***	0.39***	–	
5. Intentions to cooperate in the future	0.24***	0.39***	0.24***	0.42***	–

Source: Compiled by the authors from various internal government documents.
These are correlations between latent variables estimated within a confirmatory factor analysis model with categorial indicators. Means of all latent variables were set to zero. Variances are 0.73, 0.67, 0.80, 0.78 and 0.65 (respectively). *$p < 0.05$; **$p < 0.01$; ***$p < 0.001$.

Table 17.6 presents correlations, means, and variances of latent variables estimated within the four-factor confirmatory factor analysis model. In this instance we can see an especially strong bivariate association between trust in police effectiveness on the one hand, and procedural fairness and normative alignment on the other ($r = 0.71$).

Modeling the dynamics of police–community relations

Procedural justice theory makes specific predictions about how prior contact with the police will relate to people's willingness to cooperate with this institution in the future. From the above analysis one could reasonably proceed by using either the four-factor CFA model or the five-factor CFA model as the starting point for subsequent analysis. Figure 17.5 reports findings from a fitted structural equation modeling (SEM) that differentiates between perceived fairness and normative alignment (note that no construct is regressed onto both procedural fairness and norma-

Table 17.6 Correlations between elements of trust, legitimacy, and cooperation.

	1	*2*	*3*	*4*
1. Trust in police effectiveness	–			
2. Felt obligation to obey the police	0.25***	–		
3. Trust in police procedural fairness and normative alignment with the police	0.71***	0.38***	–	
4. Intentions to cooperate in the future	0.24***	0.24***	0.39***	–

Source: Compiled by the authors from various internal government documents.
These are correlations between latent variables estimated within a confirmatory factor analysis model with categorial indicators. Means of all latent variables were set to zero. Variances are 0.74, 0.77, 0.75, and 0.65 (respectively). *p < 0.05; **p < 0.01; ***p < 0.001.

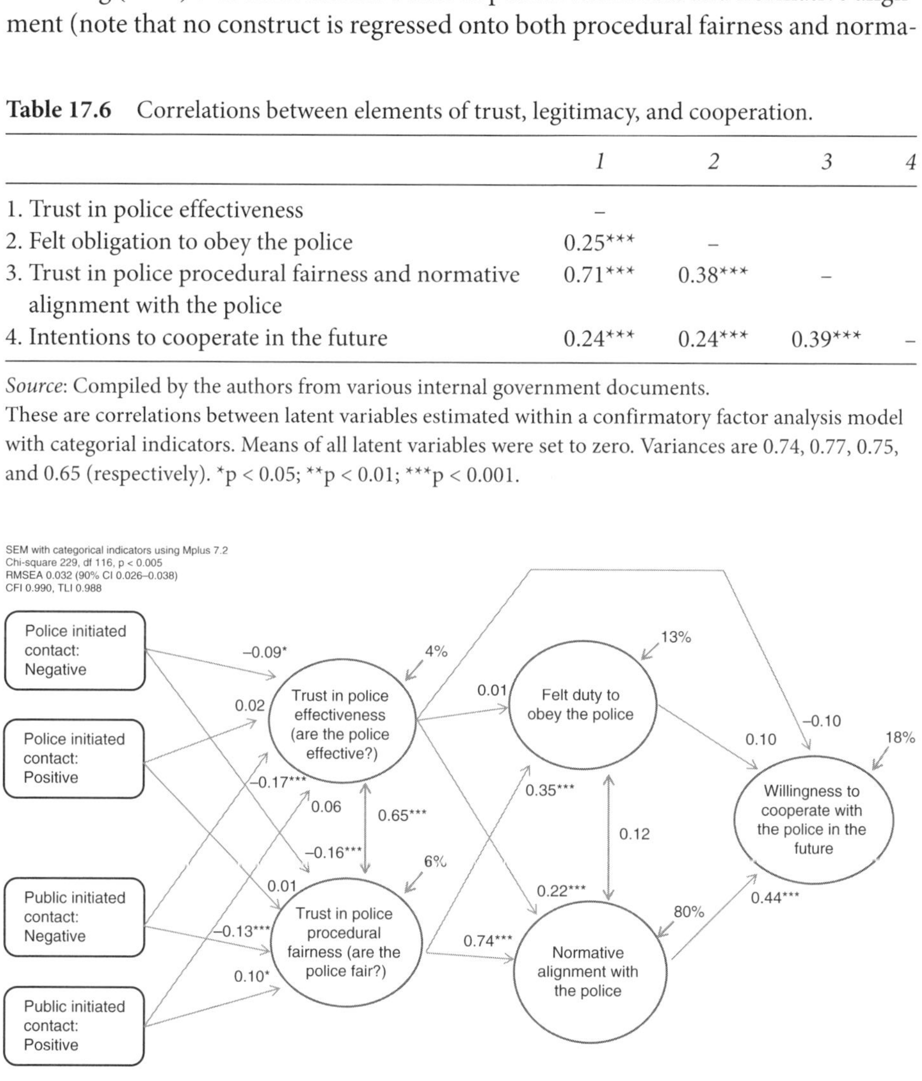

Figure 17.5 Testing procedural justice theory. *Source*: Compiled by the authors from various internal governmental documents.

*p < 0.05; **p < 0.01; ***p < 0.001. For visual ease, measurement models not presented. Standardized regression coefficients are presented. Four dummy variables for contact are used, the reference category being no contact.

tive alignment, in part to avoid multicollinearity). Starting at the right-hand side of the model, we can see that 18 percent of the variation in cooperation is explained by a linear combination of felt obligation, normative alignment, and trust in police effectiveness. Normative alignment is a strong predictor of cooperation ($B = 0.44$, $p < 0.001$), while felt obligation and police effectiveness are not ($B = 0.10$ and $B = -0.10$). Those who believe that the police share their values are more likely to say that they will proactively assist the police than those who do not feel such alignment (net of their felt obligation to obey the police and their trust in police effectiveness).

Turning to the predictors of felt obligation and normative alignment, trust in procedural fairness is a much stronger predictor than trust in effectiveness ($B = 0.74$, $p < 0.001$ compared to $B = 0.22$, $p < 0.001$). The more people believed that the police are procedurally fair, the greater the expected levels of felt obligation and normative alignment were. Particularly striking is that 80 percent of the variation in normative alignment is explained by the two predictors (mostly by procedural fairness). Less variation in felt obligation is explained by procedural fairness and effectiveness, although procedural fairness is a significant predictor ($B = 0.35$, $p < 0.001$).

On the left-hand side of the model we have contact with the police. Compared to "no contact," negatively experienced encounters with police officers are associated with lower levels of trust in procedural fairness ($B = -0.16$, $p < 0.001$ for police-initiated contact, and $B = -0.13$, $p < 0.001$ for public-initiated contact); negatively experienced public-initiated encounters are associated with lower levels of trust in effectiveness ($B = -0.09$, $p < 0.05$ for police-initiated contact; $B = -0.17$, $p < 0.001$ for public-initiated contact); and positively experienced public-initiated encounters with police officers are associated with higher levels of trust in procedural fairness ($B = 0.10$, $p < 0.05$).

Note that the model has two mediating layers between contact and cooperation. Table 17.7 presents the statistically significant indirect pathways from contact to cooperation, which were estimated using the effect decomposition function in

Table 17.7 Indirect statistical effects of contact on obligation to obey, moral alignment, and willingness to cooperate.

PATHWAY FROM	VIA ... TO COOPERATION	*B*	se	*B*/se
Public-initiated, *positively* received contact	Procedural fairness to normative alignment to cooperation	0.032*	0.014	2.34
Public-initiated, *negatively* received contact	Procedural fairness to normative alignment to cooperation	−0.044***	0.015	−0.296
Public-initiated, *negatively* received contact	Effectiveness to normative alignment to cooperation	−0.016*	0.005	−2.96
Public-initiated, *negatively* received contact	Procedural fairness to normative alignment to cooperation	−0.054***	0.015	−3.56
Police-initiated, *negatively* received contact	Effectiveness to normative alignment to cooperation	−0.009*	0.004	−2.00

Source: National Policing Improvement Agency Survey, 2009.
Standardized coefficients are estimated within the structural equation model (see Figure 17.4).
B = standardized regression coefficient; se = standard error.

MPlus 7.2. Three things are of note. First, there is asymmetry in the estimated statistical effects of contact. negatively received encounters is related to lower fitted willingness to cooperate, and only positively received public-initiated contact is particularly related to higher fitted willingness to cooperate. Second, all the effects run via normative alignment. Third, trust in police fairness has stronger indirect statistical effects than trust in police effectiveness.

Finally, Figure 17.6 presents findings from a SEM in which procedural fairness and normative alignment are combined into one latent construct. Note that little changes in terms of substance. The real difference here is conceptual; one does not estimate pathways from contact to trust to normative alignment to cooperation because one treats judgments about procedural fairness and the normative appropriateness of the police as one latent construct.

Mind the gap between constructs and measures

Throughout this chapter we have discussed reflective and formative approaches to measurement. In the second section we illustrated a hybrid approach when we derived a categorial index of fear of crime. We employed latent class analysis to choose the number of latent classes and to assign to one of the six classes combinations of the answers received for the four survey questions. We then used some logical rules to "tidy up" the cell definitions (hence the combination of reflective and formative).

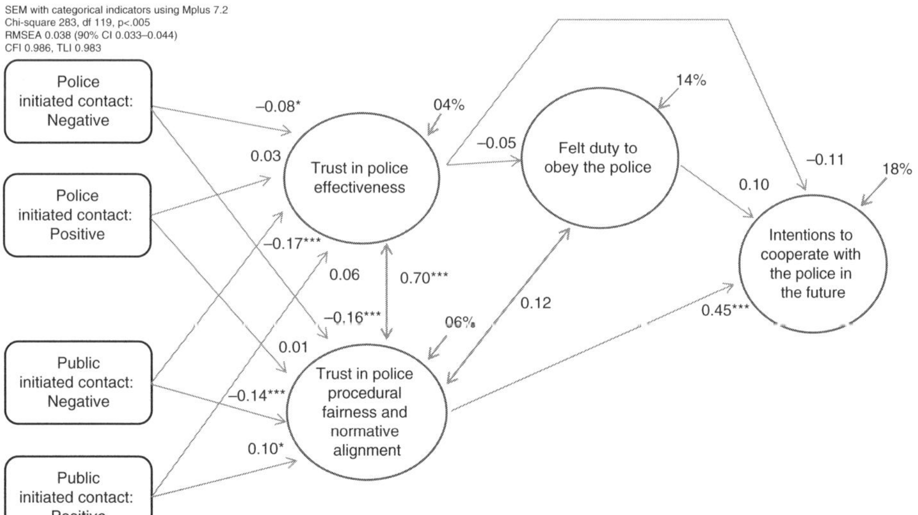

Figure 17.6 Testing procedural justice theory: An alternative model specification. *Source*: Compiled by the authors from various internal governmental documents.

*p < 0.05; **p < 0.01; ***p<0.001. For visual ease, measurement models are not presented. Standardized regression coefficients are presented. There are four dummy variables for contact, the reference category being no contact.

Next we demonstrated an entirely formative approach, whereby a categorial index was constructed using theoretically informed distinctions between different types of emotion, different effects of emotion, and different levels of frequency and impact. In the last section we used an entirely reflective approach. We used CFA to assess the dimensionality of relevant indicators of public trust and institutional legitimacy and SEM to estimate associations between manifest and latent variables.

We would like to close the chapter with some comments on what one can and cannot do with latent variable modeling techniques like CFA. We use a recent paper by Tankebe (2013) by means of illustration. His paper tells an interesting conceptual story about the nature of police legitimacy. But it also gives a warning about what latent variable modeling cannot say about the fundamental meaning of a given concept. Let us begin with the interesting conceptual story.

Tankebe (2013) proposes a new definition of police legitimacy (cf. Bottoms and Tankebe, 2012). Like other scholars in the field, he defines legitimacy as the perceived right to exercise power. But, in a departure from prior definitions, Tankebe measures legitimacy by asking people whether they think the police are effective, procedurally fair, distributively fair, and lawful. He argues that the first three dimensions render a sense of shared values (namely that the police seem to share the values of the public) while the fourth dimension renders a sense of the legality of police action – a sense that they "play by the rules."

While prior research on procedural justice and legitimacy has treated people's perceptions of the effectiveness and fairness of the police as *predictors* of legitimacy, as we did in our previous analysis, Tankebe states that, when the police are seen to be ineffective, for example, this reflects a direct belief about illegitimacy. If the police cannot be trusted to deal effectively with drug dealing and drug use, then this is a direct expression that the police do not have the right to exercise power. Communicating effectiveness to members of the public (by demonstrating that they – the police – can be trusted or relied upon to catch criminals, turn up quickly in emergency, and so forth) is not to activate instrumental motivations to cooperate and comply, as is posited by procedural justice theory. Rather it is to directly activate legitimacy in the eyes of the policed. Similarly, if one believes that the police do not treat people fairly and do not distribute their outcomes fairly throughout society, then this is a direct belief about the legitimacy and right to power of the police. Procedural justice does not activate status, respect, and identification (Tyler and Blader, 2003; Blader and Tyler, 2009), which then generate legitimacy, according to Tankebe. Procedural justice (or at least the belief that the police are procedurally fair) *is* legitimacy.

Why might people's beliefs or assumptions about the intentions and competence of the police – its being effective and fair – constitute legitimacy? Earlier on we called these beliefs and assumptions "trust judgments." But, for Tankebe (2013, p. 12), perceptions of effectiveness and fairness reflect "shared beliefs and values specify and institutionalize the rightful source of power and define the qualities appropriate to the assumption and exercise of that power." People hold basic beliefs and ideals about how a legitimate police force must act; they assess the extent to which the police meet these basic beliefs and ideals; and when the police act effectively and fairly, this accords to basic beliefs and values that legitimate their holding of power. Similarly, when people believe that the police act lawfully, this accords with the idea that the police have acquired power and exercise it in ways constituent with "principles of due process and equality, with equality being secured through the generality of the law" (Tankebe, 2013, p. 6). Legitimacy emerges when institutions demonstrate to citizens that they are effective, fair, and lawful and when citizens acknowledge this. At the aggregate level, then, when police officers demonstrate their trustworthiness (i.e., the fact that they can be relied upon to be effective, fair, and lawful) and citizens believe that the police are effective, fair, and lawful, this constitutes a right and proper basis of power and authority. This sociological approach conceives of legitimacy as a collective property (aggregated up to groups, subpopulations, and populations) where police action demonstrates (or not) that the police as an institution has the right to power, and citizen reception determines whether subordinates agree.

We do not wish to engage in further conceptual debate. (Needless to say, this is all interesting stuff; for further discussion, see Tyler, 2003; Reisig, Bratton, and Gertz, 2007; Hawdon, 2008; Gau, 2011, 2014; Bottoms and Tankebe, 2012; Tyler and Jackson, 2013; Hough, Jackson, and Bradford, 2013; Johnson, Maguire, and Kuhns, 2014; Tankebe, Reisig, and Wang, 2015; Jackson and Gau, 2015.) What we want to focus on here is how Tankebe interpreted the findings from CFA as testing "the hypothesis that the contents of the multiple dimensions of police legitimacy comprise procedural fairness, distributive fairness, lawfulness, and effectiveness" (Tankebe, 2013, p. 103). First, he found that a four-factor model that distinguished between lawfulness, effectiveness, procedural fairness, and distributive fairness fitted the data reasonably well. If one finds the above conceptual claim plausible, then one can reasonably infer that legitimacy (thus defined) has four dimensions (rather than three or two, for example). Given the constraints in the fitted CFA model (e.g., conditional independence of items once the four latent factors are estimated and included in the model), it seems that one can treat these four judgments as distinct, albeit extremely highly correlated (the correlations between procedural fairness, distributive fairness, and lawfulness were all above 0.8).

Tankebe then fitted a three factor CFA model without the effectiveness indicators; found that it fitted reasonably well; and ran a chi-square difference test to compare the relative fit of the three-factor and four-factor models. Noting that both the three-factor model (when indicators of procedural fairness, distributive fairness, and lawfulness are included) and the four-factor model (when indicators of effectiveness, procedural fairness, distributive fairness, and lawfulness are included) fitted the data,[1] he claimed:

> Effectiveness has to be viewed as a component of legitimacy; police organizations that seek legitimacy must demonstrate effectiveness as a normative requirement. Coicaud … has put this well: "Every political ruler who seeks to prove he possesses the right to govern [that is, is legitimate] has to satisfy, to try to satisfy, or to pretend to satisfy the

> needs of the members of the community." For the police, those needs include safety and security. (Tankebe, 2013, p. 121)

Moreover,

> Overall, the findings suggest that what police researchers have persistently tended to use as predictors of legitimacy (procedural fairness, distributive fairness, lawfulness, and effectiveness) are rather the constituent parts of legitimacy … The results of the confirmatory factor analysis presented in this study suggest that the debate [about whether legitimacy causes procedural justice or procedural justice causes legitimacy] might be redundant because procedural fairness is a constituent part of legitimacy rather than something apart from it. (Tankebe, 2013, p. 125)

It seems, then, that we have empirical evidence on what exactly police legitimacy *is*. Legitimacy is not the felt obligation to obey legal authorities – as Tyler (2006a, 2006b) would claim. Legitimacy is effectiveness, procedural fairness, distributive fairness, and lawfulness.

Yet we should pause before jumping to any such conclusion. Can latent variable modeling really be used to test whether one has, *in the first place*, measured the "correct" constituent parts of legitimacy? Imagine swapping the measures of effectiveness, procedural fairness, distributive fairness, and lawfulness with measures of duty to obey, institutional trust, normative alignment, and legal cynicism. These are subscales commonly used in the procedural justice literature to measure legitimacy (for a review. see Jackson and Gau, 2015). If one ran the same CFA models and got the same results, would this "prove" that police organizations need to instill in citizens a duty to obey, a sense of institutional trust, a feeling of normative alignment, and a belief that the law is binding presence in their lives if they are to be seen by citizens as legitimate? The answer to this question is, in our view, no; this remains a conceptual claim.

Legitimacy is an unobservable psychological construct. One cannot directly measure *it*; one has to infer both its existence and its meaning. One begins with a set of conceptual claims about its nature; one fields survey indicators that map onto the various assumed domains of meaning; and one can use some statistical technique like CFA to assess the underlying dimensionality of the items (if one adopts a reflective approach to measurement). But CFA says nothing directly about whether one can call these domains of meaning "legitimacy" in the first place – whether the domains of meaning be (1) effectiveness, procedural fairness, distributive fairness, and lawfulness or (2) duty to obey, institutional trust, normative alignment, and legal cynicism.

Finally, we hope that Figure 17.7 illustrates our point. The top two diagrams represent key aspects of Tankebe's (2013) modeling. Note on the left-hand side that legitimacy is defined along four different dimensions (see the "legitimacy box" placed over these four variables, denoting the conceptual claim that they represent legitimacy). Note also that these four dimensions predict both felt obligation to obey the police and willingness to cooperate, and that felt obligation also predicts

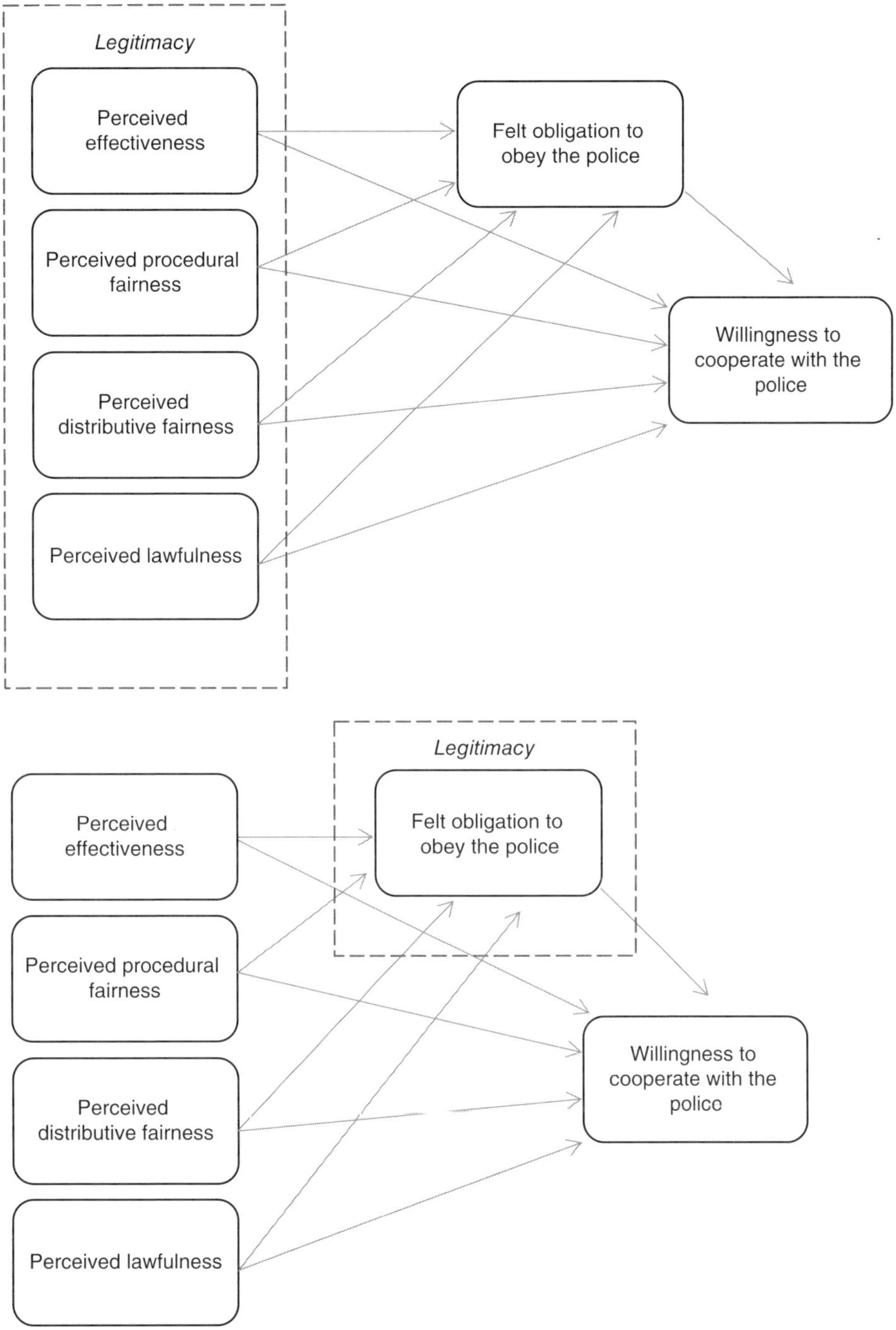

Figure 17.7 Where put the "legitimacy box"?

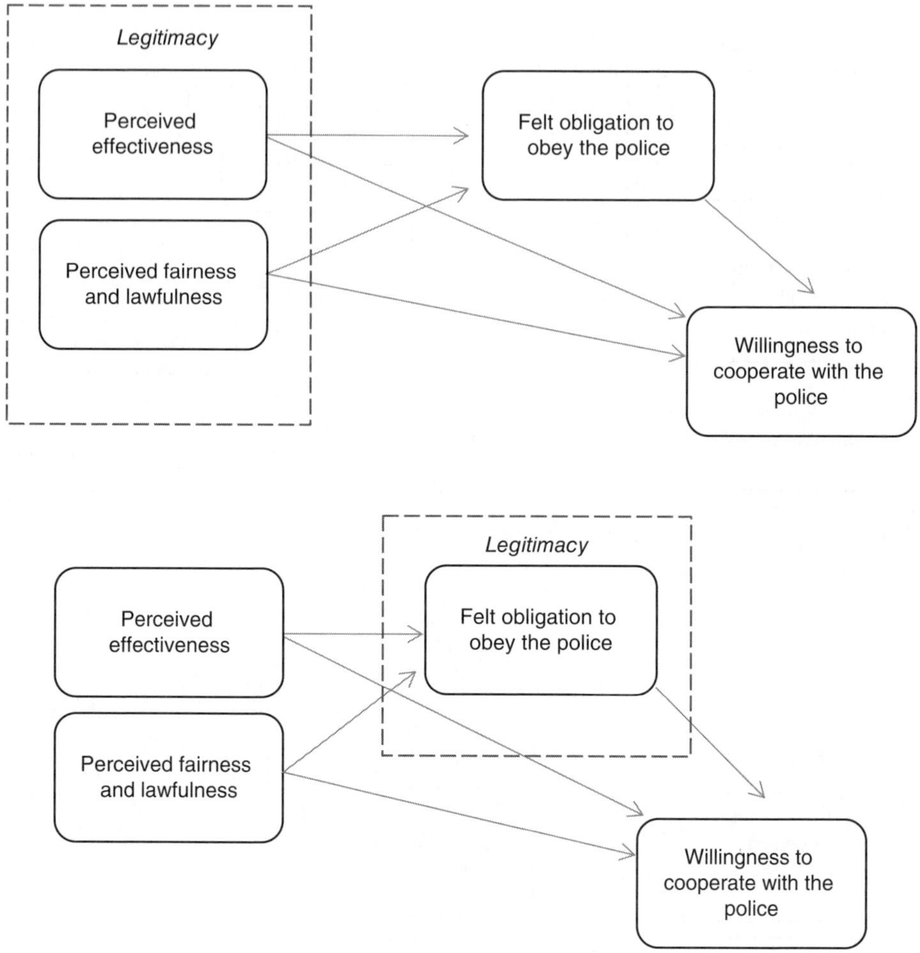

Figure 17.7 (*Continued*)

cooperation.[2] Now, note in the diagram to the right that the "legitimacy box" has moved to cover felt obligation – which reflects a key tenet of procedural justice theory, namely that legitimacy is partly felt obligation and that procedural justice creates a sense of felt obligation. The data and findings have not changed. But what, the researcher claims, *is* legitimacy has changed. Both claims are reasonable.

The bottom two diagrams in Figure 17.7 reflect Maguire and Johnson's (2014) re-analysis of Tankebe's (2013) data. They found that a two-factor model fitted the data reasonably well (and they argued that a two-factor model was to be preferred, because three out of the four constructs in the four-factor model were extremely highly correlated). Effectiveness loaded on one factor and procedural fairness, while distributive fairness and lawfulness loaded on the other factor. They then used effectiveness and fairness or lawfulness to predict felt obligation and cooperation. But, again, the "legitimacy box" can reasonably be put in the same two places.

Finally, on what basis might we claim that felt obligation is a constituent part of legitimacy? If one added the felt obligation items into the CFA and found felt obligation to be distinct from the other factors, would this say anything about the idea that obligation is part of the domain of meaning of legitimacy? The answer, again, is clearly no. This is largely a conceptual claim about whether or not obligation, consent, and authorization are part of the psychological state of legitimacy (Tyler, 2006a, 2006b; Jackson et al., 2015). Of course, one would want to be clear that the question's wording adequately stresses *truly free consent* (for a discussion, see Tyler and Jackson, 2013; Jackson and Gau, 2015). For instance, if one wanted to stress willing constraint, one should avoid questions like Tankebe's (2013, p. 116): "People like me have no choice but to obey the directives of the police" – and use instead questions like: "I feel a moral obligation to obey the police" (Bradford et al., 2015, p. 17).

Final Words

In this chapter we began by reviewing some measures of public attitudes toward crime and criminal justice commonly fielded in national opinion polls. We then used illustrative examples from criminological research into fear of crime and public attitudes toward the police to demonstrate how theory can guide measurement by (1) defining more precisely the central construct, (2) making predictions about the dynamics of the phenomenon over time (and thus guiding the development of a more sensitive measurement scheme), and (3) making predictions about antecedents and consequences. A key theme has been reflective and formative approaches to measurement. In the final stages of the current chapter we discussed the fundamental gap between unobservable psychological constructs and the measures we use to "capture" these constructs. We hope our discussion has helped to illustrate some of the fundamental links between theories, concepts and measures.

Notes

1 Although the chi-square difference test is inappropriate since these are not nested models; indeed they would not be nested even if the same indicators had been used.
2 Note that Tankebe (2013) says that felt obligation is not legitimacy because people can feel obligation to obey the police for reasons other than truly free consent (for discussion, see Bottoms and Tankebe, 2012; Tyler and Jackson, 2013; Johnson et al., 2014).

References

Acuña-Rivera, M., Brown, J., and Uzzell, D. 2014. Risk perception as mediator in perceptions of neighbourhood disorder and safety about victimisation. *Journal of Environmental Psychology*, 40: 64–75. doi: 10.1016/j.jenvp.2014.05.002.
Agresti, A. 2002. *Categorical data analysis*. New York: Wiley.

Berenbaum, H. 2010. An initiation–termination two-phase model of worrying. *Clinical Psychology Review*, 30 (8): 962–975.

Blader, S., and Tyler, T. R. 2009. Testing and expanding the group engagement model. *Journal of Applied Psychology*, 94: 445–464.

Borsboom, D., Mellenbergh, G. J., and Van Heerden, J. 2003. The theoretical status of latent variables. *Psychological Review*, 110: 203–219.

Borsboom, D., Mellenbergh, G. J., and Van Heerden, J. 2004. The concept of validity. *Psychological Review*, 111: 1061–1071.

Bottoms, A., and Tankebe, J. 2012. Beyond procedural justice: A dialogic approach to legitimacy in criminal justice. *Journal of Criminal Law and Criminology*, 102 (1): 119–170.

Bradford, B., Hohl, K., Jackson, J. and MacQueen, S. 2015. Obeying the rules of the road: Procedural justice, social identity and normative compliance. *Journal of Contemporary Criminal Justice*, 31: 151–170. doi: 10.1177/1043986214568833.

Bromley, R. D. F., and Stacey, R. J. 2012. Feeling unsafe in urban areas: Exploring older children's geographies of fear. *Environment and Planning, A*, 44: 428–444.

Cheng, K. K. Y. 2015. Prosecutorial procedural justice and public legitimacy in Hong Kong. *British Journal of Criminology*. doi: 10.1093/bjc/azv106.

Cohn, E. S., Trinkner, R. J., Rebellon, C. J., Van Gundy, K. T., and Cole, L. M. 2012. Legal attitudes and legitimacy: Extending the integrated legal socialization model. *Victims & Offenders*, 7 (4): 385–406.

Cook, C., and Fox, K. 2012. Testing the relative importance of contemporaneous offenses: The impacts of fear of sexual assault versus fear of physical harm among men and women. *Journal of Criminal Justice*, 40 (2): 142–151.

Cops, D., and Pleysier, S. 2011. "Doing gender" in fear of crime: The impact of gender identity on reported levels of fear of crime in adolescents and young adults. *British Journal of Criminology*, 51: 58–74.

Custers, K., and Van den Bulck, J. 2013. The cultivation of fear of sexual violence in women: Processes and moderators of the relationship between television and fear. *Communication Research*, 40 (1): 96–124.

Dirikx, A., and van den Bulck, J. 2014. Media use and the process-based model for police cooperation: An integrative approach toward explaining adolescents' intentions to cooperate with the police. *British Journal of Criminology*, 54 (2): 344–365.

Edwards, J. R., and Bagozzi, R. P. 2000. On the nature and direction of relationships between constructs and measures. *Psychological Methods*, 5: 155–174.

ESS (European Social Survey) Round 3. 2006. Data file edition 3.1. Norwegian Social Science Data Services, Norway. Data Archive and Distributor of ESS Data.

Fagan, J., and Piquero, A. R. 2007. Rational choice and developmental influences on recidivism among adolescent felony offenders. *Journal of Empirical Legal Studies*, 4 (4): 715–748.

Fagan, J., and Tyler, T. R. 2005. Legal socialization of children and adolescents. *Social Justice Research*, 18 (3): 217–241.

Farrall, S., Bannister, J., Ditton, J., and Gilchrist, E. 1997. Questioning the measurement of the fear of crime: Findings from a major methodological study. *British Journal of Criminology*, 37: 657–678.

Farrall, S., Jackson, J., Gray, E. 2009. *Social order and the fear of crime in contemporary times*. Oxford: Oxford University Press.

Fisher, B. S., and Sloan, J. J. 2003. Unraveling college women's fear of crime: A test of Ferraro's shadow hypothesis. *Justice Quarterly*, 20: 301–327.

Gau, J. 2011. The convergent and discriminant validity of procedural justice and police legitimacy: An empirical test of core theoretical propositions. *Journal of Criminal Justice*, 39 (6): 489–498.

Gau, J. M. 2014. Procedural justice and police legitimacy: A test of measurement and structure. *American Journal of Criminal Justice*, 39 (2): 187–205.

Geller, A., Fagan, J., Tyler, T. R., and Link, B. 2014. Aggressive policing and the mental health of young urban men. *American Journal of Public Health*, 104 (12): 2321–2327.

Girling, E., Loader, I. and Sparks, R. 2000. *Crime and social control in Middle England: Questions of order in an English town*. London: Routledge.

Gladstone, G., and Parker, G. 2003. What's the use of worrying? Its function and its dysfunction. *Australian and New Zealand Journal of Psychiatry*, 37: 347–354.

Gray, E., Jackson, J., and Farrall, S. 2008. Reassessing the fear of crime. *European Journal of Criminology*, 5 (3): 363–380.

Gray, E., Jackson, J., and Farrall, S. 2011. Feelings and functions in the fear of crime: Applying a new approach to victimisation insecurity. *British Journal of Criminology*, 51: 75–94.

Hale, C. 1996. Fear of crime: A review of the literature. *International Review of Victimology*, 4: 79–150.

Hawdon, J. 2008. Legitimacy, trust, social capital, and policing styles: A theoretical statement. *Police Quarterly*, 11: 182–201. doi: 10.1177/1098611107311852.

Hawdon, J., Vuori, M., Räsänen, P., and Oksanen, A. 2013. Social responses to collective crime: Assessing the relationship between crime-related fears and collective sentiments. *European Journal of Criminology*, 11 (1): 39–56.

Hinkle, J. C. 2014. Emotional fear of crime vs. perceived safety and risk: Implications for measuring "fear" and testing the broken windows thesis. *American Journal of Criminal Justice*. doi: 10.1007/s12103-014-9243-9.

Hollander, J. A. 2001. Vulnerability and dangerousness: The construction of gender through conservation about violence. *Gender and Society*, 15: 83–109.

Hough, M., Jackson, J., and Bradford, B. 2013. Legitimacy, trust and compliance: An empirical test of procedural justice theory using the European Social Survey. In *Legitimacy and Criminal Justice: An International Exploration*, edited by J. Tankebe and A. Liebling, 326–352. Oxford: Oxford University Press.

Howell, R. D., Breivik, E., and Wilcox, J. B. 2007. Is formative measurement really measurement? *Psychological Methods*, 12: 238–245.

Hu, L. T., and Bentler, P. M. 1999. Cutoff criteria for fit indexes in covariance structure analysis: Conventional criteria versus new alternatives. *Structural Equation Modeling*, 6: 1 55.

Huq, A. Z., Tyler, T. R., and Schulhofer, S. J. 2011a. How do the purposes and targets of policing influence the basis of public cooperation with law enforcement? *Psychology, Public Policy and Law*, 17: 419–450.

Huq, A. Z., Tyler, T. R., and Schulhofer, S. J. 2011b. Mechanisms for eliciting cooperation in counterterrorism policing: A study of British Muslims. *Journal of Empirical Legal Studies*, 8: 728–761.

Innes, M. 2004. Signal crimes and signal disorders: Notes on deviance as communicative action. *British Journal of Sociology*, 55 (3): 335–355.

Ireland, J. L. 2011. The importance of coping, threat appraisal, and beliefs in understanding and responding to fear of victimization: Applications to a male prisoner sample. *Law and Human Behavior*, 35 (4): 306–15.

Jackson, J. 2011. Revisiting risk sensitivity in the fear of crime. *Journal of Research in Crime and Delinquency*, 48 (4): 513–537.

Jackson, J. 2015a. Cognitive Closure and Risk Sensitivity in the Fear of Crime. *Legal and Criminological Psychology*, 20 (2): 222–240.

Jackson, J. 2015b. On the dual motivational force of legitimate authority. In *Cooperation and compliance with authority: The role of institutional trust*, edited by B. H. Bornstein and A. J. Tomkins, 145–166. (Nebraska Symposium on Motivation 62.) New York: Springer.

Jackson, J., and Gau, J. 2015. Carving up concepts? Differentiating between legitimacy and trust in public attitudes towards legal authority. In *Interdisciplinary perspectives on trust: Towards theoretical and methodological integration*, edited by E. Shockley, T. M. S. Neal, L. PytlikZillig, and B. Bornstein, 49–69. New York: Springer.

Jackson, J., and Gray, E. 2010. Functional fear and public insecurities about crime. *British Journal of Criminology*, 50: 1–21.

Jackson, J., and Kuha, J. 2014. Worry about crime in a cross-national context: A model-supported method of measurement using European Social Survey data. *Survey Research Methods*, 8 (2): 109–126.

Jackson, J., Bradford, B., Hough, M., Myhill, A., Quinton, P., and Tyler, T. R. 2012. Why do people comply with the law? Legitimacy and the influence of legal institutions. *British Journal of Criminology*, 52 (6): 1051–1071.

Jackson, J., Bradford, B., Kuha, J., and Hough, M. 2015. Empirical legitimacy as two connected psychological states. In *Improving legitimacy of criminal justice in emerging democracies*, edited by G. Meško and J. Tankebe, 137–160. London: Springer.

Jackson, J., Bradford, B., Stanko, E. A., and Hohl, K. 2012. *Just authority? Trust in the police in England and Wales*. London: Routledge.

Johnson, D., Maguire, E. R., and Kuhns, J. B. 2014. Public perceptions of the legitimacy of the law and legal authorities: Evidence from the Caribbean. *Law and Society Review*, 48 (4): 947–978.

Kruglanski, A. W., and Webster, D. M. 1996. Motivated closing of the mind: Seizing and freezing. *Psychological Review*, 103 (2): 263–283.

Long, J. S. 1997. *Regression models for categorical and limited dependent variables*. Thousand Oaks, CA: Sage.

Long, J. S., and Freese, J. 2006. *Regression models for categorical dependent variables using Stata*. College Station, TX: Stata Press.

Lorenc, T., Clayton, S., Neary, D., Whitehead, M., Petticrew, M., Thomson, H., … and Renton, A. 2012. Crime, fear of crime, environment, and mental health and wellbeing: Mapping review of theories and causal pathways. *Health & Place*, 18: 757–765.

Maguire, E. R., and Johnson, D. 2014. Rethinking the dimensions of public perceptions of police legitimacy. Unpublished manuscript, American University, Washington, DC.

Mazerolle, L., Bennett, S., Antrobus, E., and Tyler, T. R. 2013. Shaping citizen perceptions of police legitimacy: A randomized field trial of procedural justice. *Criminology*, 51 (1): 33–63.

Moustaki, I., and Knott, M. 2000. Generalized latent trait models. *Psychometrika*, 65: 391–411.

Murphy, K., Sargeant, E., and Cherney, A. 2015. The importance of procedural justice and police performance in shaping intentions to cooperate with the police: Does social identity matter? *European Journal of Criminology*, 12 (6): 719–738.

Murphy, K., Tyler, T. R., and Curtis, A. 2009. Nurturing regulatory compliance: Is procedural justice effective when people question the legitimacy of the law? *Regulation and Governance*, 3 (1): 1–26.

Murphy, T., Bradford, B., and Jackson, J. 2016. Motivating compliance behavior among offenders: Procedural justice or deterrence? *Criminal Justice & Behavior*, 43 (1): 102–118.

Pain, R. 2001. Gender, race, age and fear in the city. *Urban Studies*, 38: 899–913.

Papachristos, A., Meares, T., and Fagan, J. 2012. Why do criminals obey the law? The influence of legitimacy and social networks on active gun offenders. *Journal of Criminal Law and Criminology*, 102 (2): 397–439.

Quinton, P. 2010. *The impact of information about crime and policing on public perceptions: The results of a randomised controlled trial.* London: National Policing Improvement Agency.

Rader, N. E., and Cossman, J. S. 2011. Gender differences in US college students' fear for others. *Sex Roles*, 64: 568–581.

Ramirez, M. D. 2013. Americans changing views toward crime and punishment, *Public Opinion Quarterly*, 77 (4): 1006–1031.

Reisig, M. D., Bratton, J., and Gertz, M. G. 2007. The construct validity and refinement of process-based policing measures. *Criminal Justice and Behavior*, 34 (8): 1005–1027.

Shaw, G. M., and Brannan, K. E. 2009. The polls-trends: Confidence in law enforcement, *Public Opinion Quarterly*, 73: 199–220.

Shaw, G. M., Shapiro, R. Y. Lock, S., and Jacobs, L. R. 1998. The polls-trends: Crime, the police, and civil liberties, *Public Opinion Quarterly*, 62: 405–426.

Shinew, K. J., Stodolska, M., Roman, C. G., and Yahner, J. 2013. Crime, physical activity and outdoor recreation among Latino adolescents in Chicago. *Preventive Medicine*, 57 (15): 541–544. doi: 10.1016/j.ypmed.2013.07.008.

Spearman, C. 1904. General intelligence, objectively determined and measured. *American Journal of Psychology*, 15: 201–293.

Stafford, M., Chandola, T., and Marmot, M. 2007. Association between fear of crime and mental health and physical functioning. *American Journal of Public Health*, 97: 2076–2081.

Stoutland, S. E. 2001. The multiple dimensions of trust in resident/police relations in Boston. *Journal of Research in Crime and Delinquency*, 38: 226–256.

Sunshine, J., and Tyler, T. R. 2003. The role of procedural justice and legitimacy in public support for policing. *Law and Society Review*, 37 (3): 513–548.

Tallis, R., Davey, G. C. L., and Capuzzo, N. 1994. The phenomenology of non-pathological worry: A preliminary investigation. In *Worrying: Perspectives on theory, assessment and treatment*, edited by G. C. L. Davey and F. Tallis, 61–89. London: Wiley.

Tankebe, J. 2013. Viewing things differently: The dimensions of public perceptions of legitimacy. *Criminology*, 51 (1): 103–135.

Tankebe, J., Reisig, M. D., and Wang, X. 2015. A multidimensional model of police legitimacy: A cross-cultural assessment. *Law and Human Behavior*. doi: 10.1037/lhb0000153.

Trinkner, R., and Cohn, E. S. 2014. Putting the "social" back in legal socialization: Procedural justice, legitimacy, and cynicism in legal and nonlegal authorities. *Law and Human Behavior*, 38 (6): 602 617. doi: 10.1037/lhb0000107.

Tyler, T. R., and Blader, S. L. 2003. The group engagement model: Procedural justice, social identity, and cooperative behaviour. *Personality and Social Psychology Review*, 7: 349–361.

Tyler, T. R. 2003. Procedural justice, legitimacy, and the effective rule of law. In *Crime and justice: A review of research*, edited by M. Tonry, vol. 30, 431–505. Chicago, OL: University of Chicago Press.

Tyler, T. R. 2006a. Legitimacy and legitimation. *Annual Review of Psychology*, 57: 375–400.

Tyler, T. R. 2006b. *Why people obey the law*. New Haven, CT: Yale University Press.

Tyler, T. R., and Huo, Y. J. 2002. *Trust in the law: Encouraging public cooperation with the police and courts*. New York: Russell Sage Foundation.

Tyler, T. R., and Jackson, J. 2013. Future challenges in the study of legitimacy and criminal justice. In *Legitimacy and criminal justice: An international exploration*, edited by J. Tankebe and A. Liebling, 83–104. Oxford: Oxford University Press.

Tyler, T. R., and Jackson, J. 2014. Popular legitimacy and the exercise of legal authority: Motivating compliance, cooperation and engagement. *Psychology, Public Policy and Law*, 20 (1): 78–95.

Tyler, T. R., Fagan, J. A., and Geller, A. 2014. Street stops and police legitimacy: Teachable moments in young urban men's legal socialization. *Journal of Empirical Legal Studies*, 11 (4): 751–785.

Tyler, T. R., Jackson, J. and Mentovich, A. 2015. On the consequences of being a target of suspicion: Potential pitfalls of proactive police contact. *Journal of Empirical Legal Studies*, 12 (4): 602–636.

Tyler, T. R., Schulhofer, S. J., and Huq, A. Z. 2010. Legitimacy and deterrence effects in counter-terrorism policing: A study of Muslim Americans. *Law and Society Review*, 44: 365–401.

White, M. D., Mulvey, P., and Dario, L. M. 2015. Arrestees' perceptions of the police exploring procedural justice, legitimacy, and willingness to cooperate with police across offender types. *Criminal Justice and Behavior*. doi: 10.1177/0093854815602501.

Wolfe, S. E., Nix, J., Kaminski, R., and Rojek, J. 2015. Is the effect of procedural justice on police legitimacy invariant? Testing the generality of procedural justice and competing antecedents of legitimacy. *Journal of Quantitative Criminology*. doi: 10.1007/s10940-015-9263-8.

Yang, S., and Hinkle, J. C. 2012. Issues in survey design: Using surveys of victimization and fear of crime as examples. In *The handbook of survey methodology in social sciences*, edited by L. Gideon, 443–462. New York: Springer.

Further Reading

Bradford, B., Jackson, J., and Stanko, E. 2009. Contact and confidence: Revisiting the impact of public encounters with the police. *Policing and Society*, 19 (1): 20–46.

Bradford, B. 2014. Policing and social identity: Procedural justice, inclusion and cooperation between police and public. *Policing and Society*, 24 (1): 22–43.

Bradford, B., Huq, A., Jackson, J., and Roberts, B. 2014. What price fairness when security is at stake? Police legitimacy in South Africa. *Regulation and Governance*, 8 (2): 246–268.

Bradford, B., Murphy, K., and Jackson, J. 2014. Officers as mirrors: Policing, procedural justice and the (re)production of social identity. *British Journal of Criminology*, 54 (4): 527–500.

Ferraro, K. F. 1995. *Fear of crime: Interpreting victimization risk*. New York: SUNY Press.

Hand, D. J. 2004. *Measurement theory and practice: The world through quantification*. London: Arnold.

Hough, M. 1995. *Anxiety about crime: Findings from the 1994 British Crime Survey*. (Home Office Research Study No. 147.) London: Home Office.

Jackson, J. 2009. A psychological perspective on vulnerability in the fear of crime. *Psychology, Crime & Law*, 15 (4): 365–390.

Rousseau, D. M., Sitkin, S. B., Burt, R. S. and Camerer, C. 1998. Not so different after all: A cross-discipline view of trust. *Academy of Management Review*, 23 (3): 393–404.

Skogan, W. G. 2006. Asymmetry in the impact of encounters with the police. *Policing and Society*, 16 (2): 99–126.

Tyler, T. R., and Trinkner, R. 2015. Learning about the law: Legal socialization in an era of mistrust. Unpublished manuscript.

Warr, M. 2000. Fear of crime in the United States: Avenues for research and policy. *Criminal Justice*, 4: 451–489.

18

Measuring the Cost of Crime

Matt DeLisi

Introduction

By definition, for a behavior to be criminal, it must produce or cause some harm. The harm can pertain to a person – it can be, for example, a bloody nose and scrapes during an assault; to property – for example, damage to one's vehicle or home; or to society at large – for example, the blight caused by nuisance offending or drug use. In relation to criminal harm, the subjective seriousness of crime is largely reflected in criminal statutes. Legislatures enact criminal codes with specified punishment upon conviction, and that punishment largely reflects the harm that was done through the criminal offense. Thus murder, rape, and kidnapping are punished very harshly – by death, life imprisonment, or a lengthy sentence of determinate duration. Moderately serious crimes such as arson, burglary, and robbery are punished by imprisonment or intermediate sanctions, while crimes like traffic violations and petty offenses are punished by nominal fines. Systems of criminal law are predicated on the notions of offense, harm, and punishment as a means to rectify the damage caused by antisocial behavior. No harm, no foul – the saying goes.

Another way to understand the harm caused by a criminal offense is to view it as a cost (for early investigations into this theme, see Avi-Itzhak and Shinnar, 1973; Hann, 1972; Hawkins and Waller, 1936; Martin and Bradley, 1963; Morris and Tweeten, 1971; Shinnar and Shinnar, 1975; Smith, 1901). To use the aforementioned examples, a bloody nose and scrapes from an assault might result in a hospital visit for medical treatment. Damage to one's property produces insurance costs and out-of-pocket expenditures designed to repair the damage. And crimes against society impose costs such as lower property values, decreased quality of life, avoidant

The Handbook of Measurement Issues in Criminology and Criminal Justice, First Edition.
Edited by Beth M. Huebner and Timothy S. Bynum.

behaviors, and private security outlays. In other words, crime produces tangible costs. Indeed local, state, and federal criminal justice systems produce operating costs in excess of $200 billion each year (Kyckelhahn, 2011, 2012), and the direct costs to crime victims are estimated at approximately $100 billion annually (Cohen, 1988). International estimates are similarly large. The annual burden of crime is estimated at approximately $32 billion in Australia (Mayhew, 2003) and at £60 billion in the United Kingdom (Brand and Price, 2000). However, crime also imposes intangible costs that center on the pain, suffering, and negative burden that the offense places on the victim, along with the fear of potential criminal victimization. When intangible factors are also considered, the annual burden of crime has been estimated at a staggering $1 trillion (Anderson, 1999).

Here the literature on the costs of crime will be reviewed. Although monetization studies of crime are a relatively small area of scholarship, this niche is important because it demonstrates the fiscal, human, and social costs of antisocial behavior. Methodological and substantive challenges to monetizing crime costs will be discussed, including the central issue of whether crime costs can be effectively monetized at all. In addition, suggestions for future research will be made: linkages to cost–benefit analyses of prevention and criminal justice system programs, the incorporation of criminological theory that can inform what was heretofore an entirely empirical area, the embracing of qualitative research designs and qualitative data with a view to unearthing new constructs and measures, an expansion of willingness-to-pay estimates in order to accurately quantify crime costs, and consideration of the public's willingness to invest in all forms of criminal punishment (beyond rehabilitation) so as to effectively neutralize serious criminal offenders.

The Costs of Crime

The costs of crime are measured along four general dimensions relating to the type of cost and the party that bears the burden of that cost. Concerning the first of these two factors, there are two types of costs. Tangible costs encompass concrete expenditures such as treatment for medical care and health loss; work, compensation, and productivity losses; security measures for home and person; insurance costs; and costs that are incurred through changes in behavior. Changes in behavior reflect any behavioral decision where an extra measure was taken to reduce one's potential for victimization. Driving one's vehicle in order to avoid using public transportation during certain times of day or night or taking a cab instead of walking on the street are examples. Intangible costs relate to the physical and psychological strains that are associated with criminal victimization and the fear of it. These include changes in behavior, loss of quality of life, reduced perceptions about public safety, or more negative view of society (Anderson, 1999; Cohen, 1988, 2005; Doland and Peasgood, 2007; Moore and Shepherd, 2006; Smith, 1901).

Direct and indirect costs are best understood when imagining a horrifying crime, such as the Sandy Hook Elementary School shooting of December 2012, in which 20 children and six adults were murdered (the perpetrator also murdered his own mother, then committed suicide as law enforcement responded to the mass murder). The mass murder created immediate direct costs associated with the violence – costs in terms of medical care and physical and psychological treatment. However, the event was so shocking that it imposed a psychological toll that weighed on people across the United States and around the world. It has a psychogenic effect. As Alvarez and Bachman (2003, p. 204) suggested:

> The high rates of murder that our society endures annually affect us all. Even those of us who have never been personally touched by lethal violence are aware of the widespread presence of this violence in our communities. The ever-present fear that we or someone we love may be killed is but another form of psychic violence that we must all endure.

Whatever sorrow, pain, and distress was produced by the Sandy Hook shooting to persons not immediately involved was intangible, but was certainly real and profound. This example reveals the two parties that bear the burden of crime: the victim and the general public, or society at large. The point to take away is that the direct victim – and indeed anyone – can feel the consequences of a criminal event, and those consequences can be tangible or intangible.

There is no gold-standard methodology or standard measure of the costs of crime. However, there is general agreement that monetization estimates should include tangible and intangible costs, and costs to the specific victim and society as a whole. Moreover, researchers were primarily interested in the assorted costs that were imposed by a single type of offender, or in the costs imposed by a single type of crime. One of the most replicated methodological approaches to studying the cost of crime was developed by Mark Cohen and colleagues (Cohen, 1998, 2005; Cohen, Miller, and Rossman, 1994; Miller, Cohen, and Wiersema, 1996), who devised a formula for monetizing a criminal career in order to determine its lifetime external costs. The formula is:

$$\Sigma_{ij}(1-\beta)^{j-1}\lambda_{ij}\left[VC_i + CJ_i + CI^{*}T_i + W^{*}T_i\right]$$

where λ = mean number of offenses, VC = victim costs of crime, CJ = costs of criminal justice investigation, arrest, adjudication, CI = cost of incarceration in days, T = average time served, β = discount rate, W = opportunity cost of offender's time, I = crime 1 through crime I, j = year 1 through year J of crime.

This formula produces assorted cost estimates for specific criminal offenses in order to monetize the costs of a criminal career and, conversely, the savings due to prevention efforts. Victim costs include tangible costs, intangible costs, and risk of death where applicable, as in the case of homicide. Criminal justice costs are also produced and include the annualized costs of investigation, legal defense, incarceration, parole, and probation. Lost earnings equal the average yearly income lost due to incarceration (Cohen, 1998).

In his seminal paper on the costs of one high-rate juvenile offender, Cohen (1998) calculated that the total external costs of a life of crime range approximately from $1.5 to $1.8 million. The costs were spread across a range of areas, 50 percent of the total cost relating to lost quality of life, about 25 percent being tangible victim costs, 20 percent being criminal justice system costs, and 5 percent coming from losses in work productivity. Cohen's work is important because it puts a price tag on the sheer fiscal cost and negativity associated with the development of a youth into a serious, violent, and chronic juvenile offender. Moreover, it translates into financial terms the value of primary, secondary, and tertiary prevention efforts to preclude the development of a serious, violent, and chronic juvenile offender.

That a single serious, chronic, and violent juvenile delinquent imposes costs between $1 million to $2 million should also be understood in another way. Most youth – the majority of whom are predominantly conventional in their behaviors and have little delinquent involvement and likely none with the juvenile justice system – impose crime costs of approximately $0. By contrast, severely antisocial youth are emotionally, cognitively, and behaviorally discrepant from their peers (Cohen, Piquero, and Jennings 2010a, 2010b; DeLisi and Vaughn, 2014; Farrington and Welsh, 2007; Vaughn et al., 2014; Walters, 2011), and they are even *more discrepant* from them in sheer dollars and cents.

Subsequent researchers have employed similar methodologies and in many respects replicated Cohen's finding that a single serious offender costs in excess of $1 million. Using data from a highly antisocial sample of 500 adult habitual criminals with at least 30 career arrests, DeLisi and Gatling (2003) replicated Cohen's research by estimating the assorted victimization costs of career criminals, expressed in US dollars at their value in 2002. They found that the average career of an offender imposed more than $831,000 in victim costs, nearly $275,000 in criminal justice system costs, and more than $29,000 in lost productivity. The mean cost imposed per offender was more than $1.14 million. However, some of the offenders in the DeLisi and Gatling sample were extraordinarily antisocial and amassed criminal records with hundreds of arrests, convictions, and sentences. The most recidivistic offenders in their sample created more than $10 million in costs. Drawing on data from the Pittsburgh Youth Study, Welsh and colleagues (2008) examined the costs of delinquent careers among 503 boys. They found that the 10 percent most serious and chronic delinquents – who were essentially life-course-persistent offenders (Moffitt, 1993) – imposed approximately $800,000 to $900,000 in victim costs during adolescence alone.

Building on this work, Cohen and Piquero (2009) advanced the understanding of the monetary costs of criminal careers by using expanded offense and cost estimates and a much larger sample. Their analyses of 27,186 participants from the 1958 Philadelphia birth cohort (Tracy, Wolfgang, and Figlio, 1990; Tracy and Kempf-Leonard, 1996) produced several important findings. First, the present value of saving a high-risk youth ("saving" designates preventive value: it indicates how much money and victimization would be prevented if an offending career was forestalled) was estimated at something between $2.6 million and $5.3 million at the age of 18 (at the value of the US dollar in 2007). Second, the costs were higher at the age of 10 ($3.2 to $5.5 million) and at the age of 14 ($3.2 million to $5.8 million), which indicates the importance of detecting the early onset of criminal careers. This is meaningful because the most severe offenders often begin accumulating police contacts or arrests during childhood (DeLisi et al., 2013).

Third, Cohen and Piquero (2009) reported thatthe present cost (calculated at the value of the US dollar in 2007) of saving a high-risk youth ranged from $2.6 million to $4.4 million. Overall, monetization studies are concordant with criminal career research, which indicates that a small number of offenders impose a disproportionate burden in terms of criminal offenses along with a commensurate fiscal burden on crime victims, criminal justice systems, and the general public (DeLisi and Gatling, 2003; French et al., 2004; Miller et al., 2006; Welsh et al., 2008).

Another contribution is that monetization procedures were bolstered to include estimates of public willingness to pay. Willingness to pay is a concept that attempts to quantify the pain and suffering that crime creates, even though "pain and suffering" is not a construct that can be readily bought and sold (unlike tangible goods and services). Essentially, willingness-to-pay estimates capture public concern about crime and public willingness to assist in crime prevention. Willingness to pay is measured by analyzing criminal justice policies or government programs that are designed to prevent crimes (see Cohen, 2005, pp. 25–29). Willingness-to-pay estimates significantly increase cost estimates associated with serious criminal offenders, but they are important to include because they tap the intangible societal concern about crime. Cohen and colleagues (2004) calculated willingness-to-pay estimates on the basis of a nationally representative sample and found that they were between 1.5 and 10 times higher than previous estimates of the costs of crime, because they encompassed collateral costs. These costs covered prevention expenditures for personal security, avoidant behaviors to safeguard against victimization, third-party costs of insurance, and government welfare programs. To put the monetary costs of a single chronic offender in its proper context, the addition of willingness-to-pay estimates would increase total costs potentially to nearly $20 million per offender.

Some researchers have examined the targeted costs associated with a specific criminal's offenses (see Cohen, 1990; Corso, Fang, and Mercy, 2011; McCollister, French, and Fang, 2010; Miller, Cohen, and Rossman, 1993; Miller, Fisher, and Cohen, 2001). Miller and colleagues (1993) examined the monetary costs and reduced quality of life that resulted from death or nonfatal injury – which in turn resulted from serious felony victimization. They produced the following average costs per offense: murder ($2.4 million), rape ($47,000–60,000), robbery ($19,000), assault ($15,000–25,000), and arson ($25,000–50,000). Drawing on state-level data selected from Pennsylvania, Miller and colleagues (2001) produced estimates of specific forms of violence committed by and against juveniles. Considering medical care costs, lost future earnings, public program costs, property damage and losses, and quality of life losses, the average cost of a murder of a juvenile was nearly

$4.2 million in urban areas and more than $4.3 million in rural areas. The average cost of a murder of an adult in urban Pennsylvania was nearly $3.5 million and less than $3 million in rural areas.

McCollister and colleagues (2010) used more recent data and produced generally higher estimates for index offenses. The produced the following average unit costs per offense: murder, $8.9 million; rape, $240,776; assault, $107,020; robbery, $42,310; motor vehicle theft, $10,772; and arson, $21,103. In a study exclusively dedicated to murder, DeLisi and colleagues (2010) replicated the crime estimates developed by Cohen and Piquero (2009) on a sample of convicted homicide offenders selected from eight states. They found that each murder cost more than $5.16 million in direct costs and over $12 million in willingness-to-pay costs for a combined cost of $17.25 million per murder. In addition, because murderers in their sample were also convicted of other crimes, the average murderer in their data produced costs of approximately $24 million. Singly, the most violent and chronic offenders in their data produced costs in the range of $150 million (DeLisi et al., 2010).

To summarize, monetization studies of the costs of crime have produced a handful of important findings. First, the cost of crime is enormous when tangible and intangible features are considered. The fiscal burden of crime reaches easily billions of dollars annually, and some estimates are as high as $1 trillion per year (Anderson, 1999). For many years, to judge from poll data, crime was the paramount social concern among Americans, and the sheer costs of it justify the amount of public concern. While critics can quibble with the sometimes wide-ranging estimates across studies for the same offense (compare Alda and Cuesta, 2011; Byrnes, Doran, and Shakeshaft, 2012; Clark and Davis, 2011; Cohen, 2005; Cohen et al., 2010a, 2010b), monetization research nevertheless places a dollar figure on specific crimes.

Second, the costs of crime strongly align with offense seriousness in terms of legal criteria and subjective assessments. Murder and rape estimates are dramatically higher than estimates for less serious crimes, such as property and nuisance offending. In this way monetary cost estimates for criminal offenses are roughly commensurate with their perceived and legal seriousness. Third, monetization studies demonstrate asymmetry in offending – the highest costs are imposed by the most violent and chronic offenders. Consequently, prevention and correctional efforts can be effectively promoted for their cost-saving effects when the most serious offenders are considered (Cohen et al., 2010a, 2010b; Farrington and Welsh, 2007; Welsh, 2004; Welsh and Farrington, 2012, 2013).

Fourth and finally, measuring the costs of crime permits inquiry into the psychological, social psychological, and spiritual harms that result from antisocial behavior. By considering tangible and intangible costs and by including both the specific victim and society at large, monetization studies represent an important method by which the negative consequences of offending are realized. Of course, no scholarly area is perfect, and there are important methodological and substantive problems in this kind of research too. These challenges are examined next, together with possible future directions.

Methodological and Substantive Challenges

Although there are similarities across research designs in monetization studies, estimates of the cost of various crimes can be widely different at times. However, there is a more general methodological and substantive problem with estimating the cost of crime – namely whether it can be done effectively at all. Consider this quotation from Hawkins and Waller nearly 80 years ago:

> Instead of attempting to discover the cost of crime, *an enterprise foredoomed to some absurdity*, we need to study the economic effects of crime. We need to know the nature and magnitude of the probable immediate results of a crime crusade. We need to be more cognizant of the permanent consequences of crime as an organic part of our society. (Hawkins and Waller, 1936, p. 694, italics added)

Published studies on the costs of crime often attract significant media and public attention (e.g., Bialik, 2010; Blow, 2010) and, while some of this scrutiny is appreciative of the findings, another part of it is quite skeptical about the monetary values that are placed on specific crimes – and on crime generally (see Zimring and Hawkins, 1995).

At least two substantive considerations challenge the veracity of cost estimates of crime. First, victimization is not universally experienced by crime victims. A group whose members have the highest level of victimization, and hence the greatest risk of becoming victims of violent crime, is that of active criminal offenders. Yet active criminal offenders have numerous antisocial peers, are immersed in a criminal lifestyle, and generally view the threat of victimization as part and parcel of a life of crime (Copes, Hochstetler, and Cherbonneau, 2012; Hochstetler, Copes, and Williams, 2010; Walters, 1990, 2011). From this angle, crime is not generally perceived to be a cost; indeed crime is pursued and perpetrated by active street offenders because it offers many psychological, emotional, and financial benefits. For instance, criminological research (Wilson and Abrahamse, 1992) and theory (Gottfredson and Hirschi, 1990) indicates that many criminal offenses are short-term solutions to an immediate desire on the part of the offender. Thus crime appears in a positive light because its negative consequences are not truly considered.

Fear of crime also tends to be inversely related to risk of victimization (Mears and Stewart, 2010; Moore and Shepherd, 2006; Rader, Cossman, and Porter, 2012; Scarborough et al., 2010), such that the elderly, women, and whites often report greater fear despite their comparatively low victimization by comparison to that of the young, men, and nonwhites. For instance, an assault between adolescent males who are fighting during a hockey game is likely not even viewed as an assault by either party. Conversely, an assault against an older adult might be highly upsetting, even traumatic. Thus a particular crime does not have the same "cost" for every victim. Indeed, in the event of a mutually combative assault, the assault could be viewed in positive terms from the perpetrator's perspective. Second, given sharp socioeconomic differences across individuals, the notion that crimes have a fixed monetary value is questionable. For instance, the burglary of a dwelling that is valued at $10,000 likely is not, in terms of cost, the same as the burglary of a dwelling that is valued at $500,000. Hence crime estimates need to reflect the differential values that life and property have in society.

A methodological and substantive challenge is that the harm imposed by crime is incalculable, not because estimates are methodologically incorrect or artificially produced, but because of the human suffering that is involved in crime, and especially in serious violence. The literature on co-victims of homicide – family and friends of a murder victim – is illustrative. Co-victims of homicide experience a range of profound negative emotions that persist and are often lifelong. These include bereavement, maladaptive coping, post-traumatic stress disorder, and, at times, intense anger and dissatisfaction with the criminal justice system (Armour, 2002, 2007; Rinear, 1988; Stretesky et al., 2010; Vollum and Longmire, 2007). It would be difficult to place a monetary value on the pain, suffering, and anguish experienced by the victims of the most violent crimes, regardless of the data produced by actuarial tables. This point bears repeating. The harm produced by murder, or rape, or kidnapping, or burglary is extraordinary and often difficult to overcome. That emotional content most probably cannot be quantified in such a way as to link the human suffering to a cost estimate.

There are other questions that have been raised about monetization studies of crime. There is ample variation within and across legal jurisdictions in terms of the costs of criminal justice system operations (Kyckelhahn, 2011, 2012). From a systems perspective, crime sets in motion a rather lengthy chain of events – police contact and arrest, booking and interview by pre-trial service personnel, posting of bond and potential interaction with bondspersons (and, later, perhaps bounty hunters) – and people – sheriff's deputies and other jail staff, including nurses, psychologists, and various law enforcement technicians, public defenders or private counsel, prosecutors, judges, bailiffs, pre-trial treatment personnel, and others. If the offender is convicted, then there is, subsequently, possible contact with probation officers, day reporting officers, jail staff, prison staff and correctional officers, parole officers, and others. Each of these careers presupposes a salary and benefits that generate costs, and these costs vary around the country. Thus a crime "costs" more in an expensive jurisdiction than in an area with a lower operational criminal justice system cost. Concomitantly, there are massive geographic differences in crime rates: many large cities (for instance, Chicago) experience several times more homicides than entire states (for instance, Iowa). Of course, more densely populated urban centers with higher crime rates will generate greater costs than more sparsely populated areas and areas with lower crime rates.

It is common to calculate (or make estimates for) lost productivity for individual offenders; however, this approach masks the extraordinary variation in earning potential across the human population. Given the relatively low human capital and education of the modal criminal offender (DeLisi, 2013; DeLisi and Vaughn, 2014; Walters, 1990, 2011; Wilson and Herrnstein, 1985), it is incorrect to assert that a typical street offender will potentially forestall the career earnings of a more prosocial individual. In terms of life chances and career earnings potential, the typical street offender is dramatically lower than the typical functional member of society. Moreover, the lost productivity estimates are usually significantly smaller than victim and criminal justice system costs, and should bedropped.

Future Research Directions

As mentioned before, measuring the cost of crime is a niche – a relatively small area of research, and one that is not widely studied by criminologists. As a result, in terms of research design and measurement, there has perhaps not been as much innovation here as in more popularly studied areas of criminological inquiry – such as biosocial criminology, the study of delinquent peers, general strain theory, self-control theory, and many others. Nevertheless, there are exciting opportunities for new approaches to measuring the cost of crime.

First, the literature on measuring the cost of crime has been, to date, essentially comprised of studies such as the ones reviewed here: studies of the cost of specific offenses, the cost of specific types of offenders (e.g., career criminals), and studies of the cumulative burden of crime. However, there is also an important, allied literature that examines the cost–benefit of various prevention programs, correctional policies, and criminal sanctions (see Armstrong et al., 2011; Klietz, Borduin, and Schaeffer, 2010; Roman, 2004; Welsh, Farrington, and Sherman, 2001; Welsh, Sullivan, and Olds, 2010). A frequent finding is that prevention and other innovative programs can often produce dramatic savings in standard criminal justice operations, and thus can reduce costs. Many also have the advantage of reducing crime. For instance, Yeh (2010) analyzed national prisoner data to examine potential cost savings obtained from monitoring parolees and probationers with electronic monitoring. He estimated that more than 781,000 crimes could be averted annually, which would save more than $481 billion. For every dollar invested on the proposed intervention, nearly $13 were saved. Yeh's study is important because it demonstrates the practical importance of knowledge on the costs of crime. Greater efforts should be made to integrate the costs-of-crime literature that focuses on specific offenders or offenses with cost–benefit analyses of real programs in the justice system. This would help to counter the criticism that that costs-of-crime studies are artificial statistical estimates by demonstrating the implications on the fiscal realities of police, courts, and corrections.

Sometimes the cost–benefits of various criminal justice policies are far less than expected. Downey and Roman (2014) analyzed data from the National Institute of Justice's Multisite Adult Drug Court Evaluation and compared drug court participants to a control group of probationers on a variety of outcomes such as social productivity, criminal justice system costs, crime and victimization, service use, and financial support use. Overall, drug court participants were significantly less expensive than standard probationers in two areas: crime and victimization and service use. Although drug court participants cost $5,680 less than standard probationers, the difference was not statistically significant.

Second, costs-of-crime studies are almost entirely devoid of criminological theory. This is unfortunate, because in this way potential linkages between an empirical area of research and conceptual perspectives that could guide research findings are omitted and ignored. Several studies have shown that the most violent and recidivistic offenders are also the most costly ones (Cohen and Piquero, 2009; Cohen et al., 2010a, 2010b; Piquero, Jennings, and Farrington, 2013; DeLisi and Gatling, 2003; DeLisi et al., 2010). Future research could employ theoretically derived measures to assess predictors of costs of crime. There are many research questions to consider – questions that span the criminological theory canon. Are psychopathic offenders more costly than nonpsychopathic offenders? Which facets of the psychopathic personality are most predictive of greater costs? What is the relationship between self-control and an offender's subsequent fiscal burden? Do delinquent peers increase the costs of crime? How do social bonds reduce the costs of crime? Do delinquent become more costly in their antisocial behavior when they experience general strain? Do the costs of crime over an offending career comport with Moffitt's developmental taxonomy? Do social supports serve to attenuate the costs of crime among former prisoners? Are there protective factors that reduce the potential criminal costs of delinquents or adult criminals?

It is probable that the causes and correlates of serious criminal offending will also be associated with greater social and fiscal burden. But these are not simply academic questions. If theoretically meaningful constructs are found to consistently predict increased crime costs, they could serve as targets for treatment and correctional programs. For example, Klietz and colleagues (2010) studied the cost–benefits of multisystemtic therapy versus individual therapy among a sample of delinquent youth and followed them up for nearly 15 years. They found that between $9.51 and $23.59 corresponded, in savings, to every dollar spent on multisystemtic therapy. Identifying the specific features of youth who respond well to programs like these is an important goal.

Additionally, costs-of-crime studies could be integrated with epidemiological research that produces latent groupings of offenders on the basis of the severity of externalizing behavior (Vaughn, DeLisi, et al., 2011; Vaughn et al., 2010; Vaughn, Fu, et al., 2011; Vaughn et al., 2014) and is informed by theory (Moffitt, 1993). This would allow quantitative estimates of the various costs of types of individuals (e.g., abstainers from delinquency, adolescence-limited offenders, life-course-persistent offenders), which could in turn facilitate cost–benefit analyses of various sanctions and programs that serve these offenders. Research on abstainers from delinquency could be particularly meaningful if dynamic factors – prosocial peers, high conscientiousness, social support, decision-making, impulse control, and many others – associated with abstainer status were identified. These protective traits serve as treatment targets, in other words they should be bolstered in offenders who currently lack them (Heckman, 2006).

Third, monetization studies of the cost of crime are by definition quantitative. However, it is likely that qualitative research designs would prove very useful by helping develop themes among crime victims and criminal offenders that broaden the scope of constructs often included in cost estimates. For instance, focus groups with various types of crime victims, such as victims of sexual assault, domestic violence, burglary, identity theft, and many others would probably reveal the multitudinous ways in which victimization has reduced their well-being and overall quality of life. Interviews with crime victims could also reveal the various academic, employment, economic, and relationship problems that stem from their victimization. It is probable that tangible victim costs are much broader than has traditionally been measured.

Qualitative data could also shed further light on the real and perceived secondary victimization that victims feel when the legal system fails to arrest or prosecute their victimizer. In addition to the bereavement that accompanies the violent death of a loved one, family survivors of crime victims also sometimes face the incompetence and lack of interest of a criminal justice system that fails to close the case with an arrest (Malone, 2007; Stretesky et al., 2010). Although a variety of factors outside of the control of criminal justice system agents influence whether a case will go unsolved (e.g., witnesses who are unwilling to testify, witnesses and victims of the crime who are themselves active offenders and refuse to cooperate with police, timeliness of reporting of the original crime, evidentiary issues), the family of crime victims nevertheless often feels tremendous frustration and outrage toward the justice system. For example, homicide cases involving victims who were transient (e.g., the homeless, runaways, prostitutes) are less likely to be cleared than homicide cases involving victims with greater resources and socioeconomic backgrounds (Keel, Jarvis, and Muirhead, 2009; Regoeczi and Jarvis, 2013). In this way qualitative criminologists could collect data on the cascade of victimization costs that accompany open and cold cases. Moreover, there is room to extend the literature on miscarriages of justice by focusing on what happens to the families of crime victims and to the crime victims themselves – in addition to focusing (as is the case in this literature) on offenders who were the victims or wrongful arrest, prosecutorial misconduct, and other errors in the justice system.

There is a rich ethnographic body of research on criminal offenders, but here too there are opportunities to mine the existing data or collect new data on offenders that reveal additional costs brought about by, or implicit in, a criminal lifestyle. For instance, Vaughn and colleagues (2010) have shown that individuals with various psychiatric conditions, particularly conduct-related disorders such as antisocial personality disorder, also impose a significant social burden in terms of social welfare receipt, above and beyond the costs that are created from criminal justice system interventions. Delving into the daily lives of serious criminal offenders would likely produce new focal areas for scholars to identify as sources of additional costs of crime.

Fourth, the use of willingness-to-pay estimates, which measure the public's willingness to invest in various criminal justice programs and policies toward crime prevention, is a controversial area in monetization of crime studies, and likely one that is in need of measurement innovation (see Bishop and Murphy, 2011; Cohen, 2005; Piquero et al., 2013). Several issues are involved here. First, the incorporation of willingness-to-pay estimates significantly increases the total costs of crime, and the increases are acutely higher for specific offenses, such as murder. For example, in one recent study (DeLisi et al., 2010), willingness-to-pay estimates comprised 70 percent of the total costs for murder, 66 percent of the total costs for rape, 85 percent of the total costs for armed robbery, 60 percent of the total costs for aggravated assault, and 87 percent of the total costs for burglary. To put this into perspective, about $12 million of the approximately $17 million price tag for murder were coming from a willingness-to-pay estimate. From one angle, this accurately reflects the extremity of murder and the sheer costs associated with it and with the co-victims of murder. From another angle, it is an artificial inflation.

It is difficult to reconcile these positions, which is precisely why more researchers are needed to potentially devise new approaches to measuring willingness-to-pay estimates. Although they inflate total cost estimates, willingness-to-pay estimates nevertheless seem to capture the human concern about crime prevention and the overall compassion for crime victims. For example, Corso and colleagues (2011) recently calculated that respondents are willing to pay $15 million to prevent one case of child maltreatment resulting in death. This estimate is close to the homicide estimate produced by DeLisi and colleagues (2010). Philosophically and spiritually, dramatically high willingness-to-pay estimates for homicide seem appropriate when we consider the value of human life. More critical methodologists might have difficulty countering this argument. On the other hand, more conservative measures produce much more conservative estimates of the cost of homicide. For example, Mayhew (2003) calculated the individual cost for homicide at $1.6 million, on the basis of data from Australia. On the basis of data from England and Wales, Brand and Price (2000) estimated that each homicide costs £1.1 million. Taken together, these international estimates do not include willingness-to-pay criteria and are a fraction of the putative costs of a single homicide in the United States.

Willingness-to-pay estimates are primarily focused on humanistic goals toward prevention and rehabilitation; but there are large substantive areas that have barely been studied. The criminal justice system treats and supervises criminal defendants according to a range of punishment philosophies that include not only rehabilitation and deterrence, but also retribution and incapacitation. Put simply, most people are willing to pay – and presumably willing to pay enormous amounts in public expenditures toward the punitive supervision of serious offenders (for instance, there is no public outcry about outlays for the criminal justice system, as there are for general concerns about outlays for other governmental services; see Levitt, 2004). Indeed Baker and colleagues (2013) recently found that participants with greater fear of crime and more punitive views about crime were willing to pay more for harsh punishments of juvenile offenders. Criminologists should consider all of the philosophical bases for criminal punishment (beyond the kinder, gentler forms like rehabilitation) to see how much the public is willing to invest in the justice system.

Finally, one could also make the claim that, although criminal justice system costs are ideally kept as low as possible, there is also benefit for more expensive processing costs. In other words, *higher costs* is sometimes a good thing. A recent study employing a randomized experimental design is revealing. Roman and colleagues (2009) examined the effectiveness of DNA analysis in investigating serious property crimes, such as residential burglary. Drawing on a sample of several hundred cases in five American cities where DNA evidence was collected, the investigators randomly assigned the cases to a treatment group where DNA processing was added to traditional investigative techniques – the only ones used in the control group. They found that the use of DNA processing increased the cost of each arrest by $4,000 to $14,000. However, a suspect was identified in 31 percent of cases and an arrest was made in 22 percent of cases in the treatment group. In the control group, a suspect was identified in only 13 percent of cases and an arrest was made in just 10 percent of cases. In other words, using moderately more expensive DNA processing increased the yield of capturing a serious burglar more than twofold. Given that residential burglaries are commonly committed by high-rate offenders who also commit various other crimes, the arrest of one can significantly reduce the incidence of residential burglary along with that of the other crimes in that offender's repertoire. In this regard, the higher costs associated with using DNA processing appear well worth investing. Thus criminologists should not be timid in making claims that, like in many areas of life, in the specialized processing of the criminal justice system, too, you get what you pay for.

Conclusion

Crime produces victims. The victims of crime encompass not only the immediately proximal individual who was victimized by the offender, but also that individual's family and friends, community, and society at large. Murder, rape, robbery, and burglary affect the murdered, raped, robbed, and burgled along with their family, friends, and neighbors. Research on the cost of crime has shown that there are expensive negative consequences – tangible and intangible, direct and indirect – to every criminal harm. The fiscal burden of crime easily mounts to billions, perhaps trillions, each year (Anderson, 1999; Cohen, 2005; Levitt, 2004). The most chronic and serious criminal offenders individually impose costs in the tens of millions – and, in the case of multiple homicide offenders, in the hundreds of millions. And the bereavement and suffering that accompanies some forms of criminal victimization are frankly incalculable, regardless of the large cost estimates that are assigned to each specific offense.

References

Alda, E., and Cuesta, J. 2011. A comprehensive estimation of costs of crime in South Africa and its implications for effective policy making. *Journal of International Development*, 23: 926–935.

Alvarez, A., and Bachman, R. 2003. *Murder: American style*. Belmont, CA: Wadsworth.

Anderson, D. A. 1999. The aggregate burden of crime. *The Journal of Law and Economics*, 42: 611–642.
Armour, M. P. 2002. Experiences of covictims of homicide implications for research and practice. *Trauma, Violence, & Abuse*, 3: 109–124.
Armour, M. P. 2007. Violent death: Understanding the context of traumatic and stigmatized grief. *Journal of Human Behavior in the Social Environment*, 14: 53–90.
Armstrong, G. S., Armstrong, T. A. Webb, V. J., and Atkin, C. A. 2011. Can financial incentives reduce juvenile confinement levels? An evaluation of the Redeploy Illinois Program. *Journal of Criminal Justice*, 39: 183–191.
Avi-Itzhak, B., and Shinnar, R. 1973. Quantitative models in crime control. *Journal of Criminal Justice*, 1: 185–217.
Baker, T., Cleary, H. M. D., Pickett, J. T., and Gertz, M. G. 2013. Crime salience and willingness to pay for child saving and juvenile punishment. *Crime and Delinquency*. doi: 10.1177/0011128713505487.
Bialik, C. 2010. The pitfalls of calculating bad behavior's true cost. *Wall Street Journal*. Accessed March 20, 2014. http://online.wsj.com/news/articles/SB10001424052748704353504575596302906347986?mg=reno64wsj&url=http%3A%2F%2Fonline.wsj.com%2Farticle%2FSB10001424052748704353504575596302906347986.html.
Bishop, K. C., and Murphy, A. D. 2011. Estimating the willingness to pay to avoid violent crime: A dynamic approach. *American Economic Review*, 101: 625–629.
Blow, C. M. 2010. High cost of crime. *The New York Times*. Accessed March 20, 2014. http://www.nytimes.com/2010/10/09/opinion/09blow.html?_r=4&hp&.
Brand, S., and Price, R. 2000. *The economic and social costs of crime*. London: Home Office Economics and Resource Analysis Unit.
Byrnes, J. M., Doran, C. M., and Shakeshaft, A. P. 2012. Cost per incident of alcohol-related crime in New South Wales. *Drug and Alcohol Review*, 31: 854–860.
Clark, J. R., and Davis, W. L. 2011. A human capital perspective on criminal careers. *Journal of Applied Business Research*, 11: 58–64.
Cohen, M. A. 1988. Pain, suffering, and jury awards: A study of the cost of crime to victims. *Law and Society Review*, 22: 537–555.
Cohen, M. A. 1990. A note on the cost of crime to victims. *Urban Studies*, 27: 139–146.
Cohen, M. A. 1998. The monetary value of saving a high-risk youth. *Journal of Quantitative Criminology*, 14: 5–33.
Cohen, M. A. 2005. *The costs of crime and justice*. New York: Routledge.
Cohen, M. A., Miller, T. R., and Rossman, S. B. 1994. The costs and consequences of violent behavior in the United States. In *Understanding and preventing violence*, vol. 4: *Consequences and control*, edited by Albert J. Reiss, Jr. and Jeffrey A. Roth, 67–166. Washington, DC: National Academy Press.
Cohen, M. A., and Piquero, A. R. 2009. New evidence on the monetary value of saving a high-risk youth. *Journal of Quantitative Criminology*, 25: 25–49.
Cohen, M. A., Piquero, A. R., and Jennings, W. G. 2010a. Estimating the costs of bad outcomes for at-risk youth and the benefits of early childhood interventions to reduce them. *Criminal Justice Policy Review*, 21: 391–434.
Cohen, M. A., Piquero, A. R., and Jennings, W. G. 2010b. Studying the costs of crime across offender trajectories. *Criminology & Public Policy*, 9: 279–305.
Cohen, M. A., Rust, R. T., Steen, S., and Tidd, S. T. 2004. Willingness-to-pay for crime control programs. *Criminology*, 42: 89–110.

Copes, H., Hochstetler, A., and Cherbonneau, M. 2012. Getting the upper hand scripts for managing victim resistance in carjackings. *Journal of Research in Crime and Delinquency*, 49: 249–268.

Corso, P. S., Fang, X., and Mercy, J. A. 2011. Benefits of preventing a death associated with child maltreatment: Evidence from willingness-to-pay survey data. *American Journal of Public Health*, 101: 487–490.

DeLisi, M. 2013. Pandora's box: The consequences of low self-control into adulthood. In *Handbook of life-course criminology*, edited by Chris L. Gibson and Marvin D. Krohn, 261–273. New York: Springer.

DeLisi, M., and Gatling, J. 2003. Who pays for a life of crime? An empirical assessment of the assorted victimization costs posed by career criminals. *Criminal Justice Studies*, 16: 283–293.

DeLisi, M., Kosloski, A., Sween, M., Hachmeister, E., Moore, M., and Drury, A. 2010. Murder by numbers: Monetary costs imposed by a sample of homicide offenders. *The Journal of Forensic Psychiatry & Psychology*, 21: 501–513.

DeLisi, M., Neppl, T. K., Lohman, B. J., Vaughn, M. G., and Shook, J. J. 2013. Early starters: Which type of criminal onset matters most for delinquent careers? *Journal of Criminal Justice*, 41: 12–17.

DeLisi, M., and Vaughn, M. G. 2014. Foundation for a temperament-based theory of antisocial behavior and criminal justice system involvement. *Journal of Criminal Justice*, 42: 10–25.

Dolan, P., and Peasgood, T. 2007. Estimating the economic and social costs of the fear of crime. *British Journal of Criminology*, 47: 121–132.

Downey, P. M., and Roman, J. K. 2014. *Cost–benefit analysis: A guide for drug courts and other criminal justice programs*. Washington, DC: US Department of Justice, Office of Justice Programs, National Institute of Justice.

Farrington, D. P., and Welsh, B. 2007. *Saving children from a life of crime: Early risk factors and effective interventions*. New York: Oxford University Press.

French, M. T., McCollister, K. E., Alexandre, P. K., Chitwood, D. D., and McCoy, C. B. 2004. Revolving roles in drug-related crime: The cost of chronic drug users as victims and perpetrators. *Journal of Quantitative Criminology*, 20: 217–241.

Gottfredson, M. R., and Hirschi, T. 1990. *A general theory of crime*. Stanford, CA: Stanford University Press.

Hann, R. G. 1972. Crime and the cost of crime: An economic approach. *Journal of Research in Crime and Delinquency*, 9: 12–30.

Hawkins, E. R., and Waller, W. 1936. Critical notes on the cost of crime. *Journal of Criminal Law and Criminology*, 26: 679–694.

Heckman, J. J. 2006. Skill formation and the economics of investing in disadvantaged children. *Science*, 312: 1900–1902.

Hochstetler, A., Copes, H., and Williams, J. P. 2010. "That's not who I am": How offenders commit violent acts and reject authentically violent selves. *Justice Quarterly*, 27: 492–516.

Keel, T. G., Jarvis, J. P., and Muirhead, Y. E. 2009. An exploratory analysis of factors affecting homicide investigations examining the dynamics of murder clearance rates. *Homicide Studies*, 13: 50–68.

Klietz, S. J., Borduin, C. M., and Schaeffer, C. M. 2010. Cost–benefit analysis of multisystemic therapy with serious and violent juvenile offenders. *Journal of Family Psychology*, 24: 657–680.

Kyckelhahn, T. 2011. *Justice expenditures and employment, FY 1982–2007: Statistical tables*. Washington, DC: US Department of Justice, Bureau of Justice Statistics.

Kyckelhahn, T. 2012. *State corrections expenditures, FY 1982–2010*. Washington, DC: US Department of Justice, Bureau of Justice Statistics.

Levitt, S. D. 2004. Understanding why crime fell in the 1990s: Four factors that explain the decline and six that do not. *Journal of Economic Perspectives*, 18: 163–190.

Malone, L. 2007. In the aftermath: Listening to people bereaved by homicide. *Probation Journal*, 54: 383–393.

Martin, J. P., and Bradley, J. 1963. Design of a study of the cost of crime. *British Journal of Criminology*, 4: 591–602.

Mayhew, P. 2003. *Counting the costs of crime in Australia*. Canberra: Australian Institute of Criminology.

McCollister, K. E., French, M. T., and Fang, H. 2010. The cost of crime to society: New crime-specific estimates for policy and program evaluation. *Drug and Alcohol Dependence*, 108: 98–109.

Mears, D. P., and Stewart, E. A. 2010. Interracial contact and fear of crime. *Journal of Criminal Justice*, 38: 34–41.

Miller, T. R., Cohen, M. A., and Rossman, S. B. 1993. Victim costs of violent crime and resulting injuries. *Health Affairs*, 12: 186–197.

Miller, T. R., Cohen, M. A., and Wiersema, B. 1996. *Victim costs and consequences: A new look*. Washington, DC: US Department of Justice, Office of Justice Programs, National Institute of Justice.

Miller, T. R., Fisher, D. A., and Cohen, M. A. 2001. Costs of juvenile violence: Policy implications. *Pediatrics*, 107 (1): e3.

Miller, T. R., Levy, D. T., Cohen, M. A., and Cox, K. L. C. 2006. Costs of alcohol and drug-involved crime. *Prevention Science*, 7: 333–342.

Moffitt, T. E. 1993. Adolescence-limited and life-course-persistent antisocial behavior: A developmental taxonomy. *Psychological Review*, 100: 674–701.

Moore, S., and Shepherd, J. P. 2006. The cost of fear: Shadow pricing the intangible costs of crime. *Applied Economics*, 38: 293–300.

Morris, D., and Tweeten, L. 1971. The cost of controlling crime: A study in economies of city life. *The Annals of Regional Science*, 5: 33–49.

Piquero, A. R., Jennings, W. G., and Farrington, D. 2013. The monetary costs of crime to middle adulthood findings from the Cambridge Study in Delinquent Development. *Journal of Research in Crime and Delinquency*, 50: 53–74.

Rader, N. E., Cossman, J. S., and Porter, J. R. 2012. Fear of crime and vulnerability: Using a national sample of Americans to examine two competing paradigms. *Journal of Criminal Justice*, 40: 134–141.

Regoeczi, W. C., and Jarvis, J. P. 2013. Beyond the social production of homicide rates: Extending social disorganization theory to explain homicide case outcomes. *Justice Quarterly*, 30: 983–1014.

Rinear, E. E. 1988. Psychosocial aspects of parental response patterns to the death of a child by homicide. *Journal of Traumatic Stress*, 1: 305–322.

Roman, J. 2004. Can cost–benefit analysis answer criminal justice policy questions, and if so, how? *Journal of Contemporary Criminal Justice*, 20: 257–275.

Roman, J. K., Reid, S. E., Chalfin, A. J., and Knight, C. R. 2009. The DNA field experiment: A randomized trial of the cost-effectiveness of using DNA to solve property crimes. *Journal of Experimental Criminology*, 5: 345–369.

Scarborough, B. K., Like-Haislip, T. Z., Novak, K. J., Lucas, W. L., and Alarid, L. F. 2010. Assessing the relationship between individual characteristics, neighborhood context, and fear of crime. *Journal of Criminal Justice*, 38: 819–826.

Shinnar, S., and Shinnar, R. 1975. The effects of the criminal justice system on the control of crime: A quantitative approach. *Law and Society Review*, 9: 581–611.

Smith, E. 1901. *The cost of crime*. Washington, DC: US Government Printing Office.

Stretesky, P. B., O'Connor Shelley, T., Hogan, M. J., and Unnithan, N. P. 2010. Sense-making and secondary victimization among unsolved homicide co-victims. *Journal of Criminal Justice*, 38: 880–888.

Tracy, P. E., and Kempf-Leonard, K. 1996. *Continuity and discontinuity in criminal careers*. New York: Plenum.

Tracy, P. E., Wolfgang, M. E., and Figlio, R. M. 1990. *Delinquency careers in two birth cohorts*. Chicago, IL: University of Chicago Press.

Vaughn, M. G., DeLisi, M., Gunter, T., Fu, Q., Beaver, K. M., Perron, B. E., and Howard, M. O. 2011. The severe 5%: A latent class analysis of the externalizing behavior spectrum in the United States. *Journal of Criminal Justice*, 39: 75–80.

Vaughn, M. G., Fu, Q., Beaver, K. M., DeLisi, M., Perron, B. E., and Howard, M. O. 2010. Are personality disorders associated with social welfare burden in the United States? *Journal of Personality Disorders*, 24: 709–720.

Vaughn, M. G., Fu, Q., Wernet, S. J., DeLisi, M., Beaver, K. M., Perron, B. E., and Howard, M. O. 2011. Characteristics of abstainers from substance use and antisocial behavior in the United States. *Journal of Criminal Justice*, 39: 212–217.

Vaughn, M. G., Salas-Wright, C. P., DeLisi, M., and Maynard, B. R. 2014. Violence and externalizing behavior among youth in the United States: Is there a severe 5%? *Youth Violence and Juvenile Justice*, 12: 3–21.

Vollum, S., and Longmire, D. R. 2007. Covictims of capital murder: Statements of victims' family members and friends made at the time of execution. *Violence and Victims*, 22: 601–619.

Walters, G. D. 1990. *The criminal lifestyle: Patterns of serious criminal conduct*. Thousand Oaks, CA: Sage.

Walters, G. D. 2011. *Crime in a psychological context: From career criminals to criminal careers*. Thousand Oaks, CA: Sage.

Welsh, B. C. 2004. Monetary costs and benefits of correctional treatment programs: Implications for offender reentry. *Federal Probation*, 68: 9–13.

Welsh, B. C., and Farrington, D. P. 2012. Science, politics, and crime prevention: Toward a new crime policy. *Journal of Criminal Justice*, 40: 128–133.

Welsh, B. C., and Farrington, D. P. 2013. Preventing crime is hard work: Early intervention, developmental criminology, and the enduring legacy of James Q. Wilson. *Journal of Criminal Justice*, 41: 448–451.

Welsh, B. C., Farrington, D. P., and Sherman, L. W., eds. 2001. *Costs and benefits of preventing crime*. Boulder, CO: Westview.

Welsh, B. C., Loeber, R., Stevens, B. R., Stouthamer-Loeber, M., Cohen, M. A., and Farrington, D. P. 2008. Costs of juvenile crime in urban areas: A longitudinal perspective. *Youth Violence and Juvenile Justice*, 6: 3–27.

Welsh, B. C., Sullivan, C. J., and Olds, D. L. 2010. When early crime prevention goes to scale: A new look at the evidence. *Prevention Science*, 11: 115–125.

Wilson, J. Q., and Abrahamse, A. 1992. Does crime pay? *Justice Quarterly*, 9: 359–377.

Wilson, J. Q., and Herrnstein, R. J. 1985. *Crime and human nature: The definitive study of the causes of crime*. New York: Simon & Schuster.
Yeh, S. S. 2010. Cost–benefit analysis of reducing crime through electronic monitoring of parolees and probationers. *Journal of Criminal Justice*, 38: 1090–1096.
Zimring, F. E., and Hawkins, G. 1995. *Incapacitation: Penal confinement and the restraint of crime*. New York: Oxford University Press.

Further Reading

Moffitt, T. E. 2008. A review of research on the taxonomy of life-course persistent versus adolescence-limited antisocial behavior. In *Taking stock: The status of criminological theory*, edited by Francis T. Cullen, John Paul Wright, and Kristie R. Blevins, 277–311. New Brunswick, NJ: Transaction.

19

School Crime and Safety

Thomas Mowen, John Brent, and Aaron Kupchik

In recent years the topic of school crime and safety has received increasing attention from the public and researchers. Among researchers, scholars have directed their focus to topics such as rates of school crime and violence (Brady, Balmer, and Phenix, 2007; Denenberg, Denenberg, and Braverman, 1998; Dinkes et al., 2006; Snyder, 2004), the presence of criminal justice-based practices in schools (Casella, 2006; Chandler, 2004; Kupchik, 2010; Skiba, 2000; Verdugo, 2002), the effectiveness of these measures in reducing student delinquency (Cook, Gottfredson, and Na, 2009; Greene, 2005; Pagliocca and Nickerson, 2001; Skiba and Noam, 2001), and the unintended consequences of relying on harsh punishments (Cook et al., 2009; Greene, 2005; Hirschfield, 2008; Pagliocca and Nickerson, 2001; Skiba et al., 2000; Welch and Payne, 2010), among others. As evidence of concern about this issue among the public, consider the fact that, in December 2012, the US Senate Committee on the Judiciary held a hearing regarding the "school-to-prison pipeline" – a national trend in which youth become enmeshed in the criminal justice system as a result of security practices. This hearing, hosted by the Subcommittee on the Constitution, Office of Civil Rights, and Human Rights, examined the effects that relying almost exclusively on security measures for the maintenance of safety is having on students and on the larger school environment. More recently, the Obama administration has issued new recommendations regarding school discipline, specifically suggesting that practices such as behavioral counseling and restorative justice be used instead of reliance on suspension and arrest (US Department of Education, 2015).

In this chapter we provide an overview of both the substantive and the methodological developments in research on school crime and safety. We first explore trends in school crime and safety; here we rely on official sources of school data as well as

The Handbook of Measurement Issues in Criminology and Criminal Justice, First Edition.
Edited by Beth M. Huebner and Timothy S. Bynum.

on reports of important policy changes that have affected schools in this matter. Next we outline important methodological considerations that confront social scientists who engage in research within the school setting. Finally, we offer some ideas on how research in schools may continue to evolve.

Trends in School Crime

Contextualizing school crime

Prior research reveals that, in the 1930s and 1940s, schools' concerns about student misbehavior included very minor infractions, such as youth speaking out of turn and littering (Goldstein, Apter, and Harootunian, 1984; Stouffer, 1952). There is little evidence to suggest that school officials were concerned with any policies intended to deter threats from outside the school, and school officials' concerns over serious problem behavior within the school was relatively nonexistent (Stouffer, 1952).

Moving into the 1960s, the United States experienced an increase in rates of crime victimization (see Garland, 2001). In addition, social unrest – highlighted by the civil rights movement, protests to the Vietnam War, and other social movements – increased citizens' insecurity and fear of crime (Simon, 2007). One response was that criminal justice systems began to rely more on formal punishment, as evidenced by increasing incarceration rates. Similarly, at this time schools began to target more aggressive forms of problem behavior, such as physical confrontations between students (Phaneuf, 2009). School policies aimed at reducing drug use and gang activity also began to emerge (Crews and Montgomery, 2001).

Transitioning into the 1980s and early 1990s, as the United States Department of Justice intensified its war on crime, schools and policymakers became increasingly concerned with guns, gang violence, and drug violence in schools. Because of this rise in concern, zero-tolerance policies (which will be outlined in subsequent sections) became popular and have continued to dominate educational policy since. In more recent years we have seen a number of highly sensationalized school shootings – including Columbine (1999), Virginia Tech (2007), and, more recently, the 2012 shootings at an elementary school in Newtown, Connecticut. Although it is unclear whether these tragedies have had much of an independent effect on actual school policies, they have certainly helped fuel public concern, causing school safety and crime to become one of the dominant themes of discussion on the education system in the United States.

Trends in school crime: How do we know what we know?

Because school crime can be a highly sensitive and political matter, policymakers, scholars, and researchers have developed many instruments for measuring it. Many of these instruments, for instance the *Indicators of School Crime and Safety* report, are developed and used by the United States government or by governmental departments that have a specific focus on school crime. Other efforts – such as the Educational Longitudinal Study (ELS) – ask questions about school crime through surveys that address a host of other issues as well, while yet other instruments – such as the National Longitudinal Survey of Youth (NLSY) – are designed by research institutions or large universities and focus on some aspects of school crime and victimization.

Since the 1990s, the US federal government has provided statistics on crime trends that are used in much of the research on this topic. One publication, the *Indicators of School Crime and Safety* report (ISCR) (Dinkes et al., 2006), summarizes the results of data collection efforts with schools on the topic of student and staff victimization. The ISCR is a joint effort between the National Center for Education Statistics (NCES, part of the Institute of Education Sciences, which is within the Department of Education) and the Bureau of Justice Statistics (BJS); it is published annually. The ISCR includes results from multiple nationally representative, repeated cross-sectional surveys, for example the School Crime Supplement of the National Crime Victimization Survey (in which students report on whether they were victims, at school and elsewhere) and the School Survey on Crime and Safety (in which school administrators report on levels of crime within their schools). This report typically covers victimization, injury, bullying, weapons, drugs and alcohol, gang activity, and various student and teacher perceptions of safety within the school.

The most recent data reveal that in 2011 there were approximately 1.25 million nonfatal victimizations in US schools, the majority of which were thefts. This is a slight increase from 2010, but still far lower than the number of victimizations in prior years. Overall, the total victimization rate is about 49 victimizations for every 1,000 students aged 12–18. During the 2010–2011 schools year there were 11 homicides and three suicides of school-age youth at school. Much like other criminal indicators (e.g., Puzzanchera, 2013), the NCES consistently finds that males are more likely than females to report being involved in criminal activity and misbehavior, with the exception of some measures of bullying.

In addition to student indicators, the NCES also reports on events involving teachers. The most recent available data concerning teachers (2007–2008) find that teachers in an urban setting are more likely to report being threatened with victimization than teachers in suburban or rural schools. Moreover, teachers in urban schools report a higher likelihood of being physically attacked. Similarly, teachers in urban schools generally report higher levels of fear for their safety than their suburban and rural counterparts. Much as we see in the case of the students, rates of victimization for teachers have decreased over the past decade.

Moving beyond teacher and student information, the NCES also collects school environment data. For example, 85 percent of all public schools report that one or more criminal incidents had occurred on their premises, and 60 percent of schools reported to the police at least one criminal incident in the 2010–2011 school year. About 23 percent of public schools reported that bullying was a weekly or daily occurrence, which is an increase from prior years.

The NCES finds, and other research supports (Wike and Fraser, 2009; Fox and Burnstein, 2010), that school crime has been consistently declining since the 1980s. For example, the percentage of public schools reporting having to take at least one serious disciplinary action (such as suspension for 5 or more days, transfers to a specialized school, or expulsion) for the 2009–1010 school year was 39 percent, by comparison to 54 percent one decade earlier, in 1999–2000. Drug use, gang activity, violent crime, theft, and vandalism have all generally decreased since at least 1999. Table 19.1 illustrates this overall trend by showing the rate of total victimization and violent victimization per 1,000 students aged 12–18, from 1992 to 2011, as reported in the ISCR (see Robers et al., 2013, Figure 2.1).

In addition to the NCES, there are many other types of national-level surveys used to explore trends in school crime. For example, the ELS is a nationally representative survey of 10th graders in 2002, with a follow-up wave in 2004 and, again, in 2006. These data are collected by the Department of Education and have been a popular resource for scholars who explore trends in crime. The ELS data include data collected from students, administrators, teachers, parents, and librarians in schools throughout the United States. Due to the longitudinal nature of this data set, it provides researchers with the opportunity to explore trends over time and encompasses measures such as bullying, drug use, alcohol consumption, gang activity, and other forms of delinquency within the school setting.

Table 19.1 Yearly rate of total violent victimizations per 1,000 students aged 12–18.

Year	*Victimization Rate All Offenses*	*Victimization Rate Violence*
1992	182	67.9
1993	194	91.4
1994	188	89.3
1995	172	75.6
1996	158	73.8
1997	137	61.9
1998	121	60.2
1999	117	52
2000	84.9	35.8
2001	92.3	42.9
2002	75.4	36
2003	87.6	39.3
2004	67.2	26.6
2005	63.2	30.2
2006	67.5	35.3
2007	67.8	34
2008	54.3	29.8
2009	51	28
2010	34.9	16.5
2011	49.2	23.6

There are also data sets outside of the Department of Education that explore trends in school crime as part of their broader methodological mission; two examples are the NLSY and the National Longitudinal Study of Adolescent Health (Add-Health). Both of these surveys rely on nationally representative probability samples, and both include survey responses from parents and children. One of the major benefits of data sets like the NLSY or Add-Health is that youth are identified through their school, and therefore these data sets provide excellent indicators of self-reported crime, delinquency, and school aspirations as well as information about school crime and safety. These types of surveys allow scholars to compare officially reported data – like those collected by the NCES – to self-reported types of data, in order to explore how different methods for data collection yield different results. This can often be a fruitful endeavor in that it allows researchers to explore the disjuncture between official data sources and self-reported data. These types of data sets also allow researchers to explore how other life factors (age, family situation, geographic location, self-perceptions, peer networks), may relate to school crime and crime rates.

Trends in School Safety Practices

Despite the fact that school crime has been decreasing fairly steadily for twenty years, schools across the United States are employing more types of school safety measures than ever before. Such measures include school resource officers (SROs), which are police officers stationed at the school, as well as metal detectors, surveillance cameras, clear book bags, random drug tests, the use of drug-sniffing dogs, and other practices. Some researchers have found that the impetus for these changes began in the 1980s (Casella, 2006), while policymakers and school officials generally cite the 2002 Safe School Initiative as the force behind the current expansion in the use of school security measures (US Secret Service and US Department of Education, 2004). In what follows we discuss in detail both these school safety practices and their possible causes and consequences.

Columbine aftermath: A new era?

On April 20, 1999, 14 students (including the perpetrators) and one teacher were killed and many others severely injured when two students engaged in a premeditated takeover of Columbine High School before committing suicide. This event reverberated throughout the nation and brought issues of school security and school shootings promptly into the public arena. In turn, lawmakers and school administrators called for a review of the guidelines used to maintain the safety of schools in the United States. The outcome was the Safe School Initiative (SSI). The goal of the SSI was to explore past violence in schools and to implement a series of best practices for schools to engage in in order to reduce the risk of school shootings in the future.

The SSI, a collaboration between the National Threat Assessment Center, the US Department of Education, and the US Secret Service, is one of the most ambitious and lengthy studies on school safety in the United States to date. The study examined 37 lethal shootings involving 41 attackers that occurred in schools between 1974 and 2000. The research teams examined school records, existing school security practices, demographic data, and other pertinent details that shed light on these acts of school violence. In sum, the report concluded that (1) targeted violence in schools is rarely the result of impulsive acts, (2) other individuals generally were aware of the perpetrators' plans, (3) the attackers did not threaten their targets directly prior to the attack, (4) there is no such thing as a "profile" for students who engage in targeted school violence, (5) most attackers had considered or attempted suicide, (6) bullying was generally a factor, (7) attackers had access to weapons, (8) other students were involved to some degree, and (9) most incidents were not stopped by law enforcement intervention.

Overall, the conclusions of the SSI suggest that many of the attacks could have been prevented. The Department of Education concludes that schools should actively and continuously engage in threat assessment and develop strategies to prevent the occurrence of attacks on them; such strategies should include the increased presence and availability of mental health professionals, school security measures at higher levels, and a greater concentration of attention on students' antisocial behavior and misbehavior.

Explaining the rise of school security

At the same time, some researchers have argued that the event at Columbine was not a cause of contemporary school disciplinary and security strategies, since it occurred when the buildup of school discipline and security was already well underway. Perhaps the most common explanation for contemporary school discipline and security concerns is fear. This explanation interprets the criminalization of school discipline as a sociopolitical response to anxieties concerning school crime and broader insecurities (Hirschfield, 2008), reflecting observations on the rise of crime control practices more broadly (see Garland, 2001; Simon, 2007). For example, Beck (1992) and Giddens (1991) argue that modern societies have been gripped by a pro found sense of insecurity regarding their safety. In their view, individuals' fears have become a generalized concern, which pressures social institutions into implementing enhanced security. A growing literature has begun to demonstrate that this demand for security has transformed schools (Kupchik, 2010; Simon, 2007).

A more recent treatment of fear links school discipline to broader anxieties about crime that are embedded in contemporary social and political structures. This kind of work builds on the views of those who interpret modern crime control practices alongside broader cultural and structural shifts in society. Recent theorizing, much like Garland's (2001) work, attempts to understand contemporary crime control in the context of large-scale social, cultural, and political shifts. Garland argues that the "penal welfarism" that characterized the state during the early to mid-twentieth century has been dismantled because it failed to protect the public from the risks connected with crime. A new crime control initiative has risen in its place – one that has ushered in a bourgeoning "culture of control."

This framework is also noticeable in Jonathan Simon's (2007) seminal text *Governing through Crime*. His work offers an in-depth account of how politicians capitalize on popular fears and insecurities in order to gather support for legislation in a new era of social governance. He proposes that, after the 1960s, the collective trust in the state as provider of security and social welfare faded due to rising crime rates, the collapse of a progressive political agenda, and the fall of the New Deal political order. In order to alleviate this crisis of legitimacy, politicians and legislators exploited people's escalating awareness and fear of crime; crime allowed them to frame citizens as (potential) victims and thereby to garner support for new and often more punitive legislation. In essence, individuals become "governed through crime," under an increasingly penal system.

Within the context of education, widespread insecurity coupled with anxieties about youth vulnerability have forced schools to take a proactive stance toward preventing the occurrence of violent acts on their premises (see Casella, 2003; Johnson, 1999; Kupchik, 2010; Lawrence, 1998). Here violence in schools, or the potential for violence, overwhelmed the fearful schools and encouraged them to expand and intensify both punishments for students and links between the school and the criminal justice system (see Hirschfield, 2008; Kupchik, 2010; Kupchik and Monahan, 2006; Lyons and Drew, 2006). Principals and policymakers thus adopted punitive disciplinary practices and various criminal justice-oriented security measures.

Instruments of safety

One of the major recommendations of the SSI was continued implementation and use of school security measures. According to the ISCR, as of 2010, 92 percent of all schools in the United States – up from 75 percent in 1999 – control access to their grounds through check-in areas. Approximately 46 percent of schools – up from 34 percent ten years before – maintain a closed campus during the entire school day, requiring students to stay within the school, and 63 percent of all public schools – up from just 25 percent in 1999 – now require faculty to wear ID badges. Approximately 61 percent of all public schools in the United Sates use security cameras to monitor activities within the school – an increase of 32 percent since 1999, and 74 percent of all classrooms are equipped with telephones or electric communication to a central office, compared to just 45 percent in 1999. A total of 19 percent of all schools require students to wear uniforms – an increase from 12 percent in the previous decade. In addition, 21 percent of all schools have metal detectors at the entrance of the school; 69 percent use random drug sweeps on the student body to search for contraband; and approximately 55 percent of all schools have a police or school resource officer. In sum, schools have expanded the types of security measures used as well as the total number of security measure used across the board.

It's important to highlight that the types of school safety instruments used vary by region, school type, and school size. Larger schools are more likely than smaller ones to utilize any instrument of school security measure outlined above. This is due, in part, to the budget of the school, as well as to location. Similarly, public schools – which tend to be larger than private schools – by and large employ more instruments of school security. Urban schools, as opposed to rural and suburban schools, are the most likely to utilize instruments of school security. Finally, schools in the southern United States are more likely to use instruments of school security compared to schools in the Midwest or Northeast regions of the United States.

Contemporary research has largely found that students in US schools are mostly accustomed to the presence of security measures in the school, although this reaction does tend to vary by race and ethnicity (Bracy, 2010). Yet researchers have also questioned the negative effect that these measures may have on students, such as increasing the arrest rate of children within schools. Some argue that problem behavior that used to be handled by the administration in past years, before the ascendancy of such measures, is now handled by security staff and school resource officers (Kupchik, 2010). The result is that students are often disciplined and removed from the classroom for minor misdeeds.

In addition to the use of school security instruments, school administrators and policymakers also rely on the use of detentions, suspensions, and, in the most severe cases, expulsions as a means of regulating the behavior of students. During the 2009–2010 school year, of the 433,800 serious disciplinary actions taken and reported to the Department of Education, 74 percent resulted in suspensions for 5 or more days, 20 percent resulted in transfers to a specialized school, and 6 percent resulted in expulsions from the school for at least the remainder of the school year. As of 2006, approximately 6.9 percent of all students in the United States had received a suspension at some point over the course of their schooling.

Zero tolerance and school punishment

More so than any other policy geared toward increasing school safety and decreasing school crime, zero-tolerance policies gained swift popularity in the early 1990s as a way to combat student misbehavior. Zero-tolerance policies operate under the assumption that student misbehavior, no matter how minor, that falls into predefined categories must be dealt with quickly and uniformly. Zero tolerance policies were prompted by increased awareness of and attention given to the threat of gangs and gun violence in the hallways of American schools, and the late 1980s saw the ascendancy of such policies. By 1989, nearly half of all state school systems had adopted a zero-tolerance perspective on drugs and gangs, and by 1990 nearly 80 percent of all public school systems in the United States employed some level of zero tolerance (Phaneuf, 2009).

Zero tolerance involves showing no leniency for particular crimes; that is, punishments become required at a minimum for particular offenses. For example, zero tolerance requires that a penalty for a weapons offense be automatically applied for carrying not just knives and guns, which are likely to be used to harm other students, but also pocket knives, razor blades that may have been left in a student's backpack accidentally, and even cake knives, which were brought into school with birthday cakes. The goal of zero tolerance is twofold. First, it sends a clear message to students that no behavior that falls within the broad categories of an offense will be tolerated. Second, it ensures uniform punishments for a given category of offense. It attempts to deter offending while it provides uniformity in discipline, hence creating a sense of equality among diverse student bodies. Because of this, forms of zero tolerance exist in nearly all schools across the United States.

In 1994, with the passage of the Gun-Free Schools Act, public schools in the United States became legally required to expel students from school for no less than one year if those students were found with a gun on school grounds. The law, as it was originally drafted by the United States' Congress, was narrowly focused on dangerous weapon possessions – such as guns and explosives – within the school property. However, by 1995, most schools had voluntarily expanded the scope of this bill to include other weapons such as daggers, knives, brass knuckles, and lighters. As other scholars highlight, many schools also voluntarily expanded zero tolerance to the destruction of property, to repeated nonviolent defiance of school authority, to the possession of over-the-counter pain relievers, to toy guns, and to minor classroom disruption (Phaneuf, 2009).

Unintended effects of school security and zero tolerance

Although these strategies have become popular for managing school crime, growing evidence suggests the practices currently reconfiguring school discipline are often excessive and can be harmful to students in a variety of ways. First, these practices are influenced by and exacerbate existing social inequality. At the school level, research finds that schools serving racial–ethnic minority youth may be more likely to have criminal justice-oriented security practices such as the use of metal detectors, or exclusionary punishments (e.g., Irwin, Davidson, and Hall-Sanchez, 2013; Nance, 2013; Payne and Welch, 2010; Welch and Payne, 2010; Kupchik and Ward, 2014). As a result, these youth are more likely than others to be subject to punitive security measures, to be punished more harshly, and to become susceptible to the "school-to-prison pipeline" (Heitzeg, 2009).

At the student level as well, recent work has uncovered inequality in the distribution of school punishment. For similar misbehaviors, black and Hispanic students are significantly more likely to be expelled or suspended than white students (Eitle and Eitle, 2004; Skiba et al., 2006). In addition, black males are more likely to be punished for minor misbehavior than males of any other race (Raffaele Mendez and Knoff, 2003). Not surprisingly, studies have also found that black students are more likely than white students to perceive that discipline is applied unfairly (Kupchik and Ellis, 2008). Certainly, the literature reveals that racial–ethnic minority and economically disadvantaged students are more likely than their counterparts to receive harsh punishments (see Ferguson, 2001; McCarthy and Hoge, 1987; Skiba et al., 2000).

Second, others have become concerned with the authoritarian nature of school security and policies. For example, many researchers and scholars argue that the modern school focuses on establishing adults' authority over youth, often to the detriment of students' social, emotional, and academic growth. This literature suggests that the criminalization of school discipline has reoriented school practices, to the extent that members of staff view all students as potential criminals; thus students have been reconstructed as possible threats to school security and are managed as such. For example, Kupchik (2010) illustrates how a rigid school authority does little to solve students' social, emotional, or academic problems and asserts instead the school's power over students, who are perceived to be out of control or dangerous.

Finally, there is evidence that new disciplinary measures such as zero-tolerance policies have negatively influenced student performance and the overall school environment. For example, schools with harsher disciplinary practices experience lower levels of performance and higher dropout rates (Gottfredson, 2001; Gottfredson et al., 2005). Brady and colleagues (2007) also find that the use of criminal justice tactics in schools has the effect of decreasing rates of student attendance, exam taking, and student engagement. In that same vein, mounting evidence shows that such tactics have the ability to create an undesirable school climate (Ayers, Dohrn, and Ayers, 2001; Brady et al, 2007; Lewis et al., 2008; Lyons and Drew, 2006; Webber, 2003), which negatively impacts the quality of education (see Elliot et al., 1998; Hazler, 1998; Lawrence, 1998) and student participation in extracurricular activities (Mowen and Manierre, 2015). Finally, although research shows that strict discipline can help curb student misbehavior (Arum, 2003), there is no clear evidence that the criminalization of school discipline is effective at preventing school violence (Addington, 2009; Cook et al., 2009; Greene, 2005; Pagliocca and Nickerson, 2001; Skiba et al., 2000). Studies actually suggest that excessive disciplinary practices may have the adverse effect of increasing student misconduct (Gottfredson, 2001; Gottfredson et al., 2005).

Clearly these bodies of literature do not suggest that there should be no school security measures or that misbehavior should attract no consequences on the perpetrator; both security measures and consequences are important for student safety and learning. Instead, these scholars show that there may be important side effects to zero-tolerance and similar policies, which seek to exclude students from school, arrest them, or increase the presence of the criminal justice system within the school.

Methodological and Substantive Considerations

Methodological limitations

As we discuss above, the literature is fairly consistent in finding negative consequences of the criminalization of school discipline. One should have confidence in these results, given that many studies that use very different data sets and research methods and are conducted in different locations seem to converge on these results.

Yet there are important methodological limitations to many of these studies, on which we need to improve in order to have a more solid understanding of how to better maintain school safety. One problem is that many studies use small samples, or case studies, in which only a handful of schools or a single school is examined (e.g., Casella, 2003; Kupchik, 2010; Lyons and Drew, 2006; Nolan, 2011). These studies have added invaluable insight by conducting direct observation of school grounds, by engaging in in-depth interviews with school staff and students, and by collecting school-level data. Certainly these methods and data help shed light on the context of school discipline and security, on perceptions of students or school staff, and on how school practices are actually implemented. Yet such studies offer little basis for making broad generalizations.

Another limitation is that many studies use cross-sectional data, such as the School Survey on Crime and Safety that we described above (e.g., Irwin et al., 2013; Kupchik and Ward, 2014). This data set contains information about schools – levels of crime and misbehavior, security practices – that is all captured at one point in time. As a result, when researchers find that schools with police or harsh punishment policies in place have more student misbehavior, it is unclear whether the discipline is a cause or a consequence of the misbehavior. Typically, cross-sectional studies use a variety of statistical controls that factor out much of this ambiguity by controlling for variables such as student violence, drug use, gang presence, and so on and, as a result, the conclusions drawn about consequences of school discipline are reasonable. Yet without longitudinal data or, better yet, randomized experimental design studies, some doubt remains.

Even when longitudinal data are collected, methodological limitations remain. First, longitudinal surveys often suffer from attrition; that is, a respondent sampled at wave 1 "drops out" and is not sampled at wave 2 (Twisk, 2002). This can bias the results, if there is a systematic reason why the data are missing (see Boys et al., 2003). For example, if the student dropped out of school due to bullying, and the survey was administered in school and was concerned with bullying, the survey would not reach the targeted audience (students who have been bullied), because they no longer participate in the study. Second, longitudinal surveys are often limited due to cost, staffing, and time. With decreases in governmental funding within the past decade (State Higher Education Executive Officers, 2013), some school surveys have had to shorten their questionnaires, recruit fewer respondents, or forgo additional longitudinal waves of collection. All these are methodological concerns presented to researchers.

A fourth limitation is that the validity, or accuracy, of schools' reports of student misbehavior can sometimes by questionable. For contemporary schools, reporting on students' misconduct is a political act: these data are now posted online for parents to view, and parents now act like consumers, "shopping" around for the best school to send their children. Further, as schools come under increasing scrutiny for racial disparities in punishment, they may adjust their reporting. School administrators therefore have a stake in making their schools seem safer than they really are. While most are unlikely to blatantly lie, there are clear incentives for them to creatively redefine incidents or school actions. For example, if a school removes a youth from class for days at a time, but keeps her in a punishment room within the school, it may not have to report an out-of-school suspension. The political stakes of honest reporting may cause a problem of accuracy in school reports, but we do not currently know the extent to which this impacts research on school safety efforts.

Research on school safety is also very difficult given the different perspectives taken by stakeholders. Students, teachers, administrators, parents, grandparents, communities, policymakers, and all other members who interact with the educational institution tend to have very different perspectives on school problems and the worth of different solutions. Often the goals of these parties vary with respect to particular topics, especially school crime and safety. Social scientists are tasked with navigating between different viewpoints in order to empirically represent issues at hand. The difficulty of assessing similarities and differences, of respecting these diverse views, and of producing a set of research findings can result in questionable validity of school safety research, another limitation to our knowledge on the subject.

Ethics, IRB and gaining access

In addition to methodological limitations, our knowledge of school safety is also limited by barriers to conducting research on school crime and school safety practices. For example, researchers must go through a reviewing process whereby their studies are deemed ethically acceptable prior to their engaging in the research; this process is directed through institutional review boards (IRBs), which ensure the safety of subjects and researchers in the course of a study. An IRB is also tasked with ensuring that more vulnerable members of the population, such as the disadvantaged or the incarcerated, are not being taken advantage of or exploited. Children are considered a "special class" as they do not have the legal ability to consent to taking part in a scientific study without their parents' permission. At the same time, schools can give consent for students to complete state and federally mandated questionnaires, thereby providing institutional consent (called passive consent) in lieu of parental (active) consent. The issue of consent is particularly impactful when attempting to study lower income youth and youth of color, as their parents are more likely to be distrustful of the school and researchers, and less likely to give consent for their children's participation in a research study. Because of this, it can be difficult to engage in some types of studies that involve children. This includes work in schools, particularly in marginalized areas, where youth are most affected by school punishment.

Ethical research typically involves a guarantee of anonymity to research respondents as well. This means that, although the researcher will describe what a research participant does in the researcher's presence or says to her, the researcher has an obligation to not identify that participant. But what if the researcher is observing the behavior of a principal, who is obviously identifiable by position, even if her name is withheld? The researcher might respond by not reporting the name of the school under study, or even of the state in which the research has occurred; yet others, most importantly those who work with that principal, would know about the research and could read the published results that stem from it. Thus the participant's anonymity would be violated. Again, the challenges of ethical research in schools can limit researchers' ability to perform certain types of studies.

Another limitation to research access may be caused by a school's or school district's desire for privacy. Before conducting research in a school setting or collecting data from students or school staff, the researcher must first receive permission from the school and from the school district. School administrators and officials are not compelled to give access and may be reluctant to do so. This is especially true given the pressure put on schools in an area of school choice, or given the proliferation of "charter schools" in the United States. Schools must present themselves in a positive light, so that parents – particularly parents of high-performing students – choose them and send their children to those schools. A school or school district may be wary of the negative publicity that could arise from the presence of a researcher or from the research report that follows, and deny access. Indeed many administrators regard outsiders as potential liabilities (Coon, 2007).

Public scrutiny

As outlined in previous sections, school shootings often result in nationwide coverage from the media, local and state governments, and national political figures and entities such as Congress – or even the president of the United States (Addington, 2009). These reactions highlight just how much reverberation such events have at the national level. School shootings are enormously important events, which capture the nation's attention and scare us all (Rocque, 2012). It is very difficult to conduct impartial, objective research on events that cause such fear and to effectively communicate the results of research on a controversial, fear-inducing topic.

At the same time, school shootings are very rare events. While this does little to console the individuals who are affected by these tragedies, it presents both methodological and substantive difficulties for researchers. One challenge is that it is very difficult to understand the causes, consequences, and means of effective prevention of very rare events. There are (thankfully) so few data – so few instances of mass school shootings – that it is impossible to diagnose them and find causal factors with the degree of certainty that may allow one to claim that the occurrence of such horrific incidents can be prevented in the future. Another challenge is that it can be difficult to objectively analyze data on frightening events while still respecting the emotions that these events create in the public at large. For example, arguing that school violence should not be a large concern because it is at historically low rates and is, overall, very rare may be offensive to those whose children have been directly affected by it. One can imagine that a parent whose child has been seriously bullied would probably not be receptive to researchers who advocated for less punitive discipline, since schools are relatively safe. This need to show sensitivity to victims' experiences and to the broad fear of victimization at school poses additional challenges to school researchers.

The Future of School Crime and Safety Research

There can be little doubt that the topic of school safety and security will remain an important issue for social scientists, policymakers, school officials, and the larger public. As old trends fade and new developments emerge, there are a number of lines for prospective research in this area. One possible subject of future research is the ripple effect of discipline outside of school settings. As discussed above, the United States has seen substantial increases in security measures, strict disciplinary standards, punitive punishments, and zero-tolerance policies. This rising "new American school," marked by the criminalization of school discipline, places a premium on intensified forms of control (Kupchik, 2010). More broadly, a better understanding of how practices that emphasize school discipline affect the family institution – parents, siblings, and other relatives – could help reduce the collateral damage of punitive policies while bringing about more effective ones. Recent work, for instance, attempts to examine parental involvement with the school when considering the presence of school security measures, and findings suggest that parents may be less likely to engage in schools with certain forms of security measures (Mowen, 2015). Yet the extent to which this applies to discipline, disciplinary policy, and school security tactics remains unclear. Future work needs to further explore the broader consequences and implications of school disciplinary strategies on students, parents, families, and communities.

Comparative research would be particularly helpful here. Comparative studies, especially those that seek to better understand school crime and safety from an international perspective, would greatly help our understanding of how school safety works, what social factors produce what kinds of policies and practices, and how school safety practices influence youth and schools. To our knowledge, there are few such studies (see Kupchik, Green, and Mowen, 2015), perhaps because the topic of school discipline and security has received substantially more attention among researchers in the United States than among researchers in other countries.

Another area in need of attention is that of scrutiny over the criminalization of school discipline. Whether brought to popular attention by media reports, congressional hearings, or national reports, the topic of harsh disciplinary practices within education has increasingly come into public awareness. Evidenced by investigations lead by the American Civil Liberties Union and the Office of Civil Rights, schools across the nation are under significant pressure to abandon practices that create racial disparities in punishment, the school-to-prison pipeline, and failing school environments. As a result, school officials and legislators are beginning to reform practices and policies regarding how to best respond to student misconduct. Research will be instrumental in documenting, evaluating, and uncovering these policy reforms. More specifically, the next wave of school crime, safety, and discipline research may focus on what policy reforms are being enacted, how they take form within schools, whether they are corrective, and how they influence students and the larger school environment. This line of scholarship would essentially attempt to study the "after the storm" of an era marked by a criminalizing school discipline.

A final line of future research to be mentioned here builds on the need for more evaluations as to which discipline and security practices are effective and how they can best be implemented. For example, given the need to reform school discipline, many advocates have called for more training of SROs and other security or disciplinarian staff. Yet to our knowledge there are currently no evaluation studies that assess what officers are taught in school-specific trainings, to what degree such trainings improve school climate, how they are perceived among students, and whether they reduce school crime and misconduct. Continuing the calls for reforming school discipline alongside increased demands for more SROs in school, research in this area will be vital for assessing their effectiveness and what can be done to improve upon current conditions.

Conclusion

The goal of this chapter is to explore the historical and contemporary issues within the literature on school discipline and safety and to examine the methodological problems that present themselves to researchers who work with schools. Given the unequal distribution of school punishment along racial and class lines and the increased public scrutiny of school crime and discipline, this area of research will remain a pressing one for social scientists. Students, parents, teachers, school officials, policymakers, and politicians all cite the importance of the school system in the United States. Because of this, researchers within this realm will need to continue to develop innovative methods of collecting and analyzing data, of presenting reports and findings, and of using these findings so as to guide future research projects.

References

Addington, L. A. 2009. Cops and cameras: Public school security as a policy response to Columbine. *American Behavioral Scientist*, 512: 1426–1445.

Arum, R. 2003. *Judging school discipline: The crisis of moral authority*. Cambridge, MA: Harvard University Press.

Ayers, W., Dohrn, B., and Ayers, R. 2001. *Zero tolerance: Resisting the drive for punishment in schools*. New York: Free Press.

Beck, U. 1992. *Risk society*. London: Sage.

Boys, A., Marsden, J., Stillwell, G., Hatchings, K., Griffiths, P., and Farrell, M. 2003. Minimizing respondent attrition in longitudinal research: Practical implications from a cohort study of adolescent drinking. *Journal of Adolescence*, 26 (3): 363–373.

Bracy, N. L. 2010. Students perceptions of high-security school environments. *Youth & Society*, 43: 365–395.

Brady, K. P., Balmer, S., and Phenix, D. 2007. School–police partnership effectiveness in urban schools: An analysis of New York City's Impact School Initiative. *Education and Urban Society*, 39 (4): 455–478.

Casella, R. 2003. Zero tolerance policies in schools: Rationale, consequences, and alternatives. *Teachers College Record*, 105: 872–892.

Casella, R. 2006. *Selling us the fortress: The promotion of techno-security equipment for schools.* New York: Routledge.

Chandler, K. 2004. *Crime and safety in America's public schools: Selected findings from the school survey on crime and safety.* US Department of Education, National Center for Education Statistics. (NCES 2004–370). Washington, DC: US Government Printing Office.

Cook, P. F., Gottfredson, D. C., and Na, C. 2009. School crime control and prevention. *Crime and Justice*, 39 (1): 313–440.

Coon, J. K. 2007. *Security technology in US public schools.* New York: KFB Scholarly Publishing.

Crews, G. A., and Montgomery, R. H. 2001. *Chasing shadows: Confronting juvenile violence in America.* Upper Saddle Rivers, NJ: Prentice Hall.

Denenberg, T. S., Denenberg, R. V., and Braverman, M. 1998. Reducing violence in US schools: The role of dispute resolution. *Dispute Resolution Journal*, 53: 28–35. Accessed January 30, 2007. www.wps.org/Reducing-Violence-InUS-Schools.rtf.

Dinkes, R., Forrest, E., Kena, G., and Baum, K. 2006. *Indicators of school crime and safety: 2006.* US Departments of Education and Justice. Washington, DC: US Government Printing Office.

Eitle, T., and Eitle, D. 2004. Inequality, segregation, and the overrepresentation of African Americans in school suspension. *Sociological Perspectives*, 47 (3): 269–287.

Elliott, D. S., Hamburg, B. A., and Williams, K. R. 1998. *Violence in American schools: A new perspective.* New York: Cambridge University Press.

Ferguson, A. A. 2001. *Bad boys: Public schools in the making of black masculinity.* Ann Arbor: University of Michigan Press.

Fox, J. A., and Burstein, H. 2010. *Violence and security on campus: From preschool through college.* Denver, CO: Praeger.

Garland, D. 2001. *The culture of control: Crime and social order in contemporary society.* Chicago, IL: University of Chicago Press.

Giddens, A. 1991. *Modernity and self-identity: Self and society in the late modern age.* Cambridge: Polity.

Goldstein, A. P., Apter, S. J., and Harootunian, B. 1984. *School violence.* Englewood Cliffs: Prentice Hall.

Gottfredson, D. C. 2001. *Schools and delinquency.* New York: Cambridge University Press.

Gottfredson, G. D., Gottfredson, D. C., Payne, A. A., and Gottfredson, N. C. 2005. School climate predictors of school disorder: Results from a national study of delinquency prevention in schools. *Journal of Research in Crime and Delinquency*, 42: 412–444.

Greene, M. B. 2005. Reducing violence and aggression in schools. *Trauma, Violence and Abuse*, 6: 236–253.

Hazler, R. J. 1998. Promoting personal investment in systemic approaches to school violence. *Education*, 119 (2): 222–231.

Heitzeg, N. A. 2009. Education or incarceration: Zero tolerance policies and the school to prison pipeline. *Forum on Public Policy*, 2: 1–22.

Hirschfield, P. 2008. Preparing for prison: The criminalization of school discipline in the USA. *Theoretical Criminology*, 12: 79–101.

Irwin, K., Davidson, J., and Hall-Sanchez, A. 2013. The race to punish in American schools: Class and race predictors of punitive school-crime control. *Critical Criminology*, 21: 47–71.

Johnson, I. A. 1999. School violence: The effectiveness of a school resource officer program in a southern city. *Journal of Criminal Justice*, 27 (2): 173–192.

Kupchik, A. 2010. *Homeroom security: School discipline in the age of fear*. New York: NYU Press.

Kupchik, A., and Ellis, N. 2008. School discipline and security: Fair for all students? *Youth & Society*, 39 (4): 549–574.

Kupchik, A., Green, D. A., and Mowen, T. J. 2015. School punishment in the US and England: Divergent frames and responses. *Youth Justice*, 15 (1): 3–22.

Kupchik, A., and Monahan, T. 2006. The new American school: Preparation for post-industrial discipline. *British Journal of Sociology of Education*, 27 (5): 617–631.

Kupchik, A., and Ward, G. 2014. Race, poverty, and exclusionary school security: An empirical analysis of US elementary, middle, and high schools. *Youth Violence and Juvenile Justice*, 12 (4): 332–354.

Lawrence, R. 1998. *School crime and juvenile justice*. New York: Oxford University Press.

Lewis, R., Romi, S., Katz, Y. J., and Qui, X. 2008. Students' reaction to classroom discipline in Australia, Israel, and China. *Teaching and Teacher Education*, 24: 715–724.

Lyons, W., and Drew, J. 2006. *Punishing schools: Fear and citizenship in American public education*. Ann Arbor, MI: University of Michigan Press.

McCarthy, J. D., and Hoge, D. R. 1987. The social construction of school punishment: Racial disadvantage out of universalistic process. *Social Forces*, 65: 1101–1120.

Mowen, T. J. 2015. Parental involvement in school and the role of school security measures. *Education and Urban Society*, 47 (7): 830–848.

Mowen, T. J., and Manierre, M. J. 2015. School security measures and extracurricular participation: An exploratory multi-level analysis. *British Journal of Sociology of Education*. doi: 10.1080/01425692.2015.1081091.

Nance, J. 2013. Students, security and race. *Emory Law Journal*, 63 (1): 1–57.

Nolan, K. 2011. *Police in the hallways: Discipline in an urban high school*. Minneapolis: University of Minnesota Press.

Pagliocca, P. M., and Nickerson, A. B. 2001. Legislating school crisis response: Good policy or just good politics? *Law and Policy*, 23: 373–407.

Payne, A. A., and Welch, K. 2010. Modeling the effects of racial threat on punitive and restorative school discipline practices. *Criminology*, 48: 1019–1062.

Phaneuf, S. W. 2009. *Security in schools: Its effect on students*. El Paso, TX: LFB Scholarly Publishing.

Puzzanchera, C. 2013. *Juvenile arrests, 2010*. Washington, DC: Office of Juvenile Justice and Delinquency Prevention.

Raffaele Mendez, L., and Knoff, H. M. 2003. Who gets suspended and why: A demographic analysis of schools and disciplinary infractions in a large school district. *Education and Treatment of Children*, 26 (1): 30–51.

Robers, S., Kemp, J., Truman, J., and Snyder, T. D. 2013. *Indicators of school crime and safety: 2012* (NCES 2013-036; NCJ241446). Washington, DC: US Department of Education, Department of Justice.

Rocque, M. 2012. Exploring school rampage shootings: Research, theory, and policy. *The Social Science Journal*, 49 (3), 304–313.

Simon, J. 2007. *Governing through crime: How the war on crime transformed American democracy and created a culture of fear*. New York: Oxford University Press.

Skiba, R. J. 2000. *Zero tolerance, zero evidence: An analysis of school disciplinary practice*. Indiana: Education Policy Center, Research Report SRS2.

Skiba, R., Michael, R. S., Nardo, A. C., and Peterson, R. 2000. *The color of discipline: Source of racial and gender disproportionality in school punishment* (Report No. SRS1). Bloomington, IN: Indiana Education Policy Center.

Skiba, R. J., and Noam, G. G. 2001. *Zero-tolerance: Can suspension and expulsion keep schools safe?* (New Directions for Youth Development 92.) New York: Josey Bass.

Skiba, R. J., Reynolds, C. R., Graham, S., Sheras, P., Conoley, J. C., and Garcia-Vazquez, E. 2006. *Are zero tolerance policies effective in the schools? An evidentiary review and recommendations* (Report by the American Psychological Association Zero Tolerance Task Force.) Washington, DC: American Psychological Association.

Snyder, H. N. 2004. *Juvenile arrests 2002*. Washington, DC: Office of Juvenile Justice and Delinquency Prevention.

State Higher Education Executive Officers (SHEEO). 2013. State higher education finance, FY 2012. CollegeBoard Publishers. Accessed December 17, 2015. http://www.sheeo.org/sites/default/files/publications/SHEF-FY12.pdf.

Stouffer, G. A. 1952. Behavior problems of children as viewed by teachers and mental hygienist, a study of present attitudes as compared with those reported by E. K. Wickman. *Mental Hygiene*, 36: 271–285.

Twisk, J. 2002. Attrition in longitudinal studies: How to deal with missing data. *Journal of Clinical Epidmiology*, 55: 329–337.

US Department of Education. 2015. School climate and discipline. Accessed December 16, 2015. http://www2.ed.gov/policy/gen/guid/school-discipline/index.html.

US Secret Services and US Department of Education. 2004. The final report and findings of the Safe School Initiative: Implications for the prevention of school attacks in the United States. Washington, DC. Accessed January, 12, 2016. https://www2.ed.gov/admins/lead/safety/preventingattacksreport.pdf.

Verdugo, R. R. 2002. Race–ethnicity, social class, and zero tolerance policies: The cultural and structural wars. *Education and Urban Society*, 35 (1): 50–75.

Webber, Julie A. 2003. *Failure to hold: The politics of school violence*. New York: Rowman and Littlefield.

Welch, K., and Payne, A. A. 2010. Racial threat and punitive school discipline. *Social Problems*, 57: 25–48.

Wike, T., and Fraser, M. W. 2009. School shootings: Making sense of the senseless. *Aggression & Violent Behavior*, 14: 162–169.

20

Traffic Stops, Race, and Measurement

Kyle McLean and Jeff Rojek

The history of police relations within predominantly racial and ethnic minority communities in the United States has often been contentious, particularly the relationship between police and the African American community. The underlying concern of criminal justice observers and of some members of these communities is whether the police are carrying out their duties fairly across everyone they contact; and there is particular focus on who is likely to be stopped, investigated, arrested, and so forth. One of the most notable areas of worry has been racial bias in traffic stops – or what is commonly termed racial profiling. Public and political attention to racial bias in traffic stops emerged in the late 1990s, as a result of high-profile lawsuits against the Maryland State Police and New Jersey State Police in which troopers from these two agencies were accused of disproportionately stopping minority drivers on stretches of highways. Subsequent opinion surveys revealed that African American and Hispanic citizens felt that racial bias in traffic stops was a widespread practice (Carlson, 2004; Newport, 1999) – which, as Tyler and Wakslak (2004) have found, undermines perceptions of police legitimacy.

This interest soon spurred voluntary and involuntary data collection efforts by law enforcement agencies to provide transparency in law enforcement traffic stop activity, and what some hoped would be a foundation for identifying agencies that were engaging in racial bias. However, analyzing law enforcement data to detect the presence of racial bias has proven to be a difficult task. This chapter provides a review of the methodological approaches and issues related to the analysis of traffic stops, particularly vis-à-vis determining racial bias. After a review of the different strategies of data collection designed to capture traffic stop information, attention is given to examining different strategies for determining whether a population of

The Handbook of Measurement Issues in Criminology and Criminal Justice, First Edition.
Edited by Beth M. Huebner and Timothy S. Bynum.

drivers stopped by the police reflects a disparity that may be an indication of bias. We then review the methods for evaluating patterns of post-stop activity (e.g., searches, citations, arrests), which has largely become the focus of scholars in debating the presence of racial bias, given the limitations to evaluating patterns of bias in who is stopped. The concern for racial bias in police action, and particularly in traffic enforcement, is not unique to the United States (Miller et al., 2008; Satzewich and Shaffir, 2009; Jobard and Levy, 2011; Bruce-Jones, 2015). However, the focus on measuring racial bias in policing has largely been dominated by empirical work done in the United States. In consequence, the discussion provided here on the methodology for examining police racial bias comes from research conducted in the United States, yet it has clear implications for empirical efforts conducted in other countries.

Data Collection Elements

The implicit issue of concern in the examination of traffic stops is the fact that officers are acting in a biased manner by conducting stops on the basis of animus against a racial or ethnic group, or on the basis of stereotypes that associate criminal activity with a racial or ethnic group and thereby motivate them to stop individuals from that group disproportionately. Ideally, the goal of efforts to address racial bias in traffic stops is to identify this intent in officers and to take corrective action to reduce its occurrence. However, directly collecting data from officers or agency leaders through surveys or interviews meant to capture self-admission or observation of such bias-based actions is likely a fruitless endeavor, given its legal, political, and public relations implications. As a result, the examination of racial bias in traffic stops has largely relied on citizen surveys and law enforcement traffic stop records.

Citizen survey data

Police–citizen contact naturally requires another person besides the officer to be present at the incident, providing an alternative data source to surveying officers. The Bureau of Justice Statistics periodically conducts a supplement to the National Crime Victimization Survey (NCVS) called the Police–Public Contact Survey (PPCS), which asks citizens about their contact with law enforcement personnel. More direct surveys can examine police–public contact in a given jurisdiction in greater detail. For example, Tyler and Wakslak (2004) used a variety of survey instruments to measure attitudes toward the police and perceptions of racial profiling among citizens of New York City. This method allowed the researchers to examine attitudes directed specifically at the New York City Police Department (NYPD) in conjunction with experiences of racial profiling. The use of the PPCS in measuring racial profiling is common (e.g., Lundman and Kaufman, 2003; Gilliard-Matthews, Kowalski, and Lundman, 2008), and all five iterations of the PPCS since its original administration in 1999 have captured traffic stop-related questions (Bureau of Justice Statistics, n.d.).[1]

One of the benefits of using the PPCS is that it offers a nationality representative sample of citizens. The PPCS is administered to all the participants in the NCVS aged 16 or older. The Bureau of Justice Statistics randomly selects a sample of households for participation in the NCVS. Once the sample is selected, every member of the household is surveyed every six months for three years. Given that the PPCS is only conducted every three years, this means that no one is surveyed twice during his or her time as a participant in the NCVS. The survey covers a battery of questions on the characteristics of the stop and on post-stop actions regarding search, citations, arrest, and the use of force. It also contains questions on the racial characteristics of the officers, which provide the opportunity to explore implicit assumptions about the interactions between citizen and officer on the matter of race. Lastly, the survey asks respondents to evaluate the legitimacy of the officer's reasoning in stopping, citing, searching, arresting, and using force. Another benefit of using the PPCS is that it does not require the inclusion of additional data for analysis. Law enforcement-supplied data, as discussed below, require a researcher to obtain additional information in order to compare individuals who are stopped to individuals who are not stopped. The PPCS data already contain both of these populations and can be used to generate findings on the distribution of traffic stops and post-stop actions. Additionally, the PPCS has the capacity to treat respondent and event characteristics as independent variables that predict dependent outcomes such as being stopped, searched, or arrested. For example, Gilliard-Matthews and colleagues (2008) examined the impact of the officer's race on decisions to ticket drivers. The researchers found that black officers were much more likely to ticket black drivers in the 1999 version of the PPCS, but in the 2002 version the data showed that black officer–black driver interactions were indistinguishable from white officer–white driver interactions.

One of the limitations of the data, however, is that they only provide a national picture, given the sampling design. As a result, they do not help determine whether there is a racial disparity that could point to bias in traffic stop activity in specific agencies or specific officers – which has been the interest of parties calling for the analysis of traffic stops. Additionally, when looking at data from citizen surveys (PPCS or others) of police contact, it is important to remember what is actually being measured by the survey, particularly in relation to questions about the legitimacy of officers' actions or the attribution of racial bias. Citizen surveys of police contact do not actually measure the level or prevalence of racial bias. Instead they measure the perceived prevalence of racial bias. "While it may be highly likely that feeling profiled is related to being profiled, this is not always necessarily the case" (Tyler and Wakslak, 2004, p. 276). This is important to note, as it would be inappropriate to conclude that a law enforcement agency engages in any type of racial bias solely on the basis of the findings of citizen surveys. Racial bias in policing inherently involves the perceptions of citizens by police officers. It is impossible for the citizen to conclusively know the thought process and perceptions that prompt an officer to pull the citizen over.

Furthermore, research in the area of citizen reports of traffic stops has found significant differences in the levels of reporting between races (Tomaskovic-Devey et al., 2006). Tomaskovic-Devey and colleagues (2006) surveyed individuals known to have been stopped for speeding in the six months prior to the survey and found that African Americans were significantly less likely to report that they had been stopped for speeding in those six months. If this finding is consistent across all scenarios, the stop rates for African Americans reported in self-report surveys such as the PPCS are likely to be significantly lower than the actual stop rate for this population. Differences between races in reporting rates on issues fundamental to measuring racial bias make it impossible to draw definitive conclusions regarding racial bias from citizen surveys.

Despite apparent weaknesses in analyzing the data from citizen surveys, there are still significant benefits to collecting data of this type. As Lundman (2004) notes, there is a solid evidentiary basis for using citizen surveys in order to analyze racial profiling. Supplementing the data provided by law enforcement with data obtained from citizen surveys can yield greater strength to the conclusions drawn from studies of racial bias (Lundman, 2004). Additionally, in an era of community-policing, citizen survey data can help draw important conclusions about the relationship that a police agency has with its community. Engel's (2005) analysis of the PPCS found that African Americans and Hispanics were much more likely than whites to have lower perceptions of procedural justice and to believe that traffic stops were conducted illegitimately. These findings emphasize how lower perceptions of procedural justice in a traffic stop can influence the belief that traffic stops are illegitimate and potentially the result of racial profiling. Important as the realities of racial profiling are, citizen perceptions may be just as important in creating effective law enforcement policy. Tyler and Wakslak (2004, p. 276) succinctly address the importance of citizen perceptions in researching racial profiling by stating that "efforts to eliminate profiling must obviously deal with preventing its occurrence, but attention must also be focused on the psychological factors affecting people's interpretations of their interactions with police." An improved understanding of why individuals feel that they are profiled by the police can help to improve police–community relations in minority neighborhoods.

Law enforcement traffic stop data

An alternative, and in fact a predominant, data source for examining racial bias in traffic stops is law enforcement stop records. Unlike interviews or surveys of officers, stop records come from a contact card that officers complete after each traffic stop. Agencies collect data on traffic stops for a variety of reasons. Some police departments have taken a proactive approach to concerns about racial bias and civil rights violations. For example, San Diego Police Department was the first major police department in the United States to voluntarily institute a traffic stop data collection system as the issue of racial bias was coming into prominence (Walker, 2001).

Other agencies have been forced to begin collecting data on police–citizen contact through consent decrees. In 1994 the Department of Justice was given the power to sue individual law enforcement agencies over patterns or practices of activity that violate constitutional amendments or civil rights (Davis et al., 2002). Typically these court cases result in the law enforcement agency entering into a consent decree with the federal government. The consent decree establishes the police department's consent to being monitored by federally appointed observers on issues relevant to the initial lawsuit. This can be seen in the Pittsburgh Police Department and the Los Angeles Police Department (*United States of America v. City of Los Angeles*, 2000; Davis et al., 2002). Both Pittsburgh and Los Angeles were required to collect and maintain data on all traffic stops and searches that their officers engaged in.

In addition to voluntary collection and collection mandated through consent decree, some law enforcement agencies have begun collecting data as a result of state legislation. States such as Missouri, Illinois, and Rhode Island have passed legislation mandating that the law enforcement agencies in each state collect data on traffic stops (Alexander Weiss Consulting, n.d.; Executive Summary for 2013 Missouri Vehicle Stops, n.d.; McDevitt, Iwama, and Bailey-Laguerre, 2014). These data can be analyzed in markedly different ways from data collected independently by individual agencies. Data are reported in a standardized format and passed from individual agencies to a larger state agency. This allows for them to be analyzed both in an aggregate method, across the whole state, and in each jurisdiction (see Rojek, Rosenfeld, and Decker, 2004 for an example of jurisdiction comparisons; see Hernandez-Murillo and Knowles, 2004 for an example of using the whole state). While comparisons of potential racial bias across jurisdictions may be insightful, care should be taken in drawing any definitive conclusions from these comparisons. The format for reporting traffic stop data may be consistent across the jurisdictions, but other important variables that influence the likelihood of being stopped may not be. For instance, a jurisdiction with a major interstate running through it may be more likely to engage in aggressive traffic enforcement than smaller jurisdictions with few major roads.

Regardless of the motivation for collecting traffic stop data, there are pragmatic questions and considerations that agencies have to address in order to engage in this effort. While the focus of this chapter is on the data collection and analysis methodologies of traffic stops research, it cannot be overlooked that instituting a data collection process within law enforcement agencies is a time-consuming process that increases costs as well as the work burden on agency personnel. As a result, it is important for the design of data collection on traffic stops to be efficient in gaining officer compliance in completion, yet effective in capturing key data for analysis. Early efforts typically had officers completing paper forms on their activity in addition to any other citation or arrest form, but agencies are increasingly using mobile data computers in patrol cars in order to allow officers to record this information as they clear it from their traffic stop.

Once a data collection protocol is established, the next step is determining what data to collect. Decisions must be made regarding which type of stops to collect data on and what variables should be included in the collection protocol. Analyses of police–citizen contact should focus on discretionary activity, as this type of activity is most susceptible to racial bias. This concept makes traffic stops, as opposed to other measures of police activity that may be influenced by calls for service, a prime target for studying racial bias in policing (Walker, 2001). Traffic stops are inherently discretionary, as the decision to pull a car over is not based on a citizen's request for action but rather on the officer's judgment. It is important to note that the collection protocol should not include or exclude stops on the basis of their outcomes. It may be appealing to law enforcement agencies to include only stops that result in a citation, as these stops already require paperwork. However, stops that do not result in formal action are more likely to be discretionary in nature and to have greater potential to be influenced by implicit biases than requirements of the law or policy (Fridell, 2004).

Setting aside the data collection protocols, the central element of data to capture for the examination of racial bias in traffic stops is the race of the driver and passengers. However, operationally defining race may be more difficult than initially considered. Should race be measured by the officer who makes the stop or by the citizen him-/herself? Fridell (2004) points out that the perceived race of the citizen as identified by the officer is perhaps more important than the actual race of the citizen. After all, an officer engaging in the exercise of racial bias will practice that bias by acting on his perception of the citizen's race rather than on the unknown self-identified race of the citizen. Yet using the officer's identification of race opens up the possibility that the officer would intentionally put down the wrong race in order to prevent any racial bias from being discovered. Alpert, Dunham, and Smith (2007) addressed this concern by verifying the reported race with the Department of Motor Vehicles' driver's license photographs for a sample of the contact data. The researchers in this instance did not find any evidence to support the possibility of officers intentionally lying about a driver's race; however, this analysis certainly bolstered the validity of the race measurement.

When examining race, it is also important to understand the context of the study site, for instance its demographic make-up, the nature of its crime problem, or any other potentially influential factors not revealed in traffic stop data. Initial concerns regarding racial profiling were directed toward the phenomenon known as "driving while black" (Harris, 1999). Thus studies typically directed their focus on the differences in type and amount of police contact between blacks and whites. With a growing Hispanic population, attention should now also be directed toward this group of drivers. Racial profiling of Hispanics is especially important in the southwestern United States, where there are growing concerns regarding illegal immigration and drug-trafficking. Age and gender and other important demographic information should be collected in analyses of racial bias. Rosenfeld, Rojek, and Decker (2012), for example, have shown that there are significant interactions between age, gender, and race that impact stop activity.

In addition to demographic characteristics, it is important for data to contain information about the characteristics of the stop. The characteristics of the stop should include time of day, location of the stop, and reason for the stop. These characteristics highlight important variables that are correlated with racially biased stop outcomes. That is, the location of the stop and the time of day when the stop was conducted may influence an officer's decision to make a stop and his or her actions following the stop (see Ridgeway, 2006). The reason for the stop also allows for further analysis of the discretionary nature of the stop. Some analyses, such as Ridgeway's (2006) propensity score analysis, have used the reason for the stop as a filter for including or excluding cases into or from analysis. As mentioned previously, police–citizen contact where discretion is higher is potentially more likely to be influenced by racial bias than police–citizen contact where discretion is lower.

Finally, it is also important to measure post-stop outcomes in collecting data on racial profiling. These measurements should include any actions taken as a result of the stop (e.g., ticket, citation, arrest, search), as well as the duration of the stop. One post-stop outcome, discretionary searches, has been an important concern of social scientists looking at racially biased policing. Harris (1999) described the "driving while black" phenomenon as incidents in which the police stopped blacks for legitimate traffic violations, but used the stop as an opportunity to conduct a roadside investigation. These investigations included searches of the person and vehicle being stopped. While obtaining data on post-stop actions such as searches can be revealing, Ridgeway (2006) also found that, when comparing blacks and whites who received the same post-stop outcomes, blacks were more likely to have a stop of longer duration than similarly situated whites. Additional key data elements are the specific reason justifying search and arrest, the results of search (e.g., whether contraband was found), and specific items found during a search (e.g., drugs, alcohol, currency, weapons, stolen property).[2] These data elements have been used to further analyze racial bias that resulted in disparate post-stop outcomes without having to face the challenges of creating a comparison population (see Ridgeway, 2006; Knowles, Perisco, and Todd, 2001).

Using law enforcement agency data to analyze racial bias has important strengths. Legal requirements to collect the data, such as the consent decrees and the state-level profiling legislation discussed above, allow researchers to gain access to data without having to design a data collection protocol themselves. In addition, statewide data collections efforts provide access to police behavior across various settings, and data collection at the stop level creates the opportunity to explore patterns across individual officers. The ease of data collection does not come without limitations. Law enforcement does have a vested interest in the outcome of any data analysis conducted on racial profiling. Thus there is a possibility that data could be intentionally unreported or misreported, in order to improve the outcome for the agency. Also, compliance with data collection protocol is reliant on the individual officer's commitment to the specific study or broader initiative to provide transparency in traffic stop activity. Officers may not fill out reports on traffic stops not resulting in official action if they do not believe it is important or that it is too inconvenient. Thus, the quality of data for analysis is dependent on establishment of data integrity procedures (Ramirez et al., 2000).

Measuring Disparity in Law Enforcement Traffic Stop Data

While capturing law enforcement traffic stop data is crucial to examining racial bias, it only represents a part of the equation. For example, if 50 percent of stops in a jurisdiction are of black drivers and the remaining 50 percent are of white drivers, there is no possibility to determine on these data alone, whether this represents an equitable or a biased pattern of stop activity for either group. The researcher needs to identify a comparative population of drivers in order to determine whether this distribution is representative or unequal; and this is commonly referred to as a benchmark. The benchmark can then be used to create a disparity score that is derived by dividing the percentage of drivers stopped from a given racial–ethnic group by the percentage of this group in a representative population of drivers. A disparity score of 1 reflects that drivers being stopped are representative of the comparison population of drivers. A score greater than 1 means that the racial–ethnic group is overrepresented in traffic stops vis-à-vis the comparison population of that group, and a score of less than 1 reflects underrepresentation of the racial–ethnic group of interest (see Rojek et al., 2004).

Table 20.1 provides a simple illustration of this analysis. In agency A, 50 percent of the drivers stopped are black and 50 percent are white, and the representation of each of these groups in the population of drivers in the jurisdiction is 50 percent. As a result, the stops of each group represent parity with their representation in the comparison population of drivers, which generates a disparity score of 1.00 for each group. Alternatively, in agency B both racial groups again represent 50 percent of the stops, but black drivers only compose 20 percent of the comparison population of drivers and white drivers are 80 percent. This results in a disparity score of 2.50 for black drivers or, stated otherwise, the representation of black drivers is 2.5 times greater than we would expect, given their representation in the general comparative population of drivers. Then white drivers are underrepresented in stops by agency B with a disparity score of 0.63. Agency C

Table 20.1 Example of stop representation and disparity scores.

	Driver Race	*Percentage of Stopped Drivers*	*Representation in Comparison Driving Population*	*Disparity Score*
Agency A	Black drivers	50%	50%	1.00
	While drivers	50%	50%	1.00
Agency B	Black drivers	50%	20%	2.50
	While drivers	50%	80%	0.63
Agency C	Black drivers	50%	80%	0.63
	While drivers	50%	20%	2.50

subsequently reflects an alternative scenario where white drivers are overrepresented and black drivers are underrepresented in stops in relation to a comparison population of drivers.

What is important to keep in mind is that an overrepresentation in traffic stops represents a statistical disparity between the group under study and a comparison group and is not necessarily evidence of racial bias. As noted above, the use of traffic stop data is an indirect measure of officer intent to be biased in traffic stop activity. It is possible to have overrepresentation of a given racial or ethnic group in traffic stops for reasons not related to bias. Fridell (2004) articulates four alternative hypotheses to racial bias in the distribution of traffic stops that must be accounted for in studies of this kind:

1. Racial–ethnic groups are not equally represented as residents in the jurisdiction.
2. Racial–ethnic groups are not equally represented as drivers on jurisdiction roads.
3. Racial–ethnic groups are not equivalent in the nature and extent of their traffic law-violating behavior.
4. Racial–ethnic groups are not equally represented as drivers on roads where stopping activity by police is high. (Fridell, 2004, p. 12)

The disparity score noted above only addresses the first hypothesis proposed here. Fridell notes that the first three hypotheses consecutively narrow the necessary benchmark to a more precise measure of racial bias. This makes the first hypothesis easiest to address and the third hypothesis hardest to address. Ruling out a later hypothesis, however, automatically rules out an earlier hypothesis. For instance, if a researcher can account for differences through the race of drivers on jurisdiction roads, it is unnecessary to account for differences by resorting to the race of residents in the jurisdiction. That is, the racial composition of a neighborhood is not needed in order to determine racial bias if a better measure, such as the racial composition of drivers on the neighborhoods' roads, is available. The fourth hypothesis, however, is a little more controversial. While racial differences in the number of stops conducted can be explained by the high stopping activity of police, this could be a result of racial bias at higher levels, for example at the level of the police department. That is, police departments may, as a result of racial bias, direct higher levels of stopping activities to areas that racial minorities frequent. Thus it is important to emphasize that the fourth hypothesis only applies when the reasons for differential deployment are legitimate.

The analysis of traffic stops has been evolving over the past fifteen years; early attempts often used simple benchmark data. Fridell's (2004) four hypotheses is a reflection of these debates surrounding early analysis efforts. Nonetheless, her considerations frame the strengths and weaknesses of different population benchmarks, which persist to the present. The following is a review of the benchmarks commonly used in examining whether certain racial or ethnic groups are disproportionately represented in an agency's stops in general or in an agency's stops in a specific area – which is termed "aggregate benchmarking" here. Discussion is also given to the internal benchmarking approach, which is directed at identifying stop disparities attributable to individual officers rather than to the agency as a whole.

Aggregate benchmarking

The aggregate benchmarking method most commonly used in traffic stop analysis is to employ the census. Census data are popular in racial profiling research because they are inexpensive and very easy to obtain from the US Census Bureau. The difficulty, however, consists in attempting to effectively adjust census data in order to maintain a meaningful benchmark. Traditional census numbers on the racial makeup of the population in a geographic area that the study was conducted are insufficient to address Fridell's (2004) alternative hypotheses. That is, obtaining the racial proportions of the residential populations of the study area through census data only addresses the first of the alternative hypotheses. Thus, scholars have attempted to adjust these data to generate more meaningful conclusions.

One simple adjustment that can be made to the census data is to account for driving access. One approach to this benchmark is to adjust the census data so as to account for age. Individuals under the age required in the jurisdiction for obtaining a driver's license will not be driving and will not be at risk for being pulled over (Fridell, 2004). Thus their inclusion in the benchmark population is unnecessary and could even be misleading. For example, Smith and Petrocelli (2001) examined potential racial bias displayed by police in Richmond, Virginia by using as a benchmark the population of city residents over 16 – the driving age in the region. Harris (1999) pushed driving access one step further by using data from the National Household Transportation Survey (NHTS) to develop adjustments that were based on access to vehicles. Harris used the NHTP to determine that 21 percent of the black households did not own vehicles at that time. This meant that 21 percent of the black population did not have regular access to a vehicle they would drive, and this prevented them from being on the road and being eligible for being stopped. Therefore not adjusting for access to vehicles could create misleading conclusions.

While adjusting the census to account for driving access is important, it still deals only with individuals who reside within the geographic area where data were collected. In their study of disparity among traffic stops, Rojek and colleagues (2004, p. 135) found that law enforcement executives were concerned with analyses that used residential data "because persons who drove through their areas did not necessarily live there or resemble the race/ethnic characteristics of the local population." This hints at Fridell's (2004) second alternative hypothesis: the need to account for differences in the racial–ethnic characteristics of drivers on the road, not just of drivers living in the jurisdiction. To address these concerns, Rojek and colleagues (2004) used a method of spatial weighting that allowed the ethnic characteristics of municipalities within 20 miles of the target jurisdiction to influence the benchmark for that jurisdiction. Spatial weighting allowed the researchers to emphasize that residents were more likely than nonresidents to be drivers on jurisdiction roads, but that nonresidents could still play a significant role in representing the driving population.

Alternatively, Farrell and colleagues (2003) attempted to benchmark data collected in Rhode Island by accounting for what they termed "pushes" and "pulls." These researchers identified all cities within a 30-mile radius of the target city as contributing to that city's driving population. They then made calculations for each contributing city on the basis of the demographic makeup of the city, the percentage of residents who owned cars, the percentage of residents who drove more than 10 miles to work, and the travel time between the contributing city and the target city. These factors were deemed "pushes" – that is, factors that pushed drivers out of surrounding cities. The researchers then determined factors that would "pull" drivers into the target community. To make this determination, they considered these factors: "(1) percent of State employment, (2) percent of State retail trade, (3) percent of state food and accommodation sales, and (4) percent of State average daily road volume" (Farrell et al., 2003, p. 32). A calculation of the "pushes" of each contributing city and the "pull" of the target city allowed the researchers to create a new benchmark combining the target city's demographics with the contributing cities' demographics. These estimates, as well as those made by Rojek and colleagues (2004), improve the ability to use the census for creating benchmarks. However, they are still imperfect estimates of the driving population of interest. Unfortunately these complex calculations may be as accurate of an estimate as is possible when using census data.

In an attempt to estimate the racial and ethnic characteristics of drivers in a different way, scholars turned to an observational method. John Lamberth (1994), an expert witness in court cases involving racial profiling, used an observation-based benchmarking strategy to back his testimony regarding racial profiling on the New Jersey turnpike. Lamberth used observation teams to count the number of cars driving on the turnpike and to tally the proportion of those cars that had a black occupant. In addition, he had observation teams drive down the turnpike with cruise control set to 5 miles per hour above the speed limit and tallied the race of drivers who were speeding past the vehicle. Lamberth used these observations to estimate the number of drivers on the road who were black and the racial makeup of traffic violators on the road. Lamberth's observational analysis thus attempted to account for both the second and the third alternative hypotheses proposed by Fridell (2004). Lamberth's (1994) study found statistically significant disparities between the number of black drivers stopped and the number of black drivers who both drove on the turnpike and violated the law while doing so.

This type of observational method does not come without flaws and limitations, however. Alpert, Smith and Dunham (2004) note several of these limitations in a critique of observational studies that is based on their own experiences in conducting an observational study in Miami-Dade County (see also Alpert et al., 2007).

First, observational studies are time-intensive and very expensive to conduct. Second, limited resources force researchers to select only a handful of locations within a jurisdiction – usually a low number of intersections – where they conduct observations. Furthermore, these locations are typically selected on account of the high volume of traffic, traffic-law violations, or collisions. This makes it difficult, if not impossible, to generalize the observations to the entire area of interest. Third, researchers are usually forced to cease conducting observations at night, due to lack of visibility. Finally, some ethnic characteristics may be difficult to notice from observational posts on the side of the highway (Alpert et al., 2004). In their study, Alpert and colleagues (2007) were forced to categorize the drivers they observed into black and nonblack, due to difficulties in separating them into more specific racial categories (e.g., Hispanic or non-Hispanic white). This type of concern is especially important in geographic regions with other racial and ethnic minority populations, such as Miami-Dade County.

To move past the problems with observational benchmarks Alpert and colleagues (2004) suggested using not-at-fault traffic accident data to estimate the driving population. Drivers in two-vehicle crashes who are not at fault should represent the driving population as a whole, as their presence in the accident is due to chance, and not to any demographic selection mechanism. Some scholars have argued that not-at-fault traffic accident data do not consider the possibility that drivers "drive in ways that puts [*sic*] them in danger of accidents or travel in areas where traffic accidents are more frequent" (Farrell et al., 2003, p. 28). Alpert and colleagues' (2004) analysis, however, did not support the concern that drivers in not-at-fault accidents drive differently. When they compared the racial composition of drivers in accidents of this type in Miami-Dade County at the same intersections where they implemented an observational protocol to measure racial composition, they found no statistical difference between the observations and the not-at-fault statistics. It is important to note, however, that not-at-fault traffic data provide us with an estimate of the driving population as a whole, not of traffic violators. While this finding does not give us the aptitude to rule out Fridell's (2004) alternative hypotheses any more than the observational method does, it does prove to make racial profiling research much easier and more comprehensive. By implementing law enforcement data collection methods on not-at-fault traffic accidents during a racial profiling study, researchers can eliminate the expense of setting up observation teams and can include data on the driving population at night, when observation is much more difficult. Researchers can use agency traffic collision records, assuming that these reports collect information on the driver's race.[3]

Despite analytical advancements in modifying census data or using alternative sources of aggregate-level data such as not-at-fault accidents, there is still a general consensus among scholars that observational methods are the preferred way of benchmarking data. In fact, both the not-at-fault accident data and the spatial weighting method were validated by using observations as a comparison group (Alpert et al., 2004; Rojek et al., 2004). Rojek and colleagues accurately describe the situation by stating that, "if it [*sic*] were not expensive and time-consuming, observational data would be used to estimate the racial composition of the driving population in all studies of racial profiling based on traffic stops" (Rojek et al., 2004, p. 138). What becomes essential, then, is proper observational protocols and practicality. But it is unlikely that observations can be carried out throughout a whole jurisdiction, let alone across multiple jurisdictions. As a result, observations still suffer from pragmatic limitations.

Internal benchmarking

In response to these strong limitations to finding an accurate benchmark for the analysis of racial profiling data at the agency level, an alternative benchmarking process has been proposed: one that should take place at the level of the individual officer. Walker (2001) was concerned with the significant flaws in the attempts to find an accurate benchmark for traffic stop data at the aggregate level. He reasoned that benchmarking a police department's traffic stops against the population on the road is extremely difficult and may not be possible at all. Walker advocated for the use of an internal benchmark instead. That is, instead of comparing the police department's stop statistics to some benchmark derived from outside sources, researchers could compare individual officers' traffic stop statistics to traffic stop statistics from comparable groups of officers. In this type of analysis, an emphasis is placed on comparable groups of officers. Demographics between patrol beats and time of day can change drastically. Thus officers should only be compared to other officers who work the same or similar beats at the same or similar times.

One practical way of conducting this analysis is to take officers similarly situated by region of work and shift and compare their rates of stopping racial–ethnic driving groups of interest. Identifying outlying officers can be accomplished by locating those officers whose rates of stopping a given minority group are a standard deviation from the rates of their fellow officers (Decker and Rojek, 2002; Withrow, Dailey, and Jackson, 2008; Ridgeway and MacDonald, 2014). In essence, this approach is using the statistical measure of standard deviation from the mean to determine those officers who are stopping certain racial or ethnic groups significantly more than the norm established by their peers. It is important to keep in mind that this only represents disparity in relation to other officers, and not necessarily actual bias. The outlying identification only warrants further evaluation as there may be reasonable explanations for this pattern: specific beat assignments, hotspot activity, citizen requests for additional enforcement, community- or problem-oriented policing efforts, and other variation in officer enforcement efforts that are not bias in intent.

Internal benchmarking addresses racial bias in traffic stops in a drastically different manner from that of other benchmarking methods. In consequence, it has an entirely different set of advantages and limitations. Primary among its advantages is the ability to develop an early warning system to identify officers who may be engaging in racially biased traffic stops (Walker, 2001). Through the use of internal benchmarking, officers identified through an early warning system can be given appropriate interventions or disciplinary actions designed to prevent further racially biased behavior. Thus internal benchmarking not only identifies racial profiling issues but also provides a framework for dealing with them. Walker has shown that early warning systems and their interventions provide positive benefits for a police department; chief among these is the potential to "change the organizational climate of the department" into one of intolerance toward racial profiling (Walker, 2001, p. 87). Despite these benefits, there is a significant weakness of the internal benchmarking system. Since internal benchmarking compares officers within departments and other groups, it does not address the potential for institutionalized racial bias (Walker, 2001). For instance, if the officers who work a particular beat or shift all engage in racially biased policing, comparing the individual stop statistics to those of other officers on the same beat or shift will not yield evidence of racial bias.

Measuring Disparity in Post-Stop Action with Law Enforcement Traffic Stop Data

The major flaw in benchmarking traffic stop data is the inability to accurately assess the characteristics of the driving population as a whole. To avoid this concern, researchers have begun to analyze police actions after the traffic stop has been initiated. Post-stop analyses compare the demographic characteristics of individuals who experience some type of secondary action after the stop with the demographic characteristics of all individuals stopped. All the data necessary for analysis can therefore be collected by police officers who conduct traffic stops and no estimate of the driving population is needed, since all those who are at risk for these actions are already included in the data. This makes post-stop analyses more cost-efficient and provides a more complete benchmark for comparing the data. The focus on post-stop action is largely oriented to the differential application of coercive treatment such as citation, search, and arrest.

Post-stop analyses do not address the same question as the studies on traffic stop data mentioned earlier. That is, no post-stop analysis can draw any conclusions regarding the influence of race on an officer's decision to conduct a traffic stop. Instead post-stop analyses rely on the assumption that, if police officers are engaging in biased policing, this fact will manifest itself in other areas of police work, in addition to the decision to stop. For instance, if police officers in a jurisdiction are engaging in biased policing, they will be more likely to subject to discretionary searches individuals of a particular race, and not of another. This represents the underlying logic of racial bias discussed above in relation to stereotypes and the concept of pretextual stops, highlighted in *Whren v. United States* (1996). *Whren v. United States* established that, even if an officer has another motivation for pulling a car over, as long as the driver committed a legitimate traffic offense, the officer has not violated any individual rights. Essentially, officers are not stopping certain groups at greater rates for the sake of simply stopping them, but are doing so on the strength of a stereotype according to which the group in question is more criminally inclined.

Thus the stop, whether for a moving violation or for some minor violation that acts as a pretext, is assumed to be more likely to result in uncovering a legal violation, such as a person who is wanted for a crime or for the possession of illegal items.

Searches

Searches of drivers and passengers during traffic stops are the predominant focus of post-stop analysis. When unwarranted, searches are highly intrusive actions, which violate the sense of privacy as well as an individual's dignity (Rosenfeld et al., 2012). They also get at the heart of bias that emanates from criminal stereotypes, particularly when they are discretionary, as one goal of conducting a search is to uncover illegal behavior such as possession of drugs or firearms. With this in mind, however, the evaluation of search patterns across racial–ethnic groups is not a straightforward process with simple conclusions to be drawn.

For example, a researcher analyzes the post-stop data from jurisdiction A and finds that blacks are searched 20 percent of the time after they are stopped for a traffic violation, while whites are searched 10 percent of the time after they are stopped for a traffic violation. An easy preliminary conclusion to draw from this information is that jurisdiction A engages in racial profiling because it disproportionately searches blacks by comparison to whites. However, on average, the context of these searches across groups may not be equitable as to when and where they occurred, which suggests that there may be ecological influences that impact officers' decisions, as opposed to racial characteristics of the drivers. In addition, the distribution in the basis for searches across groups may not be the same, specifically whether the searchers are discretionary or nondiscretionary. Police department policies often mandate searches in specific situations, such as when an individual is arrested or a vehicle is going to be impounded. These mandated searches arguably leave less room for discretionary bias based on race – which is problematic for a simple comparison of searches if these are disproportionately represented in one group by comparison to another. Thus the interest in search analysis is commonly related to discretionary searches (e.g., consent searchers, reasonable suspicion searches). A great example of this problem can be found in the work of Alpert and colleagues (2007). A preliminary analysis of a driver's likelihood of being searched after a traffic stop revealed that black drivers were significantly more likely to be searched than drivers of other races. Moving beyond this conclusion, however, the researchers found that, after controlling for custody arrests – a situation that requires a driver to be searched – this statistically significant difference vanished. Thus the researchers determined that the increased likelihood of being searched was likely a function of a black driver's increased likelihood of being arrested.

To overcome these difficulties, Ridgeway (2006) proposed a propensity score analysis for interpreting post-stop data. The propensity score analysis arose out of a concern about differences between the characteristics of the stops of white drivers and those of the stops of black drivers. Ridgeway (2006) noted that these stops differed significantly by time of day of the stop and neighborhood the stop was conducted in. Thus previous analysis could have found racial differences in stop outcomes that were a function of an officer's increased suspicion, which was in turn due to the criminal nature of the neighborhood or time of the stop. For example, an individual driving through a shopping center in the middle of the day is not nearly as suspicious as an individual driving through a crime-prone neighborhood in the middle of the night. The propensity score method establishes scores for different characteristics of a stop in order to allow researchers to compare drivers with similar stop characteristics instead of making an aggregate-level comparison (Ridgeway, 2006). All black drivers who are stopped are not compared to all white drivers who are stopped. Instead, drivers stopped at similar times of day and in similar neighborhoods are compared by race. Rosenfeld and colleagues (2012) similarly used propensity score-matching to examine the interaction of race and age in discretionary searches. While the aggregate results revealed that black male drivers were more likely to be searched than white drivers, the propensity score analysis revealed that proportional search activity only impacted young male black drivers.

Propensity score tests, however, have limits too when they are used to uncover racial bias. Scores can only be developed on the basis of observed characteristics. Thus any influences that unobserved characteristics have on stop outcomes are not considered in this type of analysis (Ridgeway, 2006). Officer decisions to search are often based on citizen and vehicle cues, along with the "stories" citizens relay to officers (Engel and Johnson, 2006). Thus, because they don't systematically and accurately capture this information, propensity score-matching and other analytic techniques will miss important factors that influence discretionary search decisions; therefore such techniques have a limited capacity to attribute bias. Additionally, propensity score tests can be limited by sample size. Since only subsets of the data are being compared by race, there must be a sufficient number of stops with similar characteristics for a comparison to be conducted (Ridgeway, 2006).

Outcome test

An alternative to evaluating searches is the outcome test articulated by Knowles and colleagues (2001). The outcome test places an emphasis on the contraband hit rate in searches, which represents the number of searches that produce the identification of contraband (e.g., drugs, weapons, stolen property), divided by the total number of searches. The test assumes that unbiased police officers search for the sole purpose of finding contraband. Hence they will conduct searches in a manner that maximizes the number of searches that find contraband. If officers obey this principle, then the rate at which contraband is found among white drivers will be the same as – or at least close to – the rate at which contraband is found among black drivers. Additionally, this test is appealing to researchers because the nature of the unbiased police officer assumption makes other variables in the decision-making process irrelevant. It does not matter what factors the officer used in deciding to search, as long as he did it only to maximize the outcome. This eliminates the weakness of measuring only observed characteristics identified in the propensity score tests by Ridgeway (2006). Knowles and colleagues (2001) argued that, when hit rates equalize between races, there is an equilibrium in which the citizens being searched have equivalent crime rates across races. Put more specifically, "it [the test] … predicts that those groups that are searched – a small minority of all motorists – should have the same crime rate (if the police are unbiased)" (Perisco and Todd, 2008, p. 46). Moreover, the number of searches conducted does not matter, as long as the hit rate is the same. Thus, as a simple example, a lack of racial bias is found where 100 searches of white drivers and 500 searchers of black drivers were conducted, as long as the rates of cases that produce contraband are the same across both groups.

It is important to note that the outcome analysis is built upon a model with several large assumptions that Engel (2008) argues are untenable and prevent meaningful conclusions. While Perisco and Todd (2008) have acknowledged that their analysis only applies to discretionary searches, Engel (2008) notes that discretionary searches are not necessarily dichotomous. While not mandatory, searches based on evidence in plain view certainly involve less discretion than reasonable suspicion searches. Furthermore, the outcome model assumes that motorists' behavior during the stop is irrelevant to the decision to search them. Engel points out that research has consistently shown that officers do take into account citizens' behavior in decision-making and that citizens' behavior varies by racial and ethnic groups. That is, individuals of a particular racial group may be more likely to engage in behavior deemed by an officer to be disrespectful or noncompliant. This behavior may, in turn, influence the officer's decision to search the vehicle. Furthermore, Engel notes that officers are trained to use verbal and nonverbal clues of suspicion in order to make decisions. These clues include patterns of speech as well as the avoidance of eye contact. She further states research has also demonstrated that the clues used by police officers to establish suspicion also vary in their prevalence among blacks and whites (see Johnson, 2007). The use, by police officers, of indicators of suspicion that vary according to race invalidates the outcome test. Officers may disproportionately search members of a racial group due to the latter's tendency to present indicators of suspicious activity that the officer is trained to register. If these indicators are not consistently accurate across racial groups, there will not be equality in the hit rate for contraband despite the officer's reliance on training and not on racial bias (Engel, 2008; Johnson, 2007).

The outcome test also assumes that officer behavior is monolithic. That is, individual officers do not vary in their propensity to conduct a search during a traffic stop. Engel (2008) notes that research points in a very different direction: officers differ in their propensity to search, and they do so on the basis of their assignment and professional tastes. Finally, the outcome test relies heavily on the assumption that both citizens and officers tailor their behavior according to feedback from the system, in order to reach a point of equilibrium. Specifically, it assumes that officers are aware of the likelihood that a search of an individual of a particular race would result in a find, and that citizens are aware of the likelihood of their being searched by police (Knowles and colleagues, 2001). The point of equilibrium, where hit rates across races will be equal, requires citizens to carry contraband less if they are more likely to be searched and more if they are less likely to be searched. Similarly, police officers must search more individuals of a particular race if such individuals are more likely to be carrying contraband. Engel (2008) points out that the state of the criminal justice system makes this assumption highly unlikely to be true. She states: "Police officers are often unaware of empirical research and may rely on their limited personal experiences and collective 'war stories' to make decisions" (Engel, 2008, p. 25). She also notes that citizens are unlikely to be aware of empirical realities regarding their chances of being searched. Given the significant flaws that exist in the outcome test's underlying assumptions, analyses using this method raise questions about its validity.

Conclusion

The issue of racial bias in traffic stops emerged with special attention to terms like "driving while black" and to racial profiling, which were accusing the police of being disproportionately coercive toward minority citizens, especially African Americans, in these events. However, this is just one component in the much larger theme of the relationship between the police and minority communities in the United States, which has a long and at times tenuous history. At the same time, the explosion of data collection on traffic stops has provided an opportunity to examine patterns in interactions between the police and minority citizens in a contemporary context. It is also important to acknowledge that policing related to this issue has changed over the last century in the United States, and particularly in the past few decades. Law enforcement agencies have increasingly diversified since the early 1970s, and agencies have continuously tried to improve relations with minority communities, with varying degrees of success. Nonetheless, there is still mistrust of the police and feelings of differential treatment in minority communities, particularly among African Americans.

Against this backdrop, the matter of examining patterns of police traffic stop activity has put social science research methodology in the spotlight. Social scientists were hired by individual law enforcement agencies and other oversight bodies to develop benchmarks and to conduct the analysis of traffic stops, as well as asked to train agencies in analyzing their own data. This analytic effort, however, has proved challenging, as outlined in the review provided in this chapter. The research, to date, has consistently found an overrepresentation in minority drivers being stopped and searched. While the development of methodological approaches to examining traffic stop data has improved over time, they are still often challenged when addressing Fridell's (2004) four alternative hypotheses for disparities in stop patterns. Thus the analytic strategies need to be consolidated and refined if they are to more effectively determine whether the above patterns of disparity are reflective of racial bias.

Looking forward, the study of racial bias in policing is likely on course for a trajectory change. From 2000 to 2008, considerable attention was given to this issue, particularly to the methodological difficulties of assessing bias. However, scholarship on it in the way of publications has since declined, despite the presence of a number of unresolved methodological problems. This may be explained in part by a decline in political and public attention to the topic. There have been few public and political calls for new data collection efforts by law enforcement to evaluate racial bias by comparison to those launched a decade ago, and many of those earlier efforts have ended over time. However, recent high-profile cases that have called into question the role of citizens' race in police incidents where deadly force is being used may bring this issue back into prominence and spur new scholarship, including attempts to expand the examination of police racial bias beyond traffic stops. Evidence for a shift in this direction can be found in the formation of the President's Task Force on 21st Century Policing – which is, in part, a response to these high-profile incidents (Office of Community-Oriented Policing Services, n.d.). Two underlying themes of the task force are the relationship between the police and minority communities, and the issue of impartial and just treatment.

Notes

1 The PPCS survey years are 1999, 2002, 2005, 2008, 2011.

2 See Ramirez, McDevitt, and Farrell (2000) for a more detailed discussion of data collection strategies and elements.

3 It is also important to consider what types of collision are recorded by agencies and whether this will reflect a representative population of drivers. For example, in California, law enforcement agencies are required to complete only statewide traffic collision forms for events involving injuries and fatalities. The use of the form for noninjury collisions is encouraged, but not required. Thus agencies will record collisions using other mechanisms, or simply will not record these events but only require drivers to exchange information on a vehicle-damage event, with no police documentation.

References

Alexander Weiss Consulting. n.d. *Illinois traffic stop study: 2013 annual report.* Accessed December 12, 2015. www.idot.illinois.gov/Assets/uploads/files/Transportation-System/Reports/Safety/Traffic-Stop-Studies/2013/2013%20ITSS%20Executive%20Summary.pdf.

Alpert, G. P., Dunham, R. G., and Smith, M. R. 2007. Investigating racial profiling by the Miami-Dade Police Department: A multimethod approach. *Criminology and Public Policy*, 6 (1): 25–56.

Alpert, G. P., Smith, M. R., and Dunham, R. G. 2004. Toward a better benchmark: Assessing the utility of not-at-fault traffic crash data in racial profiling research. *Justice Research and Policy*, 6 (1): 43–69.

Bruce-Jones, E. 2015. German policing at the intersection: Race, gender, migrant status and mental health. *Race and Class*, 56: 36–49.

Bureau of Justice Statistics. n.d. Data collection: Police–public contact survey. Accessed December 12, 2015. http://www.bjs.gov/index.cfm?ty=dcdetail&iid=251.

Carlson, D. K. 2004. Racial profiling seen as pervasive, unjust. *Gallup News Service*. Accessed December 12, 2015. http://www.gallup.com/poll/12406/Racial-Profiling-Seen-Pervasive-Unjust.aspx.

Davis, R. C., Ortiz, C. W., Henderson, N. J., Miller, J., and Massie, M. K. 2002. *Turning necessity into virtue: Pittsburgh's experience with a federal consent decree*. New York: Vera Institute of Justice.

Decker, S. H., and Rojek, J. 2002. St. Louis Metropolitan Police Department traffic stop patterns. Report submitted by the University of Missouri, St. Louis to the St. Louis Metropolitan Police Department, January.

Executive summary for 2013 Missouri vehicle stops (n.d.). Accessed December 12, 2015. https://archive.org/stream/2013VehicleStopsReport/2013VehicleStopsReport_djvu.txt.

Engel, R. S. 2005. Citizens' perceptions of distributive and procedural injustice during traffic stops with police. *Journal of Research in Crime and Delinquency*, 42 (4): 445–481.

Engel, R. S. 2008. A critique of the "outcome test" in racial profiling research. *Justice Quarterly*, 25 (1): 1–36.

Engel, R. S., and Johnson, R. 2006. Toward a better understand of racial and ethnic disparities in search and seizure rates. *Journal of Criminal Justice*, 34 (6): 605–617.

Farrell, A., McDevitt, J., Cronin, S., and Pierce, E. 2003. *Rhode Island Traffic Stop Statistics Act Final Report*. Northeastern University: Institute on Race and Justice.

Fridell, L. A. 2004. *By the numbers: A guide for analyzing race data from vehicle stops*. Washington, DC: Police Executive Research Forum.

Gilliard-Matthews, S., Kowalski, B. R., and Lundman, R. J. 2008. Officer race and citizen-reported traffic ticket decisions by police in 1999 and 2002. *Police Quarterly*, 11 (2): 202–219.

Harris, D. A. 1999. The stories, the statistics, and the law: Why "driving while black" matters. *Minnesota Law Review*, 84: 265–326.

Hernandez-Murillo, R., and Knowles, J. 2004. Racial profiling or racist policing? Bounds tests in aggregate data. *International Economic Review*, 45 (3): 959–989.

Jobard, F., and Levy, R. 2011. Racial profiling: The Parisian police experience. *Canadian Journal of Criminology and Criminal Justice*, 53: 87–93.

Johnson, R. R. 2007. Race and police reliance on suspicious non-verbal clues. *Policing: An International Journal of Police Strategies & Management*, 30 (2): 277–290.

Knowles, J., Perisco, N., and Todd, P. 2001. Racial bias in motor vehicle searches: Theory and evidence. *Journal of Political Economy*, 109 (1): 203–229.

Lamberth, J. 1994. Revised statistical analysis of the incidence of police stops and arrests of black drivers/travelers on the New Jersey Turnpike between exits or interchanges 1 and 3 from the years 1988 through 1991. Accessed December 12, 2015. www.mass.gov/eopss/docs/eops/faip/new-jersey-study-report.pdf (without front page, title, and author).

Lundman, R. J. 2004. Driver race, ethnicity, and gender and citizen reports of vehicle searches by police and vehicle search hits: Toward a triangulated scholarly understanding. *The Journal of Criminal Law and Criminology*, 94 (2): 309–350.

Lundman, R. J., and Kaufman, R. L. 2003. Driving while black: Effects of race, ethnicity, and gender on citizen self-reports of traffic stops and police actions. *Criminology*, 41 (1): 195–220.

McDevitt, J., Iwama, J., and Bailey-Laguerre, L. 2014. *Rhode Island traffic stop statistics data collection study*. Northeastern University, MA: Institute on Race and Justice.

Miller, J., Gounev, P., Pap, A. L., Wagman, D., Balogi, A., Bezlov, T., Simonovits, B., Vargha, l. 2008. Racism and police stops. *European Journal of Criminology*, 5: 161–191.

Newport, F. 1999. Racial profiling is seen as widespread, particularly among young black men. *Gallup News Service*, December 9: 1–10.

Office of Community-Oriented Policing Services. n.d. President's Task Force on 21st Century Policing. Accessed February 5, 2015. http://www.cops.usdoj.gov/policingtaskforce.

Perisco, N., and Todd, P. E. 2008. The hit rates for racial bias in motor-vehicle searches. *Justice Quarterly*, 25 (1): 37–53.

Ramirez, D., McDevitt, J., and Farrell, A. 2000. A resource guide on racial profiling data collection systems: Promising practices and lessons learned. Washington, DC: United States Department of Justice, National Institute of Justice.

Ridgeway, G. 2006. Assessing the effect of race bias in post-traffic stop outcomes using propensity scores. *Journal of Quantitative Criminology*, 22 (1): 1–29.

Rojek, J., Rosenfeld, R., and Decker, S. 2004. The influence of driver's race on traffic stops in Missouri. *Police Quarterly*, 7 (1): 126–147.

Rosenfeld, R., Rojek, J., and Decker, S. 2012. Age matters: Race differences in police searches of young and older male drivers. *Journal of Research in Crime and Delinquency*, 49 (1): 31–55.

Satzewich, V., and Shaffir, W. 2009. Racism versus professionalism: Claims and counter-claims about racial profiling. *Canadian Journal of Criminology and Criminal Justice*, 51: 199–226.

Smith, M. R., and Petrocelli, M. 2001. Racial profiling? A multivariate analysis of police traffic stop data. *Police Quarterly*, 4 (1): 4–27.

Tomaskovic-Devey, D., Wright, C. P., Czaja, R., and Miller, K. 2006. Self-reports of police speeding stops by race: Results from the North Carolina Reverse Record Check Survey. *Journal of Quantitative Criminology*, 22: 279–297.

Tyler, T. R., and Wakslak, C. J. 2004. Profiling and police legitimacy: Procedural justice, attributions of motive, and acceptance of police authority. *Criminology*, 42 (2): 253–281.

United States of America v. City of Los Angeles, California, Board of Police Commissioners of the City of Los Angeles, and the Los Angeles Police Department. 2000. Consent decree. Accessed December 12, 2015. assets.lapdonline.org/assets/pdf/final_consent_decree.pdf.

Walker, S. 2001. Searching for the denominator: Problems with police traffic stop data and an early warning system solution. *Justice Research and Policy*, 3 (1): 63–95.

Withrow, B., Dailey, J. D., and Jackson, H. 2008. The utility of an internal benchmarking strategy in racial profiling surveillance. *Justice Research and Policy*, 10: 19–47.

Whren v. United States, 517 US 806 (1996).

Further Reading

Ridgeway, G., and MacDonald, J. 2014. A method for internal benchmarking of criminal justice system performance. *Crime and Delinquency*, 60: 145–162.

Part IV

Specialized Measurement Techniques

21

Self-Reported Crime and Delinquency

Scott Menard, Lisa C. Bowman-Bowen, and Yi-Fen Lu

In contemporary criminological and criminal justice research, the term *self-report* is almost always used to refer to self-report survey research, as opposed to data from biographies or autobiographies, or data from testimony, including confessions given in the context of formal processing within the justice system. Self-report survey research arose out of two concerns. One was a concern with producing data with broader and more representative coverage of a more general population than was typical in testimonial or biographical data. The second concern, and the one most frequently cited as a reason for the development of both self-report survey research and victimization studies (see Chapter 16 in this volume), was to account for illegal behavior that did not appear in official statistics on arrests or crimes known to the police, but that might allow us to better understand the distribution, correlates, and causes of illegal behavior. In self-report survey research, a probability or nonprobability sample of individuals (respondents) from some population is interviewed by using a structured interview format that asks all respondents the same questions, subject to eligibility criteria for those individuals. For example, respondents who are not married or otherwise involved in an intimate partner relationship may not be asked questions about whether they assault their spouses or intimate partners. In this chapter we examine issues related to the distinction between cross-sectional and longitudinal self-report research; whom we ask (sampling individuals); what we ask (sampling behaviors); how we measure those behaviors (scaling behaviors); the accuracy of self-report data; additional issues in longitudinal self-report studies; and needs for further study of the self-report method itself.

The Handbook of Measurement Issues in Criminology and Criminal Justice, First Edition.
Edited by Beth M. Huebner and Timothy S. Bynum.

Snapshot or Moving Picture? Cross-Sectional and Longitudinal Self-Report Research

Self-report survey research may involve either cross-sectional or longitudinal data, the latter collected either cross-sectionally (although this may seem paradoxical), by using retrospective data, or longitudinally, by using prospective data. As described in more detail in Menard (2002), cross-sectional data are data collected *for* a single time period, almost always *at* a single point in time, and do not allow us to measure or analyze change over time. Longitudinal data are data collected *for* two or more time periods and allow the analysis and measurement of change. Longitudinal data may be collected *at* a single point in time, for example by asking respondents to *retrospectively* report their illegal behavior in the past year, or separately for one or more years prior to the past year, as has been done in the later waves of the National Youth Survey (Menard and Elliott, 1990); or they may be collected by using techniques such as the life history calendar (Freedman et al., 1988) to report on illegal behavior for a series of years, from some time in the past up to the present. Although the data are longitudinal (*for* multiple years) and allow us to describe within-individual change, they are collected cross-sectionally, *at* a single time. What more commonly comes to researchers' minds when they think of longitudinal research is the collection of longitudinal data *prospectively*, *for* multiple time periods *at* multiple time periods, with at most a limited period (usually no more than one year) for which respondents are asked to recall their behavior. Strictly speaking, all self-reported data on behavior (as opposed to intentions or attitudes) are retrospective, referring to some period (often one year, six months, or 30 days) in the past; but for such short recall periods the data are regarded as prospective.

As defined in Menard (2002), longitudinal research may include, among other possibilities, repeated cross-sectional designs or longitudinal panel designs. Repeated cross-sectional designs involve measurements taken on the same population at multiple time periods in which a different sample (a cross-section) is drawn from the population at each measurement occasion. This allows us to measure and analyze change in the population as a whole, but not change within individuals (or other cases) within the population. Examples of repeated cross-sectional designs for self-report research at the national level are the annual survey of high school seniors (and, since 1991, eighth and tenth graders) in the Monitoring the Future study (MTF) (Johnston and O'Malley, 1997; O'Malley et al., 2000) and the National Household Survey on Drug Abuse (NHSDA), later renamed the National Survey on Drug Use and Health (NSDUH) (Harrison et al., 2007). In a longitudinal panel design, measurements are taken at multiple occasions on the same set of individuals or cases (the panel), barring deaths or other losses of individuals from the panel. This allows measurement and analysis of within-individual change as well as change in the population. Examples of longitudinal panel studies that include self-report data at the national level are the National Youth Survey (NYS) (Elliott, Huizinga, and Menard, 1989), later renamed the National Youth Survey Family Study (NYSFS) (Menard et al., 2011), and the National Longitudinal Study of Adolescent Health (Add-Health) (Udry, 2003).

Whom Do We Try to Measure? Sampling Individuals (or Aggregates of Individuals)

As with survey research more generally, there are a variety of sampling designs that may be employed with self-report survey research. The various designs are distinguished from one another by differences in what units are sampled, clustering within the sample, probability and nonprobability sampling, geographic coverage, time coverage, and age coverage. These distinctions give rise to considerations of age (developmental), period (historical), and cohort (generational) effects, plus questions of generalizability across space, time, developmental stages, and generations. In self-report survey research we ask individuals about their illegal behavior, but the individuals may not be the actual units sampled. In the MTF study the units sampled are schools, and all eligible students in the grades surveyed in the sampled schools are included in the sample. In the NYSFS, households were sampled, and all eligible children between 11 and 17 years old in each of the sampled households were included in the sample. The sampling of larger, aggregate units instead of individuals is relatively common, because of the cost and difficulty of obtaining complete lists of individuals, as opposed to such units as schools and households. The use of these clustered samples requires that adjustments be made to the analysis, either through more or less complex weighting schemes, such as those used in the MTF study, or through the use of models that take into account the fact that individuals are not sampled completely independently (because of their clustering within schools or households), such as multilevel modeling or other techniques for analyzing clustered samples. School-based samples have the disadvantage that they miss dropouts and students incarcerated at the time of the survey. Cross-sectional and repeated cross-sectional household-based surveys typically miss institutionalized and homeless individuals. Longitudinal panel surveys may or may not include these individuals; the NYSFS after wave 1 includes dropouts, overseas, homeless, and institutionalized (including imprisoned) respondents.

As described in Menard and Mihalic (2001), sampling issues include (1) whether the sample is a probability or nonprobability sample, (2) whether the sample is national or local in scope, (3) whether the sample includes the general population, excludes specific groups (school dropouts, institutionalized individuals), or is limited to "captive" populations such as arrestees, individuals in treatment programs, or known offenders or substance users or, in a different type of "captive" population, undergraduates in large lecture classes. For nonprobability samples, inferential statistics are generally not appropriate, and results cannot legitimately be generalized to any population other than the sample itself.

In particular, known offender, treatment, and incarcerated populations may be of great value in describing the situation faced by criminal justice agencies and changes in patterns of substance use and criminality for individuals who come into contact with the criminal justice system or treatment agencies (or both); but research by Pottieger (1981) compared on-the-street and captive samples and concluded that they were not equivalent in current criminality, current drug use, or history of drug use and crime. Studies of local populations can be very useful for assessing local needs and for setting local policy priorities, but findings from local samples cannot readily be generalized beyond the local area in which they were collected, even to other populations that may be similar. For example, Elliott et al. (2006) used neighborhood samples from Chicago and Denver to model the impact of neighborhood characteristics on problem behavior (which consisted mostly of illegal behavior) and found that, while neighborhood deterioration and the presence of illegal opportunities appeared to be significant predictors of problem behavior in Chicago, in Denver it was instead neighborhood bonding and control and normative and value consensus that were significant. In the Program of Research on the Causes and Correlates of Delinquency, Huizinga et al. (2000) found that the relationships among serious delinquency, drug use, school problems, and mental health problems varied among Denver, Pittsburgh, and Rochester (New York) samples.

Samples are also typically limited by some age restrictions, which are often related to the ability to understand the questions being asked. The NYSFS initially sampled adolescents 11 to 17 years old, and MTF is limited, not specifically by age, but by grade (eighth through twelfth). The NSDUH is a national probability sample of households that includes respondents aged 12 or over. In longitudinal data, the combination of possible variation by both age and period (developmental and historical change, or age and period effects), plus the specific effect of being a certain age at a certain historical time (experiencing the Great Depression as an adolescent or as a middle-aged adult, a cohort or generational effect), raises the issue of separating age, period, and cohort effects. As described in Menard (2002), if age is coded as years since birth, period is coded as calendar year, and cohort is coded as year of birth, then age, period, and cohort are linearly dependent. Purely statistical approaches to separate their impacts, such as dummy variable regression with equality constraints, suffer from high collinearity and produce unreliable results. If one instead uses some theoretically relevant *characteristic* of a cohort, such as cohort size, linear dependence can be eliminated and the separate effects of age, period, and cohort characteristics can be estimated.

The consideration of age, period, and cohort effects raises important issues of generalization across space, time, developmental stages, and generations. One cannot reasonably expect the correlates of and influences on illegal behavior to be identical for an adolescent and for someone entering middle age (developmental differences), a point illustrated, for example, by Menard and Mihalic's (2001) documentation that the association of illicit drug sales with violent offending is higher in adulthood than in adolescence. Neither is it safe to assume that the correlates of, or influences on, adolescent illegal behavior in the 1970s were the same as in the first years of the twenty-first century (historical or generational differences), as illustrated by the finding, in Johnson, Morris, and Menard (2012), that different aspects of strain are predictive of delinquency for different generations (peer problems and negative life events were significant influences on delinquency for adolescents in 1978, but not 2004). Also, as noted above, the correlates of or influences on illegal behavior may be different depending on whether one is in Chicago, Denver, Pittsburgh, or Rochester (geographic or spatial differences). In self-report survey data, as in other data, it is important not to try to generalize beyond the times, places, and ages actually included in the sample and to avoid generalizations from nonprobability samples.

Even if we select a broadly inclusive population and use probability sampling with the intention of securing participation from a sufficient number of respondents to provide the statistical power needed for the analyses we intend to perform, there may be random nonparticipation sufficient to substantially limit our sample size, or, worse, nonrandom nonparticipation, which not only reduces our sample size but also results in sampling bias, preventing us from legitimately making inferences from the sample to the population from which it was drawn. According to de Leeuw and de Heer (2002) there have been substantial increases over time in rates of nonresponse and refusal to participate in surveys, both in the United States and internationally. The length and detail of the consent process may be a factor affecting disclosure or nonresponse rates among self-report surveys of substance use (Fendrich and Johnson, 2001). Consent that is combined with excessive assurances "may defeat their purpose by heightening respondents' perceptions of the sensitivity or threat of the survey" (Singer, von Thurn, and Miller, 1995, p. 74). Monetary incentives have been shown to increase participation, particularly for lower income respondents, but it is unclear whether this results in disproportionate participation of lower income respondents or overcomes a bias that might otherwise exist toward lower participation on the part of these respondents (Singer and Bossarte, 2006). For juvenile respondents, particularly in school samples, a requirement of active parental consent (in which, even if there is no explicit refusal, failure of the parent to respond to the request for consent automatically excludes the child from participation in the research), as opposed to passive consent (in which the parent is given the option to refuse consent, but if the parent does not respond, the child is allowed to participate, pending his or her own consent or assent to participate in the research), results in lower participation rates and may result in sample bias and underestimates of problem behavior (Anderman et al., 1995; Esbensen et al., 1996), unless a high rate of return for the consent forms (on the order of 75 percent) is obtained (Eaton et al., 2004).

What Do We Measure? Sampling Behaviors

No self-report survey to date has asked specifically about every possible type of criminal act an individual may have committed, with the possible exception of a generic "Have you committed any other crimes?" type of question. Instead, self-report surveys have selected the behaviors about which they ask, sometimes on the basis of substantive criteria, such as a focus on substance use, and sometimes on the basis of the feasibility of obtaining sufficient data on the offense for analysis. One basis for the inclusion or exclusion of offenses is the seriousness of the offense. The earliest self-report studies (Porterfield, 1943; Wallerstein and Wyle, 1947), which included both juvenile and adult respondents, asked about a full range of offenses, from petty theft to serious assaults. Subsequent studies in the 1950s and 1960s that focused on juvenile delinquency rather than adult crime, however, tended to include relatively minor offenses, such as minor theft, minor assault, and status offenses (e.g., Short and Nye, 1957). This may have stemmed from two concerns, the first with whether respondents would actually admit to more serious behaviors, and the second an ethical concern about how to respond if they did. More recent self-report surveys have returned to asking questions about more serious offenses. Questions about homicide, however, are routinely excluded from practically all self-report survey research (and also from victimization surveys), although in the course of the interview interviewers may discover the commission of a homicide from responses to follow-up questions about specific offenses, or from information volunteered by the respondent.

Another reason for deciding whether to exclude a given offense from a self-report survey is whether one can expect to collect sufficient data on the behavior for analysis. In the first waves of the NYSFS (Elliott et al., 1989, p. 9), "[a]ny specific act that involved more than 1 percent of the UCR-reported juvenile arrests during the study period was included" among the 40 items in the self-report inventory. Note that the selection of offenses here is also age-specific. Earlier waves, when respondents were adolescents, did not include questions about white-collar offenses such as embezzlement or income tax evasion. Instead, these offenses were added at later waves of the study, when the respondents were in early to middle adulthood. In later waves, some items, for example gang fighting, were dropped because the then-adult respondents no longer reported engaging in this offense. Also relevant to the choice of offenses on the basis of the sufficiency of data for analysis is the emergence of new forms of illegal behavior. For surveys begun in the 1970s, questions about methamphetamine use and cybercrime were not included, because those types of offenses emerged later in history; and this change in offending patterns resulted in the modification of some ongoing surveys (for example, the later addition of methamphetamine use to the MTF, NSDUH, and NYSFS) or the inclusion of such questions in studies begun at later dates.

How Do We Measure? Scaling Illegal Behaviors

There are both qualitative and quantitative variations in how offenses are measured. Qualitative variations include differences in which offenses are measured, and whether the offense corresponds to one legal category, several, or only part of a legal category. Splitting and combining legal categories can be illustrated in the NYSFS (Elliott et al., 1989), which asks separately about theft under \$5, theft between \$5 and \$50, and theft over \$50; and also constructs a general theft scale that includes these three items plus stealing a motor vehicle, joyriding (temporarily taking a vehicle without the owner's permission), buying stolen goods, and breaking into a building or vehicle (burglary). The three items (theft under \$5, \$5 to \$50, over \$50) cover only a single legal offense, theft, while the general theft scale covers multiple separate legal offenses. Another dimension of qualitative variation comes from the criminal career and life-course developmental perspectives on illegal behavior (see Benson, 2013, and Chapter 27 in this volume) and makes distinctions among abstention (no involvement in illegal behavior during some period or time span), initiation (committing one's first offense), continuity or suspension (whether, after initiation, one continues or discontinues one's involvement in illegal behavior), resumption (reengaging in illegal behavior after a period of suspension), intermittency (whether one engages in an alternating pattern of suspension and resumption), and permanent desistance.

The principal quantitative variations in the measurement of illegal behavior are:

1. frequency (how many times one has committed an offense, with a minimum of zero);
2. active offender frequency (from the criminal career paradigm, frequency calculated only for individuals who are engaged in at least some illegal behavior, with a minimum of one);
3. truncated frequency (frequency measured up to some maximum number, after which all higher frequencies are recoded to that maximum);
4. transformed frequencies (for example, taking the square root or the natural logarithm of the frequency prior to analysis, which often involves transformations that compress the upper range in the frequency of offending; for an overview of such transformations, see Berry and Feldman, 1985);
5. ordinal scales with unequal intervals (for example, a five-category ordinal scale whose categories correspond to frequencies of zero, 1–2, 3–5, 6–10, and more than 10; for any ordinal scale with "more than X" or "X or more" as the last category, the intervals between categories are necessarily unequal);
6. variety scores (a count of the number of different *types* of offenses one has committed; for example, if questions are asked about shoplifting, burglary, and picking someone's pocket, the variety score could range from zero for someone who had committed none of the offenses to three for someone who had committed all of the offenses); and
7. prevalence (or, in the language of the criminal career paradigm, participation: whether or not one has committed a given offense).

All of these measures can be derived from frequency of offending, but, with the exception of transformations of frequency that preserve all of the information in the frequency data, such as the square root and logarithmic transformations, frequencies cannot generally be recovered from the other measures. In that respect, frequency of offending may be considered the most fundamental of these measures. Prevalence is most often coded simply as a truncated frequency with 1 as the maximum, and a variety score can be calculated as the sum of the prevalences for some set of offenses. Particularly but not exclusively in research on illicit drug use, instead of asking about the number of times one has used a particular drug, the respondent may be asked about the *number of days* one has used a particular illicit drug in some period (often the past 30 days or 12 months), as in the NSDUH. More generally, questions on frequency and other measures can be asked for varying time periods, including lifetime ("Have you ever ...:?"), past year ("How many times in the past year have you …?"), periods longer or shorter than one year, or, as noted above, for multiple periods in the past, using long-term retrospective recall or life history calendar approaches.

Reasons for variations in the quantitative measures used in self-report research often appear to be more methodological than substantive. One reason for using the unequal interval ordinal scales was that they had better properties for the use of some statistical techniques than did raw frequency data. In multivariate analysis, prevalence can easily be analyzed using logistic regression analysis. Frequency, however, poses problems for statistical techniques that assume symmetric distributions (including the normal distribution), such as ordinary least squares regression analysis, because offense frequency data are often highly skewed: most of the cases for most offenses are clustered at a frequency of zero, and there are outliers with very high frequencies that represent, for example, theft once a day or marijuana use three times a day, and large gaps in the distribution between the very highest and the next higher frequencies.

As demonstrated by Elliott and Ageton (1980), Elliott and Huizinga (1989), and Hindelang, Hirschi, and Weis (1981), the use of unequal interval ordinal scales with low maximum values is neither necessary nor desirable and leads not only to loss of information, particularly about high-frequency offenders, but also to distortions in the reported distribution of illegal behavior. Truncation at the low end of the scale, as illustrated above (more than 10), are especially problematic; truncation at a much higher level (for example, a cutoff at 1,000) may have little impact on substantive results. Other alternatives to unequal interval ordinal scales for making the data more amenable to statistical techniques like ordinary least squares regression include the use of alternative statistical techniques such as Poisson or negative binomial regression, which may be used for count data that satisfy certain assumptions, or the use of transformed frequencies, particularly the logarithmic transformation. Poisson and negative binomial regression may also be appropriate for the analysis of variety scores or days of offending; again, this is contingent upon satisfying the assumptions of those techniques.

The use of transformations that compress the upper range of the variable for frequency data has three possible justifications. One is to reduce the skewness (and thus to reduce the degree to which the assumption of a symmetric distribution is violated) in ordinary least squares regression or in similar statistical techniques. The second justification is to more strongly weight differences that occur at the low end of the scale than the same numerical difference at the high end of the scale; this reflects the finding by Huizinga and Elliott (1986) that test–retest reliability was higher for lower frequencies than for higher frequencies. The third justification, here with particular reference to the logarithmic transformation, is to model a nonlinear relationship in which an increase of one in a predictor does not result in an *arithmetic* increase in the dependent variable (a one unit increase in the predictor always produces a 0.5 unit increase in the outcome regardless of whether the starting point for the dependent variable is 10 or 100), but instead results in a *proportional* increase in the dependent variable (a one unit increase in the predictor results in a 5 percent increase in the dependent variable; so if the dependent variable starts at 10, the numerical increase is 0.5, but if the dependent variable starts at 100, the numerical increase is 5.0).

In some approaches, including Rasch models, item response theory, and latent variable structural equation modeling, there may be a concern with modeling a latent variable, perhaps criminal propensity, rather than observed criminal behavior. Self-reported illegal behavior may itself be described as a latent variable, but this is generally a stretch; the behavior itself is in principle observable, even if our observation (or the observer, the respondent giving the self-report) is imperfect. Rasch, item response, and structural equation models share the characteristic that they typically lose information by reducing the number of offenses or the number of categories in the dependent variable, often for more statistical than substantive or theoretical reasons (to reduce violations of assumptions of the statistical model, to help the model converge on a solution, or to produce higher indices of model fit). Osgood, McMorris, and Potenza (2002) used item response theory as an approach to the analysis of illegal behavior, but in practice this produced a "scale" very similar to, and with all the disadvantages of, an unequal interval ordinal scale with a very low maximum cutoff. If the interest is in illegal behavior itself, there is generally little justification for the assumption that self-reported illegal behavior is a latent variable, or for the loss of information typically involved in these models; but if the interest is genuinely in criminal propensity rather than in criminal behavior, and if one uses self-reports as an observed indicator of the unobservable latent propensity to crime, then the latent variable approach is justified. It should be noted, however, that which variables will be included or which cutoffs will emerge is often idiosyncratic to a specific sample and often capitalizes on random variation within the sample; hence results should be viewed with extreme caution, even more so than with other techniques, pending their replication.

How Well Do We Measure? Issues in the Accuracy of Self-Report Data

The two principal concerns regarding the accuracy of self-report data are reliability and validity. Reliability refers to obtaining the same result in the measurement process when there has been no change in what is being measured. Validity refers to measuring what we intend to measure, and not something else. Reliability is prerequisite to validity; if we get on a scale three times in a minute (and do not gain or lose any weight during that time) and we get three substantially different results for our weight, at least two of the three must be wrong. Reliability does not, however, guarantee validity; we may weigh ourselves three times with the same result, but that result may be consistently or systematically too high. In self-report research, in a study by Dentler and Monroe (1961), the same response was given to each of five items by at least 92 percent of subjects, in a test and retest two weeks apart. Farrington (1973) tested the reliability of responses over a two-year period in the Cambridge Study in Delinquent Development and found 88–94 percent agreement, depending on whether specific frequencies or patterns of responses were being tested. Huizinga and Elliott (1986) and Elliott and Huizinga (1989) reported reliabilities ranging from 70 to 90 percent for specific items and from 81 to 99 percent for multiple-item scales, except for minor assault in some demographic subgoups (50 to 67 percent), and higher reliabilities for low-frequency offenders than for high-frequency offenders. Self-reports of substance use in general population samples (Barnea, Rahav, and Teichman, 1987; Harrison, 1995), and even in known addict samples (Ball, 1967), have generally been found to be reliable.

For both illicit drug use and other forms of illegal behavior, there has been extensive research on concurrent validity (whether different measures intended to tap the same behavior agree with one another). One issue is whether interviews involve face-to-face questioning, anonymously filling out a paper survey form, or some form of computer assisted interviewing (CAI). Evidence on the distinction between anonymous and face-to-face interviewing is mixed, with some suggestion that higher rates of admitting to illegal behavior occur when questions are administered anonymously, as in MTF, as opposed to face to face, as in NYSFS, and the highest rates of admitting to illegal behavior appear to occur with self-administered CAI, as in NSDUH, although the differences are not always statistically significant (O'Malley et al., 2000; Tourangeau and Smith, 1996; Wright, Aquilino, and Supple, 1998).

Specific to illicit (and licit) drug use, self-reports have been compared to results from bioassay techniques including urinalysis and radioimmunoassay of hair (RIAH), most typically with incarcerated populations. It is necessary to caution against using urinalysis or RIAH as a "gold standard" for comparison. Harrison et al. (2007) detail some of the problems with RIAH, such as issues of potential bias from external contamination and treatment of hair and the relationship of RIAH results to hair color and type and the dosage and timing of substance use. They also note the limitations of urinalysis, particularly the short period for which urinalysis is valid (typically two to seven days, but longer periods, of about 30 days, for frequent marijuana use). There is also the issue that most of the testing for agreement between bioassay techniques has involved incarcerated populations (for an exception, see Ledgerwood et al., 2008), and their results may differ from those for a general population sample, because of the potential legal ramifications of incarcerated individuals admitting to illicit drug use (Harrison, 1995). Bearing those qualifications in mind, comparison of the results of self-report and urinalysis testing have generally indicated that they were highly concordant, with correlations in the range that one would expect for two measures of the same phenomenon (Mieczkowski, 1990); but both RIAH and urinalysis often find less use of marijuana and more use of other illicit drugs than do self-reports (Ledgerwood et al., 2008; Mieczkowski et al., 1993).

A frequent method employed in validating self-report data on offenses other than substance use has been to compare self-reports of being arrested with official records of being arrested. There are two notable disadvantages to this approach. The first is that it excludes actual illegal behavior and only examines the accuracy of the respondent's reporting of official responses to that behavior. The second is that the research comparing self-reported and officially recorded arrests implicitly or explicitly sets officially recorded arrests as the "gold standard" and regards any discrepancy between self-reported and officially recorded arrests as indicative of invalidity in the self-report data, not in the officially recorded data, a position sharply challenged by Elliott (1995) on the basis of empirical studies of the accuracy of arrest records. Also, it should be noted that although self-report and official data tend to be correlated, the typical correlation, around 0.60 (Hindelang et al., 1981; Enzmann et al., 2010), is lower than conventional cutoffs in reliability analysis for measures of the same behavior and is driven largely by agreement between the two on who is *not* involved in illegal behavior. Comparisons of self-reported with officially recorded police or court involvement (Dembo et al., 2002; Hardt and Peterson-Hardt, 1977; see also reviews in Elliott et al., 1989; Hindelang et al., 1981) have produced fairly consistent results regarding the overall accuracy of self-report data (approximately 80 percent on average), as well as low estimates – depending on the offense, sometimes well under 10 percent – of how much of the illegal behavior captured in self-report studies comes to the attention of the justice system. This 80 percent average estimate of validity for self-reports is consistent with attempts at validation through other methods, including the "threat" of discovering deception by using a polygraph (Clark and Tifft, 1966), and friends' reports of the delinquent behavior of the respondent (Gold, 1966).

There are questions about whether accuracy of reporting may be influenced by sociodemographic or behavioral characteristics or by the characteristics of the study. In different studies, males have been more truthful than females (Morris, 1965), or females have been more truthful than males (Hindelang et al., 1981), in reporting their known arrests or illegal behavior. Some studies (Hindelang et al., 1981; Huizinga and Elliott, 1986) have found that African American respondents are more likely to underreport their arrests or offenses than white respondents, but others (Farrington et al., 1996) indicated no difference in underreporting between African American and Caucasian respondents. Data from Gold (1966) suggest that underreporting is related less to sex, race, or class, than to the seriousness of the offense. A similar conclusion was reached by Maxfield, Weiler, and Widom (2000), who also found that underreporting and overreporting of arrests appear to be approximately equal across different groups. The disparities in these results suggest that differential accuracy in reporting may not be constant, but may vary across samples.

Differences in question-wording across different self-report surveys raise issues about content validity, namely whether the questions we ask in self-report surveys actually elicit reports of truly illegal behavior, and these differences may produce different estimates of rates of illegal behavior. Table 21.1 presents a comparison of question-wording for selected items from the MTF, NSDUH, and NYSFS studies for 2002–2003. Although it may be tempting to treat these measures as though they were equivalent, there are clear differences in potential meaning and interpretation for some. For example, arguing or having a fight with parents (MTF, NSDUH) may be entirely verbal, while hitting or threatening to hit them (NYSFS) clearly indicates some degree of physical aggression (but that, too, may be trivial rather than serious). Getting into "a serious fight" with someone (MTF, NSDUH) likewise may not imply physical aggression, while attacking them with the intent to hurt (NSDUH) does imply physical aggression, and attacking someone with the idea of seriously hurting or killing them (NYSFS) most closely resembles aggravated assault as defined in law. Similar issues can be raised regarding "group" as opposed to "gang" fights and having "taken" as opposed to having "stolen" something. Measures of drug use and drug sales (the last two rows in Table 21.1) are more similar across surveys and tend to produce more similar results; but even here, the context, the precise wording, and the details of the questions are associated with differences in estimated prevalence across the three surveys. To further assess content validity, Elliott and Huizinga (1989) analyzed the NYSFS to determine whether trivial events were being included in the reporting of serious offending found that, according to respondents' reports of details on follow-up questions, approximately two thirds of the felony assault and felony theft items and all of the hard drug sales items were appropriate and non-trivial. For minor assault (hitting someone), by contrast, over half of the items reported were considered trivial (unlikely to provoke an official response, even if they are technically illegal). Similar data is not available for MTF and NSDUH. Such differences in interview method, question-wording, and other aspects of survey design make attempts to establish concurrent validity by comparing studies like MTF, NSDUH, and NYSFS highly problematic.

For How Long Do We Measure? Additional Issues in Longitudinal Self-Report Studies

The issues that arise in the collection and analysis of longitudinal self-report survey data are the same as the issues that arise in longitudinal panel data more generally, with the added aspect that respondents are being asked to provide extremely sensitive information on their behavior – behavior that could, if known to others, result in severe formal (imprisonment or other punishment by the justice system) or informal (for example, retaliation by victims or their friends) negative consequences. These issues are discussed briefly here with specific reference to self-report survey research. For more general and detailed discussion, see Menard (2002). The issues include changes in measurement, changes in the relevance and meaning of measures over history and over the life course, panel retention and panel attrition, panel-conditioning, and problems with long-term recall.

As noted earlier, one may change the measures used in research as a result of history (the addition of methamphetamine use to MTF, NSDUH, and NYSFS), age (the addition of white-collar offenses for later ages in the NYSFS), or for other reasons. Patterson (1993) suggests that in the study of antisocial behavior this may be appropriate when earlier behaviors are discontinued and possibly displaced by new behaviors. A danger in changing measures, however, is that one can no longer clearly separate change in behavior from change in measurement. At the same time, if the subjective meaning of some terms, for example "hard drugs," changes for the respondent with age or history, comparability may be lost even though there is no change in measurement.

Panel retention and panel attrition refer, respectively, to the percentage of individuals interviewed at the first wave of a study who continue to be interviewed at a subsequent wave, as opposed to those who are not interviewed at a particular wave.

Table 21.1 Comparison of MTF, NSDUH, and NYSFS question-wording, selected items for adolescents.

MTF (2003): During the LAST 12 MONTHS, how often have you …	*NSDUH (2003): During the past 12 months, how many times have you …*	*NYSFS (2002): How many times in the last year have you…*
–	… attacked someone with the intent to seriously hurt them?	… attacked someone with the idea of seriously hurting or killing them?
… gotten into a serious fight in school or at work?	gotten into a serious fight at school or work?	–
… taken part in a fight where a group of your friends were against another group?	… taken part in a fight where a group of your friends were against another group?	… been involved in gang fights?
… used a knife or gun or some other thing to get something from a person?	–	… used force to get money or things from [teacher/students/ other people]
… gone into someone's house or building when you weren't supposed to be there?	–	… broken into a building or vehicle or tried to break in to steal something or just to look around?
… taken something not belonging to you worth over $50?	… stolen or tried to steal anything worth more than $50?	… stolen or tried to steal something worth [$50 to $100? over $100?]
… argued or had a fight with your parents?	… argued or had a fight with at least one of your parents?	… hit or threatened to hit one of your parents?
… sold an illegal drug?	… sold illegal drugs?	… sold marijuana or hashish? … sold hard drugs?
On how many occasions have you used marijuana (weed, pot) or hashish (hash, hash oil) [lifetime/last 12 months/ last 30 days]?	Have you ever, even once, used marijuana or hashish? [Follow-ups for first use and days of use in past year]	How many times in the past year have you used marijuana or hashish?

If panel attrition is random, the primary harm is the reduction of statistical power to detect significant relationships. If it is nonrandom, however, then a sample that was initially representative with respect to sociodemographic, attitudinal, and behavioral characteristics becomes less representative, and generalization to the population from which the sample was drawn may no longer be justified. Cordray and Polk (1983), for example, described studies with retention rates of 45 to 78 percent over 12–15 years. Menard et al. (2011) indicate that, over the 27-year span of the NYSFS, retention was over 90 percent for the first four waves, over 80 percent for waves 5–8, and over 70 percent in waves 9–11. They also cite evidence that the departure from randomness of the attrition is minimal and has little or no impact on estimates of frequency of offending or on substantive findings regarding relationships of other variables to illegal behavior (see also Bosick, 2009; Elliott et al., 1989; Jang, 1999). Laurie (2008) provides an extensive discussion of ways to minimize panel attrition, which covers tracking respondents, interviewer training, organization of survey content, monetary incentives, and techniques for converting refusals into participation.

Panel-conditioning refers to changes in responses that occur in later waves of a panel study, not because of actual changes in behavior but in response to prior experience with the survey. The form of panel-conditioning most often studied, and perhaps of greatest concern, is the initial admission and later denial of involvement in certain types of behavior, such as victimization or offending, in order to avoid the burden of being asked additional questions about that behavior. For example, in the National Crime Survey (NCS), later renamed the National Crime Victimization Survey (NCVS), and in some waves of the NYSFS, individuals are first asked a "screener" question about whether they have ever, or in the past year, been the victim or the perpetrator of a crime, which is sometimes simply phrased as "How many times in the past year have you…?" with the possibility of responding "never" or "none" if they have not been involved in the behavior. If they answer affirmatively to the screener question, they are subsequently asked a series of follow-up questions designed to obtain more detail about one or more of the occasions when they were involved in the behavior, typically the most recent or the most serious incidents. Cantor (2008) reported on studies of panel-conditioning, including the NCVS, which indicated that panel-conditioning apparently reduced reported rates of victimization after the first interview by 15 percent, and on comparisons between the MTF and the NYS, which found no significant differences that would indicate panel-conditioning in the latter. This is consistent with the more recent review of evidence regarding panel-conditioning in the NYSFS from 1977 to 2011 in Menard et al. (2011), and with the findings in Jang (1999) and Bosick (2009). Other longitudinal self-report surveys have not been examined as extensively for panel-conditioning as the NYSFS; hence, for many of the currently ongoing longitudinal self-report survey studies, the extent of panel conditioning is unknown.

There is considerable evidence that the reliability and validity of self-reports is worse for longer recall periods and for offenders with higher frequencies of offending (Elliott and Huizinga, 1989, pp. 163–169; Huizinga and Elliott, 1986, pp. 314–322; Zhang, Benson, and Deng, 2000, p. 286). Put simply, it appears that individuals tend to forget offenses that were committed a long time ago, and individuals who have committed a small number of offenses or who have had few arrests or police contacts are more likely to remember all of those offenses or encounters with the police than individuals who have committed many offenses or who have been arrested or otherwise contacted by the police many times. Table 21.2 presents a comparison of lifetime (cumulative) prevalence estimates of selected offenses. The comparison is based on prospective data and long-term retrospective data in the NYSFS. The prospective data are compiled on the basis of self-reports of the behaviors in each wave of the NYSFS. With regard to completeness, prospective data have the disadvantage of omitting years prior to the start of the survey and years between waves of the survey, in which respondents were not interviewed. The retrospective data are based on asking the respondents in wave 11 (2003) whether they had *ever* engaged in the behaviors. In principle, the long-term retrospective data should include all of the behaviors captured in the prospective interviews, plus behavior from years before or between the waves of the survey.

As is evident from Table 21.2, that is not the case. For offenses other than illicit drug use, beginning with aggravated assault and ending with hard drug sales, there are many more individuals who report the behavior on the prospective interview but not in the long-term recall data (–Retrospective, +Prospective) than vice-versa (+Retrospective, –Prospective), and sometimes more who report behavior *only* prospectively (–Retrospective, +Prospective) than who report it for both (+Retrospective, +Prospective). Of the total percentage of individuals who ever admit to being involved in the behavior (adding the percentages in the last three columns for each row), the percentage of all offenders detected by the prospective interviews (combining the percentages in the third and fifth columns) ranges from a low of 75 percent for theft of $5 to $50, to over 80 percent for all of the other offenses, and over 90 percent for about half of the offenses. For the retrospective data (combining the last two columns), the numbers range from a low of less than 10 percent for gang fighting to a high of only 60 percent for theft under $5. In other words, the prospective data capture nearly all (over 80 percent, often over 90 percent) of what is captured by the retrospective data; but the retrospective data typically capture about one third of the lifetime prevalence found in the prospective data. For illicit drug use (from marijuana to heroin), the prospective and retrospective data are in less disagreement, but the prospective data capture 82–90 percent of the total respondents admitting to the behavior, while the retrospective data capture roughly 59–72 percent, except for heroin, at only 16 percent, and marijuana, at a high of 81 percent. For all of the offenses in the table, (1) there is a statistically significant positive correlation between the prospective and the retrospective reports, which appears to be largely driven by the high degree of agreement about which respondents have *not* committed each offense, and (2) the differences in the distributions are also statistically significant, which appears to be driven mainly by the relatively high percentages in the third column (–Retrospective, +Prospective).

Similar patterns, not shown in Table 21.2, are found for self-reported arrest and self-reported victimization in the NYSFS, and these patterns appear to be the same whether we include only data on complete cases with valid data for every wave or, as in Table 21.2, we use available data and include respondents who may have failed to complete an interview at one or more waves of the study. The pattern of denying, "recanting," or, perhaps most accurately, just not reporting offending in long-term retrospective data when that behavior has previously been admitted in prospective data has also been found in other studies, including the MTF (Johnston and

O'Malley, 1997). Menard and Elliott (1990) made a comparison, similar to the one made in this chapter, between retrospective and prospective data for the years 1976–1983. If we compare the figures here to those in the earlier study, the percentages of the total captured by the prospective data are similar, as they are for retrospective data on burglary (45 percent of the total in both Menard and Elliott, 1990 and in the present chapter); but they are much higher in Menard and Elliott (1990) than in Table 21.2 for the other offenses in this chapter that were also included in the earlier study: 48 versus 30 percent for aggravated assault, 26 versus 10 percent for gang fighting, 40 versus 16 percent for sexual assault, 14 versus 10 percent for robbery, 61 versus 33 percent for auto theft, 71 versus 41 percent for theft over $50, and 67 versus 47 percent for hard drug sales. One possibility is that respondents become more reluctant to admit to offenses (even offenses to which they have previously admitted in the same study) as they get older. A more plausible alternative may be that the decline in the consistency of prospective and retrospective

Table 21.2 NYSFS long-term recall and prospective prevalence of selected offenses (percentages).

Offense[a]	*– Retrospective – Prospective*	*– Retrospective + Prospective*	*+ Retrospective – Prospective*	*+ Retrospective + Prospective*
Aggravated assault	76.0	16.8	2.4	4.8
Gang fighting	74.3	22.9	0.5	2.3
Sexual assault[b]	93.7	5.4	0.8	0.2
Robbery[c]	87.4	11.3	0.5	0.8
Hidden weapon[b]	67.6	21.7	1.5	9.2
Burglary	82.2	9.7	2.8	5.2
Auto theft[b]	93.0	4.7	0.4	1.9
Theft > $50[b]	82.0	10.6	2.9	4.5
Theft $5–50[b]	72.0	12.3	6.5	9.2
Theft < $5[b]	46.6	21.1	9.8	22.5
Stolen goods	67.9	22.1	2.5	7.5
Marijuana sales	72.1	14.1	1.8	12.1
Hard drug sales[b]	86.9	6.8	2.0	4.2
Marijuana use[c]	21.0	14.7	1.1	63.1
Amphetamine use[c]	71.8	8.2	3.9	16.1
Barbiturate use	56.6	16.3	5.0	22.2
Hallucinogen use[d]	77.1	9.2	3.9	9.7
Cocaine use	84.4	13.1	0.3	2.2
Heroin use	58.9	13.2	1.3	26.7

[a] N = 1170 unless otherwise noted; – indicates denial and + indicates admission of the offense.
[b] N = 1171.
[c] N = 1169.
[d] N = 1158.

self-reports with age reflects memory decay, as suggested by Menard and Elliott (1990; see also Rutter et al., 1998).

What More Do We Need to Measure? Future Needs for Self-Report Research

Published research on the reliability and validity of national self-report surveys like the MTF and NSDUH has been at best limited. Even for the NYSFS, the reliability data apply to the original respondents at a younger age and cover neither individuals who are currently in the adolescent years nor the original NYS respondents in their middle adult years. With respect to the reliability of self-reports of substance use and illegal behavior, then, we currently have decades-old data primarily on adolescents and young adults. Given the widespread use of self-report data for epidemiological and aetiological research, it seems somewhat alarming that we lack (1) *current* information about the test–retest reliability of self-reports for several types of illegal behavior for adolescents and young adults, (2) *any* information about the test–retest reliability for several types of illegal behavior for individuals beyond young adulthood, and (3) *any* information about reliability across *all* age groups combined. In the area of substance use, we lack recent data on short-term and moderate-term reliability for adolescents and young adults and on long-term reliability for individuals in middle adulthood (for whom long-term reliability is most pertinent). In brief, our information on the short-term and moderate-term reliability for adolescent and young adult self-reports on illegal behavior is over 20 years out of date, and, for older adults, it is virtually nonexistent. Also, we have limited current information on what influences reliability in self-reports, from sociodemographic characteristics to the length of recall and to the frequency and seriousness of the problem behavior, and this needs to be replicated and updated.

Self-report survey data provide information about the distribution and correlates of illicit drug use and other forms of illegal behavior, including victimless crimes that lie outside the purview of victimization surveys. Repeated cross-sectional self-report studies allow us to examine historical trends in these behaviors and to compare these trends with trends in official rates of illegal behavior. Longitudinal panel studies allow us to examine life-course developmental changes within individuals over time, including changes in the relationship of illegal behavior with its hypothesized causes. They also allow us to examine the sequencing of hypothesized causes and effects (see in particular Elliott et al., 1989, and Menard and Elliott, 1990), such as drug use compared to other forms of crime, or the association with delinquent friends and one's own delinquent behavior, to better test criminological theories. The inclusion of two or more generations in self-report research – for example the expansion of the NYSFS and of studies in the Causes and Correlates program to include additional generations of respondents – allows us to examine intergenerational transmission of, or similarity in, behavior between parents and their children. It also allows us to examine intergenerational differences in the correlates of illegal behavior across generations, not limited to comparisons of individual parents with their children, but also including differences between the entire parental generation (including those who do not have children) and the entire offspring generation (some of whom also will not have children) using identical measures. Extending this to multiple waves with the younger generation would also allow us to compare life-course developmental change across generations.

For all the potential advantages of self-report surveys, there are better and worse ways to implement them. On the basis of the evidence presented above, signs of a poorly designed self-report survey with little or no generalizability beyond the specific sample on which the analyses are performed, and with no justification for causal inferences of any sort, would include (1) a nonprobability sample (2) involving a "captive" population (3) with a low participation rate and (4) a high nonresponse rate to selected questions among participants, coupled with the use of (5) questions measuring illegal behavior by using an unequal-interval ordinal scale with a limited number of categories (6) for a relatively small number of relatively less serious offenses (7) in a purely cross-sectional design, with hypothesized causes measured for a time (e.g., attitudes measured at the time of the interview) *after* the time for which illegal behavior is measured (e.g., the year prior to the interview). A better designed survey will involve a high participation and a low nonresponse rate in a probability sample of individuals including but not limited to "captive" populations, coupled with the use of questions asking prospectively about frequency of offending (which can be recoded if other measures of illegal behavior are of interest), for a broad range of offenses. If there is an interest in drawing causal inferences from non-experimental research, longitudinal data allow, in addition to measures of covariation, (1) correct time ordering of the hypothesized causes and effects; and (2) the inclusion of prior levels of the dependent variable, in order to allow some substantial control for potential spurious relationships. If done well, self-report research can provide more reliable and valid data on individual illegal behavior across a wider range of illegal behaviors than other methods, and it also lends itself readily to the collection of information about other respondent characteristics – including sociodemographic characteristics, attitudes, and prosocial as well as illegal behavior – that better enable us to test theories of crime and delinquency. It is this potential that has led to the recognition of self-report surveys as a major resource in criminological and criminal justice research.

References

Anderman, C., Cheadle, A., Curry, S., Diehr, P., Shultz, L., and Wagner, E. 1995. Selection bias related to parental consent in school-based survey research. *Evaluation Review*, 19: 663–674.

Ball, J. C. 1967. The reliability and validity of interview data obtained from 59 narcotic drug addicts. *American Journal of Sociology*, 72: 650–654.

Barnea, Z., Rahav, G., and Teichman, M. 1987. The reliability and consistency of self-reports on substance use in a longitudinal study. *British Journal of Addiction*, 82: 891–898.

Benson, M. L. 2013. *Crime and the life course: An introduction*, 2nd edn. New York: Routledge.

Berry, W. D., and Feldman, S. 1985. *Multiple regression in practice*. Beverly Hills, CA: Sage.

Bosick, S. J. 2009. Operationalizing crime over the life course. *Crime and Delinquency*, 55: 472–496.

Cantor, D. 2008. A review and summary of studies in panel conditioning. In *Handbook of longitudinal research: Design, measurement, and analysis*, edited by S. Menard, 123–138. San Diego, CA: Academic Press.

Clark, J. P., and Tifft, L. L. 1966. Polygraph and interview validation of self-reported delinquent behavior. *American Sociological Review*, 31: 516–523.

Cordray, S., and Polk, K. 1983. The implications of respondent loss in panel studies of deviant behavior. *Journal of Research in Crime and Delinquency*, 20: 214–242.

de Leeuw, E., and de Heer, W. 2002. Trends in household survey nonresponse: A longitudinal and international comparison. In *Survey nonresponse*, edited by R. M. Groves, D. A. Dillman, J. L. Eltinge, and R. J. A. Little, 41–54. New York: Wiley.

Dembo, R., Wothke, W. Seeberger, W., Shemwell, M., Pacheco, K., Rollie, M., … Hartsfield, A. 2002. Testing a longitudinal model of the relationships among high-risk youths' drug sales, drug use, and participation in index crimes. *Journal of Child and Adolescent Substance Abuse*, 11: 36–61.

Dentler, R. A., and Monroe, L. J. 1961. Social correlates of early adolescent theft. *American Sociological Review*, 26: 733–743.

Eaton, D. K., Lowry, R., Brener, N. D., Grunbaum, J. A., and Kann, L. 2004. Passive versus active parental permission in school-based survey research: Does the type of permission affect prevalence estimates of risk behaviors? *Evaluation Review*, 28: 564–577.

Elliott, D. S. 1995. Lies, damn lies, and arrest statistics. Sutherland Award presentation, American Society of Criminology Meetings, Boston, Massachusetts.

Elliott, D. S., and Ageton, S. S. 1980. Reconciling race and class differences in self-reported and official estimates of delinquency. *American Sociological Review*, 40: 95–110.

Elliott, D. S., and Huizinga, D. 1989. Improving self-reported measures of delinquency. In *cross-national research in self-reported crime and delinquency*, edited by M. W. Klein, 155–186. Dordrecht, Netherlands: Kluwer.

Elliott, D. S., Huizinga, D., and Menard, S. 1989. *Multiple problem youth: Delinquency, substance use, and mental health problems*. New York: Springer.

Elliott, D. S., Menard, S., Rankin, B., Elliott, A., Wilson, W. J., and Huizinga, D. 2006. *Good kids from bad neighborhoods: Successful development in social context*. Cambridge: Cambridge University Press.

Enzmann, D., Marshall, I. H., Killias, M., Junger-Tas, J., Steketee, M., and Gruszczynska, B. 2010. Self-reported youth delinquency in Europe and beyond: First results of the second international self-report delinquency study in the context of police and victimization data. *European Journal of Criminology*, 7: 159–183.

Esbensen, F.-A., Deschenes, E. P., Vogel, R. E., West, J., Arboit, K., and Harris, L. 1996. Active parental consent in school-based research: An examination of ethical and methodological issues. *Evaluation Review*, 20: 737–753.

Farrington, D. 1973. Self-reports of deviant behavior: Predictive and stable? *Journal of Criminal Law, Criminology, and Police Science*, 64: 99–110.

Farrington, D., Loeber, R., Stouthamer-Loeber, M., Van Kammen, W. B., and Schmidt, L. 1996. Self-reported delinquency and a combined delinquency seriousness scale based on boys, mothers, and teachers: Concurrent and predictive validity for African Americans and Caucasians. *Criminology*, 34: 493–517.

Fendrich, M., and Johnson, T. P. 2001. Examining prevalence differences in three national surveys of youth: Impact of consent procedures, mode, and editing rules. *Journal of Drug Issues*, 31: 615–643.

Freedman, D., Thornton, A., Camburn, D., Alwin, D., and Young-DeMarco, L. 1988. The life history calendar: A technique for collecting retrospective data. *Sociological methodology, 1988*, edited by C. C. Clogg, 37–68. Washington, DC: American Sociological Association.

Gold, M. 1966. Undetected delinquent behavior. *Journal of Research in Crime and Delinquency*, 3: 27–46.

Hardt, R. H., and Peterson-Hardt, S. 1977. On determining the quality of the delinquency self-report method. *Journal of Research in Crime and Delinquency*, 14: 247–261.

Harrison, L. 1995. The validity of self-reported data on drug use. *Journal of Drug Issues*, 35: 91–111.

Harrison, L., Martin, S. S., Enev, T., and Harrington, D. 2007. *Comparing drug testing and self-report of drug use among youths and young adults in the general population*. Rockville, MD: Substance Abuse and Mental Health Services Administration, Office of Applied Studies.

Hindelang, M. J., Hirschi, T., and Weis, J. G. 1981. *Measuring delinquency*. Beverly Hills, CA: Sage.

Huizinga, D., and Elliott, D. S. 1986. Reassessing the reliability and validity of self-report delinquency measures. *Journal of Quantitative Criminology*, 2: 293–327.

Huizinga, D., Loeber, R., Thornberry, T. P., and Cothern, L. 2000. Co-occurrence of delinquency and other problem behaviors. *Juvenile Justice Bulletin*. Washington, DC: US Department of Justice, Office of Juvenile Justice and Delinquency Prevention. Accessed December 18, 2015. http://www.cops.usdoj.gov/html/cd_rom/school_safety/pubs/gov09.pdf.

Jang, S. J. 1999. Different definitions, different modeling decisions, and different interpretations: A rejoinder to Lauritsen. *Criminology*, 37: 695–702.

Johnston, L. D., and O'Malley, P. M. 1997. The recanting of earlier reported drug use by young adults. In *The validity of self-reported drug use: Improving the accuracy of survey estimates*, edited by L. Harrison and A. Hughes, 59–80. (NIDA Research Monograph 167.) Rockville, MD: US Department of Health and Human Services, National Institutes of Health.

Johnson, M. C., Morris, R. G., and Menard, S. 2012. Historical invariance in delinquency causation: A test of equivalent models for two generations of adolescents. *Crime and Delinquency*. doi: 10.1177/0011128712446051.

Laurie, H. 2008. Minimizing panel attrition. In *Handbook of longitudinal research: Design, measurement, and analysis*, edited by S. Menard, 167–184. San Diego, CA: Academic Press.

Ledgerwood, D. M., Goldberger, B. A., Risk, N. K., Lewis, C. E., and Price, R. K. 2008. Comparison between self-report and hair analysis of illicit drug use in a community sample of middle-age men. *Addictive Behaviors*, 33: 1131–1139.

Maxfield, M. G., Weiler, B. L., and Widom, C. S. 2000. Comparing self-reports and official records of arrests. *Journal of Quantitative Criminology*, 16: 87–110.

Menard, S. 2002. *Longitudinal Research*, 2nd edn. Thousand Oaks, CA: Sage.

Menard, S., and Elliott, D. S. 1990. Longitudinal and cross-sectional data collection and analysis in the study of crime and delinquency. *Justice Quarterly*, 7: 11–55.

Menard, S., and Mihalic, S. 2001. The tripartite conceptual framework in adolescence and adulthood: Evidence from a national sample. *Journal of Drug Issues*, 31: 905–940.
Menard, S., Morris, R. G., Gerber, J., and Covey, H. C. 2011. Distribution and correlates of self-reported crimes of trust. *Deviant Behavior*, 32: 877–917.
Mieczkowski, T. 1990. The accuracy of self-reported drug use: An evaluation and analysis of new data. In *Drugs, crime, and the criminal justice system*, edited by R. Weisheit, 275–302. Cincinnati, OH: Anderson.
Mieczkowski, T., Landress, H. J., Newel, R., and Coletti, S. D. 1993. Testing hair for illicit drug use. *National Institute of Justice Research in Brief.* Washington, DC: US Department of Justice.
Morris, R. R. 1965. Attitudes toward delinquency by delinquents, non-delinquents, and their friends. *British Journal of Criminology*, 5: 249–265.
O'Malley, P. M., Johnston, L. D., Bachman, J. G., and Schulenberg, J. E. 2000. A comparison of confidential versus anonymous survey procedures: Effects on reporting of drug issues and related attitudes and beliefs in a national study of students. *Journal of Drug Issues*, 30: 35–44.
Osgood, D. W., McMorris, B. J., and Potenza, M. T. 2002. Analyzing multiple-item measures of crime and deviance, I: Item response theory scaling. *Journal of Quantitative Criminology*, 18: 267–296.
Patterson, G. R. 1993. Orderly change in a stable world: The antisocial trait as a chimera. *Journal of Consulting and Clinical Psychology*, 61: 911–919.
Porterfield, A. L. 1943. Delinquency and its outcome in court and college. *American Journal of Sociology*, 49: 199–208.
Pottieger, A. E. 1981. Sample bias in drugs/crime research: An empirical study. In *The drugs-crime connection*, edited by J. A. Inciardi, 107–237. Beverly Hills, CA: Sage.
Rutter, M., Maughan, B., Pickles, A., and Simonoff, E. 1998. Retrospective recall recalled. In *Methods and models for studying the individual*, edited by R. B. Cairns, L. R. Bergman, and J. Kagan, 219–242. Thousand Oaks, CA: Sage.
Short, J. F., Jr., and Nye, F. I. 1957. Reported behavior as a criterion of deviant behavior. *Social Problems*, 5: 207–213.
Singer, E., and Bossarte, R. M. 2006. Incentives for survey participation: When are they "coercive"? *American Journal of Preventive Medicine*, 31: 411–418.
Singer, E., von Thurn, D. R., and Miller, E. R. 1995. Confidentiality assurances and response: A quantitative review of the experimental literature. *Public Opinion Quarterly*, 59: 66–77.
Tourangeau, R., and Smith, T. W. 1996. Asking sensitive questions: The impact of data collection mode, question format, and question context. *Public Opinion Quarterly*, 60: 275–304.
Udry, J. R. 2003. *The National Longitudinal Study of Adolescent Health (Add Health), Wave III, 2001–2002.* Chapel Hill, NC: Carolina Population Center, University of North Carolina at Chapel Hill.
Wallerstein, J. S., and Wyle, C. J. 1947. Our law-abiding lawbreakers. *Probation*, 25: 107–112.
Wright, D. L., Aquilino, W. S., and Supple, A. J. 1998. A comparison of computer assisted and paper-and-pencil self-administered questionnaires in a survey on smoking, alcohol, and drug use. *Public Opinion Quarterly*, 62: 331–353.
Zhang, S., Benson, T., and Deng, X. 2000. A test–retest reliability assessment of the international self-report delinquency instrument. *Journal of Criminal Justice*, 28: 283–295.

22

Crime and the Life Course

Lee Ann Slocum

Introduction

The study of crime over the life course has a relatively long history by criminological standards. As early as in the 1940s, researchers were beginning to follow individuals over time, with the purpose of understanding the aetiology of delinquency (Glueck and Glueck, 1950). In the 1970s and 1980s researchers began to think more explicitly about the unfolding of "criminal careers" and the collection, measurement, and analysis of data on individual-level offending over time (e.g., Wolfgang, Figlio, and Sellin, 1972). These discussions were accompanied by heated debates regarding the relationship between age and crime (Farrington, 1986; Hirschi and Gottfredson, 1983), the criminal career paradigm (Blumstein, Cohen, and Farrington, 1988; Blumstein et al., 1986; Gottfredson and Hirschi, 1986, 1988), and the value of longitudinal data (Gottfredson and Hirschi, 1987). Recent years have seen the rise of life-course criminology. This paradigm has been called the "soul" of criminology (Laub, 2006, p. 240). In his Sutherland Address, Frank Cullen stated that "life-course criminology … now is criminology" and should be the "organizing framework for the study of crime causation" (Cullen, 2011, p. 310). It is hard to deny that the life-course perspective has left its mark on the study of crime.

Life-course criminology is a person-centered approach to the study of offending. It can be distinguished from other ways of thinking about crime, in part because of the types of questions it addresses. Researchers who study crime over the life course are concerned with describing and explaining within-individual patterns of offending over time, for example the age at which offending is initiated, changes in the frequency or nature of offending, desistance, and the eventual termination of

The Handbook of Measurement Issues in Criminology and Criminal Justice, First Edition.
Edited by Beth M. Huebner and Timothy S. Bynum.

criminal behavior. This "longitudinal sequence of offenses committed by an offender" is often referred to as a "criminal career" (Blumstein et al., 1988, p. 2). Moreover, researchers are interested in identifying the processes that lead to stability and change in offending – such as the role played by human agency and social ties (Rutter, 1988; Laub and Sampson, 2003). Those who study crime over the life span are aware of the importance of timing and age. For example, they recognize that whether an experience leads to offending may depend on the age at which it occurs, on prior life experiences, on the sequencing and duration of events and states, and on historical context (Laub, 2004; Laub and Sampson, 2003).

The defining characteristic of the life-course perspective is that it attempts to portray the dynamic nature of life. This necessitates data on within-individual changes in offending and in life circumstances over time. Despite Gottfredson and Hirschi's (1987) protests to the contrary, researchers generally recognize that accurate longitudinal data are required to study offending over the life course. Thus it is not surprising that the theoretical development of life-course criminology has been closely linked to methodological advances in the collection and analysis of longitudinal data. This chapter describes the types of data that are used to study crime and its correlates over the life course and the methods used to collect these data, together with the strengths and weaknesses of the various approaches. Key data collection efforts utilizing the various designs are described throughout. The chapter ends with a discussion of the challenges faced by those who study crime over the life course and describes new methodologies that researchers are developing in order to overcome the limitations of prior work.

Data on Offending over the Life Course

Data used by those who study offending over the life course can come from several sources. The study participant can report on his or her own behaviors, experiences, and perceptions or someone who is close to the respondent may provide this information. In the Pittsburgh Youth Study (PYS) (Loeber et al., 1989, 1998), for example, respondents are asked to provide information on their delinquent behavior at multiple points in time and this information is supplemented with reports supplied by the boys' parents and teachers.[1] While this method has the advantage of capturing behavior that has not come to the attention of the legal system, the accuracy of the data depends on respondents' recall and veracity (Thornberry and Krohn, 2000).

Official records are also a valuable source of data on offending over the life course. Many studies use official arrest and conviction records to measure offending over time. For example, in the Philadelphia Cohort Study (Wolfgang et al., 1972) criminal history data up to the age of 30 were gathered for a sample of 9,945 males born in Philadelphia. This study offered some of the earliest information on criminal careers that covered age of onset, prevalence and frequency of delinquency, and desistance. Other types of official records used by researchers who want to explain patterns of offending over the life span are marriage and employment registries; however, these types of records are more commonly used by researchers who work in countries with centralized data repositories. In the Netherlands, centralized municipal data repositories house information on the residents' major life events, such as marriage, divorce, childbirth, and death. As part of the Criminal Career and Life-Course Study (CCLS), researchers have linked these data with official criminal history records in order to examine how life transitions shape offending trajectories (e.g., Blokland and Nieuwbeerta, 2005). Sweden also has centralized repositories that contain information on a wide range of life events and outcomes – including criminal convictions, socioeconomic characteristics, living location, and hospitalizations, which can be used to look at the influence of life events and circumstances on offending. Because data on all residents of Sweden are kept in these repositories, it is also possible to study how offending behavior is linked across family members of varying degrees of relatedness (e.g., identical twins, fraternal twins, siblings, cousins, and parents). This enables researchers to examine intergenerational continuity in offending, to assess how siblings influence antisocial behavior, and to explore biological influences on offending (Kendler, Larsson Lönn, et al., 2014; Kendler, Morris, et al., 2014).

Official data have several drawbacks. Unlike self-report data, official criminal history data miss crimes that are unknown to law enforcement. Moreover, the definitions and recording of crimes may differ from place to place and over time. Nevertheless, official records do not rely on respondent recall or truthfulness and may better capture some aspects of the criminal career, including the timing and sequencing of events (Blumstein et al., 1986).

Regardless of the source, Scott and Alwin (1998) divide data that are used to study the life course into three types. Event history data capture the duration, timing, and sequencing of past events, as well as transitions from one state to another. Criminologists are particularly interested in identifying the periods during which a respondent engaged in criminal behavior, dates of incarceration, or when a person transitioned from a period of drug use to abstention. Typically, event histories cover a number of life domains so that the researcher can understand how transitions or events in one domain affect those in other domains.

The second type of data identified by Scott and Alwin (1998) captures the accumulation of experiences and events and is the culmination of a person's life history. For example, number of years incarcerated, number of times arrested, and number of times engaged in robbery are variables that capture accumulated life experiences, as is the information provided by respondents on whether or not they think they can maintain a crime-free life upon leaving prison and their attitudes toward law-violating behavior.

Finally, those who study crime over the life course may be interested in collecting data on subjective evaluations and interpretations of events and experiences. Criminologists may collect this information if they want to understand how people make sense of their lives, particularly their offending. This is integral to understanding behavior because, as Maruna (2001) argues, the way people perceive reality and their self-narratives frame their interpretations of situations. Furthermore, personal narratives change over time and can serve as factors that sustain desistance.

"The development of a self-story favorable to desisting from crime could be seen as 'hardening' the individual's resolve to stay out of trouble" (Maruna, 2001, p. 42).[2]

Researchers can use a number of designs to collect data on offending over the life course. Ideally, the choice of design should be based on the research question at hand (Scott and Alwin, 1998), but practical concerns such as time and money often constrain researchers' options. The next section describes the types of design that researchers commonly use to collect longitudinal data on crime over the life course.

Research Designs Used for Collecting Longitudinal Data

Longitudinal research used to study criminal careers falls into two broad categories: prospective and retrospective designs. Prospective research designs require that the subject of study be identified before the events of interest occur, and then information be collected at multiple points, over a period of time. In comparison, in a retrospective study design the subject is identified after the event of interest has taken place. The researcher then pieces together the pathway leading to this point, often by using surveys or interviews that ask about prior life events and experiences, or by using official data. In the next section I describe the most common types of prospective and retrospective longitudinal research designs used to study offending over the life course. I highlight the benefits and limitations of each design.[3]

Prospective longitudinal data collection

Panel study There are a number of prospective research designs used for collecting longitudinal data (for an overview, see Menard, 2002). Perhaps the design most closely linked to longitudinal research is the prospective panel design, in which the same data are collected from the same set of cases at multiple time points. Generally the same questions are asked at each wave of data collection, and the questions refer to events and experiences that occurred during the period between the last survey and the present one, as well as to the respondents' current attitudes and perceptions. In this type of study, offending is typically measured through self-reports or through reports from parents or teachers. The types of behavior that are measured may change over time, in recognition of the fact that the manifestations of offending evolve as people age.

Although all panel studies involve the repeated assessment of individuals over time, they differ in the length of the period they span, the frequency with which respondents are surveyed, and the size and composition of their sample. Prospective longitudinal studies are costly and time-intensive endeavors, and therefore researchers must often make tradeoffs between sample size, length of follow-up, and the lag between data collection periods. Studies with smaller samples tend to oversample high-risk individuals in order to ensure that they obtain adequate rates of offending (e.g., Farrington, 2003; Loeber et al., 1998).

One of the earliest panel studies of delinquency is Sheldon and Eleanor Glueck's three wave prospective study titled *Unraveling Juvenile Delinquency* (see Glueck and Glueck, 1950, 1968). This study followed a matched sample of 500 delinquent and 500 nondelinquent males in Boston from 1939, when the boys were approximately 14 years old, to 1963, when they were aged 32. The Gluecks' collected extensive information about the people in their sample: self-reports, parent reports, and teacher reports of delinquency; official criminal history data; and a wealth of social, psychological, and biological information. This study produced "one of the most comprehensive longitudinal data bases in the history of criminological research" (Sampson and Laub, 1992, p. 26).

In the United States there are several ongoing prospective panel studies designed to collect individual-level data on delinquency and offending over time. For example, as part of the Program of Research on the Causes and Correlates of Delinquency, three panel studies were initiated in the 1980s for studying the causal process leading to delinquency and the consequences of this behavior (Thornberry and Krohn, 2003). These studies include the Rochester Youth Development Study (RYDS), the Denver Youth Survey (DYS), and the PYS. Other panel studies that provide a wealth of data on individual patterns of offending over time, as well as on its causes and consequences, are the National Longitudinal Study of Youth (NLSY) 1979 and its spin-offs: NLSY 1997 and NLSY 1979 Children and Young Adults (Bureau of Labor Statistics, 2014). Many of these panel studies are ongoing, and thus will be able to provide researchers with valuable information about the lives of participants and their involvement in illegal behavior and substance use in their older years. Some of the projects have even begun to span several generations, as researchers collect prospective longitudinal data on the children of the original participants.

Comprehensive panel studies of offending are being conducted outside of the United States as well. For example, 411 males from South London, mostly born in 1953, have been followed as part of the Cambridge Study in Delinquent Development (see Farrington, 2003 for an overview of the study). Since the study began in 1961, the men have been interviewed nine times and supplemental data about the sample has been collected through interviews with teachers, parents, and friends. Additional information has been gathered from hospitals, the criminal justice system, and school records. Aside from offending, data were collected on a wide range of behaviors, experiences, and personal characteristics that covered biological, social, and psychological factors. In New Zealand, the Dunedin Multidisciplinary Health and Development Study has followed a representative cohort of males and females born between 1972 and 1973. The first wave of data was collected when members of the cohort were three years of age, and the participants were surveyed every two years until they reached the age of 15. They have been surveyed five more times since then, and the last assessment was completed when the sample was approximately 38 years of age (Dunedin Multidisciplinary Health and Development Research Unit, 2014). As the name implies, data were collected on a number of different outcomes, including psychological and biological factors, health, risky behaviors, offending, and substance use. Several related studies are currently ongoing; one of these follows the children of the original sample.

Panel studies that span long periods and have short time lags between the waves – like the Dunedin Multidisciplinary Health and Development Study, the PYS, the Cambridge Study in Delinquent Development, and the NLSY – are considered by some to be the "gold standard" (Scott and Alwin, 1998). Indeed this design offers a number of advantages. It allows for the study of within-individual stability and change over time, since the same people are surveyed at multiple points in time. Data are collected concurrently with events, which reduces recall error and increases validity. In addition, information can be collected on aspirations, expectations, psychological characteristics, and mental health, which are hard to capture once time has passed – unless they are particularly salient.

But this design is not without its drawbacks. The most obvious limitations are the time and resources needed to follow respondents over long periods of time, which means that projects of this type are often beyond the reach of most researchers and research is instead consolidated among several well-funded projects (Gottfredson and Hirschi, 1986, p. 211). As respondents age and offending becomes increasingly rare, the question raises of whether "saturation" has been reached and the vast resources needed to continue funding data collection would be better spent on new projects. This issue is compounded when public access to data sets is restricted due to concerns about confidentiality (Lauritsen, 2005).

Another limitation of prospective panel studies is selective attrition, in which respondents with certain characteristics drop out of the study or fail to participate in some waves of data collection. Studies have found that "at-risk" youth (i.e., those most likely to be delinquent and/or victimized) are more likely to drop out of longitudinal studies (Thornberry, Bjerregaard, and Miles, 1993; Esbensen et al., 1999). Selective attrition has been found to bias estimates of the prevalence and frequency of offending and drug use (Brame and Piquero, 2003).

Panel studies can also introduce bias because they repeatedly survey the same people. This bias represents a testing or panel effect and can take many forms. Respondents may deliberately suppress the reporting of life events if they learn through repeated testing that reporting an event triggers a new series of questions (Lauritsen, 1998). Similarly, generalized test fatigue can predispose a respondent to become less willing to answer questions over time (Thornberry and Krohn, 2000). A second type of testing effect is changing construct validity. This occurs if respondents' interpretations of questions change as they mature, or if the meanings of questions change over time. A final type of testing bias is known as the Hawthorne effect, which results when a respondent changes his or her behavior in response to being observed.[4] A number of studies have found evidence supporting the existence of testing effects in panel studies of delinquent and criminal behavior (Bosick, 2009; Lauritsen, 1998).

Finally, researchers using a panel design must be aware that behavioral manifestations of underlying constructs, like violating the law, may change over time (Thornberry and Krohn, 2000). Alcohol consumption may be a perfectly good measure of delinquency for 10-year-olds, yet is completely inappropriate for measuring offending in 30-year-olds. Panel studies must be sure to measure constructs using age-appropriate questions. For particularly young children it may be necessary to get parent reports, although there is some evidence that children as young as seven can understand questions about, and report on, some types of deviant behavior (see Loeber et al., 1989; Slocum et al., 2011).

Accelerated panel study A variant of the panel study that can reduce both the time and the costs associated with prospective data collection, along with respondent burden, is the accelerated longitudinal design. This design "links adjacent segments of limited longitudinal data from different age cohorts to create a common long-term developmental trend" (Duncan and Duncan, 2012, p. 32). "Researchers can approximate a long-term longitudinal study by conducting several simultaneous short-term longitudinal studies of different age cohorts" (Duncan and Duncan, 2012, p. 32).

Duncan and Duncan (2012) outline a number of advantages of this design by comparison to a traditional panel study. Chief among them is shortness of follow-up periods, which decreases the cost and time associated with longitudinal data and mitigates testing effects and attrition. In addition, traditional panel studies confound age effects (changes that occur as someone ages) with period effects (changes that affect everyone in a particular period). Using an accelerated longitudinal design enables researchers to study different cohorts of the same age in different periods, which makes it possible to distinguish between age and period effects.

The National Longitudinal Study of Adolescent Health (Add Health) is a relatively recent example of an accelerated longitudinal design that has been used to study offending and other problem behaviors (see University of North Carolina Population Center, 2014). In this study, a nationally representative sample of adolescents in grades 7–12 was given a battery of surveys and tests in the 1994–1995 school year. This school-based sample was then followed through four waves of data collection, the most recent of which took place in 2008, when the sample ranged in age from 24 to 32.

Retrospective longitudinal research designs

An alternative to prospective data collection is the retrospective design. In this type of study, respondents are asked to report on life events and experiences that have already occurred. Retrospective data collection methods provide researchers with the means to avoid some of the limitations associated with prospective studies. Two common methods for collecting longitudinal retrospective data are described below.

Life history narratives One study design used to collect qualitative retrospective data over the life span is the life history narrative or the life review (see Clausen, 1998 for an overview). These are narrative accounts of the respondent's life that have been elicited by the researcher. At first glance they may look like "stories," but they are not. They often incorporate official records like criminal history data and employment records, in order to verify and supplement the information provided by the respondent. In his introduction to Clifford Shaw's (1966) *The Jack-Roller*, Howard Becker extolls the advantages of life histories. He argues that this method is particularly effective for understanding human agency and subjective interpretations of important life events such as turning points. In addition, these methods move from a strict variable-based approach to a dynamic, person-based model in which a person's life is not divided into disconnected data collection "waves." This quality enables researchers to capture patterns of continuity and change in offending behavior over time (Laub and Sampson, 2003). Maruna and Matrevers (2007) argue that life history narratives enable researchers to take into account the complexities of the inner and outer worlds and allow for an examination of how processes and mechanisms that lead to offending unfold over time. Unlike survey data, this method allows for the emergence of relationships and themes that the researcher did not identify a priori. This influx of ideas can reinvigorate a stagnant area of study, raising new questions and pointing to previously unthought of solutions to old problems (Becker, 1966).

The intended audience, the purpose, and whether the history was solicited by the researcher or based on personal documents like letters can all affect the content and quality of a life history and should be taken into account when using these types of data (Clausen, 1998). Respondents may alter what they reveal about the nature, extent, and timing of their offending – either knowingly or unknowingly – in order to fulfill expectations of the research or appear more socially desirable to the intended audience. For example, Wright and Decker (1994) suggest that incarcerated prisoners recount their criminal escapades in a manner that makes them look more rational, so as not to appear foolish in the eyes of the researchers; however, researchers have not examined this argument empirically (see Copes and Hotchstetler, 2010 for a review of research on potential incarceration effects). The age of the respondent may also influence the life history narrative. Some argue that, as people age, the need for a coherent story becomes more salient. Like in other retrospective methods, data quality can degrade the longer the reference period, due to memory decay. Respondents may also recast their prior experiences and attitudes in ways that are congruent with their present. Some researchers have also raised concerns that life histories are stories and not data, although these concerns can be mitigated by the methods used to collect the data and by supplementation with official records. Some of these critiques are less relevant if, as Maruna and Matrevers (2007) argue, narratives "hold psychological truth" in that they influence behavior because we act in ways that are consistent with our self-myths; they provide theories of reality and should not be taken as reality in and of themselves.

One of the most famous life narratives in criminology is Shaw's (1966) *The Jack-Roller*. To collect this life history, Stanley was presented with "official data" (list of arrests, contacts with social service agencies, and incarcerations) and asked to use this list as guide for writing his own story. After producing an initial life history, Shaw asked Stanley to elaborate on different aspects of his life and provided examples of what should be included, drawing from the boy's own life. This narrative offers information on when Stanley began offending, the regularity in which he engaged in illegal activity, the timing and length of periods of temporary reform, and finally desistance. Shaw links Stanley's offending to the ecological environment by presenting data on the neighborhoods in which Stanley lived and spent his time. This life history also incorporates Stanley's perceptions of how his family, peers, institutions, and "fate" contributed to his involvement in crime and delinquency.

A more recent life history narrative can be found in *Confessions of a Dying Thief* (Steffensmeier and Ulmer, 2005), which is a follow-up to *The Fence: In the Shadow of Two Worlds* (Steffensmeier, 1986). In this book Sam, an experienced thief and fence who is literally on his deathbed, gives a narrative account of his criminal career and of the inner workings of organized crime networks. Like Shaw, the researchers corroborated Sam's story through police reports, media accounts, and interviews with Sam's associates. This research joins the work of Laub and Sampson (2003) as one of the few studies that detail offending over the full life span.

Detailed academic life histories of women offenders like *The Jack-Roller* and *Confessions of a Dying Thief* are more difficult to find, but a number of studies have followed cohorts of women over time, incorporating qualitative life history data with quantitative surveys. For example, drawing on a series of studies, Giordano's (2010) *Legacies of Crime* followed girls (and boys) sampled from Ohio detention centers in 1982, when they were on average 16 years old, through 2003. Interviews were also conducted with their children. These data provide a nuanced examination of the gendered factors that are related to persistent offending and desistance, as well as to the intergenerational transmission of crime. Work by Shadd Maruna (2001) that analyzes narratives collected from British convicts from 1996 to 1998 also includes both males and females. In this book, titled *Making Good*, Maruna combines self-stories with field observations to build a phenomenology of the desistance process, but gender differences are not a focus of the analysis.

Life events calendars Retrospective longitudinal data need not be qualitative. One increasingly popular method used to collect retrospective quantitative data is the life events calendar (LEC), also known as the life history calendar (LHC). The LEC is an instrument created to facilitate the recall and recording of life histories. It is "designed to collect calendar time course information, represented as time lines, for different domains of inquiry (e.g., residential and employment histories) that extend across a predetermined reference period (e.g., since birth, since adulthood, previous 10 years, previous 2 years)" (Belli, Shay, and Stafford, 2001, p. 48). In addition to its unique format, this instrument differs from the traditional survey in that data collection "is organized around questions about streams of events … rather than around questions about isolated life events" (Caspi et al., 1996, p. 104).

As its name implies, the LEC resembles a calendar. Typically, time demarcations run horizontally across the calendar, while research domains are listed vertically, although this pattern is sometimes reversed. The researcher records information in the grid that is created. Events such as an arrest, as well as periods of activity like substance use, can be recorded in the space provided in the grid. This design enables the researcher to collect "continuous information about multiple trajectories and transition events in the respondent's life" (Caspi et al., 1996, 102). The design of the LEC is intended to improve upon the traditional self-report methodology by enhancing respondent recall, reducing recording error, improving interview quality, and enabling the recording of the sequence of contextual change.

Studies have found that LECs tend to provide reliable data for the sequence and timing of major life events when these events are either socially desirable or neutral, and also salient (e.g., when they occur infrequently, or when they form a central part of an individual's life). These domains include things like timing of marriage, employment, childbirths, and residential moves (Caspi et al., 1996; Freedman et al., 1988; Lin, Ensel, and Lai, 1997). The LEC tends to have less success in domains where events are less salient or are undesirable (Lin et al., 1997). Indeed, studies of the validity and reliability of offending and criminal history data collected using the LEC have produced mixed results. Horney and Marshall (1992) conducted an experiment in which they compared the Rand inmate self-report survey and their LEC survey. Contrary to expectations, the LEC method did not produce lower and more accurate estimates for frequency of offending, known as lambda, than the traditional Rand survey method. More recent studies using incarcerated samples have found that LECs may provide valid assessments of arrest prevalence and frequency. Data on timing are less accurate, although recall is superior when the arrest is more salient (Morris and Slocum, 2010; Roberts and Wells, 2010). Roberts and Horney (2010) provide a review of the use of the LEC in criminology, including studies that assess the validity and reliability of LEC data.

Unlike with prospective study designs, the collection of retrospective self-report data is generally cheaper, faster, and theoretically can cover a longer time span; but this comes at a price. Like in all retrospective methods, the quality of data is dependent on the respondent's recall. Thus this method may be most useful when collecting data on salient life events like marriage and childbirth. Arrest and offending may be salient for some people, but probably not for chronic offenders. It is also difficult to obtain valid information about prior plans, expectations, and feelings, unless they are particularly memorable (Offer et al., 2000). Data quality may be compromised by memory decay and because individuals may reinterpret prior attitudes and experiences through the veil of their current life circumstances and outlook. Retrospective methods may be more appropriate for collecting longitudinal data from people who live stable lives (see, e.g., Morris and Slocum, 2010). While one benefit of retrospective methods of data collection is that they do not suffer from selective attrition because respondents are interviewed or surveyed at only one point in time, they are subject to selection bias of a different type. Namely, only survivors and those individuals whom researchers can identify and convince to participate can be included in the study, a fact that leads to the selective exclusion of high-risk groups. This may be particularly problematic when studying offending, because offenders and those involved in the criminal justice system have higher rates of mortality and more health problems than other groups (Laub and Vailant, 2000; Nieuwbeerta and Piquero, 2008) or may be less willing to participate.

Mixed Designs

Some research designs do not fit neatly into the category of retrospective or prospective design, but rather are hybrids of the two. These studies attempt to maximize the benefits and minimize the limitations of these two approaches. For example, the catch-up design involves finding and re-interviewing respondents who participated in a study years earlier (Dempster-McClain and Moen, 1998). This enables researchers to link together two data points and gives them immediate access to longitudinal data. While these studies can save an enormous amount of time and resources, it can be difficult to find some participants, especially the ones that lead lives that are more chaotic. In addition, these studies raise ethical concerns if the participants did not give consent to be contacted. This may be particularly problematic when respondents are chosen based on their criminal behavior, victimization experiences or other criteria they wish to keep private (Laub and Sampson, 2003).

Perhaps one of the most ambitious catch-up studies in recent years is Laub and Sampson's (2003) study of the men who participated in the original Glueck study titled *Unraveling Juvenile Delinquency* (Glueck and Glueck, 1950; see also Sampson and Laub, 1992). Having stumbled upon the data from this study in the Harvard Law Library basement, Sampson and Laub reformatted, validated, and supplemented this original data set in order to study within-individual stability and change in offending through adulthood (see Sampson and Laub, 1992). In later work (Laub and Sampson, 2003), they combined these data with information obtained from archival records (criminal history and death records) for each of the 500 males in the original delinquent sample. They also found and collected narrative life histories and quantitative LEC data from 52 of the men in the delinquent sample when the men had reached the age of 70. This research design allowed them to study crime over the full life course in a relatively short period. It combines the advantages of using official records with the strengths of quantitative and qualitative retrospective life history data.

Other studies incorporate retrospective designs within a prospective study, in an attempt to improve recall, fill in the gaps between assessment periods, and obtain rich narrative accounts of offending. For example, within a panel study, retrospective methods like LECs might be used to capture information on events and experiences that have occurred in the period between survey waves. This method was used in the Pathways to Desistance study, which sampled delinquent youth in Pittsburgh and Arizona. Researchers followed the youth prospectively for ten years and used LECs to collect data on life events that occurred between assessments (see Mulvey, Schubert, and Piquero, 2014; Schubert et al., 2004).

Challenges in Measuring Crime over the Life Span

As should be apparent from the above discussion, the collection of valid and reliable longitudinal data is fraught with challenges. Yet researchers have begun to explore new and innovative methods to overcome these issues. The next section elaborates on some of the difficulties associated with measuring crime over the life course and presents some of the ways that researchers are beginning to overcome these challenges.

Prospective, longitudinal data collection: Improving upon the "gold standard"

One critique leveled at panel studies is that they introduce bias in measurements of offending, due to testing effects. A number of potential solutions have been proposed for mitigating testing effects, or at least for providing estimates of the extent to which this type of bias is being introduced into the data (for an overview, see Hofer, Thorvaldsson, and Piccinin, 2012). In one method, for each age group included in the study, at the second wave of data collection a new age-matched cohort is surveyed. Theoretically, the difference between the new sample (those being surveyed for the first time) and the old sample (those being sampled for the second time) will provide an estimation of testing effects. This solution is not perfect. If there is selective attrition, then the estimate of the testing effect will be biased, since it based on the select group that remained in the study. Another method is to parcel out statistically the effect of retests, which is measured as the number of assessments that have been completed by the respondent, from the effects of age by using a random effects model. This can provide an estimate of the change that would have occurred if there had not been repeated testing. However, these models can only be estimated if age and measurement periods are not perfectly correlated. This requires variability in age among the initial sample or variability in the number of retest intervals (or both). However, since the testing effects are measured as the number of times the respondent has been surveyed, these models assume that testing effects are based solely on the number of survey exposures and are not influenced by the length of time between assessments (Hoffman, Hofer, and Sliwinski, 2011).

Selective attrition is a second factor that can affect the quality of panel data. Brame and Paternoster (2003) argue: "Clearly the best solution to the missing data problem is a front-end solution – to minimize the amount of missing data" (p. 76). Schoeni and colleagues (2013) outline ways in which researchers can do just this. They argue that one of the most effective methods is to increase the amount of the incentives paid to respondents. Other methods involve keeping track of respondents' living location between waves of data collection by sending postcards that allow the respondents to update their contact information, newsletters, or Christmas cards. There are also ways to increase the number of completed surveys while in the field. These include sending letters that notify respondents of upcoming surveys and of the value of the data being collected, and using informants – usually family members – to help track down respondents' current living locations. Making the survey less onerous by shortening its length, by increasing the time between assessments, or by covering topics that interest the respondent may also reduce attrition. More research is needed to fully assess the success of these various methods.

Measuring the full life span

A second challenge to measuring offending over time is the difficulty of capturing this behavior over the full life span. With a few notable exceptions, few researchers have studied offending over the full life span. Those who have rely almost exclusively on official data or narrative accounts from relatively small or homogenous samples (e.g., Farrington et al., 2013; Laub and Sampson, 2003). Studies with small and homogenous samples raise concerns about generalizability. Relying solely on official data raises another set of issues. The researcher must assume that definitions of crime remain constant across time and place. In addition, official records may be incomplete due to the fractured nature of the criminal justice system. For example, an official records search in one state will miss any offending that occurred outside the state. Rap sheets obtained from the Federal Bureau of Investigation can help to mitigate this problem, but these do not capture all arrests. In their follow-up of the Glueck men, Laub and Sampson (2003) found that 29 percent of the men who had a record in the study state, Massachusetts, did not have an FBI rap sheet. As criminal justice databases become increasingly sophisticated and networked across jurisdictions, this issue may become less problematic.

In addition, official records may be less likely to capture certain types of offending or may miss offending by older individuals. For example, older offenders may be switching to behaviors that are still problematic, but have a lower likelihood of being captured in official records. Moreover, agents in the justice system may treat offenders differently according to their age. Werthman and Piliavin (1967, p. 75) argue that

> the police divide the population and physical territory under surveillance into a variety of categories, make some initial assumptions about the moral character of the people and places in these categories, and then focus attention on those categories of persons and places felt to have the shadiest moral characteristics.

Age is one of the factors that help to delineate these categories (see Piliavin and Briar, 1964, p. 212). Similarly, the context in which older offenders violate the law may make offenses less likely to be formally processed. For example, offenders may be more likely to engage in violence in the home.

Obtaining offending over the full life span is important, because study results and conclusions can vary according to the length of follow-up (Eggleston, Laub, and Sampson, 2004). Moreover, the correlates of offending may change as an individual ages, or even across historical contexts. It is also possible that the age-related changes in offending that have been documented in official data reflect, in part, changes in the extent to which official records capture actual offending. For example, Farrington et al. (2013) compared official records to self-reports up to age of 48 and found that the ratio of self-reported offenders to official offenders was lower at ages 15–18 than in any other age range they studied; however, the ratio of self-reported frequency of offending to official offending declined with age.

One solution to this difficulty is triangulation. The most accurate picture of offending over the life span will come from combining multiple sources – official records, self-report, and informant report. This, however, will require the collection of panel data into the later life, or creative ways of using archived data sets (see Elder and Taylor, 2009).

Funding

Research like that described above – data from multiple sources that cover the full life span – is expensive. As a result, few long-term prospective panel studies can be funded. Those that are struggle to maintain their stream of funding as time passes. This is partially because funding agencies often develop new priorities or devote a portion of their budgets to funding young investigators. Moreover, offending decreases with age, which makes studies that focus on offenders' later lives less relevant for criminal justice policy and thus less interesting to funding agencies. Regardless of whether this decrease in support is good or bad, it does create problems for the study of offending over the life course. The solution, some argue, is to be creative. Retrospective longitudinal surveys may need to take the place of panel studies or to be incorporated into panel studies with long time lags between assessments. Researchers may make better use of archival data and catch-up designs (Dempster-McClain and Moen, 1998; Elder and Taylor, 2009). Another solution is to develop new ways of collecting panel data with lower costs. The next section describes one way in which this might be accomplished.

New Horizons in Measurement and Methodologies: Telemetric Research

Researchers are developing new ways of studying crime over the life course – ways that overcome some of the challenges described above. One promising method is to incorporate technology. Given the increasing access to the Internet and smart phones, the use of telemetric methods for collecting longitudinal data is certainly on the horizon. Telemetric methods involve collecting data from afar; and they are typified by online data collection (Wilt, Condon, and Revelle, 2012). They can take many forms. Some types of telemetric techniques are similar to traditional methods, but are facilitated by the Internet and mobile phones. These types include self-report and informant surveys and open-ended questionnaires. Large-scale panel studies can incorporate Internet surveys into the data collection effort, which enables researchers to conduct some types of assessment more frequently and with little added cost. Although such methods are in the nascent stage, some researchers have begun to recruit participants and conduct multiple waves of data collection entirely online, using subject recruitment tools (Christensen and Glick, 2013). Telemetric data collection can also involve passive observation, such as voice-activated recording devices.

As detailed by Wilt and colleagues (2012), telemetric research designs have a number of advantages over other types of designs. This method makes it possible to reach large numbers of people; and with a larger sample comes increased power to detect effects and greater precision in estimates. In addition, online surveys can reach people who live all over the world, including those who may be difficult to survey through traditional techniques – for example the elderly, or those living in rural areas. However, if these populations are not specifically targeted, they may be missed by online surveys. Online surveys also reduce the time and costs associated with traditional data collection methods, since many tasks, such survey administration and data entry, are automated. This reduction in costs can free up funds for the collection of more waves of data. In addition, Wilt and colleagues argue that telemetric techniques may produce responses that are more honest; respondents may feel anonymous, and therefore may be willing to disclose sensitive information such as offending or substance use. Email responses and instant messaging are more spontaneous and perhaps less filtered. At the same time, it is possible to obtain more thoughtful and accurate responses than in interviews if respondents are not required to answer questions immediately. This enables them to give more reflective responses or to obtain the information needed to accurately respond to questions (e.g., information on the exact timing of life events like arrests or periods of incarceration).

Wilt and colleagues (2012) argue that telemetric methods can help address some of the problems with longitudinal data collection. They can reduce attrition by reducing respondent burden. For example, web-based surveys take less time to complete than paper-based surveys (Coyne et al., 2009), and respondents can complete the survey at their own convenience, without setting up a meeting with the researcher. It also removes geographical constraints. Telemetric methods make it easier to collect time-sensitive data and to collect data more frequently. Researchers can collect real-time data using text messaging. Thus recall error becomes less of a concern.

The most obvious disadvantage of collecting data via the Internet is that online surveys will miss respondents who do not use the Internet, which raises questions about the generalizability of the results. In addition, Internet surveys may produce more missing data and have higher rates of attrition than traditional face-to-face surveys; respondents may feel less committed to finishing the survey or to participating in subsequent waves, since they are not face-to-face with the researcher. But van Gelder, Bretveld, and Roeleveld (2010) argue that selective attrition and questions regarding the nongeneralizability of the data will become less of an issue as Internet usage becomes ubiquitous. The emergence of this type of research will require that researchers pay careful attention to issues of generalizability and observation bias. Some telemetric methods – including more invasive techniques like recording devices – just may not be appropriate for studying offending.

Research on the validity of data collected online indicates that the method holds promise. Studies using traditional and online methods can produce similar results (Krantz, Dalal, and Birnbaum, 2000). In their review of the use of web-based surveys in health research, van Gelder and colleagues (2010) conclude that web-based surveys produce information on many epidemiological factors like smoking, alcohol use, and oral contraception that is equally valid as (or even more so than) traditional paper surveys. We know less about whether these methods can produce valid longitudinal data regarding offending. In addition, studies relying solely on subject recruitment tools to gather longitudinal data tend to produce samples that are unrepresentative of the general population; respondents tend to be younger and better educated (Christensen and Glick, 2013). Moreover, studies of prospective longitudinal data collected via these methods have only followed respondents over relatively short periods. We do not know whether respondents will be invested enough in the survey process to continue their participation over time.

Conclusion

According to Scott and Alwin (1998), all things being equal, researchers generally consider prospective longitudinal studies to be superior to retrospective studies; yet the design of a longitudinal study involves a series of trade-offs because "*all other things* are rarely equal" (p. 100). For instance, the greater validity and reliability of prospective studies is usually coupled with problems of high cost, inability to collect data for use in the near future, and sample attrition. Although retrospective longitudinal data do not have these particular failings, they have their own distinct set of problems to overcome. While not exhaustive, this chapter reviewed some of the more prominent methods for collecting data on offending and their correlates over the life course, providing examples of different research designs. In addition, the strengths and weakness of different designs were outlined.

As Gottfredson and Hirschi (1987) make clear, theory and method are inextricably linked, and the choice of a research design must necessarily be driven by the question that is being addressed and by aetiological assumptions about the nature and causes of offending. As developmental theories of offending and life-course criminology have evolved in recent years, so have methods for collecting the types of data needed to assess these explanations of offending. Although recent years have seen the development of innovative methods for collecting longitudinal data as well as assessments of their ability to elicit accurate data, methodology still lags behind theoretical development.

In the coming years, researchers will need to develop methods for collecting data that capture the complex processes through which offending is initiated, is sustained, and declines over time. One way to do this is to integrate methods from other fields like public health, biology, and epidemiology. Criminologists should also carefully consider how technological innovations can enhance their ability to collect accurate and timely longitudinal data. This will require careful consideration of how techniques developed for the study of relatively benign topics can be adapted to the study of offending. In addition, these innovations should be coupled with extensive research on the quality of the data they produce as well as on the generalizability of their findings.

Acknowledgments

I would like to thank John Laub. I learned much of what I know about the measurement of crime over the life course as a student in his graduate seminar at the University of Maryland. This chapter, particularly the sections that describe different methods for collecting prospective and retrospective data, incorporates many of the readings and discussions from that class. I would also like to thank Elaine Doherty and David Klinger for acting as sounding boards for my ideas.

Notes

1 Thornberry and Krohn (2000) provide an excellent review of the use of self-report data in criminology.
2 As Scott and Alwin (1998) point out, some might argue that all survey and interview data fall into this category, because they require respondents to interpret their prior life experiences in light of their current circumstances.
3 A more general treatment of longitudinal research designs, which includes a review of the analysis of longitudinal data, can be found in Menard (2002).
4 For example, in his follow up of Shaw's (1968) *The Jack-Roller*, Snodgrass (1982) argues that the subject of the life history, Stanley, changed his behavior because he wanted to be the person that Shaw thought he could become. Furthermore, Shaw actually intervened in Stanley's life, providing legal assistance to Stanley when he was arrested for robbery (see Lauritsen, 1998).

References

Becker, H. S. 1966. Introduction. In *The jack-roller*, edited by C. R. Shaw, v–xviii. Chicago, IL: University of Chicago Press.

Belli, R. F., Shay, W. L., and Stafford, F. P. 2001. Event history calendars and question list surveys: A direct comparison of interviewing methods. *Public Opinion Quarterly*, 65: 45–74.

Blokland, A. A. J., and Nieuwbeerta, P. 2005. The effects of life circumstances on longitudinal trajectories of offending. *Criminology*, 43 (4): 1203–1240.

Blumstein, A., Cohen, J., and Farrington, D. 1988. Criminal career research: Its value for criminology. *Criminology*, 26: 1–35.

Blumstein, A., Cohen, J., Roth, J., and Visher, C., eds. 1986. *Criminal careers and career criminals*, vol. 1. Washington DC: National Academy Press.

Bosick, S. J. 2009. Operationalizing crime over the life course. *Crime & Delinquency*, 55 (3): 472–496.

Brame, R., and Paternoster, R. 2003. Missing data problems in criminological research: Two case studies. *Journal of Quantitative Criminology*, 19 (1): 55–78.

Brame, R., and Piquero, A. R. 2003. Selective attrition and the age-crime relationship. *Journal of Quantitative Criminology*, 19 (2): 107–127.

Bureau of Labor Statistics. 2014. National longitudinal surveys. Accessed June 25. http://www.bls.gov/nls.

Caspi, A., Moffitt, T. E., Thornton, A., Freedman, D., Ammell, J. W., Harrington, H., Smeijers, J., and Silva, P. A. 1996. The life history calendar: A research and clinical assessment method for collecting retrospective event-history data. *International Journal of Methods on Psychiatric Research*, 6: 101–114.

Christensen, D. P., and Glick, D. M. 2013. Crowdsourcing panel studies and real-time experiments in Mechanical Turk. *The Political Methodologist*, 20 (2): 27–32.

Clausen, J. A. 1998. Life reviews and life stories. In *Methods of life course research: Qualitative and quantitative approaches*, edited by Janet Z. Giele and Glen H. Elder, Jr., 189–212. Thousand Oaks, CA: Sage.

Copes, H., and Hotchstetler, A. 2010. Interviewing the incarcerated: Pitfalls and promises. In *Offenders on offending: Learning about crime from criminals*, edited by W. Bernasco, 49–67. Cullompton, UK: Willan.

Coyne, K. S., Sexton, C. C., Kopp, Z. S., Luks, S., Gross, A., Irwin, D., and Milsom, I. 2009. Rational for the study methods and design of the Epidemiology of Lower Urinary Tract Symptoms (EpiLuts) study. *British Journal of Urology International*, 104: 348–351.

Cullen, F. T. 2011. Beyond adolescence-limited criminology: Choosing our future: The American Society of Criminology 2010 Sutherland Address. *Criminology*, 49 (2): 287–330.

Dempster-McClain, D., and Moen, P. 1998. Finding respondents in a follow-up study. In *Methods of life course research: Qualitative and quantitative approaches*, edited by J. Z. Giele and G. H. Elder, Jr., 128–151. Thousand Oaks, CA: Sage.

Duncan, S. C., and Duncan, T. E. 2012. Accelerated longitudinal designs. In *Handbook of developmental research methods*, edited by B. Laursen, T. D. Little, and N. A. Card, 31–45. New York: Guilford.

Dunedin Multidisciplinary Health and Development Research Unit. 2014. Dunedin Study. Accessed June 25. http://dunedinstudy.otago.ac.nz.

Eggleston, E. P., Laub, J. H., and Sampson, R. J. 2004. Methodological sensitivities to latent class analysis of long-term criminal trajectories. *Journal of Quantitative Criminology*, 20 (1): 1–26.

Elder, G. H., Jr, and Taylor, M. G. 2009. Linking research questions to data archives. In *The craft of life course research*, edited by G. H. Elder, Jr. and J. Z. Giele, 93–120. New York: Guilford.

Esbensen, F.-A., Miller, M. H.., Taylor, T. J., He, N., and Freng, A. 1999. Differential attrition rates and active parental consent. *Evaluation Review*, 23: 316–335.

Farrington, D. P. 1986. Age and crime. In *Crime and justice*, vol. 7, edited by M. Tonry and N. Morris, 189–251. Chicago, IL: University of Chicago Press.

Farrington, D. P. 2003. Key results from the first forty years of the Cambridge Study in Delinquent Development. In *Taking stock of delinquency*, edited by T. P. Thornberry and M. D. Krohn, 137–183. New York: Kluwer Academic/Plenum.

Farrington, D. P., Auty, K. M., Coid, J. C., and Turner, R. E. 2013. Self-reported and official offending from age 10 to age 56. *European Journal on Criminal Policy and Research*, 19: 135–151.

Freedman, D., Thornton, A., Camburn, D., Alwin, D., and Young-DeMarco, L. 1988. The life history calendar: A technique for collecting retrospective data. *Sociological Methodology*, 18: 37–68.

Giordano, P. C. 2010. *Legacies of crime: A follow-up of the children of highly delinquent girls and boys*. New York: Cambridge University Press.

Glueck, S., and Glueck, E. 1950. *Unraveling juvenile delinquency*. New York: Commonwealth Fund.

Glueck, S., and Glueck, E. 1968. *Delinquents and nondelinquents in perspective*. Cambridge, MA: Harvard University Press.

Gottfredson, M., and Hirschi, T. 1986. The true value of lambda would appear to be zero: An essay on career criminals, criminal careers, selective incapacitation, cohort studies, and related topics. *Criminology*, 24 (2): 213–234.

Gottfredson, M., and Hirschi, T. 1987. The methodological adequacy of longitudinal research on crime. *Criminology*, 25 (3): 581–614.

Gottfredson, M., and Hirschi, T. 1988. Science, public policy, and the career paradigm. *Criminology*, 26: 37–55.

Hirschi, T., and Gottfredson, M. 1983. Age and the explanation of crime. *American Journal of Sociology*, 89: 552–584.

Hofer, S. M., Thorvaldsson, V., and Piccinin, A. M. 2012. Foundational issues of design and measurement in developmental research. In *Handbook of developmental research methods*, edited by B. Laursen, T. D. Little, and N. A. Card, 3–16. New York: Guilford.

Hoffman, L., Hofer, S. M., and Sliwinski, M. J. 2011. On the confounds among retest gains and age-cohort differences in the estimation of within-person change in longitudinal studies: A simulation study. *Psychology and Aging*, 26 (4): 778–791.

Horney, J., and Marshall, I. H. 1992. An experimental comparison of two self-report methods for measuring lambda. *Journal of Research in Crime and Delinquency*, 29: 102–121.

Kendler, K. S., Larsson Lönn, S., Morris, N. A., Sundquist, J., Långström, N., and Sundquist, K. 2014. A Swedish national adoption study of criminality. *Psychological Medicine*, 44: 1913–1925.

Kendler, K. S., Morris, N. A., Larsson Lönn, S., Sundquist, J., and Sundquist, K. 2014. Environmental transmission of violent criminal behavior in siblings: A Swedish national study. *Psychological Medicine*, 44: 3181–3187.

Krantz, J. H., Dalal, R., and Birnbaum, M. H. 2000. Validity of web-based psychological research. In *Psychological experiments on the Internet*, edited by M. H. Birnbaum, 35–60. San Diego, CA: Academic Press.

Laub, J. H. 2004. The life course of criminology in the United States: The American Society of Criminology 2003 Presidential Address. *Criminology*, 42 (1): 1–26.

Laub, J. H. 2006. Edwin H. Sutherland and the Michael–Adler Report: Searching for the soul of criminology seventy years later. *Criminology*, 44 (2): 235–258.

Laub, J. H., and Sampson, R. J. 2003. *Shared beginnings, divergent lives: Delinquent boys to age 70*. Cambridge, MA: Harvard University Press.

Laub, J. H., and Vailant, G. E. 2000. Delinquency and mortality: A 50-year follow-up study of 1,000 delinquent and nondelinquent boys. *American Journal of Psychiatry*, 157 (1): 96–102.

Lauritsen, J. 1998. The age-crime debate: Assessing the limits of longitudinal self-report data. *Social Forces*, 77 (1): 127–154.

Lauritsen, J. 2005. Explaining patterns of offending across the life course: Comments on interactional theory and recent tests based on the RYDS-RIS data. *The Annals of the American Academy of Political and Social Science*, 602: 212–228.

Lin, N., Ensel, W. M., and Lai, W. G. 1997. Construction and the use of the life history calendar: Reliability and validity of recall data. In *Stress and adversity over the lifecourse*, edited by I. H. Gotlib and B. Wheaton, 249–272. Cambridge: Cambridge University Press.

Loeber, R., Farrington, D. P., Stouthamer-Loeber, M., Moffitt, T. E., and Caspi, A. 1998. The development of male offending: Key findings from the first decade of the Pittsburgh Youth Study. *Studies on Crime & Crime Prevention*, 7 (2): 141–172.

Loeber, R., Stouthamer-Loeber, M., Van Kammen, W. M., and Farrington, D. P. 1989. Development of a new measure of self-reported anti-social behavior for young children: Prevalence and reliability. In *Cross-national research in self-reported crime and delinquency*, edited by M. W. Klein, 33–83. Washington, DC: US Department of Justice, Office of Justice Programs.

Maruna, S. 2001. *Making good: How ex-convicts reform and rebuild their lives*. Washington, DC: American Psychological Association.

Maruna, S., and Matravers, A. 2007. N = 1: Criminology and the person. *Theoretical Criminology*, 11: 427–442.

Menard, S. 2002. *Longitudinal research*, 2nd edn. Thousand Oaks, CA: Sage.

Morris, N. A., and Slocum, L. A. 2010. The validity of self-reported prevalence, frequency, and timing of arrest: An evaluation of data collected using a life event calendar. *Journal of Research in Crime and Delinquency*, 47: 210–240.

Mulvey, E. P., Schubert, C. A., and Piquero, A. R. 2014. Pathways to desistance: Final technical report. Accessed June 21, 2014. https://www.ncjrs.gov/pdffiles1/nij/grants/244689.pdf.

Nieuwbeerta, P., and Piquero, A. R. 2008. Mortality rates and causes of death of convicted Dutch criminals 25 years later. *Journal of Research in Crime and Delinquency*, 45 (3): 256–286.

Offer, D., Kaiz, M., Howard, K., and Bennet, E. S. 2000. The altering of reported experiences. *Journal of the American Academy of Child and Adolescent Psychiatry*, 39: 735–742.

Piliavin, I., and Briar, S. 1964. Police encounters with juveniles. *American Journal of Sociology*, 70: 206–214.

Roberts, J., and Julie Horney. 2010. The life event calendar method in criminological research. In *Handbook of quantitative criminology*, edited by A. R. Piquero and D. Weisburd, 289–312. New York: Springer.

Roberts, J., and Wells, W. 2010. The validity of criminal justice contacts reported by inmates: A comparison of self-reported data with official prison records. *Journal of Criminal Justice*, 38 (5): 1031–1037.

Rutter, M. 1988. Longitudinal data in the study of causal processes: Some uses and some pitfalls. In *Studies of psychosocial risk: The power of longitudinal data*, edited by M. Rutter, 1–28. Cambridge: Cambridge University Press.

Sampson, R. J., and Laub, J. H. 1992. *Crime in the making: Pathways and turning points through life*. Cambridge, MA: Harvard University Press.

Schoeni, R. F., Stafford, F., McGonagle, K., A., and Andreski, P. 2013. Response rates in national panel surveys. *The Annals of the American Academy of Political and Social Science*, 645: 60–87.

Schubert, C. A., Mulvey, E. P., Steinberg, L., Cauffman, E., Losoya, S. H., Hecker, T., Chassin, L., and Knight, G. P. 2004. Operational lessons from the pathways to desistance project. *Youth Violence and Juvenile Justice*, 2 (3): 237–255.

Scott, J., and Alwin, D. 1998. Retrospective versus prospective measurement of life histories in longitudinal research. In *Methods of life course research: Qualitative and quantitative approaches*, edited by J. Z. Giele and G. H. Elder, Jr., 98–127. Thousand Oaks, CA: Sage.

Shaw, C. R. 1966. *The jack-roller*. Chicago, IL: University of Chicago Press.

Slocum, L. A., Simpson, S. S., Hipwell, A. E., and Loeber, R. 2011. Young girls' and caretakers' reports of problem behavior comprehension and concordance across age, race, and behavior. *Youth & Society*, 43: 1010–1040.

Snodgrass, J. 1982. *The jack-roller at seventy: A fifty year follow-up of "a delinquent boy's own story."* Boston, MA: Lexington.

Steffensmeier, D. 1986. *The fence: In the shadow of two worlds*. Totowa, NJ: Rowman and Littlefield.

Steffensmeier, D., and Ulmer, J. T. 2005. *Confessions of a dying thief*. New Brunswick, NJ: Aldine Transaction.

Thornberry, T. P., Bjerregaard, B., and Miles, W. 1993. The consequences of respondent attrition in panel studies: A simulation based on the Rochester Youth Development Study. *Journal of Quantitative Criminology*, 9 (2): 127–158.

Thornberry, T. P., and Krohn, M. D. 2000. The self-report method for measuring delinquency and crime. In *Measurement and analysis of crime and justice*, edited by D. Duffee, R. Crutchfield, S. D. Mastrofski, L. G. Mazerolle, D. McDowall, and B. Ostrom, 85–138. Washington, DC: US Department of Justice.

Thornberry, T. P., and Krohn, M. D. 2003. The development of panel studies of delinquency. In *Taking stock of delinquency: An overview of findings from contemporary longitudinal studies*, edited by T. P. Thornberry and M. D. Krohn, 1–9. New York: Kluwer Academic/Plenum.

University of North Carolina Population Center. 2014. Add health. Accessed June 26, 2015. http://www.cpc.unc.edu/projects/addhealth.

van Gelder, M. M. H. J., Bretveld, R. W., and Roeleveld, N. 2010. *Web-based questionnaires: The future of epidemiology?* 172, 1292–1298.

Werthman, C., and Piliavin, I. 1967. *Gang members and the police*. In *The police: Six sociological essays*, edited by D. Bordua, 56–98. New York: John Wiley & Sons.

Wilt, J., Condon, D. M., and Revelle, W. 2012. Telemetrics and online data collection. In *Handbook of developmental research methods*, edited by B. Laursen, T. D. Little, and N. A. Card, 163–180. New York: Guilford.

Wolfgang, M. E., Figlio, R. M., and Sellin, T. 1972. *Delinquency in a birth cohort*. Chicago, IL: University of Chicago Press.

Wright, R. T., and Decker, S. H. 1994. *Burglars on the job: Streetlife and residential break-ins*. Boston, MA: Northeastern University Press.

Further Reading

Aisenbrey, S., and Fasang, A. E. 2010. New life for old ideas: The "second wave" of sequence analysis bringing the "course" back into the life course. *Sociological Methods & Research*, 38: 420–462.

Holleran, S. E., Whitehead, J., Schmader, T., and Mehl, M. R. 2011. Talking shop and shooting the breeze: A study of workplace conversation and job disengagement among STEM faculty. *Social Psychological and Personality Science*, 2: 65–71.

Holtzman, N. S., Vazire, S., and Mehl, M. R. 2010. Sounds like a narcissist: Behavioral manifestations of narcissism in everyday life. *Journal of Research in Personality*, 44: 478–484.

Mehl, M. R., Vazire, S., Holleran, S. E., and Clark, C. S. 2010. Eavesdropping on happiness: Well-being is related to having less small talk and more substantive conversations. *Psychological Science*, 21: 539–541.

23

Conducting Qualitative Interviews in Prison: Challenges and Lessons Learned

Kristin Carbone-Lopez

Introduction

Qualitative research has much to offer criminologists seeking to learn about the experiences of prisoners and prison culture beyond what we know. At the same time, the prison environment itself presents unique challenges for researchers in terms of "getting in." And conducting interviews with prisoners, particularly about offending and victimization histories, presents its own set of challenges, including simply developing rapport. As Schlosser (2008) noted, "interviewing in prison presents unique sets of obstacles and 'methodological landmines' of which inexperienced researchers may be unaware" (p. 1501). The purpose of this chapter is to describe some of those obstacles associated with conducting interviews with incarcerated individuals, particularly on sensitive topics, and offer possible solutions. My goal is that the chapter might serve as a reference for criminology and criminal justice researchers, whether they are new to the field or simply conducting research within a carceral setting for the first time.

Prisons are not an uncommon setting in which to undertake research, and prisoners are most certainly not an uncommon population to study. However, there are not many published guides to assist researchers who seek to do this type of work. Criminal justice research methods textbooks may (briefly) mention some of the challenges in accessing correctional institutions, but they often provide little guidance as to actually conducting research within them. A handful of guides published in the last decade or so provide more explicit advice on gaining entry into typically hard-to-access criminal justice organizations. Generally speaking, though, as Fox, Zambrana, and Lane (2011) point out, the wisdom and advice related to

The Handbook of Measurement Issues in Criminology and Criminal Justice, First Edition.
Edited by Beth M. Huebner and Timothy S. Bynum.

researching prison populations is typically learned more informally, through the mentoring process or in methods courses. As the authors also note, "mentoring styles and the content of methods courses vary widely" (p. 307) and not all students or young researchers will be exposed to this information. A chapter such as this one, then, can help make some of this advice more widely available.

What follows is a discussion of the (many) challenges that arise *after* access to the prison has already been secured. I also provide some considerations for collecting reliable and valid data on offending and victimization from prisoners in an ethical manner. While qualitative methods texts generally cover interviewing on sensitive topics, the types of questions we ask as criminologists are often extremely sensitive and deserve some mention here. These are the things I wish that I had known before my introduction to the world of interviewing in correctional facilities, as knowing them would have meant that I might have avoided some of the frustration and emotional roller coasters I endured. To be clear, these are my own experiences and, as a result, my own interpretations and suggestions, based on those experiences.

Before I begin, though, let me first explain what this chapter is *not* intended to be. First, while I will discuss the challenges of asking sensitive questions, particularly within a prison environment, I will not provide a general introduction to interviewing techniques. There are a number of very good readers that cover the basics of interview research far better than I can do here (see, for example, Kvale, 1996 and Spradley, 1979). Second, this chapter is focused only on collecting data and not on its analysis. Texts by Spradley (1979) and Charmaz (2006) provide detailed suggestions and should be consulted by all those who look to improve the rigor of their qualitative analysis. Finally, I do not wish to engage in a debate over whether data from incarcerated offenders are any better or worse than data from "active" offenders.[1] Rather, as I noted above, I intend to offer practical suggestions for novice researchers who seek to conduct qualitative or in-depth interviews with prisoners within the carceral setting.

Lessons Learned from Prior Prison Research

Despite the extensive body of work that has relied on prison populations, there have been relatively few published guides for novice researchers who seek to learn how to conduct research within prisons. And often the methodological details of prison-based research are relegated to an appendix or a few footnotes. These details also tend to focus exclusively on *successful* strategies or experiences. Indeed, it is "rare to find in-depth descriptions … of the methodological problems, ethical pitfalls, political battles, and personal dilemmas" that are involved in carrying out prison-based research (Grimwade, 1999, p. 291). Perhaps this is because such descriptions of difficulties in the field are perceived as being simply too embarrassing for researchers to share (Grimwade, 1999). Or it may be because, as scientists, we tend to "flinch from critically examining and sharing … our anxieties, personal traumas and shortcomings as human beings and as academic researchers" (Phillips and

Earle, 2010, p. 365). Nevertheless, there are important "how to" insights that can be gleaned from prior prison research. As I discuss in what follows, prior researchers have most often provided tips on entry into the prison and on establishing rapport with participants.[2]

One of the first concerns for researchers doing prison-based research is "breaking in," gaining access to the research site. On the basis of a survey of state juvenile corrections research departments, Jeffords (2007) found that gatekeepers were most concerned with whether research would benefit the agency, or at the very least would not cause "undue interference" with its operation (p. 97). Research that meets these criteria, he argued, is more likely to be approved. Similarly, Trulson, Marquart, and Mullings (2004) offer practical suggestions for researchers, not just on gaining access, but on maintaining access to criminal justice agencies. In other words, they attempt to help researchers avoid the "pitfalls that can doom a research project even before it starts" (Trulson et al., 2004, p. 453). One suggestion they offer the young researcher is to become affiliated to someone such as an established professor, who may have successfully worked with the agency in the past and can establish a newcomer's validity as a legitimate and competent researcher. Other tips for maintaining access they describe include developing and disseminating a research proposal that is appropriate for the audience, following one's proposed timeline (and being mindful of the staff members' time while one is at the agency), and requesting to debrief the agency at the conclusion of the research project.

An equally important concern for researchers is establishing a rapport with participants. One of the more common difficulties that those who conduct prison-based research face consists in assuring the prisoners their interest is strictly limited to research and that they are not on a secret mission on behalf of the prison administration (Patenaude, 2004). To build mutual trust with participants, Newman (1958) suggests that researchers explain the purpose of the research to the prisoner in plain language and make clear that nothing s/he divulges will be discussed with the prison staff or anyone else (see also Patenaude, 2004). Newman (1958) also suggests that researchers be strategic in their choice of whom they interview first, attempting to avoid initiating data collection with "unpopular" inmates in order to prevent the study from failing in the prison yard before it ever begins. He further explains that researchers who do work in prisons must keep in mind

> what is probably the most unique characteristic of prison research, namely the fact that most or all members of his [or her] sample know one another ... and will undoubtedly communicate with one another and quite probably will collectively evaluate the research project before it has really begun. It is, therefore, important that the first few respondents carry back to the [prison] yard a straight story of the research project and it is equally important that their in-prison reputations are such that the project can be evaluated accurately by other inmates. (Newman, 1958, p. 130)

Ultimately, the quality of the data collected within a carceral setting depends both on the extent to which prisoners and staff develop confidence in the researcher and on the prisoners' perceptions of the researcher's interactions with staff. Thus there is an inherent challenge in prison research: one needs the cooperation of staff in order to carry out research successfully, and therefore one must be courteous to and respectful of staff; but one must *also* gain the confidence and trust of prisoners (Giallombardo, 1966). To successfully deal with this challenge, Giallombardo (1966) suggests that researchers keep conversations with staff members to a minimum in the presence of prisoners, so that the latter do not feel as though they are in danger of having their personal information reported to prison administrators. Yet it is equally important for researchers to be courteous to staff members. In another "how to" guide on the topic, Fox and colleagues (2011) remind researchers to be professional and respectful while interacting with correctional staff; this should include using titles rather than first names, making requests rather than demands, and not flaunting one's degrees – say, by insisting on being called "Dr." even if one does have a doctoral degree. While staff in correctional institutions will vary widely in terms of their dedication to assisting with research projects, the likeability of the researchers can hopefully (positively) influence their degree of cooperation, and ultimately the quality of the data collected (Fox et al., 2011; Trulson et al., 2004).

It is here that many of the methodological descriptions and "how to" guides end, however.[3] As noted, readers of such guides are generally only given strategies that, performed correctly, should result in success, and few warnings about potential pitfalls, or even mistakes that could derail an entire research project. Such "airbrushed accounts" (Phillips and Earle, 2010, p. 374) create the illusion of complete objectivity – as if the research and the researcher had no impact on one another. Thus, while over the years these authors and scholars have offered a number of useful strategies for overcoming many of the challenges of collecting qualitative data within prisons, there has been less focus on the qualitative interview itself as a discursive or interactive process, or upon the emotions of doing such research. I address such challenges in the following pages and, more importantly, I offer ideas for managing the interpersonal experiences of conducting interviews in the carceral context and the emotions that such research can invoke.

Putting the Lessons into Context

Before presenting the challenges (or lessons), I briefly describe the studies from which I draw these examples, in order to provide some context for the reader. The first of these is the Women's Experiences of Violence (WEV)[4] project, a multisite study of incarcerated women, in which I was involved as a graduate student. This study examined the personal, situational, and community-level factors associated with women's experiences of violence, both as offenders and as victims.[5] The Minneapolis sample was drawn from the female population incarcerated in the Adult Detention Facility in Hennepin County, Minnesota, a short-term post-sentencing jail. Women were selected to be interviewed from rosters of the total jail population on the basis of the nearest approaching release dates. Female interviewers conducted all interviews in private rooms, away from correctional staff and other inmates.

The structured interviews involved the use of a life events calendar and collected data on women's incarceration and treatment experiences, routine and criminal activities, and intimate relationships in the 36 months before their current incarceration. Much of the focus of the interview, however, was on women's experiences with violence both within the 36-month reference period and in childhood.

The second study I draw from is a project on which I collaborated with Jody Miller. We conducted qualitative in-depth interviews with women serving sentences at Women's Eastern Reception Diagnostic and Correctional Center (WERDCC) in Missouri about their experiences with methamphetamine.[6] To recruit participants, I first visited the prison with the female graduate assistants; I described the research to all of the women in the treatment unit and asked for volunteers. Because many women volunteered and satisfied the criteria for the study, they were invited to participate in order of the nearest approaching release dates. Interviews were conducted in private offices within the institution, away from correctional and treatment staff and other prisoners. The interviews covered a range of topics related to their experiences with methamphetamine such as their initiation into methamphetamine and other drug use, changes in their use over time, and periods of desistance. We also asked about their use of other drugs both in adolescence and adulthood, about their involvement in criminal activity, including participation in methamphetamine markets, and about experiences of violence over their lifetime.

The final study from which I draw is a study on women's experiences with firearms, in which I collaborated with Jody Miller and Christopher Mullins. What began as a project designed to interview women on probation or parole in the St. Louis region when they met with their probation or parole officers quickly proved very difficult, as the women often missed their appointments.[7] After many frustrating months with very few interviews to show for our efforts, we made the decision to augment our original sample with interviews from incarcerated women, remaining true, however, to our original intention of including relatively "criminally embedded" women. Because we were explicitly interested in the ways in which neighborhood contexts shape women's attitudes toward and experiences with firearms, we asked women about the communities in which they lived, and we also asked them to describe the types of problems they believed existed within their neighborhoods. Given our focus on firearms, we asked specifically about whether and how frequently they heard gunshots or saw people carrying or using guns within their neighborhoods. Before we began asking more specific questions about their own experiences with guns, we asked the women to describe their personal involvement in crime; such questions covered their most recent offense. Women who had been convicted of violent offenses were asked whether a weapon was used during commission. The rest of the women were asked why they did *not* use a weapon in their most recent crime. We then asked the women a series of questions about their personal experiences with firearms, including gun victimization.

These three studies have a number of important elements in common. While the institutions differ (the first study took place in a post-sentencing jail in Minnesota while the latter studies were both completed at a prison for women in Missouri),

I would argue that they all steadfastly maintained a more rehabilitative approach to women's incarceration, even in an era when many other institutions are shifting to a more austere approach (Kruttschnitt and Gartner, 2005). The studies involved only female interviewers, the majority of whom were relatively young and came from privileged backgrounds. They also interviewed exclusively women, many of whom were women of color and decidedly *not* from privileged backgrounds.

Women prisoners, as a whole, appear to have more extensive histories of disability, disadvantage, and misfortune than their male counterparts (Kruttschnitt and Gartner, 2003) and therefore present a number of unique challenges for researchers. For example, women in carceral settings are more likely than men to be on psychotropic medications. The side effects of these medications, which include sleepiness and trouble concentrating, as well as their administration (which seems to take forever when it interrupts an interview), can present additional challenges for researchers. In addition, the location of prisons and carceral institutions for women (many states have only one or two of them) may be far away from women's homes.[8] For this and other reasons, many women in prison rarely get visitors – which can work to a researcher's advantage or create problems for him/her. On the one hand, a woman may be inclined to meet with a researcher when called, if for no other reason than simply to pass the time. On the other hand, many researchers will ask correctional officers (as I did) to simply ask the women to come with them to a visiting area because they have a visitor. When the woman realizes that it is a researcher and not a "real" visitor, she may be disappointed. These are but a few of the challenges we faced while in the field with each of the projects.

Some Lessons Learned (the Hard Way)

Presumably the aforementioned guides will help one gain access to an institution, receive permission to conduct the research from one's institutional review board (IRB), and get past the inner ring of gatekeepers – the correctional staff. In what follows I identify three additional challenges that researchers inevitably face when interviewing in prison. More experienced scholars may argue that these are challenges faced by any researcher. Of course that may be true, but I also believe that prison research is unique. It is an environment that is likely quite unfamiliar to most researchers, involves asking difficult questions of a population who may have little incentive to tell the truth (whatever that might be) or who may in fact be punished for doing so, and requires considerations of self and safety not commonly encountered in everyday life. So the normal challenges of developing rapport with one's informants, of getting valid and reliable data (i.e., the "truth") and of asking sensitive questions are magnified. In critically and reflexively examining my own research experiences, I also attempt to provide a more transparent discussion of these challenges, the emotions they invoke, and some potentially useful strategies for managing them. Reflexivity – the ability to see oneself as central to the topic selected for research, to the observations made in the field, and to the analyses and conclusions drawn from the data – can be difficult to achieve in practice. Only by focusing inwardly can researchers discover the extent to which their own interests may have been imposed on the research process, influencing who is interviewed, how the interviews are conducted, and what information is gleaned from the interviews (Phillips and Earle, 2010).

Developing Rapport

Newman (1958) aptly described the paradox researchers who do prison-based research face: on the one hand, "rapport of adequate intensity must be developed quickly"; but this "mutual trust and confidence is somewhat more difficult to come by when the respondent is incarcerated and … seemingly arbitrarily summoned for an interview he [or she] knows nothing about" (p. 129). In these circumstances, early guides such as Newman's emphasized the importance of remaining as "aloof" from prison staff as possible (Newman, 1958, p. 130; see also Giallombardo, 1966). Other researchers suggest that getting the support of key actors will facilitate the cooperation of others. Kruttschnitt and Gartner (2005), for example, met with prisoners who served on the women's advisory council within the prison in order to introduce their research and ask for assistance. Without buy-in from those women, recruitment for their study would have been more difficult. But I would argue that there is more to developing rapport with our informants than simply avoiding any appearance of conspiring with the authorities. And it is not always possible to solicit support from a group within the prison in order to prove the legitimacy of one's research.

Probably most methods textbooks pay at least cursory attention to developing rapport with research participants, but the circumstances in prison are rather unique. Researchers themselves may feel sufficiently out of their element as to have trouble engaging informants; and there are other barriers as well. Generally people in prison are not there willingly, they may be skeptical about speaking with anyone other than their own attorney (if they have one),[9] or they may fear that they will be punished by prison staff if they do or do not participate. Even one's unfamiliarity with the prison regime itself – in terms of its structure, physical layout, security, rules, and patterns of behavior – can be disconcerting and create difficulties for researchers (Grimwade, 1999).

Nevertheless, many of the general tips for developing rapport should still hold true. For example, presentation of self is important (see Berg, 2007 for a full discussion). In a prison as elsewhere, how one dresses, speaks, and acts will influence how others view one. As researchers, we want to be viewed as professional, yet not as part of the prison administration; as being there to learn about the prisoners' experiences and possibly to help, and not as being there to get anyone into trouble. I found that prisoners were generally receptive to me as a graduate student. They were eager to help me "write my paper" (dissertation) and, because I was still a graduate student and dressed like one (rather than in more businesslike attire), it looked as though they were more comfortable speaking with me. When I returned to the field as an assistant professor, I was fortunate enough to still be able to "pass" as a student, though one who had likely been in school for a while. Yet I found that what I wore made a difference to how the women reacted to me. Wearing somewhat more formal clothing seemed to put too great a barrier between us, whereas wearing somewhat more casual (but still professional) clothing opened up that space. Of course it is also important to follow the rules of the institutions, which nearly always prohibit shorts, short skirts, and sleeveless tops – among other potentially revealing clothing in the summertime. (It should go without saying that designer clothing is likely not a good choice either, because of the social distance it can create.) But thinking about one's clothing may be time well spent if it means one less distraction during that brief window of opportunity we have for building some kind of relationship.

Beyond dressing the part, in order to develop rapport, it is also important to show interest in the interviewees themselves, as individuals. No matter how many times I would meet with potential participants, I would always feel a bit nervous about meeting the next one. Usually this would go away as soon as we sat down and I introduced myself. Occasionally, though, I would encounter someone who just was not interested in speaking with me or who, despite my best efforts, simply did not want to participate. And when I got one refusal, then often I would get another. Was this simply bad luck? I believe it had a lot more to do with my attitude and level of confidence. Rather than seeing each woman as a person, I would occasionally slip into a mindset of "must finish project" and see the women as a means to an end. Recognizing my own failures as a researcher (after having women refuse to participate) would shake my confidence. Sometimes I could overcome this, but there were other times when I would simply pack up and quit for the day, hoping that a new day might bring better results.

It is also important to continue building a relationship beyond the introductions. This means being an active listener and showing interest in what the interviewees are saying (Berg, 2007). Don't merely pause, waiting for the next opportunity to ask a question. One can convey active listening by making eye contact, nodding, and reacting appropriately to emotional cues. I would argue that it is perfectly acceptable to register emotion in our faces on the basis of what the informants tell us; as Liebling (1999, p. 149) suggests, research in any human environment, particularly a prison, is "almost impossible" without emotion. Given the main theme of the interviews I conducted, I heard many horrific tales of abuse and drug use. In fact the interviews that produce the most relevant material can also be those that produce the most pain and feelings of exploitation for the researcher (Phillips and Earle, 2010; see also Bosworth, 1999). Had I not reacted to such stories with some kind of emotion, merely because I too am human, I doubt the interviews would have yielded such rich data. And, perhaps more importantly, the interviewees may have felt uncomfortable about confiding such private information to someone so devoid of emotion. However, it is also important not to assume emotions on the basis of one's own background. Indeed, for some of the women I spoke with, abuse was either something they took for granted in their lives or something they had spent years dealing with and to which they did not want to return emotionally. Trying to take one's cue from the interviewee herself, in terms of how to engage emotionally, is best.

There is also sometimes a misconception that shared social characteristics will lead to deeper and more meaningful interview experiences. For example, as Miller (2010) points out, for a long time there was an uncritical assumption that, "when women interviewed women, their shared experiences *as women* would result in identification, rapport and, consequently, the authentic revelation of 'women's experiences'" (p. 163). This creates a challenge for researchers who study people in prison, because it would seem to suggest that only those researchers who have been in prison, or at least who have been involved in criminal offending, would be able to identify with this population and collect "authentic" data.[10] Thankfully, there is evidence that social distance can, in fact, be useful in research and empowering, as it offers an opportunity for the interviewee to serve as an expert (rather than vice versa; Miller, 2010). Overidentifying with the interviewee or – worse – trying to create some kind of false connection with him/her is never a good idea. One very brief example of this will demonstrate the foolishness of trying to appear to be "in the know" – and this is only concerning terminology, not what I did or did not do in my spare time. When we were working on the methamphetamine project, Missouri was experiencing a meth problem. The media were frequently talking about "smurfs" – the people who would go from store to store to purchase pills and other supplies to make meth. I thought I would use this same term during an interview and ask a woman if she was a smurf. One can probably guess the outcome – she looked at me as though I were completely crazy. That was most certainly not a term she or her circle of friends used. Luckily my ignorance of the drug world was further proof that I desperately needed information from her, and she continued the interview. Had I tried to identify with her by pretending to be a fellow user, though, I would have been in much bigger trouble and likely the interview would have been over right then and there.

While attempting to overidentify with the interviewee is problematic, it is important to make the most of the connections one might share with him/her. These can emerge from the interview naturally, however, as long as the focus remains on the interviewee. It is natural to want to talk about one's own experiences, or even just to say "me too," but the researcher must resist that temptation. It is *not* about us. However, there are times when connections are so obvious that it is nearly impossible not to talk about them during the interview. For example, I was visibly pregnant during two of the three projects. Because so many women in prison are mothers, it became quite routine for my interviews to devote at least a few minutes to discussing how far along I was, what the baby's sex was, whether I had a name picked out, whether I had other children, and all manner of questions people feel the need to ask of pregnant women. Typically the women would follow this up with a revelation about their own children, telling me names, ages, where they were, and – most importantly – how much they missed them.[11] I can't obviously suggest becoming pregnant in order to achieve better rapport with informants, but I have to say that, overall, this feature did seem to help break the tension at the beginning of interviews. And my discomfort in the institutional chairs and frequent need to find the officers for restroom breaks provided some humorous relief to the women's days.

Finally, it is also imperative to be attentive to one's own biases and preconceived notions and not to allow them to distort what one hears during an interview – or to be reflexive enough to recognize when they do (Phillips and Earle, 2010). This is important not only in order to foster active listening so as to demonstrate to the interviewee that one is indeed listening to what *they* have to say, but also in order to cultivate the interviewing relationship. As researchers, we may be shocked or disturbed at what our informants tell us, or we may assume causal relationships where none exists. Just because the literature tells us that early victimization experiences are correlated with later offending, it does not follow that this is the truth in their case. We need to be attentive to the ways in which we might distort or misrepresent our informants' experiences as a result of our own biographical experiences (Kruttschnitt and Gartner, 2005; Phillips and Earle, 2010).

Similarly, we must take care not to communicate to our informants any kind of disapproval or disgust over their experiences, because this can very quickly shut down any communication. One final example will illustrate what I mean by this. During the WEV data collection we had an interviewer who offended an informant during an interview. The rumor was that the interviewer expressed disdain for women engaged in prostitution – nearly half of our sample were sex workers. What exactly happened during the interview I will never know. But the interviewee went back to her pod and told others about the insensitive group of researchers that was coming to "study" them.[12] My fellow interviewer and I tried for a couple of weeks to continue the interviews, but with no success. No one wanted to talk to us. Because we were collecting data in the short-term jail, the population eventually turned over and we could begin with a clean slate. Had we been in a prison, the damage may have been too extensive and our project may have been derailed.

I believe that there are three lessons here. First, it is important to examine our biases *before* beginning a project, and think carefully whether we are able to handle what we might hear and still treat our informants with respect. Second, what our research colleagues do matters as well; they can derail our work as easily as we can. Third, in hindsight, immediate damage control would probably have been our best (proactive) option. Hosting a group meeting with women in the facility in order to explain the research project in more detail and answer questions may have helped us regain legitimacy among the women in the jail more quickly.

Getting at "the Truth"

A second challenge is that, because of the sorts of questions we are asking about offending and victimization, the reliability and validity of our data may be called into question. After all, why would we expect people, even if they can remember the specifics (see Morris and Slocum, 2010), to be completely honest about something as potentially stigmatizing as how frequently they have been arrested in any given month? Or to give us details about traumatic experiences they may have experienced in childhood? As Fox and colleagues (2011, p. 324) note, offenders or prisoners may not be "characterized by society as truthful or reliable data sources." Indeed determining "the truth" is a difficult process, because the prison environment contains many actors who "occupy different social, economic and political positions and who in turn may have very different perspectives, opinions, and experiences of the prison" (Grimwade, 1999, p. 298).

One strategy for dealing with this is to simply ask interviewees not to lie. I have not personally used this strategy, but a very insightful graduate student of mine has done so in his work with active offenders. During his interviews, alongside repeated assurances that anything they said would be kept confidential, he would remind them that, rather than lie, he preferred that they would simply not answer a particular question. Of course this strategy must be accompanied by a statement in the informed consent procedure that the informant can refuse to answer a question or end the interview at any time.

While I have not specifically asked that interviewees not lie, in each of the interviews I have conducted I have always made it clear that it is okay if they skip questions they prefer not to answer. When I sense hesitation in a response, particularly after questions I know to be sensitive, I will remind the interviewee that s/he may choose not to answer questions. This gives him/her control over what s/he responds to and reassures him/her that I am more interested in him/her as an individual than I am in the data. However, while interviewees may skip questions,[13] it may be that they return to them some way or another, later in the interview.

In Hlavka, Kruttschnitt, and Carbone-Lopez (2007), we used part of the WEV data to determine whether interpersonal experiences with violence were related to interview noncompletion rates.[14] Though some interviewees chose to skip certain sections of the interview (often those related to childhood sexual abuse or rape during adulthood), many of them utilized certain coping strategies during the interview and ultimately provided some information about their experiences. For example, some of the women talked around the violence; they did not provide details of their experience but focused on another aspect of the encounter. In one case, rather than describe the rape she experienced, a woman spoke instead about the treatment she received at the hospital where she went for care. Others would refuse to answer questions at the time they were asked, but would return to them *voluntarily* at a later point in the interview or during the debriefing time. We concluded that

> participants want to talk with interviewers about a range of traumatic experiences, but for some … it needs to be on their own time and on their own terms … careful listening and attention allow the interview to become participant-oriented, provid[ing] the participant with the freedom of disclosing in a variety of ways. (Hlavka et al., 2007, pp. 914–915)

Thus, being flexible during the interview and allowing informants to talk about their experiences *when* and *how* they want to do it is imperative.

At the same time, Miller (2010, p. 165) argues that "no matter how much we strive to improve the validity of our data when interviewing 'offenders on offending,' ultimately the interview itself cannot provide authentic access to individuals' 'experiences' [because] interviews are accounts." Our social location, including our position as researchers, matters in the interview exchange and will subsequently affect the accounts our informants give to explain themselves and their experiences (Miller, 2010). As was the case during the interviews I conducted while pregnant, my position influenced the responses women gave to me. However, these accounts give a unique (perhaps the only) means by which we can understand how "people organize views of themselves, of others, and of their social worlds" (Orbuch, 1997, p. 455). The stories we construct to make sense of our lives are an attempt to situate ourselves within society (McAdams, 2008), and this is as true of prisoners as it is of anyone else. Thus, while we "need to maintain some healthy skepticism about the extent to which interviews with 'offenders on offending' provide access to unmediated 'truth' about experiences, actions and motives," we must also acknowledge that they can still provide information about the social worlds our informants inhabit (Miller, 2010, p. 165). Ultimately, we need to recognize what interviews can and cannot give us.

Asking Sensitive Questions ... and Then Leaving

The final challenge for conducting interviews in prison concerns the questions we ask as criminologists. Asking sensitive questions is challenging in any research project; but often we ask questions that not only are personally embarassing, but also could have legal ramifications for our interviewees. In the three studies higlighted here, we asked a number of questions about women's criminal offending and their experiences of victimization. As a precaution, in both the meth and the firearm studies, we advised them during the informed consent process that they ran the risk of criminal or civil liability if, during the interview, they disclosed that they planned to harm themselves or others.[15] To minimize that risk, we indicated that we would not ask any questions that would generate this kind of information and that we recommended they avoid making any statements of this kind. Finally, we reminded them that they should not use their own name or anyone else's name on the recording and, if they did accidentally, that we could stop the recorder, erase, and record over it.

Beyond precautionary measures to prevent disclosure of information that we would have been compelled to report to authorities, we also spent considerable time thinking about *how* and *when* to ask the more sensitive questions of our study. This was done in an effort to rectify what Bosworth and colleagues (2005, p. 258) describe as "the collective failure of scholars to acknowledge the pain their questions may evoke in their participants [which] reveals a continuing, albeit unacknowledged, tendency to objectify our research participants."

First, I would argue that the timing of questions matters. Rapport between interviewer and interviewee may take some time to develop. For this reason, we found it best to ask the sensitive and potentially emotional questions toward the middle of the interview, after some degree of trust had been established. At the same time, though, they should not be asked at the end of the interview. We did not want the interviewees to leave the interview right at the height of their emotions. Instead we always tried to end the interviews on a more positive note, asking about plans for the future, or at least with more neutral debriefing questions about the interview experience itself.

Second, it is important that researchers have some strategies for dealing with the questions and the answers that may come during the interview itself. One of the best I found was simply reminding informants that we could take a break or slow down a bit if they looked like they were becoming upset. I also always tried to keep tissues with me, because there is nothing like trying to comfort a crying woman with institutional paper towels. And I tried to avoid imposing the traditional hierarchical relationship between interviewer and interviewee; I did this by answering their questions, when appropriate. Usually the questions they asked were simply attempting to try and understand what I was doing there. But, more than once, women asked me whether I had been a victim of violence, or what "I thought" about an experience they described. While I made it a point of responding truthfully to the former questions, when asked to give my opinion about their experiences, I was often rendered speechless. Herein lies one of the inherent ethical "dangers" for researchers who conduct research in prisons. Accounts of such research often highlight the difficulties that emerge from immersion in the prison environment and the role of conflict that such immersion can cause. The experiences of imprisonment that we hear may "confront and conflict with [our] personal values and perspectives ... in ways that may be emotionally difficult and distressing" (Grimwade, 1999, p. 296). So how did I handle such questions? In many cases I believed that the women were in fact in violent relationships, and sometimes I even feared for their safety. But how could I tell that to a woman who may not have the same background, privilege, and access to resources as me? Over time, I became a little more adept at separating my "researcher" self from my "human" self and giving them an answer. Was I biasing the data? Was I imposing my worldview on them? Perhaps. But I was trying to make the interview a little more balanced and less hierarchical.

Prisoners – and particularly women in prison – often have lengthy victimization histories. As uncomfortable as it can be for researchers to listen to these recounted tales of violence, what can be more problematic is not knowing what the prisoner will return to when s/he leaves the interview. The research process itself, describing one's feelings and experiences, may be "personally disturbing, emotionally harrowing, and/or dangerous given the disciplined nature of prison settings" (Grimwade, 1999, p. 296). If security practices within the institution require that prisoners be searched after meeting with visitors, these episodes might trigger or exaggerate post-traumatic stress symptoms after answering questions about prior victimization. If prisoners return to their cell or pod visibly upset, they might be called out or taunted by fellow prisoners. So it is also important for us to be particularly sensitive to ethical issues such as privacy, confidentiality, minimization of harm, and the safety of our research participants (Grimwade, 1999). I would suggest that researchers also find out whether the prison has resources such as mental health professionals or counselors to deal with any issues that may present themselves among the interviewees after they leave the interview. For example, in the meth study, the women were housed in a treatment unit, and we made sure that the treatment staff was aware of the types of questions we would be asking. The staff members assured us that they would be watchful for women who seemed particularly upset. In the WEV project, because the women would be released in a relatively short time, we also provided them with information on local resources such as crisis hotlines, domestic violence counseling and shelters, homeless shelters, legal assistance, and substance abuse treatment they could access after release.

Finally, this type of research can pose particular dilemmas for the researcher personally (see Bosworth, 1999; Phillips and Earle, 2010). There can be an overwhelming sense of responsibility for the interviewees themselves, for sharing their stories, and for helping others in their situations. And the interviews can be long and exhausting, both physically and emotionally; the accounts of violence and victimization, loss and neglect that we often hear from prisoners can be "sad and deeply troubling" (Phillips and Earle, 2010, p. 365). Indeed, during the WEV project we would complete only one or two interivews during a given visit, because of their length and emotional content. Some of the things we heard simply could not be unheard and, because of confidentiality, there were few people with whom we could debrief. Probably the most important lesson to be gleaned from these experiences was stated quite eloquently by Liebling (1999): "support (and time) needs to be built in to research which makes demands on the emotional lives of the researchers. Emotional experiences can be crucial clues in the process of research." Being mindful of one's emotional limits and realistic about the time required to collect the data can go a long way toward reducing stress. Spending time talking about the research process with others can also be cathartic.

Conclusion

Previous "how to" research guides provide some excellent tips for gaining access to correctional institutions. And, while the methodological details of prison-based research are often found in appendices or footnotes, there have been some examples of scholars who weaved important methodological information – including the challenges they faced – into their work (e.g., Kruttschnitt and Gartner, 2005; Owen, 1998). But, as a whole, researchers do not often share failures with one another, so it is difficult for novices to anticipate the types of challenges they will face in general – let alone within a prison – in conducting research with prisoners. Some researchers are beginning this dialogue, however, and sharing experiences and "lessons learned." One recent example is Fox and colleagues (2011), who discussed many of the administrative and logistical maneuvers required to successfully pursue prison-based research. This chapter was intended to some extent to pick up where they left off as it focused on the more interpersonal aspects of data collection within a prison setting.

Given the possible challenges of developing rapport within a carceral context, with informants who may be even more skeptical of our motives than usual, I argued that it is important for us to carefully consider our presentation of self (see Berg, 2007). Our actions and reactions, our words, even our clothing, matter in an interview setting and can affect whether we are able to build a connection with our informants. Remaining flexible in the timing of our questions (Hlavka et al., 2007) can also help build and maintain rapport during the interview and ultimately increase the quality of the data we collect. At the same time, however, we must recognize that, although we might develop rapport with our informants even to the point where they will discuss intimate details of their lives with us, we will never move beyond an outsider status (see Owen, 1998; Phillips and Earle, 2010).

It is important for us to keep in mind that the experience of conducting research within prison walls can be intellectually (and personally) rewarding, but simultaneously emotionally draining. The interviews can be emotional for interviewer and interviewee alike (see Bosworth, 1999; Liebling, 1999; Phillips and Earle, 2010). Similarly, immersion in the prison environment and listening to countless tales of violence and neglect may conflict with our own personal and political values. Considering in advance how to deal with the possible scenarios that might present themselves and being particularly cognizant of the privacy and safety of our research participants is imperative (Grimwade, 1999). Prison-based research "is an intense, risk-laden, emotionally fraught environment [which] makes demands on fieldworkers which are at times barely tolerable" (Liebling, 1999, p. 163). Yet without such exposure to the pain of prison life our research can only be, at best, superficial (Liebling, 1999).

Perhaps these lessons, learned from my own prison-based research, will be useful for others, who enter this world for the first time. Certainly they are things I wish that I had known before my introduction to the world of interviewing in correctional facilities. However, I am confident that personal experiences will prove even more enlightening for budding researchers, and perhaps those experiences can then be shared in similar formats for future generations.

Notes

1 Frankly, though, I wonder whether those criminologists, who suggest that prison is full of "unsuccessful" criminals who are far removed from criminal lifestyles, have ever spent much time in prison. Offenders in prison use and sell drugs (sometimes openly), fight, have illicit sexual relationships, rape, steal, and exploit fellow inmates all the time in prison.

2 I focus here on some of the articles and book chapters that have been published *specifically* for the purpose of providing tips and successful strategies for researchers who seek to conduct research within prisons or to gain entry into criminal justice organizations for research purposes.

3 There are some notable exceptions. For example, both Owen (1998) and Kruttschnitt and Gartner (2005) provide rather extensive descriptions of their experiences in accessing three separate women's facilities in California. Importantly, these authors also acknowledge some of the challenges they faced with the administration and the struggles they had in building rapport with the women they interviewed.

4 The original project was supported by a grant from the National Consortium on Violence Research (NCOVR) to Julie Horney, Sally Simpson, Rosemary Gartner, and Candace Kruttschnitt. The three sites were: Baltimore, MD; Minneapolis, MN; and Toronto, ON. Each Principal Investigator employed female graduate students for daily operation of the project.

5 Additional methodological details can be found in Carbone-Lopez and Kruttschnitt, 2010; Kruttschnitt and Carbone-Lopez, 2006; and Slocum, Rengifo, and Carbone-Lopez, 2012.

6 Additional methodological details can be found in Carbone-Lopez and Miller, 2012 and Carbone-Lopez, Owens, and Miller, 2012.

7 The Missouri Department of Corrections would not allow us access to personal information such as address or contact information for the women we wished to interview. We attempted to send the women letters via their probation or parole officers, inviting them to participate in the study and to call us; only one woman did so. Aside from missing appointments, many of the women with whom we wished to speak also ended up being reincarcerated for violating their probation or parole before we could meet with them.

8 The fact that there are fewer women in prison – and therefore fewer women's prisons – may also mean that access to women's prisons is more difficult to attain for researchers (see Grimwade, 1999).

9 While skepticism seems to be a general rule among prisoners, there is often some degree of curiosity, or at least boredom, that may work in the researcher's favor. Indeed, Copes, Hochstetler, and Brown (2013) conducted interviews with 40 prisoners after the latter had been interviewed for another project; the intention was to explore the prisoners' reasons for participating and the benefits and harm they may have experienced. On the basis of their analyses, Copes and colleagues suggest that, "after long periods under the supervision of the state, daily routines become monotonous, schedules become repetitive, and the acceptable subject matter for prisoner communication can become stifling and tiresome." As a result, "inmates said it was nice to interact casually with an interested but emotionally uninvolved stranger who cared little about the norms of conversational suppression and could not perpetuate gossip" (p. 186).

10 While there have been researchers who used their employment in the prison as a means to successfully access it as a research site (e.g., Carroll, 1974; Marquart, 1986), this can create additional challenges for developing rapport with prisoners.

11 Elsewhere we discuss how my visible pregnancy may have influenced their (gendered) narratives of self, addiction, and recovery (Miller, Carbone-Lopez, and Gunderman, 2015). For example, some of the women in our sample appeared able to draw from an articulation of normative gender identities as a "resource" for "doing meth use." They framed their continued use of the drug in normatively appropriate ways by emphasizing how its pharmacology assisted them, for example, in being good mothers.

12 The interviewer quit soon after this happened.

13 In the projects described here, the questions that seemed to be most frequently skipped involved whether women had ever participated in selling, purchasing ingredients for, or

cooking meth (the meth project) or, in cases where women wanted to get a firearm, how they would they go about doing it (the gun project). In other words, these were questions about very serious felony offenses, though – interestingly – there was less reluctance to answer questions about involvement in physical violence. Despite our assurances of confidentiality, the women were afraid of federal charges for the manufacture of methamphetamine on top of their state sentences, or they were worried that we were trying to somehow entrap them because they were felons and therefore could not legally purchase or own firearms. We tried rewording the latter question many times, and even dressing it as a hypothetical situation – and this helped; but the women were still wary.

14 Our analyses suggested that women with both childhood and adult experiences of violence had higher noncompletion rates than those with child or adult only violence or with no prior victimization (Hlavka et al., 2007).

15 A similar statement was included in the WEV informed consent procedure.

References

Berg, B. L. 2007. *Qualitative research methods for the social sciences*, 7th edn. Boston, MA: Allyn & Bacon.

Bosworth, M. 1999. *Engendering resistance: Agency and power in women's prisons*. Aldershot: Ashgate Dartmouth Publishing.

Bosworth, M., Campbell, D., Demby, B., Ferranti, S. M., and Santos, M. 2005. Doing prison research: Views from inside. *Qualitative Inquiry*, 11: 249–264.

Carbone-Lopez, K., and Kruttschnitt, C. 2010. Risky relationships? Assortative mating and women's experiences of intimate partner violence. *Crime and Delinquency*, 56: 358–384.

Carbone-Lopez, K., and Miller, J. 2012. Precocious role entry as a mediating factor in women's methamphetamine use: Implications for life course and pathways research. *Criminology*, 50: 187–220.

Carbone-Lopez, K., Owens, J. G., and Miller, J. 2012. Women's "storylines" of methamphetamine initiation in the Midwest. *Journal of Drug Issues*, 42: 226–246.

Carroll, L. 1974. *Hacks, blacks, and cons: Race relations in a maximum security prison*. Toronto: Lexington Books.

Charmaz, K. 2006. *Constructing grounded theory: A practical guide through qualitative analysis*. London: Sage.

Copes, H., Hochstetler, A., and Brown, A. 2013. Inmates' perceptions of the benefits and harm of prison interviews. *Field Methods*, 25: 182–196.

Fox, K., Zambrana, K., and Lane, J. 2011. Getting in (and staying in) when everyone else wants to get out: 10 lessons learned from conducting research with inmates. *Journal of Criminal Justice Education*, 22: 304–327.

Giallombardo, R. 1966. Interviewing in the prison community. *The Journal of Criminal Law, Criminology and Police Science*, 57: 318–324.

Grimwade, C. 1999. Diminishing opportunities: Researching women's imprisonment. In *Harsh punishment: International experiences of women's imprisonment*, edited by S. Cook and S. Davies, 291–313. Boston, MA: Northeastern University Press.

Hlavka, H. R., Kruttschnitt, C., and Carbone-Lopez, K. 2007. Revictimizing the victims? Interviewing women about interpersonal violence. *Journal of Interpersonal Violence*, 22: 894–920.

Jeffords, C. R. 2007. Gaining approval from a juvenile correctional agency to conduct external research. *Youth Violence and Juvenile Justice*, 5: 88–99.

Kruttschnitt, C., and Carbone-Lopez, K. 2006. Moving beyond the stereotypes: Women's subjective accounts of their violent crime. *Criminology*, 44: 321–351.

Kruttschnitt, C., and Gartner, R. 2003. Women's imprisonment. *Crime and Justice*, 30: 1–81.

Kruttschnitt, C., and Gartner, R. 2005. *Marking time in the Golden State: Women's imprisonment in California*. Cambridge, UK: Cambridge University Press.

Kvale, S. 1996. *Interviews: An introduction to qualitative research interviewing*. Thousand Oaks, CA: Sage.

Liebling, A. 1999. Doing research in prison: Breaking the silence. *Theoretical Criminology*, 3: 147–173.

Marquart, J. W. 1986. Prison guards and the use of physical coercion as a mechanism of prisoner control. *Criminology*, 24: 347–366.

McAdams, D. P. 2008. Personal narratives and the life story. In *The Handbook of Personality*, edited by O. P. John, R. W. Robins, and L. A. Pervin, 3rd edn., pp. 242–262. New York: Guilford.

Miller, J. 2010. The impact of gender when interviewing "offenders on offending." In *Offenders on offending: Learning about crime from criminals*, edited by W. Bernasco and M. Tonry, 161–183. London: Willan Press.

Miller, J., Carbone-Lopez, K., and Gunderman, M. K. 2015. Gendered narratives of self, addiction, and recovery among women methamphetamine users. In *Narrative criminology: Understanding stories of crime*, edited by L. Presser and S. Sandberg, 69–95. New York: NYU Press.

Morris, N. A., and Slocum, L. A. 2010. The validity of self-reported prevalence, frequency, and timing of arrest: An evaluation of data collected using a life event calendar. *Journal of Research in Crime and Delinquency*, 47: 210–240.

Newman, D. J. 1958. Research interviewing in prison. *The Journal of Criminal Law, Criminology and Police Science*, 49: 127–132.

Orbuch, T. L. 1997. People's accounts count: The sociology of accounts. *Annual Review of Sociology*, 23: 455–478.

Owen, B. 1998. *In the mix: Struggle and survival in a women's prison*. Albany, NY: SUNY Press.

Patenaude, A. L. 2004. No promises, but I'm willing to listen and tell what I hear: Conducting qualitative research among prison inmates and staff. *The Prison Journal*, 84: 69S–91S.

Phillips, C., and Earle, R. 2010. Reading difference differently? Identity, epistemology and prison ethnography. *British Journal of Criminology*, 50: 360–378.

Schlosser, J. A. 2008. Issues in interviewing inmates: Navigating the methodological landmines of prison research. *Qualitative Inquiry*, 14: 1500–1525.

Slocum, L. A., Rengifo, A. F., and Carbone-Lopez, K. 2012. Specifying the strain–violence link: The role of emotions in women's descriptions of violent incidents. *Victims and Offenders*, 7: 1–29.

Spradley, J. P. 1979. *The ethnographic interview*. Belmont, CA: Wadsworth.

Trulson, C. R., Marquart, J. W., and Mullings, J. L. 2004. Breaking in: Gaining entry to prisons and other hard-to-access criminal justice organizations. *Journal of Criminal Justice Education*, 15: 451–478.

24

Spatial Analysis of Crime

Steven M. Radil

Introduction

A now well established observation in the quantitative study of crime has been that many types of crime are not randomly distributed in geographical space (Brantingham and Brantingham, 1981, 1984). This observation has been made repeatedly, both on spatially aggregated and disaggregated criminal event data and on data at different spatial scales. For example, research has demonstrated the spatial clustering of homicide rates at the local (e.g., Cohen and Tita, 1999), county (Messner et al., 1999), and national scales (e.g., Cork, 1999). Such observations about the geography of crime led to a large number of studies in criminology that attempted to explain spatial patterning through reference to the characteristics of the social environments in which crimes took place. These studies, referred to broadly as ecological studies of crime, often initially treated the spatial patterning of crime as a nuisance rather than a substantive topic; any observed spatial patterns were thought to be the result of the pregiven spatial distribution of environmental features typically associated with high levels of crime (e.g., poverty, unemployment, family structure), unobserved or omitted variables, or some combination of both (Tita, Cohen, and Enberg, 2005). However, repeated attempts to control for space in statistical models were insufficient, as the spatial clustering of crime could not be adequately controlled for or explained away. These early efforts were important as they shifted the understanding of the geography of crime away from seeing it as a nuisance for statistical modeling and toward creating substantive and growing subfields within both criminology and geography (LeBeau and Leitner, 2011; Tita and Radil, 2011).

The Handbook of Measurement Issues in Criminology and Criminal Justice, First Edition.
Edited by Beth M. Huebner and Timothy S. Bynum.

Quantitative approaches to crime now embody a wide range of spatial statistical techniques and models that explicitly give consideration to spatial properties such as location, relative spatial patterning, spatial arrangements, or distance (Bailey and Gatrell, 1995; Levine, 2006). Even at their most basic, these spatial properties make spatial statistics more complex than nonspatial statistics which creates a relatively high entry cost for those interested in spatial approaches. To help minimize such costs, this chapter provides a general overview of two primary classifications of spatial analysis relevant to criminology: areal (or area-based) and point-based spatial analyses. Areal approaches utilize information that has been aggregated into various two-dimensional geographical units, such as census blocks, police precincts, neighborhoods, and the like. Conversely, point-based approaches utilize information that has been precisely located in geographical space and represented as point locations with zero area. The differences between these two approaches are not absolute and some of the specific techniques described can be seen as belonging to both. In general, however, each approach lends itself to different research questions and employs different analytic methods.

What follows is intended to be a general guide through the broad field of spatial analysis for criminology rather than an exhaustive, or even comprehensive survey. It is worth noting that each topic described in this chapter represents a large and sometimes quite distinct area of research in its own right. With that in mind, the discussion emphasizes the overall concepts that underpin the described techniques over the presentation of any specific formulas and their variants; citations of key texts and examples are also provided that should allow researchers to develop in-depth knowledge of any particular technique. Important texts referred to through the chapter include the excellent (though typically quite technical) books on spatial analysis by Cliff and Ord (1981), Anselin (1988), Isaaks and Srivastava (1989), Cressie (1993), Bailey and Gatrell (1995), Diggle (2003), Haining (2003), Ripley (2004), and Chun and Griffith (2013). These texts, and recent handbooks and guides on spatial analysis, such as Fotheringham and Rogerson (2008) or Ward and Gleditsch (2008), are typically written from the perspective of statisticians or from disciplinary perspectives other than criminology. Some guides and reviews specific to the spatial analysis of crime exist, for example Hirschfield and Bowers (2001) and Messner and Anselin (2004), but these are partial in that they do not cover the breadth of spatial analysis. This state of affairs means that criminologists interested in spatial analysis must still largely immerse themselves in a literature that has been developed outside of the specific issues and traditions of their field. As with any import, care is needed in adapting these techniques and ideas to the primary concerns of criminology.

The rest of the chapter is organized as follows. First, the special nature of spatial data is introduced. Next follows an overview of each approach, areal and point-based, emphasizing the differences between the two and introducing the dominant techniques utilized by each. The chapter concludes with a discussion about three important conceptual and theoretical concerns for criminologists interested in spatial analysis.

The Nature of Spatial Data

Like much of social science, the analysis of crime is observational rather than experimental, which simply means that researchers do not specify the geographical location of their observations. Because of this, the location of criminal acts may be important information for researchers, particularly when the nature of the place or space in which the crime occurs is thought to affect the processes that generate crime (e.g., Morenoff, Sampson, and Raudenbush, 2001). Spatial data, then, are those with information about the location of each observation in geographical space (Haining, 2009). In criminology, data tend to be focused on events such as a criminal act, or on the social actors that commit crimes, for instance a gang. In either case, location can be seen as one of many possible attributes (or variables) of a set of events or actors.

A fundamental property of spatial data is the overall tendency for the values of a variable that are near each other to be more alike than are those that are further apart. This property has been described as the notion that "everything is related to everything else but near things are more related than distant things" (Tobler, 1970, p. 236) and is often referred to as the "first law of geography." Although Tobler's statement is more of a general truism than a universal law, it rightly points out that the spatial clustering of similar objects, events, people, and places on the surface of the earth is the norm. The spatial patterns that result from such clustering have been of intrinsic interest to many social scientists, including criminologists (e.g., Haining, 2003). This property of spatial data is called *spatial dependence* – a name designed to reflect the idea that the observed value of a variable in one location is often dependent (to some degree) on the observed value of the same variable at a nearby location.

Spatial dependence has important implications for researchers. First, the notion of distance-based dependence means that a variable observed at a particular location contains information about nearby locations. This property allows informed estimates about unobserved values of the same variable in nearby locations (e.g., spatial interpolation), which is central to the estimation of crime "hot spot" surfaces (e.g., McLafferty, Williamson, and McGuire, 2000). Second, distance-based dependence violates one of the basic assumptions for classical inferential statistical models: that random observations of a variable are independent, and therefore produce unbiased and efficient parameter estimates. As noted by Chun and Griffith (2013, p. 17), spatial dependence often inflates the variance among a set of observations; this effect can undermine the validity of inferences drawn from such data (e.g., Anselin, 1988).

Another intrinsic property of spatial data is that the underlying process that governs the values that can be assumed by a variable varies from place to place or across space. This tendency, known as *spatial heterogeneity*, is often due to limited scale processes or to location-specific effects (Fotheringham, 1997). This spatial nonstationarity has an important consequence for statistical modeling: a single global relationship for an overall region of study may not adequately model the process that governs outcomes in any given location of the study region. Further, variations in local relationships can lead to inconsistent estimates of the effect of variables at "global" levels of analysis if the relationship between the dependent variable of interest and the independent variables is characterized by a nonlinear function (Fotheringham, Charlton, and Brundson, 2002).

Exploratory spatial data analysis

Both of these properties have been central to the development of quantitative analytic techniques that assess and accommodate the nature of spatial data for both descriptive and inferential statistical analysis and modeling (e.g., Goodchild, 2004). A collection of different methods and techniques have been developed for visualizing and assessing the presence and degree of spatial dependence or heterogeneity in spatially organized data. This set of techniques have been referred to collectively as exploratory spatial data analysis (ESDA) (Anselin, 1998). The key steps of an ESDA involve describing and visualizing the presence and degree of both spatial dependence and spatial heterogeneity in one's variables of interest. ESDA typically involves calculating descriptive spatial statistics and mapping variables in order to identify atypical locations (so-called "spatial outliers"); in order to uncover patterns of spatial association (cluster analysis); and in order to assess any change in the associations between variables across space (spatial nonstationarity). A comprehensive review of the techniques of ESDA is beyond the scope of this chapter. However, there are a growing number of treatments of this topic in criminology, for both areal and point data. General introductions of ESDA can be found in Anselin (1998, 1999), while treatments of ESDA specific to criminology are presented in Chakravorty and Pelfrey (2000), Williamson et al. (2001), and Weisburd, Bernasco, and Bruinsma (2009).

Spatial dependence in located data can be assessed and measured statistically by considering the amount of *spatial autocorrelation* among the values of a single variable observed in different locations or between pairs of variables observed at identical locations. Spatial autocorrelation occurs when the measured values of a variable (or variables) sampled at nearby locations are not independent of one another (Cliff and Ord, 1981). When similar values cluster together in geographical space, the variable is said to be positively spatially autocorrelated. Alternatively, when very different values cluster, the variable is negatively spatially autocorrelated. Spatial autocorrelation may be either positive or negative. Positive spatial autocorrelation is a very common feature, particularly in the built environments that provide the setting for much of the study of crime. This is partly due to the self-segregation of people in such environments along educational, economic, political, cultural, or other similar dimensions of identity. Many similar land-use activities also cluster together in urban environments, which forms another basis for positive spatial autocorrelation. Negative spatial autocorrelation is far less commonly observed and spatial research in criminology has concerned itself only with the presence of positive spatial autocorrelation (e.g., Baller et al., 2001).

Spatial autocorrelation is an important aspect of spatially organized data for criminological research, as most inferential statistical models assume that sampled observations are independent of one another. Accordingly, the task under such circumstances is to first measure the strength of spatial autocorrelation in crime data and to test the assumption of spatial independence or randomness. Several measures of spatial autocorrelation have been developed for both areal and point data and have been implemented in a number of statistical software packages. A general review of the spatial autocorrelation techniques specific to both types of data is provided in the respective sections below.

Areal Spatial Data

Spatial data are observations on a variable or set of variables of interest where the geographical location of each observation is also recorded. Location information can be represented as occurring either within the boundaries of a discrete two-dimensional area or at the intersection of a pair of coordinates in two-dimensional space. Data located by using the former approach are described as areal data, and many different types of geographical units are commonly used to divide up and manage spaces within a city or region for a multitude of social purposes. In consequence, there are numerous areal-unit systems that can be seen as relating to the occurrence and management of crime (see Weisburd, Bruinsma, and Bernasco, 2009). Examples include political, legal, or jurisdictional boundaries like neighborhoods, census units, or policing districts. Areal data also typically consist of aggregated information: information that is grouped together on the basis of shared location within a discrete area unit, such as a neighborhood. A common example of aggregated crime data is that of crime counts, where all the instances of a particular type of crime that occurred within the boundaries of a specific areal unit are added up and assigned to that area. Crime rates – or a ratio measurement of crime counts against some other measurable feature of an areal unit, such as population or land area – are another very common type of areal data.

Spatial autocorrelation analysis

When organized spatially, areal crime data often display positive spatial autocorrelation (e.g., Gorman et al., 2001). A large number of statistical tests have been developed that are appropriate for use with areal data; the most well known and commonly utilized are the join count statistic, Moran's *I*, and Geary's *C* tests (Cliff and Ord, 1973). The join count statistic is appropriate for binary nominal data, while both Moran's *I* and Geary's *C* are appropriate for continuous interval or ratio-level measurements. These are also examples of "global" measures of spatial autocorrelation in that they summarize the total deviation from spatial randomness across a set of spatial data with a single statistic, although they do so in different ways. For example,

Moran's *I* is a cross-product coefficient similar to a Pearson correlation coefficient and ranges from -1 (perfect negative spatial autocorrelation) to +1 (perfect positive spatial autocorrelation). Geary's *C* is based on squared deviations and values of less than 1 indicate positive spatial autocorrelation, while values larger than 1 suggest negative spatial autocorrelation. As a counterpart to these global statistics, there are also local statistics that assess the presence of local spatial clusters in a study region by comparing local averages to global averages across a set of spatial units. The two most commonly used local measures of spatial autocorrelation are the *Gi** statistics (Getis and Ord, 1992) and the local Moran's *I* (Anselin, 1995).

Although the technical details vary, these types of tests all assess spatial autocorrelation against a null hypothesis of spatial randomness. At the most basic level, the way this is done is by comparing the observed values in each areal unit to those in "neighboring" units. For example, consider the join count statistic, which is used for binary nominal data (Cliff and Ord, 1970). If a set of areal units are categorized as either high crime (H) or low crime (L), the join count first sums the number of areal units adjacent to a focal unit that (1) have the same observed value as the focal unit (H adjacent to H or L adjacent to L) and (2) have the different value as the focal unit (HL or LH). When similar values cluster, there will be relatively few HL/LH outcomes. Although used for continuous rather than for nominal data, Moran's *I* and Geary's *C* tests follow a similar logic: influential neighbors are defined and a measure of spatial autocorrelation is calculated on the basis of the neighbors which is then compared to an expected value that would be realized if the data values were spatially randomly distributed.

Defining neighbors for spatial analysis

A critical first step in all of these tests is to define the conditions under which, or criteria according to which, a given spatial unit may be understood as a "neighbor" to a focal unit. This is often done through simple geometric measures of spatial adjacency or contiguity or through distance-based measures. The specification of the neighbor's conditions or criteria can impact the results of these tests, so some care is needed; the formulation of the neighbor relationship should be grounded in a particular theory or rationale that sets expectations for the spatial form of the particular process under investigation (Leenders, 2002; Tita and Radil, 2011). Once a theory about the connection between areal units is established, the number of commonly used criteria can be employed to specify the neighbor relationships.

Two geometric measures common in defining neighbor relationships are referred to as "Rook" and "Queen" contiguity. These both evoke the logic of the chessboard and the movement rules assigned to the rook and the queen respectively. Rook contiguity defines neighbors as those areal units that share non-zero length boundaries; on a chessboard, this would typically mean that each unit would have four neighbors. The Queen's case differs slightly in that neighbors may be defined through zero-length boundaries – such as a shared corner. Sticking with the chessboard analogy, the typical number of neighbors in this circumstance would be eight.

"Neighbors of neighbors" may also be considered (immediate neighbors are often described as first-order contiguous, while neighbors of neighbors would be second-order ones), as can custom formulations based on some other understanding of how and why some areal units are connected in geographical space and therefore influential. Examples here might include features that enable movement between areas, such as street networks, or perhaps other shared attributes, such as similar land use.

Distance-based measures are also commonly used in areal data but require of one to first define a single point that represents each area (typically, the approximate geographical center of the area) in order to calculate measures of the distance between units. When distance is used to define neighbors, the analyst must also decide upon a distance threshold at which the connection between units and whether to use a distance decay function that gives more weight to closer locations. A slightly hybrid approach to a distance-based logic that is also frequently used with areal data is the "k-nearest neighbor" case, where analysts can specify in advance the number of neighboring units, no matter how far away they may be in geographical space. For instance, a fourth nearest neighbor case means that every spatial unit has exactly four neighbors, even if a unit shares boundaries with more than four other units. This enables analysts to connect distant or disconnected areas to those that are nearest without pre-specifying a distance threshold for the relationship. However, this form requires some thought to the selection of the number of neighbors (Cliff and Ord, 1981).

All of these processes of establishing neighbors for areal units result in what is called a "spatial weights matrix," which is the formal construct of locational similarity required by every spatial autocorrelation test statistic. This is a square (n x n) matrix, where n is the total number of areal units and the value of each cell is interpreted as the measure of connection between a pair of units. This measure can be binary (0 for no connection, 1 for a connection) or continuous, to reflect differing degrees of connection. The matrix is used to define the set of neighbors for each focal unit, which also defines the set of values used to assess autocorrelation. If either positive or negative spatial autocorrelation is present, the basic assumption of unit independence for statistical modeling is violated, which can result in biased and inconsistent estimates for all the coefficients in the model, biased standard errors, or both (Anselin, 1988). This has led to the adoption of statistical models that model spatial dependence either by including a spatial interaction variable in the model or through the error term.

Spatial regression

Although there are many types of variants to regression models that have been developed for spatially autocorrelated data, the standard models for areal spatial data are referred to as simultaneous autoregressive (SAR) models (Anselin, 2006). SAR models typically assume one of two basic forms (Anselin, 1988, 2002; Haining, 2003). The first SAR model assumes that spatial autocorrelation is present only in the dependent variable (i.e., the response variable). To accommodate spatial autocorrelation in the dependent variable, an additional covariate is introduced to other, independent variables (i.e., predictor variables). This new variable is referred to as a "spatial lag," which is a weighted average of values for the dependent variable. Such values are calculated from the units defined as "neighbors" in the spatial weights matrix and are often used as a proxy for interaction effects across, such as contagious diffusion or travel-to-crime approaches. For example, if the dependent variable was a measure of crime activity, the new covariate would be a weighted average measure of crime activity in all "neighboring" areas. Because the new spatial lag variable introduces simultaneity into the explanatory variables (part of the value for any focal dependent unit is always present in the spatial lag variable), the regression residuals will be correlated with the spatial lag variable. This means that specialized estimation methods must be used; these are typically maximum likelihood measures.

The second SAR model addresses spatial autocorrelation in the error term. In this case, the error term is composed of a spatially autocorrelated component that is based on the spatial weights matrix and of a stochastic component; the rest is as in the spatial lag model. This resolves the simultaneity problem created by introducing a spatial lag covariate, but can be more difficult to interpret. For instance, the strength and direction of the coefficient of a spatial lag variable can be understood as the strength or intensity of interaction between a focal area and its defined neighbors. On the other hand, the spatial error component is often seen as a result of some unobserved or unmeasurable process (sometimes referred to as the "neighborhood effect"), or when the spatial unit of observation differs significantly from the spatial extent of the phenomena under study (such as highly localized events aggregated into very large areas). While the source of the autocorrelation is unknown in either circumstance, model residuals will present spatial autocorrelation and therefore can be addressed through the introduction of an additional spatial error term.

Whether the areal approach to spatial data involves descriptive statistics (measures of spatial autocorrelation) or predictive modeling (SAR models), its aggregated nature has important consequences for researchers. First, areal data are grouped from a collection of individual or discrete observations (each of which can be represented as a point location in geographical space). As a consequence, the amount of aggregation is typically a function of the relative size and configuration of the spatial areal units. Descriptive statistics of areally aggregated data have been shown to be quite sensitive to the amount of aggregation and to the inconsistent size and configuration of commonly used geographical units, like census units (Openshaw, 1984). For example, the variation of aggregated data typically decreases as the size of the set of areal units increase. These effects are collectively referred to as the modifiable areal unit problem (MAUP) and are really a series of interconnected problems concerning the spatial scale of aggregation (the "scale" problem) and the configuration of the boundaries between a system of areal units (the "shape" or "zoning" problem). A full treatment of MAUP for spatial analysis is beyond the scope of this chapter; at a minimum, researchers are encouraged to use the smallest areal units possible so as to preserve variation in the unaggregated data as much as possible (see Openshaw, 1996; Haining, 2009).

Second, and related to the above discussion, researchers often work with crime data that have been collected and aggregated by others, such as police departments, into preexisting political or jurisdictional areal units. These units typically vary in size and shape, which can exasperate the MAUP. A recommended approach is to begin with disaggregated data wherever possible and to impose a consistently sized and shaped areal system for aggregation purposes. However, many covariates to crime that are of interest to researchers, such as education or class, are themselves available only in aggregate form. This can lead to the adoption of the areal system used to report covariates as the primary spatial unit of analysis, which nearly always involves variation of the size and shape of the areal units that leads to the problems associated with MAUP.

While these problems are well documented, there are no easy and widely employed solutions. MAUP is intrinsic to spatial data, but it is also a function of how data are recorded and organized by the many different social and political entities that are involved with crime and law enforcement. Hence the presence of MAUP effects and of the alternatives available to address them are largely beyond the control of individual researchers. In the absence of full control over the amount of aggregation in crime data and in possible covariates, and over the system of spatial units used for aggregation, the best advice remains to be aware of these issues as they can limit the value of findings from research that utilizes aggregated data.

Other issues commonly encountered by researchers who use aggregated spatial data are border effects and the challenges of the ecological fallacy. Border effects refer to the fact that the often arbitrary boundaries between study regions may exclude information that affects outcomes within those regions (see Griffith, 1983). The ecological fallacy – the difficulty in inferring individual behavior from aggregate data – is ever present in many social sciences that attempt to predict individual behavior from an analysis of geographically aggregated data (see King, 1997; O'Loughlin, 2003) While well established in geography, these issues tend to resurface in other disciplines as spatial analysis becomes more prevalent (for an example, see Hipp, 2007). For a review of the treatment of some of these issues in the spatial analysis of crime see Weisburd and colleagues (2009).

Point Spatial Data

A crime event can be grouped together with other nearby events and summarized by using any sort of two-dimensional spatial areal unit. But the location of an individual event itself can also be described as the intersection of a pair of geographical coordinates. Spatial data of this type evoke the traditional "pushpin" maps used to examine the location of crime and are most often associated with "hot spot" analysis (LaVigne and Groff, 2001). When locations are precisely known, spatial point data can be used with a variety of spatial analytic techniques that go beyond the methods typically applied to areal data. Although point data can be aggregated into areal units, the reverse in infrequently true. In consequence, point data can have more utility for researchers, as they enable their own set of analytic methods while also preserving the option to pursue areal analyses as well. The set of methods unique to point data are often referred to as point pattern analysis and geostatistics (Isaaks and Srivastava, 1989), and many different approaches to detecting hot spots are summarized in a number of key texts in spatial analysis (Cressie 1993; Bailey and Gatrell, 1995; Diggle, 2003; Ripley, 2004). The most commonly utilized methods of hotspot analysis are described below.

The ESDA of point data largely has the same goal as the ESDA of areal data: to uncover both global (a single measure for a set of locations) and local (a measure for each spatial location) patterns of spatial dependence, association, or clustering. In criminology, this has most often been expressed through the notion of crime "hot spots" (Sherman, Gartin, and Buerger, 1989; Sherman and Weisburd, 1995). A hot spot is a spatial concentration of a set of discrete crime events – that is, crime events that cluster together in geographical space – over a defined time period. The goal of a hotspot analysis is to therefore consider the locational patterns of a set of events against some expected spatial pattern. Typically the expected spatial pattern is assumed to be random, which forms the null hypothesis in formal statistical tests. However, a key difference between the types of spatial clustering techniques common to areal measures described in the previous section and point-based analyses is that areal approaches typically assess the spatial distribution of the values of a variable across a set of possible locations (areal units), while point-based analysis explicitly emphasizes the location of events themselves (within a defined study area) as the primary analytic focus.

The most basic type of analysis of point data is called "point pattern analysis"; in criminology, this typically involves plotting the locations of crime events in a two-dimensional geographical space. This is done in order to search for spatial patterns in the event locations in the hope that revealing such patterns will lead to a better understanding of the processes that produced them. Of course, mapping is central to this type of analysis, and interest in point pattern analysis led to an early adoption of the use of geographical information systems in criminology – early, that is, by comparison with its adoption in other social sciences (e.g., Clarke, 1990). The examination of a point pattern map considers whether the spatial distribution of crime events displays any sort of pattern. Basic assessments of spatial point-patterning may include calculating descriptive measures of central tendency and dispersion for an entire set of points (e.g., mean center of a set of points, or the standard distance around a mean center). More commonly, such assessments involve measurements of the relative location of points to each other. Assessing the relative location of points within a study area focuses on whether the locations are clustered together in geographical space, are uniformly dispersed, or are randomly spatially distributed.

Random point patterns are patterns in which every location in the study area is equally likely to receive a point. Depending on the type of crime, this type of outcome is rare in criminology (Brantingham and Brantingham, 1993). For example, one wouldn't expect every possible coordinate pair of a city block to be equally likely to be the location of a violent crime. Nonetheless, most point pattern analyses are based on calculating the departure from some expected measure of complete spatial randomness among a set of point events. Although several approaches have been developed to address this general concern about spatial data, four of the most important techniques are summarized below: quadrat analysis, nearest neighbor analysis, and kernel density estimates.

Quadrat analysis

Quadrat analysis focuses on changes in the density of points within a defined area across a study region (Ripley, 2004). The method begins by overlaying a regularly sized grid on the study region and uses the grid cells (called "quadrats") as new analytical units. The number of points that fall within each cell is calculated and the observed frequency of points per cell can then be compared to a theoretical distribution based on spatial randomness. A clustered spatial distribution of points would be characterized by relatively few sets of cells that contain large numbers of points while a uniform distribution would be characterized by a similar number of points falling within each cell. A random spatial distribution of points across the grid would likely be neither clustered not uniform. Most commonly, a random spatial distribution is theorized as one described by a Poisson distribution for which the variance and mean of the points per cell are equal. Therefore such patterns will have a variance-to-mean ratio of 1. Clustered distributions are then those with variance-to-mean ratios greater than 1, and uniform distributions have variance-to-mean ratios approaching 0. Examples of the quadrat analysis of crime can be found in Chakravorty (1995) and Wing and Tynon (2006).

While relatively simple and intuitive, a quadrat analysis can suffer from a number of conceptual problems that have limited its usefulness in criminology. First, because in a particular type of crime the process of interest may be continuous in geographical space, how a study region is bounded may impact the fundamental nature of the observed point distribution in that region. For example, increasing or decreasing the size of the study region could introduce or remove points that might alter the overall pattern. Related to this is the notion that a dispersed pattern at one scale may be clustered as another. Increasing or decreasing the scale, and therefore the area encompassed by a study region, may change one's interpretations about the amount of clustering among a set of points. A second problem has to do with the size of the cells used in the analysis. The choice of cell size is up to the analyst, but choosing a larger cell size can smooth over variation that would be revealed if smaller cells were used. A third problem is in the shape of the cells themselves. Variants of a grid-based quadrat analysis have been developed by using circles in place of square grid cells. However, circles can oversample some spaces in the study region (where circles overlap) and undersample others (where spaces are uncovered by any circle). These various limitations have stimulated efforts to develop novel solutions, and many different versions of the basic quadrat analysis are commonly utilized as exploratory tools in criminology. For example, Wang, Liu, and Eck (2014) utilized a quadrat analysis of simulated crime data in an urban area; their analysis constrained the gridded space under examination to road networks, in order to exclude the possibility of estimating hot spots in spaces other than pedestrian and police patrol corridors.

Nearest neighbor analysis

Another problem of quadrat analysis is that it is insensitive to the spatial arrangement of points with cells. For instance, consider a set of crime events that are distributed evenly across a pair of cells but whose locations are very close to the boundary of the cells. Under such circumstances, a quadrat analysis would treat this spatial arrangement as spatially uniform. However, to the eye, the crime events would appear to be clustered, because the distances between them are relatively short. Nearest neighbor analysis provides an alternative type of point pattern analysis, one that takes into account the distance between points rather than just their distribution across a set of cells.

Nearest neighbor analysis begins by calculating the distance between each pair of points in order to derive the minimum distance between each point and its closest neighboring point. The mean of the set of minimum distances can be compared to the mean expected minimum distance of a randomly point pattern; this will produce a ratio designed to distinguish between clustered or dispersed patterns. The ratio of the observed mean minimum distance and the expected mean minimum distance (assuming randomness) is called the nearest neighbor index and ranges from 0 to 2.15. The index equals 1 for random spatial patterns, approaches 0 for clustered patterns, and approaches 2.15 for uniform patterns. Nearest neighbor analysis has been used more frequently in criminology than quadrat analysis; recent examples include hotspot analyses of the location of robberies (Van Patten, McKeldin-Coner, and Cox, 2009) and of registered sex offenders (Socia and Stamatel, 2012).

Kernal density analysis

Related to these examples of global assessments of point patterns is the use of point data to create grid-based surfaces for a study region. There is a large set of spatial interpolation techniques that use point data, in an attempt to create a continuous estimate of crime events across space (Cressie, 1993). Put another way, spatial interpolation techniques, such as inverse distance-weighting, attempt to estimate the value of a variable at unsampled locations. When applied to event locations (rather than to the value of some variable at a precise location), this type of estimation can produce continuous surfaces that estimate the density of events even where events were not observed. This approach, referred to as kernel estimation, is widely used in criminology to define the potential for crime across a study area and has become an important tool in assessing the local risk of crime on the basis of the location of a set of observed or recorded events (e.g., Liu and Brown, 2003).

Kernel estimation begins with the creation and overlay of a uniform grid across a study region – just as in a quadrat analysis. After this, a circular window is drawn around the center of each grid location. This window encompasses an area that must be defined by the analyst (this distance from the focal point that defines the area encompassed by the window is called the bandwidth of the kernel) and is used to calculate a weighted density measure of the points for each grid cell. Points within the window are weighted by their distance from the center of the window according to a distance-based function chosen by the analyst; points lying closer to the center of the window are given greater weight than points lying further away. The combination of window size and distance-weighting function is referred to as "the kernel." The kernel is applied to each grid cell, one by one (this process is known as a "moving window"), and the result is a continuously distributed estimate of crime density for each regularly spaced cell of the study area. The total result is a grid-based surface of the study region, which is often described as a "smoothed" estimate of the density of point events. Unlike the original point data from which it is derived, the kernel estimate describes event densities even across areas where no events were actually observed as points (see Cressie, 1993; Bailey and Gatrell, 1995; Ripley, 2004).

Density maps are a popular visual and descriptive tool in criminology and represent a kind of middle ground between a grid-based quadrat analysis and a distance-based nearest neighbor analysis. However, it is important to note that, unlike in quadrat and nearest neighbor analyses, here there is no pregiven global hypothesis of spatial randomness that is typically used to assess a kernel estimate. Instead the surface identifies localized clusters as areas where event are most likely to occur. A hypothesis test can be developed to assess the fit of an estimated surface to the assumptions of the underlying process thought to generate the observed pattern (Bailey and Gatrell, 1995), but this is quite different from the spatial randomness null hypothesis test associated with either quadrat or nearest neighbor analysis. In addition, because the surface is an estimate derived from observed patterns, it can also be seen as potentially sensitive to the bounding of the study area and the scale of the analysis. Kernel estimates are also sensitive to several choices required of the analyst; these include choices about the size of the window (larger sized windows can encompass more area, and therefore more points), the shape of the window (ellipse windows are possible), and the distance-weighting function (which specifies the relative importance of nearby points). Given the combination of these potential sensitivities and the popularity of these surfaces as descriptive visual tools, care must be taken in their interpretation and use.

Although a kernel estimate may be seen primarily as a descriptive tool rather than a predictive tool, it also has analytic utility, because it transforms point data into a kind of areal data. For instance, a kernel estimation surface can be used as the input for global and local spatial autocorrelation measures, including those described in the previous section. While local spatial autocorrelation measures, such as the Gi^* statistic (Getis and Ord, 1992), have been applied to kernel estimated surfaces to statistically identify crime hot spots (e.g., Ratcliffe and McCullagh, 1999), it is important to recognize the conceptual limits of such an endeavor. Kernel surfaces are estimates that can be sensitive to the decisions of the analyst, as are spatial autocorrelation statistics. To apply one to the other may exacerbate errors and stretch the limits of reliability as inputs to public policy or policing resource allocation.

Kernel density estimates require the analyst to specify a distance, or bandwidth, that defines the area used for identifying other points needed in order to interpolate the density surface. This generates a question about the appropriate distance and a concern that the estimated surface is necessarily sensitive to bandwidth choices. In other words, the assessment of clustering may be scale-dependent and any clustering detected at one scale (defined by the bandwidth) may not be detected at another – or may be detected to a different degree. An alternative approach is to use Ripley's *K* function (Ripley, 2004). Like a nearest neighbor analysis, Ripley's *K* compares the observed density of points along a given distance to an expected density for a spatially random distribution. The key difference between Ripley's *K* and other distance-based cluster tests is that multiple distance bands are used in the calculation of the *K* statistic rather than a single band. Analysts must define both the initial distance and the maximum distance, but the *K* statistic can be calculated and compared for different maximum distance values (see Bailey and Gatrell, 1995).

The advantage of Ripley's *K* is that other clustering techniques only consider predefined scales (and often very small scales) of spatial patterning; information on larger scales of patterning is therefore ignored. However, this information may not be of interest unless the process that generates an observed point pattern is thought to vary across the space of a study region. At very small scales of analysis, a city block for example, using Ripley's *K* is unlikely to yield any insight, as the process under consideration may be homogenous at that scale. Like the other techniques described above, Ripley's *K* is also sensitive to edge effects that require the use of an edge correction or the incorporation of points beyond the boundaries of the study region. Although implemented in popular spatial analysis packages like CRIMESTAT (see Levine, 2006), Ripley's *K* is not widely used in the criminology literature. A recent exception is found in Lum's (2008) analysis of the clustering of drug-related violence.

Conclusions

The concepts, methods, and techniques discussed in this chapter are among the ones most central to the spatial analysis of crime. However, this chapter is not an exhaustive survey of spatial analytic methods or of the adoption of spatial perspectives within criminology. The importance of location in the analysis of any event-based phenomenon, such as crime, means that spatial approaches are ever more likely to be utilized by criminologists. Examples of the exploration of other descriptive and predictive spatial techniques not covered in this chapter are the use of spatial measures of central tendency and dispersion, such as standard deviational ellipses (e.g., Huang and Ryan, 2014); the location quotient, a measure of spatial concentration related to the Gini coefficient (e.g., Andresen, 2007); and the exploration of how distance matters to a particular type of criminal activity (e.g., Lu, 2003). The use of spatial concepts and analytic methods in criminology continues to grow and manifests itself in a variety of forms.

This growth, which in large measure represents an adoption of ideas and methods developed for other applications than criminology, may be seen as involving some risks for practitioners. With that in mind, two distinct issues relevant to the spatial analysis of crime are raised, in order to alert those who are new to spatial analysis to potential pitfalls and problems they may encounter. These two issues are (1) the appropriate scale of analysis and (2) the meaning of distance and the related challenge of defining neighboring units. Each is discussed in turn below.

The choice of scale for a spatial analysis is often closely tied to the way in which data of interest to criminologists are collected, organized, and represented by organizations or institutions without an explicit consideration of the use of those data for scholarly analysis. This may be a significant problem for research that utilizes regression modeling. While data about crime events often record the distinct location of the event, such as a physical address, data on the suspected covariates of crime are rarely available at the same level of geographical specificity. This manifests itself most plainly in the case of areal data, where information is aggregated or assigned to arbitrary (at least from the researcher's point of view) geographical units that can vary widely in size, shape, and consistency. Under such circumstances, researchers are left with the prospect of analyzing a phenomenon at a scale not of their choice, and perhaps at a scale that has little to do with the underlying process under investigation.

For example, consider the often widely cited and spatially explicit research that explores county- or state-level covariates of crime such as homicide (i.e., Messner et al., 1999; Baller et al., 2001). Homicide is an act undertaken by a single individual in a specific and highly localized setting. Yet Messner and colleagues (1999) and similar studies explore the processes of homicide at a level of analysis that approximates neither the act of agency by the offender nor the place-specific environment within with the act occurs. Although such studies can reveal general overall patterns or trends, such as the tendency for homicide rates to be higher in the southeastern US (Messner et al., 1999), they do little to inform about the process of homicide at the level at which the phenomena actually occur. The scale of the event and that of the analysis are mismatched and the potential for new insights is thereby dramatically diminished.

What choices are available to researchers under such circumstances? Some scholars working with spatially organized scales in other fields have developed methods that attempt to use observed data at one scale in order to estimate data at another, smaller spatial scale (i.e., data "downscaling"). This practice, widespread in atmospheric and climate science, is typically only used with gridded data where the size and shape of each spatial unit is uniform. Since this feature is very unlikely to be found in criminology research, the best practical advice is to conduct research at the smallest possible spatial scale. Doing so often helps with (while not fully alleviating) the associated problems of MAUP and of the ecological fallacy. Perhaps better advice may be to encourage as much primary data collection as possible, in order to reduce reliance on data collected by others at spatial scales suited for their own specific needs. Although framed here as a practical issue associated with data-driven analysis, the advice to perform one's analysis at the smallest possible scale is also fundamentally in concert with an emerging theoretical perspective on the importance of local contexts to particular types of crime (see Fotheringham, 1997; Smith, Frazee, and Davison, 2000; Hipp, 2007; Tita and Greenbaum, 2008).

Measuring distances between spatial units, whether areas or points, is a fundamental step in nearly all of the techniques summarized in this chapter. While the geographical distance between two objects on the surface of the earth is easy to measure and interpret, the use of distance in spatial analysis is intended to represent the outer bounds of the influence that one location has on another. For example, in a point pattern analysis, distance is used in a nearest neighbor analysis to define a radius around a location that then becomes the basis upon which clustering is interpreted as either present or absent. Similarly, spatial autocorrelation measures often use distance in order to establish which spatial units are used in calculating the mean value of a variable, so as to compare it against the value of a focal unit. While much of the spatial analysis literature offers technical guidance on operationalizing distance, how should geographical distance be interpreted for use in criminology? Can two units be close geographically yet distant in other ways?

Helpfully, criminologists are well positioned to consider this question; and several studies have recently emerged that consider the use of alternative or hybrid measures of distance in conjunction with explicitly spatial methods (Mears and Bhati, 2006; Radil, Flint, and Tita, 2010; Tita and Radil, 2011). For example, measures of social distance (e.g., Cohen and Felson, 1979) and homophily (McPherson, Smith-Lovin, and Cook, 2001) may be more meaningful than geographical distance for many types of crime studies. The continued use of geographical distance as a proxy for social distance may be appropriate in some circumstances but may also be seen as a missed opportunity to theorize social interaction in a spatial setting (Leenders, 2002; Radil et al., 2010). For example, Tita and Radil (2011) compared spatial weights matrices of geographical distance measures of gang interaction against matrices based on rivalry relationships, in order to model the location of gang-related violence in Los Angeles. Distance-based measures had less explanatory power than the measures generated by modeling the actual social relationships. All of the techniques described in this chapter can accept and use alternative measures of distance, or measures that hybridize geographical distance with forms of social distance. Researchers should carefully consider whether or not geographical distance is a meaningful proxy for the type of interactions they believe to be salient to the particular type of crime under investigation.

Related to the interpretation of distance is the choice of neighbors for use in spatial autocorrelation, spatial regression, and point pattern analyses. The way in which neighbors are chosen can have impacts on the results of the analysis, which often requires that researchers invest effort in specifying and testing alternative forms, so as to assess how robust the results are against such changes. While this task is often framed as a purely technical problem (see Griffith, 1996), the problem is also a conceptual one, just as the identification of neighbors is also a formalization of the spatial structure of influence within a study region. Should influence be seen as purely a function of nearness in geographical space? Might influence be directional, or might it be conditioned by other spatial arrangements present within a region of study, such as road networks? There are no easy answers to such questions, but attending to the relevant details may provide opportunities to better understand the complexities of space, location, place, context, society, and crime.

References

Andresen, M. A. 2007. Location quotients, ambient populations, and the spatial analysis of crime in Vancouver, Canada. *Environment and Planning, A*, 39: 2423–2444.

Anselin, L. 1988. *Spatial econometrics: Methods and models*. Boston: Kluwer Academic.

Anselin, L. 1995. Local indicators of spatial association – LISA. *Geographical Analysis*, 27: 93–115.

Anselin, L. 1998. Exploratory spatial data analysis in a geocomputational environment. In *Geocomputation, a primer*, edited by P. Longley, S. Brooks, R. McDonnell, and B. Macmillan, 77–94. New York: Wiley.

Anselin, L. 1999. Interactive techniques and exploratory spatial data analysis. In *Geographical information systems*, edited by P. Longley, M. Goodchild, D. Maguire, and D. Rhind, 253–266. New York: Wiley.

Anselin, L. 2002. Under the hood: Issues in the specification and interpretation of spatial regression models. *Agricultural Economics*, 27: 247–267.

Anselin, L. 2006. Spatial econometrics. In *Palgrave handbook of econometrics*, vol. 1: *Econometric theory*, edited by T. C. Mills and K. Patterson, 901–941. Basingstoke, UK: Palgrave Macmillan.

Bailey, T. C., and Gatrell, A. C. 1995. *Interactive spatial data analysis*. Harlow, UK: Addison Wesley Longman.

Baller, R. D., Anselin, L., Messner, S. F., Deane, G., and Hawkins, D. F. 2001. Structural covariates of us county homicide rates: incorporating spatial effects. *Criminology*, 39: 561–588.

Brantingham, P. J., and Brantingham, P. L. 1981. *Environmental criminology*. Beverly Hills, CA: Sage.

Brantingham, P. J., and Brantingham, P. L. 1984. *Patterns in crime*. New York: Macmillan.

Brantingham, P. J., and Brantingham, P. L. 1993. Environment, routine and situation: Toward a pattern theory of crime. *Advances in Criminological Theory*, 5: 259–294.

Chakravorty, S. 1995. Identifying crime clusters: The spatial principles. *Middle States Geographer*, 28: 53–58.

Chakravorty, S., and Pelfrey, W. V. 2000. Exploratory data analysis of crime patterns: Preliminary findings from the Bronx. In *Analyzing crime patterns: Frontiers of practice*, edited by V. Goldsmith, P. G. McGuire, J. H. Mollenkopf, and T. A. Ross, 65–76. London: Sage.

Chun, Y., and Griffith, D. A. 2013. *Spatial statistics and geostatistics: Theory and applications for geographic information science and technology*. London: Sage.

Clarke, K. C. 1990. *Analytical and computer cartography*, vol. 290. Englewood Cliffs, NJ: Prentice Hall.

Cliff, A. D., and Ord, J. K. 1970. Spatial autocorrelation: A review of existing and new measures with applications. *Economic Geography*, 46: 269–292.

Cliff, A. D., and Ord, J. K. 1973. *Spatial autocorrelation*. London: Pion.

Cliff, A. D., and Ord, J. K. 1981. *Spatial processes, models, and applications*. London: Pion.

Cohen, L. E., and Felson, M. 1979. Social change and crime rate trends: A routine activity approach. *American Sociological Review*, 44: 588–608.

Cohen, J., and Tita, G. E. 1999. Diffusion in homicide: Exploring a general method for detecting spatial diffusion processes. *Journal of Quantitative Criminology*, 15: 451–493.

Cork, D. 1999. Examining space–time interaction in city-level homicide data: Crack markets and the diffusion of guns among youth. *Journal of Quantitative Criminology*, 15: 379–406.

Cressie, N. A. C. 1993. *Statistics for spatial data*, rev. edn. New York: Wiley.

Diggle, P. J. 2003. *Statistical analysis of spatial point patterns*, 2nd edn. London: Arnold.

Fotheringham, A. S. 1997. Trends in quantitative methods, I: Stressing the local. *Progress in Human Geography*, 21: 88–96.

Fotheringham, A. S., Charlton, M., and Brundson, S. 2002. *Geographically weighted regression: The analysis of spatially varying relationships*. New York: Wiley.

Fotheringham, A. S., and Rogerson, P. A., eds. 2008. *The Sage handbook of spatial analysis*. Thousand Oaks, CA: Sage.

Getis, A., and Ord, J. K. 1992. The analysis of spatial association by use of distance statistics. *Geographical Analysis*, 24: 189–206.

Goodchild, M. F. 2004. GIScience, geography, form, and process. *Annals of the Association of American Geographers*, 94: 709–714.

Gorman, D. M., Speer, P. W., Gruenewald, P. J., and Labouvie, E. W. 2001. Spatial dynamics of alcohol availability, neighborhood structure and violent crime. *Journal of Studies on Alcohol and Drugs*, 62: 628–636.

Griffith, D. A. 1983. The boundary value problem in spatial statistical analysis. *Journal of Regional Science*, 23: 377–378.

Griffith, D. A. 1996. Some guidelines for specifying the geographic weights matrix contained in the spatial statistical models. In *Practical handbook of spatial statistics*, edited by S. L. Arlinghaus, 65–82. Boca Raton, FL: CRC Press.

Haining, R. 2003. *Spatial data analysis: Theory and practice*. Cambridge, UK: Cambridge University Press.

Haining, R. 2009. The special nature of spatial data. In *The Sage handbook of spatial analysis*, edited by A. S. Fotheringham, and P. A. Rogerson, 4–21. Thousand Oaks, CA: Sage.

Hipp, J. R. 2007. Block, tract, and levels of aggregation: Neighborhood structure and crime and disorder as a case in point. *American Sociological Review*, 72: 659–680.

Hirschfield, A., and Bowers, K., eds. 2001. *Mapping and analysing crime data: Lessons from research and practice*. London: Taylor & Francis.

Huang, H., and Ryan, J. P. 2014. The location of placement and juvenile delinquency: Do neighborhoods matter in child welfare? *Children and Youth Services Review*, 44: 33–45.

Isaaks, E. H., and Srivastava, R. M. 1989. *Applied geostatistics*, vol. 2. New York: Oxford University Press.

King, G. 1997. *A solution to the ecological inference problem: Reconstructing individual behavior from aggregate data*. Princeton, NJ: Princeton University Press.

LaVigne, N. G., and Groff, E. R. 2001. The evolution of crime mapping in the United States. In *Mapping and analysing crime data: Lessons from research and practice*, edited by A. Hirschfield and K. Bowers, 203–221. London: Taylor & Francis.

LeBeau, J. L., and Leitner, M. 2011. Introduction: Progress in research on the geography of crime. *The Professional Geographer*, 63: 161–173.

Leenders, R. 2002. Modeling social influence through network autocorrelation: constructing the weight matrix. *Social Networks*, 24: 21–47.
Levine, N., 2006. Crime mapping and the Crimestat program. *Geographical Analysis*, 38: 41–56.
Liu, H., and Brown, D. E. 2003. Criminal incident prediction using a point-pattern-based density model. *International Journal of Forecasting*, 19: 603–622.
Lu, Y. 2003. Getting away with the stolen vehicle: An investigation of journey-after-crime. *The Professional Geographer*, 55: 422–433.
Lum, C. 2008. The geography of drug activity and violence: Analyzing spatial relationships of non-homogenous crime event types. *Substance Use & Misuse*, 43: 179–201.
McLafferty, S., Williamson, D., and McGuire, P. G. 2000. Identifying crime hot spots using kernel smoothing. In *Analyzing crime patterns: Frontiers of practice*, edited by V. Goldsmith, P. G. McGuire, J. H. Mollenkopf, and T. A. Ross, 77–85. London: Sage.
McPherson, Smith-Lovin, M., L., and Cook, J. 2001. Birds of a feather: Homophily in social networks. *Annual Review of Sociology*, 27: 415–444.
Mears, D., and Bhati, A. 2006. No community is an island: The effects of resource deprivation on urban violence in spatially and socially proximate communities. *Criminology*, 44: 509–548.
Messner, S. F., and Anselin, L. 2004. Spatial analyses of homicide with areal data. In *Spatially integrated social science*, edited by M. F. Goodchild, and D. G. Janelle, 127–144. Oxford: Oxford University Press.
Messner, S. F., Anselin, L., Baller, R. D., Hawkins, D. F., Deane, G., and Tolnay, S. E. 1999. The spatial patterning of county homicide rates: An application of exploratory spatial data analysis. *Journal of Quantitative Criminology*, 15: 423–450.
Morenoff, J., Sampson, R. J., and Raudenbush, S. 2001. Neighborhood inequality, collective efficacy, and the spatial dynamics of urban violence. *Criminology*, 39: 517–560.
O'Loughlin, J. 2003. Spatial analysis in political geography. In *A companion to political geography*, edited by J. A. Agnew, K. Mitchell and G. Ó Tuathail, 30–46. Malden, MA: Blackwell.
Openshaw, S. 1984. Ecological fallacies and the analysis of areal census data. *Environment and Planning A*, 16: 17–31.
Openshaw, S. 1996. Developing GIS-relevant zone-based spatial analysis methods. In *Spatial analysis: Modeling in a GIS environment*, edited by P. Longley, and M. Batty, 55–73. New York: Wiley.
Radil, S. M., Flint, C., and Tita, G. E. 2010. Spatializing social networks: Geographies of gang rivalry, territoriality, and violence in Los Angeles. *Annals of the Association of American Geographers*, 100: 307–326.
Ratcliffe, J. H., &. McCullagh, M. J. 1999. Hotbeds of crime and the search for spatial accuracy. *Journal of Geographical Systems*, 1: 385–398.
Ripley, B. D. 2004. *Spatial statistics*, 2nd edn. New York: Wiley.
Sherman, L. W., and Weisburd, D. 1995. General deterrent effects of police patrol in crime "hot spots": A randomized, controlled trial. *Justice Quarterly*, 12: 625–648.
Sherman, L. W., Gartin, P. R. and Buerger, M. E. 1989. Hot spots of predatory crime: Routine activities and the criminology of place. *Criminology*, 27: 27–56.
Smith, W. R., Frazee, S. G., and Davison, E. L. 2000. Furthering the integration of routine activity and social disorganization theories: Small units of analysis and the study of street robbery as a diffusion process. *Criminology*, 38: 489–523.

Socia, K. M., and Stamatel, J. P. 2012. Neighborhood characteristics and the social control of registered sex offenders. *Crime & Delinquency*, 58: 565–587.

Tita, G. E., Cohen, J., and Engberg, J. 2005. An ecological study of the location of gang "set space." *Social Problems*, 52: 272–299.

Tita, G. E., and Greenbaum. R. 2008. Crime, neighborhoods and units of analysis: Putting space in its place. In *Putting crime in its place: Units of analysis in spatial crime research*, edited by D. Weisburd, W. Bernasco, and G. J. N. Bruinsma, 145–170. New York: Springer.

Tita, G. E., and Radil, S. M. 2011. Spatializing the social networks of gangs to explore patterns of violence. *Journal of Quantitative Criminology*, 27: 521–545.

Tobler, W. R. 1970. A computer movie simulating urban growth in the Detroit region. *Economic Geography*, 46: 234–240.

Van Patten, I. T., McKeldin-Coner, J., and Cox, D. 2009. A microspatial analysis of robbery: Prospective hot spotting in a small city. *Crime Mapping: A Journal of Research and Practice*, 1: 7–32.

Wang, N., Liu, L., Eck, and J. E. 2014. Analyzing crime displacement with a simulation approach. *Environment and Planning B*, 41: 359–374.

Ward, M. D., and Gleditsch, K. S. 2008. *Spatial regression models*. Thousand Oaks, CA: Sage.

Weisburd, D., Bernasco, W., and Bruinsma, G. J. N., eds. 2009. *Putting crime in its place: Units of analysis in spatial crime research*. New York: Springer.

Weisburd, D., Bruinsma, G. J. N., and Bernasco, W. 2009. Units of analysis in geographic criminology: Historical development, critical issues, and open questions. In *Putting crime in its place: Units of analysis in spatial crime research*, edited by Weisburd, D., W. Bernasco, and G. J. N. Bruinsma, 3–31. New York: Springer.

Williamson, D., McLafferty, S., McGuire, P., Ross, T., Mollenkopf, J., Goldsmith, V., and Quinn, S. 2001. Tools in the spatial analysis of crime. In *Mapping and analysing crime data: Lessons from research and practice*, edited by A. Hirschfield and K. Bowers, 187–202. London: Taylor & Francis.

Wing, M. G., and J. Tynon. 2006. Crime mapping and spatial analysis in national forests. *Journal of Forestry*, 104: 293–298.

Further Reading

Anselin, L., Griffiths, E., and Tita, G. E. 2008. Crime mapping and hot spot analysis. In *Environmental criminology and crime analysis*, edited by R. Wortley and L. Mazerolle, 97–116. Abingdon, UK: Willan Publishing.

25

Network Analysis

Owen Gallupe

Introduction

Moreno and Jennings (1934) are usually credited as the pioneers of modern social network analysis (SNA), though Freeman (2004) notes that precursors can be traced to the thirteenth century. However, the value of SNA for criminology began to be recognized much more recently, and Krohn's (1986) examination of the influence of network multiplexity (i.e., having relationships with the same people in various spheres of life, e.g., at school, in church) and density (i.e., the interconnectedness of the network) on delinquent behavior is one of the first to explicitly employ sociometry as an analytic framework in criminology. The focus on individuals within a relational context (and on groups within broader structures of relations) and the development of network-analytic methods have allowed for the examination of dynamics otherwise not possible through traditional methods based on the general linear model – though network-derived measures are often subsequently used in regression-type analyses. This chapter will start with a basic outline of what it is that social network analysis brings to the table. Next, some of the major streams of research in criminology that rely on network methods will be discussed. That will be followed by the description of a number of major social network data collection efforts that have contributed to criminological knowledge. I will then discuss a number of key methodological issues and debates before concluding with a discussion of new directions in SNA.

The Handbook of Measurement Issues in Criminology and Criminal Justice, First Edition.
Edited by Beth M. Huebner and Timothy S. Bynum.

What Is Network Analysis?

The most fundamental idea behind SNA is that relationships are important (Papachristos, 2011). Relationships can be the reason for behavior as well as the result of it. That is, being associated with others can cause a person to act in certain ways.[1] Conversely, actions can attract or repel others. From a broadly defined social network perspective, both the structure and the content of relationships are important (Borgatti et al., 2009). "Content of relationships" refers to specific qualities of the tie between people. A familiar example for many criminologists that illustrates the importance of tie content is the association between hanging out with delinquents and individual delinquent behavior, the basis for differential association theory (Sutherland, 1947). In this instance, the content of the tie (delinquency of peers) is related to individual action (delinquency).

"Structure of relationships" refers to the pattern of ties among people in the network. In all but the smallest networks, some people are in the middle (see person A in Figure 25.1) while others are peripheral (person B). Some may be predominantly connected to people who are key figures in the network (person C), while others are mostly connected to those with little influence (person L). People occupying different structural positions in a network tend to perform different roles and have different levels of power within that network (Wasserman and Faust, 1994). Individuals located in the middle are likely to be highly visible and may be more likely than others to determine group norms. They may also be more constrained to act in ways supported by the broader network, since their behaviors tend to be noticed by the network and they have more to lose by going against group norms (e.g., Gallupe and Bouchard, 2015; Haynie, 2001). Individuals at the periphery are unlikely to determine what is acceptable, but they are also less likely to be constrained, since their low status means that they do not have as much to lose.

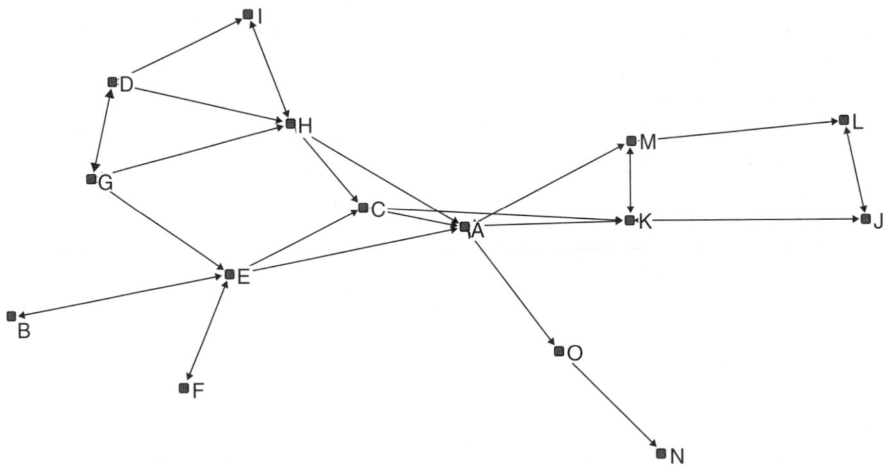

Figure 25.1 Sample network.

It is common in SNA to produce visual representations of the structure of the network. A tremendous amount of information can be conveyed simply by looking at how those in the network are related to one another. From Figure 25.1 we could safely infer that, if person O were to introduce N to A, person N would be likely to experience a gain in social status, since that person would be likely to become known to a much wider audience. Further, B and F are more likely to become friends than they would be by chance, given the tendency toward transitivity (the tendency for friends of friends to become friends; see Wasserman and Faust, 1994).

Given the dyadic focus of SNA (i.e., the focus on relationships between two entities), network data differ from traditional data structures. In traditional data matrices, each row contains the values on all variables (e.g., number of delinquent acts per year, self-esteem, age) for any single case (e.g., a survey respondent). The starting point of SNA is the sociomatrix that indicates who is connected with whom. In a sociomatrix, the same nodes (in this case, individuals) generally make up both the rows and the columns (see Table 25.1 for the sociomatrix corresponding to Figure 25.1).[2] Zeroes indicate no connection between the nodes; ones indicate that there is a tie between two particular nodes. Table 25.1 shows, for example, that persons B and E are connected to each other but persons B and D are not connected. This particular sociomatrix is undirected, in that X→Y also means Y→X. In a friendship network, this means that, if one person lists another person as a friend, there is a tie between them regardless of whether that friendship nomination is reciprocated. In other words, a friendship tie exists if one, the other, or both people state that they are friends. Therefore all information can be conveyed either above or below the diagonal in the table; the sociomatrix is symmetrical. This does not have

Table 25.1 Sociomatrix.

	A	B	C	D	E	F	G	H	I	J	K	L	M	N	O
A	0	0	1	0	1	0	0	1	0	0	1	0	1	0	1
B	0	0	0	0	1	0	0	0	0	0	0	0	0	0	0
C	1	0	0	0	1	0	0	1	0	0	1	0	0	0	0
D	0	0	0	0	0	0	1	1	1	0	0	0	0	0	0
E	1	1	1	0	0	1	1	0	0	0	0	0	0	0	0
F	0	0	0	0	1	0	0	0	0	0	0	0	0	0	0
G	0	0	0	1	1	0	0	1	0	0	0	0	0	0	0
H	1	0	1	1	0	0	1	0	1	0	0	0	0	0	0
I	0	0	0	1	0	0	0	1	0	0	0	0	0	0	0
J	0	0	0	0	0	0	0	0	0	0	1	1	0	0	0
K	1	0	1	0	0	0	0	0	0	1	0	0	1	0	0
L	0	0	0	0	0	0	0	0	0	1	0	0	1	0	0
M	1	0	0	0	0	0	0	0	0	0	1	1	0	0	0
N	0	0	0	0	0	0	0	0	0	0	0	0	0	0	1
O	1	0	0	0	0	0	0	0	0	0	0	0	0	1	0

The shaded ties on the diagonal are self-ties. They are generally excluded from calculations of network measures.

to be the case. The sociomatrix can also be directed so that ties are not necessarily reciprocated: just because X listed Y as a friend, it does not follow that Y considers X to be a friend. This would result in the sociomatrix being asymmetric (i.e., above the diagonal is not the same as below). Further, ties can be weighted to indicate particular characteristics. For example, instead of 0 = no tie present, 1 = tie present, the strength of that tie could be estimated on a scale from 1 to 5 where 1 = very weak tie and 5 = very strong tie. All of these aspects of SNA have utility for criminological research.

How Has SNA Been Used in Criminology?[3]

Much criminal behavior is social, which makes an understanding of the relationships between involved parties critical to interdiction. In some of the most applied uses of SNA in criminology, knowledge of the structure of a given illicit network can direct enforcement agencies to the highest value targets. This type of "key player" analysis can suggest which node is likely to cause the most damage to the whole network through its removal. For example, Morselli and Roy (2008) found that removing the three top brokers in two different stolen vehicle exportation networks was more effective at disrupting the networks than removing a random selection of 15 other members. Further work by Morselli (2009, chapter 9) showed that some of the most important players in what had been thought to be a street-gang-dominated drug distribution operation were actually nongang members who acted as intermediaries between various components of the network. Wu, Carleton, and Davies (2014) used network-analytic techniques to predict who is likely to replace Osama bin-Laden as the leader of al-Qaeda. While those studies relied on data collected through police or media investigations, other research has taken advantage of computer science expertise for similar purposes. For example, Westlake, Bouchard, and Frank (2011) developed a web crawler with the capacity to index the content of child exploitation websites and map out the connections between them as a way to help police focus their investigations on websites that would cause the most damage to the overall network by their removal.

Peer-influence research is another major area that has benefited from the insights and methods provided by the network perspective (Carrington, 2011). In criminology, peer-influence research is dominated by Sutherland's (1947) differential association theory (DAT) and by Akers's (2009) social learning theory (SLT). In very basic terms, DAT argues that there is a normative transfer between individuals such that those who associate with people who support criminal behavior are more likely than others to come to believe that criminal behaviors are acceptable choices of action, especially when these relationships are established early in life, last for longer periods, involve frequent contact, and are emotionally intense. SLT extends DAT by incorporating reinforcements and behavioral modeling. The key component, for the sake of this chapter, is that the peer-influence perspective in criminology is about possessing contacts to others, who are differentially involved in offending behavior.

Historically, there has been plenty of support in the empirical literature for this relationship (see, for example, Pratt et al., 2010).

Prior to the proliferation of SNA in peer-influence research, the criminogenic influence of peers was measured by asking survey respondents to report their own delinquency and then to report the delinquency of their friends. However, these types of perceptual measures came to be seen as problematic, as people generally do not know exactly how much offending behavior their associates are involved in. Some researchers view this as more than a typical example of measurement error, which is common in a field focused on actions that often generate scorn and embarrassment. When asking about sensitive topics (e.g., criminal involvement), participants may be hesitant to respond. This underreporting is not overly problematic if it is not systematically related to other factors under examination. That is, models predicting criminal behavior are still informative, even if the outcome variable is underreported, since statistically significant relationships are likely to be conservative estimates that would be found to have a stronger effect given more accurate reporting of criminal behavior. The issue with perceptual measures of peer offending is different. The primary concern is projection bias. This is when a person perceives others to be more similar to oneself than they really are. If this is the case, the correlation between peer and individual delinquency will be inflated, since those involved in high levels of delinquency indicate that their peers are also highly delinquent, while those involved in low levels of delinquency will indicate that their peers are also minimally delinquent, regardless of actual levels of peer behavior. At the extreme end, some have suggested that perceived peer delinquency "may merely be another measure of self-reported delinquency" (Gottfredson and Hirschi, 1990, p. 157).

A network approach gets around problems associated with individuals who report the criminal involvement of their peers by using "measures of peer delinquency that are based on responses from the peers themselves, rather than perceptions from respondents" (Haynie, 2001, p. 1015). To get around such problems, all members of a given network are sampled (minus missing cases, a particularly troublesome issue in SNA; more on this later in the chapter) and asked about their own delinquent behavior. They are also asked to indicate their friends from a list of network members. This allows researchers to determine who is friends with whom. They can then establish the amount of delinquency (as it results from self-reports) in any individual's friendship group. In network parlance, this is known as ego network delinquency: the amount of offending behavior reported by "alters" – people in the network other than the focal individual – connected to "ego" – the focal individual.

Figure 25.2 provides an example of a network consisting of delinquents and nondelinquents. Triangular nodes are people who self-report having been involved in delinquent behavior, while circular nodes are nondelinquents. The size of the triangular nodes is a visual indicator of the amount of delinquent behavior a given person reports having committed (larger = more delinquent). Thus, all six of person A's friends are delinquent, including some who are quite heavily involved (persons E, H, K, and M). Person H is delinquent, but, of their five friends, only two are delinquent and one is only minorly so. With this information, it is a simple task to get measures of peer

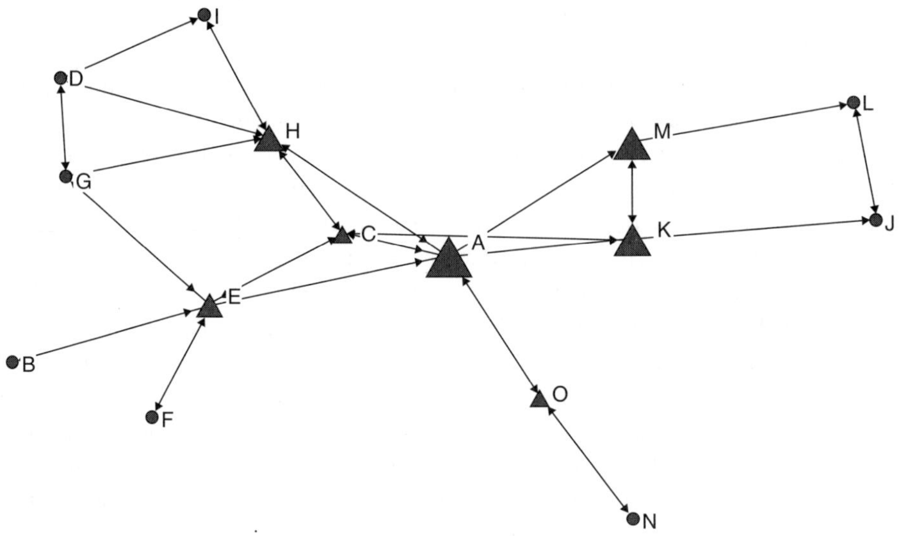

Figure 25.2 Sample network: Node shape and size by delinquency.
triangular nodes = delinquent;
circular nodes = nondelinquent;
larger nodes = more delinquent.

delinquency such as average ego network delinquency (dividing the total amount of delinquency committed by a person's friends by the number of friends he or she has), number of delinquents in the ego networks (a count of the number of friends who report any involvement in delinquency), total network delinquency (summing the amount of delinquency in the whole network), and so on. There is evidence that having more delinquent peers (as measured through network methods) is associated with higher levels of personal delinquency (e.g., Haynie, 2001). Furthermore, Payne and Cornwell (2007) use SNA to show that greater risk-taking behavior of friends of friends is related to higher individual delinquency. This means that a person can be influenced by those with whom he or she has no direct contact.

Countering the criticisms of perceptual measures of peer delinquency is the argument that perceptions are what truly matter. Akers (2009, p. 119) notes that, "even if peer behavior is misperceived as more (or less) delinquent than it actually is, the peer influence will still come through that perception." In other words, it makes little difference whether a person knows the precise amount of delinquent behavior his or her peers are involved in; what is important is the amount of delinquent behavior a person *thinks* his or her peers are involved in. Having a friend who is a frequent shoplifter is unlikely to result in higher levels of personal shoplifting if the person remains ignorant of his or her friend's behavior. Weerman and Smeenk (2005) found that perceptual and direct (network-based) measures of peer delinquency were positively correlated with personal delinquency, although the relationship was stronger for perceptual measures than for direct measures. This is consistent with the suggestion that people tend to overestimate behavioral similarity with peers. Recent work that addresses this issue by using dyadic data – that is, data in which respondents and a friend are asked about their delinquent behavior and the delinquency of their friend – generally shows the following results (e.g., Boman et al., 2012; Rebellon and Modecki, 2013; Young et al., 2015): (1) perceived peer delinquency, direct peer delinquency, and personal delinquency are separate constructs; and (2) there is a significant, positive relationship between those constructs. Together, these findings suggest that perceptual peer delinquency is not the same as direct measures of peer delinquency, but people are not completely ignorant of the behaviors of their peers either. Therefore, while network methods certainly provide more accurate measures of peer delinquency than traditional perceptual measures, claims that they are "better" are likely overblown. In fact, for peer influence research from an SLT perspective, perceptual measures maintain theoretical superiority, given Akers' emphasis on the importance of perceptions. Most importantly, it is critical that researchers be aware of what exactly these different measures are and are not capable of delivering – and design studies that get at exactly the peer influence dynamic they want to investigate.

The issue of selection versus influence is another issue of interest to criminologists that is well suited to SNA. The validity of DAT and SLT hinges on the premise that a person's associates have the power to alter that person's behavior. This is the influence perspective (also called the "socialization" perspective). The selection perspective is the idea that people choose to associate with others who are similar to themselves. In criminology, the influence perspective argues that associating with delinquents is a cause of personal delinquency, while the selection perspective argues that people who are already inclined toward delinquent behavior choose to associate with others who are predisposed to delinquency. This is a form of behavioral homophily (McPherson, Smith-Lovin, and Cook, 2001). If this is the case, the correlation between peer and individual delinquency is not due to any causal mechanism associated with peers (see Hirschi, 1969).

Recent statistical advances have paved the way to the explicit examination of selection and influence dynamics. One of the major ways in which this can be done is by using stochastic actor-oriented models (SAOMs) (e.g., Snijders, van de Bunt, and Steglich, 2010) with the Simulation Investigation for Empirical Network Analysis (SIENA) package (see http://www.stats.ox.ac.uk/~snijders/siena). The primary input of SAOMs are sociomatrices that record patterns of ties collected on the same general network at different points in time. Using this type of longitudinal network data, SAOMs have the capacity to model network change tendencies and the individual–dyadic characteristics associated with changes in tie formation or dissolution. This allows researchers to examine whether there is a tendency for ties to form on the basis of similarity in levels of delinquency (selection effect) and whether peer delinquency tends to lead to changes in individual delinquency (influence effect). Using these models, Weerman (2011) found that adolescents with more heavily delinquent peers were more likely to increase their own delinquency from time 1 to time 2 but did not find that delinquency was the basis for friendship formation. This study provided (weak) evidence for influence but not for selection. Baerveldt, Volker, and Van Rossem (2008) used a meta-analysis of SAOMs across 16 schools and found evidence that peer influence was operative in all schools, while selection processes were only evident in four. Dijkstra et al. (2010) found no evidence that friendship ties formed around similarity in weapon-carrying (no selection effect), but they did find that weapon-carrying became more in line with the behavior of their peers over time (influence effect) among a sample of mostly socio-economically low-status Hispanic male adolescents in the United States. Countering those studies, Knecht (2008), using a SAOM approach, found support for friendship ties being formed around similarity in minor delinquency but did not find any influence effects.

Network methods have also played an important role in advancing research on the diffusion of criminal activity. For example, Nash, Bouchard, and Malm (2013) noted the importance of "network bridges" – those who act as a link between people otherwise unconnected – in facilitating the spread of investments in a Ponzi scheme. Cohen and Prinstein (2006), using a sample of adolescents sociometrically found to be of average social status, demonstrated that support for aggressive or risk-taking behavior is more likely to be internalized when peers who promote associated beliefs are of high status. They suggest that status differentials are a key component in the contagion of antisocial behavior among adolescents.

Gang research is the final substantive area that I will discuss. McGloin's (2005) analysis of gangs in Newark showed that they tend to be quite sparse. Instead of tight links between all members of a gang, fewer than 10 percent of all possible within-gang ties were actually made. That is, if all members of a gang were connected to each other, 100 percent of all possible ties would be realized; however, the fact that fewer than 10 percent of ties were made indicates that gang members generally do not have personal connections to most other people in their own gang. This has implications for intervention strategies. For example, "collective accountability" in which "the gangs were informed that if one member committed violence, the [authorities] would respond to the gang as a whole" are unlikely to be very successful, since there is not enough contact among members for the message to spread adequately (p. 624). However, there are more cohesive cliques within a given gang, in which this approach may be more effective. Further, McGloin identified "cut points," individuals who act as the sole link between different groups. Authorities are more likely to ensure structural instability in the gang (while potentially disrupting illicit activities in the process) by focusing interventions on these particular people than by engaging in street sweeps or by concentrating efforts on other individuals.

Papachristos's (2009) wide-ranging study showed (among a variety of other results) that gang murders in Chicago were a product of relational forces between gangs that operate essentially independently of individuals, whose membership in gangs is often transient. This study demonstrated that gang murder is frequently reciprocal, in that a gang committing a murder has often recently experienced the murder of one of their own at the hands of the other gang. In other words, the murder of an Imperial Gangster by a Spanish Cobra (to use two arbitrarily chosen gangs listed by Papachristos) is often followed quite rapidly by the murder of a Spanish Cobra by an Imperial Gangster. Examining dynamics from both an individual- and group-level perspective, Hughes (2013) showed that more popular gang members tended to be more involved in delinquency and violence. Hughes also found that, contrary to hypotheses, higher levels of group cohesion were associated with lower levels of violence.

Major Research Efforts

Given the relative recency of the adoption of sociometric methods in criminology, there have been few large-scale studies that collect the tie nomination data necessary for SNA. Of those that do exist, most have used school-based samples. In these studies, students are given a roster of possible friends within their school or grade and asked to indicate who their friends are. These friendship nominations are used to create sociomatrices of the type displayed in Table 25.1. The most widely used study has been the recently renamed National Longitudinal Study of Adolescent to Adult Health (formerly called the National Longitudinal Study of Adolescent Health), commonly referred to as Add Health (Bearman et al., 2004; see also http://www.cpc.unc.edu/projects/addhealth). The first wave of Add Health sampled 80 high schools selected to be representative of American schools. Additionally, feeder schools (schools with a seventh grade whose students move on to the sampled high school) were included for a total of 132 schools in the core sample (over 90,000 students). From there, more extensive in-home surveys were conducted longitudinally by using students drawn from the population eligible for the in-school surveys. Four in-home waves were collected between 1994–1995 and 2007–2008. School-based social network data were collected by asking respondents to list their closest male and female friends (up to five of each).[4] The Add Health team calculated ego network attribute variables so that, for example, measures of the amount of delinquency within each individual's ego network are available.

An important design aspect of Add Health is what is referred to as the "saturation sample." This is a subsample of schools in which, for the in-home survey, an attempt was made to capture the whole school (as opposed to a sample of students within each school, as was done for the main in-home samples) and to collect friendship nominations at waves 1 and 2. This allows researchers to examine the sociomatrices for each saturation school at both waves, for use in longitudinal social network analyses and with a greater variety of attribute variables than are available in the in-school data. The saturation sample was made up of 16 schools. Of these, 14 were small (under 300 students per school), representing both urban and rural areas and private and public schools. Two of the saturation schools were large (over 3,100 students combined). One was from an ethnically diverse metropolitan area, while the other was from a moderately sized city with a mostly white student body. The saturation sample is not representative but is nonetheless one of the few large longitudinal social network data sets available.

While Add Health has been heavily used (in over 5,500 studies as of January 2016, according to http://www.cpc.unc.edu/projects/addhealth/publications/database), the potential of the Add Health saturation sample has not yet been fully exploited. Many questions of importance to criminologists could be addressed by using recent advances in network-analytic techniques (e.g., SIENA or temporal exponential random graph models) with the longitudinal saturation sample data.[5] Some studies have used only the two large saturation schools, given issues of attrition, response rates, and missing nomination data in the smaller schools: "~40 percent of respondents could only nominate one male and one female friend due to a computer error" (Simpkins et al., 2013, p. 540). Add Health is publicly available in reduced form. The total data are restricted, but researchers can apply for access.

There have been several other large, longitudinal social network data collection efforts that have built on the lessons of Add Health and are more focused on criminological issues. The Promoting School–Community–University Partnerships to Enhance Resilience (PROSPER) Peers study is one of these (e.g., Moody et al., 2011). This study collected school-based networks from 27 communities in rural Iowa and Pennsylvania where at least 15 percent of families exhibited socioeconomic risk (eligibility for free or subsidized lunch); one other community participated, but sociometric data were not collected (see Ragan, Osgood, and Feinberg, 2014). Typical of rural America, the sample was predominantly white and English-speaking. Each school in a sampled community was included, and two cohorts – the first starting in 2002–2003, the second the following year – were followed from the 6th to the 9th grade.[6] Over this four-year span, there were five data collection points: at the start and end of the 6th grade, and then at the end of every subsequent school year. Respondents were asked to indicate their two best friends and up to five other close friends within their grade. This resulted in 368 within-grade school networks (Moody et al., 2011). In most rural communities, nearly all adolescents attend the closest school; this minimizes the likelihood that close friends attend a different school and are in consequence not included in the school network. School networks in rural areas are therefore likely to give closer representations of adolescents' full peer networks than school networks are in urban areas (Osgood et al., 2013). The number and temporal consistency of data collection waves of PROSPER Peers are a clear strength by comparison to those of Add Health. This feature makes the former ideal for the examination of co-evolution patterns of network and delinquent behavior. However, the PROSPER Peers sample is less diverse than Add Health and cannot claim to be nationally representative.[7]

The final major social network data collection project that will be discussed is the School Project by the Netherlands Institute for the Study of Crime and Law Enforcement (Nederlands Studiecentrum Criminaliteit en Rechsthandhaving [NSCR]) (see Weerman, 2011; Young et al., 2014; Young et al., 2015; Young and Weerman, 2013). The NSCR study consists of two waves of data separated by one year (spring 2002 and 2003) from two cohorts – first and third grades at wave 1, equivalent to the seventh and ninth grades in the North American system – in 12 participant schools. However, network data collection measures in one school deviated from the others, while another school refused to participate at wave 2, which resulted in ten schools with usable longitudinal network data. Like PROSPER

Peers, the NSCR study focused on a "high-risk" sample by including only lower educational track schools and by oversampling inner-city areas of a major Dutch city. Additionally, approximately 30 percent of the sample attended school in one of two mid-sized cities and fewer than 10 percent were from a smaller town. This was done "to achieve substantial variation in school contexts" (Weerman, 2011, p. 260). Also like PROSPER Peers but contrary to Add Health, the NSCR study collected grade-level networks (Add Health collected school-level networks). As in Add Health, NSCR participants were asked to nominate ten friends, though no gender differentiation was employed (Add Health asked respondents to nominate up to five male and five female friends). A greater proportion of respondents in the NSCR study nominated the maximum number of friends (34 percent at wave 1, 30 percent at wave 2: Weerman, 2011, p. 261) than in Add Health (3 percent of the valid in-school network sample).

As in PROSPER Peers, the major strength of the NSCR study is its explicit focus on criminological interests. These interests ensure that a wider array of important correlates of delinquency can be incorporated into studies of adolescent networks and offending. But, also like PROSPER Peers, it lacks the scale and generalizability of Add Health (at least of the in-school network data). In all, Add Health is responsible for much of what is known about peer networks in criminology and continues to be a valuable data source, but the insights provided by PROSPER Peers and by the NSCR study have only just started to advance our knowledge of longitudinal network effects and are likely to play a major role in advancing the field in the near future. These are, however, all school-based networks. There are no known criminologically relevant data sets of comparable scale (in terms of size and attributes) that have been collected on other populations. But, regardless of the scale of the data collection effort, there are a number of methodological issues that must be considered.

Methodological Issues

I will focus on three methodological issues that network researchers must confront: (1) independence of cases; (2) longitudinal versus cross-sectional designs; (3) missing data. The first is strictly an analytic consideration, while the second and third are issues of both design and analysis.

Independence of cases

Criminological questions are often posed in ways that suggest a regression-based approach to analysis. For example, within a drug importation network, do members who occupy brokerage positions make more money than others? Calculate effective size (a measure of brokerage; see Burt, 1992) for each member of the network, obtain estimates of illicit earnings, run a regression model predicting earnings from effective size (with appropriate controls) – and your analysis is done, right? Unfortunately it is not quite that simple. One of the main assumptions of standard regression models is that respondent scores are not systematically tied to the scores of others in the analysis (Tabachnick and Fidell, 2007). However, the whole purpose of SNA is to examine between-individual dependence. That is, SNA is relational, such that we *expect* individual behaviors to be related to those with whom they are connected. For example, the density of a person's ego network is dependent upon everyone else in that person's network. If you have two friends who are not friends with each other, the density of your ego network is 0 (the one possible tie between others is not made). However, if those two friends become friends, your ego network density increases to 1 (one out of a possible one tie has been made), even though none of your direct ties has changed.

Violation of independence does not mean that questions like the one above cannot be tested using social network data. There are a number of options that can be used and revolve around bootstrapping in some way. Bootstrapping is a nonparametric method that allows for the relaxation of standard regression assumptions (Efron and Tibshirani, 1993). The basis of bootstrapping is that statistics are calculated by resampling from the existing data a large number of times. These provide accurate estimates even when data are "poorly behaved." Bootstrapping can be done in most commonly used statistical packages, which means that, to run bootstrapped models, one really only needs to know how to add them to the appropriate type of regression model within one's chosen statistical software and be prepared to wait longer for the analysis to be processed.[8]

Regression using a quadratic assignment procedure (QAP regression) can be employed to examine dyadic data (Krackhardt, 1988). This is useful for analyzing whether, for example, people who play on the same sports team and who associate outside of school are more likely than others within a school network to co-offend. To do this analysis, you would need three sociomatrices: (1) a co-offending matrix, in which a tie is indicated if two individuals are involved in the same offence; (2) a sports participation matrix, in which a tie is indicated if two individuals play on the same sports team; (3) an extramural matrix, in which a tie is indicated if two individuals associate outside of school grounds. With QAP regression, a large number of random permutations are applied to generate significance tests. In this example, a significant positive coefficient for "sports team" would mean that people who play on the same sports team are more likely than others to co-offend (controlling for extramural association). QAP regression is easily implemented in UCINET (Borgatti, Everett, and Freeman, 2002) or in the "sna" package in R (Butts, 2014).

Longitudinal versus cross-sectional

The decision to use or collect longitudinal as opposed to cross-sectional social network data is a matter of matching the data to the research question and is therefore something that each researcher must decide in the context of his or her own work. However, it is difficult to see how collecting longitudinal network data is ever a bad idea, considering that it is generally straightforward to limit analyses to a single wave, thereby making longitudinal data suitable for cross-sectional interests. The major limiting factor in the collection of large-scale longitudinal network data is the often prohibitive amount of resources that they require. Collecting longitudinal network data is much more feasible on a smaller scale. These smaller studies can be very informative, as they can be customized for specific criminological interests. But, regardless of the scale of the study, researchers must decide on the time lag between waves. Beyond practical considerations, this decision should be based on the idea that enough time must be left for network evolution to occur, while one should not allow so much time to pass that causes or effects of network change may be clouded by a host of others factors, which have exerted their influence in the interim period between data collection waves. For example, if we were interested in the effect of delinquency involvement on changes in network centrality, we would not want waves 1 and 2 to be only a day apart. There is little chance for friendship patterns to alter over the course of a day. But any influence that delinquency at wave 1 may have had on centrality could be difficult to detect five years later, given all the circumstances that arise over that time. The major school network data sets discussed above (Add Health, PROSPER Peers, NSCR) all used one-year lags, though both Add Health and PROSPER Peers have at least one shorter interval (Add Health: in-school wave to wave 1 in-home; PROSPER Peers: wave 1 to wave 2). There is a need for social network data in criminology that examine more contemporaneous relationships between networks and crime or criminogenic factors (e.g., lag times in the one- to three-month range). In terms of the number of waves collected, most longitudinal statistical techniques can be used with two waves, but more than that is preferable, as more waves would allow for time-variant network evolution processes to be examined more fully.

Missing data

The most troublesome aspect of criminological social network analysis is probably the issue of missing data. In addition to the common problem that our main research interest is often what our research participants would least like to discuss (including the fact that "dark" networks like terrorist organizations must remain undetected to be able to carry out their function), SNA has other method-specific missing data challenges. With traditional surveys, if a respondent does not answer a particular item, he or she is usually dropped from the analysis, or else his or her score is imputed. Regardless of how they are handled, these missing values (should) have no effect on the values of others in the network, since cases are independent. But with SNA, an individual's score is dependent upon the pattern of interrelations in the network (Borgatti, Carley, and Krackhardt, 2006). Therefore having a single missing case within a network can alter the scores of all other members of the network. Figure 25.3 uses the sociomatrix in Table 25.1 to provide an illustration of the effect of missing nodes on the overall network structure. The first panel displays the full

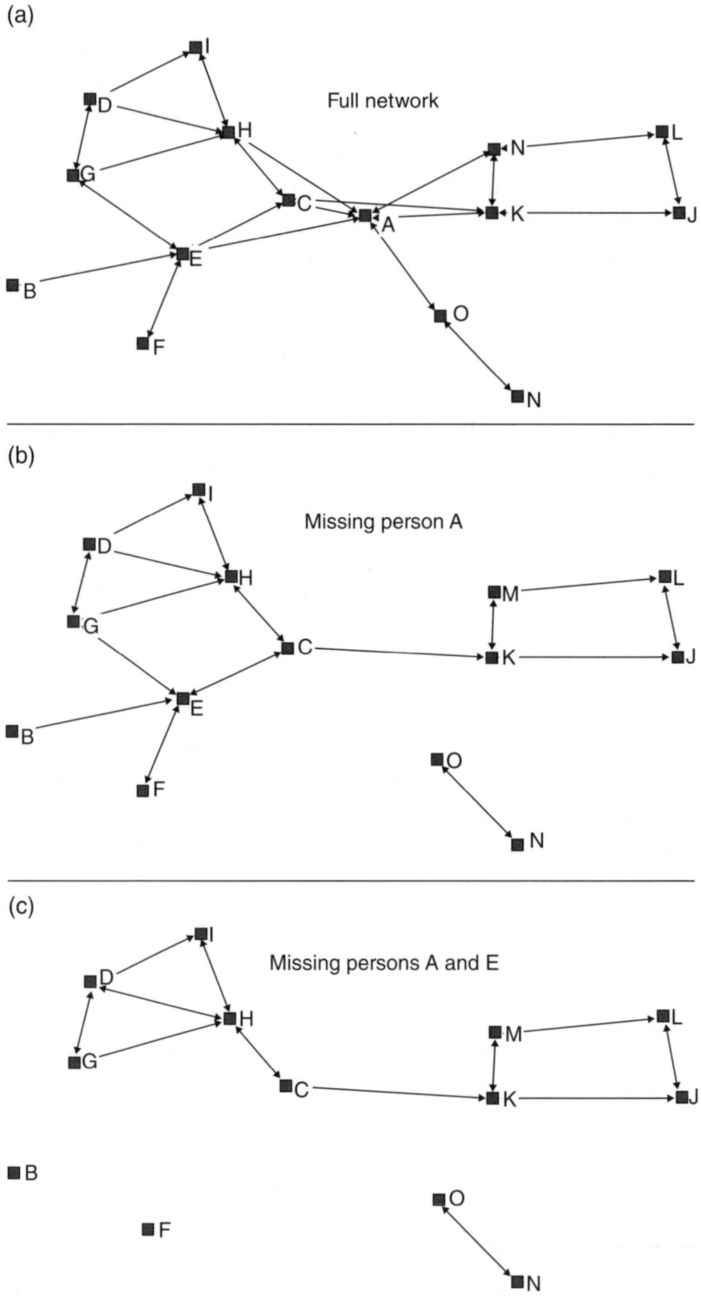

Figure 25.3 Sample network, with and without missing nodes.

network, in which everyone in the network is connected. The second panel is what the network looks like if person A is not included.[9] By removing this one person, two individuals (O and N) become disconnected from the rest of the network, and there is now a clear brokerage link between C and K (theirs is the only link between the right and left side of the network). The third panel is the network with person E also removed. This makes the network look substantially sparser. Persons B and F become "isolates" (they have no connections), while person C's brokerage characteristics change, as they no longer appear to be part of the left side of the network at all but rather act as the sole connection between the two sides.

Table 25.2 provides a statistical illustration of the dependence between cases as based on the situation in Figure 25.3. Degree and density scores (defined in the table notes) for the network as a whole decrease as the number of missing nodes increase.[10]

Table 25.2 Network and node statistics with and without missing cases.

	Full network		*Missing node A*		*Missing nodes A and E*	
	Average degree[a]	Network density[b]	Average degree	Network density	Average degree	Network density
	2.933	0.21	2.286	0.18	1.846	0.15
Node:	Degree	Ego density[c]	Degree	Ego density	Degree	Ego density
A	6	0.27				
B	1	N/C[d]	1	N/C	0	0.00
C	4	0.50	3	0.00	2	0.00
D	3	0.67	3	0.67	3	0.67
E	5	0.10	4	0.00		
F	1	N/C	1	N/C	0	0.00
G	3	0.33	3	0.33	2	1.00
H	5	0.30	4	0.33	4	0.33
I	2	1.00	2	1.00	2	1.00
J	2	0.00	2	0.00	2	0.00
K	4	0.33	3	0.00	3	0.00
L	2	0.00	2	0.00	2	0.00
M	3	0.33	2	0.00	2	0.00
N	1	N/C	1	N/C	1	N/C
O	2	0.00	1	N/C	1	N/C

Grey cells indicate nodes that have been omitted from the network.

[a] Degree is the number of ties made by a person in the network (e.g., person A has 6 friends meaning that their degree score is 6). Average degree is the mean number of ties across all members of the network.

[b] As described by Borgatti et al. (2013, 150), "density is simply the number of ties in the network, expressed as a proportion of the number possible. In an ordinary undirected non-reflexive graph, the number possible is $n(n - 1)/2$, where n is the number of nodes." Here, since $n = 15$, the number of possible nodes $15(15-1)/2 = 105$. In the full network, there are 22 ties made. This results in a network density score of 21%.

[c] According to Borgatti et al. (2013, 274), ego network density "is normally computed without ego, so it is, loosely, the proportion of ego's friends who are connected to each other. More exactly, it is the number of ties between ego's friends divided by the total number of ties possible." For example, person A has six friends. Therefore there are $6(6-1)/2 = 15$ possible ties between person A's friends. Of these, four are made. The ego network density score for person A is therefore $4/15 = 0.2667$ or 27%.

[d] N/C = not calculated. Since the denominator in the density calculation (number of possible ties) is zero for a person with only one contact, the value is undefined.
Denominator = # of possible ties = $n(n - 1)/2 = 1(1 - 1)/2 = 0$.

At the individual (node) level, ego network density for persons C, E, K, and M drops to zero when person A is not included in the network. For person G, ego network density increases when person E is not included. Everyone who is connected to either person A or person E has his or her degree score underestimated when these individuals are not included in the network. The important thing to note is how the fundamental structure of the network appears to change when missing data are present.

Missing data are often a product of the study design. Adolescent network studies generally limit peer nominations to those within the same grade (PROSPER Peers, NSCR) or school (Add Health). This artificially imposed boundary does not reflect the fact that many students have friends outside of the school (even if the majority of friends are in the same school). Boundary definitions are important in studies of illicit networks as well. These studies have often made use of publicly available (e.g., Morselli, 2001; Morselli, 2003; Wu et al., 2014) or investigative sources (e.g., Baker and Faulkner, 1993; Carrington, 2009; Morselli and Roy, 2008). When only those who have been investigated, caught, prosecuted, or convicted as part of the network are considered, network actors who were not detected are missed. These people might be more successful criminals, and therefore potentially more informative. In essence, most studies of illicit networks focus on failed criminals, the ones for which current investigative practices are successful. The ones who manage to elude detection are the ones we need to know more about in order to disrupt their illegal activities. Collecting network data on active criminals is likely to require detailed ethnographic work with a focus on keeping track of roles, behaviors, and ties among network members.

Some research has simulated how robust network statistics are to missing data. Borgatti and colleagues (2006, p. 134) found that, if a "data collection method misses 5 percent of ties, then the correlation between true and observed centrality will be in the .90s." Smith and Moody (2013, p. 652) showed that "larger, more centralized networks are generally more robust to missing data." These findings suggest that estimates of network and node characteristics are likely to be most problematic in small networks. The upside is that getting complete network information is more feasible in smaller networks, all other factors being equal. The fact that there is some indication of robustness is in no way a substitute for extremely careful data collection, and there should always be major efforts to capture as much of the network as possible.

New Directions

With increasing interest in network analysis in the social sciences (though Papachristos, 2011 argues that criminology has lagged behind on this trend), available large-scale network data (e.g., Add Health), strong recent data collection efforts (e.g., PROSPER Peers), and advances in network-analytic methods that open up the possibility for a much wider variety of questions to be answered than in the past (SIENA), there is a lot to like about the current state of affairs. However, this is not to say that we should be satisfied. There are many new directions that criminological SNA can – and should – take. Arguably the best data in terms of data quality are from adolescent school-based samples. Certainly this meets the interests of many researchers but excludes covert and adult networks, which are often of the greatest policy concern. It is my belief that the greatest criminological insights in the near future will be gained by collecting data for groups upon which little or no rigorous network research has previously been done. This may involve collaborations with other disciplines. Recent developments by Westlake and colleagues (2011) exemplify this approach. By drawing on computing science techniques and on programming skills, they have collected large-scale, dynamic data from a highly covert illicit network: child exploitation websites. In a different direction, ethnographic approaches have the potential to delve more deeply into the perceived causes of, and meanings attributed to, network activities. There is a rich history of qualitative contributions to understanding social networks in general (see Hollstein, 2011), including detailed accounts of groups involved in offending behavior (Whyte, 1943). But embedding oneself in a particular group in the ethnographic tradition can also contribute to structural analyses of covert networks. Accessing the everyday experiences of the group should produce knowledge of the pattern of relationships and power dynamics within those relationships (e.g., Adler, 1993). This does not necessitate any fundamental changes in approach on the part of the ethnographic researcher. The only thing required is an awareness of the basic ideas of SNA – the sociomatrix – and an appropriate recording of ties.

Acknowledgments

I would like to thank Rebecca Nash for her helpful comments on an earlier version of this chapter.

Notes

1 I will be referring to networks of people for the sake of convenience, but networks can refer to connections between social service agencies, companies, gangs, countries, or any other entity.

2 Another form of sociomatrix is the two-mode network (Borgatti and Everett, 1997). In this format, connections between different types of entities are measured. An example would be a cohort of probationers and their ties to social service agencies. Here a tie to an employment agency would be indicated if a person used the services of that agency, but no tie to a drug treatment facility would be indicated if the person did not receive treatment. Two-mode networks rarely have the same number of rows and columns (in this example, individuals and agencies).

3 Of the many uses of SNA in criminology, I will discuss only a select few prominent areas; within those areas, I will only discuss a few studies. This is meant to be an overview rather than an exhaustive review of criminological applications of SNA.

4 This constraint on the number of friends a person can nominate is unlikely to cause much of a problem, as only 3.15 percent of valid respondents nominated the full ten friends.

5 While these techniques are best when there are more than three waves of network data, they can be used with as few as two. However, since the in-school sample was collected before the wave 1 in-home sample and both contain sociometric data, the saturation sample allows for three waves (in-school wave, wave 1 in home, wave 2 in home).

6 According to Moody et al. (2011), data have been collected through the 12th grade but are still being prepared. At the time of writing this chapter, no known studies have used all the data covering grades 6 through 12. The recent study by Ragan et al. (2014) uses the grade 6–9 data.

7 It should be reiterated here that the Add Health saturation sample is not representative. But network measures are available for the Add Health in-school data that, in combination with appropriate sample weights, can claim representativeness.

8 In Stata, the syntax for running a linear regression model that predicts illicit income from effective size and controls for age and sex could be done using the following syntax:

```
regress illicit_income eff_size age sex
```

To run the same model, but with 2,000 bootstrap replications, the syntax would be:

```
bootstrap, reps(2000): regress illicit_income eff_size age sex
```

9 Note that this example makes the assumption that persons A and E are part of the network but are essentially not noted. There are more complicated examples, where a person may be part of the network (e.g., a school roster) but is not present on the day of survey administration. In this situation, that person's incoming ties (friendship nominations by others) will be present, but his or her outgoing ties (nominations to others) will be missing.

10 This is not a law, but rather a finding in this particular example. Both average degree and network density could increase if a missing node were peripheral. The point is that missing data in SNA influence network patterns in more complicated ways than we find in traditional surveys.

References

Adler, P. A. 1993. *Wheeling and dealing: An ethnography of an upper-level drug dealing and smuggling community.* New York: Columbia University Press.

Akers, R. L. 2009. *Social learning and social structure: A general theory of crime and deviance.* Brunswick, NJ: Transaction.

Baerveldt, C., Volker, B., and Van Rossem, R. 2008. Revisiting selection and influence: An inquiry into the friendship networks of high school students and their association with delinquency. *Canadian Journal of Criminology & Criminal Justice*, 50 (5): 559–587.

Baker, W. E., and Faulkner, R. R. 1993. The social organization of conspiracy: Illegal networks in the heavy electrical equipment industry. *American Sociological Review*, 58 (6): 837–860.

Bearman, P., Moody, J., Stovel, K., and Thalji, L. 2004. Social and sexual networks: The National Longitudinal Study of Adolescent Health. In *Network epidemiology: A handbook for survey design and data collection*, edited by M. Morris, 201–220. London: Oxford University Press.

Boman, J. H., IV, Stogner, J. M., Miller, B. L., Griffin, O. H., III, and Krohn, M. D. 2012. On the operational validity of perceptual peer delinquency: Exploring projection and elements contained in perceptions. *Journal of Research in Crime and Delinquency*, 49 (4): 601–621.

Borgatti, S. P., Carley, K. M., and Krackhardt, D. 2006. On the robustness of centrality measures under conditions of imperfect data. *Social Networks*, 28 (2): 124–136.

Borgatti, S. P., and Everett, M. G. 1997. Network analysis of 2-mode data. *Social Networks*, 19: 243–269.

Borgatti, S. P., Everett, M. G., and Freeman, L. C. 2002. Ucinet for Windows: Software for social network analysis. Harvard, MA: Analytic Technologies.

Borgatti, S. P., Mehra, A., Brass, D. J., and Labianca, G. 2009. Network analysis in the social sciences. *Science*, 323 (5916): 892–895. doi: 10.1126/science.1165821.

Burt, R. S. 1992. *Structural holes: The social structure of competition*. Cambridge, MA: Harvard University Press.

Butts, C. T. 2014. SNA: Tools for social network analysis: R package version 2.3–2. Accessed December 18, 2015. http://cran.r-project.org/web/packages/sna/sna.pdf.

Carrington, P. J. 2009. Co-offending and the development of the delinquent career. *Criminology*, 47 (4): 1295–1329.

Carrington, P. J. 2011. Crime and social network analysis. In *The SAGE handbook of social network analysis*, edited by J. Scott and P. J. Carrington, 236–255. Thousand Oaks, CA: Sage.

Cohen, G. L., and Prinstein, M. J. 2006. Peer contagion of aggression and health risk behavior among adolescent males: An experimental investigation of effects on public conduct and private attitudes. *Child Development*, 77 (4): 967–983. doi: 10.1111/j.1467–8624.2006.00913.x.

Dijkstra, J. K., Lindenberg, S., Veenstra, R., Steglich, C., Isaacs, J., Card, N. A., and Hodges, E. V. E. 2010. Influence and selection processes in weapon carrying during adolescence: The roles of status, aggression, and vulnerability. *Criminology*, 48 (1): 187–220.

Efron, B., and Tibshirani, R. J. 1993. *An introduction to the bootstrap*. (Monographs on Statistics and Applied Probability 57). New York: Chapman & Hall.

Freeman, L. C. 2004. *The development of social network analysis: A study in the sociology of science*. Vancouver, BC: Empirical Press.

Gallupe, O., and Bouchard, M. 2015. The influence of positional and experienced social benefits on the relationship between peers and alcohol use. *Rationality & Society*, 27 (1): 40–69.

Gottfredson, M., and Hirschi, T. 1990. *A general theory of crime*. Stanford, CA: Stanford University Press.

Haynie, D. L. 2001. Delinquent peers revisited: Does network structure matter? *American Journal of Sociology*, 106 (4): 1013–1057.

Hirschi, T. 1969. *Causes of delinquency*. Berkeley: University of California Press.

Hollstein, B. 2011. Qualitative approaches. In *The SAGE handbook of social network analysis*, edited by J. Scott and P. J. Carrington, 404–416. Thousand Oaks, CA: Sage.

Hughes, L. A. 2013. Group cohesiveness, gang member prestige, and delinquency and violence in Chicago, 1959–1962. *Criminology*, 51 (4): 795–832. doi: 10.1111/1745–9125.12020.

Knecht, A. 2008. *Friendship selection and friends' influence: Dynamics of networks and actor attributes in early adolescence.* Doctoral dissertation, Utrecht University, Netherlands.

Krackhardt, D. 1988. Predicting with networks: Nonparametric multiple regression analysis of dyadic data. *Social Networks*, 10 (4): 359–381.

Krohn, M. 1986. The web of conformity: A network approach to the explanation of delinquent behavior. *Social Problems*, 33 (6), S81–S93.

McGloin, J. 2005. Policy and intervention considerations of a network analysis of street gangs. *Criminology & Public Policy*, 4 (3): 607–635.

McPherson, M., Smith-Lovin, L., and Cook, J. M. 2001. Birds of a feather: Homophily in social networks. *Annual Review of Sociology*, 27: 415–444.

Moody, J., Brynildsen, W. D., Osgood, D. W., Feinberg, M. E., and Gest, S. 2011. Popularity trajectories and substance use in early adolescence. *Social Networks*, 33 (2): 101–112. doi: 10.1016/j.socnet.2010.10.001.

Moreno, J. L., and Jennings, H. H. 1934. *Who shall survive?* Washington, DC: Nervous and Mental Disease Publishing Company.

Morselli, C. 2001. Structuring Mr. Nice: Entrepreneurial opportunities and brokerage positioning in the cannabis trade. *Crime, Law, and Social Change*, 35: 203–244.

Morselli, C. 2003. Career opportunities and network-based privileges in the Cosa Nostra. *Crime, Law, and Social Change*, 39: 383–418.

Morselli, C. 2009. *Inside criminal networks.* New York: Springer.

Morselli, C., and Roy, J. 2008. Brokerage qualifications in ringing operations. *Criminology*, 46 (1): 71–98.

Nash, R., Bouchard, M., and Malm, A. 2013. Investing in people: The role of social networks in the diffusion of a large-scale fraud. *Social Networks*, 35 (4): 686–698. doi: 10.1016/j.socnet.2013.06.005.

Osgood, D. W., Ragan, D. T., Wallace, L., Gest, S. D., Feinberg, M. E., and Moody, J. 2013. Peers and the emergence of alcohol use: Influence and selection processes in adolescent friendship networks. *Journal of Research on Adolescence*, 23 (3): 500–512. doi: 10.1111/jora.12059.

Papachristos, A. V. 2009. Murder by structure: Dominance relations and the social structure of gang homicide. *American Journal of Sociology*, 115 (1): 74–128.

Papachristos, A. V. 2011. The coming of a networked criminology. In *Measuring crime and criminality: Advances in criminological theory*, edited by J. MacDonald, vol. 17, 101–140. New Brunswick, NJ: Transaction.

Payne, D. C., and Cornwell, B. 2007. Reconsidering peer influences on delinquency: Do less proximate contacts matter? *Journal of Quantitative Criminology*, 23 (2): 127–149.

Pratt, T. C., Cullen, F. T., Sellers, C. S., Winfree, L. T., Jr., Madensen, T. D., Daigle, L. E., … Gau, J. M. 2010. The empirical status of social learning theory: A meta-analysis. *Justice Quarterly*, 27 (6): 765–802.

Ragan, D. T., Osgood, D. W., and Feinberg, M. E. 2014. Friends as a bridge to parental influence: Implications for adolescent alcohol use. *Social Forces*, 92 (3): 1061–1085.

Rebellon, C. J., and Modecki, K. L. 2013. Accounting for projection bias in models of delinquent peer influence: The utility and limits of latent variable approaches. *Journal of Quantitative Criminology*, 30 (2): 163–186. doi: 10.1007/s10940-013-9199-9.

Simpkins, S. D., Schaefer, D. R., Price, C. D., and Vest, A. E. 2013. Adolescent friendships, BMI, and physical activity: Untangling selection and influence through longitudinal social network analysis. *Journal of Research on Adolescence*, 23 (3): 537–549. doi: 10.1111/j.1532-7795.2012.00836.x.

Smith, J. A., and Moody, J. 2013. Structural effects of network sampling coverage, I: Nodes missing at random. *Social Networks*, 35 (4): 652–668. doi: 10.1016/j.socnet.2013.09.003.

Snijders, T. A. B., van de Bunt, G. G., and Steglich, C. E. G. 2010. Introduction to stochastic actor-based models for network dynamics. *Social Networks*, 32 (1): 44–60.

Sutherland, E. H. 1947. *Principles of Criminology* (Vol. 4). Philadelphia: J. B. Lippincott.

Tabachnick, B. G., and Fidell, L. S. 2007. *Using multivariate statistics*, 5th edn. Boston, MA: Allyn & Bacon.

Wasserman, S., and Faust, K. 1994. *Social network analysis: Methods and applications*. New York: Cambridge University Press.

Weerman, F. M. 2011. Delinquent peers in context: A longitudinal network analysis of selection and influence effects. *Criminology*, 49 (1): 253–286.

Weerman, F. M., and Smeenk, W. H. 2005. Peer similarity in delinquency for different types of friends: A comparison using two measurement methods. *Criminology*, 43 (2): 499–524.

Westlake, B. G., Bouchard, M., and Frank, R. 2011. Finding the key players in online child exploitation networks. *Policy & Internet*, 3 (2): 104–135. doi: 10.2202/1944–2866.1126.

Whyte, W. F. 1943. *Street corner society*. Chicago, IL: University of Chicago Press.

Wu, E., Carleton, R., and Davies, G. 2014. Discovering bin-Laden's replacement in al-Qaeda, using social network analysis: A methodological investigation. *Perspectives on Terrorism*, 8 (1): 57–73.

Young, J. T. N., Rebellon, C. J., Barnes, J. C., and Weerman, F. M. 2015. What do alternative measures of peer behavior tell us? Examining the discriminant validity of multiple methods of measuring peer deviance and the implications for etiological models. *Justice Quarterly*, 32 (4): 626–652. doi: 10.1080/07418825.2013.788730.

Young, J. T. N., Rebellon, C. J., Barnes, J. C., and Weerman, F. 2014. Unpacking the black box of peer similarity in deviance: Understanding the mechanisms linking personal behavior, peer behavior, and perceptions. *Criminology*, 52 (1): 60–86.

Young, J. T. N., and Weerman, F. 2013. Delinquency as a consequence of misperception: Overestimation of friends' delinquent behavior and mechanisms of social influence. *Social Problems*, 60 (3): 334–356.

Index

Note: *b* indicates box; *f*, figure; and *t*, table.

abuse *see* child abuse; intimate partner violence
Add Health *see* National Longitudinal Study of Adolescent Health (Add Health)
adolescents, violent victimization of, 12–13
  see also juveniles
African Americans *see* minorities; traffic stops
alcohol use, by juveniles, 56
Al Qaeda in the Arabian Peninsula, 36
Anonymous (online activist group), 36
Anti-Defamation League (ADL), 133
antigay violence, 134 *see also* hate crime(s)
Arab women's pathways to crime, 195–196
arrest data, limitations of, 10–11
arrests, age-crime curve for, 11

bias crime *see* hate crime(s)
Booker, United States v., 317, 342
Bootstrapping, 566
"broken windows" policing, 282
bullying
  juveniles and, 59–65
  legal definition of, 61–62
  legislation on, 61–62
  online, 35
  required reporting of, 63

Campus Sexual Assault (CSA) study, 267
case-processing and court decision-making research
  analytical challenges in, 310–312
  data advances in, 318–320
  dependent variables in, 304–306
  difficulties in, 303
  experimental methods in, 316–317
  improvement of, 320–321
  independent variables in, 306–310
  mixed methods in, 317–318
  multilevel models in, 314
  path-analytic modeling in, 315
  quantile regression in, 313–314
  regression techniques in, 315–316
  sentencing decisions and, 340–341
  statistical matching in, 313
child abuse
  as pathway to offending by women, 183–185
  sexual

The Handbook of Measurement Issues in Criminology and Criminal Justice, First Edition.
Edited by Beth M. Huebner and Timothy S. Bynum.

definition, 71
four-factor model, 77–78
child molesters
classifications of, 73–74
rapists compared with, 82
recidivism of, 83
children *see also* gendered pathways to crime; school crime; school safety
cyberporn and, 35
pornography and, 72
victimization surveys of, 252–253
cigarette smoking *see* tobacco use
civil liberties, public opinion on, 378–380
Civil Rights Act (1968), 131, 135
Columbine High School shootings, 438
Commodities Futures Trading Commission (CFTC), 104
community disorder, 286
community policing
components of, 282–283
critical assessments of, 281
definitions of, 279–281
difficulty of measuring, 279–280
expected outcomes of, 285–287
as organizational strategy, 281–283
problem-solving *vs.* problem-oriented, 282–284
vs. professional policing model, 281
community policing and police interventions research
approaches to, 288–289
direct observation in, 295–297
emerging, 297–298
evaluation in, 292–294
experimental studies of, 289–292
police and official data in, 297
surveys and interviews in, 294–295
CompStat, 22–23, 284, 293–294
computer crime, 30, 31 *see also* cybercrime
Confessions of a Dying Thief (Steffensmeier and Ulmer), 504
Conflict Tactics Scale (CTS), 17–18, 263, 264
corporate crime *see also* white collar crime
definition of, 102
impediments to accurately measure, 102–103
improved data on, 107–108
vs. occupational crime, 102
official sources of data on, 103–105
research challenges of, 107
unofficial sources of data on, 106–107
Corporate Fraud Task Force (CFTF), 107–108
correctional interventions research *see also* rehabilitation and treatment program
background on, 352
implementation of, 359–360
logic models of, 352–354, 355*f*
recidivism and, 360–367 (*see also* recidivism)
reentry focus in, 367–371
risk-need-responsivity model in, 354, 356–359
Correctional Program Assessment Inventory, 359
costs of crime
and challenges to monetization studies, 422–424
direct and indirect, 417–418
future research in, 424–428
harm and, 416–417
monetary costs of criminal career and, 418–420
per offense, 420–421
and public's willingness to pay for prevention, 420, 426–427
summary of monetization studies of, 421
tangible and intangible, 417
crime *see also* cost of crime; fear of crime; life-course offending research
public opinion on, 378–380
Crime Act (1994), 294–295
crime clusters *see* hot spots
crime prevention, cost-benefits of, 424
Crime Survey in England and Wales (CSEW), 253
criminal behavior, risk factors for, 226–227, 227*t*
cybercrime
computer-mediated communications as data source of, 39–40
cyberdeception/theft, 32–34
cybertrespass (hacking), 31–32, 192–193
cyberviolence, 35–36
defining of, 30–31

cybercrime (*cont'd*)
future research in, 41–42
limitations of research on, 36–39
pornography and obscenity, 34–35
public awareness of, 41
self-report data of, 38
types of, 31–36

death-penalty research, victim effects in, 308
defendants, in case-processing research, 306–308
delinquency *see* juvenile crime and delinquency
Department of Justice (DOJ)
corporate crime and, 103, 104
Corporate Fraud Task Force (CFTF), 107–108
State and Local White Collar Crime Program (SLWCCP), 108
Survey of Inmates in State and Federal Correctional Facilities, 97–98, 100
differential association theory (DAT), 558, 561
digital piracy, 33–34
disorder *see* community disorder
DNA processing, cost-benefits of, 428
dosage, in rehabilitation and treatment program, 237–238
drug court, cost-benefits of, 424–425
drug dealing, by women, 186–187, 192
drug offenders, sentencing disparities and, 337–339
drug use *see* substance use
Dual Relationships Inventory-Revised (DRI-R), 241

Educational Longitudinal Study (ELS), 436
elderly, victimization surveys of, 253
emotional harm, 62
Enron, 106
ethnic minorities *see* minorities
European Social Survey (ESS) *see* fear of crime, defining and measuring of
exploratory spatial data analysis (ESDA), 538–539

fear of crime, 286–287
defining and measuring of, 380–381
combining four measures into single index for analysis, 383–386
four measures of worry about victimization, 381–383
process clarification, 389–396
using new index to estimate levels of fear, 386–389
Federal Bureau of Investigation (FBI) *see also* National Incident-Based Reporting System (NIBRS); Uniform Crime Reporting (UCR)
child-molester classification by, 73–74
Federal Justice Statistics Resource Center (FJSRC) data, 319
Federal Trade Commission (FTC), 103
Financial Crimes Report to the Public, 96
Financial Institution Fraud and Failure Report, 96
fraud, Internet (cyberdeception/theft), 32–33 *see also* white collar crime

Gall v. United States, 342
gang crime
consequences of inability to measure, 160
membership-*vs.* motivation-based definitions of, 164, 166–167
overreporting of, 168
gang research
ethnographic, 169–172
future, 176
self-report surveys in, 172–175
gang(s)
definitions of, 161–164, 165–166*b*
discriminating between nongang groups and, 161–163
disproportionate offending rates of, 159
lists of members of, 167–169
official police data on, 163–164
risk of violent offending and membership in, 13–15
social network analysis (SNA) and, 562–563
gendered pathways to crime *see also* pathways research
association with delinquent males, 186–187
ethnographic studies on, 191–193
four pathways leading to criminality, 182
future of research on, 193–197
gendered experiences leading to crime, 181

official data on, 187–189
overview of, 181–183
physical and verbal abuse, 183–185
self-report surveys on, 189–191
substance use, 185
general theory of crime, individual criminality and, 10
geography of crime *see* spatial analysis of crime
Governing through Crime (Simons), 440
group-based trajectory analysis (GBTA), 21
Gun-Free Schools Act (1994), 442

hacking (cybertrespass), 31–32, 192–193
harm
bullying and, 62
cost of crime and, 416
hate crime(s)
anti-white, 141–142
vs. "bias crime", 134–135
Canadian and European laws on, 139–140
data collection on, 132–134
definitions of, 131, 135, 138
improving data quality of, 149–151
National Crime Victimization Survey (NCVS) data on, 145–149, 146*f*, 149*f*
National Incident-Based Reporting System (NIBRS) data on, 143–144, 145*t*
number of law enforcement agencies reporting on, 141
state statutes on, 136, 137–138*t*, 138–139
Uniform Crime Reporting (UCR) data on, 131–132, 140–143, 141*f*, 148–149, 149*f*
Hate Crimes Prevention Act (HCPA, 2009), 136
Hate Crime Statistics Act (HCSA, 1990), 131, 135
Hawthorne effect, in gang research, 171
health research *see* mental health research; physical health research
Heartland Payment Systems hack, 32–33
hierarchical linear model (HLM), 314
Hispanics *see* minorities; traffic stops
hot spots, 20–21, 284–285, 290–292, 537 *see also* spatial analysis of crime
human trafficking
chain referral method of measuring, 116–117
definition of, 112
lack of empirical research on, 112–113
open-source estimates of, 113–117
overview of, 111
rapid assessment method of measuring, 116
United Nations protocol on, 112
human trafficking research
areas of future, 125
on criminal justice system's response to trafficking, 122–124
data from victim-stakeholder relationship in, 120–121
ethical concerns in, 119
focus on alternative populations in, 118–119
focus on women in, 118
on framing of human trafficking, 122–123
limitations of qualitative measurements in, 117
on long-term effects of victimization, 121–122
post hoc *vs.* real-time data in, 119–120
on social services for victims, 122
surveys *vs.* interviews in, 118
on trafficking laws, 122, 123

incest, 71–72
incident data, limitations of, 10–11
indecent exposure, 72
Indicators of School Crime and Safety, 436–437
Internet *see also* cybercrime
child pornography and, 72
widespread use of, 29
Internet Crime Complaint Center (IC3), 38
intimate partner violence, surveys on, 256
item response model, 271–272
Izz ad-Din al-Qassam Cyber Fighters, 36

Jack-Roller, The (Shaw), 503–504
judge characteristics, in court decision-making research, 308–309 *see also* sentencing disparity
juvenile crime and delinquency
bullying and, 59–65
challenges of measurement of, 64–65
geography of, 18
official data on, 51–55
police discretion and, 54

juvenile crime and delinquency (*cont'd*)
public concern about, 49–50
role of peers in, 52–53
self-report data on, 55–59
juveniles *see also* gendered pathways to crime; school crime; school safety
alcohol, tobacco, and marijuana use by, 56, 57
statutory rape and, 71
victimization surveys of, 252–253

kernel density analysis, 546–548

labeling theory, 10
labor trafficking, 114, 118–119 *see also* human trafficking
Legacies of Crime (Giordano), 504
Level of Service Inventory-Revised (LSI-R), 356
life-course offending research
challenges in, 506–509
data on offending in, 497–499
future, 511
life events calendars in, 504–505
life history narratives in, 502–504
mixed designs in, 506
overview of, 496–497
panel studies in, 499–502
telemetric, 509–511
life events calendar, 191
Los Angeles County Human Relations Commission (LACHRC), 133–134

Making Good (Maruna), 504
malware, 32
mandatory minimum-sentencing laws, 330
marijuana use, by juveniles, 56
Matthew Shepard and James Byrd, Jr. Hate Crimes Prevention Act *see* Hate Crimes Prevention Act (HCPA, 2009)
mental health research, 202
assessment of co-occurring disorders in, 208–209
conceptualization of mental illness in, 207–208
diagnostic *vs.* dimensional measurement in, 203–207
measurement of prevalence rates in, 212–213
prediction of violence in, 213–214
reviewing chart records in, 209–210
screening instruments in, 210–212
minorities *see also* hate crime(s); traffic stops
case-processing and sentencing research and, 306–307
death-penalty research and, 308
violent crime and, 19–20
modifiable areal unit problem (MAUP), 542–543
monetization studies *see under* costs of crime
Monitoring the Future (MTF), 55–56
moral panic theory, 338
Mortgage Fraud Report, 96

National College Women Sexual Victimization (NCWSV) study, 258–260, 259*b*, 262, 263
National Crime Victimization Survey (NCVS) *see also* Police-Public Contact Survey (PPCS)
bounded interviews in, 260
context of, 251, 252
cybercrime data and, 37
hate-crime data of, 145–149, 146*f*, 149*f*
juveniles and, 57, 58
panel conditioning in, 488
population samples in, 253
sample question in, 258*b*
wording of questions in, 262–263
National Crime Victimization Survey School Crime Supplement (NCVS-SCS), 57, 58
National Crime Victimization Survey, Supplemental Survey (NCVS-SS)
cyberstalking data in, 37–38
National Criminal Justice Treatment Practices Survey (NCJTP), 229–231
National Gang Center, 164
National High School Senior Survey *see* Monitoring the Future (MTF)
National Incident-Based Reporting System (NIBRS)
cybercrime data of, 36–37
hate crime data of, 143–144, 145*t*
white-collar crime data of, 95–96
National Intimate Partner and Sexual Violence Survey, 251

National Lesbian, Gay, Bisexual, Transgender, and Queer (LGBTQ) Task Force, 134
National Longitudinal Study of Adolescent Health (Add Health), 438, 563–564
National Longitudinal Survey of Youth (NLSY), 436
National Survey of Drug Use and Health, 252
National Violence against College Women (NVACW) survey, 263
National Violence against Women survey, 251–252
National White-Collar Crime Center (NW3C), 99–100
National Women's Study (NWS), 261
National Youth Gang Survey, 163
Nature and Sanctioning of White Collar Crime (Wheeler et al.), 96–97
nearest neighbor analysis, 546
network analysis *see* social network analysis (SNA)
New York City Commission on Human Rights (CCHR), 134

obscenity, online, 34–35
occupational crime, 102
offenders, adolescent-limited and life-course-persistent, 10
Office for Democratic Institutions and Human Rights (ODIHR), 139, 140
Operation Ceasefire (Boston), 23–24, 292–294
ordinary least squares regression, 314
Organization for Security and Cooperation in Europe (OSCE) Office for Democratic Institutions and Human Rights (ODIHR), 139, 140

Palestinian women's pathways to crime, 195–196
Pathways from Dependency and Neglect to Delinquency (Coleman-Davis and Forde), 188
pathways research *see also* gendered pathways to crime
  on court processing, 315
  future, 193–194
  international, 195–196
  intersectionality in, 194–195
  policy implications of, 196–197
physical health research, 214–215
physical illness, 202
piracy, digital, 33–34
Police-Public Contact Survey (PPCS), 453–454
pornography
  children and, 72
  Internet, 34–35
  sex offending and, 81
prison interviews
  and emotional impact on researcher, 530
  guidelines on, 517–518
  handling sensitive questions in, 528–529
  prisoner's mental state following, 529–530
  rapport with prisoners during, 523–526
  reflexivity in, 522–523
  reliability and validity of data from, 526–528
  researcher's concerns on, 519–520
  three studies involving, 520–522
procedural justice theory, 396–397
Project Exile (Richmond, VA), 293–294
Project Greenlight (New York), 360
Project on Policing Neighborhoods (POPN), 296–297
Promoting School-Community-University Partnerships to Enhance Resilience (PROSPER) Peers study, 564
propensity score matching, 313
prosecutorial discretion, 304–305, 330, 340–341, 344
PROSPER study *see* Promoting School-Community-University Partnerships to Enhance Resilience (PROSPER) Peers study
prostitution, online, 34–35
Public Corporation Accounting Oversight Board (PCAOB), 103–104
public indecency, 72
public opinion on police
  citizen satisfaction and, 287
  dimensionality of trust, legitimacy, and willingness to cooperate, 399–400
  dynamics of police-community relations, 401–403
  gap between psychological construct (legitimacy) and measures, 403–409
  procedural justice theory and, 396–397
  trends in, 378–380
  trust and institutional legitimacy, 397–398

quadrat analysis, 545–546
quadratic assignment procedure (QAP regression), 566
quantile regression, 313–314

racial profiling *see* traffic stops
radioimmunoessay off hair (RIAH), 484
rape, 70–71 *see also* sex crime(s)
rapists, typologies of, 74–76
reactive effect, 295–296
recidivism
  definition of, 360–361
  follow-up period in, 362–364, 364*t*
  frequency and timing of subsequent, 365–367, 366*t*
  intermittency of, 366–367, 367*f*
  measurement trends in, 364–365
  rates of, according to reoffending events, 361, 362*t*
  reoffense events in, 361–362
reentry, correctional interventions research and, 367–371
regression techniques, 315–316
rehabilitation, 223
rehabilitation and treatment program
  client-facilitator relationship in, 239–241
  client-level proximal measures of, 239–242
  client's perception of procedural justice in, 241–242
  components of, 223–224, 224*f*
  conceptual delivery models of, 234–235, 234*f*
  length and duration of sessions in, 237–238
  measuring effectiveness of
    clients, 225–228
    factors, 224–225
    setting and organizational culture, 229–231
    staffing and resources, 228–229
  progress measures in, 238–239
  standardized curricula for, 236
  strengths-based approaches in, 236
  structure of, 233–235
  targets in, 231–233, 232*t*
  theoretical orientations of, 235–236
  types of therapy in, 236–237
rehabilitation treatment program *see also* correctional interventions research
Risk, Need, Responsivity Simulation Tool, 359
Rita v. United States, 342
runaways, female, 184

Safe School Initiative (SSI), 438–439
Sandy Hook Elementary School shooting, 417–418
school crime
  context of, 435
  trends in, 435–438, 437*t*
school safety *see also* National Crime Victimization Survey School Crime Supplement (NCVS-SCS)
  instruments of, 440–441
  reasons for rising security measures for, 439–440
  trends in, 438–443
  unintended effects of, 442–443
  zero tolerance and, 441–442
school safety research
  barriers in, 445–446
  future of, 447–448
  limitations of, 443–445
  and public scrutiny of shootings, 446–447
School Survey on Crime and Safety, 57, 58, 444
self-report survey research
  accuracy of data in, 483–486
  advantages of, 491–492
  cross-sectional and longitudinal data in, 476
  limitations of, 491
  nonparticipation or low participation in, 479
  overview of, 475
  panel conditioning in, 488
  panel retention and attrition in, 486–488
  recall problems in, 488–491, 490*t*
  sampling in, 477–479
  scaling illegal behaviors for, 480–483
  selection of behaviors for, 479–480
  and traits of poorly and well-designed survey, 492
  wording of questions in, 485–486, 487*t*
sentencing data, 330–331
sentencing discretion, 329
sentencing disparity
  effects of race, ethnicity, and gender on, 336–339
  future research on, 343–345

gender and, 332–333, 335–336
indirect effects on, 340–341
liberals and conservatives views on, 329
limitations of research on, 333–334
race/ethnicity and, 334–335
sentencing legislation and, 342–343
statistics on, 333
stereotypes and, 331–332
variables related to, 331
sentencing guidelines, 342–343
Sentencing in Eight Federal District Courts (Forst and Rhodes), 97
Sentencing Reform Act (SRA, 1984), 329–330
sentencing research, 305–307
sex crime, definitions of, 69, 70
sex offender registry and notification (SORN) laws, 84–85
sex offenders
recidivism of, 82–84
registries of, 84–85
typologies of, 72–77
sex offending
developmental and situational factors in, 78–79
risk factors for, 79–81
specialization in, 81–82
theories on, 77–79
types of, 70–72
sex trade, illegal (online), 34–35
sex trafficking *see also* human trafficking
in Cambodia, 115–116
in Nepal, 116
sexual abuse
of children, 71
victimization surveys on, 256–257
sexual aggression, quadripartite model of, 76–77
sexual assault, 70
sexual battery, 70–71
simultaneous autoregressive (SAR) model, 541–543
situational crime research, 15–18
smoking *see* tobacco use
social learning theory (SLT), 558, 561
social network analysis (SNA)
future research in, 570–571
gang research and, 562–563
independence of cases in, 565–566
key players and, 558
longitudinal *vs.* cross-sectional data in, 566–567
major studies in, 563–565
missing data in, 567–570
overview of, 556–558
peer-influence research and, 558–561
sample network in, 556, 556*f*, 557
selection *vs.* influence in, 561–562
sociomatrix in, 557–558, 557*t*
sociomatrix, 557–558, 557*t*
Southern Poverty Law Center (SPLC), 133
spatial analysis of crime
areal, 536, 539–543
choice of neighbors in, 550–551
choice of scale for, 549–550
distances between spatial units in, 550
early studies in, 535
exploratory, 538–539
point-based, 536, 543–548
spatial autocorrelation, 538–540
spatial data, properties of, 537–538
spatial dependence, 537
spatial heterogeneity, 537–538
spatial techniques, 548 *see also* spatial analysis of crime
stalking, online, 37–38
State and Local White Collar Crime Program (SLWCCP), 108
statistical matching, 313
statutory rape, 71
stochastic actor-oriented model (SAOM), 561–562
street gangs *see* gang(s)
substance use *see also* drug dealing
alcohol and marijuana use by juveniles, 56
and pathway to crime by women, 185, 192
prisoner reentry and, 368–369
Survey of Inmates in State and Federal Correctional Facilities (DOJ), 97–98, 100

terrorist groups, online, 36
tobacco use, by juveniles, 56, 57
traffic stops
benchmarking data in, 460
aggregate data, 461–464
internal data, 464–465

traffic stops (*cont'd*)
citizen survey data on, 453–455
and disparity in post-stop action, 465–469
future research in, 470
measuring disparity in, 459–465
non-racially biased reasons for, 460
outcome-test evaluation of, 467–469
police data on, 455–458
searches following, 466–467

Uniform Crime Reporting (UCR)
on hate crimes, 131–132, 140–143, 141*f*, 148–149, 149*f*
on human trafficking, 124
on juvenile crime and delinquency, 51–55
policing research and, 297
on victimization, 250
on white-collar crime, 95
United States v. Booker, 317, 342
Unraveling Juvenile Delinquency (Glueck and Glueck), 500
urinalysis, 484
using new index to estimate levels of fear of crime, 386–389
US Sentencing Commission Annual Statistical Report, 96, 97

victim characteristics, in death-penalty research, 308
victimization
age and violent-crime, 12, 13*f*
European survey on worries about, 381–383
of juveniles, 58
typical measurement of, 250–251
violent-crime, 12–13
victimization research
early, 249
future, 268–272
victimization surveys
bounded interviews in, 260–261
context of, 251–252
data-collection methods in, 265–268
ordering of questions in, 264, 269
question wording in, 261–264, 269
reducing measurement errors in, 268–272
samples in, 252–253, 256–257
two-stage *vs.* one-stage measurement strategy in, 257–260
Victims of Trafficking and Violence Protection Act (TVPA), 112, 122
violence
individual level, 9–13
official data on, 10–11
online, 35–36
self-reported data on, 11–12
violent crime
ethnic minorities and, 19–20
gang membership and, 13–15
geography of, 18–21 (*see also* spatial analysis of crime)
offender-victim relationships and, 15–16, 16*t*
police interventions to reduce, 21–24
situational and contextual analyses of, 15–18
Violent Crime Control and Law Enforcement Act (1994), 136

white collar crime *see also* corporate crime
conceptual ambiguity of, 92
definitions of, 93–94
difficulty in quantifying, 92–93
improved data on, 107–108
official sources of data on, 95–98
research challenges of, 107
summary of data sets on, 101*t*
unofficial sources of data on, 98–100
Whren v. United States, 465
women *see also* gendered pathways to crime
effects of negative experiences on, 182
life histories of, 504
Women's Experiences of Violence (WEV), 520–521
Working Alliance Inventory (WAI), 240–241

youth *see* children; juveniles
Youth Risk Behavior Surveillance System (YRBSS), 57
youth violence *see* juvenile crime and delinquency